The Social Psychology
of Political Life

Duxbury Press Series in Politics

Bernard C. Hennessy
General Editor
California State College, Hayward

AMERICAN POLITICAL INTEREST GROUPS
Betty H. Zisk

THE IRONY OF DEMOCRACY, Second Edition
Thomas R. Dye and L. Harmon Zeigler

THE CONGRESSIONAL SYSTEM
Leroy N. Rieselbach

TECHNIQUES OF POLITICAL ANALYSIS
Lyman Tower Sargent and Thomas A. Zant

PUBLIC OPINION, Second Edition
Bernard C. Hennessy

AN INTRODUCTION TO THE STUDY OF PUBLIC POLICY
Charles O. Jones

A LOGIC OF PUBLIC POLICY
L. L. Wade and Robert Curry

POLITICAL LIFE AND SOCIAL CHANGE, Readings
Charles Andrain

SOCIAL PSYCHOLOGY OF POLITICAL LIFE
Samuel A. Kirkpatrick and Lawrence K. Pettit

POLITICAL LIFE AND SOCIAL CHANGE
Charles Andrain

THE PEOPLE, MAYBE
Karl Lamb

ANALYZING AMERICAN POLITICS
Walter A. Rosenbaum, John W. Spanier and William C. Burris

THE BLACK POLITICIAN
Mervyn M. Dymally

CAMPAIGN FINANCE IN AMERICA
David W. Adamany

SOCIAL AND POLITICAL INQUIRY
J. D. May and Karl J. Bemesderfer

POLITICAL IMAGES AND REALITIES
Donald Reich and Paul Dawson

SAVING APPEARANCES
Henry S. Kariel

The Social Psychology
of Political Life

Edited by

Samuel A. Kirkpatrick
University of Oklahoma

Lawrence K. Pettit
Montana State University

Duxbury Press

Belmont, California
North Scituate, Massachusetts

Duxbury Press
A division of Wadsworth Publishing Company, Inc.

L. C. Catalog Card No.: 72-83678
ISBN 0-87872-038-3
Printed in the United States of America
1 2 3 4 5 6 7 8 9 10 — 76 75 74 73 72

Contents

Preface

During the past decade social scientists have witnessed a rapid substantive, theoretical and methodological expansion of our knowledge in the general area of social psychology and politics. Research trends in political science have emphasized an explanation of political life in terms of interdisciplinary concepts which are both sociological and psychological in nature. Yet the availability of research findings organized around these concepts has remained limited. It is our goal to present a body of these major findings about political life within an integrated explanatory framework borrowing heavily from social psychology.

Although this is a book about political attitudes and behavior, it does not focus narrowly on any one explanatory factor. Attention is paid to sociological and cultural factors as well as to personality attributes. It is not limited to political socialization and personality; rather, it is comprehensive in its treatment of both structural and psychological components of political life. Our focus on the individual interacting with others and with his environment in the context of a social-psychological model will hopefully contribute some order to the chaos of unorganized substantive findings in the area of political attitudes and behavior.

In attempting a departure from the more usual explanatory categories we have relied on the constructive comments of a variety of colleagues who have influenced the organization of the book and our introductory essays: particularly Harmon Zeigler, Roberta Sigel, C. Michael Lanphier, Bernard Hennessy, Charles Andrain and John Soule. We are also grateful to Larry Hill for composing an essay especially for this volume, and to Paul Dawson and Fred Grupp for permitting us to consider the publication of their research findings prior to their acceptance in professional journals.

We are also indebted to our students who provided comments as we experimented with the organization of the book, and we are especially grateful to those who played a direct role in that process and in the editorial chores necessary for such an anthology: Mary Ann Armour, James Bromeland, Gary Cathey, Mel Jones and Larry Edwards. The capacities of secretaries are acknowledged not only in regard to typing skills, but in their useful assistance in the permission process: Eva Gunter, Vickie Craig and Cheryl Flury have endured both.

As many other authors have found, the advice and assistance of Robert Gormley at Wadsworth Publishing Company and Duxbury Press has been constant and wise. Finally, our wives, Pam and Shari, have assisted us in editorial tasks, but more important, they have survived another book.

Norman, Oklahoma   SAK
Bozeman, Montana   LKP

1

Social-Psychological
Perspectives in Politics

The primary purpose of this introductory chapter is to set forth a general statement of a social-psychological approach to the study of politics, and to elaborate a model integrating that perspective and the readings to follow. The meaning and utility of this approach is dependent on some common definitions of politics and social psychology. Our contemporary understanding of political life reflects various methods of inquiry into a broad field called "politics." What we know about politics derives essentially from our definition of the term, and our conception of political science and the political system. Definitions of what is political have varied greatly from time to time and place to place. The classic focus, and one still to be found, has been on political values and legal institutions. In contemporary political science there is a concern for individual political behavior and for what has been described as the "authoritative allocation of values" at the social level. The various definitions assumed by political scientists have recently been shaped by broader trends away from the history of political philosophy and toward a concern for political behavior. Approaches to the study of politics, sometimes treated in formalistic terms as paradigms, have included an emphasis on historical explanation, games, formal powers, organisms, processes, inputs and outputs, and many other devices used to organize and assist in our explanations of politics.[1] The concepts political scientists use are therefore shaped by the subject matter or substantive inquiry being pursued. Some paradigms are particularly suited to explanations of individual and group behavior, while

[1] For a review of these approaches see Michael Haas, "The Rise of a Science of Politics," in Michael Haas and Henry S. Kariel, eds., *Approaches to the Study of Political Science* (Scranton: Chandler Publishing Company, 1970), pp. 3–48.

1

others are clearly aimed at achieving a broad and integrative knowledge of political systems as a whole.[2]

Since this is a book about political attitudes and behavior, the research comprising the volume is found primarily at the *micro*-level. This refers to activities and actions by individuals and small collectivities of individuals within a larger political system. When political scientists study *macro* politics they are most concerned with the interaction between and the integration of various social, economic and political systems and the institutions comprising them. Although there is a basic distinction which separates our focus from broader treatments of political systems, this distinction can be misleading. It should be obvious that *both* levels of analysis are necessary for a comprehensive knowledge of political life. For example, a thorough understanding of system-level events and processes, such as international affairs, is necessarily dependent upon theories and knowledge at the micro-level. Furthermore, the meaning of individual behavior cannot be viewed apart from an understanding of the system within which that behavior occurs.

In order to impart an understanding of political life from a micro perspective, we have organized this work around a social-psychological approach. This approach is typified by a focus on individual phenomena, but beyond that focus it is as disparate as social psychology itself, and it is sufficiently general to subsume narrower paradigms and theories under a broad rubric. The collection of research represented in this volume is evidence that such an approach is not unique to our discipline at this point in time. Rather, it is the product of several decades of empirical research aimed at various levels of analysis whether social, cultural or personal, across a variety of social constructs including the group, organization, elite and community.[3]

In concept, our approach cannot be claimed as recent fare: it is deeply rooted in prescientific philosophical inquiries by ancient philosophers such as Aristotle and Plato, and by a variety of 17th- and 18th-century writers on social conduct, such as Hobbes and Behtham. Yet its primary intellectual debt is to the behavioral movement in the social sciences, and, as we speak of politics, to the behavioral tradition in political science. The research discussed here is the result of a mood emphasizing political behavior, systematic empirical research, theory, explanation and description, and interdisciplinary approaches. As political scientists searched for

[2] See John H. Kessel, George F. Cole and Robert Seddig, eds., *Micropolitics: Individual and Group Level Concepts* (New York: Holt, Rinehart and Winston, Inc., 1970), pp. 1–15; and Heinz Eulau, *Micro-Macro Political Analysis: Accents of Inquiry* (Chicago: Aldine Publishing Company, 1969), pp. 1–19.

[3] For a discussion of units and levels of analysis see Heinz Eulau, *The Behavioral Persuasion in Politics* (New York: Random House, Inc., 1963).

similarities, regularities, and explanations of behavior, they became increasingly dependent on research conducted in other social sciences. Both sociology and psychology became important reference points for this endeavor; yet our search for theory and our concern for environmental contexts of individual behavior led to an important reliance on social psychology. It is to this discipline and its components that we now turn.

A Social-Psychological Perspective on Politics

A fundamental concern for human behavior characterizes all the social sciences. Political science is unique, however, in its concern for behavior about political objects. These objects are the events, issues, institutions and actors relevant to the process of making binding decisions for society. They are political insofar as they relate to authoritative activities which prescribe sanctions and produce policies which are viewed as legitimate. Political science uses the ideas and findings of social psychology to understand the nature of the political system and public policy, and, in turn, the relationships between and among political systems. The underlying process of inquiry in both disciplines (as in all social sciences) is directed at man's relationship to man and man's relationship to his environment. But the political scientist is most interested in those interrelationships and those environmental effects which pertain to the means by which political systems make policy which is binding for society. As a consequence, the research findings of social psychology serve as a reference point for understanding attitudes and behavior; yet it is the political scientist's desire to make those findings relevant for the political process. In doing so, we must not only concern ourselves with such conventional activities as voting, but also with the less conventional processes of reaction and protest.

Social psychology is broadly concerned with the social nature of man and the close interconnection between society and the individual. People's relationships to society affect the political system and the behavior within it. Man in isolation from others does not fully develop his biological and psychological capacities. Indeed, man's life space is continually characterized by his attempt to cope with his environment and others within it. It is similarly difficult to view the individual apart from the political system, or, in turn, the political system apart from the individuals that comprise it.

The organizing approach presented throughout this volume attempts to join social and psychological perspectives, but does not assume that either perspective is useless without the other. The sociological side emphasizes social interaction and the development of norms for controlling behavior in any society. On the other hand, the psychological side emphasizes personality, stimuli and responses, habit, perceptions and cognitions. A recent statement of the state of social psychology summarizes this point of view: "Social psychology is coming to be viewed as a general approach to the study of human behavior that rests, on the one hand, on certain basic facts of perception, cognition, motivation, and learning and, on the other hand, on certain basic facts that have to do with the social context which sets boundary conditions for the behavior in the form of expectations of others."[4]

Although the public implications of a social-psychological approach are not always immediately apparent, they are hopefully forthcoming in an age of public policy shaped with social-psychological forces in mind.[5] The policy science approach has long recognized that the political system's leaders and the subsequent policy outputs of the system can only be effective in their goals insofar as these policies are based on an understanding of human behavior and attitudes. It would be naive, for example, to anticipate a set of solutions for the social and political problems of ghetto life without an understanding of those factors shaping the political personality and behavior of ghetto residents—the social, cultural and psychological factors that are so closely related to the attitudinal and behavioral posture assumed by those subjected to and socialized to ghetto life. Furthermore, all political systems have important control functions which are the antithesis of anarchy—the most visible are various forms of public policy, especially laws. Yet social control is not only achieved legally with threats of sanction; rather, there are bounded interrelationships within any system which are responsible for the system's existence, cohesion and integration. There are various agents in any society, such as the family, church, school, peer groups, which are part of a socialization process through which cultural norms are acquired. This acculturation and acquisition is a social-psychological phenomenon.

Psychological and Social Forces: Two Profiles

The ideas presented here will be elaborated and defined more explicitly in a model of attitudes and behavior. But now, concrete examples of individual perspectives may facilitate an understanding of basic concepts.

[4] Harold B. Gerard, "Social Psychology," in David L. Sills, ed., *International Encyclopedia of the Social Sciences,* Vol. 14 (New York: Crowell, Collier & Macmillan, Inc., 1968), p. 460.

[5] For linkages between opinion and policy see Norman R. Luttbeg, ed., *Public Opinion and Public Policy: Models of Political Linkage* (Homewood: The Dorsey Press, 1968).

We suggest two fictitious profiles of individuals whose political attitudes and behavior are shaped by psychological and social forces of the kind investigated by the articles in this volume.

Harry

Harry is a young lawyer on the staff of a corporate law firm in a middle-sized city in the Northeast. Born of middle class parents and reared in a nearby suburb, he graduated with honors from high school, a liberal arts college and law school. His parents were by no means wealthy, and Harry's education was a strain on them financially. Aware of his parents' financial insecurity, rooted in their unpleasant memories of the Depression, Harry valued his educational opportunities and worked diligently to prove himself worthy.

Harry's socialization process was characterized by a moderately permissive family atmosphere, a less than doctrinaire religious training and an open and participatory educational experience in high school. His college experiences reinforced his middle class values and his belief in the Protestant ethic. Aided by a reasonably keen intellect and good learning habits, Harry pursued knowledge and success with vigor. His personality structure is characterized by ego development and self-control mechanisms. Aggressive and mildly obsessive in his behavior, he always managed to stay within socially acceptable limits. As a student of liberal arts, Harry was exposed to diverse cultural patterns reinforced by religious idealism and developed a set of attitudes toward society which were basically humanitarian. He was always sympathetic with the civil rights movement and came to embrace enthusiastically a social welfare philosophy of government. His personality and education contributed to Harry's sense of personal effectiveness and self-confidence, increasing his tolerance for nonconformity.

As a professional, Harry's job requires him to deal with complex social and legal niches as civic leader and protector of legal rights. He belongs to a variety of professional, civic and private clubs, reflecting his community interests and gregarious personality. Thus Harry became adept at handling complex social roles. As a registered Democrat, he usually votes for Democratic candidates, but he often delays his decision on how he is going to vote because of conflicting social pressures from friends and fellow group members who are both Republicans and Democrats.

Harry is able to articulate a philosophy of government which is open-minded yet basically liberal in ideology; his attitudes about politics are highly interrelated. He achieves personal satisfaction from participating in politics, feels efficacious in doing so, and receives psychic rewards from his peers, the community and fellow professionals who expect him to follow the civic-leader norms of his profession. Nevertheless, Harry's views about politics are often mixed, reflecting his transition between classes and his upward occupational mobility which often confuses his views of economic liberalism, since welfare for the poor will pose an increasing economic burden for him.

Joe

Joe is a middle-aged machinist living in a small southern city where he was born and reared. His parents had lower class status during his childhood, but since then have achieved only lower middle class economic status. Joe was raised in a subculture of the South placing high value on social conformity, with well-defined behavioral proscriptions and norms which are widely shared throughout his homogeneous community. The residents of his community had similar religious, ethnic, racial and class characteristics which were predominantly white, Anglo-Saxon, Protestant and lower class. Joe never graduated from high school, and he was rarely exposed to divergent elements in his community or among his peers. The socialization process, shaping his orientation to society and politics, was characterized by an authoritarian family structure, a strict and racially segregated school system, and training in fundamentalist religious doctrines.

Joe's personality is characterized by obsessive traits, hostility, alienation and low tolerance for nonconformity, complemented by ethnocentrism which leads him to fear outsiders who do not share his or his community's social characteristics. Joe projects and externalizes, casting his own conflicts and inadequacies on others. His primary satisfactions from life are emotional and job-centered; yet achievement on the job is mainly directed toward financial rewards and the ability, therefore, to be satisfied at home. Consequently, Joe holds few attitudes about politics except those which are job-related as a function of economic rewards and his need to be liked by others in work groups and in his union. His socialization process and the cultural milieu in which that occurred, plus his inability to make fine distinctions in conceptual categories characterized by broad compartmentalization, have also shaped his attitudes on racial segregation. Both of these small sets of attitudes, however, are held with great intensity.

The remainder of his belief system is ill-defined and lacks system and pattern. Although Joe is a Democrat, his party identification is primarily a reflection of his parents' party identification, the tradition within his community and social pressures on his job. Joe rarely votes, feels that he cannot influence the political process and belongs to no political groups outside his economically oriented union.

The above profiles of both Harry and Joe are illustrative of the forces common to individual behavior. These are not in-depth case studies, and they are obviously characterized by stereotypical extremes. Indeed, we could imagine a variety of combinations of social and psychological forces, resulting in a variety of political orientations and actions. Harry and Joe could be described as influenced by those social forces presented above, yet with different psychological predispositions their attitudes and behavior would be very different. An extreme example emphasizing psychological factors might depict both individuals' socialization as characterized by ambigious cultural norms and weak situational pressures, thereby assigning greater importance to the attributes and processes of individual personality in explaining variance in behavior.

Yet despite the differential impact of social-psychological variables which create two very different individuals in the above examples, the variables are common to both profiles. They are both shaped by cultural factors and social norms somewhat unique to their own subcultures and environments. Their personality characteristics differ, and their social roles and interactions vary. The socialization process is common to the life space of Harry and Joe; yet the impact of various agents of socialization, their characteristics and their consequences vary. As a result, the structure of their belief systems about politics, as it is filtered by the process of political perception tied to personality characteristics and needs, varies in content and organization. Their political motivations are based on common processes that can be applied across a variety of individuals; yet the differential impact of these processes manifests itself in different forms of behavior.

The political systems, in which Harry and Joe are individual entities — the channels of communication, substantive content, and public policy — are influenced by political behavior. This behavior, in turn, is shaped by values, beliefs and attitudes over a set of life experiences characterizing the individual's socialization process and one's perception of objects in the political world. The nature of that perception and the structure and content of one's belief system is in turn shaped by personality, relative position in various social structures, the meaning assigned to that context and by broader cultural norms developed over time in any society or segment of society. In summary, Harry and Joe are influenced by common variables; yet the products are quite different. The meaning of these variables is explored in greater detail immediately below and throughout the book.

A Model of Political Attitudes and Behavior

We have mentioned the linkages between social psychology and political science and the general components of a social-psychological approach to politics; yet those components have not been elaborated in any detail.

Our primary focus is on the explanation of political attitudes and behavior, and the processes and stimuli suggested by a perspective useful for that understanding. A concern for attitudes and behavior pervades the research reported throughout this volume. While there are no separate chapters on political behavior, it is an important dependent variable for most of that research. Our preferred approach is based on two fundamental and interrelated concepts: *field theory* and a *stimulus-organism-response paradigm.*

In general, the field component views the individual within a larger set of social and cultural forces. It represents the interaction between the individual (and implicitly, his biological and hereditary characteristics) and his environment.[6] The context of one's behavior and attitudes toward politics and political objects is within a larger environmental field of forces which the individual perceives, orders and evaluates in order to cope with the occurrences of everyday life. The process of political socialization is the means by which the individual learns about this larger field, gives it meaning, and attempts to control it. Whereas traditional political science was concerned with the formal and legal aspects of political decision making, a field approach explicitly considers a host of informal influences surrounding each individual and political actor. Political behavior is explained, therefore, by a set of interdependent environmental and personal characteristics.

More specifically, the individual as an organism (O) with basic psychological and personality traits is influenced by a stimulus environment (S) which in turn produces a behavioral response (R). The S-O-R paradigm focuses on the perceptions and meaning attributed to stimuli, subsequent behavior, and its meaning. This pattern occurs within an interactional framework where the "self" and the "other" are both important. The following model is dependent upon, and this volume is organized around, this set of concepts.

Political Personality

We begin at the individual level with an emphasis on personality characteristics. Conceptually, this includes a broad set of needs, drives, ego-defense mechanisms and resultant personality types. On the most general level, personality is the sum-total of behavior patterns as they are shaped by heredity and environment. Personality develops through the interaction of a set of elements into which behavior patterns are organized: abilities (such as intelligence), temperament (ego strength) and ergic ten-

[6] See J. Milton Yinger, *Toward a Field Theory of Behavior* (New York: McGraw-Hill Book Company, Inc., 1965).

sions (motivational traits such as assertiveness and curosity).[7] These elements are integrated with physical characteristics to constitute an open system of psycho-physical relationships which are in turn shaped by environmental forces.

The environment in which the individual exists is particularly important for subsequent expressions of behavior. This environment does not simply act as a multiple force on the individual; rather, there is a constant flow of interrelationships from the environment to the individual, and from the individual to the environment via his behavior. This behavior is a vital link since the different qualities of personality must be inferred through observable phenomena. The research reported in Chapter 2 focuses on these personality attributes and manifestations of them, such as misanthropy, cynicism, alienation and authoritarianism, as they relate to politics.

Social Forces

One set of primary environmental stimuli which influences the organism and its personality, and interacts with it to shape attitudes and behavior, is basically social. Yet our primary interest in these social stimuli is from a social-psychological perspective. Usual sociological variables such as race, religion, ethnicity, class and status are important influential factors for behavior; yet the primary meaning is within an interactional focus. While social structure is itself important, the meaning given to it by the individual, his role within various structures, his interaction with others and the subsequent conflicts, strains and pressures are of vital importance. The individual is exposed to, and is a part of, many groups — whether formal or informal. Some of these groups are common to a great number of people (family and school), while others are job related (work groups, unions, professional organizations) or the result of conscious choices in a political climate (political clubs and organizations).

The individual's role in these complex group structures is shaped by his perception of his own expectations and those expectations of others. Whether he is an interested citizen, a political actor, or a political leader, his political life is shaped by the interpersonal relations within a set of groups and within a complex set of social structures and institutions. These groups and structures are closely tied to personality needs fulfilled by group membership, for instance, the need for belonging and social

[7] Raymond Cattell, "Cultural and Political-Economic Psychology," in Cattell, ed., *Handbook of Multivariate Experimental Psychology* (Chicago: Rand McNally, 1966), pp. 769–89. Also see Ralph W. Dreger, *Fundamentals of Personality* (London: Routedge and Kegan Paul, 1962), p. 21.

adjustment and the providing of life perspective to the individual. The characteristics of others in the group, the cohesion of the group, its purpose and its leaders not only influence the individual's decision to join or remain in a group, but they influence larger decisions which relate to political objects (candidates, parties). Furthermore, under the influence of social conflict, inconsistencies in status, class mobility and cross pressures, the individual will react to politics in predictable ways. The role of interaction, structure and conflict is the primary theme of Chapter 3.

Culture and the Individual

To this point we have progressed from a primary focus on the individual level (Chapter 2) to a concern for the individual within specific groups and social structures (Chapter 3). We now turn to the individual within a larger collectivity that we call *culture*. This collectivity represents sets of social values, customs, myths, mores, traditions, and learned beliefs which are shared by members of society or by subgroups (subcultures) of societies. In this larger set of collective relationships cultural norms are developed through individual roles and expectations which define the limits of behavior and the nature of social and political values within a culture. These learned cultural proscriptions and prescriptions shape the more specific attitudes and behavior that individuals exhibit toward political objects. The characteristics of a culture are shaped by its traditions, individual expectations and the degree of diversity within that culture. In our earlier examination of Joe's profile it became evident that the political and social traditions of a particular subculture, the expectations that one has of others and of the system and the homogeneity of the subculture, are all important factors influencing one's behavior. When we speak of political culture we refer more specifically to the boundaried set of values which are politically relevant (for instance, for political leadership, decision making, conflict). The interaction between these larger sets of values and the individual produces a variety of perspectives toward politics and one's role and behavior within the political system. These cultural factors, for example, influence the level of salience of politics for the individual and even the broader political authority relationships within a society.

Socialization and Perception

Within the field theory framework, individual personality characteristics and psychological factors interact with and are shaped by, sets of environmental stimuli, both social and cultural. Political belief systems are shaped by these factors as the individual relates to various political objects in the environment. These social, cultural and political stimuli are filtered by personality attributes and, more specifically, by the processes of political socialization and political perception. For political objects to have meaning, they must be learned and perceived. The process of socialization, or the learning of political values, is influenced by the individual personality, and together they enable the assimilation of broader cultural stimuli. The individual lives within a complex set of social roles which are represented by various agents of the socialization process. The agents are often the family, church, school and peer groups within which the individual learns social values which shape his political predispositions and behavior. For him to acquire sets of political attitudes and behavior, relevant political object-specific stimuli must be perceived. These are objects that are part of the political system and therefore part of the value-allocation process, for instance, political parties and candidates, decisions (issues), political groups, events, political institutions and authoritative decision makers. Each individual has a perceptual screen that filters environmental stimuli and permits their assimilation and the attribution of meaning by the individual. Physical and psychological factors limit this degree of assimilation and the accuracy of perception. When we spoke of Joe's ethnocentric characteristics, we fashioned him with perceptual blinders. His personality, his role within social structures, the subculture characteristics of his environment and his socialization shaped his perceptual screen such that those outside his immediate environment were incorrectly perceived. These factors enable any individual to perceive selectively certain political objects and events, and subsequently retain and assimilate only a portion of them. These perceptual factors and the socialization process are the basic foci for Chapters 5 and 6.

An important dependent variable in much contemporary research in political science is the *political opinion* of individuals and collectivities of individuals. We have emphasized previously that these opinions, as well as political behavior, are treated throughout the research reported in this volume. Many political scientists have been interested in the basic properties of public opinion, as well as its relationship to public policy. These properties are generally threefold:[8] (1) *direction* — the feeling that the individual has toward political objects, that is, whether he approves or disapproves of particular public policies, whether he is liberal or conservative in his evaluation of political issues, whether he favors the Republican or Democratic candidate; (2) *intensity* — the degree of feeling toward political objects, that is, how strongly one approves/disapproves of policy, how firmly liberal or conservative opinions are held; and (3) *stability* — longitudinal shifts in direction and intensity, or the extent to which one's evaluation of political objects and the intensity of that evaluation remain the same over time.

[8] For an elaboration see Robert E. Lane and David O. Sears, *Public Opinion* (Englewood Cliffs: Prentice-Hall, Inc., 1964), pp. 5ff.

Each of these properties is an important variable in political research; yet a social-psychological approach is more comprehensive. It argues for a consideration of political belief systems as a complex entity for study; a system directed at political objects that is the product of the processes of political socialization and perception in interaction with the personality and environmental social and cultural stimuli. Although we may still speak of a belief system's aggregate direction, intensity or stability, the notion of an integrated set of beliefs occurring together in less than random fashion raises questions which are more unique to a social-psychological approach. These are basically questions of the function, structure, and conflict of belief systems.

Although the idea of "belief systems" has become popular in political behavior research, a social-psychological definition entails more than just beliefs. For us, the system is an interrelated set of opinions toward political objects; these opinions reflect more generalized attitudes, yet they are sharpened, focused and directed at specific political objects. Both attitudes and opinions can be further decomposed into cognitive and affective components. The cognitive dimension primarily refers to knowledge, intellect, perceptions of fact, and what is commonly called *beliefs*. On the other hand, the affective component is a value-laden and emotionally-oriented preference or statement of good/bad, likes/dislikes that are commonly called *feelings*.

These components are themselves complex and their interrelationships shape attitudes, which are in turn complexly woven into a system of attitudes or opinions (popularly, a "belief system"). A social-psychological approach recognizes this complexity and attempts to treat (1) the functions or needs that are served by a particular system, especially its relationship to personality; (2) the structure of that system and the extent to which it is integrated, cohesive or constrained; and (3) the conflict between components of attitudes and between attitudes themselves within a total system. The functions, the nature of the structure and the characteristics of conflict, each have implications for direction, intensity and stability, as well as for resultant behavior. Furthermore, considerations of conflict, inconsistency and dissonance are closely tied to explanations of attitude change, as are the functions which that change performs for the individual. These characteristics of belief systems are explored in Chapters 7 and 8.

Political Motivation

A social-psychological perspective assumes a close interrelationship between opinions and behavior; yet that interrelationship is dependent upon a necessary degree of motivation for behavior. Every opinion about political objects is not necessarily followed by behavior, and if behavior does follow, there are instances in which it may not be consistent with opinions. The existence of this behavior and its consistency with the belief system is dependent on the individual's motivation for behavior.

In a general sense, this threshold of motivation for behavior is dependent on the same stimuli that shape attitudes and opinions. Social and cultural stimuli, personality attributes, political socialization, the nature of political perception and the characteristics of one's belief system all influence this process of translation into behavior. Particular subcultures may accept opinions (such as racial bigotry), yet cultural norms for behavior may inhibit the translation into overt action (such as efforts at racial segregation). That is, cultural norms may vary for opinions and behavior. One's role in the social structure or within particular groups may necessitate behavior in the presence of others that is inconsistent with held opinions. Sometimes the rewards for behavior may be economic as they reflect social status. But personality attributes play an important role in this motivation process. Although actual inducements from the social and economic sphere may indeed be real, they are often based on more fundamental needs (such as social adjustment, or power) tied to personality and anticipated satisfaction derived from overt behavior. As "filters" for these stimuli, the political socialization and perception processes aid in the development of predispositions to act.

The impact of these factors on behavior, however, is mediated by the *belief system*. The structure of that system, the needs fulfilled by it, the conflicts within it and the level of intensity immediately shape one's motivation to act. If the structure is highly integrated and constrained, and if the needs fulfilled are those which require externalization and projection onto others or onto the political system, overt action is likely to result. If there is conflict within the belief system, behavior may follow from and be consistent with only an intensely held subset of that system.

Furthermore, attitudinal conflict may best be resolved through overt action. This action or inaction is dependent upon psychological factors and mechanisms available to the individual which, therefore, justify no action or a particular set of actions, such as, rationalization or avoidance. The level of motivation, of course, varies by types of behavior, for instance, it appears easier to cross the motivational threshold through the act of voting than through the act of running for political office. Some of these influencing factors directed at several political objects are treated in Chapter 9.

Each of the factors present in a model of political opinions and behavior are summarized in Fig. 1. The model depicts the role of social and cultural (environmental) stimuli, personality attributes, and the process of political socialization and perception in shaping political belief systems. This sys-

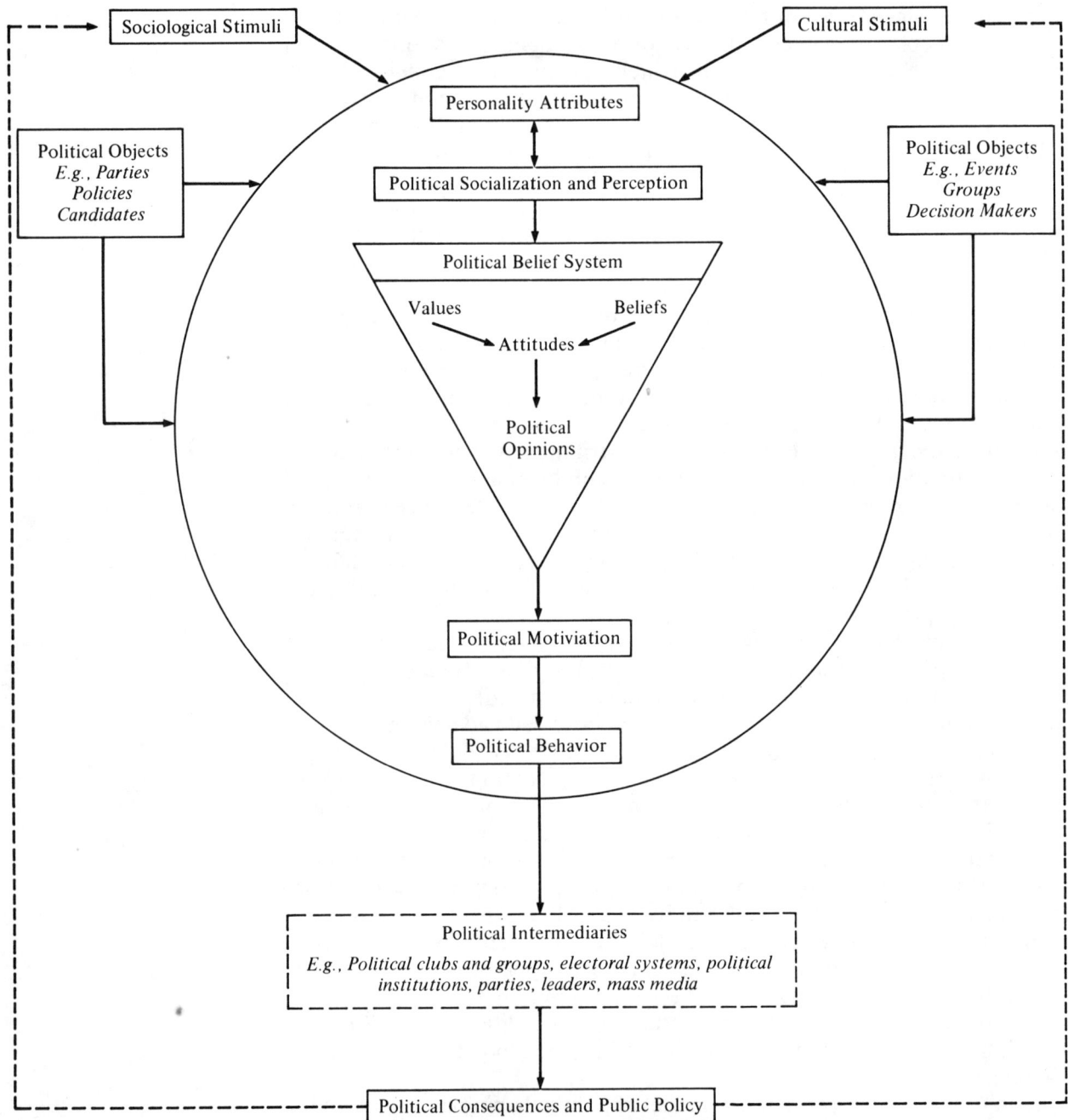

Fig. 1.   A Social-Psychological Model of Political Opinion and Behavior

tem is directed toward political objects which give political opinions their specific focus. The environmental stimuli exist outside the large circle, and, although they may enter the process at various stages, the arrows represent primary points of linkage.

In Fig. 1, subsequent opinion and behavior are placed within the larger context of the political system by recognizing that behavior is mediated by and works through a layer of political structures, groups and leaders which play an influential role in shaping the political consequences of the system and public policy. These policy outputs in turn, become a part of the set of larger environmental stimuli that influence the individual and serve as points of reference for political behavior. The political system, its channels of communication, its substantive content and its public policy are influenced by one's political opinions and behavior closely linked to values, beliefs and attitudes learned over a set of life experiences shaped by perceptions of objects in the political world. The nature of that perception, and the structure and content of one's belief system, is also influenced by the individual's personality, by his relative position in various social structures, by the meaning attributed to them, and by broader cultural norms developed over time in any society.

2

Personality Attributes

"Personality" is one of those residual terms for which precision of definition is impossible, but which is pregnant with connotations suggestive of a person's habits, appearance, style, beliefs and preferences. Psychologists have not developed a consensus on a definition of the term, and few political scientists have been willing to devote time to defining the total concept. Nevertheless, the possible nexus between personality attributes and political beliefs and behavior has intrigued a number of scholars in the United States at least since the 1930's. For the most part, political scientists have homogenized a variety of psychological perspectives—Freud's psychoanalytic theory, Maslow's intrinsic needs approach, and the work of several cognitive theorists—in an effort to identify personality traits that might have political consequences.[1]

Of compelling interest has been the question of the relationship between personality disorders and social and political maladies. Does personality help to explain why some persons are more susceptible to extremist overtures in both religion and politics? Are Nazis and Communists similar or disimilar in their personality characteristics? How do feelings of prejudice and intolerance relate to overt political activity? Are the highly nationalistic beliefs and behavior of the "superpatriot" compensatory actions motivated by identifiable personality deprivations? To what extent is one's sexuality related to postures of tolerance/intolerance or assertiveness/submissiveness in politics?

[1] For a review see Fred I. Greenstein, *Personality and Politics* (Chicago: Markham Publishing Company, 1969), Chapter 1.

Belief and Attitude Functions

One approach in relating attitudes to personality has involved an assessment of what *functions* certain beliefs and attitudes perform for the personality. Put another way, the question is, What personality needs are fulfilled by such attitudes as intolerance, prejudice or hostility? M. Brewster Smith discusses categories of needs which can be satisfied in part by the formation and perpetuation of certain beliefs and attitudes. We might group these needs into three categories as follows: (1) meaning, (2) self-anchoring, and (3) ego defense.

Personality Types

While the larger term remains only vaguely defined, considerable work has been done by social scientists on the measurement of personality *types*. For example, such *attributes* as misanthropy, cynicism, and "tough-mindedness" have been used by researchers in efforts to relate personality to political beliefs and behavior. Clusters of attributes which seem to coexist help to identify personality types. For example, what has been called "the authoritarian personality" is one that exhibits such attributes as unnecessarily perceiving threats in his environment, having "ego-alien impulses" (socially forbidden urges that he refuses to acknowledge or projects onto others), being generally misanthropic, being hostile toward and suspicious of those unlike himself, and preferring hierarchy and order, where "everything is in its place." The authoritarian is prejudiced, intolerant of human weakness, and generally conservative in his political and economic beliefs.[2]

Another classification of personality types which ensues from Freudian psychology is the anal/oral distinction. Over thirty years ago Harold Lasswell suggested that in politics the *anal* type (compulsive, relating to others only through rules and regulations, rigid and methodical) is likely to be an *administrator,* and that the *oral* type (expansive, outgoing, seeking immediate gratification and the approbation of others) is likely to be an *agitator.* In Lasswell's scheme the politician's life is focused on the pursuit of power, and there is a static group of values which are pursued more or less fervently by all persons, with personality types being revealed on the basis of which value (wealth, power, well-being, rectitude, etc.) is emphasized more than the others.

Lasswell's *Psychopathology and Politics, The Authoritarian Personality*

[2] For a review of this extensive literature see John P. Kirscht and Ronald C. Dillehay, *Dimensions of Authoritarianism: A Review of Research and Theory* (Lexington: University of Kentucky Press, 1967).

by T. W. Adorno and others, and Herbert McClosky's "Conservatism and Personality"[3] — all alluded to several times by the authors represented in this anthology — are three of the classics in the study of personality and politics. McClosky devised a scale to measure Burkean, philosophical conservatism, and then related respondents' scores on the conservatism scale to their scores on scales which measured clinical and nonclinical personality attributes. He found conservatives to be more hostile, suspicious and paranoid, and less intellectual and intelligent than nonconservatives. Not surprisingly, the McClosky study engendered some controversy.

Personality and Environment

By now it is a commonplace that multivariate explanations are necessary in the social sciences, and that, correspondingly, personality and social environment seldom act independently of one another in affecting political attitudes and behavior. Greenstein, in his selection below, makes the point that "environmental stimuli are mediated through the individual's psychological predispositions," but that one's psychological predispositions are to a large extent environmentally determined. Of course, this does not obviate the need to study either personality or social environment as causes of political style, but emphasizes the requirement of understanding each within the context of the other. Lasswell underlines the utility of the developmental approach,[4] in which the "ruling characteristic" on one's personality is seen as deriving from the "critical experiences in the antecedent life of the individual which dispose him to set up a certain mode of dealing with the world." The joint effect of environment and personality is acknowledged also by St. Angelo and Dyson in their study, reported below, which found that the effect of personality on political belief was modified by environmental conditions — namely, subcultural differences associated with race and status.

The selections that follow provide several good examples of how personality attributes are first ascertained and then related to political beliefs and behavior.

Ego control. St. Angelo and Dyson employ as a personality attribute the tendency to overcontrol or undercontrol one's ego, and relate this characteristic to political efficacy and political attitudes. The overcon-

[3](Chicago: University of Chicago Press, 1930); (New York: Harper and Row, 1950); *American Political Science Review* 52 (1958): 27–45.

[4]See Harold D. Lasswell, "A Note on 'Types' of Political Personality: Nuclear, Co-Relational, Developmental," *Journal of Social Issues* 24 (1968): 89–91.

trollers in their study (roughly similar to Lasswell's anal type) are more likely to be rural, and of lower education and income. Undercontrollers (roughly similar to Lasswell's oral type) are conversely urban, of higher education and higher income. The overcontrolled scored lower in political efficacy and more conservative on the policy indices.

Alienation. Aberbach's study of alienation and political behavior is an attempt to systemitize the discussion of *alienation* as a concept and a personality attribute. "Alienation" has become a popular term in the current setting of student and black protests, and growing disaffection between citizens and the dominant features of the political system. As with so many social science concepts which suddenly enter the popular lexicon, popular usage has nearly drained the term "alienation" of any particular meaning. It is used to imply whatever vague notions anyone wants to impute to it at any given time.

The most fundamental point that has to be made with respect to alienation is that it is a *psychological* concept, denoting a feeling of estrangement from something on the part of an individual. This distinguishes contemporary social science usage of the term from the way it has been used by Marx, Fromm and others. Note, secondly, that Aberbach refers to various "forms" — or what we might call "dimensions" — of alienation in order to consider the question, "Do various forms of alienation lead to different types of behavior?" The forms used by Aberbach are "trust" and "efficacy." The measure of political behavior which the author employs is the respondent's vote in the 1964 presidential election.

As a group the selections below provide the reader a succinct introduction to typical conceptualization and measurement in the study of personality and politics.

Selected Additional Readings

Adorno, T. W., et al. *The Authoritarian Personality.* New York: John Wiley & Sons, Inc., 1964.

Agger, Robert E., Marshall Goldstein and Stanley Pearl. "Political Cynicism: Measurement and Meaning." *Journal of Politics* 23 (1961): 477–506.

Barber, James D. *The Lawmakers.* New Haven: Yale University Press, 1965.

Davies, James O. *Human Nature in Politics.* New York: John Wiley & Sons, Inc., 1963.

DiRenzo, Gordon J. "Professional Politicians and Personality Structures." *American Journal of Sociology* 73 (1967): 217–25.

DiRenzo, Gordon J. *Personality, Power and Politics: A Social-Psychological Analysis of the Italian Deputy and His Parliamentary System.* Notre Dame: University of Notre Dame Press, 1967.

Dittner, Lowell. "The German NPD: A Psycho-Sociological Analysis of Neo-Naziism." *Comparative Politics* 2 (1969): 79–111.

Edinger, Lewis. *Kurt Schumacher: A Study in Personality and Political Behavior.* Stanford: Stanford University Press, 1965.

Eysenck, H. J. "The Psychology of Politics and the Personality Similarities Between Fascists and Communists." *Psychological Bulletin* 59 (1956): 431–38.

Farris, Charles D. "Selected Attitudes on Foreign Affairs as Correlates of Authoritarianism and Political Anomie." *Journal of Politics* 22 (1960): 50–67.

Finifter, Ada W. "Dimensions of Political Alienation." *American Political Science Review* 64 (1970): 389–410.

George, Alexander L., and Juliette L. *Woodrow Wilson and Colonel House: A Personality Study.* New York: John Day, 1956.

Greenstein, Fred I. *Personality and Politics*. Chicago: Markham Publishing Company, 1969.

Horton, John, and Wayne Thompson. "Powerlessness and Political Negativism: A Study of Defeated Local Referendums." *American Journal of Sociology* 68 (1962): 485–93.

Kirscht, John P., and Ronald C. Dillehay. *Dimensions of Authoritarianism: A Review of Research and Theory*. Lexington: University of Kentucky Press, 1967.

Lane, Robert E. *Political Thinking and Consciousness*. Chicago: Markham Publishing Company, 1969.

Lasswell, Harold D. *Psychopathology and Politics*. New York: Viking Press, 1960.

Lasswell, Harold D. *Power and Personality*. New York: Viking Press, 1962.

Lipset, Seymour M. "Democracy and Working Class Authoritarianism." *American Sociological Review* 24 (1959): 482–502.

Litt, Edgar. "Political Cynicism and Political Futility." *Journal of Politics* 25 (1963): 312–23.

McClosky, Herbert. "Conservatism and Personality." *American Political Science Review* 52 (1958): 27–45.

McClosky, Herbert, and John H. Schaar. "Psychological Dimensions of Anomy." *American Sociological Review* 30 (1965): 14–40.

McDill, Edward L., and Jeanne C. Ridley. "Status, Anomie, Political Alienation and Political Participation." *American Journal of Sociology* 68 (1962): 205–13.

Milbrath, Lester W., and Walter W. Klein. "Personality Correlates of Political Participation." *Acta Sociologica* 6 (1962): 53–66.

Muller, Edward N. "Cross-National Dimensions of Political Competence." *American Political Science Review* 64 (1970): 792–809.

Rogow, Arnold. *James Forrestal: A Study of Personality, Politics and Policy*. New York: Macmillan, 1963.

Rogow, Arnold A., ed. *Politics, Personality, and Social Science in the Twentieth Century*. Chicago: University of Chicago Press, 1969.

Rokeach, Milton. *The Open and Closed Mind*. New York: Basic Books, 1960.

Rosenberg, Morris. "Misanthropy and Political Ideology." *American Sociological Review* 21 (1956): 690–95.

Rosenberg, Morris. "Misanthropy and Attitudes Toward International Affairs." *Journal of Conflict Resolution* 1 (1957): 340–45.

Rosenberg, Morris. "Self-Esteem and Concern with Public Affairs." *Public Opinion Quarterly* 26 (1962): 201–11.

Rutherford, Brent M. "Psychopathology, Decision-Making and Political Involvement." *Journal of Conflict Resolution* 10 (1966): 387–408.

Schoenberger, Robert A. "Conservatism, Personality and Political Extremism." *American Political Science Review* 62 (1968): 868–78.

Seeman, Melvin. "Alienation, Membership and Political Knowledge: A Comparative Study." *Public Opinion Quarterly* 30 (1966): 353–68.

Templeton, Frederic. "Alienation and Political Participation: Some Research Findings." *Public Opinion Quarterly* 30 (1966): 249–62.

Wolfenstein, E. Victor. *Personality and Politics*. Belmont, Calif.: Dickenson Publishing Company, 1969.

The Impact of Personality on Politics:

An Attempt to Clear Away Underbrush

Fred I. Greenstein

There is a great deal of political activity which can be explained adequately only by taking account of the

Fred I. Greenstein, "The Impact of Personality on Politics: An Attempt to Clear Away Underbrush," *American Political Science Review* 61 (1967): 629–41. Reprinted with permission.

personal characteristics of the actors involved. The more intimate the vantage, the more detailed the perspective, the greater the likelihood that political actors will loom as full-blown individuals influenced by all of the peculiar strengths and weaknesses to which the species *homo sapiens* is subject, in addition to being role-players, creatures of situation, members of a culture, and possessors of social characteristics such as occupation, class, sex, and age.

To a non-social scientist the observation that individuals are important in politics would seem trite. Undergraduates, until they have been trained to think in terms of impersonal categories of explanation, readily make assertions about the psychology of political actors in their explanations of politics. So do journalists. Why is it that most political scientists are reluctant to deal explicitly with psychological matters (apart from using a variety of rather impersonal psychological constructs such as "party identification," "sense of political efficacy," and the like)? Why is political psychology not a systematically developed subdivision of political science, occupying the skill and energy of a substantial number of scholars?

A partial answer can be found in the formidably tangled and controversial status of the existing scholarly literature on the topic. I am referring to the disparate research that is commonly grouped under the heading "personality and politics": e.g., psychological biographies; questionnaire studies of "authoritarianism," "dogmatism," or "misanthropy"; discussions of "national character"; and attempts to explain international "tensions" by reference to individual insecurities. The interpretations made in psychological biographies often have seemed arbitrary and "subjective"; questionnaire studies have encountered formidable methodological difficulties; attempts to explain large-scale social processes in personality terms have been open to criticism on grounds of "reductionism." And beyond the specific shortcomings of the existing "personality and politics" research, a variety of arguments have been mounted suggesting that there are *inherent* shortcomings in research strategies that attempt to analyze the impact of "personality" on politics. It is not surprising that most political scientists choose to ignore this seeming mare's nest.

If progress is to be made toward developing a more systematic and solidly grounded body of knowledge about personality and politics, there will have to be considerable clarification of standards of evidence and inference in this area.[1] My present remarks are merely a prolegomenon to methodological clarification of "personality and politics" research. It will not be worthwhile to invest in explicating this gnarled literature with a view to laying out standards unless there is a basis for believing that the research itself is promising. Therefore I shall attempt to clear away what seem to be the main reason for arguing that there are inherent objections—objections in principle—to the study of personality and politics.

Clearing away the formal objections to this *genre* can serve to liberate energy and channel debate into inquiry. More important, several of the objections may be rephrased in ways that are substantively interesting—ways that move us from the vague question "Does personality have an important impact on politics?" to conditional questions about the circumstances under which diverse psychological factors have varying political consequences. As will be evident, the several objections are based on a number of different implicit definitions of "personality." This is not surprising, since psychologists have never come close to arriving at a single, agreed-upon meaning of the term.[2]

I. Objections to the Study of Personality and Politics

A bewildering variety of criticisms have been leveled at this heterogeneous literature. The criticism has been so profuse that there is considerable accuracy to the sardonic observation of David Riesman and Nathan Glazer that the field of culture-and-personality research (within which many of the past accounts of personality and politics fall) has "more critics than practitioners."[3]

The more intellectually challenging of the various objections asserting that *in principle* personality and politics research is not promising (even if one avoids the methodological pitfalls) seems to fall under five headings. In each case the objection is one that can be generalized to the study of how personality relates to any social phenomenon. Listed rather elliptically the five objections are that:

1. Personality characteristics tend to be randomly distributed in institutional roles. Personality therefore "cancels out" and can be ignored by analysts of political and other social phenomena.

2. Personality characteristics of individuals are less important than their social characteristics in influencing behavior. This makes it unpromising to concentrate research energies on studying the impact of personality.

3. Personality is not of interest to political and other social analysts, because individual actors (personalities) are severely limited in the impact they can have on events.

4. Personality is not an important determinant of behavior because individuals with varying personal characteristics will tend to behave similarly when placed in common situations. And it is not useful to study personal variation, if the ways in which people vary do not affect their behavior.

5. Finally, there is a class of objections deprecating the relevance of personality to political analysis in which "personality" is equated with particular aspects of individual psychological functioning. We shall be concerned with one of the objections falling under this heading—*viz.*, the assertion that so-called "deep" psychological needs (of the sort that sometimes are summarized by the term "ego-defensive") do not have an important impact on behavior, and that therefore "personality" in this sense of the term need not be studied by the student of politics.

The first two objections seem to be based on fundamental misconceptions. Nevertheless they do point to interesting problems for the student of political psychology. The final three objections are partially well taken. These are the objections that need to be rephrased in conditional form as "Under what circumstances?" questions. Let me now expand upon these assertions.

II. Two Erroneous Objections

The Thesis That Personality "Cancels Out"

The assumption underlying the first objection seems, as Alex Inkeles points out, to be that "in 'real' groups and situations, the accidents of life history and factors other than personality which are responsible for recruitment [into institutional roles] will 'randomize' personality distribution in the major social statuses sufficiently so that taking systematic account of the influence of personality composition is unnecessary." But, as Inkeles easily shows, this assumption is false on two grounds.

First, "even if the personality composition of any group is randomly determined, random assortment would not in fact guarantee the *same* personality composition in the membership of all institutions of a given type. On the contrary, the very fact of randomness implies that the outcome would approximate a normal distribution. Consequently, some of the groups would by chance have a personality composition profoundly different from others, with possibly marked effects on the functioning of the institutions involved." Secondly,

there is no convincing evidence that randomness does consistently describe the assignment of personality types to major social statuses. On the contrary, there is a great deal of evidence to indicate that particular statuses often attract, or recruit preponderantly for, one or another personality characteristic and that fact has a substantial effect on individual adjustment to roles and the general quality of institutional functioning.[4]

The objection turns out therefore to be based on unwarranted empirical assumptions. It proves not to be an obstacle to research, but rather—once it is examined—an opening gambit for identifying a crucial topic of investigation for the political psychologist: How are personality types distributed in social roles and with what consequences?

The Thesis That Social Characteristics Are More Important Than Personality Characteristics

The second objection—asserting that individuals' social characteristics are "more important" than their personality characteristics—seems to result from a conceptual rather than empirical error. It appears to be an objection posing a pseudo-problem that needs to be dissolved conceptually rather than resolved empirically.

Let us consider what the referents are of "social characteristic" and "personality characteristic." By the latter we refer to some inner predisposition of the individual. The term "characteristic" applies to a state of the organism. And, using the familiar paradigm of "stimulus→organism→response," or "environment→ predispositions→response," we operate on the assumption that the environmental stimuli (or "situations") that elicit behavior are mediated through the individual's psychological predispositions.[5]

But we also, of course, presume that the individual's psychological predispositions are themselves to a considerable extent environmentally determined, largely by his prior social experiences. And it is these prior environmental states (which may occur at any stage of the life cycle and which may or may not persist into the present) that we commonly refer to when we speak of "social characteristics." Social "characteristics," then, are not states of the organism, but of its environment. (This is made particularly clear by the common usage "*objective* social characteristics.")

It follows that social and psychological characteristics are in no way mutually exclusive. They do not compete as candidates for explanation of social behavior, but rather are complementary. Social "characteristics" can cause psychological "characteristics"; they are not substitutes for psychological characteristics. The erroneous assumption that social charac-

teristics could even in principle be more important than psychological characteristics probably arises in part from the misleading impression of identity fostered by the usage of "characteristics" in the two expressions.[6]

This confusion also very probably is contributed to by the standard techniques used by social scientists to eliminate spurious correlations, namely, controlling for "third factors" and calculating partial correlations. Control procedures, when used indiscriminately and without reference to the theoretical standing of the variables that are being analyzed, can lead to the failure to recognize what Herbert Hyman, in the heading of an important section of his *Survey Design and Analysis,* describes as "The Distinction Between Developmental Sequences or Configurations and Problems of Spuriousness."[7]

For an example of how this problem arises, we can consider the very interesting research report by Urie Bronfenbrenner entitled "Personality and Participation: The Case of the Vanishing Variable."[8] Bronfenbrenner reports a study in which it was found that measures of personality were associated with participation in community affairs. However, as he notes, "It is a well-established fact that extent of participation varies with social class, with the lower classes participating the least." Therefore, he proceeds to establish the relationship between personality and participation controlling for social class (and certain other factors). The result: "Most of the earlier . . . significant relationships between personality measures and participation now disappear, leaving only two significant correlations, both of them quite low."

One common interpretation of such a finding would be that Bronfenbrenner had shown the irrelevance of personality to participation. But his finding should not be so interpreted. Hyman's remarks, since they place the problem of relating social background data to psychological data in its more general context, are worth quoting at some length.

. . . the concept of spuriousness cannot *logically* be intended to apply to antecedent conditions which are associated with the particular independent variable as part of a developmental sequence. Implicitly, the notion of an uncontrolled factor which was operating so as to produce a spurious finding involves the image of something *extrinsic* to the . . . apparent cause. Developmental sequences, by contrast, involve the image of a series of entities which are *intrinsically* united or substituted for one another. All of them constitute a unity and merely involve different ways of stating the same variable as it changes over time. . . . Consequently, to institute procedures of control is to remove so-to-speak some of the very cause one wishes to study. . . . How shall the analyst know what antecedent conditions are intrinsic parts of a developmental sequence? . . . One guide, for example, can be noted: instances where the "control" factor and the apparent explanation involve *levels of description from two different systems* are likely to be developmental sequences. For instance, an explanatory factor that was a personality trait and a control factor that was biological such as physique or glandular functions can be conceived as levels of description from different systems. Similarly, an explanatory factor that is *psychological* and a control factor that is *sociological* can be conceived as two different levels of description, i.e., one might regard an attitude as derivative of objective position in society as leading to psychological processes such as attitudes. Thus, the concept of spuriousness would not be appropriate.[9]

In the Bronfenbrenner example, then, an individual's "objective" socio-economic background (as opposed to such subjective concomitants as his sense of class consciousness) needs to be analyzed as a possible social determinant of the psychological correlates of participation, taking account of the fact that, as Allport puts it, "background factors never directly cause behavior; they cause attitudes [and other mental sets]" and the latter "in turn determine behavior."[10] A more general lesson for the student of psychology and politics emerges from our examination of the second objection. We can see that investigators in this realm will often find it necessary to lay out schemes of explanation that are developmental—schemes that place social and psychological factors

in the sequence in which they seem to have impinged upon one another.

III. Three Partially Correct Objections

The three remaining objections bear on (a) the question of how much impact individual actors can have on political outcomes, (b) the question of whether the situations political actors find themselves in impose uniform behavior on individuals of varying personal characteristics, making it unprofitable for the political analyst to study variations in the actors' personal characteristics, and (c) the numerous questions that can be raised about the impact on behavior of particular classes of personal characteristics—including the class of characteristics I shall be discussing, the so-called "ego-defensive" personality dispositions. In the remainder of this essay, I shall expand upon each of these three questions, rephrase them in conditional form, and lay out a number of general propositions stating the circumstances under which the objection is or is not likely to hold. As will be evident, the propositions are not hypotheses stated with sufficient precision to be testable. Rather, they are quite general indications of the circumstances under which political analysts are and are not likely to find it desirable to study "personality" in the several senses of the term implicit in the objections.

When Do Individual Actors Affect Events ("Action Dispensability")?

The objection to studies of personality and politics that emphasizes the limited capacity of single actors to shape events does not differ in its essentials from the nineteenth and early twentieth century debates over social determinism—that is, over the role of individual actors (Great Men or otherwise) in history. In statements of this objection emphasis is placed on the need for the times to be ripe in order for the historical actor to make his contribution. Questions are asked such as, "What impact could Napoleon have had on history if he had been born in the Middle Ages?" Possibly because of the parlor game aura of the issues that arise in connection with it, the problem of the impact of individuals on events has not had as much disciplined attention in recent decades as the two remaining issues I shall be dealing with. Nevertheless, at one time or another this question has received the attention of Tolstoy, Carlyle, Spencer, William James, Plekhanov, and Trotsky (in his *History of the Russian Revolution*). The main attempt at a balanced general discussion seems to be Sidney Hook's vigorous, but unsystematic, 1943 essay *The Hero in History*.[11]

Since the degree to which actions are likely to have significant impacts is clearly variable, I would propose to begin clarification by asking: *What are the circumstances under which the actions of single individuals are likely to have a greater or lesser effect on the course of events?* For shorthand purposes this might be called the question of *action dispensability*. We can conceive of arranging the actions performed in the political arena along a continuum, ranging from those which are indispensable for outcomes that concern us through those which are utterly dispensable. And we can make certain general observations about the circumstances which are likely to surround dispensable and indispensable action. In so reconstructing this particular objection to personality explanations of politics we make it clear that what is at stake is not a psychological issue, but rather one bearing on social processes on decision-making. The question is about the impact of action, not about its determinants.

It is difficult to be precise in stipulating circumstances under which an individual's actions are likely to be a link in further events, since a great deal depends upon the interests of the investigator and the specific context of investigation (the kinds of actions being studied; the kinds of effects that are of interest). Therefore, the following three propositions are necessarily quite abstract.

The impact of an individual's actions varies with (1) the degree to which the actions take place in an environment which admits of restructuring, (2) the location of the actor in that environment, and (3) the actor's peculiar strengths or weaknesses.

1. *The likelihood of personal impact increases to the degree that the environment admits of restructuring.* Technically speaking we might describe situations or sequences of events in which modest interventions can produce disproportionately large results as "unstable." They are in a precarious equilibrium. The physical analogies are massive rock formations at the side of a mountain which can be dislodged by the motion of a single keystone, or highly explosive compounds such as nitroglycerine. Instability in this sense is by no means synonymous with what is loosely known as political instability, the phrase we typically employ to refer to a variety of "fluid" phenomena — political systems in which governments rise and fall with some frequency, systems in which violence is common, etc. Many of the situations commonly referred to as unstable do not at all admit of restructuring. In the politics of many of the "unstable" Latin American nations, for example, most conceivable substitutions of actors and actions would lead to little change in outcomes (or at least in "larger" outcomes). Thus, to continue the physical analogy, an avalanche in motion down a mountainside is for the moment in stable equilibrium, since it cannot be influenced by modest interventions.

The situation (or chain of events) which does not admit readily of restructuring usually is one in which a variety of factors conspire to produce the same outcome.[12] Hook, in *The Hero in History*, offers the outbreak of World War I and of the February Revolution as instances of historical sequences which, if not "inevitable," probably could not have been averted by the actions of any single individual. In the first case the vast admixture of multiple conflicting interests and inter-twined alliances and in the second the powerful groundswell of discontent were such as to make us feel that no intervention by an single individual (excluding the more far-fetched hypothetical instances that invariably can be imagined) would have averted the outcome. On the other hand, Hook attempts to show in detail that without the specific actions of Lenin the October Revolution might well not have occurred. By implication he suggests that Lenin was operating in an especially manipulable environment. A similar conclusion might be argued about the manipulability of the political environment of Europe prior to the outbreak of World War II, on the basis of the various accounts at our disposal of the sequence of events that culminated with the invasion of Poland in 1939.[13]

2. *The likelihood of personal impact varies with the actor's location in the environment.* To shape events, an action must be performed not only in an unstable environment, but also by an actor who is strategically placed in that environment. It is, for example, a commonplace that actors in the middle and lower ranks of many bureaucracies are unable to accomplish much singly, since they are restrained or inhibited by other actors. Robert C. Tucker points out what may almost be a limiting case on the other end of the continuum in an essay on the lack of restraint on Russian policy-makers, both under the Czars and since the Revolution. He quotes with approval Nikolai Turgenev's mid-nineteenth century statement that "In all countries ruled by an unlimited power there has always been and is some class, estate, some traditional institutions which in certain instances compel the sovereign to act in a certain way and set limits to his caprice; nothing of the sort exists in Russia."[14] Elsewhere, Tucker points to the tendency in totalitarian states for the political machinery to become "a conduit of the dictatoral psychology"[15]—that is for there to be a relatively unimpeded conversion of whims of the dictator into governmental action as a consequence of his authoritarian control of the bureaucratic apparatus.

3. *The likelihood of personal impact varies with the personal strengths or weaknesses of the actor.* My two previous observations can be recapitulated with an analogy from the poolroom. In the game of pocket billiards the aim of the player is to clear as many balls as possible from the table. The initial distribution of balls parallels my first observation about the manipulability of the environment. With some

arrays a good many shots are possible; perhaps the table can even be cleared. With other arrays no successful shots are likely. The analogy to point two—the strategic location of the actor—is, of course, the location of the cue ball. As a final point, we may note the political actor's peculiar strengths or weaknesses. In the poolroom these are paralleled by the player's skill or lack of skill. The greater the actor's skill, the less his initial need for a favorable position or a manipulable environment, and the greater the likelihood that he will himself subsequently contribute to making his position favorable and his environment manipulable.[16]

The variable of skill is emphasized in Hook's detailed examination of Lenin's contribution to the events leading up to the October Revolution. Hook concludes that Lenin's vigorous, persistent, imaginative participation in that sequence was a necessary (though certainly not sufficient) condition for the outcome. Hook's interest, of course, is in lending precision to the notion of the Great Man. Therefore he is concerned with the individual who, because of especially great talents, is able to alter the course of events. But for our purposes, the Great Failure is equally significant: an actor's capabilities may be relevant to an outcome in a negative as well as a positive sense.

When Does Personal Variability Affect Behavior ("Actor Dispensability")?

Often it may be acknowledged that a particular action of an individual is a crucial node in a process of decision-making, but it may be argued that this action is one that might have been performed by any actor placed in a comparable situation, or by anyone filling a comparable role. If actors with differing personal characteristics perform identically when exposed to common stimuli, we quite clearly can dispense with study of the actors' personal differences, since a variable cannot explain a uniformity. This objection to personality explanations of political behavior—and here "personality" means personal variability—is illustrated by Easton with the example of political party leaders who differ in their personality characteristics and who are "confronted with the existence of powerful groups making demands upon their parties." Their "decisions and actions," he suggests, will tend "to converge."[17]

The task of rephrasing this objection conditionally and advancing propositions about the circumstances under which it obtains is not overly burdensome, since the objection is rarely stated categorically. Exponents of the view that situational pressures eliminate or sharply reduce the effects of personality usually acknowledge that this is not always the case. Similarly, proponents of the view that personality *is* an important determinant of political behavior also often qualify their position and note circumstances that dampen the effects of personal variability. These qualifications point to an obvious reconstruction of the question. *Under what circumstances, we may ask, do different actors (placed in common situations) vary in their behavior and under what circumstances is behavior uniform?* We might call this the question of *actor dispensability*.[18]

The question of under what circumstances the variations in actors' personal characteristics are significant for their behavior has received a good bit of intermittent attention in recent years. The several propositions I shall set forth are assembled, and to some extent reorganized, from a variety of observations made by Herbert Goldhamer, Robert E. Lane, Daniel Levinson, Edward Shils, and Sidney Verba, among others.[19] But before proceeding to lay out these propositions, it will be instructive to consider a possible objection to the notion of actor dispensability.

The circumstances of actor dispensability are those in which, as Shils puts it, "persons of quite different dispositions" are found to "behave in a more or less uniform manner."[20] A personality-oriented social analyst might attempt to deny the premise that behavior *ever* is uniform (and indeed, Shils says "behave in a *more or less* uniform manner.") The objection is, of course, correct in the trivial, definitional sense: every different act is different. The objection is also empirically correct in that, if we inspect actions with sufficient care, we can always detect dif-

ferences between them—even such heavily "situation-determined" actions as "the way in which a man, when crossing a street, dodges the cars which move on it"[21] vary from individual to individual. Nevertheless, the objection—if it is meant to invalidate Shils' assertion—is not well taken, since it denies the principle (necessary for analytic purposes) that we can classify disparate phenomena, treating them as uniform for certain purposes. Furthermore, a significant sociological proposition follows from Shils' point: "To a large extent, large enough indeed to enable great organizations to operate in a quite predictable manner, . . . [different individuals] will conform [i.e., behave uniformly] despite the conflicting urges of their personalities."[22]

Yet the objection leads to an important observation. What we mean by uniform behavior depends upon our principle of classification, which in turn depends upon the purposes of our investigation. If our interests are sufficiently microscopic, we are likely to find variability where others see uniformity. Nor, it should be added, is there anything intrinsically unworthy about being interested in microscopic phenomena—in nuances and "small" variations.

Even if one *is* interested in the macroscopic (major institutions, "important" events), the irrelevance of microscopic variations introduced by actors' personal characteristics cannot be assumed, since action dispensability and actor dispensability are independent of each other. Small actor variations may lead to actions with large consequences. Thus, for example, there might be relatively little room for personal variation in the ways that American Presidents would be likely to respond to the warning system that signals the advent of a missile attack, but the consequences of the President's action are so great that even the slightest variations between one or another incumbent in a comparable situation would be of profound interest.

In noting the conditions under which actors' personal characteristics tend to be dispensable and those under which they tend to be indispensable, we may examine conditions that arise from the *environmental situations* within which actions occur, from the *pre-*

dispositions of the actors themselves, and from the *kinds of acts* (responses) that are performed—that is, from all three elements of the familiar paradigm of E → P → R (or S → O → R). The propositions I shall list under these headings are neither exhaustive nor fully exclusive of each other, but they do serve to pull together and organize crudely most of the diverse observations that have been made on the circumstances that foster the expression of personal variability.

1. *There is greater room for personal variability in the "peripheral" aspects of actions than in their "central" aspects.* Examples of "peripheral" aspects of action include evidences of the personal *style* of an actor (for example, his mannerisms), the *zealousness* of his performance, and the *imagery* that accompanies his behavior at the preparatory and consummatory phases of action (for example, fantasies about alternative courses of action).

By "central" I refer to the gross aspects of the action—for example, the very fact that an individual votes, writes a letter to a Congressman, etc.

Lane suggests that "the idiosyncratic features of personality" are likely to be revealed in the "images" political actors hold "of other participants." There also is "scope for the expressions of personal differences," Lane points out, in "the grounds" one selects "for rationalizing a political act," and in one's style "of personal interaction in a political group."[23]

Shils, after arguing that "persons of quite different dispostions" often "will behave in a more or less uniform manner," then adds: "Naturally not all of them will be equally zealous or enthusiastic. . . ."[24]

Riesman and Glazer point out that although "different kinds of character" can "be used for the same kind of work within an institution," a "price" is paid by "the character types that [fit] badly, as against the release of energy provided by the congruence of character and task."[25]

2. *The more demanding the political act—the more it is not merely a conventionally expected perform-*ance—*the greater the likelihood that it will vary with the personal characteristics of the actor.*

Lane suggests that there is little personal variation in "the more conventional items, such as voting, expressing patriotic opinions and accepting election results as final." On the other hand, his list of actions which "reveal . . . personality" includes "selecting types of political behavior over and above voting":[26] writing public officials, volunteering to work for a political party, seeking nomination for public office, etc.

3. *Variations in personal characteristics are more likely to be exhibited to the degree that behavior is spontaneous—that is, to the degree that it proceeds from personal impulse, without effort or premeditation.*

Goldhamer refers to "a person's . . . casual ruminations while walking along the street, sudden but perhaps transient convictions inspired by some immediate experience, speculations while reading the newspaper or listening to a broadcast, remarks struck off in the course of an argument. . . . If we have any theoretical reason for supposing that a person's opinions are influenced by his personality structure, it is surely in these forms of spontaneous behavior that we should expect to find the evidence of this relationship."[27]

We may now consider two propositions about actor dispensability that relate to the environment in which actions take place.

4. *Ambiguous situations leave room for personal variability to manifest itself.* As Sherif puts it, "the contribution of internal factors increases as the external-stimulus situation becomes more unstructured."[28] (A classically unstructured environmental stimulus, leaving almost infinite room for personal variation in response, is the Rorschach ink blot.)

Budner[29] distinguishes three types of ambiguous situations. Each relates to instances which have been given by various writers of actor dispensability or indispensability. Budner's three types of situations include: (a) a *"completely new situation in which there are no familiar cues."*

Shils comments that in new situations "no framework of action [has been] set for the newcomer by the expectations of those on the scene. A new political party, a newly formed religious sect will thus be more amenable to the expressive behavior of the personalities of those who make them up than an ongoing government or private business office or university department with its traditions of scientific work."[30]

Goldhamer argues that the public opinion process moves from unstructured conditions admitting of great personal variability to more structured conditions that restrain individual differences. Immediate reactions to public events, he argues, reflect personal idiosyncrasies. But gradually the individual is constrained by his awareness that the event has become a matter of public discussion. "There is reason to believe that, as the individual becomes aware of the range and intensity of group preoccupation with the object, his orientation to it becomes less individualized, less intimately bound to an individual perception and judgment of the object. . . . [He] is drawn imperceptibly to view this object anew, no longer now as an individual percipient, but as one who selects (unconsciously, perhaps) an 'appropriate' position in an imagined range of public reactions . . . a limitation is thus placed on the degree to which the full uniqueness of the individual may be expected to influence his perceptions and opinions."[31]

The second type of ambiguity referred to by Budner is (b) *"a complex situation in which there are a great number of cues to take into account."*

Levinson suggests that the availability of "a wide range of . . . socially provided . . . alternatives" increases "the importance of intrapersonal determinants" of political participation. "The greater the number of opportunities for participation, the more the person can choose on the basis of personal congeniality. Or, in more general terms, the greater the richness and complexity of the stimulus field, the more will internal organizing forces determine

individual adaptation. This condition obtains in a relatively unstructured social field, and, as well, in a pluralistic society that provides numerous structured alternatives."[32]

Finally, Budner refers to (c) *"a contradictory situation in which different elements suggest different structures."*

Several of Lane's examples fall under this heading: "Situations where reference groups have politically conflicting points of view. . . . Situations at the focus of conflicting propaganda. . . . Current situations which for an individual are in conflict with previous experience."[33]

5. *The impact of personal differences on behavior is increased to the degree that sanctions are not attached to certain of the alternative possible courses of behavior.*

"The option of refusing to sign a loyalty oath," Levinson comments, "is in a sense 'available' to any member of an institution that requires such an oath, but the sanctions operating are usually so strong that non-signing is an almost 'unavailable' option to many who would otherwise choose it."[34]

The foregoing environmental determinants of actor dispensability suggest several aspects of actors' predispositions which will affect the likelihood that any of the ways in which they differ from each other will manifest themselves in behavior.

6. *The opportunities for personal variation are increased to the degree that political actors lack mental sets which might lead them to structure their perceptions and resolve ambiguities.* The sets they may use to help reduce ambiguity include cognitive capacities (intelligence, information) that provide a basis of organizing perceptions, and pre-conceptions that foster stereotyping.

Verba, in an essay on "Assumptions of Rationality and Non-Rationality in Models of the International System," comments that "the more information an individual has about international affairs, the less likely it is that his behavior will be based upon non-logical influences. In the absence of information about an event, decisions have to be made on the basis of other criteria. A rich informational content, on the other hand, focuses attention on the international event itself. . . ."[35]

Wildavsky, in an account of adversary groups in the Dixon-Yates controversy, points to ways in which the preconceptions of members of factions lead them to respond in predictable fashions that are likely to be quite independent of their personal differences. "The public versus private power issue . . . has been fought out hundreds of times at the city, state, county, and national levels of our politics in the past sixty years. A fifty year old private or public power executive, or a political figure who has become identified with one or another position, may well be able to look back to twenty-five years of personal involvement in this controversy. . . . The participants on each side have long since developed a fairly complete set of attitudes on this issue which have crystallized through years of dispute. . . . They have in reserve a number of prepared responses ready to be activated in the direction indicated by their set of attitudes whenever the occasion demands. . . ."[36]

7. *If the degree to which certain of the alternative courses of action are sanctioned reduces the likelihood that personal characteristics will produce variation in behavior, then any intense dispositions on the part of actors in a contrary direction to the sanctions increase that likelihood.*

"Personality structure . . . will be more determinant of political activity when the impulses and the defenses of the actors are extremely intense"—for example, "when the compulsive elements are powerful and rigid or when the aggressiveness is very strong."[37]

8. *If, however, the disposition that is strong is to take one's cues from others, the effects of personal variation on behavior will be reduced.* Personality may dispose some individuals to adopt uncritically the political views in their environment, but as a result,

Goldhamer comments, the view adopted will "have a somewhat fortuitous character in relation to the personality and be dependent largely on attendant situational factors."[38] (Dispositions toward conformity are, of course, a key variable for students of political psychology. The point here is merely that these dispositions reduce the impact of the individual's other psychological characteristics on his behavior.)

9. *A situational factor working with individual tendencies to adopt the views of others to reduce personal variation is the degree to which the individual is placed in a group context in which "the individual's decision or attitude is visible to others."*[39]

Another predispositional determinant:

10. *The more emotionally involved a person is in politics, the greater the likelihood that his personal characteristics will affect his political behavior.*

Goldhamer comments that "the bearing of personality on political opinion is conditioned and limited by the fact that for large masses of persons the objects of political life are insulated from the deeper concerns of the personality." [But, he adds in a footnote], "this should not be interpreted to mean that personality characteristics are irrelevant to an understanding of the opinions and acts of political personages. In such cases political roles are so central to the entire life organization that a close connection between personality structure and political action is to be expected."[40]

Levinson argues that "[t]he more politics 'matters,' the more likely it is that political behavior will express enduring inner values and dispositions. Conversely, the less salient the issues involved, the more likely is one to respond on the basis of immediate external pressures. When a personally congenial mode of participation is not readily available, and the person cannot create one for himself, he may nominally accept an uncongenial role but without strong commitment or involvement. In this case, however, the person is likely . . . to have a strong potential for change toward a new and psychologically more functional role."[41]

The final proposition has reference to political

roles and does not fit neatly into any of the three elements of the Environment → Predispositions → Response formula.

11. *Personality variations will be more evident to the degree that the individual occupies a position "free from elaborate expectations of fixed content."*[42] Typically these are leadership positions. We have already seen that such positions figure in the conditions of action indispensability; their importance for the student of personality and politics is evident a fortiori when we note that the leader's characteristics also are likely to be reflected in his behavior, thus meeting the requirement of actor indispensability.

The military leader, it has been said, may have an especially great impact. "Even those who view history as fashioned by vast impersonal forces must recognize that in war personality plays a particularly crucial part. Substitute Gates for Washington, and what would have happened to the American cause? Substitute Marlborough or Wellington for Howe or Clinton, and what would have happened? These are perhaps idle questions, but they illustrate the fact that the course of a war can depend as much upon the strengths and failings of a commander-in-chief as upon the interaction of geography and economics and social system."[43]

Under What Circumstances Are Ego-Defensive Needs Likely to Manifest Themselves in Political Behavior?

The final objection to explanations of politics in terms of personality is one in which the term "personality" denotes not the impact of individuals on social processes (action dispensability), or the mere fact of individual variability (actor dispensability), but rather the specific ways in which "personalities" vary. Once we have found it necessary to explain political behavior by referring to the ways in which political actors vary, objections can be made to whatever specific personality variables we choose to employ. (Objections falling into this final category might be summarized under the heading "actor characteristics.")

Some choices of variables are particularly controversial, especially the variables based on "depth" psychology that have so commonly been drawn upon in such works as Lasswell's *Psychopathology and Politics,* Fromm's *Escape from Freedom,* and *The Authoritarian Personality.*[44] It is the deep motivational variables that many commentators have in mind when they argue that "personality" does not have an important impact on politics. It is sometimes said, for example, that such personality factors do not have much bearing on politics, because the psychic forces evident in the pathological behavior of disturbed individuals do not come into play in the daily behavior of normal people. Rephrasing this assertion conditionally, then, we arrive at the question: *Under what circumstances are ego-defensive[45] needs likely to manifest themselves in behavior?* It should be emphasized that my selection of this particular question about actor characteristics carries no implication that "personality" should be conceived of in psychodynamic terms, or that it should be equated with the unconscious, the irrational, and the emotional. It simply is convenient to consider this class of personality characteristics, because psychoanalytic notions have guided so much of the personality and politics literature and have antagonized so many of the literature's critics.

Much of what I have said about actor dispensability also applies to the present question. Wherever the circumstances of political behavior leave room for individuality, the possibility exists for ego-defensive aspects of personality to assert themselves. These circumstances include "unstructured" political situations; settings in which sanctions are weak or conflicting, so that individuals of diverse inclinations are not coerced into acting uniformly; and the various other considerations discussed under the previous heading. These circumstances make it *possible* for ego-defensive personality needs to come to the fore. They do not, of course, make it necessary—or even highly likely—that behavior will have a significant basis in ego defense.

Given the foregoing circumstances, which make ego-defensive behavior possible, what, then, makes it likely (or at least adds to the likelihood) that deeper psychodynamic processes will be at work? We may briefly note these three classes of factors, locating them conveniently in terms of environment, predispositions, and response.

1. *Certain types of environmental stimuli undoubtedly have a greater "resonance" with the deeper layers of the personality than do others.* These are the stimuli which evoke "disproportionately" emotional responses—people seem to be "over-sensitive" to them. They are stimuli which politicians learn to be wary of—for example, such issues as capital punishment, cruelty to animals, and, in recent years, fluoridation of drinking water. Often their stimulus value may be to only a rather small segment of the electorate, but their capacity to arouse fervid response may be such that a Congressman would prefer to confront his constituents on such knotty matters as revision of the tariff affecting the district's principal industry than on, in the phrase of the authors of *Voting,* a "style issue"[46] such as humane slaughtering.

One element in these sensitive issues, Lane and Sears suggest, is that they touch upon "topics dealing with material commonly repressed by individuals. . . . Obvious examples are war or criminal punishment (both dealing with aggresion) and birth control or obscenity legislation (both dealing with sexuality). Socially 'dangerous' topics, such as communism and religion, also draw a host of irrational defensive maneuvers. The social 'dangers' that they represent frequently parallel unconscious intra-psychic 'dangers.' For example, an individual with strong unconscious hatred for all authority may see in Soviet communism a system which threatens intrusion of authoritarian demands into every area of his life. His anti-communism may thus stem more from a residual hatred for his father than for any rational assessment of its likely effects on his life."

Lane and Sears also suggest that, "Opinions dealing with people (such as political candidates) or social groups (such as 'bureaucrats,' 'blue bloods,' or the various ethnic groups) are more likely to invite irrational thought than opinions dealing with most domestic economic issues. Few people can give as clear an account of why they like a man as why they like an economic policy; the 'warm'—'cold' dimension seems crucial in many 'person perception' studies, but the grounds for 'warm' or 'cold' feelings are usually obscure. Studies of ethnic prejudice and social distance reveal the inaccessibility of many such opinions to new evidence; they are often compartmentalized, and usually rationalized; that is, covered by plausible explanation which an impartial student of the opinion is inclined to discount."[47]

2. *The likelihood that ego-defensive needs will affect political behavior also is related to the degree to which actors "have" ego-defensive needs.* This assertion is not quite the truism it appears to be. We still have very little satisfactory evidence of various patterns of psychopathology in society[48] and even less evidence about the degree to which emotional disturbance tends to become channelled into political action.

Although it is not a truism, the proposition *is* excessively general. It needs to be expanded upon and elaborated into a series of more specific hypotheses about types of ego-defensive needs and their corresponding adaptations as they relate to political behavior. For example, one of the more convincing findings of the prejudice studies of a decade ago was an observation made not in the well-known *The Authoritarian Personality* but rather in the somewhat neglected *Anti-Semitism and Emotional Disorder* by Ackerman and Jahoda.[49] Personality disorders which manifested themselves in depressive behavior, it was noted, were not accompanied by anti-semitism. But anti-semitism was likely if the individual's typical means of protecting himself from intrapsychic conflict was extra-punitive—that is, if he was disposed to reduce internal tension by such mechanisms as projection. There is no reason to believe that this hypothesis is relevant only to the restricted sphere of anti-semitism.

3. *Finally, certain types of response undoubtedly provide greater occasion for deep personality needs*

to find outlet than do others—for example, such responses as affirmations of loyalty in connection with the rallying activities of mass movements led by charismatic leaders and the various other types of response deliberately designed to channel affect into politics. Both in politics and in other spheres of life it should be possible to rank the various classes of typical action in terms of the degree to which the participants take it as a norm that affective expression is appropriate.

IV. Summary and Conclusions

My purpose has been to reconsider a topic that too often has been dealt with in a rather off-hand (and sometimes polemical) fashion: "Is personality important as a determinant of political behavior?" Five of the more intellectually challenging assertions about the lack of relevance of "personality" to the endeavors of the student of politics have been considered. Two of these seem to be based on misconceptions, albeit interesting ones. The three additional objections can be rephrased so that they no longer are objections, but rather provide the occasion for advancing propositions about how and under what circumstances "personality" affects political behavior.

In rephrasing these objections we see three of the many ways in which the term "personality" has been used in statements about politics: to refer to the impact of individual political actions, to designate the fact that individual actors vary in their personal characteristics, and to indicate the specific content of individual variation (and, particularly, "deeper," ego-defensive, psychological processes). It therefore becomes clear that the general question "How important is personality?" is not susceptible to a general answer. It must be broken down into the variety of sub-questions implied in it, and these—when pursued—lead not to simple answers but rather to an extensive examination of the terrain of politics in terms of the diverse ways in which "the human element" comes into play.

Notes

[1] In my own efforts to do this I find that much of the existing research can be considered under three broad headings: psychological studies of single political actors, such as political biographies; studies which classify political actors into types, such as the literature on authoritarianism; and aggregative accounts, in which the collective effects of personality are examined in institutional contexts—ranging from small aggregates such as face-to-face groups all the way through national and international political processes. Needless to say, it is one thing to suggest that clarification of such diverse endeavors is possible and another thing actually to make some progress along these lines.

[2] A standard discussion by Allport notes a full fifty *types* of definition of the term (apart from colloquial usages): Gordon Allport, *Personality* (New York: Holt, 1937), 24–54.

[3] David Riesman and Nathan Glazer, "The Lonely Crowd: A Reconsideration in 1960," in Seymour M. Lipset and Leo Lowenthal (eds.), *Culture and Social Character* (New York: The Free Press of Glencoe, 1961), p. 437. For examples of discussions that are in varying degrees critical of personality and politics writings see the essays by Shils and Verba cited in note 17, Reinhard Bendix, "Compliant Behavior and Individual Personality," *American Journal of Sociology* 58 (1952): 292–303, and David Spitz, "Power and Personality: The Appeal to the 'Right Man' in Democratic States," *American Political Science Review* 52 (1958), 84–97.

[4] Alex Inkeles, "Sociology and Psychology," in Sigmund Koch (ed.), *Psychology: A Study of A Science* 6 (New York: McGraw-Hill, 1963): 354.

[5] It is a matter of convenience whether the terms "personality" and "psychological" are treated as synonymous (as in the present passage), or whether the first is defined as some subset of the second (as in my discussion of the fifth objection). Given the diversity of uses to which all of the terms in this area are put, the best one can do is to be clear about one's usage in specific contexts.

[6] My criticism of the second objection would of course not stand in any instance where some acquired inner characteristic (such as a sense of class consciousness) was being defined as a social characteristic, and it was being argued that this "social" characteristic was "more important" than a "personality" characteristic. In terms of my usage this would imply an empirical assertion about the relative influence of two types of psychological, or "personality" variables. My remarks in the text on the meaning of terms are simply short-hand approaches to clarifying the underlying issue. They are not canonical efforts to establish "correct" usage.

[7] Herbert Hyman, *Survey Design and Analysis* (Glencoe, Ill.: The Free Press, 1955), 254–257.

[8] Urie Bronfenbrenner, "Personality and Participation: The Case of the Vanishing Variables," *Journal of Social Issues* 16 (1960): 54–63.

[9] Herbert Hyman, *Survey Design and Analysis* (Glencoe, Ill.: The Free Press, 1955), 254–57. Italics in the original. Also see Hubert Blalock, "Controlling for Background Factors: Spuriousness Versus Developmental Sequences," *Sociological Inquiry* 34 (1964): 28–39, for a discussion of the rather complex implications of this distinction for data analysis.

[10] Gordon Allport, review of *The American Soldier, Journal of Abnormal and Social Psychology* 45 (1950): p. 173. Nothing in this discussion is intended to gainsay the use of controls. "I am not, of course, arguing against the use of breakdowns or matched groups," Allport adds. "They should, however, be used to show where attitudes come from, and not to imply that social causation acts automatically apart from attitudes." Often a control, by suggesting the source of a psychological state, helps explain its dynamics and functions. A good example can be found in Hyman and Sheatsley's well-known critique of *The Authoritarian Personality*. The critique shows that certain attitudes and ways of viewing the world which the authors of *The Authoritarian Personality* explained in terms of a complex process of personal pathology are in fact typical of the thought processes and vocabulary of people of lower socioeconomic status. Hyman and Sheatsley are therefore able to suggest that such attitudes may be a learned part of the respondents' *cognitions* rather than a psychodynamic manifestation serving ego-defensive functions. It should be clear from what I have said in the text, however, that Hyman and Sheatsley's thesis cannot legitimately be phrased as an argument that such attitudes are social (or cultural) rather than psychological: Herbert Hyman and Paul B. Sheatsley, "The Authoritarian Personality—A Methodological Critique," in Richard Christie and Marie Jahoda (eds.), *Studies in the Scope and Method of "The Authoritarian Personality"* (Glencoe: The Free Press, 1954), pp. 50–122.

[11] Sidney Hook, *The Hero in History* (Boston: Beacon Press, 1943).

[12] Compare Wassily Leontief's interesting essay "When Should History be Written Backwards?" *The Economic History Review* 16 (1963): 1–8.

[13] For an account of European politics in the 1930's that is consistent with this assertion see Alan Bullock, *Hitler: A Study in Tyranny* (New York: Harper, rev. ed., 1962). Needless to say, any attempt to seek operational indicators of environments that "admit of restructuring" in order to restate the present proposition in testable form could not take the circular route of simply showing that the environment *had* been manipulated by a single actor.

[14] Robert C. Tucker, *The Soviet Political Mind* (New York: Praeger, 1963), 145–65; quotation from Turgenev at p. 147.

[15] Robert C. Tucker, "The Dictator and Totalitarianism," *World Politics* 17 (1965): 583.

[16] In other words, the skill of the actor may feed back into the environment, contributing to its instability or stability. To the degree that we take environmental conditions as given (i.e., considering them statically at a single point in time), we underestimate the impact of individuals on politics. For examples of political actors shaping their own roles and environments see Hans Gerth and C. Wright Mills, *Character and Social Structure* (London: Routledge and Kegan Paul, 1953), Chapter 14.

[17] David Easton, *The Political System* (New York: Knopf, 1953), p. 196.

[18] Strictly speaking, it is not the actor who is dispensable in this formulation, but rather his personal characteristics. In an earlier draft I referred to "actor substitutability," but the antonym, "non-substitutability," is less successful than "indispensability" as a way of indicating the circumstances under which an explanation of action demands an account of the actor. On the other hand, "substitutability" is a very handy criterion for rough and ready reasoning about the degree to which the contribution of any historical actor is uniquely personal, since one may easily perform the mental exercise of imagining how other available actors would have performed under comparable circumstances.

[19] Robert E. Lane, *Political Life* (Glencoe, Ill.: The Free Press, 1959), pp. 90–100; Edward A. Shils, "Authoritarianism: 'Right' and 'Left'," in Richard Christie and Marie Jahoda, (eds.), *op. cit.*, pp. 24–49; Herbert Goldhamer, "Public Opinion and Personality" *American Journal of Sociology* 55 (1950): 346–354; Daniel J. Levinson, "The Relevance of Personality for Political Participation," *Public Opinion Quarterly* 22 (1958): 3–10; Sidney Verba, "Assumptions of Rationality and Non-Rationality in Models of the International System," *World Politics* 14 (1961): 93–117.

[20] Shils, *op. cit.*, p. 43.

[21] This is a quotation from a well-known passage in Karl Popper's *The Open Society and Its Enemies* (New York: Harper Torchbook edition, 1963), II, p. 97, arguing that sociology is an "autonomous" discipline because psychological evidence is so often of limited relevance—compared with situational evidence—to explanations of behavior. For a critique of Popper's analysis see Richard Lichtman, "Karl Popper's Defense of the Autonomy of Sociology," *Social Research* 32 (1965): 1–25.

[22] Shils, *op. cit.*, p. 44.

[23] Lane, *op. cit.*, p. 100.

[24] Shils, *op. cit.*, p. 43.

[25] Riesman and Glazer, *op. cit.*, pp. 438–39.

[26] Lane, *op. cit.*, p. 100.

[27] Goldhamer, *op. cit.*, p. 349.

[28] Muzafer Sherif, "The Concept of Reference Groups in Human Relations," in Muzafer Sherif and M. O. Wilson (eds.), *Group Relations at the Crossroads* (New York: Harper, 1953), p. 30.

[29] Stanley Budner, "Intolerance of Ambiguity as a Personality Variable," *Journal of Personality* 30 (1960): 30.

[30] Shils, *op. cit.*, 44–45.

[31] Goldhamer, *op. cit.*, 346–47.

[32] Levinson, *op. cit.*, p. 9.

[33] Lane, *op. cit.*, p. 99.

[34] Levinson, *op. cit.*, p. 10.

[35] Verba, *op. cit.*, p. 100. By "non-logical" Verba means influences resulting from ego-defensive personality needs, but his point applies generally to personal variability.

[36] Aaron Wildavsky, "The Analysis of Issue-Contexts in the Study of Decision-Making," *Journal of Politics* 24 (1962): 717–32.

[37] Shils, *op. cit.*, p. 45.

[38] Goldhamer, *op. cit.*, p. 353.

[39] Verba, *op. cit.*, p. 103.

[40] Goldhamer, *op. cit.,* p. 349.

[41] Levinson, *op. cit.,* p. 10.

[42] Shils, *op. cit.,* p. 45. The term "role" is commonly used so as to have both an environmental referent (the prevailing expectations about his duties in a role incumbent's environment) and a predispositional referent (the incumbent's own expectations). For a valuable discussion see Daniel Levinson, "Role, Personality, and Social Structure in the Organizational Setting," *Journal of Abnormal and Social Psychology* 58 (1959): 170–180.

[43] Henry Wilcox, *Portrait of a General* (New York: Knopf, 1964), ix-x.

[44] Harold D. Lasswell, *Psychopathology and Politics,* originally published in 1930, reprinted in *The Political Writings of Harold D. Lasswell* (Glencoe, Ill.: The Free Press, 1951); Erich Fromm, *Escape From Freedom* (New York: Rinehart, 1941); T. W. Adorno, et al., *The Authoritarian Personality* (New York: Harper, 1950).

[45] For the present purposes a detailed conceptual side-trip into the meaning of "ego-defensive needs" will not be necessary. In general, I am referring to the kind of seemingly inexplicable, "pathological" behavior that classical, pre-ego psychology psychoanalysis was preoccupied with. A rough synonym would be needs resulting from "internally induced anxieties," a phrase that appears in Daniel Katz's remarks on ego-defense. "The Functional Approach to the Study of Attitudes," *Public Opinion Quarterly* 24 (1960): 163–204. Also see Fred I. Greenstein, "Personality and Political Socialization: The Theories of Authoritarian and Democratic Character," *Annals* 361 (1965): 81–95.

[46] Bernard Berelson, et al., *Voting* (Chicago: University of Chicago Press, 1954), p. 184.

[47] The quotations are from Robert E. Lane and David O. Sears, *Public Opinion* (Englewood Cliffs, New Jersey: Prentice-Hall, 1964), p. 76. Also see Heinz Hartmann, "The Application of Psychoanalytic Concepts to Social Science," in his *Essays on Ego Psychology* (New York: International Universities Press, 1964), p. 90f. Lane and Sears also suggest that "irrational" opinion formation is fostered where the "referents of an opinion" are "vague," where the issue is "remote" and it is "difficult to assess its action consequences," and where the "terms of debate" are "abstract." These are points which, in terms of the present discussion, apply generally to the possibility that personal variability will affect behavior (actor dispensability), as well as more specifically to the possibility that ego-defense will come to the fore.

[48] But see Leo Srole et al., *Mental Health in the Metropolis,* (New York: McGraw-Hill, 1962).

[49] Nathan W. Ackerman and Marie Jahoda, *Anti-Semitism and Emotional Disorder* (New York: Harper, 1950).

A Map for the Analysis of Personality and Politics

M. Brewster Smith

Progress in the social and behavioral sciences has in general not been marked by major theoretical "breakthroughs." As those of us who profess one or another of these disciplines look upon the succession of research and theoretical interests that capture the center of the stage, we may sometimes wonder if there is indeed any progress at all. Particularly if we are fixated on the physical sciences as models of what a good science should be,[1] we can easily become discouraged. As therapy for this depressive mood, however, one has only to scan the textbooks of former

M. Brewster Smith, "A Map for the Analysis of Personality and Politics," *Journal of Social Issues* 24 (1968): 15–28. Reprinted with permission.

generations and some of the earlier landmark contributions to our fields: the fact of progress, of the cumulativeness of understanding that is the hallmark of science, is immediately apparent.

The progress that we see, however, is not on the pattern according to which Einstein included and supplanted Newton, or even on that by which the modern theory of the chemical valence bond makes sense of Mendeleyev's descriptive table of elements. In addition to the development and refinement of research methods and accretion of facts, our kind of progress has involved developing some more or less satisfactory "theories of the middle range" (Merton, 1957), and, especially, a steady increase in the sophistication of the questions that we ask and in our sensitivity to the variables that are likely to be relevant to them.

To codify this kind of progress, and to make our gains readily accessible as we face new problems of research and application, we need something other than grand theory in the old literary style: we are not ready for genuinely theoretical integration, and to pretend that we are is to hamper rather than to aid us in attacking new problems with an open mind. Rather, it often seems most useful for particular purposes to attempt to link the islands of knowledge turned up in the pursuit of middle-range theories and to sort out the kinds of variables that appear likely to be relevant, by means of mapping operations that have only modest theoretical pretensions. When the variables are drawn from the home territory of different academic disciplines, as is bound to be the case in the study of any concrete social problem and is also true of many facets of a context-defined field like political science, ventures in mapping become particularly important. They are the best we can do toward interdisciplinary integration, which in these instances is required of us by the nature of the task.

This essay sketches such a map for the analysis of personality and politics, an outgrowth of my attempts to apply the approach developed in *Opinions and Personality* (Smith, Bruner and White, 1956; Smith, 1958) to the analysis of various social problems involving social attitudes and behavior, particularly McCarthyism, civil liberties and anti-Semitism.[2] While it obviously bears the marks of its origins, I have had to go considerably beyond the range of variables, mainly psychological ones, that Bruner, White and I were dealing with.

A map like this is *not* a theory that can be confirmed or falsified by testing deductions against evidence; it is rather a heuristic device, a declaration of intellectual strategy, that is to be judged as profitable or sterile rather than as true or false. I have found it personally useful in coming to grips with topics that were new to me, and in organizing what I think we know for my students in teaching. Placing particular variables and relationships as it does in larger context, it may have the further virtue of counteracting one's natural tendency to stress the exclusive importance of the variables or theories that one happens to be momentarily interested in. Many persisting disputes in the social sciences are like the story of the Blind Men and the Elephant. A good map helps us to keep the whole Elephant in view.

The Schematic Map

Schematic as it is, the map is too complicated to take in at a glance. Figure 1 presents the gross outlines—the continents in their asserted relationships.

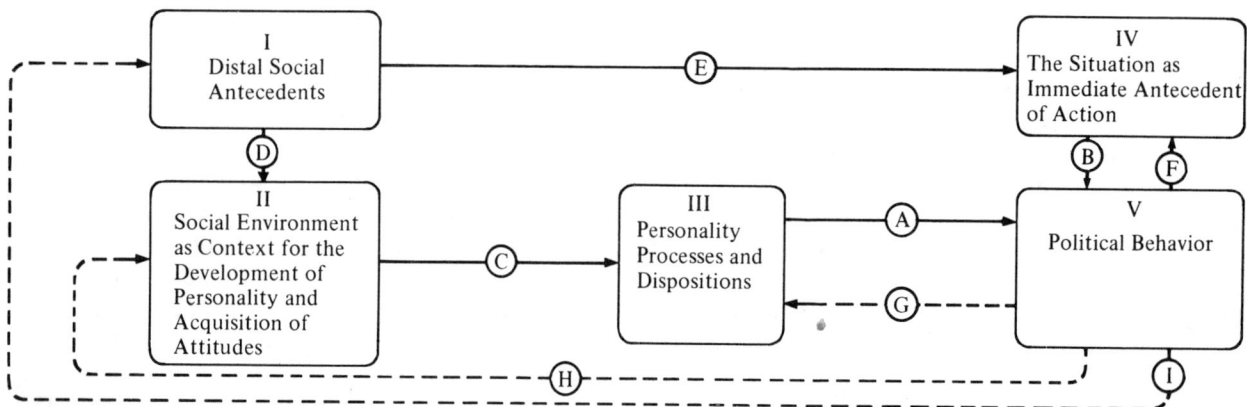

Fig. 1

In Figs. 2 and 3, we will look in more detail at particular segments of the terrain. The full map, given in Fig. 4, should then become intelligible. Certain intentional omissions and simplifications must finally be noted by way of qualification. Illustrations will be provided casually en route, for the most part without documentation from the literature.

The Map in Its Simplest Form

Figure 1 diagrams the major components of a framework for the analysis of personality and politics in terms of five major panels. In keeping with the psychological focus of the map, Panel III (which indicates types of variables relating to the processes and dispositions of personality) occupies the center of the stage. Causal relationships are indicated by arrows. Because we are used to reading from left to right, I have put the payoff in actual behavior (Panel V) at the extreme right. This panel is concerned with personal political decisions as carried into action: voting, information-seeking, policy formation or implementation, influence attempts or—the source of much of our psychological data—question-answering. The data that come from our observations of people, what they say as well as what they do, belong here; only by reconstruction and inference do we arrive at the contents of the central personality panel.

Panel IV represents the person's behavioral situation as an immediate antecedent of action; Panel II includes features of the person's more enduring social environment to which we turn to explain how he has happened to become the sort of political actor that we find him to be; and Panel I represents the more remote or distal facts of politics, economics, history, etc., that contribute to the distinctive features of the environment in which he was socialized and of the immediate situations in which he acts. From the standpoint of the behaving individual, the contents of Panel I are conceptually distal but may be temporally contemporaneous: a political system, for example (Panel I), affects (Arrow E) the political norms about democracy, authority, legitimacy, etc., to which a person is socialized (Panel II); it also affects (Arrow E)

the structure of the immediate situations of action that he is likely to encounter (Panel IV)—the alternatives offered on a ballot, the procedural rules in a legislative body, etc. Temporally distal determinants are also assigned to Panel I: thus the history of slavery, the plantation economy, the Civil War and Reconstruction as determinants of the poltically relevant environments in which participants in Southern politics have been socialized, and of the immediate situations that comprise the stage on which they perform as political actors.

If we start with behavioral outcomes in Panel V, the arrows (marked A and B) that link them with Panels III and IV represent the methodological premise emphasized by the great psychologist Kurt Lewin: all social behavior is to be analyzed as a joint resultant of characteristics of the *person,* on the one hand, and of his psychological *situation,* on the other. The behavior of a single political actor may differ substantially as he faces differently structured situations; conversely, different persons who face the same situation will respond differently. Both the contribution of the person and that of his situation, in interaction, must be included in any adequate analysis.

For long, there was a disciplinary quarrel between psychologists and sociologists about the relevance and importance of personal dispositions (primarily *attitudes*) versus situations in determining social behavior. To take this feature of our map seriously is to regard the argument as silly and outmoded: both classes of determinants are jointly indispensible. The study of "personality and politics" cannot afford to neglect situational factors, which must in principle be taken into account if we are to isolate the distinctive contributions of personality. In concrete cases in which analysis along these lines is undertaken so as to guide social action, one may ask, of course, whether the personal or the situational component is more *strategic* in terms of accessibility to major influence. It may be more feasible, for example, to influence the normative structure that pertains to interracial relations than to carry through the program of mass psychoanalysis that might be required in order to reverse authoritarian personality trends that predispose people toward prejudice and discriminatory behavior. The practical question of strategic importance and accessibility does not seem to be as charged with disciplinary *amour-propre* as are the theoretical issues that still tend to divide the proponents of personality-oriented and of situational approaches.

The dotted arrows of relationship that leave the behavioral panel require special mention. Political behavior has consequences as well as causes, and for the sake of formal completeness some of these are suggested by the dotted "feedback loops" in the map. As Leon Festinger has argued on the basis of considerable evidence, self-committing behavior may have effects in turn upon a person's attitudes (Arrow G) (Festinger, 1957, Brehm and Cohen, 1962). A political actor who adopts a position for expedient reasons may be convinced by his own rhetoric, or—similar in result though different in the process that is assumed—he may shift his attitudes to accord with his actions in order to reduce feelings of "dissonance." The dotted Arrows F, H and I merely recognize that individual behavior also has effects in the social world. What the person does in a situation may immediately change it (Arrow F); as we integrate across the behavior of many individuals, the joint consequences of the behavior of the many eventually alter the social environments that shape and support the attitudes of each (Arrow H). In the longer run (Arrow I), the behaviors of individuals constitute a society and its history.

To be sure, this is a psychologist's map that focuses on the attitudes and behavior of individual persons. A political sociologist would have to give explicit attention to matters that remain implicit in the feedback arrows—to the social structures according to which individual behaviors are integrated to have political effects. His map would necessarily be differently centered and elaborated than the present one.

Panels III and IV

With the broad framework laid out, we can now look at the details of Panels III and IV, still working from the proximal to the distal determinants of be-havior (see Fig. 2). The contents of Panel IV (The Situation as Immediate Antecedent of Action) remind us that an important component of any behavioral situation is the set of norms or prescriptions for behavior that are consensually held to apply in it. Students of political behavior at the various levels of governmental organization are concerned with recurring types of situations that confront the citizen as constituent, voter or petitioner: the legislator, the executive, the administrative functionary, the party leader. Much of the variation in personal behavior, not only across types of situations but within the same type in different political structures and different historical periods, will be attributable to differences and changes in the norms that prevail. Apart from the norms, there are of course many other situational features that are also important as codeterminants of action—among them, the competitive or cooperative relations that hold with other actors who participate in the situation, the degree of urgency with which decision or action is required, the contingencies of cost and benefit that obtain (see Thibaut and Kelley, 1959). Lore about the relevant features of political situations is a principal currency of political science.

Turn now to Panel III, Personality Processes and Dispositions. We are concerned here with inferred dispositions of the person that he brings to any situation he encounters, and with their basis in his experience and motivational processes. Social psychologists have come to use the term *attitudes* to refer to such dispositions, when they represent integrations of cognitive, emotional and conative tendencies around a psychological object such as a political figure or issue. Our problem is a dual one: to formulate how a person's attitudes come to bear on his political behavior and how these attitudes arise and are sustained in relation to their part in the ongoing operations of the person's psychological economy.

A first point suggested in Fig. 2 is that we cannot take for granted just which of a person's attitudes will become engaged as a codeterminant of his behavior in a political situation. Political scientists are probably less naive than psychologists about this. A citizen's presidential vote for one or another candidate de-

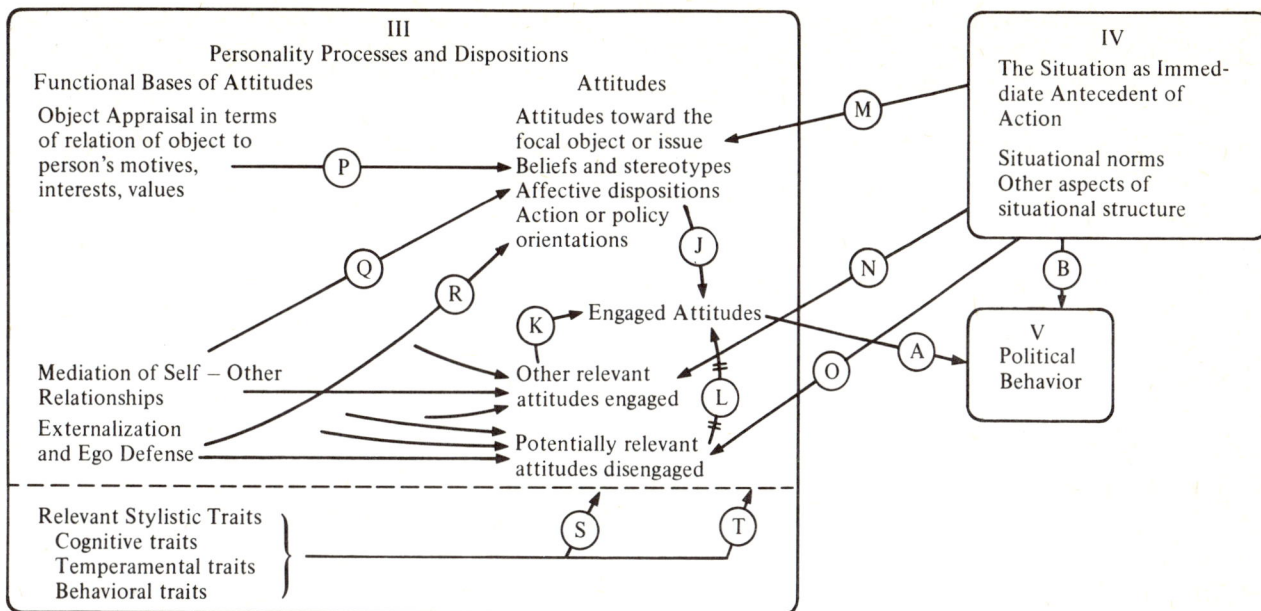

Fig. 2

pends, as we know (Campbell, Converse, Miller, and Stokes, 1960), not only on his focal attitude toward that candidate, but also on attitudes toward the alternative candidates, toward party and toward issues. A legislator's vote on a bill will depend not only on situational factors (including whether or not a roll call is involved) and on his attitudes toward the focal issue but also on other relevant attitudes that become engaged—toward tangential issues, toward the party leadership, toward political survival or whatever. The situation plays a dual role here: both as a codeterminant, together with his engaged attitudes, of what he does (B) (the legislator may want to vote for a bill but not dare to), and as differentially activating certain of the actor's attitudes (M and N) while allowing or encouraging other potentially relevant attitudes to remain in abeyance (O). In recent years, issues concerning Negro civil rights have come to be posed in the Congress and elsewhere in such pointed terms that political actors probably find it less feasible than formerly to isolate their attitudes of democratic fair

play from engagement—attitudes embodied in the American Creed (Myrdal, 1962) to which most citizens have been socialized to some degree.

Social psychological research may elect to measure and manipulate one attitude at a time for good analytic reasons, but people rarely behave in such a piecemeal fashion. What gets into the mix of a person's engaged attitudes, and with what weighting, makes a big difference. Given the complexity of these relationships, there is no reason to suppose that people's political behavior should uniformly correspond to their attitudes on the focal issue. It is surprising that some psychologists and sociologists have been surprised at the lack of one-to-one correspondence between single attitudes and behavior and have questioned the validity of attitude measurement on these irrelevant grounds.

Moving toward the left of Panel III, we turn from the problem of how attitudes are differentially aroused to that of how they are formed and sustained. The approach taken here is the functional one which posits that a person acquires and maintains attitudes and other learned psychological structures to the extent that they are in some way useful to him in his inner economy of adjustment and his outer economy of adaptation. The scheme for classifying the functional basis of attitudes is one that I have discussed in greater detail elsewhere (Smith, Bruner and White, 1956; Smith, 1968). It answers the question, "Of what use to a man are his opinions'??, under three rubrics: *object appraisal, mediation of self-other relationships* and *externalization and ego defense.*

Object Appraisal

Under object appraisal, we recognize the ways in which a person's attitudes serve him by "sizing up" significant aspects of the world in terms of their relevance to his motives, interests and values. As Walter Lippmann long ago (1922) made clear, all attitudes, not just "prejudice," involve an element of "prejudgment"; they are useful to the person in part because they prepare him for his encounters with reality enabling him to avoid the confusion and inefficiency of appraising each new situation afresh in all its complexity. In the most general way, holding *any* attitude brings a bit of order into the flux of a person's psychological world; the specific content of a person's attitudes reflects to varying degrees his appraisal of how the attitudinal object bears upon his interests and enterprises. This function involves reality testing and is likely to be involved to some minimal degree in even the least rational of attitudes — which on closer examination may turn out to be relatively reasonable within the person's own limited framework of appraisal.

Mediation of Self-Other Relationships

A person's attitudes not only embody a provisional appraisal of what for him is significant reality; they also serve to mediate the kind of relationships with others and the kind of conception of self that he is motivated to maintain. Is it important to the decision maker to think of himself as a liberal Democrat? Then his adopting a liberal stand on any of a variety of issues may contribute to his self regard. Does he rather set much stock in being right in the light of history? Such motivation, by orienting him toward an ideal reference group, may make him relatively independent of immediate social pressures. To the extent that by self-selective recruitment politicians are disproportionately likely to be "other directed" in Riesman's sense (1950), however, they may be predisposed by personality to be especially vulnerable to such pressures.

Externalization and Ego Defense

Finally comes the class of functions to which psychoanalytic depth psychology has given the closest attention, here labelled externalization and ego defense. This is the functional basis to which Lasswell (1930) gave exclusive emphasis in his classic formula for the political man: private motives displaced onto public objects, rationalized in terms cf the public interest. It also underlies the conception of the "authoritarian personality" (Adorno, Frenkel-Brunswik, Levinson, and Sanford, 1950) — a posture in which an essentially weak ego puts up a facade of strength that requires bolstering through identification with the strong, the conventional and the in-group, and rejection of the weak, the immoral, the out-group. Given the appeal of depth interpretation in the study of personality and politics, there is little need to expand on these themes; it is more necessary to insist that externalization and ego defense are only part of the story.

The arrows P, Q and R raise the functional question about the motivational sources of any attitude that a person holds. Arrows S and T, near the bottom of the panel, reflect on their part a different kind of relationship. A person's attitudes and the way they engage with particular political situations bear the mark of his stylistic traits of personality as well as of the purposes that they serve for him. Intelligence or stupidity, Kennedy incisiveness or Eisenhower vagueness, zest or apathy, optimism or pessimism, decisiveness or hesitation—cognitive, temperamental and behavioral traits like these may have their own history in the residues of the person's previous motivational conflicts, but their immediate relevance for his political attitudes and behavior is hardly motivational. His attitudes and actions in the sphere of politics, as in other realms, inevitably reflect such pervasive personal qualities, which can have momentous behavioral consequences. A purely functional account is likely to neglect them.

Panel II

The foregoing analysis provides us with leverage for identifying aspects of the person's social environment that are relevant to the development, maintenance and change of his political attitudes and his stylistic personality traits, as we turn to Panel II at the left of our map (Fig. 3). To the extent that a person's attitudes in a particular political context reflect

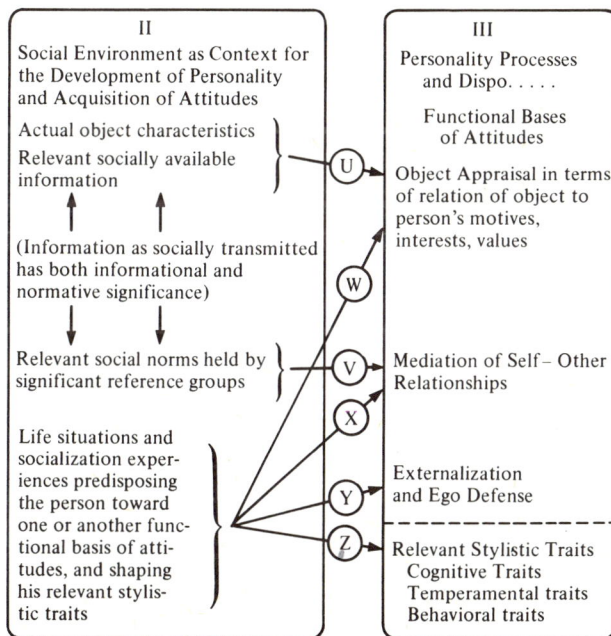

Fig. 3

processes of object appraisal, he should be responsive to the information that his environment provides about the attitudinal object or issue (Arrow U). The actual facts about it will be important in this connection only as they affect the information that is socially available to him, and as we know, the quality and quantity of this information vary widely from issue to issue and across the various niches that people occupy in society.

The information on a topic that reaches a person through the channels of communication has a dual relevance, as the internal arrows in Panel II are intended to suggest: not only does it feed into his processes of object appraisal, but it carries further information—a second-order message, so to speak—about the social norms that prevail. When discussions of birth control begin to percolate through Catholic channels, or debates about the pros and cons of China policy through American ones, not only is new grist provided for object appraisal; the important news is conveyed that these previously taboo topics have become moot and discussable. As Arrow V indicates, the second motivational basis of attitudes—the mediation of self-other relations—then may lead to attitudinal consequences that point to a different resultant in behavior. It becomes safe to think in new ways.

Besides providing the environmental data that the first two attitudinal functions can work with to generate new attitudes or to sustain or change established ones,[3] the person's life situation and socialization experiences may predispose him—in general, or in a particular topical domain—toward one or another of the functional bases of attitudes (Arrows W, X and Y). What makes the rational man, in whom the first function predominates? The Utopia has not yet arrived in which we know the answer, but recent studies of socialization are beginning to become relevant to the question, and it is a good guess that part of the story is rearing by loving and confident parents who give reasons for their discipline. In the shorter run, environments that augment one's self esteem and allay one's anxiety should also favor object appraisal. Research in the wake of Riesman (1950), including the Witkin group's studies of field dependence-independence (Witkin et al, 1962) and Miller and Swanson's (1958, 1960) work on child rearing and personality in entrepreneurial and bureaucratic families, contains suggestions about the sources of primary orientation to the second function, mediation of self-other relationships. As for externalization and ego defense, again the picture is not clear, but conditions that subject the developing person to arbitrary authority, that deflate self esteem, that arouse vague anxiety, that provoke hostility but block its relatively direct expression toward the source of the frustration, seem likely sources.

The final arrow Z is drawn not to complete the alphabet but to make place for the findings of personality research, as they emerge, concerning the determinants in socialization of personal stylistic traits.

The entire map can now be reassembled in Fig. 4.

Arrows U to Z, taken together, replace Arrow C in Fig. 1.

Some Omissions and Simplifications

The usefulness of a map and its inherent limitations are two sides of the same coin: its status as a simplification and schematization of reality. There are many complexities that the present map does not attempt to handle. Some of the major omissions, which I note briefly here, arise from the fact that the role of the basic psychological apparatuses and processes of motivation, perception and learning is assumed implicitly rather than explicitly delineated.

The triadic functional classification attempts to sort

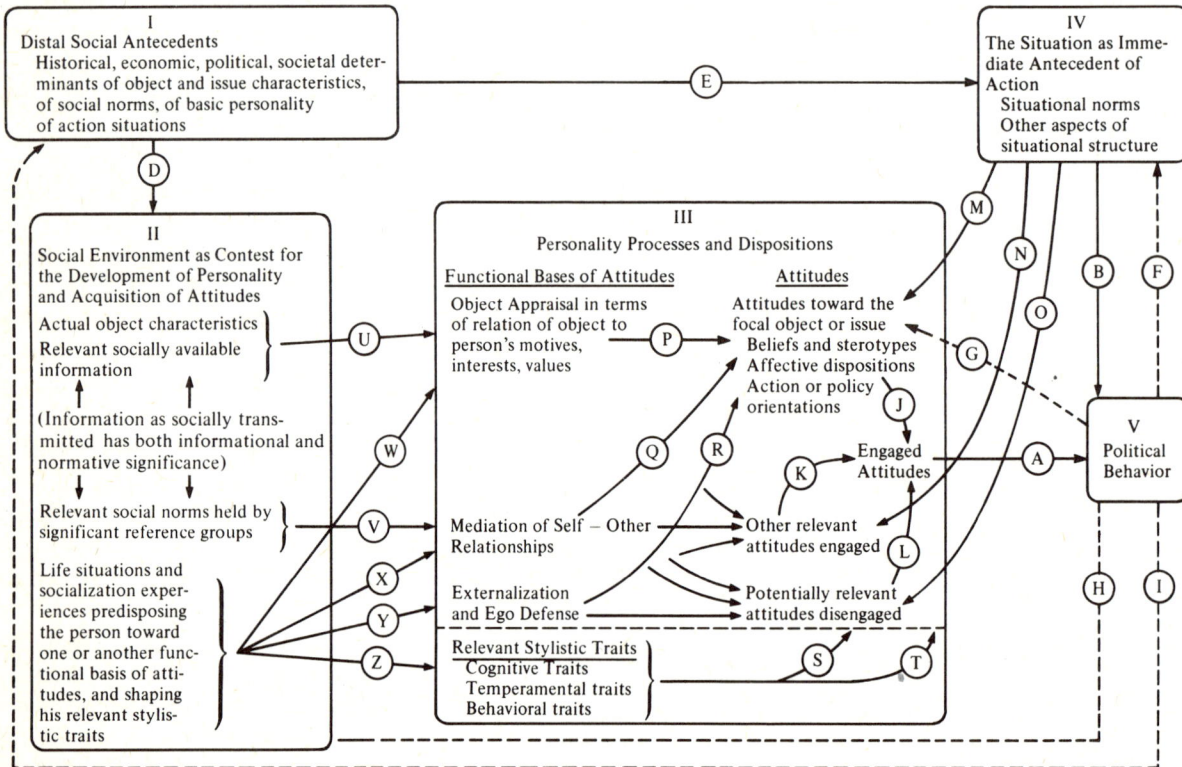

Fig. 4

out the ways in which a person's attitudes are rooted in his underlying motives and their fusions and transformations, whatever they may be. It assumes but does not spell out a conception of human motivation.

As for perception, it would elaborate the map to an incomprehensible tangle to give due recognition to what we know about perceptual selectivity, the ways in which a person's existing expectations, motives and attitudes affect what he will attend to and how he will register and categorize it. A perceptual screening process intervenes between the environmental facts (Panel II) and what the person makes of them (Panel III); likewise between the immediate behavioral situation as it might appear to an objective observer (Panel IV) and how the person defines it for himself, which in the last analysis is the guise in which it affects his behavior.

In regard to learning, the present formulation makes the broad functionalist assumption that people in general acquire attitudes that are useful, that is, rewarding to them. But it ignores the details of the learning process, and such consequences of learning as the persistence of learned structures beyond their original point of usefulness. Much of the content of political attitudes, moreover, may be acquired by an individual quite incidentally, in his unfocused, only mildly attentive effort to make sense of his world. The culture says, in effect, "This is how things are with (Russia) (China) (Republicans) (Southerners) (Negroes) (socialized medicine)," and in the absence of better information, he takes note. Such incidentally learned, psychologically marginal "information" may at the time have little real payoff in object appraisal or social adjustment (the person may have no occasion for dealing with the object or issue, and it may not matter enough to his significant reference groups to become part of the currency of his self-other relationships), yet, should the occasion arise, the basis for resonance to certain political positions rather than others has been laid.

References

Adorno, T. W., Frenkel-Brunswick, Else, Levinson, Daniel J. and Sanford, R. Nevitt. *The Authoritarian Personality*. New York: Harper, 1950.

Brehm, Jack W. and Cohen, Arthur R. *Explorations in Cognitive Dissonance*. New York: Wiley, 1962.

Campbell, Angus, Converse, Philip E., Miller, Warren E. and Stokes, Donald E. *The American Voter*. New York: Wiley, 1960.

Festinger, Leon. *A Theory of Cognitive Dissonance*. Chicago: Row, Peterson, 1957.

Lasswell, Harold D. *Psychopathology and Politics*. Chicago: University of Chicago Press, 1930.

Lippmann, Walter. *Public Opinion*. New York and London: Macmillan, 1922.

Merton, Robert K. *Social Theory and Social Structure* (rev. ed.). Glencoe, Illinois: The Free Press, 1957.

Miller, Daniel R. and Swanson, Guy E. *The Changing American Parent*. New York: Wiley, 1958.

Miller, Daniel R. and Swanson, Guy E. *Inner Conflict and Defense*. New York: Holt, 1960.

Myrdal, Gunnar. *An American Dilemma* (rev. ed.). New York: Harper, 1962.

Riesman, David. *The Lonely Crowd*. New Haven: Yale University Press, 1950.

Smith, M. Brewster. "Opinions, Personality, and Political Behavior." *American Political Science Review*, 1958, 52, 1–17.

Smith, M. Brewster. *Determinants of Anti-Semitism: A Social-Psychological Map*. New York: Anti-defamation League of B'nai B'rith. N.D. (1965).

Smith, M. Brewster. "Attitude Change." *International Encyclopedia of the Social Sciences*. New York: Macmillan and Free Press, 1968.

Smith, M. Brewster, Bruner, Jerome S., and White, Robert W. *Opinions and Personality*. New York: Wiley, 1956.

Stouffer, Samuel A. *Communism, Conformity, and Civil Liberties*. Garden City: Doubleday, 1955.

Thibaut, John W. and Kelley, Harold H. *The Social Psychology of Groups*. New York: Wiley, 1959.

Witkin, Herman A., Dyk, R. B., Faterson, Hanna F., Goodenough, Donald R. and Karp, Stephen A. *Psychological Differentiation. Studies of Development*. New York: Wiley, 1962.

Notes

[1] Other than meteorology, which in some respects offers such an appropriate model that I am puzzled that social scientists have not picked it up.

[2] In the area of McCarthyism and civil liberties, I prepared an unpublished memorandum for Samuel A. Stouffer in connection with planning for the studies leading to his book on the subject (Stouffer, 1955). The application to anti-Semitism is embodied in a pamphlet (Smith, 1965) on which I draw heavily in the present essay, with gratitude to the Anti-Defamation League of B'nai B'rith for support in the project of which it was a by-product.

[3] Environment data play a much more incidental and erratic role in relation to the function of externalization and ego defense.

Personality and Political Orientation

Douglas St. Angelo

James W. Dyson

Attempting to understand the nature of political ideology presents a persistent challenge to political scholars. In recent decades some of the interest in political ideology has focused upon development of theories which relate ideological belief systems to personality constructs.[1] These efforts have been sufficiently successful to keep alive interest in the relationship of personality to ideology. Even so, the efforts to date leave much, and perhaps most, of the relationship unexplained.

This paper is part of a continuing effort which seeks an expansion of the theoretical knowledge concerning personality and political ideology. The paper attempts to show how certain personality dimensions relate to political ideology. Its main thrust is directed at the effect of environmental conditioning upon the personality-ideological relationship. The environmental factors utilized here are normally identified as con-stituting subcultural differences. The primary subcultural differences which we utilize are race and status. This study seeks to test two major hypotheses: (1) personality is related to political belief, and (2) subcultural differences modify the relational patterns between personality and political belief.[2]

Two streams of research undergird this analysis. The first of these is the extended effort to isolate behavioral and social correlates of various "liberal-conservative" continua.[3] Multidimensionality is a confounding problem in determining the behavioral and social correlates of liberal-conservatism. Various liberal-conservatism scales with high reproducibility coefficients are not always highly intercorrelated.[4] This may mean that different liberal-conservatism scales measure different aspects of liberal-conservative attitudes and that general scales do not separate liberals from conservatives, but rather they distinguish liberals in certain respects from conservatives in certain respects.

The second stream of research proceeds from the concern among scholars of attitude testing and measurement regarding the problem of "response set." It has been suggested recently[5] that new findings in

Douglas St. Angelo and James W. Dyson, "Personality and Political Orientation," reprinted from the *Midwest Journal of Political Science* 12 (1968): 202–24, by permission of the Wayne State University Press. Copyright 1968, by Wayne State University Press.

"response set" research have provided additional information on the personality differences of individuals defined politically as either liberal or conservative. This suggestion provides the basis for the tests reported in this paper.

The "Acquiescence Response-Set"

World War II intensified interest in the prevalence of fascist and authoritarian tendencies in our society. Following the publication of *The Authoritarian Personality*,[6] the focal work of this research, evidence mounted indicating that many respondents displayed an acquiescent tendency, i.e., a tendency to agree rather than disagree with test items. The acquiescent tendency embodies at least two dimensions. On the one hand it reflects a personality characteristic of respondents. On the other hand, it generates a "response set" which can have the effect of bringing into question the validity of a scale. Moreover, the acquiescent tendency is complemented by the finding that certain respondents manifest a tendency to disagree with items. The tendencies to agree and to disagree have been studied as indicators of personality types.

Arthur Couch and Kenneth Keniston undertook a major study to determine the differences between respondents exhibiting tendencies to agree and to disagree with scale items.[7] Using a limited sample, they administered a battery of "paper and pencil tests" over an extended period of time and extensively interviewed the deviant cases. Their evidence indicated distinct differences in personality types between the two groups of respondents. "Yeasayers" were found to be expressive types, the sort of people who responded to stimuli quickly and enthusiastically. They possessed little ego control and yielded to and enjoyed immediate, situational, short-term forces. In short, they were outgoing, enthusiastic, and unrestrained. The "naysayers," on the other hand, exhibited strong personality control. They avoided exclamatory phrases, colloquial slang and enthusiastic

statements. Their preference was for qualified and hesitant statements. The dominant effort among this group was for ego control, and the group tried to minimize the internal and external forces which sought expression.

Couch and Keniston did not include political content in their study. It was Lester Milbrath[8] who added the political dimension. He found that among forty-seven Washington lobbyists, Democrats were more likely to turn up in the positive response-set (10–7) and Republicans were more than likely to turn up in the negative response-set (15–5). In checking this response-set tendency with 1956 Survey Research Center data Milbrath found that the pattern persisted for Democrats and Republicans in the survey. He also found that liberals were more often in the positive response-set and conservatives in the negative one.

Response-set has an equivalent dimension in psychological studies of personality. Some behavioral psychologists who study personality believe that a number of traits serve as the basis of a personality system. One of these traits is referred to as personal control. Personal control has two extreme dimensions: overcontrol and undercontrol. An overcontrolled person is restrained in personal relationships, while the undercontrolled person is outgoing and impetuous in personal relationships. Psychologists reason that the control system is one of the determinants of how one performs in social situations.[9]

The overcontrolled individual is consistently "aloof" and his state of aloofness sometimes renders him inept in his attempt to cope with unanticipated situations. The undercontrolled person is one who usually feels involved. While this may be an asset in many situations in an "other-directed" culture, it can cause one to overreact to unwanted outcomes. The overcontrollers may be portrayed as relatively unresponsive to situational demands. Undercontrollers may be seen as "at the mercy of their environments."[10]

The psychological characterization of overcontrollers and undercontrollers parallel the Couch and Keniston descriptions of naysayers and yeasayers. This parallelism led us to explore personality impacts on political outlooks through the use of a control scale weighted against the naysaying-yeasaying response set. We attempted to find restraint types by agreement responses (instead of naysaying) and impetuous types by disagreement responses (instead of yeasaying).

The procedure of ascertaining personality types by loading the items against a predicted response tendency entails the risk of including naysayers with impetuous types and yeasayers with restraint personalities. However, a test of responses to selected items did not indicate that a response set bias was present for overcontrollers or undercontrollers.

So even though we did not control for response set by scoring half the items for agreement and half for disagreement, we used a procedure that should be at least sufficient. We loaded the items against a predicted response set bias. This precaution may not overcome this source of error, but it can reduce it.

The lack of congruency between yea–nay-sayers and over–undercontrolled may be explained. Perhaps the parallel characterization of nay–yea-sayers and over–under-controllers does not mean that a yeasayer, for example, is a direct counterpart of an undercontroller. There may be underlying differences in behaviors that are described as impetuous. The differences may be related to other dimensions of a total personality system.

Before one can assess the influence of personality control on political attitude sets, certain social characteristics of respondents must be related to overcontrol and undercontrol. The purpose of this step is to ascertain the social dimensions associated with types of control systems. The literature on control systems, and on yeasayer-naysayers, leads us to infer that the relationships of social characteristics with the control system are straightforward. Those who grew up in rural environments, received little formal education, and earn low incomes will tend to be overcontrollers. Those who grew up in urban environments, received

Table 1
Personal Characteristics, Personality Control, and Race[a]

| | | Place Size* | | | | Income** | | | | Education*** | | | |
| | | Small | | Large | | Under $6000 | | $6000 or More | | HS or Less | | More than HS | |
		N	%	N	%	N	%	N	%	N	%	N	%
Whites	Over	63	31.2	18	10.7	33	28.0	43	18.1	39	30.0	32	14.3
	Middle	72	35.6	69	41.1	44	37.3	92	38.7	55	42.3	80	35.7
	Under	67	33.2	81	48.2	41	34.7	103	43.3	36	27.7	112	50.0
Negroes	Over	64	57.1	26	43.3	77	57.0	04	15.4	63	62.4	13	25.0
	Middle	23	20.5	14	23.3	28	20.7	08	30.8	18	17.8	16	30.8
	Under	25	22.3	20	33.3	30	22.2	14	53.8	20	19.8	23	44.2
Total	Over	128	40.6	44	19.3	111	43.7	47	17.8	102	44.2	46	16.6
	Middle	95	30.2	83	36.4	72	28.3	100	37.9	73	31.6	96	34.7
	Under	92	29.2	101	44.3	71	28.0	117	44.3	56	24.2	135	48.7

Total

$*x^2 = 19.06$; Pr $< .001$[b]

$**x^2 = 41.56$; Pr $< .001$

$***x^2 = 53.27$; Pr $< .001$

[a] x^2 values are reported without regard to the race variable. When race produces a chi-square value significantly different from the overall value the relevant chi-square by race is reported.

[b] For Negroes $x^2 = 3.38$; Pr $> .05 < .10$.

at least some training beyond high school, and earn high incomes will tend to be undercontrollers. These relationships are reported in Table 1.

In the course of research it was discovered that race made a large difference in distribution patterns. As a consequence, cross-classifications are given by race. It was found, in addition, that Negro females were more likely to be overcontrolled than Negro males. However, this difference did not turn up among whites, and as it was not particularly large ($X^2 = 1.90$; $P > .10$ and $< .20$) with the Negro subgroup, it has been disregarded in this study.

Personality Control Scale

This paper contains an attempt to test further the suggestions deriving from research in response sets. The difference between previous research and this study is the use of a four-item scale to separate personality types. The items on the scale are as follows with the undercontrolled response indicated after each question:[11]

1. I would say that the best thing is to be proper in behavior and not really loosen up in social situations.   (disagree)

2. It is best not to ever let others see how you really feel about something.   (disagree)

3. A person should be forward and speak his mind in all social situations.   (agree)

4. It is best to bring up children by continually telling them what they should and should not do. (disagree)

Three variables have been selected to establish the background characteristics of the overcontrolled and the undercontrolled respondents. These are population of childhood environment (called place size), income, and education. Place size divides respondents who grew up on farms or in towns from those reporting that they grew up in cities. The two-part educational variable divides those with a high school education or less from those who have more than a high school education, such as high school education and some

special training (barber school, business school, etc.) or some degree of college education. Income is used to divide the sample into those earning less than $6,000 and those earning $6,000 or more. We might point out again that cross-classifications are given by race.

Whites more often scaled in the undercontrolled classification than did Negroes. Of the white respondents, about 40 percent are classified as being undercontrolled. Only 26 percent of Negroes are so classified. This racial difference is not compatible with the stereotyped conception of the Negro subculture. The relatively large number of overcontrolled Negroes suggests that the image of the Negro as "happy-go-lucky" is not an accurate portrait.

Childhood community size is an important variable in both racial groups. Respondents from rural areas and small towns are more likely to be overcontrolled than those raised in cities. This difference is greater for whites than for Negroes; in fact, this variable generates one of the larger differences among whites. The relatively large influence of place size on control for white respondents is probably due to the closer division of whites on the control scale.

Dividing respondents into those over and those under $6,000 annual family income also produces differences on the control variable. The high-income group is more often undercontrolled than the low-income group. With whites and Negroes the difference is about the same, though it is more striking for whites than Negroes. The income variable produces a larger variation among whites than Negroes on the control scale.

Education is also directly related to undercontrol. With both Negro and white respondents, the more highly educated segments are more often undercontrolled. However, the difference is more marked for Negroes than for whites.

These data permit only speculation on the reason for this condition: it may well be that more highly educated Negroes have greater mobility and have experienced greater assimilation into the white community. Such occurrences probably mitigate the influence of earlier subcultural conditioning.

The composite picture of the *undercontrolled* indicates that such a person is either a white who has been raised in a fairly large community, has attained more than a high school education and has received a larger than average family income, or that he is a Negro male with a high degree of education. Moreover, Negro undercontrollers are more likely than Negro overcontrollers to group under high family income.

The *overcontrolled* respondent appears most often to be a white person, or a Negro female, who was raised in a rural setting and who has not attained a high degree of education.

Personality Control and Political Efficacy

We hypothesized that personality control is related to feelings of political effectiveness. The data in Table 3 demonstrate that the more outgoing, enthusiastic, and impetuous style of the undercontrolled person does relate more positively to political efficacy than the more reserved, hesitant and cautious style of the overcontrolled individual.

In testing this relationship a political efficacy scale very similar to the Survey Research Center's efficacy scale was used.[12] The four political efficacy items utilized in this study are (with the most efficacious response indicated) as follows:

1. People like me have very little say about what the government does. (disagree)
2. Voting is one way that people like me can have some sort of say about what the government will do. (agree)
3. Usually politics and government seem so complicated that a person like me can't really understand what's going on. (disagree)
4. Nothing I ever do seems to have any effect upon what happens in politics. (disagree)

The scoring on this scale requires three or four responses in the same direction to be scored as efficacious or inefficacious. That is, to be classified as effi-

cacious the respondent has to give three or four efficacious answers (such response is called high efficacy herein) and to be classified as inefficacious the respondent has to supply three or four inefficacious responses (such response is called low efficacy herein). The remaining respondents are treated as falling at the middle of the efficacy continuum.

Table 2 shows the efficacious map of the entire sample and of the sample controlled for race. The table indicates that the total sample is more often low (43.9 percent) than high (34.9 percent) in efficacy. The racial differences, however, are significant. Fewer whites achieve a low efficacy rating (37.4 percent) than Negroes (57.8 percent). In explaining this difference, several plausible reasons can be offered. Efficacy is highly associated with relatively high education, and whites in Tallahassee have a much higher median education than Negroes.[13] Moreover, there is the simple problem of reality. It is obvious that in this community, as in most American communities, whites do have greater impact upon and access to government than do Negroes. Indeed if the data did not demonstrate a racial difference we would be suspicious of its validity.

When the efficacy variable is cross-classified with the personality control variable a significant change occurs in the racial differences of overcontrolled respondents. Overcontrolled respondents of both races are low rather than high in efficacy. However, a higher percentage of overcontrolled Negroes than overcontrolled whites are low in efficacy. This finding is one indication that the relationship of political values and personality similarities can be modified by subcultural experiences.

Table 2
Efficacy and Race

Efficacy	White N	%	Negro N	%	Total N	%
Low	139	(37.4)	100	(57.8)	239	(43.9)
Middle	89	(23.9)	26	(15.0)	115	(21.1)
High	143	(38.5)	47	(27.1)	190	(34.9)
	371	(99.8)	173	(99.9)	544	(99.9)

$x^2 = 19.7$; Pr $< .001$

Table 3
Personality Control, Race, and Efficacy

Overcontrolled

	White		Negro		Total	
Efficacy	*N*	*%*	*N*	*%*	*N*	*%*
Low	47	(58.0)	70	(77.8)	117	(68.4)
Moderate	20	(24.7)	10	(11.1)	30	(17.5)
High	14	(17.3)	10	(11.1)	24	(14.0)
	81	(100.0)	90	(100.0)	171	(99.9)

Middle

	White		Negro		Total	
Efficacy	*N*	*%*	*N*	*%*	*N*	*%*
Low	50	(35.2)	19	(50.0)	69	(38.3)
Moderate	39	(27.5)	05	(13.2)	44	(24.4)
High	53	(37.3)	14	(36.8)	67	(37.2)
	142	(100.0)	38	(100.0)	180	(99.9)

Undercontrolled

	White		Negro		Total	
Efficacy	*N*	*%*	*N*	*%*	*N*	*%*
Low	42	(28.4)	11	(24.4)	53	(27.5)
Moderate	30	(20.3)	11	(24.4)	41	(21.2)
High	76	(51.4)	23	(51.1)	99	(51.3)
	148	(100.1)	35	(99.9)	193	(100.0)

$x^2 = 75.8$; $Pr < .001$

The most significant fact that emerges from this cross-classification is the direct relationship between the efficacy measure and the personality control measures. The hypothesis that overcontrol would relate to inefficacy and undercontrol to efficacy is demonstrated. Of the total sample 68.4 percent of the overcontrolled respondents are also designated as low in efficacy while 27.5 percent of the undercontrolled respondents are located in the inefficacious grouping. These highly significant distributions occur in spite of the fact that both scales were deliberately weighted against the possibility of naysaying tendency by overcontrollers and yeasaying tendency by undercontrollers.

Overcontrolled whites are more than three times as likely to be low as high in efficacy (58.0 percent), while undercontrolled whites are almost two times as likely to be high as low in efficacy. A subcultural difference is demonstrated in respect to overcontrolled Negroes, but the pattern follows the expected direction. Overcontrolled Negroes are markedly more inefficacious than overcontrolled whites. However, as has already been noted, the subcultural difference disappears among the undercontrolled Negroes. There is virtually no difference between their efficacious percentage and that of the undercontrolled whites. We will have more to say on the point of subcultural differences and the personality control variable in the discussion of the conservative-liberal dimension.

Conservatism-Liberalism and Personality Control

In order to provide a more rigorous test of the Milbrath suggestion that restrained and impetuous types are related respectively to conservatism and liberalism a scale measuring this dimension was developed from topical items relevant to the political conflict at the time of the survey. A topical approach was chosen for its simplicity and in order to avoid the uncertainty and ambiguity of other approaches such as status quo-change, corporatism-individualism, and altruism.[14] The scale used in this study was limited to domestic items to reduce the multidimensionality that often occurs in testing with international items.[15] Racial items were excluded for the same reason. Multidimensionality on racial questions is clear, particularly in southern communities.[16] However, several racial items were included in the schedule to test for the effect of personality control and these results are presented separately.

The items utilized in the Conservatism-Liberalism Scale (with the conservative response indicated) are as follows:[17]

1. Do you think the government in Washington should try to give everyone a chance to live in decent housing? (no)

2. Should able-bodied people on welfare be made to work by the government in Washington? (yes)

3. Do you feel the government in Washington ought to try to help everybody who wants to work to get a job? (no)

4. Actually, if you want to control crime we have got to allow policemen to use more force than is now allowed in dealing with people. (agree)

Table 4 presents the breakdown of conservatism and liberalism for the sample and by race. The conservative tendency found in these results is hardly startling, considering the geographic location of the sample. It could even be argued that a conservatism tendency was manifested in spite of the fact that the items skew the scores to liberalism because they are easy to agree with, but this was counterbalanced by "loading" the questions with the phrase "the government in Washington." This phrase is supposed to be a factor generating conservative type responses among Southerners. On this test the area is more conservative than liberal, though neither segment dominates, on domestic questions.

Once again the data indicate racial subcultural differences. While white respondents occupy the conservative classification by a wide margin of two to one there are only eighteen Negroes who fit the conservative category. Consequently, regardless of any variable controls that are introduced in this study the Negro respondents emerge as overwhelmingly liberal. We disregard Negroes in studying the relationship of liberalism and conservatism with personality because Negroes are liberal whether they are undercontrolled or overcontrolled. The personality control variable does not relate to this group's topical liberalism. Apparently Negro subcultural forces are so strong on topical liberalism that they override the effect of the personality control scale.

The data are not clear and forceful on the relationship between political ideology and personality control. However, some tentative findings can be stated.

Table 4
Liberal-Conservatism and Race

| | Race | | | | | |
| | White | | Negro | | Total | |
Liberal-Conservatism	N	%	N	%	N	%
Liberal	103	(27.7)	85	(49.1)	188	(34.5)
Moderate	92	(24.7)	70	(40.4)	162	(29.7)
Conservative	176	(47.4)	18	(10.4)	194	(35.6)
	371	(99.9)	173	(99.9)	544	(99.8)

$x^2 = 67.68$; Pr $< .001$

Table 5
Personality Control, Race, and Liberalism-Conservatism

Overcontrolled

Liberalism-Conservatism	White		Negro		Total	
	N	%	N	%	N	%
Liberal	13	(16.0)	33	(36.7)	46	(26.7)
Moderate	33	(40.7)	46	(51.1)	79	(46.5)
Conservative	35	(43.2)	11	(12.2)	46	(26.7)
	81	(99.9)	90	(100.0)	171	(99.9)

Middle

	White		Negro		Total	
	N	%	N	%	N	%
Liberal	34	(23.9)	24	(63.2)	58	(32.2)
Moderate	34	(23.9)	11	(28.9)	45	(25.0)
Conservative	74	(52.1)	03	(07.9)	77	(42.7)
	142	(99.9)	38	(100.0)	180	(99.9)

Undercontrolled

	White		Negro		Total	
	N	%	N	%	N	%
Liberal	56	(37.8)	28	(62.2)	84	(43.5)
Moderate	25	(16.9)	13	(28.9)	38	(19.7)
Conservative	67	(45.3)	04	(08.9)	71	(36.8)
	148	(100.0)	45	(100.0)	193	(100.0)

$x^2 = 38.34$; Pr $< .001$

Among whites there is, in this sample, a clear tendency for undercontrolled respondents to be significantly more liberal than overcontrolled respondents. The relationship is there and it is measurable. Proportionately more than twice as many undercontrollers are liberals. The absence of a similar relationship among Negroes suggests that personality may be less significant where overriding subcultural conditions prevail. Such conditions may be so immediate and forceful in the lives of the subcultural members that personality factors do not affect political action or political attitude set. If this is the case, and these data indicate that this is so, further research into personality relationships and political attitudes and actions will have to control for the social conditions that are inherent in subcultural identification.

Racial Attitudes and Personality Control

Questions centering on civil rights were cross-classified with the personality control variable and two of these cross-classifications are presented and analyzed in this section.

The first question was designed to test attitudes toward desegregation of public facilities[18] and was stated in the following manner:

The 1964 "Civil Rights Act" says that all persons regardless of race should be served in public places such as hotels, restaurants, theaters, and similar establishments. Would you like to see this law enforced, strictly enforced, or not enforced at all?

The enforced and strictly enforced responses are collapsed in Table 6. The table shows that, as in the case of the conservatism and liberalism test, the condition of being overcontrolled or undercontrolled also affects the relationship of the respondents' choices on the public facilities question. Once again, however, it is necessary to scrutinize the subcultural differences to see the impact of control on the dependent variable. Negroes, regardless of control characteristics, are overwhelmingly in favor of enforcement of the Act. The overcontrolled Negroes express this reaction at the level of 87.3 percent while the uncontrolled Negroes only slightly exceed this proportion (91.1 percent). In the Negro subculture the personality variable is muted by the presence of homogeneous subcultural goals. Among whites this is not the case. White support for the Act is clearly related to the personality control variable. Overcontrolled whites oppose enforcement of the Act by about a two-to-one margin; undercontrolled whites take just the opposite stance. They favor enforcement of the Act by better than a two-to-one margin. The proportionate difference between white overcontrollers and undercontrollers is even more striking here than on the conservative-liberal measure. In sum, we find that the white overcontrolled group is more likely to be in *opposition* to enforcement of the 1964 Civil Rights Act than to be conservative, and the undercontrolled whites are more often in favor of enforcement of the Act than liberal.

The second civil-rights types question related to the personality control variable attempts to measure a more personal reaction to racial intermingling and equality:

Table 6
Personality Control and Race by Desired Degree of
Civil Rights Act Enforcement

Overcontrolled

Attitude	White N	%	Negro N	%	Total N	%
Enforced	27	(35.1)	75	(87.2)	102	(62.6)
Not Enforced	50	(64.9)	11	(12.8)	61	(37.4)
	77	(100.0)	86	(100.0)	163	(100.0)

Middle

Attitude	White N	%	Negro N	%	Total N	%
Enforced	66	(49.6)	34	(94.4)	100	(59.1)
Not Enforced	67	(50.4)	02	(05.6)	69	(40.8)
	133	(100.0)	36	(100.0)	169	(99.9)

Undercontrolled

Attitude	White N	%	Negro N	%	Total N	%
Enforced	90	(66.7)	41	(91.1)	131	(72.8)
Not Enforced	45	(33.3)	04	(08.9)	49	(27.2)
	135	(100.0)	45	(100.0)	180	(100.0)

$x^2 = 7.66$; Pr $< .025$[a]

[a] For the Negro subgroup $x^2 = 1.56$; Pr $> .40$.

Table 7
Personality Control and Race by Attitudes toward
Working for a Negro Boss

| | Overcontrolled | | | | | |
| | White | | Negro | | Total | |
Attitude	N	%	N	%	N	%
Yes	29	(39.2)	82	(93.2)	111	(68.5)
No	45	(60.8)	06	(06.8)	51	(31.5)
	74	(100.0)	88	(100.0)	162	(100.0)

| | Middle | | | | | |
| | White | | Negro | | Total | |
Attitude	N	%	N	%	N	%
Yes	80	(61.5)	34	(97.1)	114	(69.1)
No	50	(38.5)	01	(02.9)	51	(30.9)
	130	(100.0)	35	(100.0)	165	(100.0)

| | Undercontrolled | | | | | |
| | White | | Negro | | Total | |
Attitude	N	%	N	%	N	%
Yes	99	(72.8)	41	(93.2)	140	(77.8)
No	37	(27.2)	03	(06.8)	40	(22.2)
	136	(100.0)	44	(100.0)	180	(100.0)

$x^2 = 4.6$; $Pr = .10$[a]

[a] For whites $x^2 = 22.8$, $Pr < .001$; for Negroes $x^2 = .77$, $Pr > .90$.

Would you work on a job where a colored person is the boss?[19]

The relationship of the personal control scale produces a very little difference between the first and second questions. This small difference indicates that a few more whites, both over and undercontrolled, are willing to work for a Negro boss than approve of enforcement of the Civil Rights Act. However, overcontrollers are against working for a Negro boss and undercontrollers are not against it. Among Negroes, again regardless of the personality control variable, a slightly larger percentage say that whites should work under the direction of a Negro boss than favor enforcement of the Civil Rights Act.

In general, it appears that white civil rights attitudes are related significantly to personality overcontrol and undercontrol.

Fourth Order Relationship of Personality and Belief

We began this analysis of the relationship of personality to status indicators and political dimensions hypothesizing that personality control was related to status and dimensions like efficacy and liberal-conservatism. The expected relationships were obtained. The weaker relationship uncovered with the impact of personality on belief system (liberal-conservatism). It was also found that status was weakly related to belief system. For example, 24 percent of low income whites and 30 percent of high income whites were liberal. Race had a relatively high impact on belief system: whites were much more likely to be conservative than liberal, while Negroes were overwhelmingly liberal.

We found that in spite of the belief system distributions imposed by race, personality control modified the relationship. Overcontrolled Negroes were more apt to be *conservative* than undercontrolled Negroes, and undercontrolled whites were more apt to be *liberal* than overcontrolled whites. So far we have not demonstrated the relationship of personality and race to belief system while holding constant each of the status indicators (income, education and place size). In holding constant race along with each of the status indicators we found that the relationship of belief system and personality is present though the relationship is affected differently by the three status indicators.

Tables 8 and 9 present the relationship of belief system and personality when race and education and race and place size are held constant. In the first set of circumstances personality is operative on belief system for highly educated respondents; in the latter case the relationship obtains when place size is small. When education is low and place size is large the influence of personality is muted for both whites and

Negroes. However, even in a fourth order relationship it is important to note that personality is not muted at one end of each of the status indicators.

The relationship of personality and belief system with race and income held constant is clearer. Table 10 shows these relationships. For two of the four subtables chi-square values indicate the difference is not a chance one. In all the subtables personality has some impact on belief system, but, for highly educated Negroes the relationship is not substantially different from a chance one. However, the small number of overcontrolled high income Negroes in the sample places restrictions on chi square. If there were, say, 20 overcontrolled high income Negroes, and the pattern persisted, chi square would be significant beyond .05. The dissolution of N in this subset prohibits straightforward interpretation.

The data in these tables lead us to conclude that personality is related to belief system even when race and status indicators are held constant. The lack of a strong relationship is due in part to the distributions of respondents on the belief system dimension. White

Table 8
Control and Liberalism-Conservatism with Education and Race Held Constant

Whites

| | Low Education (N = 130) | | | | | | | | High Education (N = 224) | | | | | | | |
| | Over Control | | Middle | | Under Control | | Total | | Over Control | | Middle | | Under Control | | Total | |
	%	N	%	N	%	N	%	N	%	N	%	N	%	N	%	N
Liberal	30.4	(7)	34.8	(8)	34.8	(8)	100.0	(23)	7.6	(6)	31.6	(25)	60.8	(48)	100.0	(79)
Middle	41.3	(19)	39.1	(18)	19.8	(9)	100.0	(46)	22.2	(8)	33.3	(12)	44.4	(16)	99.9	(36)
Conservative	21.3	(13)	47.5	(29)	31.1	(19)	99.9	(61)	16.5	(18)	39.4	(43)	44.0	(48)	99.9	(109)

$x^2 = 6.086$, Pr $< .20 > .10$ $x^2 = 8.117$, Pr $< .10 > .05$

Negro

| | Low Education (N = 101) | | | | | | | | High Education (N = 52) | | | | | | | |
| | Over Control | | Middle | | Under Control | | Total | | Over Control | | Middle | | Under Control | | Total | |
	%	N	%	N	%	N	%	N	%	N	%	N	%	N	%	N
Liberal	52.5	(21)	27.5	(11)	20.0	(8)	100.0	(40)	18.9	(7)	32.4	(12)	48.6	(18)	99.9	(37)
Middle	71.4	(35)	10.2	(5)	18.4	(9)	100.0	(49)	30.0	(3)	40.0	(4)	30.0	(3)	100.0	(10)
Conservative	58.3	(7)	16.7	(2)	25.0	(3)	100.0	(12)	60.0	(3)	20.0	(1)	20.0	(1)	100.0	(5)

$x^2 = 5.223$, Pr $< .30 > .20$ $x^2 = 4.806$, Pr $< 40 > .30$

Table 9
Control and Liberalism-Conservatism with Place Size and Race Held Constant

Whites

Small Place Size (N = 202)

	Over Control %	Over Control N	Middle %	Middle N	Under Control %	Under Control N	Total %	Total N
Liberal	15.2	(7)	28.3	(13)	56.5	(26)	100.0	(46)
Middle	46.8	(29)	32.3	(20)	21.0	(13)	100.1	(62)
Conservative	28.7	(27)	41.5	(39)	29.8	(28)	100.0	(94)

$x^2 = 21.248$, Pr $< .001$

Large Place Size (N = 168)

	Over Control %	Over Control N	Middle %	Middle N	Under Control %	Under Control N	Total %	Total N
Liberal	10.5	(6)	36.8	(21)	52.6	(30)	99.9	(57)
Middle	13.8	(4)	44.8	(13)	41.4	(12)	100.0	(29)
Conservative	9.8	(8)	42.7	(35)	47.6	(39)	100.1	(82)

$x^2 = 1.247$, Pr $< .80 > .70$

Negro

Small Place Size (N = 112)

	Over Control %	Over Control N	Middle %	Middle N	Under Control %	Under Control N	Total %	Total N
Liberal	46.2	(24)	25.0	(13)	28.8	(15)	100.0	(52)
Middle	64.6	(31)	16.7	(8)	18.8	(9)	100.1	(48)
Conservative	75.0	(9)	16.7	(2)	8.3	(1)	100.0	(12)

$x^2 = 5.494$, Pr $< .30 > .20$

Large Place Size (N = 60)

	Over Control %	Over Control N	Middle %	Middle N	Under Control %	Under Control N	Total %	Total N
Liberal	28.1	(9)	34.4	(11)	37.5	(12)	100.0	(32)
Middle	68.2	(15)	13.6	(3)	18.2	(4)	100.0	(22)
Conservative	33.3	(2)	16.7	(1)	50.0	(3)	100.0	(6)

$x^2 = 9.653$, Pr $< .05 > .02$

Table 10
Control and Liberalism-Conservatism with Income and Race Held Constant

Whites

Low Income (N = 118)

	Over Control %	Over Control N	Middle %	Middle N	Under Control %	Under Control N	Total %	Total N
Liberal	17.2	(5)	34.5	(10)	48.3	(14)	100.0	(29)
Middle	40.5	(15)	29.7	(11)	29.7	(11)	99.9	(37)
Conservative	25.0	(13)	44.2	(23)	30.8	(16)	100.0	(52)

$x^2 = 6.781$, Pr $< .20 > .10$

High Income (N = 238)

	Over Control %	Over Control N	Middle %	Middle N	Under Control %	Under Control N	Total %	Total N
Liberal	11.1	(8)	33.3	(24)	55.6	(40)	100.0	(72)
Middle	30.6	(15)	42.9	(21)	26.5	(13)	100.0	(49)
Conservative	17.1	(20)	40.2	(47)	42.7	(50)	100.0	(117)

$x^2 = 12.770$, Pr $< .02 > .01$

Negro

Low Income (N = 145)

	Over Control %	Over Control N	Middle %	Middle N	Under Control %	Under Control N	Total %	Total N
Liberal	44.3	(27)	29.5	(18)	26.2	(16)	100.0	(61)
Middle	66.7	(40)	15.0	(9)	18.3	(11)	100.0	(60)
Conservative	71.4	(10)	14.3	(2)	14.3	(2)	100.0	(14)

$x^2 = 7.824$, Pr $< .10 > .05$

High Income (N = 26)

	Over Control %	Over Control N	Middle %	Middle N	Under Control %	Under Control N	Total %	Total N
Liberal	6.3	(1)	31.3	(5)	62.5	(10)	100.1	(16)
Middle	33.3	(2)	33.3	(2)	33.3	(2)	99.9	(6)
Conservative	25.0	(1)	25.0	(1)	50.0	(2)	100.0	(4)

$x^2 = 3.124$, Pr $< .70 > .50$

respondents were much more likely to be conservative than liberal, and Negro respondents were much more likely to be liberal than conservative. Once the limitations imposed by this distribution are accepted the data indicate that personality differences relate to liberal-conservatism when income is held constant.

Summary and Conclusions

In this study, we have attempted to develop and test an attitudinal scale based upon personality characteristics. The personality feature was first made relevant to politics through studying the difference between persons with a tendency to respond positively and those with a tendency to respond negatively to attitudinal questions. Our efforts to carry this research into the area of political phenomena depart from previous efforts in that the measurement of personality types was accomplished with a scale rather than by segregating agreement and disagreement tendencies. We conclude, on the basis of the data presented, that the two approaches arrive at similar findings. The common finding is that personality control does relate to political and social attitudes. But the scale procedure which we employ indicates that personality control is independent of the yeasayer's tendency toward acquiescence.

We have found that personality control is related to background and personal characteristics, to feelings of political efficacy, to topical conservatism and

liberalism, and to attitudes toward civil rights. These findings emerged even though impetuous persons were forced to give negative responses and restraint respondents had to respond positively. In sum, the relationships of control to ideology and to efficacy are present without the aid of response-set tendencies.

Analysis of the data strongly indicates that the personality control scale is related to political and social variables. While the Negro subculture overrides personality control in some respects, a difference is evident between overcontrolled and undercontrolled white respondents on all measures. Negro respondents, unlike whites, are overwhelmingly in favor of the civil rights items regardless of their personality control classification. This finding leads us to believe that future research on psychological and personality correlates to political phenomena must carefully control for subcultural differences.

Clearly this entire area requires, and deserves, further research. Some of the relationships studied with this data are strong, but none of them is complete. This study does not permit us to explain why the largest segment of white undercontrolled respondents are liberal. We cannot be fully comfortable with the rule until we can explain these exceptions. In spite of these qualifications, the data and the analysis support our theoretical framework. There is a relationship between personality and political ideology. Moreover, this analysis suggests that personality-political belief theory is made more meaningful when controls are included in tests of the theoretical framework.

Notes

The authors gratefully acknowledge support to this project from the Institute of Governmental Research and the Computing Center of Florida State University. We would also like to thank our colleague, Vincent Thursby, for helpful comments on an early draft of the paper.

[1] For some of the major works on political ideology and personality see: T. W. Adorno, Else Frenkel-Brunswick, Daniel I. Levinson, and R. Nevit Sanford, *The Authoritarian Personality* (New York: Harper, 1950). Hans J. Eysenck, *The Psychology of Politics* (London: Routledge and Kegan Paul, 1954). Eric Hoffer, *The True Believer* (New York: Mentor, 1958). Robert E. Lane, *Political Ideology: Why the American Common Man Believes What He Does* (New York: The Free Press, 1962). Milton Rokeach, *The Open and Closed Mind* (New York: Basic Books, 1960). M. Brewster Smith, Jerome S. Bruner, and Robert White, *Opinions and Personality* (New York: Wiley, 1956). Samuel A. Stouffer, *Communism, Conformity and Civil Liberties* (Garden City, N.Y.: Doubleday, 1955).

[2] The data for this study are drawn from a randomly selected sample of 538 adults in Tallahassee, Florida. Of this number, 173

were Negroes who were interviewed by Negro interviewers. Income, education, race and age distributions in the sample closely approximated the census data on Tallahassee.

[3] For a topical domestic welfare scale of these concepts, see V. O. Key, Jr., *Public Opinion and Democracy* (N.Y.: Knopf, 1961), Appendix 2. For a status quo-change approach see Herbert McClosky, "Conservatism and Personality," *The American Political Science Review* (March, 1958): pp. 27–31. On the extensiveness of ideology see Angus Campbell et al., *The American Voter* (N.Y.: Wiley & Sons, 1960), pp. 227–34.

[4] Walter Owens, "An Operationalized Conceptualization of Selected Ideological Variables in the Perspective of Liberalism and Conservatism" (unpublished Ph.D. dissertation, Dept. of Government, The Florida State University), pp. 28–36.

[5] Lester Milbrath, "Latent Origins of Liberalism-Conservatism and Party Identification: A Research Note," *The Journal of Politics* (November, 1962): 679–88.

[6] Adorno et al., *op. cit.*

[7] Arthur Couch and Kenneth Keniston, "Yeasayers and Naysayers: Agreeing Response Set as a Personality Variable," *Journal of Abnormal and Social Psychology* 60 (March, 1960): 151–75.

[8] Milbrath, *op. cit.*, p. 680ff.

[9] For a brief and lucid discussion of control, see E. Earl Baughman and George Schlager Welsh, *Personality: A Behavioral Science* (Englewood Cliffs: Prentice-Hall, Inc., 1962), pp. 217–19. In this connection Theodore Sarbin points out that the role construct should be supplemented by the idea of self. See Theodore R. Sarbin, "Role Theory," in Gardner Lindzey (ed.), *The Handbook of Social Psychology* (Reading: Addison-Wesley, 1954), p. 248.

[10] Baughman and Welsh, *op. cit.*, 219. In essence, the control mechanism links ego to temperament, and its particular form emerges out of the process of socialization. It is because of control's relationship to socialization that we argue that subcultural influences can override its influence. For a discussion of ego and control, see Baughman and Welsh, *op. cit.*, 266–67.

[11] The items in the three scales differentiate between respondents within a range of 52 to 78.4 percent, except for one item in the efficacy scale. The Guttman CR for the Personality Control Scale is .83 and MCR is .57. Guttman scale scores of three and four represented the middle group. Guttman scores of one and two represent one extreme group and five represents the other. The Guttman four scorers were included in the middle group because 39 of the 40 cases in this category gave two responses in each direction. Of those scoring one and two on the Guttman scale only nine respondents gave two responses going in two directions. Of the respondents with a Guttman scale score of five only eight respondents gave two responses going in two directions.

[12] The Guttman CR score for the Efficacy Scale is .94 and the MCR is .62. Guttman scale scores of four and five were used to represent low efficacy. Of respondents so scoring only 27 scored five. Of the 212 cases scoring four 60 gave responses going in two directions. A Guttman scale score of one represented high efficacy. All respondents with a score of one on the Guttman scale gave at least three responses going in the same direction.

[13] The median years of education for whites and nonwhites in Leon County is 12.0. The similar figure for nonwhites is 7.2. (The 12.0 figure deflates the white educational level as it includes all of the nonwhites as well. Consequently, the educational difference between the races is greater than these two figures indicate.) The Bureau of the Census, *U.S. Census of Population: 1960, General Social and Economic Characteristics, Florida*, PC(1)-11C, p. 235, p. 259.

[14] Owens, *op. cit.*, pp. 11–18.

[15] On this point see Key, *op. cit.*, pp. 154–62, and Campbell, *op. cit.*, pp. 197–98.

[16] Herbert Doherty, Jr., "Liberal and Conservative Voting Patterns in Florida," *The Journal of Politics* 14 (August, 1952): 403–17.

[17] The Guttman CR score on the Conservatism-Liberalism Scale is .89 and MCR is .60. Guttman scale scores of one and two represented liberal responses. All liberals gave at least three responses going in one direction. Guttman scores of four and five represented conservative responses. Thirty-five respondents who scaled four gave responses going in two directions. All classified as five on the Guttman scale gave at least three responses going in the same direction.

[18] Prior to the passage of the 1964 Civil Rights Act only a few Tallahassee public facilities served Negroes. Since the 1964 Act virtually all facilities are open to Negroes.

[19] The interview schedule utilized for Negro respondents reads: "Do you think white people ought to work on jobs where a Negro is the boss?"

Alienation and Political Behavior

Joel D. Aberbach

I. Introduction: Alienation

Alienation is both one of the most popular and vague concepts used by contemporary social scientists. Scholars often cite Robert Nisbet's statement that alienation is basically a perspective.[1] The current age is said to be one of alienation, or writers declare alienation to be the fundamental interpretive concept for explaining deviant behavior. One author has even gone so far as to say that definition is unnecessary because we can all feel what "it" is in our very bones. Indeed, if we don't understand it intuitively we are alienated by definition.[2]

Recently, there have been a series of attempts to clarify the meaning of the term. Daniel Bell, commenting on the uses of the concept alienation in the works of Marx, distinguishes *estrangement* ("a socio-psychological condition") from *reification* ("a philosophical category with psychological overtones").[3] For research purposes, the fundamental difference between these meanings lies in the criteria which are applied in determining whether an indivudal is alienated. The existence of estrangement is determined by investigating the attitudes of individuals; reification is measured against "objective" standards about the quality of human life established by the investigator.

The reification (objective) tradition has many strong exponents.[4] It offers a potentially powerful concept to an analyst wishing to evaluate the human condition in terms of explicitly stated criteria of what man *ought*

Joel D. Aberbach, "Alienation and Political Behavior," *American Political Science Review* 62 (1969): 86–99. Reprinted with permission.

to be in his social and personal relationships. Most of the contemporary scholarly work, however, is concerned with estrangement, and my own interest also lies in the individual's perception of the situation he faces.

Merely limiting ourselves to determining the existence or degree of alienation by gauging the attitudes of individuals is but a small step forward in clarifying what we mean by the term. Fortunately, two contemporary scholars have laid a solid foundation for a more adequate conceptualization. Melvin Seeman's "On the Meaning of Alienation" systematically isolates five "basic ways in which the concept of alienation has been used" in the literature.[5] He suggests an effort to explore the interrelationships between operational measures of these variants and also the causes and consequences of them.[6] Kenneth Keniston, in a very concise appendix to his study of alienated youth, suggests that[7]

... while the concept of alienation in every variation suggests the loss or absence of a previous or desirable relationship, it requires further specification in at least four respects:

1. *Focus:* Alienated from what?
2. *Replacement:* What replaces the old relationship? (This might more crisply be referred to as the *form* of the alienation.)
3. *Mode:* How is the alienation manifest?
4. *Agent:* What is the agent (cause) of the alienation?

It is evident, as Keniston points out, that these four questions "provide a basis for a virtually limitless number of varieties of alienation."[8] A person must naturally wonder if it might not simply be better to discard the term. This solution is quite appealing, but Keniston speaks of the certainty in this case "that the same problems of definition would crop up again and again with some cognate term like estrangement, disaffection, or detachment."[9] An even more important reason for at least temporarily retaining the term, I think, is that it has been employed in a great number of widely used theories and one task of scholars at this point should be to clarify when and how various forms of alienation do serve as important independent or intervening variables and whether these attitudes are meaningfully structured in people's minds. The Keniston scheme is valuable for empirical and theoretical purposes because it stimulates definitional and measurement refinements (i.e., looking at alienation in terms of form [subject] and focus [object]), and emphasizes the place of the various types of alienation in a chain of sources and consequences.

In this paper I have taken operational measures of two commonly accepted forms of alienation (trust and efficacy),[10] in each case provided two foci for each form, and examined the relationship between individuals' scores on these indicators and their political behavior. I am trying to discover the value of measuring alienation in this way—i.e., do the various forms of alienation lead to different types of behavior and does the focus of the measurement make a difference?

While a test of the utility of Keniston's scheme in empirical research is valuable in itself, there is a broader set of questions raised in the existing literature on alienation and political behavior. Basically, these concern the conditions which stimulate the political mobilization of the alienated. Therefore, before presenting the data, I will review the relevant literature, giving special attention to discussions of the political settings in which attitudes of alienation are important determinants of behavior and to contradictions in research findings which appear to result from inadequate consideration of the forms and foci of alienation. This review emphasizes the literature on American political behavior since it is the subject matter of the most systematic research and also the setting for the data employed here. I begin with authors who do not use direct measures of both aliena-

tion and behavior in establishing relationships and then consider those who do.

II. Some Views in the Literature

One prominent interpretation is that the alienated (the term is usually very broadly defined) are quiescent under ordinary circumstances, but subject to mobilization into mass movements (or at least support of extremist, demagogic and/or authoritarian political leaders) when the material or psychological circumstances are proper and the right leader presents himself.[11] Empirical studies done in the United States on support for extremist leaders and groups do not present a very clear picture. Thus, while Nelson Polsby found that Senator McCarthy gathered the bulk of his support in areas "where the Republican Party was strongest"[12] and that his reputed influence on elections outside of Wisconsin had no basis in fact, Michael Rogin's study of George Wallace's 1964 Democratic presidential primary campaign in Wisconsin demonstrated that Republican crossover voters (particularly in middle- and upper-class districts) gave him substantial support.[13] The implication of the first study is that McCarthy's impact on the behavior of voters was negligible, but the second indicates that many Republicans may compose a natural reservoir of support for classic American demagogues.[14] Some substantiation of the latter point is found in the Wolfinger, et al., study of Christian Anti-communist Crusaders where the most salient characteristic of respondents studied was that they were Republicans.[15]

A more general principle may do something to reconcile any surface contradictions in these studies: In clearly structured general elections, standard reference symbols like party and group govern the direction of voting behavior; but in situations where these symbols provide no clear guide (primaries, nonpartisan elections, decisions to join movements of various types), other factors can assume great importance. In the Rogin (Wallace) case, many Republicans were people prone to "express their general resentment against outside interference in their lives—from government as well as Negroes"[16] and gave this feeling free reign (along with certain working-class Democrats) in a primary where an issue appropriate to this sentiment was raised, while in the Polsby (McCarthy) case voting was more clearly on party lines and motivations based in resentment were more obscure.

Support for this interpretation can be found in the literature on the impact of personality on politics ably summarized by Greenstein.[17] Drawing on the writings of Lane, Shils, Christie and Jahoda, Levinson and others in the field, Greenstein stresses that an unambiguous environment reduces the opportunities for personal variations in behavior. Where the situation is clearly structured—for example, an attractive reference group takes a clear and definite stand, or strong sanctions are attached to certain behavior alternatives—the scope for personality to affect behavior is severely limited. However, where salient reference groups have conflicting points of view, or "current situations . . . are in conflict with previous experience," etc., the individual's clues are not clear and personality factors can play a key role.[18]

Writers employing psychological measures of alienation present evidence which appears to confirm this general principle. For example, detailed investigations of referendum voting consistently emphasize the negativism of the politically alienated "lead [ing] to an attitude on a given issue which represents a protest against the existing structure in the community."[19] The alienated, therefore, tend to express their resentment in negative votes on bond issues and the like. This could, of course, also explain the behavior of certain Republicans in the Wallace primary.

A more detailed look at these studies is in order because of the nature of the measures employed and the different arenas (foci) considered. In some cases combined (composite) measures of political distrust (cynicism) and powerlessness are used.[20] The focus of the measurement items in these cases is clearly the local government and the dependent variable is vote in a local referendum. Composites are useful devices for either obtaining a more homogenous and precise measurement of a variable or for obtaining a better device for predicting another variable.[21] However,

forming them on an *ad hoc* basis (i.e., without either of the above purposes clearly in mind) may disguise the relationship of some of the components with outside variables or otherwise distort the results.[22]

My argument is not that it is illegitimate to base an operational definition of political alienation on an assertion that alienation "really" means, for example, a state in which an individual is powerless and distrusts those who govern, but that using an *ad hoc* composite to measure political alienation is self-defeating and leaves unanswered a series of nagging questions. Just how are the indicators related? Which part of the composite index is causing the relationships described or, better, how does each indicator relate to the various dependent variables? Perhaps they operate in the same way, maybe only one plays a significant role, or perhaps there are interesting interactions between the indicators which are significant theoretically and empirically.[23] The fundamental reason for defining alienation as a combination of distrust and powerlessness is the expectation that the joint occurrence of the two attitudes produces a unique behavioral tendency[24] and this should be established rather than, as in the case of these authors, assumed.

Other researchers in this area have used powerlessness measures alone in their work or have made some incomplete tests on the independent effects of powerlessness and distrust. Horton and Thompson, for example, emphasize that "referendums may serve as institutional outlets for protest . . . on the part of the powerless and ordinarily apathetic members of the community."[25] They operationally define political alienation as a feeling of powerlessness and an identification of an appropriate power center as a controlling agent.[26] They not only find the expected relationship between the composite index of powerlessness and negative voting, but they present some evidence that the feeling of powerlessness by itself has an independent effect on voting behavior in this instance.[27] They do have a direct measure of the distrust of local government, but it is unfortunately not discussed in terms of political behavior.

William Gamson's work on attitudes toward water fluoridation proposals is also germane here. He cites

Coleman's suggestion that this issue gives citizens an opportunity to vent their frustrations against local administrators who introduce the idea.[28] Gamson attempted to gauge ideological differences between respondents in his Cambridge, Massachusetts sample, but found that "overt differences in ideology concerning individual rights and government intervention have little to do with the average voter's position on fluoridation in this Cambridge precinct."[29] However, alienation measures were useful as predictors. Indicators of powerlessness and meaninglessness did successfully discriminate opponents of fluoridation from proponents,[30] but measures of distrust did not. Unfortunately, the measures of powerlessness were political and those of distrust were not, but we can see that distrust is not necessarily related to issue negativism.

Clearly, on these local issues, a perceived sense of powerlessness does lead to negative voting or to opposition to certain controversial programs. However, it is not certain just what effect distrust of local government exerts and how it interacts with feelings of powerlessness.

It is also still not clear that attitudes of alienation (of any form) play a role in voting in all types of referendums. One author has suggested that alienation is important in determining direction of vote only in referendums where "vague emotion-laden symbols are employed"[31] and that the alienated may turn out in large numbers in other types of referendums and vote like other citizens. There is, obviously, still a great need for research on the whole question of turnout, alienation and vote in local referendums and, for that matter, in local partisan elections.

If research and knowledge on the relationship between alienation and vote are somewhat confused and definitely incomplete on local elections, they are virtually non-existent on national elections. Templeton found alienation, in this case measured by Srole's Anomia scale,[32] unrelated to respondents' party identification or voting behavior in 1956 and 1960.[33] However, following Levin and Eden,[34] he finds some inferential support for the notion that the "quality" of the vote cast by an alienated voter may be different, i.e., that he tends to vote negatively and is most inspired when issues are perceived in terms of good and evil. Since, under most circumstances, "both major parties present themselves as 'responsible' national voices and both are in fact committed to the established political system . . . neither provides the citizen with the opportunity to validate his personal rejection of the political system."[35] As a result of this, says Templeton, the alienated citizen tends to withdraw from participation in the national political process. He manifests this through inconsistent voting (vacillating between the parties), and low political knowledge and interest,[36] although no evidence is presented of unusual nonparticipation in voting per se. According to this view, the whole process of national politics as usually practiced in this country serves to insulate us from a direct impact of the alienated feelings of part of the electorate.

Reported data on political efficacy are replete with findings of nonparticipation, low interest, etc., on the part of the inefficacious,[37] but there is no evidence that they are "protest voters" in national elections. Again, this may well be a function of the choices and symbols presented in these contests where party and group identifications provide such strong guides to behavior.

An analysis by Donald E. Stokes of the public's "basic evaluative orientations toward the national government"[38] (political trust) based on the SRC 1958 election study failed to turn up any very exciting positive information. Political trust was virtually unrelated to direction of party identification (and vote), but associated with rejection of the party system as indicated by failure to identify oneself along the partisan spectrum.[39] There was a relationship with sense of political efficacy (which Stokes sees as lying behind the individual's attitude toward government) and a slight tendency for poorly educated respondents scoring low on political trust to participate less frequently than others. Stokes feels that those who are low in trust have no articulate commitment to a fundamental change in the political order or to extremist movements or leaders, but that their negative orientation "must . . . be seen as latent support that might be tapped by parties or factions or individual political leaders whose stance is hostile to the prevailing order."[40] The basic and unresolved issue is still when and if this latent support can be tapped in elections given the role of the institutions of our political system in dampening the behavioral effects of attitudes of alienation.

A graphic example of this can be seen in investigations using the murky variable, authoritarianism. These yield some evidence that this attitude, which contains a strong element of hositility, has a much weaker impact on behavior in general elections than its effect on candidate preferences might indicate. While Lane, using SRC data, found a small relationship between authoritarianism and both Republican party identification and vote for Eisenhower in 1952,[41] Milton's study of the presidential preferences of University of Tennessee students in 1952 demonstrated that neither Eisenhower nor Stevenson received strong support from authoritarians, although Eisenhower was clearly preferred to Stevenson. With a more varied slate of nominees presented to them, authoritarian students opted heavily for Taft and MacArthur, two candidates whose names were not on the official ballot.[42] Two basic points in the Milton study should be noted: (1) There was a strong correlation "between the authoritarianism attributed to aspirants for candidacy and the F-scale scores of students preferring each man"[43] in this preference test without partisan structure; and (2) The actual nominees were those least attractive to authoritarians, although one candidate (Eisenhower) was preferred.

Given the above, to provide some satisfactory test of the effects of attitudes of alienation on political behavior in national elections we need an appropriate set of stimuli. For science, the 1964 election was a blessing.

III. Setting and Procedures

In 1964 the Republicans nominated a candidate widely labelled as an "extremist,"[44] a man who offered people "a choice, not an echo," and whose covert appeal to racism (in addition to an overt appeal to the old American values) was at least given credence in the mass media if it was not based in his own

Table 1
Alienation Items

A. Interpersonal Trust (Trust in People)

1. Generally speaking, would you say that most people can be trusted or that you can't be too careful in dealing with people?
2. Would you say that most of the time people try to be helpful or that they are mostly just looking out for themselves?
3. Do you think most people would try to take advantage of you if they got a chance or would they try to be fair?

B. Political Trust (Prefaced by the following statement: Now I'd like to talk about some of the different ideas people have about the government in Washington and see how you feel about them. These opinions don't refer to Democrats or Republicans in particular but just to the government in general. For example:)

1. Do you think that quite a few of the people running the government are a little crooked, not very many are, or do you think hardly any of them are crooked at all?
2. Do you think that people in the government waste a lot of money we pay in taxes, waste some of it, or don't waste very much of it?
3. How much of the time do you think you can trust the government in Washington to do what is right—just about always, most of the time, or only some of the time?
4. Do you feel that almost all of the people running the government are smart people who usually know what they are doing, or do you think that quite a few of them don't seem to know what they are doing?
5. Would you say the government is pretty much run by a few big interests looking out for themselves or that it is run for the benefit of all the people?

C. Personal Efficacy (Personal Effectiveness)

1. Have you usually felt pretty sure your life would work out the way you want it to, or have there been times when you haven't been very sure about it?
2. Do you feel that you are the kind of person who gets his share of bad luck or do you feel that you have mostly good luck?
3. When you make plans ahead do you usually get to carry out things the way you expected, or do things usually come up to make you change your plans?

D. Political Efficacy (Agree—Disagree Statements)

1. Voting is the only way that people like me can have a say about how the government runs things.
2. People like me don't have any say about what the government does.
3. Sometimes politics and government seem so complicated that a person like me can't really understand what's going on.
4. I don't think public officials care much what people like me think.

intentions. This represented a major opportunity for investigating the relationship between attitudes of alienation and direction of voting behavior in a situation conducive to the joint variation of the two in a national election. The 1964 election study of the Survey Research Center at the University of Michigan provides a vehicle for such an investigation.

Fortunately, this study contained four separate measures of alienation as well as rich information on political attitudes and voting behavior. There were indicators of political trust (a slightly modified version of the Stokes scale) and interpersonal trust (trust in people),[45] political efficacy and personal efficacy (personal effectiveness).[46] In other words, we have measures of two forms (subjects) of alienation and two foci (objects) for each form. As Table 1 indicates, the items in the trust-in-people and personal-efficacy measures refer to the self and the environment in a very general way; they ask about "most people," "luck," and "life" working out, etc. The political trust items, on the other hand, refer to the government in Washington very specifically and the political efficacy questions have a manifest political content.[47] A factor-analytic test shows that these items, as predicted, fall empirically on distinct psychological dimensions, although the factors are positively correlated.[48] Available evidence, therefore, points to the fact that thinking about alienation in terms of form and focus should be useful empirically as well as conceptually.

I have constructed separate standardized indices for each factor in the form of T-scores (i.e., with a mean of 50 and a standard deviation of 10) and, for purposes of this analysis, consolidated the scales so that each value represents a standard deviation unit. These scales are then related to vote in the 1964 election and, where results indicate the utility of further exploration, are correlated with additional variables

under controlled conditions. Sometimes comparisons are made to relationships in other elections. The goal is always to illuminate, in as much depth as a secondary analysis permits, the conditions under which these attitudes of alienation are relevant to behavior.

The analysis is limited to white respondents because of one stark fact: there is simply no meaningful variation in the direction of Negroes' votes in 1964. This comes as no surprise in light of the issues involved, but illustrates the general principle that when a highly salient reference group's interests are threatened in a political contest, its members behave in a uniform manner if a clear behavioral option is open.[49]

IV. Findings

A look at the relationship in Table 2 between the different attitudes of alienation measured here and the direction of vote in 1964 reveals rather clearly that *only* political trust was a viable zero-order predictor of vote in this election.[50] Table 3 illustrates the true strength of this relationship. The others are substantively trivial. Even interpersonal trust, which is seen by many as the fundamental underpinning of political trust,[51] did not successfully predict the candidate chosen by the electorate on this occasion. Clearly, both the form and focus of alienation are important factors to consider in any study.

An immediate question arises as to whether political trust, as measured here, is really just a proximal partisan attitude of the type used so successfully by the authors of *The American Voter* in predicting vote.[52] This is not the case. Campbell, *et al.* found

Table 2
T_c Correlations between Attitudes of Alienation and Vote, 1964

Attitude	Interpersonal Trust	Political Trust	Personal Efficacy	Political Efficacy
Vote* (1 = Johnson) (0 = Goldwater)	−.01	.39	−.03	−.05

* A positive coefficient indicates that the higher the person's score on the index (high score equals positive attitude or allegiance), the more likely he was to vote for the Democrat.

Table 3
Political Trust and Vote, 1964

Political Trust*	0	1	2	3	4	5
Vote Goldwater	62.7%	52.3%	36.5%	29.9%	20.9%	13.5%
Johnson	37.3%	47.7%	63.5%	70.1%	79.1%	86.5%
N =	185	149	104	197	215	156

* In T-score terms (i.e., a mean of 50 and standard deviation of 10):

0 = Below 40	3 = 51–55
1 = 40–45	4 = 56–60
2 = 46–50	5 = Above 60

party identification very strongly related to each of the partisan attitudes they described,[53] but in 1964 political trust was only mildly related to party identification ($T_c = .15$, i.e., Republicans were less trusting than Democrats). The strength of the relationship between political trust and vote ($T_c = .39$) goes well beyond what one might expect from the measure of association given for party identification.

It is useful to compare the relationships between party identification, political trust, and vote in 1958 and 1964. It would probably be better to make a direct comparison of two Presidential elections,[54] but when I did this analysis these were the only election studies available where the relevant data were gathered, and there is reasonable evidence that the 1958 data are not atypical on the relationship of political trust to both party identification and vote. In 1958, political trust was negatively correlated with Democratic party identification ($T_c = -.06$, i.e., the Democrats were slightly more distrustful) and Democratic vote for Congress ($T_c = -.08$). There is, then, some evidence that a mild partisan element is captured by the measure of political trust since the followers of the party *out* of power tend to be less trusting,[55] but the behavioral relevance of this attitude in 1964 went well beyond this. The special significance of the 1964 election in this regard is manifested in the correlation between political trust (measured, you will recall, in 1964) and respondent's memory of his 1960 vote. As one might expect, respondents disproportionately remember voting for Kennedy (61.1 percent), but the correlation between reported Kennedy vote and politi-

cal trust is only .14 (compared to .39 with Johnson vote). There is *no* relationship between 1958 political trust scores and recalled vote for Eisenhower in 1956. In respect to the relationship of political trust to vote, then, 1958 appears to be a fairly typical year and 1964 a very unusual one.

If we examine the relationship between political trust and vote for the two years in more detail the situation becomes even clearer. Controlling for party identification virtually eliminates even the small relationship between distrust and Democratic vote for Congress in 1958, but the pattern in 1964 is striking. As Table 4 demonstrates, the most strongly identified partisans in 1964 were least affected in their voting behavior by the extent of their political distrust, while independents voted very heavily for Goldwater if they were distrustful. In this case, as with Negroes, a strong attachment to a reference group (here party) inhibited the effects of cynicism on the direction of the vote—only the least trusting Strong Democrats broke ranks to vote for Goldwater and only the most trusting Strong Republicans were able to support Johnson with their ballots.[56] It should also be noted that these relationships were stronger for the Republican identifiers than for the Democrats. This is probably because of the added pressures on these individuals to break party ranks in this election[57] as reflected here by the sensitivity of T_c coefficients to the slopes of relationships. The 1964 campaign, then, served to activate feelings of political hostility in a meaningful way for all but the most strongly identified partisans, and even these people were not totally immune.

Table 4

T_c Correlations between Political Trust and Democratic Vote by Party Identification and Year

Party Identification:	Strong Democrat	Democrat	Independent Democrat	Independent	Independent Republican	Republican	Strong Republican
Year 1958	−.03	.00	−.08	.03	*.37	.04	−.02
1964	.09	.25	.20	.49	.41	.34	.12

*This deviant coefficient is a function of the Democratic votes of 6 of the 9 Independent Republicans with the lowest scores on political trust. It is difficult to assess its substantive importance.

Even primary voters were strongly affected in their 1964 general election behavior by feelings of political trust or distrust. As one might suspect, primary voters are even more strongly identified with one of the two parties than other members of the electorate[58] and party identification provides them with an even stronger guide to electoral behavior than it does other voters. As Table 5 indicates, however, voters in the Republican primaries who were high in political trust split their votes between Goldwater and Johnson in the national election, while forty percent of the Democratic primary voters who were low in trust cast their ballots for Barry Goldwater. This table illustrates very plainly the fact that a larger proportion of the Republican than Democratic primary voters were politically distrustful and shows the influence of party on vote, but it also gives a clear indication of the importance of political trust in determining voter defections in this election,[59] even among the more active members of the electorate.

Without carrying this much further, it should be noted that people who engaged in activities beyond voting (attending political meetings, working in a campaign, writing letters, giving money) were more likely than others to support Goldwater in 1964, and the relationship between political trust and vote direction grew progressively stronger for the more active groups. The Republicans who could not support Goldwater tended to withdraw from active participation in the campaign. There is no evidence, however, that Goldwater was able to mobilize substantial numbers of politically distrustful voters who were previously politically inactive.[60]

Was there an interaction between political powerlessness and distrust in this election? Did individuals who saw themselves as politically powerless *and* distrustful of the national government flock to the Goldwater banner in unusual numbers? Clearly, as Table 6a shows, the powerless voted less often than the powerful in this election, regardless of their level of political trust. In addition, as both Tables 6a and 6b demonstrate, the distrustful were more likely to vote

Table 5

Political Trust by Voting Behavior for 1964 Primary Voters by Party Primary

		Voters in the 1964 Primaries					
		Republican Primary			Democratic Primary		
Political Trust		Low (0–1)	Medium (2–3)	High (4–5)	Low (0–1)	Medium (2–3)	High (4–5)
General Election Voting	Goldwater	·87%	74%	50%	40%	13%	7%
	Johnson	13	26	50	60	87	93
		100%	100%	100%	100%	100%	100%
		(N = 89)	(N = 51)	(N = 40)	(N = 88)	(N = 83)	(N = 127)

Table 6a
Political Powerlessness and Distrust by Voting Preference and Behavior,
1964

Alienation:*	Powerless and Distrustful %	Powerful and Distrustful %	Powerless and Trustful %	Powerful and Trustful %
Voted Democratic	45%	43%	60%	67%
Non-voter, Democratic Preference	20	10	26	16
Voted Republican	28	43	11	15
Non-voter, Republican Preference	7	4	3	2
	100%	100%	100%	100%
	(N = 296)	(N = 341)	(N = 300)	(N = 600)
No answer, Refuse or Don't Know on Voting Preference or Behavior	(N = 10)	(N = 3)	(N = 10)	(N = 8)

Table 6b
Political Powerlessness and Distrust among Voters Only

Alienation:*	Powerless and Distrustful %	Powerful and Distrustful %	Powerless and Trustful %	Powerful and Trustful %
Voted Democratic	61%	50%	85%	82%
Voted Republican	39	50	15	18
	100%	100%	100%	100%
	(N = 218)	(N = 293)	(N = 213)	(N = 496)

Percentages are down

* The powerful and trustful are defined as those above the sample mean (i.e., T > 50).

Republican, no matter how powerful or powerless they felt. In fact, individuals who felt powerless and distrustful were somewhat more likely to vote *against* Goldwater than persons who felt powerful as well as distrustful. This is the exact opposite of what those who stress an interaction between powerlessness and distrust would predict.

If a feeling of powerlessness does not act as a stimulus to voting for an extremist candidate among the distrustful, what does? While I cannot attempt to give a complete answer to this question here, the emphasis in the literature on negativism and protest among the alienated deserves some attention. The 1964 election heightened the tendency for people holding conservative attitudes to vote Republican,[61] but the more interesting phenomenon for our purposes is the inter-action between attitudinal negativism, political distrust and protest voting which occurred in *both* 1958 and 1964 (the two years for which we have data).

Table 7 is a comparison of the T_c coefficients relating political trust and Democratic vote in 1958 and 1964 within opinion categories of representative issues. For purposes of presentation only the correlations for the strongly favorable and strongly opposed categories are given,[62] but the magnitudes of the coefficients are usually ordered across the opinion spectrum. What emerges is a very interesting pattern (with one exception) where those strongly opposing a liberal policy position tend to vote against the party in power (in this case defined as the party holding the Presidency) if they are distrustful politically. Conservatism (or at least negative attitudes) and political

Table 7

T_c Correlations between Political Trust and Democratic Vote by Issue Attitude, and Year

	Issue Attitude (Direction)			
	1958	1964	1958	1964
1. Federal Aid to Education	.01	.21	−.17	.47
2. Government Enforced School Integration	.01	.27	−.16	.47
3. Government Enforced Equal Job Opportunity	.05	.25	−.25	.36
4. ⎰ Foreign Aid	*	.30	*	.46
Trade with Communist Nations	*	.21	*	.43
Internationalism**	−.08	**	.00	**

*Question not asked in 1958.

**Questions not asked in 1964. This general item was the only close approximation: "This country would be better off if we just stayed home and did not concern ourselves with problems in other parts of the world."

distrust interact to produce a behavioral negativism.

In 1958, politically distrustful people with conservative policy attitudes tended to vote Democratic and in 1964 similar individuals went heavily for the Republicans. The situation in 1964 was different, of course, in that the relationship between political distrust and vote held for those with positive (liberal) attitudes too, but the relationships here were much lower in magnitude than for the conservatives. These data suggest a modification of the hypothesis that there is a connection between alienation (at least in the form of political distrust) and protest voting. They suggest that attitudinal negativism on political issues is an important contextual factor which stimulates the relationship.[63] They show in addition, of course, that a candidacy like Goldwater's also makes political distrust behaviorally relevant for individuals with positive policy attitudes.

Certain important questions remain. First, are these issue attitudes important contextual factors in defining the relationship between other forms of alienation (or trust with a different focus) and behavior? The general answer, based on the measures available to me, is no. The only interesting differences are found in the relationship between political efficacy and vote, and here those with negative issue attitudes tended to vote disproportionately for Goldwater if they felt highly efficacious.[64] This is not only the exact opposite of the situation with political trust (since aliena-

tion is related to a Johnson vote in the efficacy case), but the magnitudes of the coefficients are exceedingly small (below .10) and it is hard to attach much substantive significance to them.

A second question concerns the meaning of issue conservatism here. Are the relationships found a reflection of an interaction between deeply held attitudes or are we merely dealing with a cumulation of negative feelings, some of which are shallow in content? The fact that the very vague item on internationalism asked in 1958 was the only one which did not stimulate a relationship between political distrust and negative voting leads one to suspect that there may be something to an interpretation which puts some emphasis on the substance of the particular issues involved, but this is certainly an open question at this point.[65] What is required now is research on the structure and stability of issue attitudes for the trustful and distrustful and an investigation of the cumulative effects of negative issue attitudes as they interact with political distrust in influencing the vote.

V. Political Alienation and the Political System: The Moderating Role of Institutions

In the American political system, basic issues are usually muted in elections and debate. Candidates for office seek the middle ground to gain marginal support, legislative personnel do the same to build winning coalitions, parties are composed of "wings" representing divergent points of view, etc. When this delicate system is upset, the patterns of people's responses to the stimuli presented also change. Motivations which are usually of limited importance in determining the direction of voting behavior can come strongly to the fore. This is especially true for individuals who are not very strongly committed to either of the established parties currently operating.

We have seen in the preceding pages a vivid example of the role of political institutions in moderating the effects of political hostility, and what can happen when this system does not function effectively. Goldwater's appeal was not unrecognized and did not go unheeded by large groups of people who were cynical about the personnel and operations of government. The basic issues and appeals in this election were, in one sense at least, *less* ambiguous than usual—the usual smoke screen laid down by fundamental agreement between traditional party candidates was missing—and voters responded accordingly. Party loyalties were partly set aside by basic orientations to the political system. The fact that Goldwater was so unsuccessful does not eliminate this fact, nor the possibility that a more able candidate could make better capital out of the potential manifested in this situation.[66]

It seems that the importance of a variable like political trust in governing the direction of vote is not determined solely by whether elections are structured contests between standard parties or non-structured (primaries, referendums, etc.), but by what appeals are made and how clearly they are perceived. In some cases party or group is a more relevant variable for organizing whatever perceptions exist and for making choices as to the direction of behavior than in others. The political system of the United States, as it traditionally operates, serves to dampen the relevance of attitudes like political trust, but this is not an inevitable by-product of partisan elections, even in a two-party system.

It is also apparent that attitudes of alienation are not equally relevant in each situation. Political trust was a powerful determinant of vote in 1964, but interpersonal trust, personal efficacy, and political efficacy were virtually irrelevant. The utility of speaking of alienation in terms of focus as well as form is amply demonstrated by the fact that the correlation between vote and scores on trust in people in 1964 was nonexistent ($T_c = -.01$) in spite of the extreme relevance of political trust. Goldwater's partisans, no matter what their party affiliation, were quite selective in the object of their distrust.

Evidence in the literature clearly suggests that politically inefficacious people vote negatively in referendums and there is inferential material to support the notion that the powerless are hostile to local authorities and express their distrust in this way. In 1964 there is absolutely no support for a model which holds that perceived powerlessness leads to political distrust which, in turn, leads to voting against the prevailing order (negative voting) or even for the simpler idea that attitudes of powerlessness and distrust interact in affecting behavior in national elections. The evidence is that political distrust alone (or, better, distrust interacting with negative policy attitudes) spurs negative voting in national elections, especially under certain favorable conditions which heighten the relevance of distrust to the voting choice. Feelings of powerlessness influence turnout, but *not* the voter's choices.

Why wasn't perceived political powerlessness a stimulus to negative voting in the 1964 election? One possibility, I think, is the nature of the Goldwater appeal. It was against a major governmental role in the society—opposed to a backdrop of social and economic security provided or supported by government. This kind of appeal might ring true to those who distrust government, but the politically powerless would, if anything, tend to feel that they need this protection. Therefore, the finding that those who felt politically powerless and distrustful were more likely to vote for Johnson than people who felt powerful and distrustful. If a populist-type candidate were to present himself to the electorate this might be reversed. In such a setting, powerlessness and distrust could conceivably interact significantly. Survey data on Wallace voters in the 1968 election will soon be available for testing this hypothesis.

Notes

This article is adapted from my doctoral dissertation prepared at Yale University under the supervision of Professor Robert E. Lane. I am grateful to Professor Lane for his invaluable help at every stage of the research and I would also like to thank Paul Conn and my colleagues M. Kent Jennings, Robert A. Schoenberger and Jack L. Walker for comments on an earlier draft of this paper. The data used here are from national surveys conducted by the Survey Research Center at The University of Michigan and made available through the Inter-University Consortium for Political Research.

[1] Robert A. Nisbet, *Community and Power* (New York: Oxford University Press, 1962), p. 15.

[2] Gerald Sykes (ed.), *Alienation: The Cultural Climate of Our Time* (New York: George Braziller, 1964), vol. 1, p. xiii.

[3] Daniel Bell, "The Rediscovery of Alienation: Some Notes Along the Quest for the Historical Marx," *Journal of Philosophy* 56 (1959): 933–34.

[4] See, for example, Erich Fromm's introduction to Erich Fromm (ed.), *Marx's Concept of Man* (New York: F. Ungar Publishing Co., 1961); and C. Wright Mills, *White Collar* (New York: Oxford University Press, 1951).

[5] Melvin Seeman, "On the Meaning of Alienation," *American Sociological Review* 24 (1959): 783. The five "variants" (as Seeman calls them) are: (1) Powerlessness; (2) Meaninglessness; (3) Normlessness; (4) Isolation; and (5) Self-Estrangement.

[6] Several of Seeman's students and others inspired by him have been particularly interested in empirical investigations of the dimensionality of these variants. See, in particular, Dwight G. Dean "Alienation: It's Meaning and Measurement," *American Sociological Review* 26 (1961): 753–58; and Arthur G. Neal and Salomon Rettig, "On the Multidimensionality of Alienation," *American Sociological Review* 32 (1967): 54–64.

[7] Kenneth Keniston, *The Uncommitted: Alienated Youth in American Society* (New York: Harcourt, Brace and World, Inc., 1965), p. 454.

[8] *Ibid.*, p. 454.

[9] *Ibid.*, p. 452.

[10] For an extended discussion of the forms of alienation commonly used in the literature and a critique of Seeman's article, see Joel D. Aberbach, *Alienation and Race* (unpublished Ph.D. Dissertation, Yale University, 1967), especially pp. 7–12 and 71–4.

[11] See, for the best known example, William Kornhauser, *The Politics of Mass Society* (Glencoe: Free Press, 1959). For Kornhauser, alienation is described rather indiscriminately in several forms. He employs operational measures of political inefficacy, social distrust and low ego strength in his secondary analyses and alludes to expressions of hostility and resentment against established insitutions in the text. (See, among others, pp. 109–12, 148 and 166.) Economic dislocation, social shock caused by events like defeat in war and/or social confusion accompanied by demogogic attack on the existing political system can arouse the public susceptible to mass appeals. The mass man (who suffers from "a lack of proximate attachments") lacks internalized standards and is, therefore, politically volatile. When there are no clear signals available his anxiety is mixed with political apathy, but spasmodic "flights into activity" are also characteristic. Precise predictions about the behavioral and psychological results of alienation are not made by the theory except at the extremes of a continuum which runs from no signals (resulting in apathy) to appeals in time of acute societal distress (yielding active mass movements).

[12] Nelson W. Polsby, "Toward an Explanation of McCarthyism" in Nelson W. Polsby, Robert A. Dentler and Paul A. Smith (eds.), *Politics and Social Life* (Boston: Houghton Mifflin Company, 1963), p. 816.

[13] Michael Rogin, "Wallace and the Middle Class: The White Backlash in Wisconsin," *Public Opinion Quarterly* 30 (1966): 98–109. On page 100 he says that "In Wisconsin, a state where Republicans can vote in the Democratic primary, Wallace's vote closely resembled the normal Republican vote." This analysis involves ecological correlations and thus all of the risks which go with it but Polsby's basic technique is similar.

[14] *Ibid.*, p. 106. Rogin, it should be noted, points to the fact that there were some differences in the support attracted by Wallace and McCarthy. Wallace was stronger in working-class areas, while McCarthy did much better in rural areas. But he emphasized that "each was strong among conservative Republicans" (p. 105). This is a deduction supported by some reasonable evidence, but Rogin discounts the unpopularity of Governor Reynolds who stood in for Johnson in the primary and the possibility that Republicans crossed over to vote for Wallace in order to embarrass the Democrats. These data, of course, cannot be used to make a definitive conclusion in this area.

[15] Raymond E. Wolfinger, Barbara Kaye Wolfinger, Kenneth Prewitt, and Sheilah Rosenhack, "America's Radical Right: Politics and Ideology," pp. 262–93, in David E. Apter (ed.), *Ideology and Discontent* (New York: The Free Press of Glencoe, 1964). See especially, p. 288. The subjects in this study felt quite efficacious politically (and, therefore not alienated in the powerlessness sense), were fundamentalist Goldwater supporters and "old-fashioned individualists."

[16] Rogin, *op. cit.,* p. 106.

[17] Fred I. Greenstein, "The Impact of Personality on Politics: An Attempt to Clear Away Underbrush," this REVIEW 61 (1967): 629–42. Personality is not defined by Greenstein because psychologists themselves have not come close to an agreed-upon meaning of the term and, more importantly, because he is really talking about "psychological factors" (p. 630) which is a very broad category indeed. This broad focus is forced upon him by the content of the literature being reviewed as much as by any personal preference.

[18] Robert E. Lane, *Political Life* (Glencoe: Free Press, 1959), p. 99.

[19] Wayne E. Thompson and John E. Horton, "Political Alienation as a Force in Political Action," *Social Forces* 38 (1960): 195.

[20] *Ibid.;* and Edward L. McDill and Jeanne Claire Ridley, "Status, Anomia, Political Alienation and Political Participation," *American Journal of Sociology* 68 (1962): 205–14. No test of unidimensionality is reported.

[21] Edwin E. Ghiselli, *The Theory of Psychological Measurement* (New York: McGraw-Hill, 1964), p. 184. When the analyst wishes to make his measurement of a variable more homogenous and precise he chooses elements which have relatively high intercorrela-

tions. One does not greatly increase the correlation between a composite variable and an outside variable if the components added to form the composite are highly correlated. However, when a composite is developed for purposes of prediction, the components will probably be correlated at a low level with each other and the addition of each element will greatly increase the level of correlation with the outside variable. The goal in this case, then, is a composite formed of relatively independent components each highly correlated with the outside variable we wish to predict.

[22] See Richard F. Curtis and Elton P. Jackson, "Multiple Indicators in Survey Research," *American Journal of Sociology* 68 (1962): 195–204.

[23] This argument is made in detail in Aberbach, *op. cit.*, Ch. 2. I am currently preparing an article which reviews the literature on alienation in these terms.

[24] Clarence N. Stone makes a similar point in "Local Referendums: An Alternative to the Alienated-Voter Model," *Public Opinion Quarterly* 29 (1962): 213–22.

[25] John E. Horton and Wayne E. Thompson, "Powerlessness and Political Negativism: A Study of Defeated Local Referendums," *American Journal of Sociology* 67 (1962): 485.

[26] There is an implied, but not explicit, element of distrust in the second element of the definition.

[27] Horton and Thompson, *op. cit.*, p. 490, Table 1.

[28] William Gamson, "The Fluoridation Dialogue," *Public Opinion Quarterly* 35 (1961): 533; citing James Coleman, *Community Conflict* (Glencoe: Free Press, 1957).

[29] Gamson, *op. cit.*, p. 531.

[30] *Ibid.*, p. 535. As in the other studies, these relationships hold with social status controlled.

[31] Stone, *op. cit.*, p. 222. He includes school bonds in this category along with fluoridation and charter elections. More "concrete" issues which Stone hypothesizes draw large turnouts, but do not activate feelings of alienation, include such things as water supply, fire protection, etc. This is the familiar distinction between style and position issues.

[32] Fredric Templeton, "Alienation and Political Participation," *Public Opinion Quarterly* 30 (1966): 252. In light of our discussion of alienation in terms of form and focus it should be noted that Templeton believes "it . . . unlikely that the present findings would be appreciably modified by using one of the other currently available measures of alienation."

[33] *Ibid.*, pp. 254–55.

[34] Murray B. Levin and Murray Eden, "Political Strategy for the Alienated Voter," *Public Opinion Quarterly* 26 (1962): 47–63, cited in Templeton, *op. cit.*, p. 255.

[35] *Ibid.*, p. 256. Note that Templeton believed the 1964 election might constitute a "partial exception to this generalization."

[36] *Ibid.*, p. 256.

[37] See, for example, Angus Campbell, Philip E. Converse, Warren E. Miller and Donald E. Stokes, *The American Voter* (New York: John Wiley & Sons, 1960), pp. 103–5.

[38] Donald E. Stokes, "Popular Evaluations of Government: An Empirical Assessment" in Harlan Cleveland and Harold D. Lass-

well (eds.), *Ethics and Bigness: Scientific, Academic, Religious, Political and Military* (New York: Harper and Brothers, 1962), p 64.

[39] *Ibid.*, p. 69. Stokes is referring to the small number of people who fall into the SRC a-political category and not to those who classify themselves as independents.

[40] *Ibid.*, p. 72.

[41] Robert E. Lane, "Political Personality and Electoral Choice," *American Political Science Review* 49 (1955): 173–90. See Table IV on p. 181 and the conclusion, p. 190.

[42] O. Milton, "Presidential Choice and Partisan Performance on a Scale of Authoritarianism," *The American Psychologist* 7 (1952): 597–8. The reference is from Richard Christie, "Authoritarianism Re-examined," pp. 123–97 in Richard Christie and Marie Jahoda (eds.), *Studies in the Scope and Method of "The Authoritarian Personality"* (Glencoe: The Free Press, 1954).

[43] *Ibid.*, p. 146.

[44] This was a part of the rhetoric of the campaign in the primaries as well as the national election, but was also accepted by less directly partisan individuals. See, for example, Robert A. Dahl, "The American Oppositions," pp. 65–8 in Robert A. Dahl (ed.), *Political Oppositions in Western Democracies* (New Haven: Yale University Press, 1966), where he discusses the response of the "Alienated Right" (p. 66) to both Joe McCarthy and Barry Goldwater. Both, he says, wished to "shake off the shackles of two-party pragmatic, compromising politics and offer a radical and uncompromising alternative."

[45] Morris Rosenberg, "Misanthropy and Political Ideology," *American Sociological Review* 21 (1956): 690–5, developed the basic scale.

[46] Angus Campbell et al., *op. cit.*, pp. 516–17, developed this measure as an "agree-disagree' scale. It has since been modified.

[47] It would be better to have political efficacy questions which focus on the federal government also. See Edgar Litt, "Political Cynicism and Political Futility," *The Journal of Politics* 25 (1963): 312–23, for an example of the potential importance of this. I am currently conducting a study designed, in part, to check the relevance of focus in measuring efficacy.

[48] Principal component factors with eigen-values (amount of variance explained) greater than one were rotated using both orthogonal and oblique criteria. The four factors extracted explained about 65 percent of the variance of all variables. The clarity of structure was marked, with the items for each measure showing strong loadings on separate factors. An oblique factor analysis using the biquartimin solution recommended by Harmon (see Harry Harmon, *Modern Factor Analysis* (Chicago: University of Chicago Press, 1960), pp. 261–337) yielded the following correlations between the primary factors:

	Trust in People	Political Trust	Political Efficacy	Personal Efficacy
Trust in People	—	.16	.11	.13
Political Trust		—	.07	.12
Political Efficacy			—	.05
Personal Efficacy				—

See Aberbach, *op. cit.*, pp. 75–101 for a full discussion. These findings will be reported in detail in an article I am now writing. Similar findings are reported in Arthur G. Neal and Salomon Rettig, "On the Multidimensionality of Alienation," *American Sociological Review* 32 (1967): 54–64.

[49] Negro bloc-voting is not uncommon, even in less dire situations. John C. Legget, for example, studied the 1958 gubernatorial election in Michigan using a sample of 375 Detroit blue-collar workers. He found that class consciousness and union militance had a strong influence on white workers' voting behavior (the more militant voted for the reform candidate), but that Negroes voted for the reform candidate regardless of militance or union membership. See John C. Legget, "Working Class Consciousness, Race and Political Choice," *American Journal of Sociology* 69 (1963): 171–77.

[50] The ordinal correlation used here is Kendall's tau_c (T_c). It ranges between 0 and 1, but reaches unity when all cells are empty except those in the diagonal. Since this rarely happens, T_c seldom approaches unity and is a very conservative (although sensitive) measure of association. See Maurice G. Kendall, *Rank Correlation Methods* (London: C. Griffin, 1955), Chs. 1 and 3; and Hubert M. Blalock, *Social Statistics* (New York: McGraw Hill, 1960), pp. 321–24.

[51] See, for example, Morris Rosenberg, *op. cit.*, pp. 690–5; Robert E. Lane, *Political Life* (Glencoe: Free Press, 1959), p. 164; and Gabriel Almond and Sidney Verba, *The Civic Culture* (Princeton: Princeton University Press, 1963), p. 285.

[52] Campbell, et al., *op. cit.*, Chs. 3, 14, 19.

[53] *Ibid.*, pp. 128–33.

[54] Presidential, as compared to Congressional, elections usually stimulate turnout. This was true in 1964 as compared to 1958, although it is not always the case. See Angus Campbell, "Surge and Decline: A Study of Electoral Change," *Public Opinion Quarterly* 24 (1960): 397–418.

[55] The 1966 SRC election study, now available for analysis, had items comparable to those asked in 1958 and 1964 and results of a quick analysis confirm what is reported throughout the body of this article. On the particular point at issue here, Democrats (with their party in power) were slightly more trusting than Republicans (T_c = .13) and the trusting voted for the Democratic candidates for Congress (T_c = .16). Again the other alienation measures were totally irrelevant in predicting the voters' choices.

[56] It is interesting to note that *Gamma* coefficients are less sensitive to this fact, but give a better indication of the fact that a relationship exists for every group of identifiers. These coefficients are as follows:

Strong Democrat	.49
Democrat	.48
Independent Democrat	.63
Independent	.75
Independent Republican	.66
Republican	.42
Strong Republican	.45

[57] see Philip E. Converse, Aage R. Clausen and Warren E. Miller, "Electoral Myth and Reality: The 1964 Election," *American Political Science Review* 59 (1965): 321–37; and Donald E. Stokes, "Some Dynamic Elements of Contests for the Presidency," *American Political Science Review* 60 (1966): 19–29, especially pp. 21–3.

[58] It should be noted that very few members of the troublesome Wisconsin electorate are represented in the 1964 SRC sample since only Sheboygan was in the sampling frame. A study done in Wisconsin (Austin Ranney and Leon D. Epstein, "The Two Electorates: Voters and Non-Voters in a Wisconsin Primary," *Journal of Politics* 28 (1966): 598–617), however, demonstrated that even there (p. 613) "primary voters, far more than party identifiers who did not vote in primaries, merited the description 'the party faithful'" since they (primary voters) did not defect as much from their party in general elections as non-primary voters and were more active politically.

[59] Unfortunately, the SRC data do not indicate who the individual voted for in the particular primaries.

[60] In Stokes, *op. cit.*, there is very minor evidence of a relationship between past voting participation and political distrust, i.e., the greater the distrust, the less regular a person's voting turnout. There is no evidence of this in the Goldwater election. This not only negated a part of his electroal strategy, but goes against notions about the mobilization of the alienated non-voter in certain electoral situations.

[61] The correlations between Republican identification and issue attitudes also increased.

[62] SRC asked respondents to rate their agreement with an attitude statement on a five-point Likert scale ranging from "Agree Strongly" to "Disagree Strongly" in 1958, and in 1964 asked them opinions on an issue first and then assessed opinion intensity.

[63] The 1966 election data reveal a similar pattern.

[64] In contrast, the highly efficacious voters with positive issue attitudes tended to vote for Johnson.

[65] See Campbell et al., *op. cit.*, Chs. 8 and 9, and Philip E. Converse, "The Nature of Belief Systems in Mass Publics," pp. 206–62 in David E. Apter (ed.), *Ideology and Discontent* (New York: Free Press of Glencoe, 1964). Given the research reported by these scholars, an ideological interpretation must be approached with great caution.

[66] See Philip E. Converse et al., *op. cit.*, pp. 321–36. They point out how poor Goldwater's appeal was on most policy issues and how fear of his position on non-racial issues often muted the so-called "white-backlash" which did exist as a powerful potential. A more effective candidate with his views who could avoid labels like "trigger-happy" might have done considerably better. Certainly, these data indicate that an appreciable increase in the number of people holding strongly negative issue opinions would increase the vote totals of a Goldwater-type candidate.

3

Social Interaction, Structure and Conflict

In attempting to understand political actions and orientations to political objects many political scientists have relied heavily on a sociological paradigm emphasizing one's position within the social structure. This position is usually operationalized as class or socioeconomic status, and it has been used to explain variance in a host of political variables. Despite the "power" of status-related independent variables, the social-psychological basis of identifications within structures is one that has been frequently ignored. We propose to focus on the basis of these identifications, the interactions that occur within groups and conflicts between groups and statuses. Each of these notions has a more secure tie to social-psychological interpretations than status per se.

When contemporary scholars refer to the "political system", they mean a system of *behavior,* with a network of interrelated *roles,* bound together by their relationship to a common set of goals and functions which are defined as "political." In David Easton's terms, the political aspect of human activity is that which affects ". . . the authoritative allocation of values for a society."[1] The systems perspective leads to a focus on the dynamics of politics and enables the observer to view the political world in terms more encompassing than just governmental institutions.

[1] *A Systems Analysis of Political Life* (New York: John Wiley & Sons, Inc., 1965), Chapter 2.

Role

The basic component of a system of behavior is the role, which in turn can be defined as *the behavioral element of status or position.* For example, one can occupy the status of father, husband, legislator, etc. The behavior he engages in with respect to any of his positions follows in part from one's interpretation of his role. Any role in society will have a set of expectations associated with it. That is, the norms of society (and in some cases formal rules) will prescribe and proscribe certain types of behavior for such roles as father, husband and legislator. The expectations in this sense can be thought of as "cultural oughts."

Within society there are many *role structures*—sets of functionally interrelated roles. At a very broad and diffuse level, the total political system may be conceptualized as a role structure. At the more concrete and specific level, we may view a court, for example, as a role structure, incorporating the roles of judge, prosecutor, plaintiff, defendant, and so on. Similarly, we can view legislatures, legislative committees, interest groups and executive departments and bureaus as role structures within the political system, and as "subsystems" of the larger political system. Of course, as the selection by Patterson below indicates, a political role structure may be as small as a three-person friendship clique within a legislative assembly.

Role Potential

Social scientists have developed a set of concepts to help identify and analyze the variety of factors which determine the character of one's role performance, and which provide a context of competing expectations as one performs in several roles simultaneously. To anticipate, to some extent, what we shall be saying below about the effects of social class on political behavior, we can begin with the concept of *role potential.* We might fairly assume that the various persons entering a legislative body, where the behavioral expectations are rather equally applied, will differ significantly in their role potentials, and that this difference will account for differences in role interpretation and performance. To continue the legislative example, one's role potential is a composite of the human ecology of his constituency; short-run situational factors, such as the tone and character of his election campaign; the composition of his supporting coalition; his own socioeconomic characteristics and background; and his personality. Taken together, these variables act to restrict a legislator's range of options, and help to determine for him which forms of legislative activity and which issue areas it will be most efficacious for him to engage in. In this sense, no one is completely a free agent in determining the political roles he will play and the manner in which he will play them.

Role Performance

Obviously *role performance* is inextricably related to role potential. Political norms and formal rules are seldom so rigid and explicit as not to allow for differences in individual performance. Usually the degree of deviance permitted before sanctions are applied is an empirical question, and some political structures, such as the United States Senate, in recent years have begun to tolerate wider diversity of styles in role performance. The differences in style reflect to a large degree differences in role potential: some senators are more comfortable fading into the background and working "behind the scenes": others prefer to emphasize the oratorical and adversary qualities of the role, basking in public attention, even at the risk of alienating their colleagues. In a now classic study, Ralph Huitt discussed the conscious choice by Senator William Proxmire of Wisconsin to play the so-called "outsider" role, because it corresponded more than the "insider" role to his personality, background, and conceptualization of the role of senator—all elements of his role potential.[2]

Role Conflict

Role strain and *role conflict* are additional important concepts which are discussed cogently by Mitchell in his article in this section. Strain occurs as one experiences adjustment problems in trying to fulfill role expectations which cannot be met fully. Note that Mitchell suggests a variety of sources of role strain among elected political officials.

Role conflict—in the form of competing or contradictory expectations—occurs because of the inevitability of our having to perform a variety of roles, some of which on occasion are difficult to reconcile. A variant of role conflict often takes place after a change in roles. Mitchell hypothesizes about the role conflict which would attend a scholar, clergyman, or military man as any one of them becomes an elected public official. An obvious problem, cited by Mitchell, is the need in such an instance to adapt to a totally different notion of authority.

Groups

Groups, as a type of role structure, have been an object of social science research for generations. Political scientists, sociologists and psychologists have studied small group behavior in both simulated and on-going

[2] "The Outsider in the Senate: An Alternative Role," *American Political Science Review* 60 (1961): 566–75.

groups. Many political scientists have investigated the normative constraint, behavior patterns and level of integration of legislative committees, executive bureaus and city councils. Others have focused their inquiry on political interest groups and attitude groups.

All groups have a formal role structure, which allocates specialized
tasks and leadership positions. It is usually the formal role structure and
its patterns of communication and influence which are the objects of social
science analysis. But we know that informal patterns of communication
and influence evolve also during the life cycle of a group, and that these
often are as important to policy outcomes as are the formal definitions of
leader-follower relationships.

Patterson, in the selection below, discusses informal friendship groups,
or "cliques," in the Wisconsin Assembly. Using sociometric techniques
similar to those developed by Bales in his frequently-cited *Interaction
Process Analysis*,[3] Patterson was able not only to discern the existence
of informal cliques, but also to describe leadership structures within some
of them. Not unlike other research findings that had been reported up to
that time, Patterson's study found leaders to be "prototypes" of their
groups: norm models, ideological prototypes and loyal to group-defined
goals.

"Groupings" and Social Class

Groups, as identifiable role structures, are distinguishable from
groupings in society, in that the latter do not denote organization or structure, but are categories used by political scientists and sociologists to
classify persons. Groupings, thus conceived, exist in terms of race, ethnicity, status, age, sex, residence, and so forth. It is in this sense that
political scientists conceptualize *class* as an important variable in explaining political attitudes and behavior, and as a factor in determining political role potential. Americans have an aversion to open discussions of
social class. Our heritage is officially that of a classless society, and our
self-conception as a people is ironically one of a single, large amorphous
middle class, but with perceived status distinctions which generate status
insecurity and status striving.

The United States has never had an authentic upper class in the sense
of an aristocracy with successive generations of cumulative advantages.
In fact, there is a frightfully low correspondence between background and
wealth in the United States. Moreover, when compared to other developed industrial democracies, the United States deviates from the usual

[3] R. R. Bales, *Interaction Process Analysis: A Method for the
Study of Small Groups* (Cambridge, Mass.: Addison-Wesley, 1950).

pattern in its failure to develop a self-conscious working class, or a socialist or labor political party of any consequence.

In the absence of authentic class politics, students of American politics look for differences in socioeconomic status (or "SES" in abbreviated form) for partial explanations of political differences. SES is usually defined as a composite of three attributes: level of education, prestige of occupation and level of income. Persons can be arrayed on a status continuum, with the two extremes being those who are high on all three measures and those who are low on all three. Although any particular status may offer explanations of politics, concepts of conflict in statuses and group affiliations reflect both social and psychological effects.

Social Conflict and Personality Stress

We have suggested previously that such sociological stimuli as group and class identification have a direct bearing on political attitudes and behavior, but our focus here is on a set of intervening variables that mediate the influences of social structure. These intervening variables relate to conflicts between different group identifications and between different status positions in society. While the transmission of political values through an important primary group, such as the family, has a direct bearing on political behavior, a social-psychological focus and the interactional paradigm encourage us to examine behavior and attitudes, as they reflect interactions between *sets* of primary group identifications.

Similarly, behavior and attitudes are linked to singular notions of class (such as education); yet the interaction of various dimensions of class (such as education and race) intervenes to influence attitudes and behavior. When there are conflicting primary group cues and identifications, we speak of *cross-pressures*. But when there are conflicting status positions, we refer to *status inconsistency*. The two concepts are closely related, as are concepts of attitudinal consistency treated later (Chapter 8); yet cross-pressures occur within the context of a primary group or intimate environment, while status inconsistencies occur at a broader level of social strata.

Why should these forms of conflict have an impact on one's orientation to politics or his political behavior? On its face, the theme which suggests an answer is a relatively simple theoretical notion; yet, as we shall see, any conflict paradigm yields a complex network of interrelationships which must treat various combinations of values and objects of orientation.

In its basic form, the explanatory theme maintains that conflicting sociological stimuli (and the psychological attachments inherent in them) create pressures on, or stress within, the individual subjected to them, and that this stress is basically uncomfortable. The individual may then react in a variety of ways: he may use psychological mechanisms to reduce the stress (such as rationalization); he may avoid the source or selectively misperceive it; he may withdraw from situations which recall the stress; he may change his opinions because of it; or he may overtly behave so as to reduce it. By no means is this an exhaustive list of consequences, and, as we shall see in Chapter 9, the processes are analogous to attitudinal conflict as well. In general, one's political opinion and behavior at any one point in time are partially dependent upon these sources of stress and the mechanisms by which one attempts to reduce stress. These sources are not sole causes, nor should it necessarily follow that all individuals have similar desires to reduce stress.

Cross-Pressures

The concept of cross-pressures was first introduced to political science in two landmark voting studies, *The People's Choice* and *Voting*.[4] Both were partially concerned with group contacts of the individual voter and the tendency for people to discuss politics with those who share political orientations and thereby reinforce the individual's political convictions. These early studies found such reinforcement to be particularly salient in primary group contacts where close interpersonal ties exist. When conflict occurs in this intimate context, the stress is particularly significant. The nature of social interaction at this level and conflicts that may be associated with it, such as conflicting political views from the family and peer groups, yield a variety of consequences. Findings from the early voting studies indicated that an individual subjected to conflicting group pressures is more likely to withdraw from politics, to alter his vote intention and waver during the campaign and to make up his mind late in the campaign. This set of findings, however, should not imply that situations of cross-pressure or, for that matter, inconsistencies in status or in attitudes, prevail among a majority of the electorate. The findings reported in this chapter and in our subsequent analysis of attitudinal conflict suggest that, of necessity, theories about the consequences of inconsistency must apply only to a subset of individuals. Indeed, there has been a prevailing stability in American politics and electoral behavior because of the tendency for social groups not only to have different interests, but also social differentiation from other groups, continuity between generations

[4] Paul F. Lazarsfeld, Bernard Berelsen and Hazel Gaudet, *The People's Choice* (New York: Columbia University Press, 1948); Bernard Berelsen, Paul F. Lazarsfeld and William McPhee, *Voting* (Chicago: University of Chicago Press, 1954).

and in-group contacts, which aid in the transformation of political interests into rather stable social traditions.

Variations on the cross-pressures' theme are examined in the Merelman article. Merelman treats political inconsistency in the primary group environment of college students and one's conflicting tendencies for withdrawal, ideological overcompensation and politicization. Although most research has isolated withdrawal as a consequence of cross-pressures, role conflict theory suggests an alternative. Cross-pressures cause stress in the individual's ability to play his perceived role; and, rather than withdrawing from politics, he may conform to *one set* of roles and subsequently develop an ideology to justify that choice. By focusing on two intimate groups, parents and friends, Merelman postulates three environments: one of role congruence and nonexistent cross-pressures where friends and parents support the same political party; a cross-pressured environment which is politicized, i.e., friends support one party and parents another; and an environment of limited congruence, where only one group gives party identification cues to the individual. He finds that those in the first environment are most interested and involved in politics, but that those in a conflicted but politicized environment are more involved than those in a conflicted but depoliticized environment. These findings are elaborated and presented in the context of a revised cross-pressures theory.

Status Inconsistency

The concept of *status inconsistency* is not unlike that of cross-pressures; yet it occurs in a context beyond the intimate environment. It is based upon the notion, first elaborated by Lenski,[5] that status has more than a vertical dimension (i.e., low to high) but a horizontal dimension which cuts across the vertical dimension at various points. That is, one has a variety of statuses (i.g., education, wealth, occupational prestige) each of which has a vertical dimension. The inconsistencies between statuses, the types of these statuses and the relative visibility and stability of each help to shape political attitudes and behavior.

The earlier findings about this phenomenon dealt primarily with inconsistencies between statuses rather than with types, visibility or stability. Lenski found that respondents with high status inconsistency differ in their political attitudes and behavior from those with low status inconsistency. Specifically, status inconsistency is associated with liberal support for social-welfare domestic issues and support for the Democratic party. If an individual is inconsistent, that is, high on one status dimension but lower on another, he tends to view himself as high status; yet he is

[5] Gerhard E. Lenski, "Status Crystallization: A Non-Vertical Dimension of Social Status," *American Sociological Review* 19 (1954): 406.

often treated as low status by others. This produces social stress and, as a consequence, the individual supports political parties and candidates which favor social change; i.e., he seeks to change a political system which makes his lower status relevant. This linkage between inconsistency and political liberalism has been found to hold across several nations.[6] Yet it does not necessarily follow that left-wing tendencies are the only form of extremism associated with inconsistency. For example, it has been found that right wing extremism results from combinations of low education and high occupation or income, but that left-wing extremism is a consequence of higher education and low occupational prestige and income.[7]

The basic findings have been refined by distinctions between types of status. This distinction is basically twofold: achieved status (occupation, education, income) and ascribed status (race, ethnicity, religion). When there are discrepancies between these types of status, the inconsistencies are even more influential for political attitudes and behavior.

From this base, Segal develops a set of refinements. He argues that when there is inconsistency between an achieved and ascribed status, the stress will be particularly disturbing to the individual. Yet some ascribed statuses are more visible than others (for instance race vs. religion). If the status is not visible (such as a Catholic businessman) political events (Catholic candidate) might make it visible and stressful to the individual. Therefore, under some conditions of status pressure, the individual will support the progressive party, but in other instances he will withdraw. He is most likely to support the party if he has low and visible ascribed status and a high achieved status, but when conflicting pressures are less visible, internal and transient, he is more likely to withdraw.

If a nonvisible status is made relevant by a political campaign, the individual will withdraw unless one alternative is more attractive than the other. When differences between alternatives are large, he will favor the more attractive candidate (for instance, one's Catholicism is aroused in the context of the 1960 election). An important contention is that inconsistency between low visibility statuses leads to intrapsychic stress that is resolved in a nonvisible manner (nonpartisanship). A further refinement of these ideas suggests that the stressfullness of achieved versus ascribed status inconsistencies is proportional to crystallization of statuses (fixed or variable).[8] Both stress and liberalism increase with fixed statuses as the individual attempts to cope with his rather immobile position, that is, he is more fervent in his desire to change the system.

[6] Lenski, "Status Inconsistency and the Vote: A Four Nation Study," *American Sociological Review* 32 (1967): 298.

[7] Gary R. Rush, "Status Consistency and Right-Wing Extremism," *American Sociological Review* 32 (1967): 87.

[8] Thomas S. Smith, "Structural Crystallization, Status Inconsistency and Political Partisanship," *American Sociological Review* 34 (1969): 907–22.

Selected Additional Readings

Bales, Robert F. *Interaction Process Analysis: A Method for the Study of Small Groups.* Reading: Addison-Wesley, 1950.

Barber, James D. *Power in Committees.* Chicago: Rand McNally & Company, 1966.

Bell, Roderick. "The Determinants of Psychological Involvement In Politics: A Causal Analysis." *Midwest Journal of Political Science* 13 (1969): 237–54.

Berelson, Bernard, Paul F. Lazarsfeld, and William McPhee. *Voting.* Chicago: University of Chicago Press, 1954, *passim.*

Biddle, Bruce, and Edwin J. Thomas, eds. *Role Theory: Concepts and Research.* New York: John Wiley & Sons, Inc., 1966.

Borgatta, Edgar F. "Role and Reference Group Theory." In *Social Science Theory and Social Work Research,* pp. 16–25. National Association of Social Workers, 1960.

Brandmeyer, Gerard. "Status Consistency and Political Behavior: A Replication and Extension of Research." *Sociological Quarterly* 6 (1965): 241–57.

Broom, Leonard, and F. Lancaster Jones. "Status Consistency and Political Preference: The Australian Case." *American Sociological Review* 35 (1970): 989–1000.

Campbell, Angus, et al. *The American Voter.* New York: John Wiley & Sons, Inc., 1960, *passim.*

Chiricos, Theodore G., Michael A. Pearson, and James M. Fendrich. "Status Inconsistency, Militancy and Black Identification Among Black Veterans." *Social Science Quarterly* 51 (1970): 572–86.

Eitzen, D. Stanley. "Social Class, Status Inconsistency and Political Attitudes." *Social Science Quarterly* 51 (1970): 602–09.

Fenno, Richard F., Jr. "The House Appropriations Committee as a Political System: The Problem of Integration." *American Political Science Review* 56 (1962): 412–36.

Golembiewski, Robert T. *The Small Group.* Chicago: University of Chicago Press, 1962.

Goode, William. "A Theory of Role Strain." *American Sociological Review* 25 (1960): 483–96.

Gouldner, Alvin W. "Cosmopolitans and Locals: Toward an Analysis of Latent Social Roles." *Administrative Science Quarterly* (December, 1957 and March, 1958): pp. 281–306, 444–80.

Gross, Neal C., W. S. Mason, and W. W. McEachern. *Explorations in Role Analysis.* New York: John Wiley & Sons, Inc., 1959.

Grossman, Joel B. "Role Playing in the Analysis of Judicial Behavior." *Journal of Public Law* (1962): pp. 285–309.

Homans, George C. *The Human Group.* New York: Harcourt, Brace and World, Inc., 1950.

Huitt, Ralph K. "The Outsider in the Senate: An Alternative Role." *American Political Science Review* 55 (1961): 566–75.

Hunt, Larry L., and Robert G. Cushing. "Status Discrepancy, Interpersonal Attachment and Right-Wing Extremism." *Social Science Quarterly* 51 (1970): 587–601.

James, Dorothy. "Role Theory and the Supreme Court." *Journal of Politics* 30 (1968): 160–87.

Kelly, K. Dennis and William Chambliss. "Status Consistency and Political Attitudes." *American Sociological Review* 31 (1966): 375–81.

Kemper, Theodore D. "Reference Groups, Socialization and Achievement." *American Sociological Review* 33 (1968): 31–45.

Kenkel, William F. "The Relationship Between Status Consistency and Politico-Economic Attitudes." *American Sociological Review* 21 (1962): 365–68.

Kornberg, Allan. "Rules of the Game in the Canadian House of Commons," *Journal of Politics* 26 (1964): 358–80.

Lazarsfeld, Paul F., Bernard Berelson, and Hazel Gaudet. *The People's Choice,* pp. 52–69. New York: Columbia University Press, 1948.

Lenski, Gerhard E. "Status Inconsistency and the Vote: A Four-Nation Test." *American Sociological Review* 32 (1967): 298–301.

McClosky, Herbert, and Harold E. Dahlgren. "Primary Group Influence on Party Loyalty." *American Political Science Review* 53 (1959): 757–77.

Meller, Norman. "Representational Role Types." *American Political Science Review* 61 (1967): 474–78.

Prewitt, Kenneth, Heinz Eulau, and Betty Zisk. "Political Socialization and Political Roles." *Public Opinion Quarterly* 30 (1966–67): 569–83.

Rothman, Stanley. "Systematic Political Theory: Observations on the Group Approach." *American Political Science Review* 54 (1960): 15–33.

Segal, David R. and David Knoke. "Social Mobility, Status Inconsistency and Partisan Realignment in the United States." *Social Forces* 47 (1968): 154–58.

Smith, Thomas S. "Structural Crystallization, Status Inconsistency and Political Partisanship." *American Sociological Review* 34 (1969): 907–22.

Truman, David B. *The Governmental Process.* New York: Alfred A. Knopf, 1951.

Verba, Sidney. *Small Groups and Political Behavior.* Princeton: Princeton University Press, 1961.

Wahlke, John, et al. *The Legislative System.* section IV. New York: John Wiley & Sons, Inc., 1962.

Weiner, Myron. "Traditional Role Performance and the Development of Modern Political Parties: The Indian Case." *Journal of Politics* 26 (1964): 830–49.

Patterns of Interpersonal Relations

in a State Legislative Group:

The Wisconsin Assembly

Samuel C. Patterson

Traditionally, legislative bodies have been studied in terms of the formal structure of the legislative group—the structure of formal leadership or of committee organization, and legislative decision-making typically has been analyzed in terms of "pressures" or "vectors" which influence the decision-making process. The pattern of informal organization of legislative groups based on a variety of interpersonal relationships among legislators has been frequently recognized, but seldom investigated systematically.

The Assembly, the lower house of the Wisconsin State Legislature, consists of one-hundred members elected from single-member districts apportioned on the basis of population. Assemblymen are elected in November of even-numbered years, and the Assembly meets in biennial session for about six months in odd-numbered years. The formal organization of the Wisconsin Assembly with respect to the election and powers of elected officers, the organization of committees, and the formal legislative procedure is similar in most respects to the practices in many other states.

During the months of February, March, and April 1958, members of the 1958 session of the Wisconsin Assembly were systematically interviewed by means of a schedule of questions.[1] Seventy percent of the

members were interviewed personally, and an additional 17 percent were interviewed by mail. Data were therefore available for 87 percent of the members of the 1957 Assembly.

With respect to the patterns of interpersonal relations in the Assembly, sociometric techniques were employed to determine (1) what the informal pattern of organization was in the 1957 Assembly, and (2) whether, as other social-psychological research has indicated, legislators who have leadership status tend to receive more friendship choices than non-leaders; that is, whether leaders tend to be "overchosen."

The method employed by some social scientists to identify and analyze the interpersonal relations of members of a social group is that of interaction process analysis, a technique which was developed by Bales.[2] Interaction process analysis is, however, fairly strictly limited in its application to small-group research and certainly would be a monumental, if not an impossible, task for a researcher with limited facilities if it were attempted on a body as large as the Wisconsin Assembly.

The outstanding illustration of an effort to analyze the interpersonal relationships of members of a legislative group in the literature of political science is the classic study of Routt, who counted the number of interactions between members during the first fifteen minutes of each daily session of the 1937 Illinois Senate.[3] Routt's analysis was confined to a sample of

Samuel C. Patterson, "Patterns of Interpersonal Relations in a State Legislative Group: The Wisconsin Assembly," *Public Opinion Quarterly* 23 (1959): 101–9. Reprinted with permission.

eleven senators, and interactions were counted during eighty-six sample periods. This technique is, as Routt himself maintained, limited in its utility to a small group of members who could be observed manageably by the researcher.

Systematic interviewing of members of a legislative body provided an opportunity, however, to analyze the interpersonal relations among members by means of sociometric techniques which have been highly developed by the social psychologists.[4] In the Wisconsin study, members were asked to nominate their closest personal friends within the Assembly—members whom they liked the best and spent the most time with outside the legislative chamber. The analysis of the data was accomplished by the manipulation of a matrix which indicated the friendship choices of members. Members were listed on the top and on the side of the matrix, and friendship choices were then plotted on the matrix. The matrix was squared to reveal mutual choices between members and, finally, cubed to reveal cliques. The procedure is not difficult even with a 100-man legislative group, and is fully and adequately described in Festinger *et al., Social Pressures in Informal Groups.*[5]

The sociometric, or friendship, score for each member was computed simply by totaling the number of sociometric choices for the member. These data were utilized to show a relationship between high friendship scores and leadership status.

The Role of Friends

Friendship is not a well-defined concept, and for the most part Assemblymen were encouraged to define it for themselves in designating their closest friends in the Assembly. Clearly, friendship among members of any social group can develop in a variety of ways. In the Assembly some friendships develop between members from the same geographical areas in the state who regularly ride together from their homes to the capitol. Others are developed between seatmates—members who sit next to each other in the Assembly.[6] The most important friendships for

this analysis are those that reflect a community of interests and attitudes among members who share norms.

Legislators have the usual expectations with respect to their friends. They expect them to be honest with them, keep their confidences, and demonstrate compatible psychological characteristics. With respect to the legislative process, by and large Assemblymen expect their friends to support their bills unless there is some compelling reason why they cannot. If a member cannot support a friend's bill, he is expected to tell his friend why he cannot "go along" before he votes against the bill, and to explian why he must vote as he does. Otherwise, his friend will most likely automatically "count" on him, and an unwarned adverse vote may sever the friendship relationship. Since members tend to select persons of like minds as their friends, this problem does not create serious difficulty. A member will be most frequently "forgiven" for voting against his friend if his reason is based on the nature of his district, that is, if he cannot "go along" because of district pressure.

The Informal Substructure of the Assembly

The analysis of perception of friends in the Assembly revealed a total of 81 mutual choices between members, that is, in 81 cases members chose each other reciprocally. In 18 percent of these cases, the members who chose each other were seatmates, so that it can be hypothesized that friendships in the Assembly are sometimes a function of sitting together in the chamber. In a few other cases friendships can be attributed to the fact that the members often rode back and forth together from Madison to their homes, although these friendship relationships probably did not result in a high frequency of interaction while the members were in Madison. One instance of this kind resulted in a three-way choice, which can be schematically illustrated by means of a simple sociometric diagram (Fig. 1).[7] These three members were all from the Green Bay area, one a Democrat and two Republicans.

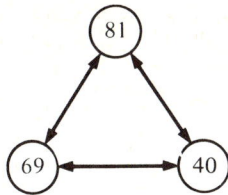

Fig. 1. Sociometric Diagram of Members from Green Bay Area

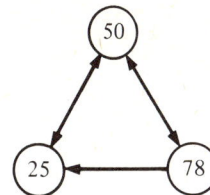

Fig. 3.   Sociometric Diagram of Other Milwaukee Democrats

The most interesting sub-groups, or cliques (which is the term the Assemblyman uses), revealed by an analysis of reciprocal choices are those among Democrats.[8] A third of the members of the 1957 Assembly were Democrats. The Democratic membership of the Assembly was divided into two principal cliques: the Milwaukee County clique and the Dane County clique. The Milwaukee County clique consisted of six Democrats who were referred to by members as the "Unholy Six," and included the Democratic floor leader (Fig. 2). The Unholy Six were Democrats who tended to see their role as one of cooperating with the majority party as much as possible in order to get their own legislation passed. Also, these members expected the floor leader to play down partisanship and cooperate with the Republican leadership. The Unholy Six were limited partisans. Three other Milwaukee Democrats comprised an additional sub-clique which was often allied with the Unholy Six (Fig. 3). In some respects, however, this smaller clique represented a dissident element among Milwaukee Democrats, expressing some dissatisfaction with the party leadership.

The Dane County clique was composed of the four Democratic members from the county in which the captiol is located, plus their allies (Fig. 4). Both the Democratic assistant floor leader and the caucus chairman were members of this clique. These members were more partisan in their role expectations, and tended to see the floor leader as a "party hatchet man." This group was able to defeat Pellant of the Unholy Six, the 1955 session assistant floor leader, for re-election and elect Hardie, one of their allies. The Dane County clique saw Molinaro, the caucus chairman, as the "real" party leader, although he is himself from Kenosha. Molinaro was the Democratic candidate for speaker of the 1957 session, and he lost by a straight party vote to the Republican candidate, Marotz. In addition to the Dane County members, the clique included one Assemblyman from Racine, one from Kenosha, and two from northwestern rural Wisconsin.

An examination of roll-call votes indicates considerable difference in the voting behavior of the Dane

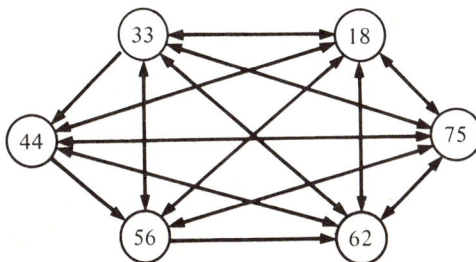

Fig. 2. Sociometric Diagram of the "Unholy Six"

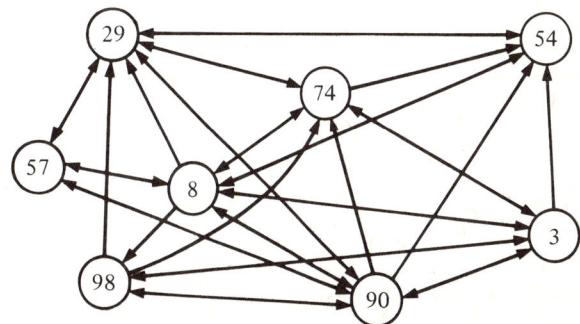

Fig. 4.   Sociometric Diagram of the Dane County Clique

County clique and the Unholy Six. The Dane County members were strongly influenced, and to some extent limited, by the editorial policy of one Madison newspaper, *The Capitol Times,* and were less likely to vote for legislation introduced by Republican members than were the Unholy Six. The same was true to a lesser extent of the northwestern Wisconsin Democrats in areas where the circulation of that newspaper is considerable.

The clique structure of the Democratic contingent in the 1957 Assembly reflects the statewide division between Milwaukee County and the rest of the state in the political behavior of Democratic activists. In this way the state Democratic convention is regularly divided, both in terms of platform policy and, to a greater extent, in the election of officers and the support of candidates.

The friendship clique structure of Republican members was not as spectacular. Interestingly enough, there were no three-way choices among the six members of the Republican steering committee, the group which comprised the primary Republican leadership of the Assembly, although these members met regularly as a group. The best-defined Republican clique had its own name: "Murderers' Row" (Fig. 5). This clique was composed of members who sat together in the Assembly, who voted together most of the time, and who "caucused once in a while" if a member of the clique "got out of line." Three pairs of seatmates made up the clique, plus one other mutual choice and four single choices. Two of these members were chairmen of important committees, and one was Assembly chairman of the powerful joint finance committee.

Another Republican clique consisted of what might be referred to as the younger leadership group, which had as its center the relationship among Grady, the floor leader, Pommerening, Heider, and Bidwell (Fig. 6). This clique had friendship ties with other cliques close to the center of leadership in the Assembly. In terms of friendship expectancies, the clique was related to Rice, the powerful chairman of the agriculture committee, and through him to Stone, chairman of the finance committee and member of Murderers' Row. Heider, one of the members of this clique, sometimes sat in on meetings of the steering committee when one of the regular members was not able to attend. Also, most of the members of this clique had supported Grady for speaker in the initial Republican caucus when Grady lost the speakership election to Marotz. Pommerening was Grady's campaign manager. These members constituted the core of the members who had, during the 1955 session, opposed the dominating tactics of Speaker Catlin, and these members believed at the opening of the 1957 session that the Catlin influence was being continued under the speakership of Marotz, who had been floor leader when Catlin was speaker.

Another clique of young Republican members which can be identified from the friendship patterns in the Assembly is a group, principally of new members, who were not related to the leadership by friendship ties and who were critical of certain aspects of the way the leaders performed (Fig. 7). This "new member" clique consisted of Assemblymen who had not been affected by the Catlin leadership in the As-

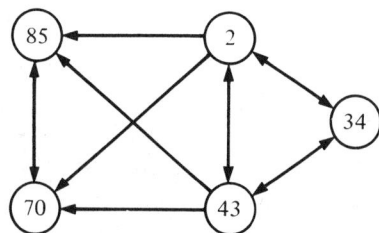

Fig. 5.   Sociometric Diagram of "Murderers' Row"

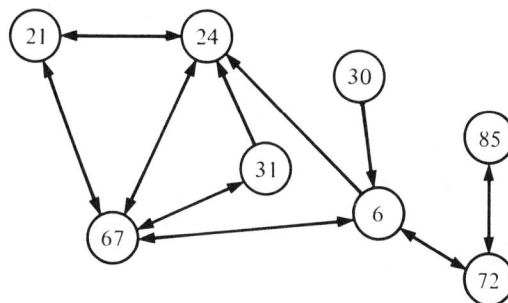

Fig. 6.   Sociometric Diagram of Young Republican Leader Clique

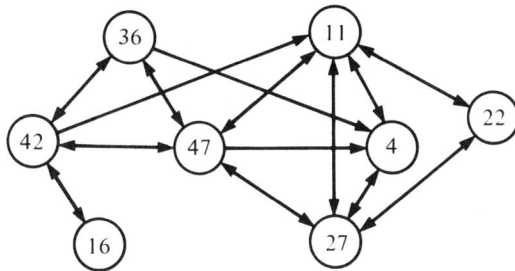

Fig. 7. Sociometric Diagram of the New Member Clique

sembly, and who thought the legislative process was too cumbersome and inefficient. They believed that it was largely because of the unwillingness of older members that it had not been streamlined and at the end of the 1957 session members of this clique suggested the possibility of new leadership and the necessity for reforms in legislative procedure.

The remaining Republican clique as determined by friendship patterns illustrates a different kind of relationship among members who mutually perceive each other in the role of friend. This clique consisted of Rice, former speaker and chairman of the agriculture committee, and two other southern Wisconsin farmer-legislators (Fig. 8). These two farmer-legislators were new members, and one had been urged to run for the Assembly by Rice, with whom he was well-acquainted before he bacame an Assemblyman. For these two members Rice was, in effect, a role model. He "took them under his wing" during the session.

These patterns of interpersonal relationships in the Assembly in terms of friendship choices illustrate the structure of the informal organization of the legislative group. But the data with respect to friendship choices can be used not only to illustrate the patterns

of influence and communication in a group, but also to indicate what kinds of individuals tend to get the most choices.

Friendship and Leadership

The data on sociometric choices among legislators can be used to test the hypothesis: If a member has leadership status, then he will tend to be chosen as a friend by more members than will a non-leader. Leaders in the Assembly tend to be the prototypes of their group in a variety of ways: they tend to function as norm models, they tend to be the ideological prototypes of their group, and they tend to be more loyal to group-defined goals.[9] Since they also occupy positions of higher status in the legislative group than non-leaders, it should follow that leaders are perceived as friends by more members than are non-leaders.

Such a hypothesis is supported by the data from the Wisconsin Assembly. There is a clear relationship between the extent of friendship perception and leadership. Among members of both parties, leaders are seen as friends by more members than are the rank-and-file party members. Table 1 shows that more members selected Republican steering committee members (primary leaders) for the role of friend than other Republican members.

Table 1
Relationship between Republican Leadership and Friendship Perception (N = 67)

Leadership Status	6 or More Friends	Fewer than 6 Friends
Steering committee	5	1
Other Republicans	8	53

$x^2 = 12.9$; p. $< .001$

The same relationship is true of the Democratic party members in the Assembly (Table 2). Democratic leaders are seen in friendship roles by more members then rank-and-file Democrats.[10] It appears likely that members identify psychologically with their leaders and thus frequently see them not only as leaders but also as friends.[11]

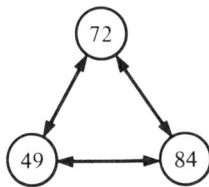

Fig. 8. Sociometric Diagram of the Rice Clique

Table 2

Relationship between Democratic Leadership and Friendship Perception (N = 33)

Leadership Status	6 or More Friends	Fewer than 6 Friends
Leaders	3	1
Other Democrats	2	27

$x^2 = 7.9$; p. $< .01$

Conclusion

Friendship roles are functional roles in the legislative group. No social group can be maintained if there are not significant and persistent interpersonal relations among members, and large groups like a legislature tend to be broken down into sub-groups on a friendship basis.[12] Friendship roles designated by the reciprocal choices among friends can be used to explore the informal organization of a legislative group. Perception of friendship by members can be related to leadership in the sense that leaders will tend to be perceived as playing friendship roles by more members than non-leaders.

Friendship roles are not only functional for the maintenance of the legislative group but also for the resolution of political conflict. The legislator is not simply the "pawn of contending forces" who seek access to the legislative group in order to get their concepts of the public interest accepted as public policy. The legislator brings to the decision-making process not only his own sociological and psychological make-up and his multiple-group memberships, but also his informal social structure of the legislative group, and is affected by the norms of these informal groups in his own decision-making behavior.[13]

Individuals who assume the legislative role have diverse backgrounds and diverse social, political, and economic experience, and different reference groups are salient for them. The informal friendship structure of the legislature tends to lessen such differences, to mitigate against the development of potential conflicts, to provide channels of communication and understanding among members who share goals, and to facilitate logrolling.

Notes

[1] The complete study is reported in Samuel C. Patterson, "Toward a Theory of Legislative Behavior: The Wisconsin State Assemblymen as Actors in a Legislative System," unpublished Ph.D. dissertation, Madison, Wis., University of Wisconsin, 1958.

[2] Robert F. Bales, *Interaction Process Analysis: A Method for the Study of Small Groups* (Cambridge, Mass.: Addison-Wesley, 1950).

[3] Garland C. Routt, "Interpersonal Relationships and the Legislative Process," *The Annals of the American Academy of Political and Social Science* 195 (1938): 129–36.

[4] Sociogram analysis is, of course, far more refined than the simple application of it here illustrated. The principal reference is J. L. Moreno, *Who Shall Survive?* (New York: Beacon House, 1953).

[5] Leon Festinger, Stanely Schachter, and Kurt Back, *Social Pressures in Informal Groups: A Study of Human Factors in Housing* (New York: Harper, 1950), pp. 132–50.

[6] This analysis of friendship in the legislative group considers primarily the question of who tends to form friendships with whom, and not the process through which these patterns develop. An attempt to study friendship as a process rather than a product is illustrated by the studies of Paul F. Larzarsfeld and Robert K. Merton, "Friendship as Social Process: A Substantive and Methodological Analysis," in Morroe Berger, Theodore Abel, and

Charles H. Page, editors, *Freedom and Control in Modern Society* (Princeton, N.J.: Van Nostrand, 1954), pp. 18–66.

[7] The numbers in the diagrams refer to interview code numbers.

[8] A clique is operationally defined as any combination of three or more members who mutually choose each other, plus other related members.

[9] These are general characteristics of leadership, but they are borne out in the Wisconsin Assembly. See Patterson, *op. cit.*, Chap. 9, "Leadership Roles in the Assembly."

[10] Similar findings with respect to other kinds of social groups can be found in the literature of social psychology. See Henry W. Riecken and George C. Homans, "Psychological Aspects of Social Structure," in Gardner Lindzey, editor, *Handbook of Social Psychology*, vol. 2 (Cambridge, Mass.: Addison-Wesley, 1954), 786–832.

[11] Routt found that interpersonal contacts "tended to center around individuals who by other indices were shown to play important roles in the process of legislation." See *op. cit.*, p. 132.

[12] A variety of related social-psychological research is analyzed in Harold H. Kelley and John W. Thibaut, "Experimental Studies in Group Problem Solving and Process," in Lindzey, *op. cit.*, pp. 761–70.

[13] In this connection, see the very valuable recent study of David B. Truman, "The State Delegations and the Structure of Party Voting in the United States House of Representatives," *American Political Science Review* 50, no. 4 (1956): 1023–45.

Occupational Role Strains:

The American Elective Public Official

William C. Mitchell

An important subject for behavioral research is the interplay between organizational structure and personality, between the peculiar conditions or demands of given occupations and the kinds of accommodations that individuals make to them. This analysis is concerned with the strains and conflicts associated with elected political office in the United States. Unfortunately Weber's classic essay on politics as a vocation has not been widely read, nor is it influential among American political scientists.[1] Politics is widely and intensively studied, but the practice of politics as an occupation has received little more than anecdotal treatment by journalists.[2] In this study role theory and role analysis are used to explore certain facets of the elective public official's occupational role. More precisely the paper is concerned with the development of a "middle-range" conceptual scheme for the analysis of the strains engendered by elective public office.

Role Strains

Briefly, we can define strain as the resultant of attempts to meet expectations that cannot be fully met either by a person or a social system. Neither social systems nor persons can ever be free of the problems of adjustment to new and difficult situations. Strain

William C. Mitchell, "Occupational Role Strains: The American Elective Public Official," *Administrative Science Quarterly* 3 (1958): 210–28. Reprinted with permission.

in some form will therefore accompany the process of adjustment.

The strains to which a person is subject are not randomized in the social system. Rather these strains are patterned along the structure of the roles or norms that make up the system. All incumbents of a particular role will therefore be subject to the same role strains, even though they may respond quite differently to them. If we know the role or norm structure of a given social system we ought to be able to predict where and how role strains will occur.

Whether a particular occupational strain is consciously felt by a given individual is problematical. Some politicians may recognize the existence of a strain for a colleague but not be personally bothered by that same strain. Certain personality types may demonstrate an immunity to strains that cause great anxiety among others. But even in the case of the person who does not recognize or admit to being disturbed by some strain, we have to recognize the possibility that his failure to do so is itself a response to the strain. Self-awareness of a role strain is not a criterion of its existence. If it were, psychoanalysis would have little to do.

The role strains of politics are not simply acquiesced in by the politician any more than is the case with other persons in the social structure. A variety of responses is possible, including passive acceptance and deviance; but typically the politician attempts to effectuate some control over the situation, even if only a partial form. Efforts, of course, are also made to reform the situation so that the strain can be eliminated, but for the most part politicians attempt to gain only a partial control as the more realistic course of action. Periodically rather full-scale transformations of the political situations are completed; one such transformation was the Legislative Reorganization Act of 1946, which made some significant changes in the situation of congressmen and senators.

I shall consider seven general sources of strain for the elected public official. The categories used are by no means exhaustive, but they are primary in the sense that any other role strains are products of those selected for discussion. In the order in which they will be analyzed they are: (1) insecurity of tenure; (2) conflict among public roles; (3) conflict of private and public roles; (4) ambiguities in political situations; (5) diffused responsibility and limited control of situations; (6) time and pressure of demands; (7) and status insecurity. Finally, it should be clear that I am writing not as a psychologist, but as a political sociologist. No attempt will be made, therefore, to analyze the effects of role strains upon the personality. My concern is solely with sources.

Sources of Strain

Insecurity of Tenure

No occupational role guarantees perfect security of tenure, least of all, perhaps, that of the politician. The turnover in the ranks of elected public officials is very great as the investigations of Charles S. Hyneman have demonstrated.[3] His findings respecting tenure in ten state legislatures over a period of ten years (1925–1935) indicate that in only four of the twenty chambers studied had as many as 50 percent of the members completed three sessions. And in seven chambers less than 25 percent could show experience in three previous sessions. In "Tribulations of a State Senator" Duane Lockard claimed that "roughly half of the six thousand legislators you are going to elect will be entering the legislature for the first time. Most legislators cannot afford to serve more than one

term."[4] Regardless of the reason fragmentary evidence indicates that tenure is far from being guaranteed in politics.

Although the insecurity of public office is a fact, it does, however, require an explanation. Whenever an occupational role is part of a competitive situation — as it normally is in politics — insecurity of tenure is bound to be felt. Tenure, of course, refers to the role itself and not to any other roles the person may occupy. A politician may have a guaranteed income from other sources so that his economic anxieties are allayed; yet his insecurity as a politician will force him to reduce the tensions of the political role. And this will not necessarily be done for selfish reasons. The reduction of tension will be an indicator of success as a politician, meaning that his work is being done more effectively. A person who has to devote considerable time and energy to the security of his tenure will be more responsive, both consciously and subconsciously, to the wishes of those governing his tenure than one who does not. The politician is in this position because he is elected. He is therefore peculiarly sensitive to the currents of public opinion in his constituency. The fickle nature of the crosscurrents of opinion adds to his insecurity, for the number of issues on which the constituency can be unified into significant, clear-cut majorities is rather small. The politician's mandate, then, is ambiguous on most issues and his insecurity heightened for that reason. No politician can ignore public opinion. Even when he feels it to be wrong, it is still a fact that he has to calculate when attempting to rule.

The strains of insecurity then stem from the periodic, usually rather short, terms of office that a politician can attain only by winning elections. Much of what a politician does can be viewed as varying forms of response to political insecurity. The very fact that American politicians respond more quickly and willingly to the demands of their constituencies than to those of their parties is a recognition, by them, of the source of the insecurity.[5] In devoting their attentions to the constituencies, they are hoping to relieve tension and its consequences.

Increases in salary and pension plans are also

means of coping with the problem. Control over elections—ranging from the purely legal ones of intense campaigning and gerrymandering to the illegal buying of votes—are additional responses. Among the better-known means of control has been the resistance of politicians to the adoption of open primaries. Since the primary adds another hurdle, many politicians obviously opposed it; when they could no longer prevent its development, they then moved to minimize its effects. They were aided in this by an indifferent electorate. No politician encourages competition, and certainly not at the primaries. There the effort is to eliminate as many potential competitors as possible before the formal election and to reduce the effectiveness of those who escape during the campaign.

Democratic forms of procedure, however, are designed to promote competition so that the politician can never be said to have complete control over his fate. And, as stated above, forces from without the constituency can and do affect tenure. Great social forces—and such well-known phenomenon as the "coattail" effect—all impinge upon the politician's tenure of office.[6] They are, almost of necessity, imponderable forces and difficult for the practical politician to control.

Role Conflicts

The fact that most politicians serve in more than one role as elective public officials guarantees conflicts among norms of performance. Expectations emanating from a variety of sources impinge upon the politician every time he is to make a decision. Various persons and groups constantly attempt to influence the decisions and the premises of the politician so that the actual decision will satisfy the interests of the persons specifying the premises or decisions.

Talcott Parsons' pattern-variable scheme enables us to categorize the premises of decisions in terms of five dichotomous choices on the part of the actor in orienting himself to his situation.[7] Different orientations mean different decisions on the part of the politician—hence the great concern in shaping the politi-

cians' orientation by other persons. If a politician chooses to accept or be guided in his decision making by one role in preference to another, he is forced to de-emphasize other roles he might be expected by some to perform. This matter of choosing certain premises rather than others brings out the problem of role conflict.

We can illustrate the point by characterizing two roles, the administrative and the partisan. When these roles are analyzed in terms of the pattern variables, one can readily see that the expectations concerning performances are contrary at every relevant choice point. The premises of action in each role are opposed. Whereas the administrator is expected to be affectively neutral, the partisan is expected to be affectively involved in the situation. Whereas the administrator's role is functionally specific, the partisan's is diffused. The administrator is expected to employ universalistic standards; the partisan, to employ particularistic criteria. Whereas administrators are expected to be achievement-oriented, the partisan has to be ascriptively oriented. And, finally, partisans are expected to be self-oriented, while administrators are expected to be collectivity-oriented.

The norms or premises of action expected by others of the politician are not always in conflict. At some of the relevant junctures in decision making, the premises may be the same so that no role conflict ensues. We know that administrative and the judicial roles have much in common. The one role which, perhaps, conflicts the most with each of the other roles is that of the partisan. One should not deduce, therefore, that the partisan role is dysfunctional and to be suppressed. Whether it ought to be is a value judgment and not a scientific one.

The conflicts that theoretically exist among the four roles of the polity can be simply presented in tabular form. This means of presentation has the merit of bringing out the relationships among the norms in a clearer fashion. Table 1 illustrates the role structure and possible areas of conflict. Read horizontally, Table 1 describes in terms of the pattern variables the premises or norms of each of the four possible roles constituting an office. If instead of the rows the col-

Table 1
The Pattern-Variables and Role Conflict

Role	1	2	3	4	5
Admin.	Specific	Affective neutrality	Universalistic	Collectivity orientation	Achievement
Executive	Diffuse	Affective neutrality	Universalistic	Collectivity	Achievement
Partisan	Diffuse	Affective	Particularistic	Self-orientation	Ascription
Judicial	Specific	Affective neutrality	Universalistic	Collectivity	Ascription

ums are read, we are presented with the points at which conflicts among the norms or premises of decisions are found. Thus in the first column the conflicts are found between the administrative role and both the executive and partisan roles. Again, the executive role conflicts with the judicial. In total there are four possible conflicts at this juncture in the decision-making process. One can proceed down the other columns in the same way and list the conflicts.

A fruitful question to pose at this time is: Under what conditions are role conflicts most likely to occur? On an impressionistic basis alone the answer suggests that the major variables are the office, the structure of the constituency, and the incumbent of the office.

Obviously those offices which combine the greater number of roles will engender the most conflicts, whereas the offices with the fewest number of roles develop the fewest conflicts. Offices such as the presidency, governorships, and mayoralties of the large cities are likely to be the source of more conflicts than both legislative and judicial offices. In the latter case litigants and interested persons or groups have conflicting expectations about the outcome of a particular trial or decision, but the role of the justice is so clear-cut, so isolated from the other role, and so protected from the public and retribution that role conflicts are minimized. The legislative and executive offices are not so protected; but since the legislator generally has fewer roles to play, he has fewer conflicts. His conflicts are of another type involving the same role, usually the partisan, in conflict with other partisans rather than with other roles. Republican and Demo-

cratic congressmen apply the same premises of action but come out with opposing decisions on a particular piece of legislation. One votes "yes" and the other "no."

It stands to reason that in the matter of constituencies, those districts which have the greatest heterogeneity in the voting population will cause the greatest number of conflicts for their elective public officials to resolve. Some voters will expect their officeholders to act as executives, and others will emphasize other roles. Generally speaking, the larger the constituency in terms of population, the greater will be the heterogeneity and the subsequent number of conflicts. Senators probably face more role conflicts than do congressmen, assuming other factors are constant. Because of the districting process some congressmen have larger constituencies than do many senators, so the former's problems may be magnified as a result. Congressman Celler is a good example, as he has more constituents than many western seantors do. Among the executive offices role conflicts are greater on the national level than on the state and local levels.

Private versus Public Roles

The type of role conflict discussed in the previous section dealt with conflicts originating within or among the various roles that constitute an elective public office. But these are not the only role conflicts a politician must face. The fact is that politicians while fulfilling public office must also play private roles, i.e., roles without formal public responsibilities. The distinction between the two types of roles is a convention, as are all roles, but it is a convention of the greatest significance in a democracy and especially in America.

In short, behavior which is regarded as acceptable or even admirable in private life may not be so regarded in public office. Let us compare, e.g., the role of the businessman with that of an elected public officeholder. The former is not only permitted to attempt to maximize his financial returns but is encouraged to do so; the public official, on the other hand, is not only discouraged from doing so but is sometimes required to divest himself of financial holdings. The politician is expected to work directly and at all times for the public interest, whereas the businessman is encouraged to serve his own ends. This contradiction between private, economic, and political roles would not be important if the politician could simply play one or the other role. In reality he must generally play both roles because public office seldom provides the incumbent his sole income. Insecurity of tenure and low salaries often force the politician to maintain other sources of income. As a result the politician has to live by a dual set of norms. To honor one set may mean the dishonoring of the other.

I should now like to consider another type of strain, one arising from this same source in the conflict of private and public roles. The previous illustration was one of a private and a public role conflict stemming from simultaneous adherence to both roles. Another type of strain results when a person transfers from one role to another but has difficulty in shedding his previous role and adopting the new one. This is particularly the case when at least one of the roles is sharply defined. A scholar, a military man, or a minister will probably have great difficulty in adjusting to the roles of a politician. Each role is not only sharply defined but defined in a way that is quite different from those of political life. Consider the notion of authority in each of these roles: the politician is expected to honor majorities; the minister the word of God; the scholar the canons of science; and the military man

superior office or rank. A person who has devoted many years of obedience to any one set of these norms and who suddenly finds that he is expected to honor a new set is faced with very intense problems of adjustment. Political life subjects the person not only to a new set of norms but to different occupational problems which it is not easy to prepare for through education or any other kind of experience. To be successful in a private role does not automatically guarantee success in public office. Illustrations are hardly necessary.

Ambiguities in Political Situations

Lest the discussion suggest that most political situations are characterized by clear-cut conflicting expectations, let me emphasize the fact that as many or even more are dominated by ambiguity. Instead of being pulled in opposite directions by well-known forces, the elected official is often in the position of a lost hunter seeking direction.

Both the administrative and partisan roles share in the ambiguity, but the latter experiences a somewhat different type. The ambiguities of the administrative role stem from a lack of knowledge concerning means, and the partisan has difficulty defining the goals of the community. Theoretically the former admit of scientific resolution; the latter only of compromise or power. Goals are, by definition, preferences, and in a democracy individual preferences are ideally weighted equally, as is testified by the practice of one man, one vote. While an administrator is concerned with the efficiency of means, the partisan focuses on the moral question of whether efficiency is the desired norm to apply. In a democracy efficiency may not be the proper end of societal action.

Yet the value problems confronted by the politician are not insoluble. Politicians do have some relatively stable reference points in the American value systems. The problem is one of the practical application of general norms to specific social problems. The task is not easy because standards change, constituency pressures are conflicting and powerful, and the authoritative documents, like the Constitution, are not always crystal clear. Politicians lack the certainty of scientifically valid answers, because political situations are concerned with values that do not admit of scientific treatment.[8]

Response to ambiguous situations is uncertain response, whereas response to conflicting but unequal forces is generally certain. Politicians often have "no comment" to make when confronted by the former case. They are "waiting for the dust to settle," for the situation to clarify itself in terms of expectations and possibilities. Those situations in which the greatest amount of ambiguity exist are those in which both the greatest amount of strain and perhaps freedom are present. Depending upon the incumbent, the politician can either be immobilized or creative. Well-structured situations can permit independent action, as in a constituency where a given problem is of little concern; such is the case in many northern districts where the "Negro problem" is unimportant. But they may also deter independent action when the expectations are overwhelming in one direction. Such is the case with politicians in the South when faced with race issues.

Politicians react to ambiguity by attempting to reduce it. Public opinion polls, newspaper commentary, personal contact with constituents, reports from advisers, research bureaus, investigating committees, and "trial balloons" are a few of the methods used to counteract uncertainty. But while politicians are utilizing more scientific process to gather factual data for the structuring of situations, in the final analysis the data is never complete, nor can it resolve value questions, because logically an "ought" statement cannot be deduced from an "is" statement. The politician's responsibility to define system goals will always be fraught with ambiguity.

Diffused Responsibility and Limited Controls

Though the politician has to define his own sense of responsibility to some extent, it is probably safe to say that responsibility in all offices which have an executive role to play is diffused regardless of how the incumbent decides to structure his own role.[9] Executive responsibility is generalized rather than specific —as in most administrative roles or other nonpolitical, specialized roles. The focus in such a role is upon relationships with other persons rather than upon technical goals to be reached by the most efficient means. Men are to be treated less as instruments for the creation of things than as ends in themselves whose co-operation has to be sought before anything can be done. In a democracy diffused responsibility and limited controls over the situation are built into the situation of the leader. While the politician is often held responsible by someone for practically everything, he cannot control many of the variables that affect the outcome of the situation and its demands. This is, of course, more true of the executive role than of any other, and of national than of state and local offices. But politicians from all levels complain about the limited control they have to effectuate goals.

Most of the strain that comes from this disparity of responsibility and control relates to the structure of government in the United States. The American polity disperses power to such an extent that no one official is able to accomplish a task without the co-operation of several other officials, who may have different values and goals and may, in addition, belong to a different party. Because the formal means for securing co-operation are not always sufficient, many informal means have grown up. I need not specify these means here, but merely indicate that role strains have encouraged them.

Politicians are constantly attempting to improve their control over their situations. Proposals are always being advanced to give the President more control, the Congress more control, the governors more control, and so on. I might quote a few politicians on the subject. Note how they claim inability to meet their functions as presently defined by themselves. Notice, too, that a simple reform of the structure of government is expected to improve their control. In general, while politicians always have good things to say about the American polity, they seldom deceive themselves about their own position within it. The governmental system, though outmoded in many respects, is never outmoded fundamentally. Efficiency can be introduced by enacting the necessary reforms.

Senator Kefauver has been quite articulate concerning reform of the governmental structure. In fact, he wrote a book on the subject, though restricting his analysis to the situation of congressmen. In the opening pages appears a straightforward statement about the strains of politics:

> Like many an average freshman congressman, I had my ideals and plans for worthwhile legislation. . . . I was anxious that Congress be equipped for the part it would have to play.
>
> As the years passed, the results were disappointing. I found that the outmoded legislative machinery made it difficult to get much done. I soon realized that the Congress, intended by the Founding Fathers to be the predominate branch of the government, was ill-equipped to chart the legislative program of the nation and was surrendering too many treasured powers to the Executive. I also discovered that the numerous other services expected of a congressman left me little time to study or analyze legislation.[10]

Later, Senator Kefauver speculates on the reasons why men leave active political careers. One of the reasons was the "feeling of frustration due to the inefficiency that results from trying to run a twentieth-century Congress without adequate tools." The frustrations of office outweighed the contributions one could make.

The volume of work and responsibility is simply too taxing for the legislator to accept his job with equanimity. Practically every student of the legislative process has commented upon this fact and suggested reforms to improve the condition. Senator Kefauver was one of these people. Senator La Follette was another.[11] Those who assisted La Follette and Senator Monroney in the legislative reorganization of Congress in 1946 also wished to reduce the demands upon the legislator stemming from organizational sources.

Time and the Pressure of Demands

A persistent complaint of politicians at all levels is related to the number of demands being made on their time and influence. Voters commonly overestimate the influence of politicians; consequently they ask them to do the impossible. More burdensome are their time-consuming requests; the politician often feels this time could better be devoted to more important matters. Local politicians expect to perform chores and usually do not complain to the same extent as do politicians who are concerned with more significant policy matters. Senator Downey of California gives a vivid portrait of the burdens of a senator, burdens which, incidentally, are increasing:

> Each day Senators have matters come before them which could, if they could spare the time, occupy their attentions for months . . . yet here we are compelled to dispose of weighty and complicated matters after being able to listen to arguments only for perhaps an hour or two. . . . Observe for a moment the volume of business that is done in my office alone. It is so great as almost to break me and my whole staff down. In mail alone we receive from 200 to 300 letters every 24 hours. And this in addition to telegrams and long-distance calls and personal visits. We do the best we can. We try to have every letter answered the day it is received. My staff is departmentalized. That is, each girl is an expert in some particular field. . . . If the office were not so organized, we could not possibly begin to carry the load. Yet, Mr. Chairman, I can say to you truthfully that even if I had four times the amount of time I have I could not possibly perform adequately and fully the duties imposed upon me as ambassador from my state. In the departments of government there are always delays or injustices or matters overlooked in which a Senator can be of very great assistance to his constituents. The flood of duties in my office has reached such proportions, and is so steadily increasing, that I am almost totally unable to enter into the study of any legislative matters. That means that frequently I have to inform myself concerning matters of importance by listening to arguments on the floor of the Senate. And yet even my presence on the floor is only

intermittent, so great is the burden of my office duties if I am to efficiently carry out my responsibilities with respect to the state of California.[12]

Senator Fulbright adds his lament in the following words:

But the fact is that the multitude of requests for minor personal services comes close to destroying the effectiveness of a great many capable representatives. The legislator finds himself in a dilemma. If he refuses to see the constant stress of visitors or to give personal attention to their requests, they may become offended and withdraw their support. In addition, it is personally gratifying to be able to be of help to one's friends. On the other hand, if he does give his attentions to these matters, he literally has no time left for the intelligent study and reflection that sound legislation requires.[13]

The senator further states that voters often will not accept the services of secretaries but insist on the personal attention of the politician. "They [the voters] feel that they elected the Senator and they are, therefore, entitled to his personal attention."[14] Senator Kennedy adds:

If we tell our constituents frankly that we can do nothing, they feel we are unsympathetic or inadequate. If we try and fail—usually meeting a counteraction from other Senators representing other interests—they say we are like all the rest of the politicians. All we can do is retreat into the cloakroom and weep on the shoulder of a sympathetic colleague—or go home and snarl at our wives.[15]

Several of the quotations just given suggest rather strongly that politicians, at least those on the congressional level, feel frustrated in their mission by the press of time and conflicting demands in their situation. The politician often feels that he has a job of considerable responsibility and that petty demands prevent him from making the contribution which he was elected to do and ought to do. Young politicians are frequently disillusioned about politics in this respect. Senator Neuberger, then a newly elected state legislator in Oregon, wrote: "I arrived at our new marble Capitol expecting to spend most of my time considering momentous issues—social security, taxes, conservation, civil liberties. Instead, we have devoted long hours to the discussions of regulations for the labeling of eggs."[16]

Status Insecurities

Adequate performance on the part of role incumbents requires some form of compensation or appreciation for the services rendered. Most men like to believe that what they are doing is a contribution to others and that the relevant others know this and are grateful. Politicians are no different in this respect than are other people; if anything, they are even more sensitive to opinion about their work than are many other groups in the community. Although politicians occasionally voice dissatisfaction with their monetary rewards, more often the complaint is about an assumed low social status. According to T. V. Smith and L. D. White, "The politician's faith in himself has been impaired by the people's distrust of him."[17] I have some doubts about the assumption of a low status for the politician, but the important point is the assumption in the case of the politicians themselves. If they feel they are appreciated, they may act accordingly. "If he [the politician] believes in himself he'll devote himself to his high mission," Smith and White conclude.[18]

Senator Robert La Follette, Jr., voiced a common complaint in respect to the status of Congressmen:

Congress has been a favorite target for the disgruntled, the disappointed, the intellectual snobs, and the doubters of democracy alike. But most of this criticism is not constructive. It springs from personal prejudice, political bias, and above all from an utter lack of knowledge of the workaday problems with which a great legislative body must deal.[19]

After stating that "a legislator, like other people, has an ego that requires expression and recognition if it is to avoid becoming warped and eccentric," Senator Fulbright went on to say:

Honorable men in public life can take the abuse that is heaped upon them by the public so long, and then they succumb to a sense of futility and frustration. It is true that some of the frustration that afflicts the Member of Congress is due to the antique and obsolete organization of the Congress itself, and it should be remedied. But of far greater influence upon the decision of good men to remain in politics is the attitude of those whom they seek to serve.[20]

Senator Neuberger has also been quoted as saying the vilification of politics is "one of the nation's basic problems."[21]

Status insecurities thus grow out of the ambivalent status accorded the politician by the voters. The politician is never quite certain whether he has a position of respect or not. If he is convinced that he has, he is still unsure about the reason for it. The reasons may not be particularly admirable ones, for the politician is subject to much selfish flattery. Some he can recognize, but not all. As a result many politicians are likely to manifest forms of behavior that indicate doubt about their prestige.

The foregoing quotations indicate some of the responses of the politician to his status insecurity. The first response is to give verbal expression to the fact, writing articles about the plight of the public official. Note, too, that the writers assert vigorously that the politician is mistakenly abused and that he serves a vital function in society. Typical in this respect is an article by Governor Bradford of Massachusetts entitled, "Politicians Are Necessary Too."[22] A congressman and scholar has written an article on "The Magnitude of the Task of the Politician" to prove that the politician deserves better treatment.[23] In *Profiles in Courage,* John Kennedy has defended the politician by citing historical examples of great politicians who lived up to their principles. There is a certain defensiveness about such articles and books, indicating that the politician is not only interested in correcting the

public's view of him but in sustaining his own conception of himself as a useful member of society.

Status insecurity can take other forms. One of the more obvious is for the politician simply to leave the realm of active politics. As noted earlier, Senator Kefauver believes some excellent congressmen are leaving government for precisely this reason. I have no statistics on the matter, but it seems certain that status insecurity does lead some men to leave politics. The writer knows of two individuals who participated in local politics but decided, with the approval of their wives, that they had taken enough abuse from unappreciative voters. Their resentment is considerable, even though other politicians have taken more abuse during the same period and in the same area.

Politicians form a sort of informal mutual admiration society to compensate for their insecurities. The often exaggerated deference that politicians show for one another, in spite of party affiliations, suggests a latent function in terms of maintaining morale. The politicians who appear on television and radio to debate various issues always pay high tributes to their opponents and colleagues. The same is true of much of the debate that takes place in legislative assemblies. The contributions of one politician are always cited by other politicians in their public appearances. Incidentally the politician generally refers to his colleagues as "statesmen," and seldom, except during a campaign and only in regard to the opposition, as "politicians."

Still another means of coping with status insecurity is for the politician to adopt a cynical attitude toward those who are responsible for his situation, the voters. Not infrequently, the politician becomes tough-minded and cynical. By distrusting other people and their motives, he immunizes himself from criticism and disappointment. The politician may attempt to convince himself that he is uninterested in the attitudes of others. In fact, he cannot be, but the delusion is comforting.

Some politicians adopt a stoic view to handle their status problems. Presidents Roosevelt, Truman, and Eisenhower have all been known to say that the varying degrees of abuse to which each has been subjected is petty and unimportant compared to the criticism suffered by some of the greatest of American Presidents. The detractors are, so Truman is reported to have once said, soon forgotten. The historical-minded politician is more concerned with what future generations will think of him than what his contemporaries do. The conviction that what one is doing will be of lasting importance sustains the politician through the rocky present.

The role of humor ought not to be underestimated as a means for handling the strains of politics, including that of status insecurity. Politicians like the late Senator Barkley were not only renowned for their gift of humor but also honored for the use which they made of it during times of great stress. The politician, as Senator Wiley has shown, is quite capable of laughing at himself.[24] The fact that he can and does may constitute an effort to minimize the difficulties of political life.

Conclusion

I have indicated some of the major sources of strain in the occupation of the elected public official. Instead of summarizing them, I want, now, to list a few propositions or, better, hypotheses about role strains in the hope that others may be stimulated to further research. The hypotheses are stated in an unqualified manner and without supporting evidence.

Hypothesis 1. The more complex the social system, the more numerous are the possible sources of role strains.

Hypothesis 2. The more sharply roles are defined in a system the more intense will be the resultant strains where role conflict occurs.

Hypothesis 3. In the American polity executive offices are subject to more role strains than are legislative and judicial offices.

Hypothesis 4. Legislative offices are subject to more role strains than are judicial offices.

Hypothesis 5. The higher the office, i.e., in terms of the local, state, and national division, the more numerous the role strains.

Two further subjects deserve emphasis. The first concerns the practical use of any information which might result from further studies in the area of occupational role strains in politics. We know very little about the way in which public officials respond to the conditions under which they labor. Yet, as democrats, we want them to perform their functions in a responsive and responsible manner. Traditional political theory has not offered much help in devising conditions that will produce the desired behavior. Since much of political behavior is conditioned by the strains to which it is subject, we might inquire into those strains, their sources, and the resultant behavior. If we can understand and, perhaps, control the strains, we will be in a better position to make the ideals of democratic rule possible. I do not wish to be understood as pleading for a reduction of the strains of politicians, if indeed that were possible. American democratic theory has always emphasized the desirability of subjecting public officials to various strains, and no doubt there is much to be said for this position. But empirical evidence on the point is rare, and the problem remains. In any case it is worth entertaining the view that the elected official's work, like that of other organizational members, might be improved by bettering his conditions of employment.

The final point I want to make relates to research on role strains. Relationships need to be established — if there are any — among types of offices, personalities, awareness of strains among politicians, and their behavior. The research apparatus of the social sciences is sufficiently advanced to handle most of the problems involved. Questionnaires and interviews can be used quite effectively in getting at a politician's awareness of his occupational problems and frustrations. Harold Lasswell long ago demonstrated some of the possibilities. More recently certain political scientists have shown how legislators respond to conflicting expectations when they cast their votes. And, of course, we have a rich background of historical and biographical writing from which to derive hypotheses and data. Burns's study of Roosevelt and the Georges' personality analysis of Wilson contain excellent material on the role strains of these two Presidents.

Notes

[1] A translation of Weber's "Politik als Beruf" can be found in H. H. Gerth and C. Wright Mills, eds. and trs., *From Max Weber* (London: 1948).

[2] The best but by no means the only writings of this type are those of Frank Kent, *Political Behavior* (New York: 1928), and J. H. Wallis, *The Politician* (New York: 1935).

[3] Tenure and Turnover of Legislative Personnel, *Annals* 195 (Jan. 1938): 21–31.

[4] Tribulations of a State Senator, *Reporter* (May 17, 1956), pp. 24–8.

[5] Julius Turner, *Party and Constituency: Pressures on Congress* (Baltimore: 1951), p. 179.

[6] See V. O. Key, Jr., *American State Politics: An Introduction* (New York, 1956), chs. ii and viii; Samuel Lubell, *The Future of American Politics* (New York, 1951).

[7] The pattern-variable scheme is dealt with in most of Parsons' recent work. The best introduction, however, is contained in the volume edited by Parsons and Edward A. Shils, *Towards a General Theory of Action* (Cambridge, 1952), pp. 76–91.

[8] The assertion is premised upon the notion that political systems are primarily concerned with the specification of societal goals and the mobilization of support for their implementation. And, finally, it is maintained that such goals are statements of preference and not factual assertions about reality.

[9] See Talcott Parsons, *The Social System* (Glencoe, Ill., 1951), p. 100.

[10] Estes Kefauver and Jack Levin, *A Twentieth Century Congress* (New York: 1947), p. vii.

[11] Robert M. La Follette, Jr., "A Senator Looks at Congress," *Atlantic Monthly* 172 (July 1943): 91–6.

[12] George B. Galloway, *Congress at the Crossroads* (New York: 1946), p. 279.

[13] J. William Fulbright, The Legislator: Duties, Functions, and Hardships of Public Officials, *Vital Speeches of the Day* 12 (May 15, 1946): 470.

[14] *Ibid.*

[15] *New York Times Magazine*, Dec. 18, 1955, p. 34.

[16] I Go to the Legislature, *Survey Graphic* 30 (July 1941): 374.

[17] *Politics and Public Service: A Discussion of the Civic Art in America* (New York, 1939), p. 228.

[18] *Ibid.*, p. 229.

[19] La Follette, *op. cit.*, p. 92.

[20] Fulbright, *op. cit.*, p. 472.

[21] Quoted by Maurice Klain, "'Politics'—Still a Dirty Word," *Antioch Review* (Winter 1955–1956): 464.

[22] *Harvard Business Review* 32 (Nov.–Dec. 1954): 37–41.

[23] Frederich M. Davenport, in *Harvard Business Review* 11 (July 1943): 468–77.

[24] *Laughing with Congress* (New York: 1947).

Intimate Environments and Political Behavior

Richard M. Merelman

Introduction

It is by now a truism that contemporary political scientists have rediscovered the primary group.[1] The

Richard M. Merelman, "Intimate Environments and Political Behavior," reprinted from the *Midwest Journal of Political Science* 12 (1968): 382–400, by permission of the Wayne State University Press. Copyright 1968, by Wayne State University Press.

pioneering research of Lazarsfeld, Berelson and their associates brought the primary group to the attention of students of electoral behavior. The early voting studies indicated clearly the extent to which campaign influences on electoral behavior are mediated through the primary groups which compose an individual's intimate environment.[2] Primary groups have since been examined as part of inquiries into such diverse subjects as partisan identification,[3] the mass media,[4] the Supreme Court,[5] committee behavior,[6] and group decision-making.[7]

The primary groups of which a person is a part make up his intimate environment. Within this environment he takes the steps which lead him either into or away from political involvement, social action and productive citizenship. This study investigates the effects of differing intimate environments on the political behavior and attitudes of a large group of college students. We will rely on two major bodies of literature which handle the subject of intimate environments in differing ways.

The relevant literature most familiar to the political scientist is that on the problem of cross-pressures. One form of cross-pressures exists when the individual is exposed to and perceives incompatible primary group demands. For example, his friends may want him to vote democratic and his parents Republican. Or he may wish to vote Republican, but his friends and/or his parents disagree.

Berelson, Lazarsfeld and McPhee claim that cross-pressured people behave distinctively during election campaigns. "People under cross-pressures . . . change their vote during the campaign more than people in homogeneous circumstances. . . . People under cross-pressures . . . come to their final vote decision later than people in homogeneous circumstances. . . ." Furthermore, "The more intimate the conflict (as between family and friends), the later the decision."[8] McCloskey and Dahlgren extend these findings considerably, noting that though it is the family which is primarily responsible for the growth of party loyalty, people whose friends do not share the family's party preference are likely to defect from the family's choice. Furthermore, such individuals have lower levels of political awareness.[9]

Therefore, emerging from the cross-pressures literature is a theme of political hesitancy and withdrawal. As Lane puts it, "Conflicts between primary group references . . . may increase withdrawal tendencies."[10] This is not to say that all those who are cross-pressured vacillate in or actually leave the political arena, but rather that they are more likely than others to do so.

However, a wider perspective, encompassing role conflict theory, yields another view of this problem. According to Banton, "Every member of a social unit . . . has one or more parts to play. He has tasks to perform and is entitled to receive services from other people in recognition of his contributions. These clusters of rights and obligations constitute roles."[11] Social systems define many roles, such as son or daughter or friend. In other cases, as Turner stresses,[12] individuals create their own roles and the obligations that accompany them. In our society, the stance a person assumes *vis a vis* the political world is not socially determined, but is partially constructed by the individual himself. However, this formulation of a political identity is affected by the socially defined roles the individual already plays.

People occupy and play multiple roles in complex social systems. Often these roles conflict with each other and produce stress. A major source of such role stress are the cross-pressures exerted by incompatible primary group demands in the intimate environment. Cross-pressures create stress both because they make it difficult for the person to play his prescribed roles in his intimate environment and because they circumscribe his ability to produce new roles for himself.

Role conflict theory suggests *two* major ways in which an individual can resolve or manage his role conflicts and cross-pressures. Stouffer states that "(1) He can conform to one set of role expectations and take the consequences of nonconformity to other sets." Or, "(2) He can seek a compromise position by which he attempts to conform in part, though not wholly, to one or more sets of role expectations, in the hope that the sanctions applied will be minimal."[13] Alternative Two is merely a restatement of the withdrawal and compromise reaction observed in the cross-pressures literature. Alternative One, however, is something else.

Because an individual is exposed to cross-pressures in his intimate environment, it does not follow that he must withdraw. As Stouffer suggests, he may choose one of the horns of his dilemma, thereby exposing himself to the assault of the other horn. The person who chooses a position, rather than withdraw, takes on a psychological burden. Within his intimate environment he will suffer strong disagreement with his position. He must arm himself for the assault to come. According to the theory of cognitive dissonance, such preparation may often take the form of sophisticated rationalization of his choice.[14] Commitment to a position which produces strong and intimate opposition should force the individual to produce an ideology justifying his choice. Thus, to the politically role conflicted individual, either withdrawal or choice followed by ideological overcompensation may seem a reasonable strategy. Our first major hypothesis is that both responses occur.

But a second question arises. Which intimate environment is more likely to produce withdrawal from politics, that one which is cross-pressured or that one which is depoliticized? Is it more debilitating for a person to inhabit an intimate environment in which primary groups disagree or an intimate environment where primary groups do not give solidary, strong partisan political cues? We might hypothesize that a person who plays a role in two primary groups, each of which is united within itself politically but politically hostile to the other, will still be more involved politically than a person who belongs to two primary groups, of which one one is united and politically and therefore able to send him forceful partisan political cues. Our second major hypothesis, therefore, is that the cross-pressured person is more likely to remain politically involved than the person who gets fewer solidary partisan political cues. Both the agreement of and the number of politically partisan solidary primary groups produce political involvement, with the latter factor being more important than the former.

The intimate environments of young men and women are characterized by two major primary group attachments: to parents and to friends. When parents and friends are in agreement on political party identification, we may say that in many respects the individual lives in a congruent political environment. Though party identification in the United States does not tie one tightly to a party line or ideology, it is at least a rough index of attitudes on major political issues.[15]

Therefore, in the case of parent-peer agreement on party choice, the youth's roles as friend and child are mutually reinforcing politically. This happy arrangement facilitates the construction of a stable, active political identity. On the other hand, the young person's intimate environment may place him in a political role conflict. His parents may agree on one party identification and his friends on another. Parent-peer political differences make it risky and problematic for him to construct a political role. Finally, the youth may exist in an intimate environment which, with respect to these other two environments, is depoliticized. Only one of his salient primary groups, either his parents or his friends, passes him partisan political cues. Either his parents of his friends agree among themselves on a party identification, while from the other primary group he receives no consistent partisan direction. Thus, an individual may inhabit one of three intimate environments: (1) Role Congruence, characterized by parents and friends who support the same party; (2) Role Conflict, in which parents agree on one party and friends on another; (3) Limited Congruence, in which only one primary group, parents or friends, have a solidary party identification.[16]

Major Operational Hypotheses

Responses to Role Conflict

We will, for convenience, specify our operational hypotheses in terms of the role conflict environment and role conflicted individuals. As suggested above in our first general hypothesis, we expect two major responses to political role conflicts.

Withdrawal. Specifically, the role conflicteds will cope by actively avoiding political involvement. Therefore, we should expect them to have less general interest in politics when compared to congruents. On the other hand, given our second general hypothesis, we would also expect the role conflicteds to evidence more interest in politics than the limited congruents.

Specific withdrawal techniques will involve information, communication and partisanship. The role conflicteds should have lower levels of information on political matters than the congruents, but more than the limited congruents. We should also expect the role conflicteds to manage their incongruent political environments by avoiding in conversation the sources of stress, namely politics. As Kahn, et al. put it, in their meticulous study of role conflict in organizations:

> People communicate less with their associates when under strong conflicts than when they are relatively free of them. This would be expected, considering the weakening of such affective interpersonal bonds as trust, respect, and attraction. There is also a direct instrumental reason for this curtailment of communication. Role pressures are exerted for the most part by oral communications from role senders. When these inductions prove stressful, the stress can be reduced by withdrawing from the inducers, by avoiding interaction with those who create the conflict.[17]

According to our two general hypotheses, the role conflicteds should communicate less about politics when compared to the role congruents, but should communicate more than the limited congruents.

Finally, we expect the role conflicteds to have a lower rate of partisan identification than the congruents. Since much of the role conflicted's stress centers on the fact that his friends are of one party identification and his parents another, the role of partisan should be threatening to him. Therefore, he is likely to consider himself as an Independent or take no party identification at all. Role congruents, on the other hand, have every reason to adopt the party identification so vigorously reinforced by their primary groups. Limited congruents, having fewer solidary partisan political cues, should have the lowest amount of partisan choice, given our second general hypothesis.

Partisan choice and rationalization. While withdrawal among the role conflicteds is predicted by the cross-pressures literature, role conflict theory and theories of cognitive dissonance suggest partisan choice and ideological rationalization as a second means of coping. Though fewer of the role conflicteds than the congruents may choose a partisan identification, the former's choice, when it does occur, will have interesting consequences. To choose a Democratic identification when one's friends are Republican or to choose a Republican identification when one's parents are Democrats is to invite what the Gullahorns term "status-produced role conflict."[18] Here the conflict erupts from occupancy of a single status—in this case, partisan identifier—which an important primary group in the intimate environment opposes. Because of this self-imposed stress, partisans among the role conflicteds should defend themselves through ideological rationalization. Specifically, the reasons party identifiers among the role conflicteds give for adherence to their party should be more politically sophisticated than those given by either the limited congruent or the full congruent partisans.[19] Congruent partisans, of course, should be more ideologically sophisticated than limited congruent partisans.

Prediction of Conflict Resolution

Gross, et al. demonstrate that the mode of role conflict resolution is predictable if one can measure three variables: (1) the extent to which the groups producing the conflict for the individual are perceived by him as willing to exercise sanctions for non-conformity to their position; (2) the extent to which the individual views the demands put on him by his conflicting primary groups as being legitimate; (3) his own role orientation, i. e., his disposition to respond more strongly to either the legitimacy dimension or the sanctions dimension or to both equally.[20] Using these three dimensions in their examination of school superintendents, Gross and his associates were able to predict correctly the resolution of 91 percent of their subjects' role conflicts.[21]

The measurement of role orientation (variable 3)

used by Gross, et al, involves the application of a 37-item instrument. In our own research, no such elaborate estimate of role orientation was feasible. Therefore, in an effort to predict the resolution of stress for the role conflicteds, an alternative, but less satisfying, expedient was devised. We hypothesized that those who were goaded toward identification with either parents' or friends' party by the legitimacy and sanction pressures would choose the relevant party for themselves. On the other hand, those who found pressures closely balanced between parents and friends would opt for Independence or no identification. But we also expected that the unmeasured dimension—role orientation—would become most important in closely balanced cases. Therefore, we expected to have reduced success in predicting the partisan identifications of those subjected to equal pressures from parents and friends, although we hypothesized higher rates of Independence in this group.

Questionnaires designed to test the hypotheses were distributed to undergraduates in introductory history, economics, anthropology and geology courses at UCLA. Only students below the age of 21 were examined, since it was felt that voting experience might distort, in unforeseeable ways, the process to be examined. The act of voting constitutes for some a commitment, regardless of previous behavior or attitudes. Demographic controls were placed on the findings at the analysis stage in order to assure that differences in the composition of the three categories or respondents did not contaminate results.[22]

Findings

Responses to Role Conflict

As the following tables indicate, while the general pattern of findings fits and supports our two major hypotheses, results are not consistently statistically significant. Therefore, it is the general *positioning* of the environments in relation to each other, rather than the quantitative differences between them which must carry the burden of our argument.

Withdrawal. Table 1 indicates the interest in politics our respondents report.

Though differences are not significant, they are in the hypothesized direction. Congruents seem able to reach a higher level of confidence and interest in politics than do the others. On the other hand, the role conflicteds, despite the stress they face in their environments, appear slightly more able than the limited congruents to manifest interest in the political world.

The lowered rates of interest in politics evidenced by both the limited congruents and the role conflicteds should, we hypothesize, take the more specific form of avoiding political information. In order to investigate this hypothesis, a six-question political information test, which focused on domestic politics, was devised. Table 2 indicates that only our first general hypothesis, but not our second, is supported. While the role conflicteds meet our expectations with refer-

Table 1
Interest in Politics in Three Intimate Environments

Amount of Interest	Congruent	Environment Role Conflicted	Limited Congruent	Total
Rather and quite interested	66% (115)	60% (28)	57% (115)	61% (258)
Not very and somewhat interested	34% (57)	49% (19)	43% (87)	39% (163)
Totals	100% (172)	100% (47)	100% (202)	100% (421)

$X^2 = 3.5$, not significant

Table 2
Comparison of Mean Political Information Scores in Three
Intimate Environments

	Environment			
Congruent	Role Conflicted	Limited Congruent	t Value	Significance
2.92 (172)	2.29 (47)		2.33	.02
	2.29 (47)	2.47 (200)	.70	not
2.92 (172)		2.47 (200)	2.77	.1

Total mean = 2.65 (419)

ence to the congruents, they also fall below the limited congruents in their political knowledge. Clearly, however, the congruents are in a superior position to gather information than are the inhabitants of the other two environments.

When the party identification of respondents is controlled, interesting refinements appear.

Only among Independents are there statistically significant differences. Inspection of Table 3 indicates that Independents from congruent environments have the highest information score of any subgroup. On the other hand, the lowest score for all sub-groups, 1.44, is also made by Independents, this time among

the role conflicteds. How can we explain this paradox? The answer may lurk in the differing implications of Independence in role conflicted and congruent intimate environments. In the case of the role conflicteds, Independence represents a withdrawal from choice in a threatening environment. Independence is a shaky compromise designed to avoid commitment, yet mollify both parents and friends. Therefore, withdrawal from political information might be expected to accompany this choice. On the other hand, Independence in a congruent partisan environment represents revolt against both parents and peers, and, as with most revolt, considerable stress is entailed. This strain

Table 3
Comparison of Mean Political Information Score in Three Intimate
Environments with Party Identification Controlled

	Environment			
Congruent	Role Conflicted	Limited Congruent	t Value	Significance
	Republican Party Identification			
2.76 (30)	3.35 (14)		1.01	not
2.76 (30)		2.61 (53)	.43	not
	3.35 (14)	2.61 (53)	1.48	not
	Democratic Party Identification			
2.75 (98)	2.31 (16)		1.04	not
2.75 (98)		2.50 (60)	1.03	not
	2.31 (16)	2.50 (60)	.42	not
	Independent and None			
3.44 (44)	1.44 (17)		4.58	.0001
3.44 (44)		2.38 (87)	3.53	.001
	1.44 (17)	2.38 (87)	2.32	.02

Total mean = 2.65 (419)

for Independents in congruent environments may well force the Independent to defend himself with political knowledge. In the role conflicted environment, however, Independence does not represent a stressful response, but party identification does. It is therefore understandable why Independence in the role conflicted environment should not encourage the growth of political knowledge. We see, though, that when the stressful choice is made in the role conflicted environment and a party identification is chosen, political information rises to a level comparable to that of party identifiers in the other environments. The mean information score of party identifiers among the role conflicteds is 2.80, slightly higher than the mean information score for the sample as a whole.

These findings suggest that the proverbial political ignorance of Independents may bear reinterpretation.[23] Independence itself need not necessarily be associated with a dearth of political information. Much may depend on the intimate environment in which Independence occurs. When Independence represents a withdrawal from stress, the Independent may indeed be uninformed, but when Independence represents actual choice of stress, the Independent may be quite knowledgeable.[24]

Our third hypothesized withdrawal reaction to a conflicted intimate political environment involves party identification. Table 4 lends support both to the hypothesis that the role conflicteds will have lower

rates of party identification than the congruents and to the hypothesis that the role conflicteds will have higher rates of party identification than the limited congruents.

Despite the hindrances of cross-pressures, the role conflicted environment contains sufficient political cues to produce a moderate amount of party identification. On the other hand, the limited congruent environment is not sufficiently politicized to motivate as great a rate of party identification. Again, both the agreement of and sheer number of politically solidary primary groups contribute to political involvement.

Following the lead of Kahn et al. we hypothesized that the role conflicteds would further manifest withdrawal by discussing politics less with both friends and parents than would the congruents. On the other hand they should be more talkative than the limited congruents. Tables 5 and 6 indicate that our prediction of the role conflicted-congruent relationship is marginally supported for friends, but not at all for family. On the other hand, in both cases the limited congruents are somewhat less politicized than are either the role conflicteds or the congruents.

As far as the role conflicteds are concerned, the avoidance of communication hypothesis enjoys little support. It is, of course, possible that the role conflicteds may employ in discussion many techniques of perceptual distortion and psychological compartmentalization which would contribute to an inhibited

Table 4
Party Identification in Three Intimate Environments

Party Identification	Congruent	Role Conflicted	Limited Congruent	Total
Have Party Identification (Republicans and Democrats)	72% (128)	63% (30)	54% (109)	64% (267)
No Party Identification (Independents, and None)	28% (43)	37% (17)	46% (93)	36% (153)
Totals	100% (171)	100% (47)	100% (202)	100% (420)

$X^2 = 11.5, p < .01$

Table 5
Frequency of Discussing Politics with Friends in Three Intimate
Environments

Frequency	Congruent	Environment Limited Congruent	Role Conflicted	Totals
Never	3% (4)	5% (9)	6% (3)	4% (16)
Occasionally	61% (105)	72% (147)	64% (30)	67% (282)
Frequently	36% (62)	23% (47)	30% (14)	29% (123)
Totals	100% (171)	100% (203)	100% (47)	100% (421)

$X^2 = 6.6$, not significant

Table 6
Frequency of Discussing Politics With Parents in Three Intimate
Environments

Frequency	Congruent	Environment Limited Congruent	Role Conflicted	Totals
Never	7% (9)	16% (33)	8% (4)	12% (46)
Occasionally	66% (114)	66% (134)	66% (12)	66% (279)
Frequently	27% (48)	18% (35)	26% (12)	22% (95)
Totals	100% (171)	100% (202)	100% (47)	100% (420)

$X^2 = 11.1$, p. $< .02$

communication process. However, our data do not deal with this problem. Most clearly, however, Tables 5 and 6 indicate again that the number of solidary political cues in the intimate environment may be more important than the conflict within that environment.

Party choice and rationalization. Our second hypothesized response to political role conflict was party choice coupled with ideological rationalization, such that the sophistication of the role conflicteds' adherence to party, when it occurred, would surpass that of the other two groups. In order to test this hypothesis, respondents were asked to explain in their own words the reasons for their choice of party, Independence, or no identification. Three graduate students of political science coded responses inde-

pendently on a scale of 0 to 4, where 0 represented total absence of reasoning and 4 represented the most sophisticated ideological response. Each respondent was assigned a mean score compiled from the coders' ratings, and mean ideological sophistication scores for each environment were calculated. Table 7 reports the results.

Both our major hypotheses gain some support from the positioning of the environments evident in Table 7. Those among the role conflicteds who identify themselves as Republicans or Democrats have developed relatively high levels of ideological sophistication. Neither the congruents nor the limited congruents develop such sophistication, though, as expected, the congruents surpass the limited congruents. The stress encountered by the role conflicteds who choose a party seems to motivate ideological rationali-

Table 7

Comparison of Mean Sophistication of Response among Partisans in Three
Intimate Environments

	Environment			
Congruent	Role Conflicted	Limited Congruent	t Value	Significance
1.85 (128)	2.05 (30)		1.19	not
1.85 (128)		1.71 (109)	1.31	not
	2.05 (30)	1.71 (109)	2.19	.03

Total Mean = 1.84 (267)

Intercoder coefficient of realiability = .670

zation. Controls placed on the data for party choice did not alter the relationship between environments.

Prediction of Conflict Resolution

Finally, using the legitimacy and sanctions dimensions of Gross, et al.'s investigation, we attempted to predict the role conflicted respondent's resolution of his conflict. We hypothesized that role conflicted respondents would adopt the party identification of that primary group exerting the greatest pressure. Respondents who faced a balanced field of forces would choose according to role orientation dimensions not investigated, with a strong tendency to opt for Independence. In order to investigate this hypothesis, we first measured the sanctions dimension by asking respondents how much their friends and parents cared about the respondent's political beliefs. We reasoned that if a group was perceived as caring it would also appear likely to penalize for nonconformity. We then assessed the legitimacy dimension by asking respondents how much right their parents and friends had to concern themselves with the respondent's political beliefs. Each respondent was given four choices on each question. A respondent who reported that his parents both cared very much about his beliefs and had every right to do so, while his friends neither cared nor had the right to care was given a +8 score, the highest pro-parents score possible. Scores run to a possible −8 pro-friends score at the other end of the continuum, with a 0 score representing a relatively balanced field of forces.

In general, our hypothesis is supported. Of the 17 role conflicted respondents who reported pressure equal to or greater than ±2, 14 identified with the predicted party. Thus, simply knowing the balance of forces on two dimensions — perceived sanctions and legitimacy — made it possible to predict correctly the direction of party choice for 82% of those respondents pushed strongly toward parents or friends. The breaking point in predictive accuracy, however, lies at ±1. Of the 29 respondents in a relatively balanced field of forces, scoring from −1 to +1, prediction was correct in only 12 cases. This low rate of correct prediction is attributable to the fact that a ±1 score does not have nearly the pushing power that a score of ±2 or more has. However, using ±1, rather than 0, as a boundary for a relatively balanced field of forces yields a good prediction of Independence. Of the 16 Independents among the role conflicteds, 14 or 88% had fields of forces of no more than ±1. We can conclude that when strong pressures of legitimacy and sanctions push the individual toward parents' or friends' party identification, he will yield to those pressures at a high level of predictability. But when relatively equal pressures from both sides exist, his choice of Independence or party identification depends on other factors. Independence, itself, however, is most likely to be characteristic of the equal pressures range.[25]

Summary and Conclusion

Let us first summarize the data relevant to our first major hypothesis which relates the behavior of the role conflicteds to the congruents. Then let us focus on the findings relevant to the second major hypothesis.

All of our hypotheses about the lower politicization of the role conflicteds *vis a vis* the congruents gain some support. The role conflicteds are more likely to withdraw from politics than are the congruents. They express less interest in politics, and this fact is reflected in their lower rates of political information and partisan identification. On the other hand, they are only slightly less likely than the congruents to discuss politics in their intimate environment. Finally, partisan conflicteds rationalize their party identification more completely than both partisan congruents and partisan limited congruents. The Independent response, characterized by extreme role stress for the congruents is accompanied by high levels of information about politics. However, Independents among the role conflicteds have entered a half-way house that mollifies both parents and friends. Role conflicted Independents, therefore, are less motivated to assimilate political information.

Our second major hypothesis, which predicted greater political motivation among the role conflicteds than among the limited congruents, was also generally, though less strongly, supported. Role conflicteds had somewhat higher rates of political interest, partisanship and conversation than did limited congruents. Furthermore, their choice of party, when it occurred, had greater ideological significance for them than did a similar choice among limited congruents. Although role conflicteds also had slightly lower amounts of political information than did limited congruents we may tentatively conclude that while political conflict is missing for the limited congruents, so is a politicized intimate environment. Therefore, differences between the role conflicteds and the limited congruents generally favor the former. It would appear that the sheer number of politically solidary groups in the intimate environment may be slightly more important than the conflicts within that environment, though both factors contribute to sustained political motivation. If our formulation is correct, it suggests that a re-evaluation of traditional theories of cross-pressures and political motivation may be needed.

It would have been impossible to predict accurately the resolution of cross-pressures among the role conflicteds or to account for ideological sophistication among role conflicted partisans without an expansion of this study's perspective to encompass role conflict theory. In that sense, this paper represents the convergence of theory, research, and speculation from a number of different literatures. However, role conflict theory particularly suffers from some major substantive and methodological difficulties which limit its present utility for the political scientist. Two problems in particular bear mention.

Role conflict theorists are not at all agreed on the meanings of role and the inferences that should be drawn from role playing. Roughly speaking, role conflict theorists are divided between those who conceive of roles as individual dramaturgical presentations and those who view roles as tightly structured, socially determined positions in formal and informal organizations. While the first group emphasizes the ability of the individual within broad limits to create his own, idiosyncratic roles, the second group argues that tightly patterned, socially validated and formally organized roles restrict the behavior of incumbents.[26] This division makes it hazardous for the political scientist to thread his way though the field, picking out usable data and theory.

In addition, intimate environments are much more complicated than many role conflict theorists acknowledge. The number of possible roles played and the number of important primary groups and reference individuals in any intimate environment will vary from person to person. They may, in fact, be so multitudinous as to defeat our attempts to encompass them in one theory. In this paper, parents and peers were the two primary groups singled out, and friend, child, and political animal were the roles involved. However, we know that these roles hardly exhaust the intimate environments of our respondents. It must be admitted that role theory as a whole has not fully met the complex challenges of intimate environments. For this reason, role theory does not yet offer us a compelling new approach to political behavior.

Despite these problems, however, role conflict theory has afforded us some fresh insights into the problems of cross pressures and primary groups in politics. In this sense, the present effort must be understood only as a first step in applying all of role theory to an understanding of politics.

Notes

[1] I am particularly indebted to Professors Leo Snowiss, James Guyot, and Peter Orleans for their careful and perceptive comments on a previous draft of this paper and to Douglas Madsen and Bolivar Lamounier for their help in calculations.

[2] See Paul Lazarsfeld, Bernard Berelson and Hazel Gaudet, *The People's Choice* (New York: Columbia University Press, 1944), chaps. 15 and 16. Also, Bernard Berelson, Paul F. Lazarsfeld, and William McPhee, *Voting* (Chicago: University of Chicago Press, 1954), chaps. 6 and 7. For a recent, imaginative application of primary group theory to problems of local political behavior and identification, see Robert D. Putnam, "Political Attitudes and the Local Community," *American Political Science Review* 60, no. 3 (September, 1966): 640–55.

[3] Herbert McClosky and Harold E. Dahlgren, "Primary Group Influence on Party Loyalty," *American Political Science Review* 53, no. 3 (September, 1959): 757–77.

[4] Joseph T. Klapper, *The Effects of Mass Communication* (Glencoe: The Free Press, 1960), passim. The fullest statement of the role of primary groups in mass communication is Elihu Katz and Paul F. Lazarsfeld, *Personal Influence* (Glencoe: The Free Press, 1955).

[5] E. C. Snyder, "The Supreme Court as a Small Group," *Social Forces* 36, no. 3 (March, 1958): 232–8.

[6] Richard F. Fenno, Jr., "The House Appropriations Committee as a Political System," in *New Perspectives on the House of Representatives,* eds. Robert L. Peabody and Nelson W. Polsby (Chicago: Rand McNally; 1966), pp. 79–109. Also, James David Barber, *Power in Committees* (Chicago: Rand McNally, 1966).

[7] Sidney Verba, *Small Groups and Political Behavior* (Princeton: Princeton University Press, 1961).

[8] Berelson, Lazarsfeld, and McPhee, *op. cit.,* 148.

[9] McClosky and Dahlgren, *loc. cit.*

[10] Robert E. Lane, *Political Life* (Glencoe: The Free Press, 1959), 202.

[11] Michael Banton, *Roles* (New York: Basic Books, 1965), p. 2.

[12] Ralph Turner, "Role Taking: Process versus Conformity," in *Human Behavior and Social Processes,* Arnold Rose, ed., (Boston: Houghton Mifflin, 1962), pp. 20–40.

[13] Samuel A. Stouffer, "An Analysis of Conflicting Social Norms," *American Sociological Review* 25, no. 6 (December, 1949): 707–17, 707. For other hypotheses on means of resolving role conflicts see Jackson Toby, "Some Variables in Role Conflict Analysis," *Social Forces* 30, no. 3 (March, 1952): 323–7; Stewart E. Perry and Lyman C. Wynne, "Role Conflict, Role Redefinition, and Social Change in a Research Organization," *Social Forces* 38, no. 3 (October, 1959): 62–5; also, William Goode, "A Theory of Role Strain," *American Sociological Review* 25, no. 3 (June, 1960): 483–96.

[14] Leon Festinger, *A Theory of Cognitive Dissonance* (Stanford: Stanford University Press, 1957), p. 83. The consequences of stress are also taken up by studies of status inconsistency. People who are status inconsistent do not occupy congruent status ranks on all dimensions. For example, an individual may have little education, but much money. Though status inconsistency pressures may not manifest themselves in the intimate environment through primary groups, they may have considerable impact through the more distant reference groups to which an individual orients himself. Some evidence exists to indicate a major response to status inconsistency is ideological overcompensation and political activism. For an introduction to the debate, see Gerhard Lenski, "Status Crystallization: A Non-Vertical Dimension of Social Status," *American Sociological Review* 19, no. 2 (August, 1954): 405–13; Irwin W. Goffman, "Status Consistency and Preference for Change in Power Distribution," *Ibid.* 22, no. 3 (June, 1957): 275–81; William F. Kenkel, "The Relationship Between Status Consistency and Politico-Economic Attitudes," *Ibid.* 21, no. 3 (June, 1956): 365–8; K. Dennis Kelly, and William J. Chambliss, "Status Consistency and Political Attitudes," *Ibid.,* vol. 31, no. 3, June, 1966, 375–82; Gerard Brandmeyer, "Status Consistency and Political Behavior: A Replication and Extension of Research," *Sociological Quarterly* 6, no. 3 (Summer, 1965): 241–57. Political observers attempting to explain the growth of the radical right have also been intrigued by the status consistency problem. See Richard Hofstader, "The Pseudo-Conservative Revolt," in *The Radical Right,* ed., Daniel Bell, (Garden City: Doubleday Anchor Books, 1964), pp. 75–97, and Seymour Martin Lipset, "The Sources of the Radical Right," in *Ibid.,* pp. 307–73.

[15] The interesting research on "party image" corroborates this conclusion. See Donald R. Matthews and James W. Prothro, "The Concept of Party Image and Its Importance for the Southern Electorate," in *The Electoral Process,* eds. M. Kent Jennings and L. Harmon Zeigler (Englewood Cliffs, N.J.: Prentice-Hall, 1966), pp. 139–175. See also Angus Cambell, et al., *The American Voter* (New York: Wiley, 1960), chap. 3. For a theoretical investigation into the meaning of ideology in a mass society, see Philip E. Converse, "The Nature of Belief Systems in Mass Publics," in *Ideology and Discontent,* ed., David Apter, (New York: The Free Press of Glencoe, 1964), pp. 206–62.

[16] There may be a fourth environment, characterized by neither

parents nor friends who have a solidary party identification. How-ever, examination of this environment is unnecessary to test our two major hypotheses and would have added additional theoretical burdens to the paper. Hence, it was excluded from the analysis.

[17] Robert L. Kahn, et al., *Organizational Stress: Studies in Role Conflict and Ambiguity*, (New York: Wiley, 1964), pp. 68–9.

[18] John T. and Jeanne E. Gullahorn, "Role Conflict and its Reso-lution," *Sociological Quarterly* 4, no. 1 (Winter, 1963): 32–48, 38.

[19] This possibility is suggested by much sociological speculation. For example, Sutton, et al. claim that American business ideology finds its origin in the need of the businessman to manage the status-produced conflicts in his role. Having chosen the business role, the executive is expected to produce profits for his company. On the other hand, society expects from him behavior which may be in-compatible with the company's demand for profits. The business ideology, which attempts to reconcile these conflicts, is the result. As the authors put it, "Ideology is a patterned reaction to the pat-terned strains of a social role. We have seen . . . that explicit thought about action is typically a response to conflict. Where a role in-volves patterns of conflicting demands, the occupants of that role may respond by elaborating a system of ideas and symbols, which in part may serve as a guide to action, but chiefly has broader and more direct functions as a response to strain." Francis X. Sutton, et al., *The American Business Creed* (New York: Schocken Books, 1962), pp. 307–8. Similarly, Carper and Becker suggest that fledg-ling physiologists elaborate a set of ideological rationalizations to justify to themselves and to society at large their switch from a medical career. James W. Carper and Howard S. Becker, "Adjust-ments to Conflicting Expectations in the Development of Identi-fication with an Occupation," *Social Forces* 36, no. 1 (October, 1957): 51–6, 52. Becker describes elsewhere how occupational deviants, such as jazz musicians, react to the stress of their non-conformity by elaborating an occupational and social ideology. Howard Becker, *Outsiders* (Glencoe: The Free Press, 1963), chap. 5. In addition, as fn. 14 makes clear, status inconsistency and theories of cognitive dissonance would predict the same response.

[20] Neal Gross, Alexander W. McEachern, and Ward S. Mason, "Role Conflict and Its Resolution," in *Role Theory: Concepts and Research*, eds. Bruce J. Biddle and Edwin J. Thomas (New York: Wiley, 1966), pp. 287–97.

[21] *Ibid.*, 296.

[22] The questionnaires were administered by the investigator to the sample classes of students during class periods. The investigator informed the students of his interest in getting at some "factors which affect the way college students view politics." This extremely general explanation was designed to prevent the students from dis-covering the actual hypotheses under examination and thereby contaminating the study. Because the administration occurred dur-ing class time, response rate of those students present approached 100%. Classes in the social sciences and history were picked for the bulk of the administration in order to insure obtaining subjects who had at least some probable prior interest in politics. However, political science classes were excluded to prevent the inclusion of too many highly politicized students, who might be atypical of the general student population. The geology class was used when no further cooperation from instructors of introductory social science classes could be elicited. Only 50-odd students were in this class.

The use of other sorts of students, *i.e.*, from the natural sciences or the fine arts, might have produced somewhat different findings, but it would be difficult to predict the directions these differences might take.

There were 236 boys and 183 girls in the sample; controls for sex within environments yielded no changes in the order of rela-tionships between environments. The sample was over 80% from homes where the breadwinner held a white collar job. This was not an unexpected result. Students from blue collar backgrounds did not cluster in any single environment. In terms of religion, 270 of the students were non-Jewish, of whom the great bulk (over 80%) were Protestant; the remaining 150 were Jewish. Because 101 of the Jews clustered in the congruent environment, it was feared that religion might be a source of possible spuriousness. Controls for the effects of religion within environments eliminated this possibility, however.

The two questions used to group the students in their environ-ments were:

> Would you say that most of your current friends are: Repub-licans, Democrats, Neither, Both, Don't Know?

> Would you say that your parent(s) are: Republicans, Demo-crats, Neither, Both, Don't Know?

The congruent environment was composed of all those who re-sponded that their parents and most of their friends were Republi-cans or Democrats. The role conflicted environment consisted of all those who said either that their parents were Democrats and most of their friends Republicans or vice-versa. The limited Congruent environment was composed of all those who said that their parents or their friends were either Republican or Democratic, while the other primary group was neither Republican nor Democratic both Republican and Democratic, or not perceived in political terms ("Don't Know"). When one of the groups was both Democratic and Republican, neither (presumably Independent or partisan-Inde-pendent), or unknown politically, it conveyed no solidary major party identification to the student. It should be noted that at the time of the study (Spring, 1967) neither the American Independent nor the Peace and Freedom Party had been formed in California. Thus, there was little chance for third party identifications to in-trude on the analysis.

[23] I take this to be a direction in which the late V. O. Key was moving. See his *The Responsible Electorate* (Cambridge: Harvard University Press, 1966). An earlier consideration of the Inde-pendent which points to a revocation of the view that Independents are less interested and informed than others is Alan S. Meyer, "The Independent Voter," in *Public Opinion and Congressional Elec-tions*, William A. McPhee & William A. Glaser, eds. (New York: The Free Press of Glencoe, 1962), pp. 65–78. The earlier view of the marginal role of Independents may be found particularly in Campbell, et al., *op. cit.*, 143. See also, Berelson, Lazarsfeld and McPhee, *op. cit.*, pp. 25–7; and Robert Agger, "Independents and Party Identifiers: Characteristics and Behavior in 1952," in *Ameri-can Voting Behavior*, eds. Eugene Burdick and Arthur G. Brodbeck (Glencoe: The Free Press, 1959), pp. 308–30.

The problem of the "Independent," as Key correctly points out, is partly terminological. That is, there is no commonly accepted definition of Independence. Key's switchers, it seems to me, are at least independent in their voting behavior if not in their self-definition. However, while Key recognizes the ambiguity surrounding Independence as a category, he does not come near resolving it, for his own categories neither include it nor meet the problem headon. For Key's remarks on Independence, see *op. cit.*, pp. 92–3.

[24] Our data also indicate the vital contribution of a congruent environment to the stability of party identification, as the following table indicates:

Party Identification in Congruent and Limited Congruent Environments

Respondents' Party Identification

Environment	Democrat	Republican	Independent	Totals
Congruent Democrat	69% (97)	3 (4)	28 (40)	100 (141)
Congruent Republican	10% (3)	84 (26)	6 (2)	100 (31)
Limited Congruent Democrat	55% (67)	6 (7)	39 (44)	100 (118)
Limited Congruent Republican	6% (5)	51 (39)	43 (34)	100 (78)
	47% (172)	20% (76)	33% (120)	100% (368)

As the table indicates, the limited congruent environment succeeds in keeping respondents from defecting to the other party. However, it is not as efficient as the congruent environment at preventing defections to Independence.

[25] Sutcliffe and Haberman found in their investigation of role conflict resolution that personality characteristics and role orientation also became important primarily when there were relatively equal pressures on the individual from both sides. See J. P. Sutcliffe and M. Haberman, "Factors Influencing Choice in Role Conflict Situations," *American Sociological Review* 21, no. 6 (December, 1956): 695–703. For another investigation of role conflict resolution and personality, see Daniel Solomon, "Adolescents' Decisions: A Comparison of Influence from Parents with that from Other Sources," *Marriage and Family Living* 23, no. 4 (November, 1961): 393–6. Miller and Shull attempt, in another context, to replicate Gross, *et al's* findings. See Delbert C. Miller and Fremont A. Shull, Jr., "The Prediction of Administrative Role Conflict Resolutions," *Administrative Science Quarterly* 7, no. 2 (September, 1962): 143–61. Another extension of Gross, *et al's* findings is Howard J. Ehrlich, James W. Rinehart, and John C. Howell, "The Study of Role Conflict: Explorations in Methodology," *Sociometry* 25, no. 1 (March, 1962): 85–97. See also Elliot G. Mishler, "Personality Characteristics and the Resolution of Role Conflicts," *Public Opinion Quarterly* 17, no. 1 (Spring, 1953): 115–35; and Samuel Stouffer and Jackson Toby, "Role Conflict and Personality," *American Journal of Sociology* 56 (1950–1): 395–407.

[26] The first group generally takes its theoretical cues from Meadian social psychology, while the second group is much influenced by the Lintonian view of culture. For an excellent statement of these problems, see Turner, *loc. cit.*

Status Inconsistency, Cross Pressures, and American Political Behavior

David R. Segal

Partisanship and Non-Voting

A great deal of research in the field of political behavior has been devoted to explorations of the social correlates of political partisanship. (See for example

David R. Segal, "Status Inconsistency, Cross Pressures, and American Political Behavior," *American Sociological Review* 34 (1969): 352–59. Reprinted with permission of the author and the American Sociological Association.

This research was supported in part by the National Institute of Mental Health under grant MH–13783–01. I am indebted to the Inter-University Consortium for Political Research for making the data contained herein available to me. Mary Tassier and Stephen H. Wildstrom provided much appreciated research assistance. Mady W. Segal contributed important insights on the applicability of psychological consistency theories to the phenomenon of status inconsistency. James C. Moore, Jr. and Thomas Smith provided helpful criticism of an earlier draft of this paper.

Janowitz and Segal, 1967.) Numerous studies have shown that in the United States, members of minority religious and ethnic groups, and persons of low occupational, financial, or educational status, tend to support the Democratic Party, while members of "core" Protestant churches, and persons of high status, generally tend to support the Republican Party.

A second major concern in the field of political behavior has been the factors associated with nonvoting. By and large, the characteristics related to such political inactivity are similar to those related to support of the Democratic Party — particularly, low educational and occupational status (Lane, 1959; Milbrath, 1965).[1]

Research on the correlates of partisanship has assumed, either implicitly or explicitly, at least one of two dynamics to explain the linkage between social and political variables. On the one hand, rational self-interest on the part of the voter may be used as the basis for such arguments as "Each citizen in our model votes for the party he believes will provide him with a higher utility income than any other party during the coming election period," (Downs, 1957: 3). On the other hand, processes of social pressure are often cited as the intervening mechanism. "The higher the identification of the individual with the group, the higher the probability that he will think and behave in ways which distinguish members of his group from non-members," (Campbell et al., 1960: 37; cf. Bendix and Lipset, 1957; Lindenfield, 1964). We shall see below that formulations of status inconsistency may similarly be differentiated on the basis of whether they reflect an individual's own evaluation of the relevance of his statuses, or the ease with which he may be identified by others as a member of some reference group.

Most research on political behavior has focused on zero-order relationships between social characteristics and political choice. Conclusions derived from such studies are essentially probability statements dealing with the relative likelihood of two individuals at different points on the same social dimension supporting the same political party. For example, the argument is often found in the literature on the correlates of social class that, *ceteris paribus,* people in white-collar occupations are more likely to vote Republican than are people in blue-collar occupations.

At a somewhat higher level of theoretical and methodological sophistication, some researchers have recognized that other things are rarely equal, and have dealt with first-order relationships between social and political variables by holding some third variable constant. Campbell et al. (1960: 367), for example, in controlling for the effect of region, found that "[status] polarization [the relationship between social class and party choice] is lower in the South than in other regions of the nation."

While the search for intervening variables is becoming more common in behavioral research, the study of the interactions existing among social variables is a relatively underdeveloped part of our science. Two notable exceptions exist to this rule, and these define very different expectations in very similar situations.

Cross Pressures and Status Inconsistency

As a result of data obtained in their study of presidential voting in Erie County, Ohio, in 1940, Lazarsfeld et al. (1948: 60), proposed that "whatever the source of the conflicting pressures, whether from social status or class identification, from voting traditions or the attitudes of associates, the consistent result was to delay the voter's final decision." In a follow-up study conducted in Elmira, New York, in 1948, Berelson et al. (1954: 200) found that "a few cross-pressured voters act like the proverbial donkey and do not vote at all," while other cross-pressured voters were able to resolve the issue by assigning weights to the relevant pressures. More recent research has suggested that withdrawal of psychological affect from political symbols is one method of resolving cross pressures (Lipset, 1963: 211).

Studies of the cross-pressure phenomenon, however, are not unanimous in their support of the proposition that persons under cross pressures are less partisan than others. Although they initially assumed its validity, Pool et al. (1965: 76) found that the cross-pressure hypothesis was not supported by the 1960 presidential election. The Republican Catholic, for example, was likely to vote for Kennedy rather than stay away from the polls.

Lenski's theory of status inconsistency provides a related model of political process. Lenski (1966: 87) argues that when an individual is of high status on one dimension and low status on another, he tends to think of himself in terms of the higher status, while other people treat him in terms of the lower one. This is, for the individual involved, a continual source of stress. Lenski proposes that the individual will react to these frustrations by supporting political parties that favor social change. In the United States, this would be viewed as the Democratic Party (Lenski, 1967).

The effects of status inconsistency are most strongly felt, Lenski argues, when they occur between achieved and ascribed statuses, rather than two achieved or two ascribed statuses. Data presented by Segal and Knoke (1968) support this proposition.[2] Such status inconsistencies may be seen as one manifestation of the more general cross-pressure phenomenon, and, given the inconclusive results of earlier studies, we may hypothesize that the political effects of such inconsistencies may be either support of the Democratic Party or withdrawal of affect from politics.

Status Relevance and Status Inconsistency

We derive from Lenski's formulation one qualification that does not appear in the general cross-pressure hypothesis. In the true status inconsistency situation, stress is derived from interpersonal relations, and can in fact be translated into a variant of Heider's (1958) system of interpersonal relations. In terms of Heider's general conceptualization, a person, P, has an affective relationship with another person, O, and one of the bases of this relationship is agreement on the evaluation of some object, X. There are three links in Heider's triangle: (1) between P and X, (2) between O and X, and (3) between P and O. If signs are placed on these links, i.e., specification of positive (+) and negative (−) relationships, then the system is said to be balanced if there is an even number of negative links. This condition is achieved, for example, if P likes O, P likes X, and O likes X (no negative links), or if P likes O, but neither P nor O likes X (two negative links).

In the present case, X is a person's status, and O is in fact a series of others $O_1, O_2, \ldots O_n$. There is not necessarily an affective bond between P and O, but there is a nexus of interaction that we may define as a positive link. Through the interaction between P and a series of O's, each constituting a triangular system, P learns that he differs with each O in his evaluation of X, his status, and thus, each triangle is unbalanced. This imbalance is a source of stress, but cannot be resolved in the modes most commonly associated with Heider's theory. P cannot terminate his relationship with O, since O is, in effect, the social system. Neither can he change his evaluation of X, his own status, since he is utilizing objective achievement criteria. He hence seeks to change the system that makes his lower status relevant and supports political parties that promise to change the system. Similarly, the individual of high ascribed and low achieved status is identified in some cases in terms of his lower status and will also feel the strains of status inconsistency. However, in a society where assembly-line workers wear white shirts to work and change at the factory, low ascriptive statuses tend to be more highly visible than low achieved statuses, and the contribution of this latter case to the total effect would be presumed to be less.

It is important to note that for this interpersonal influence to occur, O must identify P's lower status. Thus, the true case of status inconsistency arises only when P's low status is visible in some meaningful way: through skin color, physical features, accent, etc. (see Allport, 1958). Thus, for example, the American who has black skin may readily be treated in terms of his ascriptive status, and if he is of higher achieved status, this will only serve to heighten his awareness of being discriminated against.

There are cases, however, where P's lower status is not visible to O; if it becomes relevant to his political choice, it is due solely to his perception of the political world. The Catholic businessman, for example, is in most cases not readily identifiable as a member of a minority religious group, and people relate to him in terms of his achieved occupational status, which Lenski predicts that he himself will define as relevant. The Protestant manual worker, on the other hand, to the extent that he leads a seemingly middle-class existence, is under no direct social pressure to abandon the political party of his co-religionists.

Insofar as the Catholic businessman is identified by society as a businessman, and thus identifies himself, he may support the Republican Party with impunity, feeling that it best represents his financial interests. If, however, his Catholicism is made relevant through specific political events such as the issue of government aid to parochial schools being raised, or a Catholic candidate running for office, and the Democratic Party is on the pro-Catholic side of the ledger, then affective and cognitive political notions will be aroused which are inconsistent with those associated with his occupational status (for a discussion of these dynamics see Rosenberg et al., 1960: 112–163). This is clearly a cross-pressure situation, but, in the absence of interpersonal precipitating factors, it does not truly fit Lenski's status inconsistency formulation. Moreover, this latter case, unlike true status inconsistency, is a transient state, since the individual's low ascribed status ceases to be relevant to his political choice when religion ceases to be a political issue.

Democratic Support and Withdrawal of Affect As Functional Alternatives

The cross-pressured Catholic voter is in a stressful situation. In 1948, he seems to have resolved the stress by not voting, while in 1960, he resolved it by voting Democratic. Pool (1965) attributes this difference to the fact that in 1948, the Democratic Party was not a very attractive alternative. Truman himself was a relatively unimpressive candidate, and the party had been tainted by the image of communism through the Harry Dexter White scandal. Thus, while the individual under cross-pressures might have been motivated by that fact to lean toward the Democratic Party, the party itself did not reinforce this tendency. In 1960, on the other hand, the Democrats, aside from having a strong liberal platform, had an attractive candidate, one that cross-pressured Catholics would be strongly identified with. Thus the "push," generated by the cross-pressure situation, was reinforced by the "pull," generated by the party.

On the basis of these considerations, it may be argued that the reason for contradictory findings in research on both cross-pressures and status inconsistency is that there are two different processes going on that cross-cut both fields of research. Where such pressures involve the system's persisting identification of the individual in terms that he finds distasteful, he will seek to effect social change. However, where the conflicting pressures are internal to the individual and transient in nature, he may withdraw affect from the political arena completely, unless one of the alternatives that he is forced to consider is clearly a more attractive short-term choice. Thus, considering cross-pressures in general, it is our first hypothesis that under some conditions of cross-pressure, people will react by supporting the political party that offers the more progressive program, while under other conditions of cross-pressure, people will react by withdrawing from politics. The alternative hypothesis that must be considered is that in any given situation of cross-pressure some people will react by supporting the progressive political party, while others will withdraw from political activity.

The argument presented above also provides some basis for predicting which alternatives will be chosen under given conditions. We hypothesize that where an individual is visibly of low ascribed status but is also of high achieved status, he will feel the strains of status-inconsistency and support the Democratic Party. If, however, he is not identified by those around him in terms of his lower status, but that status is made relevant by issues or candidates in a particular election, then the choice between withdrawal and partisanship will be based on the difference in attractiveness of alternatives. Where the difference is small, the cognitive inconsistency will be resolved by withdrawal. Where the difference is large, however, the inconsistency will tend to be resolved in favor of the more attractive alternative.

The Data

Tests of these hypotheses were conducted through the secondary analysis of data collected from a sample of the American electorate in March, 1960, as part of a cross-national study of civic involvement (see Almond and Verba, 1963: 47, 519–525). We are concerned here with inconsistencies between either of the two ascribed statuses (religion and race) and any of the three achieved statuses (occupation, income and education). Support of a progressive political party has been defined as expressing a preference for the Democratic Party, while withdrawal of affect from politics is defined as expressing support of no political party.

Expectations

1. *Functional alternatives.* It was anticipated that under conditions of status inconsistency associated with Democratic preference, failure to choose a political party would be minimal. On the other hand, where a high degree of non-partisanship existed, it would be at the expense of the Democratic Party.

2. *Effects of race.* Americans whose skin color is other than white are readily identified as being of low racial status, and inconsistencies with achieved statuses can only serve to increase their awareness that they are being discriminated against. It was expected that among non-white Americans in 1960, status inconsistency would increase support for the Democratic Party.

3. *Effects of religion.* Previous research has shown

that members of minority religious groups tend to support the Democratic Party, but that there is some differentiation on the basis of occupational status, with white-collar workers being somewhat less "Democratic" than blue-collar workers (Segal, 1967). Hence, it was expected that John F. Kennedy's announced attempt to attain the Democratic nomination for the presidency would create cross-pressures for middle-class Catholics. Their occupational status caused them to identify with the Republican Party, while Kennedy's candidacy made their religious status relevant and caused them to attach affect to the Democratic Party.

The attractiveness of the Democratic Party, however, was lessened by the fact that in early March, 1960, few Catholics felt that a Roman Catholic had a chance to be elected president.[3] Given the relevance of Catholicism, the fact of status inconsistency, and the widespread belief that the United States was not yet ready to elect a Catholic to the presidency, it was expected that white-collar Catholics would in fact hesitate to state a party preference. Note that this expectation was not generalized to Catholics of high financial or educational status, because earlier research had failed to yield political differentiation among Catholic along these status dimensions when the effects of occupation were accounted for.

Results

Tables 1 and 2 present the effect of status inconsistency upon Democratic preference and upon failure to choose a political party respectively. Each cell in Table 1 represents a four-fold table, in which the percentage of Democrats in the consistent cells (two high statuses or two low statuses) have been subtracted from the percentage of Democrats in the inconsistent cells (one high status and one low status).[4] A positive difference indicates a surplus of Democrats in the inconsistent cells. Table 2, similarly, represents the difference in percent expressing no party preference in the consistent and inconsistent cells.

Table 1
Effect of Status Inconsistency upon Democratic
Preference*

	Occupation	Income	Education
Religion	−6.2	20.5	12.1
Race	12.4	−6.7	12.3

* Each cell entry is based on the entire sample of N = 970 cases.
For explanation see Footnote 4.

Table 2
Effect of Status Inconsistency upon Failure to Choose
a Political Party*

	Occupation	Income	Education
Religion	19.5	−6.5	.3
Race	−9.7	5.3	−5.2

* Entries based on 970 cases.

The first hypothesis is supported by the data. For those inconsistent situations where support is shown for the Democratic Party, surpluses of people preferring no political party fail to appear. However, in the two instances where there are fewer Democrats in the inconsistent cells than in the consistent cells, there is a surplus of respondents who failed to state a party preference.[5] As Fig. 1 shows graphically, there is an inverse relationship between incidence of Democratic

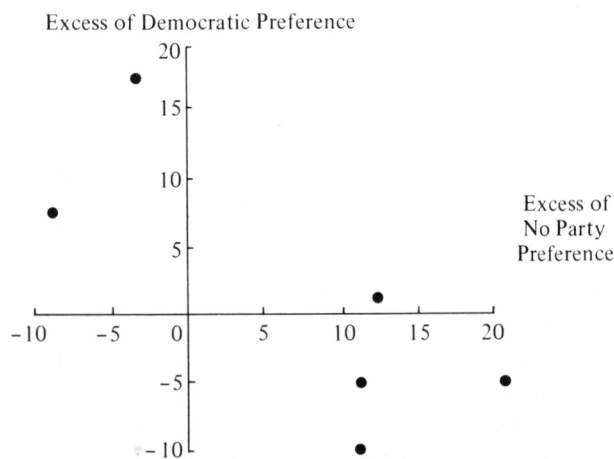

Fig. 1. **Excess of Democratic Preference by Excess of No Party Preference for Inconsistent Cells**

preference and incidence of no party preference in status-inconsistent situations. Clearly preferring the Democratic Party and refusing to choose a party are functional alternatives, appearing in different situations of status inconsistency.

Let us now look at the instances in which the two types of reaction occurred. It had been hypothesized that the effects of inconsistency between racial and achieved variables would be increased support for the Democratic Party. Indeed, in two of the three tests of racial-achieved inconsistencies, Democratic support was more than 12% higher in inconsistent than in consistent cells. In the third case, where inconsistencies between race and income are considered, respondents who were status-inconsistent were less likely to be Democrats and more likely to prefer no political party. Table 3 presents the set of data from whence this deviant case was derived. Clearly, the lowest proportional support for the Democratic Party and the highest rate of no party preference is found among high-income non-whites. This is strange, since our data indicate that non-whites of high educational or occupational status do support the Democratic Party and have relatively low rates of no preference. Indeed, we may infer from these data that those high-income non-whites who voice no preference are of low educational and occupational status. It may well be that the results in this table are a reflection of a segment of the non-white community that has found lucrative employment in domestic service but has not been integrated into the body politic. Whether or not this truly explains this deviant case, the data on inconsistencies involving racial status in the main support our expectations.

Table 3
Democratic Preference and No Party Preference, by Race and Income*

Race	Income	% Democratic	% No Preference
White	Low	36.4	39.7
White	High	36.6	42.1
Non-white	Low	39.8	52.3
Non-white	High	33.3	60.0

* Entries based on 970 cases.

The data on religion similarly confirm our expectation. Inconsistencies between religion and income or education yielded only the Democratic affiliation generally associated with minority religious status. Catholics with middle-class occupations, however, were cross-pressured by the candidacy of a Catholic in the Democratic Party which deterred them from their customary middle-class identification with the Republican Party. However, for the most part, they believed that Kennedy could not win the election, and rather than support a loser or oppose a Catholic, they withdrew affect from the political arena and claimed non-partisanship. As Table 4 shows, the middle-class Catholics who claimed identification with the Democratic Party in the 1950's, excluding those who called themselves independent but leaned toward the Democratic Party, were less than 50 percent. By March, 1960, the percent of Democrats *and* of Republicans decreased, and the percent claiming no preference increased. After March, 1960, during which month John F. Kennedy polled a record 45,000 votes in the New Hampshire Democratic primary, the percent supporting the Democrats soared, reaching 70 percent in the Fall. In 1964, when their religious status was no longer politically relevant, some middle-class

Catholics returned to the Republican Party, although a small majority still called themselves Democrats.

Conclusion

Lenski's conceptualization of status inconsistency has been shown to subsume two different aspects of cognitive imbalance, only one of which meets the specifications of Lenski's own formulation. Where an individual defines his own status as high and others define his status as low, he suffers from status inconsistency, and tends to support the Democratic Party. This situation assumes that his lower status is, in some sense, visible. On the other hand, an individual may feel cross-pressured because two statuses which become salient to him in the absence of interpersonal pressures involve conflicting expectations. In this situation, the individual may withdraw from the political arena until such time as one of the troublesome statuses becomes politically irrelevant. However, if one of the alternative sets of expectations has greater short-term pay-off value, then that alternative will be chosen.

Table 4
Percent of Middle-Class Catholics Identifying with Democratic
Party, 1952–1964

*Fall, 1952**	*Fall, 1956**	*March, 1960***	*Fall, 1960**	*Fall, 1964**
43%	49%	38%	70%	53%
(N = 1614)	(N = 1731)	(N = 970)	(N = 3021)	(N = 1489)

* Survey Research Center (SRC) Presidential Election Survey.
** Almond-Verba Survey.

References

Allport, Gordon W. *The Nature of Prejudice.* Garden City: Doubleday, 1958.

Almond, Gabriel A. and Sidney Verba. *The Civic Culture.* Princeton: Princeton University Press, 1963.

Bendix, Reinhard and Seymour Martin Lipset. "Political Sociology." *Current Sociology* 6: 82–87. 1957.

Berelson, Bernard R., Paul F. Lazarsfeld and W. N. McPhee. *Voting.* Chicago: University of Chicago Press, 1954.

Campbell, Angus, P. E. Converse, W. E. Miller and D. E. Stokes. *The American Voter.* New York: Wiley, 1960.

Downs, Anthony. *An Economic Theory of Democracy.* New York: Harper and Row, 1957.

Heider, Fritz. *The Psychology of Interpersonal Relations.* New York: Wiley, 1958.

Janowitz, Morris and David R. Segal. "Social Cleavage and Party Affiliation: Germany, Great Britain and the United States." *American Journal of Sociology* 72 (May 1967): 601–18.

Kelly, K. Dennis and William J. Chambliss. "Status Inconsistency and Political Attitudes." *American Sociological Review* 31 (June 1966): 375–82.

Lane, Robert E. *Political Life*. Glencoe: Free Press, 1959.

Lazarsfeld, Paul F., Bernard Berelson and Hazel Gaudet. *The People's Choice*. New York: Columbia University Press, 1948.

Lenski, Gerhard. *Power and Privilege*. New York: McGraw-Hill, 1966. "Status Inconsistency and the Vote." *American Sociological Review* 32 (April 1967): 298–301.

Lindenfield, Frank. "Economic Interest and Political Involvement." *Public Opinion Quarterly* 28 (Spring 1964): 104–11.

Lipset, Seymour Martin. *Political Man*. Garden City: Doubleday, 1963.

Milbrath, Lester W. *Political Participation*. Chicago: Rand McNally, 1965.

Pool, Ithiel de Sola, R. P. Abelson and S. L. Popkin. *Candidates, Issues and Strategies*. Cambridge: M.I.T. Press, 1965.

Rosenberg, Milton J., C. I. Hovland, W. J. McGuire et al. (eds.) *Attitude Organization and Change*. New Haven: Yale University Press, 1960.

Segal, David R. "Classes, Strata and Parties in West Germany and the United States." *Comparative Studies in Society and History* 10 (October 1967): 66–84. "Partisan Realignment in the United States: the Lesson of the 1964 Election." *Public Opinion Quarterly* 32 (Fall 1968): 441–44.

Segal, David R. and David Knoke. "Social Mobility, Status Inconsistency and Partisan Realignment in the United States." *Social Forces* 47 (December 1968): 154–58.

Notes

[1] It might be argued that non-voting among the types of people who consider themselves Democrats is functional for the viability of the two-party system in America, since in recent years, the Democrats have claimed the allegiance of a much larger proportion of the electorate than the Republicans. If indeed as large a proportion of Democrats as Republicans appeared at the polls on Election Day, elections as such would cease to be contests between competing parties, candidates and policies, and would serve as window dressing to legitimize a persisting Democratic administration. Assuming equal turnout, the Republicans could win elections only if nominal Democrats bolted across party lines with greater frequency than is likely (cf. Segal, 1968).

[2] Many of the early criticisms of Lenski's formulation are invalid because, although they fail to show relationships between status inconsistency and political attitudes, they tend to focus on inconsistencies between two achieved statuses. (See for example Kelly and Chambliss, 1966.)

[3] Two-thirds of the subscribers who replied to a poll conducted by *Jubilee*, a Roman Catholic publication, for example, held that if nominated, Kennedy would not win the election because of a bias against Catholics.

[4] If we imagine each cell representing a table showing status on 2 dimensions thus:

| | | Status 1 | |
		Low	High
Status 2	Low	II	I
	High	III	IV

then if the cell entries are percent Democratic, the inconsistency effect is equal to $(I + III) - (II + IV)$.

The relevant dichotomies for the status attributes were:

	Religion	Race	Occupation	Income	Education
Low	Catholic and Jewish	Non-white	Blue-collar	$4,999–	11 years or less
High	Protestant	White	White-collar	$5,000+	12 years or more

[5] That is, the corresponding cells of Tables 1 and 2 are in all cases of opposite sign with one exception; inconsistency between religion and education, the sole exception, has an excess of non-identifiers of 0.3.

4

The Psycho-Cultural Context
of Politics

In this next section of the book our level of analysis shifts from the individual, the group and social structure, to a larger collectivity. Here we focus on the *configuration* of psychological attributes which have political meaning for a society, and a set of related cultural stimuli which comprise part of the individual's environment. "Political culture" has been defined in a variety of ways, but most modern scholars agree that a central element of political culture is denoted by the definition used by Gabriel Almond and Sidney Verba: the pattern of politically relevant orientations in a society.[1] The concept stems from Parsons'[2] theorizing about the social system where the individual and his role orientations are a unit of analysis, and where human action is organized in terms of meanings and orientations to objects in the environment. The cultural component, in interaction with personality, defines a normative orientation to action, i.e., desirable actions, goals and standards of behavior. When we speak of political culture, we refer primarily to the goals and norms developing over a set of cultural and historical experiences which shape sets of orientations toward political objects. These orientations have cognitive (such as perceptions and knowledge), affective (emotional attachment) and evaluative (values and preferences) characteristics,[3] and they are learned over time through the process of political socialization. Political culture therefore affects the performance of political roles in the system,

[1] *The Civic Culture: Political Attitudes and Democracy in Five Nations* (Boston: Little, Brown and Company, 1965).

[2] For a review of these theories and their relationship to political science see William C. Mitchell, *Sociological Analysis and Politics: The Theories of Talcott Parsons* (Englewood Cliffs: Prentice-Hall, Inc., 1967).

[3] Gabriel A. Almond, "Comparative Political Systems," *Journal of Politics* 18 (1956): 395.

and it affects political behavior by defining the scope of politically relevant action, the mode of that action, the intensity of involvement and
expectations of the system. It represents the "psychological and subjective dimensions of politics . . . rooted in public events and private experiences."[4] The utility of political culture as a concept is that it serves to
link analytically psychological and political phenomena, and to enable
us to study the predominant feelings and beliefs that a people display
toward their government. The factors which determine the degree of
psychological support that a political system receives are rooted in the
political culture. As a link between micro and macro analysis it provides
a tool which can be used to relate the politically relevant attitudinal structures of individuals to the performance and characteristics of the total
system.

Political Culture

Abinski and Pettit discuss political culture as having "structural"
components—in the form of important historical events, patterns of settlement, ethnic and religious divisions, the pattern of interest group activity,
etc.—in addition to the attitudinal or psychological dimensions alluded to
above.[5] Our total view of political culture is similar to that conception,
but here we mean to focus on the psychological dimensions, consonant
with the theme of the book. That there are also structural elements in
political culture, is a notion that the reader should be aware of as he ex-
amines the selections to follow.

Certainly one attribute of a political culture is the degree to which the
citizens feel a sense of political efficacy, or believe themselves to have the
ability and opportunity to participate and to have some effect on political
decision-making. In this case, as with the others which we shall mention
below, there are obvious individual differences within any culture; nonetheless, political societies will differ in terms of the distribution or pattern
of individual sentiments and beliefs. In this sense, the collective psychology of a people is linked to political arrangements and performance. We
should expect that a sense of political efficacy would be highest in the
more democratic, participatory societies—Britain and the Scandinavian
countries, for example,—and that it would be relatively lower in totalitarian regimes.

[4] Lucian Pye, *Politics, Personality and Nation-Building* (New
Haven: Yale University Press, 1962), p. 321.

[5] Henry S. Albinski and Lawrence K. Pettit, eds., *European
Political Processes: Essays and Readings* (Boston: Allyn and
Bacon, 1968), Chapter 1.

Other dimensions of political culture include system affect, political role conceptions, and the pattern of expectations citizens have in relating to political authority. System affect concerns the degree to which there are positive sentiments directed toward the political system per se and agreement on the values which are fundamental to it. Are the basic governmental arrangements regarded as good or bad in comparison with those of other nations? Is politics regarded as a high calling or as a game of intrigue for scoundrels? Are the basic assumptions of the political system (such as equality, democratic accountability and so forth) passively accepted or questioned? In sum, system affect has to do with whether one has a positive or negative feeling toward the political system of which he is a part.

The way in which one conceives of his political role is closely related to the idea of efficacy. Here we are concerned with a person's appraisal of his own actual or expected political activity: does he conceive of himself as a participant, involved in the maelstrom of political decision-making, or does he conceive of himself as subject to governance, but powerless to affect the behavior or fate of the governors? Similarly, when a citizen is confronted by agents of public authority, or when he seeks them out to petition for change or redress, what kind of treatment does he expect from them? Will he be treated fairly and dispassionately, in the same manner generally as other citizens? Or will some categories of citizens receive preferential treatment and others be dismissed as unimportant? Again, political societies will reveal different patterns of citizen attitudes with respect to these dimensions of political culture as they are shaped by the long term development of cultural norms and myths which the individual assimilates over time.

Culture and Personality

Although political culture reflects a variety of interest dimensions to political scientists, a social-psychological perspective is particularly concerned with psycho-cultural relationships. Both David Singer and Larry Hill, in their selections below, allude to personality as a component of political culture. Singer regards personality, along with attitudes and opinions, to be one of the psychological attributes which "join man to his political environment," and thus constitute components of political culture. Hill, in going a step further, calls for the use of a new concept, that of "political culture-and-personality." Hill agrues that a society will reveal typical personality traits such as tenderness or egoism, which in turn ". . . may be relevant to the individual's structuring of certain political culture data. . . ." He suggests that a dominant personality characteristic among New Zealanders, for example, is a "mild" authoritarian submissiveness, which helps to explain governmental stability in the face of widespread political participation. Singer, similarly, mentions the possibility of detecting "national character," as a composite of dominant personality types and political orientations in a society.

Much more research needs to be conducted on the prospect of incorporating personality as a component of political culture, but we may suppose that certain personality traits coexist with certain political orientations, and that in time scholars will be able to identify clusters of dominant personality traits and political attitudes which will define types of political cultures.

Selected Additional Readings

Albinski, Henry J., and Lawrence K. Pettit. *European Political Processes*. Chapter 1. Boston: Allyn and Bacon, 1968.

Almond, Gabriel A., and Sidney Verba. *The Civic Culture*. Boston: Little, Brown & Company, 1965.

Almond, Gabriel A. *The American People and Foreign Policy*. 2nd ed. New York: Praeger, 1960.

Czudnowski, Moshe M. "A Salience Dimension of Politics for the Study of Political Culture." *American Political Science Review* 61 (1968): 878–88.

Inkeles, Alex, and Daniel Levinson. "National Character: The Study of Modal Personality and Socio-Cultural Systems." In *Handbook of Social Psychology*. 2nd ed., 4: 418–506. Gardner Lindzey and Elliot Aronson, eds. Reading, Mass.: Addison-Wesley, 1969.

Inkeles, Alex. "National Character and Modern Political Systems." In *Psychological Anthropology: Approaches to Culture and Personality*, pp. 172–208. Edited by Francis L. K. Hsu. Homewood: Dorsey Press, 1961.

Kaplan, Bert, ed. *Studying Personality Cross-Culturally*. Evanston: Row, Peterson, 1961.

Kim, Young. "The Concept of Political Culture in Comparative Politics." *Journal of Politics* 26 (1964): 313–36.

Kluckhohn, Clyde. "The Study of Culture." In *The Policy Sciences*, pp. 86–101. Daniel Lerner and Harold Lasswell, eds. Stanford, Ca.: Stanford University Press, 1951.

Kluckhohn, Clyde. "Culture and Behavior." In *Handbook of Social Psychology*, pp. 921–68. Edited by Gardner Lindzey. Cambridge: Addison-Wesley, 1954.

Leites, Nathan. "Psycho-Cultural Hypotheses About Political Acts." *World Politics* 1 (1948): 102–19.

Lipset, Seymour Martin. *Revolution and Counterrevolution: Change and Persistence in Social Structures*. New York: Basic Books, 1968.

McClosky, Herbert. "Consensus and Ideology in American Politics," *American Political Science Review* 58 (1964): 361–82.

Mitchell, William C. *The American Polity*. New York: The Free Press, 1962.

Patterson, Samuel C. "The Political Cultures of the American States." *Journal of Politics* 30 (1968): 187–210.

Pye, Lucian. *Politics, Personality, and Nation Building*. New Haven: Yale University Press, 1962.

Pye, Lucian and Sidney Verba. *Political Culture and Political Development*. Princeton: Princeton University Press, 1965.

Pye, Lucian. *The Spirit of Chinese Politics: A Psychocultural Study of the Authority Crisis in Political Development*. Cambridge: M.I.T. Press, 1968.

Man and World Politics:

The Psycho-Cultural Interface

J. David Singer

In every discipline, the would-be theorizer must eventually come to grips with the age-old issue of the parts-versus-the-whole, or the components-versus-the-system. This issue divides, in turn, into two fairly distinguishable subissues. First, what is the relative importance of each for explanatory purposes? Can we develop a satisfactory general theory without any regard for the parts, the particles, the particular? Is inclusion of them desirable, necessary, sufficient? How much attention can we pay to micro-level entities and phenomena without invading an unfamiliar discipline, without becoming extreme reductionists? These questions cannot, of course, be answered in even the most tentative fashion until we devise an acceptable solution to the second subissue: what sort of conceptual scheme permits us to embrace parts as well as whole, or allows us to explicitly ignore one or the other? Can we develop a paradigm which gets at the interplay between micro- and macro-level phenomena? How is the interface between them best formulated and described?

For the social scientist, the issue—in one way or another—is that of relating the individual to all those social groups of which he is a member, as well as

J. David Singer, "Man and World Politics: The Psycho-Cultural Interface," *Journal of Social Issues* 24 (1968): 127–56. Reprinted with permission.

The organization of this paper and the development of its argument have benefited from the comments and criticism of Fred I. Greenstein, Karl W. Deutsch, Guy E. Swanson, Harry Gollob and Michael Wallace; the final revision is, of course, my responsibility and not theirs.

understanding the relationship between the smaller of these groups and the larger. In sociology and psychology, the hybrid discipline of social psychology has largely emerged in response to this set of questions. In anthropology, the personality-and-culture approach represented a serious, if not fully successful, effort to cope with the matter (Cohen, 1961; Hsu, 1961; Kluckhohn and Murray, 1953). In economics, the impression is that all but a handful of brave, but nonempirical, theorists have preferred to ignore the problem for the present, with the consumer, the firm and the market generally serving to identify the separate fields of interest. In political science, it has indeed been a traditional preoccupation, with man-versus-the-state and individual freedom-versus-public order very much on our minds. But as we have shifted from prescientific to more rigorous methodologies, we seem to have suffered from the same sorts of separatist tendencies as the economists, even to the extent that the philosophical issues in the discipline have been defined in so irrelevant a fashion as that of the "behaviorists" (usually at the individual level) versus the "institutionalists."

In the world politics field, the picture is much the same. Some of us concentrate on individuals (or at least their attitudes and opinions) and others concentrate on the foreign policies of the nations, with a smaller third group focussing upon the international system.[1] Even the psychologists and sociologists who have lately ventured into the world politics field, despite their many valuable and promising contributions, have tended to shy away from any systematic effort to integrate psychological and societal phenomena.[2]

Rejoining Men with Their Political System

In order to get on with theory building and hypothesis testing it is necessary to bring the parts and the whole together, but in a more rigorous fashion than has been evident in the past. This need for rejoining men and their political systems is essential for at least two reasons. First, without paradigms that embrace both the micro- and macro-levels, we cannot advance very far in answering the question: how much latitude do individual citizens and decision making elites enjoy in world politics? Or to put it another way, what is the relative potency of men vis-a-vis their institutions?[3] Second, we can seldom get very far in answering more specific theoretical and policy questions if we work with paradigms that leave out either the individual or the larger environment. By definition, any paradigm which ignores one or the other remains woefully incomplete.[4]

While the behavior of men or of social systems may be *described,* and perhaps even *predicted,* without recourse to such variables, no satisfactory *explanation* is possible until we understand the psychological link which joins man to his sociopolitical environment, and through which each impinges on the other. In the absence of a judicious and well-balanced conceptual scheme, moreover, we will continue to suffer from two extremes of misinterpretation. On the one hand, there is the traditional view which sees individuals — be they members of an elite or of a mass public — as more or less irrelevant to an understanding of world politics. On the other, there is the tendency to anthropomorphize and to describe nations in such personal terms as aggressive, intro-punitive, sadistic, narcissistic, ego-defensive and the like. Closely related to this is the tendency to assume that any character trait which is widely distributed within the population provides a sufficient basis for understanding that nation's foreign policies.

The purpose of this paper, then, is to examine the interface between individual man and the larger societal environment, from a world politics point of view, and at the same time avoid both types of pitfall. My intent is to do this via a concentration on those variables which join man to that environment: psychological variables. Given the centrality of this problem to any potential theory of world politics, and the relative inattention to it to date, my hope here is to address it in a fashion which may clarify some of the conceptual problems and at the same time increase our capacity to move toward such theory in a more operational and data-based fashion. With these objectives in mind, let me first outline a general taxonomy of world politics which hopefully is not only quite susceptible to operational treatment, but is also neutral regarding the inclusion of variables which would bias it toward either the individual autonomy or ecological determinist point of view.

What is offered here is not a theory, but a taxonomy within which a range of theories might be developed. Moreover, it is only a static taxonomy, since space limitations preclude any attention to the dynamic interaction of the variables which are discussed. That is, all I can hope to do in this paper is describe certain components of the "global machine" in a state of rest; in a forthcoming study, I hope to describe what occurs when they are combined with other components and the entire apparatus is set in motion. As a further concession to spatial limitations, I summarize in only the briefest fashion those nonpsychological variables, which, while essential to the completeness of the scheme, have already been elaborated elsewhere (Singer, 1968).

A General Framework

In addition to the above specific requirements for any taxonomy which is addressed to the individual-versus-society issue, a framework for the understanding of global politics must also satisfy at least four other criteria: first, it must embrace both institutional and behavioral classes of variables; second, it must be a developmental scheme in the sense that it can handle a wide range of historical periods in the evolution of the global system; third, it must be sufficiently a-theoretical (or multi-theoretical) to permit the sort of integration and synthesis most appropriate to the present state of our discipline; and fourth, it must be stated in terms that permit operational definition and measurement. Elsewhere, I hope to spell out a fairly complete scheme (Singer, 1968) but here let me merely sketch in the outlines of that framework, and indicate that it relies heavily upon a general systems approach.[5]

Entities and Their Attributes

Whereas most laymen and most foreign policy practitioners tend to organize their ideas on world politics around a variety of social *entities,* many social scientists increasingly tend to build their schemes around *roles* and *relationships.*[6] In my judgment, this represents a regressive step, moving us away from conceptual clarity and operational measurement with no trade-off in the form of enhanced explanatory power. To the contrary, by subdividing an entity's roles into those appropriate to the economy, the polity or the society, we reduce the probability of ever seeing the entity in anything approximating its entirety. By focussing on only one portion of the relationships of these multipurpose entities, how can we expect to describe and understand their behavior in that isolated role, no less in their other roles? While many of the notions in common use are indeed theoretically misleading and scientifically nonoperational, a fair number may easily be refined and salvaged; therefore, the burden of proof ought to be on those who would reject the more familiar concepts and intellectual frameworks.

Thus, let me begin by specifying the classes or levels of entity around which the present paradigm is organized. These are: (a) national states; (b) such subnational entities as: political parties, pressure groups (latent as well as manifest), labor and professional associations, and family, tribal, religious and ethnic groups; and (c) such extranational entities as associations of the above sorts of subnational groups, international intergovernmental organizations, and international nongovernmental organizations.

Once the social entities are specified — and the paradigm permits selection of those most appropriate to a given researcher's theoretical interests — we find that all relevant entities may be identified, measured and compared according to three sets of attributes. First, there are the obvious *physical* attributes, including elements of geography, demography and technology; for the purposes of this paper, no further elaboration of these attributes is necessary. The second set of attributes falls into the *structural* class, and may be conventionally (if not readily) divided into the formal and the informal, or better still, placed on a formal-informal continuum. Toward the formal end are those attributes based on observation and description of what political scientists usually refer to as institutions, and would include such phenomena as the types and powers of legitimate political and economic institutions handling legislative, administrative, judicial, banking, commercial-industrial regulation, social welfare, military, information control and related functions. Toward the informal end are those structural attributes based on the observation of: urban-rural distribution; social mobility, kinship and marriage patterns; citizen access to and influence over the decision-making process; size, centralization and scope of political parties and other unofficial or quasi-official associations (including pressure groups); number, power and role of religious, ethnic and linguistic groupings and the like. Also relevant as aspects of informal structure might be the extent of pluralistic cross-cutting ties, and the general coalition configurations which develop among the system's many component subsystems.

The final attributes are what might be called the *cultural* ones; being central to this paper, they will be developed in more detail in later sections. Here, let me merely point out that I use culture in a much narrower sense than do those anthropologists who

permit it to embrace everything from belief in an
after-life to technological artifacts, often including
social structure as well. The usage here is similar to
that found in some of the recent comparative politics
literature (Almond and Verba, 1963; Pye and Verba,
1965; Banks and Textor, 1963). Note further that
these cultural attributes are all strictly nonbehavioral,
or more accurately, both postbehavioral and prebehavioral in the sequential or causal sense. We will
return to them in due course.

Relationships Among Entities

Before moving from the identification of entities
and their attributes to their behavior and interaction,
an intermediate set of variables needs to be delineated.
Reference is to the relationships that exist between
and among our relevant entities, and in addition to
describing some illustrative types of relationships it
is necessary to clarify two definitional points. First,
relationships exist not only among entities at the *same*
level of analysis (i.e., among pressure groups, among
nations, among international organizations) but also
among those at *different* levels of analysis. Second,
relationships are of two types. One type deals with
the *similarity* or dissimilarity of attributes while the
other deals with degrees of *interdependence* and con-
nectedness. On the similarity side, we first decide on
the attributes which interest us, next measure or scale
each entity's rank or interval score on that attribute
dimension, and then compute the discrepancy or
"distance" between the two. And while such distances
are usually measured on only one attribute dimension
at a time, it is quite feasible to locate nations or other
entities within a certain conceptual space on the basis
of multidimensional distances, as in Rummel (1965).
On the interdependence side, we are again concerned
with the concept of closeness and distance, but in
terms of interdependence, interpenetration, connect-
edness, dominance and the like. Needless to say, there
is no necessary correlation between the similarity
and the interdependence of a given pair of entities.

Behavior and Interaction Among Entities

A final aspect of our taxonomy is the distinction
between relationship (in the sense of interdependence)
and *interaction*. In brief, whenever a nation[7] *behaves*
vis-a-vis another nation (or any other entity) and the
second nation responds to that behavior, we may
speak of an interaction. Of course, we require evidence that the two behavioral events or acts are somehow linked causally if we are to identify them as an
interaction; if not, we merely have two isolated acts.
When we observe a fairly long series of causally connected acts and responses, we may speak of an interaction sequence.

It should be noted, then, that two or more entities
may display both relationships and interactions, and
despite the tendency in our literature to use relationship and interaction interchangeably, it seems imperative to differentiate between an essentially static pair-
wise phenomenon and a highly dynamic one. To put
it differently, relationships change slowly and are
described in highly spatial terms, whereas interactions
occur in a brief interval and are highly temporal in
nature. Obviously, relationships affect interactions,
and vice versa, and are causally quite connected; one
often *observes* a sequence of interactions in order to
infer a relationship. Thus, after observing a large
number of behavioral events and interactions, such
as the exchange of many threatening diplomatic messages, we may infer the existence of a hostile relationship.

Conversely, one may often predict an interaction
sequence or a single behavioral event on the basis
of a recognized relationship. For example, if we infer
a relationship such as high economic interdependence,
we may predict a continuing succession of direct or
indirect cargo shipments between the two nations
under consideration. But since all these export and
import actions happen to leave a relatively reliable
trace, via standard bookkeeping procedures, it is more
efficient to measure the economic interdependence
between these entities by examining periodic records
of aggregate shipments and transfers; we need not
dispatch research assistants to all the ports of entry

and departure. On the other hand, there are a great many relationships which can be inferred only by direct observation of interaction sequences, especially interactions between individuals and between less formal social entities. And there are, likewise, many interactions which cannot be readily observed — especially in diplomacy — and these must be inferred by observing changes in relationship.

Dimensions / Attributes	Generality	Durability	Observability
Personality Attitude Opinion	High Medium Low	High Medium Low	High Medium Low

Fig. 1. **Postulated Ordering of Psychological Attitudes on Three Descriptive Dimensions**

Psychological Attributes: The Individual Level

Given this fairly general framework, the next step in articulating the role of psychological variables in world politics is to direct our attention to the individual level of analysis and to certain psychological attributes of the single human being, both normal and deviant. My effort here will be to impose some order on a bewildering melange of constructs such that the political scientist or other macro-social scientist can put them to greater use. I recognize that others, in and out of psychology (Smith et al., 1956), have tried before with only moderate success, but the possible payoffs seem worth the effort, and I therefore trust that our behavioral science colleagues will be understanding in their appraisal, and if necessary, gentle in their disapproval of this intruder's temerity.

In the view outlined here, there are three basic and differentiable psychological properties of individuals which are of interest to the societal scientist. These properties or constructs may be labeled: (a) personality, (b) attitude and (c) opinion. Further, they may be roughly scaled on three different dimensions. First, there is the generality dimension; second, there is durability; and third, there is the observability dimension. In the verbal descriptions of these three types of psychological attribute, these ranges will become more apparent, but the ordering may be graphically summarized here.

Perhaps more critical than the hypothesized ways in which personality, attitude and opinion may scale on the above dimensions is the nature of the subject matter with which all intra-psychic activities are concerned. There would seem to be three very general substantive areas. The first of these concerns beliefs about reality in the individual's life space: how he responds, cognitively and affectively, to the way "things *are* done" or used to be done. The second concerns the way things *should* be done, in both the present and future, as well as the way they should have been done in the past; this category is quite similar to what we often refer to as values. The third concerns the way things *will* be done in the future or *might* have been done in the past. These may be thought of as the perceptual, the preferential and the predictive dimensions. These three dimensions, it would seem, are largely undifferentiated at the personality level, moderately differentiated at the attitudinal level, and rather clearly differentiated at the opinion level. Thus, if we treat personality as a reservoir of predispositions, we need not expect that any sharp distinctions between present and future, or between "is" and "ought," will be found. That is, we look to general personality traits and their configurations as a major *source* of (and perhaps predictor of) preconscious and unverbalized attitudes and opinions, rather than as the *location* of these more specific and differentiated psychic attributes. When we move to attitudes, the distinctions between and among what is, what ought, and what will, should be expected to take on greater clarity. And at the level of opinions, the distinctions may well be quite clear and perhaps might even become specific enough to be stated by the individual in relatively operational terms.

Given these general remarks on the relationships among personality, attitude and opinion, we may now turn to a more detailed consideration of each in turn. Note again that whereas most social psychologists tend to treat attitudes and/or opinions as components, aspects or levels of personality, the approach here is to treat all three as separate—but causally interdependent—psychological attributes of the individual.

Personality

Of all the terms using the psychological literature, none causes more difficulty than personality, and at least two reasons come to mind. First, and on this there seems to be a strong consensus, personality is the most inclusive and all-embracing psychological property attributed to the human being.[8] Second, there is an overwhelmingly long list of schemata and taxonomies by which an individual's personality may be compared with another's, or with itself over time.[9] One's choice of scheme here is less important than the fact that these (and other) formulations are attempts to classify and measure fairly basic internal predispositions toward action of normal, as well as mentally ill, people. As Cattell (1950, 2) puts it, "personality is that which permits a prediction of what a person will do in a given situation." And typically, these predispositions are thought of as a consequence of biological inheritance, the near-universal infancy experience, and the varying experiences of puberty and adulthood. A paraphrase of Allport's view is illustrative:

> The newborn babe lacks the characteristic organization of psychological systems, and has a *potential* personality that develops within the skin. The givens of personality are an idiographic complex of physique, temperament and intelligence, motivated in infancy by essentially biological and nutritional drives. As the infant matures and interacts with the social and physical environment, he develops a personality. Once beyond the infantile stage, this personality cannot be understood in terms of biological motives alone (Bertócci, 1965, 302).

An equally important aspect of personality is that we generally see it as the organizing and integrating framework within which all other intrapsychic attributes are embraced. In addition to its generality, post-adolescent personality is thought of as showing only the most gradual change over time, at least in the "normal" individual who has essentially "normal" experiences during a lifetime. Finally, despite the availability, demonstrated reliability, and apparent validity of many of the tests (projective and otherwise) by which we observe and measure personality, the inferential leap between the measuring instrument and the intellectual construct is so great that personality must be treated as the least observable of our three psychological variables.[10] In short, personality is defined here as a hypothetical construct embracing and structuring the individual's total reservoir of behavioral predispositions.

Attitudes

Shifting to a somewhat more restricted, malleable and observable cluster of individual attributes, we come next to what will be called *attitudes*.[11] While attitudes are largely shaped by the personality which organizes and embraces them, they are also seen as responsive to and modifiable by immediate (or even moderately distal) experience; more particularly, an individual's attitude on any matter may best be viewed as resulting from the interplay of personality and experience (Brim and Wheeler, 1966).

In the taxonomy employed here, attitudes (as well as personality and opinion) fall into the three subclasses outlined earlier: the individual's perceptions of the way things *are* done in his "life space," his preferences for the way things *should* be done, and his predictions as to the way things probably *will* be done. Attitudes, then, are defined here in a literal—if broad—sense to mean the partially structured disposition to act in a certain way; the meaning is highly analogous to that used when we describe the attitude of an astronaut's capsule moving in space, or that of a dancer prior to or during a singe routine or even that of the Leaning Tower of Pisa. The notion may be further conveyed by terms such as posture or stance.

That is, an entity's attitude markedly affects its probability of acting or moving in a given, and—depending on the state of our theory—predictable direction.

An individual's attitudes may differ from his neighbor's not only in their content, but in their degree of generality, in their durability, in the amount of affective loading with which their holder invests them, and in the extent of their structure, integration and coherence (Converse, 1964). The interdependence between personality and attitudes will be explored further, but a more orderly procedure would be to move on next to our third and final set of psychological attributes: opinions.

Opinions

While much of the literature tends to treat opinions and attitudes as more or less interchangeable, it seems worthwhile to preserve the distinction, even at the risk of raising some difficult problems of operationalization. Thus, I would define opinions as considerably more specific than attitudes, markedly more transitory and appreciably more susceptible to systematic observation and measurement. At the same time, they may be divided into the same subclasses as attitudes: perceptions, preferences and predictions. To illustrate in regard to specificity (durability and observability will be discussed below), we can classify a person's *general* approval or disapproval of strong supra-national organizations—for instance—as *attitudinal*. He may perceive those organizations now in existence as weak, may prefer that they become stronger and may (for example) predict that they will not become stronger in some relevant future. This attitudinal cluster should, of course, predict fairly well to his *opinions* on a particular aspect of the general problem. Thus, during the Congo crises of 1960, this individual might hold the opinions that the Secretary General was not exploiting the full latitude voted him by the General Assembly, that he should have assumed wider powers and that, if certain governments acquiesced in the original range of assumed authority, Mr. Hammarskjold would gradually try to expand that range. Whether the problem was sufficiently salient to the individual to convert the general attitude into a specific set of opinions is, of course, in doubt, as is the extent to which the attitudinal and opinion clusters were each internally consistent as well as logically compatible with one another.[12]

The Interplay of Psychological Attributes

Let me now return to a somewhat more detailed consideration of the interplay between and among all three of these psychological attributes. More particularly, what are the ways in which personality relates to both attitude and opinion? There would seem to be two different types of relationship here. First, there is the generally understood notion that a certain personality type will hold attitudes and opinions whose content is largely predictable from, and shaped by, his personality. For example, the parochial or provincial *personality* is associated with negative *attitudes* toward outsiders and with *opinions* which favor policies designed to keep such groups in a distant, if not subordinate, position.

But there is a second type of interrelationship at work here, and it tends to get less attention. Reference is to the way in which personality affects the structuring and the durability of attitudes and opinions, regardless of their substantive *content*. Of course, the personality syndrome as defined here is such that its content will not be independent of its structure and durability, but these qualities may be, for analytical convenience, treated separately. At the attitudinal level, if we look at perceptions, preferences and predictions, it should immediately be evident that there is a fair degree of interdependence among them. Perceptions and preferences will both affect predictions, perceptions and predictions will affect preferences, and preferences and predictions will affect perceptions; all three attitudinal components are highly interconnected. Moreover, the way in which any two of these combine in order to affect the third is very much a function of the more fundamental personality traits.

Let me illustrate each of these three combinational effects. For example, a normal and concerned individual who perceives his nation to be following a given diplomatic stategy and who prefers that it be reversed, will—depending upon the strength of the preference—be more likely to predict such reversal than will his counterpart who prefers continuation of the present strategy. But most of the variance in the prediction will probably be a function of the personality dimension which embraces optimism and pessimism. The optimistic personality might even be defined operationally by the extent to which his predictions coincide with his preferences; the extreme optimist might be called the "wishful thinker" and the person whose preferences and predictions are usually far apart appears in the role of Cassandra.

In the second and more interesting case, when perceptions and predictions combine to shape preferences, the effect of personality becomes more striking. The inner-directedness dimension or trait is central here, with strongly inner-directed personalities tending to hold onto their preferences even though they see little chance of those preferences being realized. To put it in different language, certain personality types can tolerate a much greater degree of dissonance or incongruence between the way they *expect* things to be and the way they *prefer* them to be. Those who are (a) less inner-directed, or (b) have a lower tolerance for such dissonance, find a fairly convenient solution; they tailor their preferences so as to make them more "realistic."[13] Turning to the third case— preference and prediction combining to shape perceptions—this is probably the sector which most social psychologists have emphasized when examining international politics. They are, quite rightly, struck by the frequency with which citizens and elites either construct, or accept, the most outrageous distortions of past or present reality. Here, again, a personality typical of many societies takes its toll. Whether we call it other-directedness or something else, these attitudinal misperceptions just could not be so universal and so pronounced were it not for the prevalence in America and elsewhere of the socially acquiescent personality. While I know of no hard

evidence to this effect, every indication is that—and this is almost definitional—very few citizens are deviant enough to resist the cumulative distortion of perception (Livant, 1963) and perpetuation of arbitrary judgments (Jacobs and Campbell, 1961) which social pressures are able to generate.[14]

Personality may be thought of not only as a predictor of the way in which attitudes are structured and modified, but also as a predictor of the way in which opinions will combine and change. Again, we will merely scratch the surface here, as the intent is only to demonstrate that all three attributes are highly interdependent, and that from the observation of an individual's opinion, we may make some reasonable inferences about his personality. In the most obvious sense, we generally expect that a so-called authoritarian personality would tend to correlate with opinions that perceive relationships very much in terms of superior-subordinate, and that prefer clearcut lines of authority, well-defined roles and boundaries, and vigorous law enforcement, for example. Similarly, closed-minded personality types will find it difficult to change their opinions in the face of new evidence, but might nevertheless be expected to change such opinions when authority figures express an opinion contrary to the one originally held by the subject. To put it another way, many of the personality measures and classifications used today are based on the kind of opinions and attitudes expressed or admitted to by the respondent or subject, and we should therefore not be surprised that those constructs which we call personality traits would correlate strongly with opinions and attitudes. Further, the way in which an individual structures and integrates his opinions and attitudes will also provide important indicators of, and be responsive to, the basic personality traits.

Cultural Attributes: The Societal Level

Having summarized and/or hypothesized the general relationships among personality, attitude and opinion at the individual level, let me now shift to the societal level, be it a subnational, national, or extra-national entity which concerns us. The central thesis here is that, even though no social group can be properly thought of as having a personality, an attitude or an opinion, we may nevertheless attribute certain properties to a group on the basis of the distribution and configuration of these psychological properties. In other words, I would hold that the aggregation of individual *psychological* properties provides a quite sufficient base for describing the *cultural* properties of the larger social entity which is comprised of those individuals.

The Aggregative-Emergent Argument

This position brings me face to face with the ancient, and still open, issue of aggregative versus emergent properties. If the issue can still arouse controversy between the defenders of "organismic" and "mechanistic" approaches in disciplines ranging from biology to astronomy, we need not be surprised by its durability in the social sciences.[15] In my view, however, there is a relatively straightforward solution to the problem, such that the reductionist or aggregative position taken here need not appear as foolish and simplistic as it is often made out by advocates of the "emergent properties" school. That solution requires, however, a somewhat more refined taxonomy and more selfconscious epistemology than is often found among the occasionally mystical "gestaltists" in sociology, political science and anthropology.

First, it requires that we define levels of analysis along only one dimension, or at least, only one at a time. If we want to treat the economic, the political and the social *sectors* of society, and the cultural and the structural *attributes* of society as different "levels of analysis" (as does Smelser in this issue, for example) there may be no serious harm, but to shift from a horizontal back to a vertical axis and to also include the physiological and the psychological in the scheme (as do many, including Smelser) is to court conceptual chaos. It would seem more in keeping

with the symbolism associated with "levels" and with conceptual clarity were we to adhere to the vertical axis alone and base our levels of analysis on the size and complexity of the entities which we are considering at the moment; e.g., from cell to organ to organism or individual to family to nation. This and closely related points are made succinctly by Coleman (1964, 84):

One important measurement problem in sociology concerns the two levels on which sociologists must work: the level of the individual and that of the group. We have observations at two levels, concepts at two levels, and relationships at two levels. Furthermore, it is necessary to shift back and forth: measuring group-level concepts from individual data; or inferring individual relationships from group-level relations.

A second distinction of importance in this epistemological issue is that between structure and culture. Even though the structure and the culture of a social system are causally linked in a most intimate fashion, they are by no means identical; nor does it enhance our clarity to ignore the boundary between them. In the taxonomy proposed here, the *structure* of a system is defined as that set of properties which we attribute to it on the basis of the observed *relationships* among the entities (individuals or groups) which comprise the system. *Culture,* on the other hand, is defined as the set of properties we attribute to the system by observing the distribution of *psychological attributes* among the individuals who comprise the system. The problem is one of distinguishing between the construct or verbal representation which we use for descriptive and explanatory purposes and the operations by which we ascertain that construct's presence or absence, strength or direction of change. While there are many exceptions, a large number of system properties can only be defined and measured by observing subsystem phenomena, and on that basis, the distinction between structure and culture should not be too difficult to observe.

The third and equally critical clarification that is required is that between behavioral phenomena and essentially static phenomena of a pre- or post-be-havioral nature. For example, much of the social science literature concurs that the *structure* of a social system is a property we attribute to the system on the basis of observing relationships among its subsystems. But since little of the literature distinguishes between *relationship* (marital, friendly, heirarchical, alliance, etc.) and *interaction* (embrace, fight, speak, exchange, etc.) we end up by confusing the formal or informal *structure of* a system with the behavioral and inter-actional regularities which *occur within* that system. To be sure, we may infer relationships by observing interactions and we often predict interactions from known relationships, but they are — and deserve to be treated as — quite distinct classes of phenomena.

The Linkage Between Subsystems

A final distinction of importance, and one which appears to lie at the heart of the aggregative versus emergent confrontation is that between the procedures we use to *describe* a social system and those we use to *explain* how it "got that way." We may, quite legit-imately, observe the distribution of subsystem attri-butes, the relationships among the subsystems, and the interactions among them, and on the basis of these offer a fairly full *description* of that system.[16] But until we have observed and demonstrated the linkage be-tween and among subsystem attributes, relationships, and interactions, we can not *explain* and account for the properties, behavior or relationships of the system itself. Admittedly the line between scientific explana-tion and description begins to blur as that description becomes more complete, but the intellectual opera-tions are sufficiently different to merit explicit de-marcation.

As one reads the philosophers of science as well as the critics of the position taken here, it turns out that the ancient argument against reductionism and in favor of organic or holistic epistemologies rests largely on the inability of a reductionist model to *account for* the system's properties or behavior; we cannot, they

remind us, explain or predict the behavior or future states of the system solely on the basis of the proper-ties of its constituent elements. But even here, knowl-edge of the components' properties can carry us a fair part of the way from description to explanation. To illustrate, we can pour pellets of steel into a container until it is full, with little qualitative change in the aggre-gate; it merely becomes larger. But if we do the same thing with pellets of enriched uranium under appro-priate conditions, we will eventually arrive at the "critical mass" threshold, with important qualitative change in the aggregate as a result. In such a case, the emergent properties of the system are largely explica-ble in terms of the properties of its component parts. In the same vein, observation of the placement or relationships among components may enhance our understanding of the system's behavior. For example, a society which becomes involved in a limited war and has a large number of citizens who are intolerant of ambiguity may move quickly into all-out war in the "drive for closure." The same result could come about, even if such a personality trait were infrequent in that society, but typical of its elites or only of its chief of state. My point, then, is that while knowledge of subsystem or component properties, or relations or interactions among these components may not al-ways suffice for explanatory, or even predictive, pur-poses, such knowledge constitutes a major basis for *describing* the larger system. And while explanation and operational description must be distinguished, the latter is not so plentiful in social science that we can afford to dismiss it as trivial.

Once any of these four distinctions become blurred, we are much more likely to reject the view outlined here and retreat into some sort of metaphorical and pre-operational formulation. That is, unless levels are arranged on one set of dimensions only, unless struc-ture and culture are distinguished, unless behavioral and nonbehavioral phenomena are differentiated and unless the needs of explanation kept distinct from those of description, we have almost no choice but to accept the organic-emergent position. By explicitly recognizing these distinctions, however, it becomes possible to devise social science taxonomies within which data may be gathered and the testing of alternative theories may go forward.

Having digressed for this unavoidable epistemological-ontological excursion, let me now return to the psycho-cultural interface by which we might better comprehend the relationships between man and world politics. To reiterate, the position taken here is that the cultural properties of any subnational, national or extranational system may be described in a strictly aggregative fashion, by observing the distribution and configuration of individual psychological properties.[17]

National Character, Ideology and Climate of Opinion

The most straightforward, if not the only, way to convert the distribution of individual properties into social system properties is to let each of the three *psychological* variables serve as the basis for a distinct *cultural* variable. Choosing that path, let us treat *personality* as the basis for national (or any other social system's) *character, attitude* as the basis for *ideology,* and *opinion* as the basis for *climate.* That is, when we have ascertained which individuals score where on one or more personality, attitude or opinion scales, we have the basis for descriptive statements about the culture (or portions thereof) of the entity which they constitute. In this manner, then, the three societal "equivalents" would rank the same way as their psychological "counterparts" on the three dimensions used earlier. National character (or basic personality, as it is often called) would be the most general of the three cultural variables, most durable, and least accessible to direct observation and measurement.[18] At the other end, climate of opinion would be most specific, most transitory, and most observable; ideology would fall in the middle range on all three dimensions. Let me now say a few words about each of these cultural attributes of national, subnational, and extra-national entities and then go on to a discussion of their measurement and statistical description.

There are many approaches to the study of national character but two stand out in the literature; one tends toward the *organismic* and the other toward the aggregative and *statistical.* The former often attributes certain individual personality traits to the society as a whole, usually anthropomorphizing to some extent. This approach usually rests either on the assumption that there is near-uniformity of personalities within the social system or that the social structure impinges upon and molds diverse personalities in such a way as to produce highly uniform attitudes, opinions or behavior. The statistical approach is obviously the one taken here, and it coincides with the definition offered by Inkeles and Levinson (1954, 983): "national character refers to relatively enduring personality characteristics and patterns that are modal among the adult members of a society." Whether we speak of national character or of basic personality, the theme is almost always an aggregative and additive one, in which we look for the ways in which certain personality traits are distributed throughout a given population. There is, of course, no assurance that we will find only one modal personality in a given entity; the possibility of bi- or multi-modal types is always present (Levinson, 1957).

Moving from personality and national character to attitude and its societal counterpart, *ideology,* we come to that cultural attribute which is perhaps most central in understanding a nation's foreign policy. Neither as remote from policy concerns as personality, nor as evanescent as opinion, attitudinal configurations provide the most salient nonmaterial incentives and constraints within which nations decide upon their behavior in world politics. When we speak of ideology, it is important to distinguish among the various ways in which it is defined. A formal institution such as political party, pressure group or government usually has both an official or articulated ideology, as reflected in speeches and documents, and an operative ideology, which actually guides the group's behavior. The latter may not even be fully known to the group's own members, but it inevitably differs from the official ideology, especially as the time lag since the articulation or revision of the official ideology increases. There are few more serious errors in science, or in policy, than to assume that the official and the operative ideologies are identical; yet it occurs with alarming frequency.[19] Not only is it crucial to distinguish between the formal and the operative ideology of an elite group, but to distinguish between both of these and the ideology of the larger social entity for which the elite claims to act. This distinction is often most evident when we contrast opinions to attitudes. That is, the elite may hold, or merely express, a given set of attitudes, and may try to bring the general public's attitudes into line with either of these. Unfortunately, there has been little research on the congruence between elite and mass ideology, but the impression is that the effort is not always successful. The several publics may well express, and even hold, *opinions* which coincide with those urged by the elite, but never internalize them sufficiently to qualify as attitudes.[20]

Ideology is crucial in foreign policy not only because it provides the matrix within which the present is interpreted, the past recalled, and the future anticipated, but because it provides the boundaries within which the climate or distribution of opinion can range. Within that range, opinion distributions for given sectors of a society will respond to behavioral events and information about them.

On the basis of what we now know about the malleability of most people's *opinions,* it is safe to say that political elites and/or mass media can—if they have a fairly accurate picture of the attitudinal configuration or ideology within their society—generate an impressively wide range of opinion changes. There are important constraints on such manipulation, including the climate of opinion at the moment, the ideology of the period, and the more slow-moving national character, but the degree of malleability is remarkable as well as alarming. More specifically, the would-be engineer of opinion change needs to know how many individuals in what particular classes (from mass to elite, from indifferent to attentive, etc.) hold what attitudes and opinions with what tenacity on what issues. In other words, he must know in some detail what the ideology and the climate of opinion

look like at some particular point in time. This consideration leads us, then, to the problems of observation, measurement and description by which such distributions and configurations may be ascertained.

The Observation and Description Problem

The statistical description of a nation's character, ideology, or climate of opinion—all combining to constitute its cultural attributes—are not only of interest to those who would modify or exploit that state of affairs. Until we have progressed further along this road, social scientists will also have a most incomplete understanding of the dynamic processes which occur within and between those entities, from small groups to the global system, which constitute our major theoretical focus.

In the sections above, I contended that opinions were most susceptible to observation, that personality traits were least susceptible, and that attitudes would fall somewhere between. Such a statement may misleadingly suggest that all three phenomena can—or must be—measured via direct observation alone. If we bear in mind that all psychological, and therefore, all cultural (in the restricted sense used here) phenomena are literally intrapsychic, it is evident that we must *always* make an inferential leap from those events which can be observed directly to the variable which we seek to measure. To return to an epistemological theme which is central to the whole scheme developed here, we need to be ingenious in looking for the traces and indicators of our variables, but we must remember that the traces, and the variables they reflect, are seldom the same thing. If this were not so, the problem of validity in social science measurement would be considerably less vexatious; that is we would be less concerned with the question of whether we are measuring that which we claim to be measuring. As difficult as the problem is in other sectors of social science, it is even more troubling at the intrapsychic level, where few of our observations are made in the natural setting and most occur in the artificial and contrived laboratory or interview setting. In addition to this type of danger, validity is also threatened by the rather standard practice whereby we not only observe such behavioral events as verbal response in order to tap opinion, for example, but move back and forth (or up and down) among all three variables by inferring attitudes from opinions and personality from attitudes, and by predicting opinions from attitudes and attitudes from personality.[21]

To continue at the individual level, it seems to me that social scientists have all too often tended to assume that directly elicited verbal behavior represents the major—or even the only—avenue to understanding and measuring individual traits. Thus, in order to get at personality, we generally ask for written or oral responses to such stimuli as Rorshach blots, TAT pictures or incompleted sentences. To get at attitudes, we present our subjects with rather lengthy questionnaires, many of whose items seem to have little face validity, and then tote up the responses. To get at opinions, we usually organize a survey, replete with its myriad costs and problems of sampling, fielding an interview team, and then laboriously coding the alleged responses.[22]

It is certainly not my intention to reject these observational methods, but it is worth emphasizing their several shortcomings and suggesting the availability of alternative strategies. First of all, it cannot be emphasized too often that the assumed directness of these methods is generally overstated. The inferential leap from verbal response back to imputed trait is a long and elusive one at best. As to projective tests, there is the subjectivity of the coding criteria, illustrated by the amount of training and experience required before the interpreter is considered qualified and before we get any satisfactory degree of intercoder agreement. Whereas a cardinal rule in the search for reliability is to reduce coding procedures to a highly routinized algorithm, the projective tests are of limited value except in the hands of an insightful, artistic and trained expert. And even as the personality scales gradually reach satisfactory levels of reliability across time and across subjects, they still leave unanswered a number of serious questions on the validity side. On too many occasions we hear the assertion of the hyper-operationalist: "The _____ syndrome is what this scale is designed to measure, and what it measures is, therefore, the _____ syndrome"! Worth consideration, too, in both the paper-and-pencil and the face-to-face situations are the dangers of systematic error resulting from interviewer or experimenter induced bias, the unnatural setting, the low salience of the questions, respondent indifference and faulty recording (Remmers, 1954). Whether we are interrogating publics or elites, whether we seek to measure something as deep and general as a personality trait or as close to the surface and specific as an opinion, the inferential leap is a long one, marked by a variety of hurdles, only some of which we fully understand.

An Alternative

Are there any alternatives to the direct verbal expression route, and are they any less problematical? One option which political scientists are now using with some regularity is the search for behavioral rather than prebehavioral or merely verbal indicators. Thus, we ask respondents—or find out through informants or public records—which political party they belong to, how they have voted or plan to vote, which pressure groups and professional associations they belong to and in what capacity, whether they write to their newspapers or legislators, and so forth. By and large, these provide somewhat more reliable information, but they too pose certain problems of validity. If we want to tap psychological attributes it is usually in order to use such data for predicting to _behavior,_ and it may be risky to observe behavior, infer back to alleged psychological predispositions and then predict to the very behavior which has been observed. The danger of tautological explanations is very much with us in this sort of research design, but as more varied psychological and behavioral data become available, the opportunities for cross-validation will inevitably increase. The same problems remain even if we shift from interrogation to behavior-inducing experiments, or if we observe more natural or field-setting behavior, since we must still infer personality, attitude and opinion phenomena from the more directly observable — but not easily codeable — behavioral phenomena.

Having emphasized the pitfalls, let me now retreat somewhat and recognize that often we have no alternative other than direct interrogation or experimentally induced behavior, and that social scientists have shown remarkable ingenuity and rigor in seeking to minimize the misleading effects of these methods. Moreover, it is worth reiterating that there really is no such thing as a *directly observable* variable in social science; we always have an inferential leap of some magnitude between the event or condition on the one hand and the repertorial representation on the other. Thus, despite the danger to validity and reliability, any serious research on personality, attitude and opinion will continue to depend on the resourcefulness and precision with which we apply and develop the basic research strategies already in use. The only place where dramatic improvement seems both necessary and possible is at the personality level, where much of our knowledge depends upon the psychiatrist's protocols and reports, and the clinical psychologist's investigations. The consensus, which I largely share, is that the intra-psychic probings of these researchers (especially the former) leave a great deal to be desired when it comes to the operationalization of their variables; intuition is absolutely essential to scientific discovery, but it is seldom sufficient.[23]

Despite the central argument here — that we can and should employ the distribution and aggregation of individual attributes in order to measure certain social attributes — it does not necessarily follow that we can *only* do so by *observing* individual responses. That is, we seem to have underestimated the extent to which the distribution of intrapsychic phenomena within a population may be inferred via observation of *collective* phenomena.[24] Not only does this strategy avoid the artificialities of many interview and experimental situations, but it even provides an economical

route for getting at macrophenomena in a more direct fashion. Thus, we may follow the anthropological approach and merely observe a great deal of social interaction, and on the basis of the way things are done and discussed, infer the nature of the personalities, attitudes and opinions of those who constitute the entity under investigation. Another tack widely used in anthropology is to examine the physical or artistic artifacts of the entity and treat them as indicators of these same phenomena; whether pottery or poetry, conference chambers or constitutions, and whether recent or ancient, these products may serve as manifestations or traces of the way in which a population views or did view many phenomena of interest to us.[25] Likewise, such phenomena as elections, mass movements, migration, market behavior, social mobility, and so forth, may all provide the empirical base from which we might infer back to the underlying culture.

When we observe societal and collective phenomena in order to tap the distribution of individual psychological attributes, however, there is again the danger of circularity in our reasoning. Thus, unless we have sufficient understanding of the social structure (roles and relationships) within which these interactions occur, and unless the state of our theory is relatively advanced, inferences about national character, ideology and opinion distributions can be quite wide of the mark. Another way to avoid unwitting circularity is to opt, quite consciously, for the cyclical model in which feedback is explicitly introduced; in such models, each set of variables serves the dependent, the independent, and the intervening role, in turn. Moreover, with some of the more recent tools of path analysis, and causal inference (Blalock, 1964), we can discover which particular sequence offers the most powerful explanation in the process, thus settling many of the old issues as to which is cause and which is consequence in sequences that can only be understood within a feedback framework (Deutsch, 1963).

Turning from problems of observation to the ways in which we might report and describe our observations, the standard tools of descriptive statistics seem quite appropriate to the task at hand. What are the familiar ways in which a frequency (or probability) distribution is portrayed, so that the dominant characteristics of the configuration are best illuminated? First of all, we generally want to know something about the central tendency of a set of observed frequencies, and the median, mode and mean all have their uses in this regard. Beyond these, important aspects of an aggregate can be graphically portrayed via the histogram (bar graph), the frequency polygon (line graph), or the cumulative frequency curve, especially if individual scores on a given psychological dimension are collapsed into grouped frequency distributions. Nor should the factor analysis approach be overlooked (Cattel, 1955). While these graphic representations offer an economical overall picture of the dispersion, as well as the central tendency, of an aggregative distribution, we can get a more precise indication of the former by computing the variance or the standard deviation. Going a step further, the asymmetry of the distribution is precisely measured by computing the magnitude and direction of its skewness, and another measure of the curve's deviation form normality is found in its kurtosis (peakedness). To demonstrate the application of these familiar statistical descriptors is neither necessary nor appropriate here, but their relevance to the many empirical studies (many of which are cross-cultural) of personality, attitude, and opinion distributions should be self-evident. Nor is this the place to suggest the theoretical purposes to which such descriptions might be put.[26]

The Individual

Up to this point, I have tended to treat every individual's personality traits, attitudes and opinions in an undifferentiated fashion, ignoring the obvious fact that some individuals exercise a far greater impact on world politics than others. Let me now recognize, if not rectify, that omission by way of a brief digression. While research on the strength and direction of differences between elites and others has not yet led to many universal generalizations, the evidence does point to the regular existence of certain mass-versus-elite discrepancies. In the work of Lasswell (1948), Dicks (1950), and others, we find suggestions of data which would permit the construction of cultural profiles which take explicit account of such discrepancies.[27] One might, for example, superimpose on the histogram for some trait or cluster of traits in the general population, similar profiles of the groups from which foreign policy or military elites are drawn. It might well turn out that the isomorphism or lack thereof between the two configurations would predict to that nation's behavioral tendencies or correlate strongly with the types of relationships it forms. Or, in line with the "two-step flow" hypothesis (Katz, 1957), a useful inquiry into the identity and potency of community influentials could be mounted. That is, if the foreign policy opinion profile for a general population sample and for several alternative reference groups could be ascertained on perhaps a weekly basis, and the various media could be content analyzed, one might be able to trace the path along which information and influence tend to move. Space limitations preclude further pursuit of these research possibilities, but the options are many and the need is great.

In Conclusion

Between the familiar regions of individual behavior and the dimly perceived ones of world politics lies a *terra incognita* into which few social scientists have yet begun to venture. Given the inadequacy of our maps, it is little wonder that we have given those regions a wide berth. My purpose here was to draw up a tentative map, preliminary to more thorough exploration. The map is largely conjectural, but may possibly have profited from the missteps and false starts of those who have explored comparable regions in other disciplines.

On the basis of those not dissimilar experiences, certain caveats seem justified. First, the map should identify the entities which exist in the region, and next, provide operational descriptions of their major attributes. Once these entities are recognized and described, we may safely inquire into their various roles and relationships vis-a-vis one another. Then, if we can resist the temptation to assign them all sorts of goals, purposes and functions, and treat the whole matter as an empirical question, we might get on to the next item on our agenda. That item, of course, is not explanation, but description. Until we have described a range of phenomena, we cannot explain it, and the main purpose of the map drawn here is to help us describe and measure now that which we hope to explain later.

Leaving the map-making metaphor behind, the scheme proposed explicitly rejects the need for an "emergent properties" concept when the description of social entities is the matter at hand. Conversely, it urges that we can be both operational and relevant by defining and measuring the *cultural* properties of a subnational, national, or extranational entity strictly in terms of the *psychological* properties of those individuals who constitute that particular system. It

does not deny the possibility that the interaction of individual properties (both within and among single humans) may produce emergent effects, but it insists that: (a) those effects are either structural of behavioral, and (b) if they are not in either of these two classes, but are indeed themselves cultural, then the effects can be observed in the form of individual psychological properties.

In sum, while the nature of the man-society conjunction has been debated and discussed for years, no satisfactory formulation has yet emerged. I have, therefore, taken not only a very explicit, but fairly extreme, aggregative position here, in the hope that if it accomplishes little more, this paper will have served to clarify and sharpen the methodological and theoretical issues. In the interim, I should like to believe that this type of formulation will carry us some distance toward a fuller understanding of the psycho-cultural interface by which man's role in world politics might be more fully comprehended.

References

Adcock, C. J. and Ritchie, J. E. "Intercultural Use of Rorschach." *American Anthropologist* 60 (1958): 881–92.

Adorno, T. W. et al. *Authoritarian Personality.* New York: Harper and Row, 1950.

Allport, G. W. and H. S. Odbert. "Trait Names: A Psycho-Lexical Study." *Psychological Monographs* No. 211, 1936.

Almond, Gabriel and Sidney Verba. *The Civic Culture.* Princeton: Princeton University Press, 1963.

Angell, Robert C. "Governments and Peoples as Foci for Peace-Oriented Research." *Journal of Social Issues* 11 (1955) no. 1: 36–41.

Atkinson, John. *Motives in Fantasy, Action, and Society.* Princeton: Van Nostrand, 1958.

Banks, Arthur S. and Robert B. Textor. *A Cross-Polity Survey.* Cambridge, Mass.: M.I.T. Press, 1963.

Bertocci, Peter A. "Foundations of Personalistic Psychology." In Benjamin Wolman (ed.), *Scientific Psychology.* New York: Basic Books, 1965.

Blalock, Hubert M. *Causal Influence in Nonexperimental Research.* Chapel Hill, N.C.: University of North Carolina Press, 1964.

Brim, Orville G. and Stanton Wheeler. *Socialization after Childhood.* New York: John Wiley, 1966.

Campbell, Donald T. "Common Fate, Similarity, and Other Indices of the Status of Aggregates of Persons as Social Entities." *Behavioral Science* 3 (1958) no. 1: 14–25. Reprinted in J. David Singer (ed.), *Human Behavior and International Politics.* Chicago: Rand McNally, 1965.

Campbell, Donald T. and D. W. Fiske. "Convergent and Discriminant Validation by the Multitrait-Multimethod Matrix." *Psychological Bulletin* 56 (1959): 81–105.

Cattell, Raymond B. "Concepts and Methods in the Measurement of Group Syntality." University of Illinois Press, 1953.

Cattell, Raymond B. *Personality: A Systematic Theoretical and Factual Study.* New York: McGraw-Hill, 1950.

Cattell, Raymond B. "Concepts and Methods in the Measurement of Group Syntality." *Psychological Review* 48 (1955) no. 1: 48–63. Reprinted in J. David Singer (ed.), *Human Behavior and International Politics.* Chicago: Rand McNally, 1965.

Cohen, Yehudi, A. (ed.). *Social Structure and Personality.* New York: Holt, Rinehart and Winston, 1961.

Coleman, James S. *Introduction to Mathematical Sociology.* New York: The Free Press, 1964.

Converse, Philip E. "The Nature of Belief Systems in Mass Publics." In David Apter (ed.), *Ideology and Discontent*. New York: Free Press, 1964.

Deutsch, Karl W. *The Nerves of Government*. New York: The Free Press, 1963.

Dicks, Henry V. "Personality Traits and National Socialist Ideology." *Human Relations* 3 (1950): 111–54.

Frenkel-Brunswik, Else. "Intolerance of Ambiguity as an Emotional and Perceptual Personality Variable." *Journal of Personality* 18 (1949): 108–43.

Freud, Sigmund. *Introductory Lectures on Psychoanalysis*. Trans. Ivan Riviere. London Allen and Unwin, 1922.

Grinker, Roy (ed.). *Toward a Unified Theory of Human Behavior*. New York: Basic Books, 1956.

Hsu, Francis L. K. (ed.). "Psychological Anthropology." Homewood, Ill.: Dorsey, 1961.

Hyman, Herbert, et al. *Interviewing in Social Research*. Chicago: University of Chicago Press, 1954.

Inkeles, Alex and Daniel J. Levinson. "National Character: The Study of Modal Personality and Sociocultural Systems." In Gardner Lindzey (ed.), *Handbook of Social Psychology*. Cambridge, Mass.: Addison-Wesley, 1954.

Jacobs, Robert C. and Donald T. Campbell. "The Perpetuation of an Arbitrary Tradition Through Several Generations of a Laboratory Microculture." *Journal of Abnormal and Social Psychology* 62 (1961): 649–58. Reprinted in Singer (ed.), *Human Behavior and International Politics*. Chicago: Rand McNally, 1965.

Jung, Carl G. *Psychological Types*. New York: Harcourt, Brace, 1923.

Kahn, Robert and Charles Cannell. *The Dynamics of Interviewing: Theory, Techniques, and Cases*. New York: John Wiley, 1957.

Kaplan, Bert (ed.). *Studying Personality Cross-Culturally*. Evanston, Ill.: Row, Peterson, 1961.

Katz, Elihu. "The Two-Step Flow of Communications." *Public Opinion Quarterly* 21 (1957): 61–78.

Kelman, Herbert C. "Compliance, Identification, and Internalization: Three Processes of Attitude Change." *Journal of Conflict Resolution* 2 (1958) no. 1: 51–60.

Kelman, Herbert C. *International Behavior: A Social-Psychological Analysis*. New York: Holt, Rinehart and Winston, 1965.

Kish, Leslie. *Survey Sampling*. New York: John Wiley, 1965.

Klineberg, Otto. *Human Dimension in International Relations*. New York: Holt, Rinehart and Winston, 1964.

Kroeber, Alfred L. and Clyde Kluckhohn. "Culture: A Critical Review of Concepts and Definitions." *Papers of the Peabody Museum* 47 (1952) no. la: 643–56.

Kluckhohn, Clyde and Henry Murray. "A Critical Review of Concepts and Definitions." *Papers of the Peabody Museum* 47 (1952) no. la: 643–56.

Lasswell, Harold D. *Power and Personality*. New York: W. W. Norton, 1948.

Leites, Nathan C. *Operational Code of the Politburo*. New York: McGraw-Hill, 1951.

Levinson, Daniel, J. "Authoritarian Personality and Foreign Politics." *Journal of Conflict Resolution* 1 (1957) no. 1: 37–47.

Livant, William P. "Cumulative Distortion of Judgment." *Perceptual and Motor Skills* 16 (1963): 741–45.

Macoby, Eleanor and Nathan Macoby. "The Interview: A Tool of Social Science," In Gardner Lindzey (ed.), *Handbook of Social Psychology*. Cambridge, Mass.: Addison-Wesley, 1954.

McCary, J. L. (ed.). *Psychology of Personality: Six Modern Approaches*. New York: Logos Press, 1956.

McClelland, David. *The Achievement Motive*. New York: Appleton-Century-Crofts, 1958.

McClelland, David. *The Achieving Society*. Princeton: Van Nostrand, 1961.

McCloskey, Herbert. "Conservatism and Personality." *American Political Science Review* 52 (1953): 27–45.

McGranahan, Donald and Ivor Wayne. "German and American Traits Reflected in Popular Drama." *Human Relations* 1 (1948): 429–55; reprinted in J. David Singer (ed.), *Human Behavior and International Politics*. Chicago: Rand McNally, 1965.

Milgram, Stanley. "Nationality and Conformity." *Scientific American* 205 (Dec. 1961) no. 6: 45–51.

Miller, James G. *Living Systems*. New York: John Wiley, 1968.

Mitchell, William. *Sociological Analysis and Politics: The Theories of Talcott Parsons*. Englewood Cliffs, N.J.: Prentice-Hall, 1967.

Murphey, Gardner (ed.). *Human Nature and Enduring Peace*. Boston: Houghton Mifflin, 1945.

Nagel, Ernest. *The Structure of Science*. New York: Harcourt, Brace, 1961.

Pye, Lucian and Sidney Verba (eds.). *Political Culture and Political Development*. Princeton: Princeton University Press, 1965.

Raser, John R. "Personal Characteristics of Political Decision Makers: A Literature Review." *Peace Research Society Papers* 5 (1966): 161–81.

Remmers, H. H. *Introduction to Opinion and Attitude Measurement*. New York: Harper and Row, 1954.

Rieselbach, Leroy. "Personality and Political Attitudes: Available Questionnaire Measures." Ann Arbor: University of Michigan, 1964. Mimeo.

Robinson, W. S. "Ecological Correlations and the Behavior of Individuals. *American Sociological Review* 15 (1950): 351–57.

Rokeach, Milton. *The Open and Closed Mind.* New York: Basic Books, 1960.

Rosenau, James N. "Private Preferences and Political Responsibilities: The Relative Potency of Individual and Role Variables in the Behavior of U.S. Senators." In J. David Singer (ed.), *Quantitative International Politics: Insights and Evidence.* New York: Free Press, 1968.

Rosenberg, Morris. "Misanthropy and Attitudes Toward International Affairs." *Journal of Conflict Resolution* 1 (1957) no. 4: 340–45.

Rummel, Rudolph J. "A Social Field Theory of Foreign Conflict." New Haven: Yale University Press, 1965. Mimeo.

Singer, J. David. "The Level-of-Analysis Problem in International Relations." *World Politics* 14 (1961) no. 1: 77–92.

Singer, J. David, "Soviet and American Foreign Policy Attitudes: A Content Analysis of Elite Articulations." *Journal of Conflict Resolution* 8 (1964) no. 4: 424–85.

Singer, J. David (ed.). *Human Behavior and International Politics: Contributions from the Social-Psychological Sciences.* Chicago: Rand McNally, 1965.

Singer, J. David. "The Global System and its Subsystems: A Developmental View." In James N. Rosenau (ed.), *Linkage Poli-*

tics: Essays on the Convergence of National and International Systems. 1968.

Singer, J. David. *Behavior and Interaction in the Global System.* Englewood Cliffs, N.J.: Prentice-Hall, 1969.

Smith, M. B., J. S. Bruner, and R. W. White. *Opinions and Personality.* New York: John Wiley, 1956.

Sprout, Harold and Margaret Sprout. *The Ecological Perspective on Human Affairs with Special Reference to International Politics.* Princeton: Princeton University Press, 1965.

Stratton, George M. *Social Psychology of International Conduct.* New York: D. Appleton and Co., 1929.

Wallace, Anthony, F. C. *The Modal Personality Structure of the Tuscarora Indians.* Washington, D.C.: Government Printing Office, 1952.

Wallace, Anthony, F. C. *Culture and Personality.* New York: Random House, 1961.

Waltz, Kenneth. *Man, the State, and War.* New York: Columbia University Press, 1959.

Webb, Eugene, et al. *Unobtrusive Measures: Nonreactive Research in the Social Sciences.* Chicago: Rand McNally, 1966.

Wolfers, Arnold. "The Actors in International Politics." In William T. R. Fox (ed.), *Theoretical Aspects of International Relations.* Notre Dame, Ind.: University of Notre Dame Press, 1959.

Notes

[1] Among those who *have* concerned themselves with the micro-macro issue, either explicitly or implicitly, there seems to be the familiar division into two schools of thought; one might be called the ecological determinist school, exemplified in the thoughtful analysis developed by Waltz (1959), and the other might be called the individual autonomy viewpoint. Among the handful of explicit but pre-operational efforts to synthesize these viewpoints are Sprout and Sprout (1965), Wolfers (1959), and Singer (1961).

[2] Two exceptions come to mind. One is an early article by Angell (1955) and the other is the recent anthology edited by Kelman (1965), especially his own opening and closing chapters. See also Stratton (1929), Murphy (1945), and Klineberg (1964).

[3] An important study on this issue is Rosenau's research into the relative potency of role constraints versus "personal preference" in the foreign policy behavior of U.S. Senators in the Acheson and Dulles eras (1968).

[4] I am certainly not urging that all research must come to a halt until we have solved these problems, or that inquiries which sidestep them are of no value. I am merely urging that anything approximating a coherent and complete theory must ultimately be sufficiently molecular to embrace the behavior of men and sufficiently molar to embrace their environment.

[5] That approach is best exemplified in the articles found in the

Yearbook of the Society for General Systems Research, published annually since 1956, and the most integrated single effort is James Miller's forthcoming *Living Systems* (1968). In my judgment we have not yet developed a general systems theory; hence the word "approach."

[6] Perhaps most instrumental in this movement is Talcott Parsons, whose theoretical views are synthesized for a political science audience in Mitchell (1967). For those who think I misinterpret Parsons, there is this quote: "the unit of a partial social system is a role, and not the individual. . . . A social system is a behavioral system. It is an organized set of behaviors of persons interacting with each other: a pattern of roles. The roles are the units of a social system" Grinker, (1956, 328). Two compelling discussions from the entity-oriented viewpoint are Cattell (1955) and Campbell (1958), both of which are reprinted in Singer (1965).

[7] To keep an already complex paper somewhat simpler, I will often refer only to national entities from now on, but it is understood that the reference could always be to subnational and extra-national ones as well.

[8] A useful compendium, albeit a decade in age, is McCary's *Psychology of Personality: Six Modern Approaches* (1956).

[9] Over thirty years ago, Allport and Odbert (1936) pointed out that over 17,000 personality trait names could be identified in western literature. A more recent scanning of the personality literature reveals such dimensions as: high or low on the need for achieve-

ment, affiliation or power (McClelland, 1958, and Atkinson, 1958); authoritarian (Adorno et al., 1950); conservative (McCloskey, 1953); open- or closed-minded (Rokeach, 1960); misanthropic (Rosenberg, 1957); intolerant of ambiguity (Frenkel-Brunswik, 1949); provincial or cosmopolitan (Levinson, 1957); introverted (Jung, 1923); narcissistic and/or egoistic (Freud, 1922); optimistic or pessimistic; altruistic; exhibitionist; apathetic; dominant; dependent; sadistic or masochistic; manic-depressive; inner-directed or other-directed; and so on.

[10] Two possible paths to improvement in the measurement of personality come to mind. First, the clinical psychology and psychiatry subcultures could profitably borrow and adapt the more rigorous and operational methods already in use in other social sciences; there seems to be room for considerable modification in coding, classifying and scaling procedures. Second, some tentative evidence seems to be emerging that we might find occasional correlations between mental state or personality and certain biochemical or electro-physiological indicators.

[11] A fairly complete survey of the measures for those which are most relevant to political science is in Rieselbach (1964).

[12] It has become something of a ritual for political scientists to note how uninterested and/or uninformed the bulk of the world's citizens are in regard to politics, and while the evidence seems compelling, it may be somewhat beside the point for students of foreign policy. Overlooking, for the moment, the ways in which elite foreign policy articulations and arguments may easily lead to public cynicism and indifference, the fact is that those members of the public who *are* attentive and/or informed are generally those whose opinions do exercise some impact on the policy-making process.

[13] This normative flexibility—because it is a widespread personality trait in the industrial societies of today—may well account for (i.e., acquiesce in) a great deal of the incompetence and inhumanity found in modern foreign policies. Seeing no feasible way of changing things, many citizens merely revise their notions as to what constitutes acceptable (or justifiable) diplomacy or strategy.

[14] Such manipulability could be expected to vary from one society to another, and one study (Milgram, 1961) found that a French sample was significantly more resistant to such pressures than a matched Norwegian sample. We must be careful, however, not to confuse that "decent respect for the opinions of mankind" which might be more prevalent in a society characterized by high mutual trust, with high suggestibility; conversely, the distrust of others may not be equivalent to inner-directedness.

[15] Perhaps the most balanced and thorough treatment of the issue, from a physical science point of view, is in Nagel (1961) 336–97.

[16] My impression is that this view does not run afoul of the stricture which Wallace (1961, 43) and others keep returning to. He inveighs against the "statistical fallacy, which offers an enumeration of the properties of individual persons as if it were a description of a social or cultural system. . . ." Given the context, he is presumably concerned about those "personality and culture" authors who treat psychological factors as all, and nearly ignore the structural attributes of the society. Nor do we seem to be committing Robinson's (1950) "ecological fallacy" in which one infers individual attributes from group attributes for which only the marginals are known.

[17] As suggested earlier, my definition of cultural properties is considerably narrower than that used by most anthropologists, whose consensus is approximated in Kroeber and Kluckhohn (1952); the classical and global definition is Taylor's: "That complex whole which includes knowledge, belief, art, morals, law, custom, and any other capabilities and habits acquired by man as a member of society."

[18] It is certainly not my intention to suggest that ease of direct observation necessarily guarantees that our measures will be high on both reliability and validity. As Campbell and Fiske (1959) as well as others, have pointed out, it is difficult to actually *achieve* construct validity but easy to believe that it has been achieved. Reliability is, however, an essential precondition for validity and while it may often be necessary to make trade-offs between the two, our selection of variables cannot be insensitive to the observation and measurement problem. These issues are discussed more fully in the next section.

[19] A particularly distressing example is Leites' *Operational Code of the Politburo* (1951) based largely on the "holy scriptures" of Marxism-Leninism. The saving grace of the study is its open-endedness, in which an extremely wide range of behavioral patterns is predicted from a given cluster of formal articulations.

[20] Highly suggestive in this context is Kelman's "Compliance, Identification, and Internalization: Three Processes of Attitude Change" (1958). Despite the fact that he does not distinguish among attitude, opinion and behavior, his scheme meshes in a general way with the one proposed here. The "compliance" process may be thought of as producing opinion change but little more, with identification and internalization both affecting attitudes and internalization perhaps even impinging on personality.

[21] This inferential strategy is particularly risky in a cross-cultural research setting, inasmuch as variations in social structure—or differential rates of change therein—may impinge upon essentially similar modal personalities and "produce" appreciably different ideologies.

[22] For a valuable discussion of the many problems involved in the opinion survey approach, see Kahn and Cannell (1957), Kish (1965), and Maccoby (1954). An early study which concentrates on the sources of error is Hyman et al. (1954).

[23] Interestingly enough, some of the most rigorous research on personality variables is that of the anthropologists. Some imaginative and persuasive methods of data-acquisition and analysis via Rorschach blots are reported in Wallace (1952) and in the anthology compiled by Kaplan (1961). On the cross-cultural use of Rorschach see Adcock and Ritchie (1958).

[24] An excellent discussion, with examples, of alternative methods for getting at such social phenomena is in the volume of *Unobtrusive Measures* (Webb et al., 1966).

[25] One approach is represented in the McGranahan and Wayne (1948) analysis comparing popular drama in Germany and the United States during the late 1920's. And despite certain acknowledged inadequacies in his methods, David McClelland has demonstrated the possibilities of systematic examination of such cultural artifacts as textbooks and tapestry for generating politically relevant data (1961).

[26] A few possibilities, might, however, merit a footnote. We

could, for example, search for the amount of symmetry in the way two populations perceive one another as well as themselves, in order to ascertain which of the many combinations of these four attitude configurations best predicts to the relations and interactions between the entities which they comprise. Some basic data can be found in Cantril and Buchanan (1953) and in Singer (1964). Another possibility might be a longitudinal analysis, in which any observed convergence or divergence in cultural profile could be examined to ascertain whether cultural differences and similarities associate with various types of interdependence, friendly or hostile, in any regular fashion.

[27] A systematic and carefully coded survey of much of the literature on the social background and personality traits of modern political elites is in Raser (1966).

Political Culture-and-Personality: Theoretical Perspectives

on Democratic Stability from the New Zealand Pattern

Larry B. Hill

Such terms as political ideology, national character or ethos, *Weltanschauung,* the political formula, public opinion, etc. have long been used by political analysts to refer to phenomena that are social-psychological in nature. In 1956 Gabriel Almond introduced a new term, political culture, which was destined to become a part of the vernacular of practicing political scientists, "Every political system," he claimed, "is imbedded in a particular pattern of orientations to political action."[1] Citing Parsons and Shils in *Towards a General Theory of Action,*[2] he identified three components of political culture—the perceptive, the affective, and the evaluative.

The impact of Almond's original formulation can easily be discerned in the usages of three highly prestigeous and visible works that followed. First, in 1958,

This is the first publication of this article. All rights reserved. Permission to reprint must be obtained from the publisher and author. This is a slightly revised version of a paper presented at the 1970 Convention of the Southwestern Political Science Association. I am grateful to Oliver Benson, Moshe Czudnowski, Alex Inkeles, and Samuel Kirkpatrick for critical comments on that paper. This is a preliminary overview of research in progress; full responsibility is assumed for the ideas expressed.

Samuel Beer described the concept as "the particular distribution of patterns of orientation toward political objects among the members of the nation." Furthermore, "the principal components of the political culture are *values, beliefs,* and *emotional attitudes."*[3] Second, in 1965, Sidney Verba said, "the political culture of a society consists of the system of empirical beliefs, expressive symbols, and values which defines the situation in which political action takes place,"[4] Third, Lucian Pye wrote as follows in the *International Encyclopedia of the Social Sciences:*

> Political culture is the set of attitudes, beliefs, and sentiments which give order and meaning to a political process and which provide the underlying assumptions and rules that govern behavior in the political system.[5]

These conceptualizations are obviously quite similar; and, though there may often be important problems in scholars' attempts to operationalize political culture, it is clear from the popularity of the term among practitioners that they have become much more sensitive to these "orientations" than they were previously. The major research study undertaken in this genre,

The Civic Culture, has empirically grounded the concept, particularly to the extent of showing what was meant by political culture, as well as providing a useful set of data for secondary analysis.

Political Culture-and-Personality

Despite the general acceptance of the term, I wish to propose an alternative: political culture-and-personality. Three justifications for such an addition to our vocabulary are offered. First, this concept focuses upon the personality as the unit of analysis. Normally, neither the theoretical expositions of the term political culture nor its operationalizations subaggregate their findings at the level of the political actor (or nonactor) before investigating "the particular distribution of patterns of orientation toward political objects among the members of the nation."[6] That is, a mere study of the distribution of various political attitudes over the society might obscure important configurations of them within individual personalities. To explicate this distinction it may be useful to refer to a content analysis of the tables and figures in the *Civic Culture.* Of the total 140, 49 were reports of simple percentage variations in questionnaire responses among the four countries. A further 50 introduced a demographic variable (more than one was seldom used, and sex and education seemed to appear most often). Eleven tables were cross-tabulations of the behavioral[7] variable, party vote, and of perceptions of various parties. A total of 29 tables concerned an analysis of responses on the composite scale of subjective political competence. Nineteen of them were cross-tabulations with other demographic and/or behavioral variables.[8] The remaining ten tables were the only ones in which two explicitly psychological variables were pitted against each other.[9] Thus, this quantitative analysis reveals that in *The Civic Culture* only a relatively small amount of attention was accorded to the search for political attitude configurations within particular individuals; also this limitation has been generally characteristic of the approach.

Personality is, of course, a much debated concept, but the intended usage can be summed up in Singer's identification of it[10] as "the organizing and integrating framework within which all other intrapsychic attributes are embraced." Similarly, he later says, "personality is defined here as a hypothetical construct embracing and structuring the individual's total reservoir of behavioral predispositions." We are interested in any aspects of personality that might have an impact upon political behavior. Thus, a society's distribution of traits such as tenderness or egoism, may be relevant to the individuals' structuring of certain political cultural data; these traits then merit our consideration even if they are not overtly political.

Second, the term political culture-and-personality, which is adapted from the culture-and-personality school of anthropology, is broader than political culture, for it may encompass the analysis of political behavior. Francis L. K. Hsu has described the core concerns of culture-and-personality as follows:

> Culture-and-personality deals with human behavior primarily in terms of the ideas which form the basis of the interrelationship between the individual and his society. On the one hand, it deals with ideas shared by a considerable portion of any society [and] how these and other ideas held by the individuals are rooted in the diverse patterns of culture in which they grow up. On the other hand, culture-and-personality deals with characteristics of societies: reactions to conquest and disaster, internal or external impetuses to change, militarism and pacifism, democratic or authoritarian character; it deals with how these and other characteristics consistently associated with some societies may be related to such things as the aspirations, fears, and values held by a majority of the individuals in these societies.[11]

It will be observed that especially the last part of this definition includes behavioral and institutional phenomena that are not normally included under the category of political culture.

In their search for more rigorous conceptualizations, theorists of political culture usually have been adamant that one cannot study the orientations in which they are interested through inferring them from either behavior or artifacts, such as political institutions. Some form of direct measurement was required and mass interviews seemed most reliable.[12] David Singer has described some of the deficiencies of survey data and recommended:

> We may follow the anthropological approach and merely observe a great deal of social interaction, and on the basis of the way things are done and discussed, infer the nature of the personalities, attitudes and opinions of those who constitute the entity under investigation. Another tack widely used in anthropology is to examine the physical or artistic artifacts of the entity and treat them as indicators of these same phenomena; whether pottery or poetry, conference chambers or constitutions, and whether recent or ancient, these products may serve as manifestations or traces of the way in which a population views or did view many phenomena of interest to us.[13]

This orientation is especially amenable to the exploration and description of the important intersectices between man, his society, his culture, and his political institutions. Thus, this analysis assumes a political system level of analysis, rather than concentrating almost exclusively upon inputs as does political culture. Therefore, it focuses on the linkages between micro-and macro-levels of analysis.[14]

A third reason for proffering this new term is that the research methods of the culture-and-personality tradition are more congruent with the financial and other resources most often available to political scientists than are those of political culture. Certainly, there are pitfalls in inferring psychological characteristics from behavior, for individuals do possess logically inconsistent beliefs, act in ways that are contrary to them, and support institutions that are opposed to them. However, I would submit that these drawbacks have in some cases had the effect of inhibiting research, where money, organizational support, and so on were not available to conduct a large survey. It should be pointed out that few examples of political culture surveys exist within single nations,[15] that the *Civic Culture* study remains one of two cross-national studies using national probability samples yet published,[16] and that funding for political research seems to be in a depression.

Thus, the more flexible methods of culture-and-personality researchers are worth consideration. They are best described as eclectic and innovative. Usually a variety of procedures is utilized, such as participant observation, interviewing, the administration of psychological tests, and the analysis of social institutions, in order to provide as rich a basis as possible for interpreting the phenomena under analysis. Of course, one cannot be blind to the dangers of such eclectic methods, particularly to the problems of the reliability of intersubjective evaluations and of inferring culture-and-personality from behavior and institutions. Nevertheless, it is possible to minimize error through careful observation, through cautious borrowing from previous treatments of the subject,[17] and through the development of innovative and economical research strategies.

Perhaps the following simplified paradigm will add clarity to the mode of analysis suggested here:

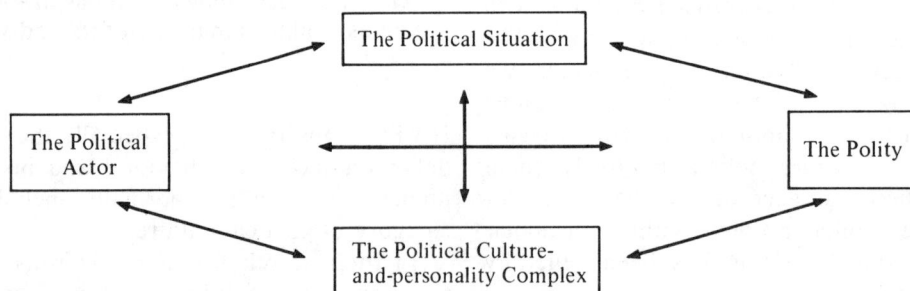

The basic concern is with the political system level of analysis; and, although this particular treatment stresses the actor's role, the elements of the system are conceived of as interacting in a reciprocal fashion; patterns of influence are viewed as constantly changing. From the point of view of the political actor at either the mass or elite level, it is first assumed that his objective sociological situation, in terms of his abilities, resources, and so on, structures his opportunities and limitations for political action. Second, the society's political culture-and-personality complex makes available to him both its repertoire of political attitudes, values, and beliefs and a selection of basic orientations to social and political life. Through the process of political socialization, particular elements are selected from the political culture-and-personality complex and are internalized by the actor. Once they are institutionalized they will affect his interpretation of his sociological situation and of the political situation as well as his interactions with the polity. Particular distributions of political culture-and-personality configurations, not necessarily uni-modal ones, are presumed to exist in various polities.[18] From the point of view of the polity, it may act to structure the political situation within narrow confines and it may overtly influence the political culture-and-personality complex. Further, the pattern of relationships established between the polity's output structures and their subjects may or may not be congruent with those of the political culture-and-personality complex. Such reciprocal relationships are thus viewed as prime objects of analysis.

Scope and Research Design

Having adumbrated the political culture-and-personality approach, this paper's intent is to consider some theoretical problems of democratic stability from the perspective of the New Zealand polity, employing a political culture-and-personality focus. The questions may arise, Why study New Zealand? What can the study of small countries contribute to our political understanding? The latter question has been so adequately answered by Harry Eckstein[19] that I will not comment here, but will focus on the former.

Despite New Zealand's smallness[20] and her isolation from the Western World (even Australia is 1200 miles away), it is generally acknowledged that New Zealand has become a modern "developed" society. In fact, comparative studies commonly rank her near or even at the top of these developed societies. For example, Buck and Jacobson rank New Zealand first among 50 countries on a "social evolution" scale derived from Parsonian theory.[21] David C. McClelland rates New Zealand third after Sweden and the United States on his scale that attempts to measure achievement level.[22] Haywood R. Alker and Bruce M. Russett[23] place New Zealand in the mid-range of what they have determined from a combination of nine social and economic variables to be "high mass-consumption" societies. The point is that New Zealand is big enough and complex enough to warrant consideration.

Further, New Zealand's very extensive homogeneity can be advantageous for our analysis. Some aspects of it will be discussed below, but at this point we will note that in New Zealand, there are no important ethnic divisions (as in Switzerland), social divisions (as in Great Britain), economic divisions (as in the United States) regional divisions (as in Italy), religious divisions (as in Germany), ideological divisions (as in France), or linguistic divisions (as in Canada). The most usual pattern of research on these countries is to focus upon these divisions; since they are relatively unimportant in New Zealand we are, in effect, using them as control variables. Therefore, New Zealand can be looked at as a laboratory[24] in which the political scientist has a particularly wide scope for investigating such notions as the nature of "political man," the conditions for stable democracy, and so on. Of course, it remains difficult to set up experimental conditions anywhere in the real political world, but results obtained in New Zealand come closer to the conditions in Kurt Lewin's laboratory than they do anywhere else.

The data presented here are from a variety of

sources. The survey data were gathered in a post-election survey conducted by the School of Political Science and Public Administration of the Victoria University of Wellington in 1963.[25] The findings reported here are from random samples of two electorates near Wellington, Karori (an upper-middle-class suburb) and Miramar (a partly rural area). It is thought that the two are reasonably representative of New Zealand opinion. My colleagues at the school, to whom I am indebted for access to the data, indicate that these data are congruent with those gathered in a large rural sample.

For almost two years, 1967–68, I researched New Zealand politics and taught at the Victoria University. During that time, I attended a large proportion of the parliamentary session, did research in government departments, and immersed myself in New Zealand politics as a participant-observer. Much of these data are not yet analysed; some results of my interviews with all 80 members of Parliament, with all the ministers of the Crown, and with the administrative heads of the major bureaucratic departments are reported here. In addition, the views and data of previous scholars and other "softer" data are reported.[26]

It is the thesis of this paper that New Zealand is a stable democracy and in all probability the most stable example thereof. Harry Eckstein has defined the ideal type of such a democracy as follows:[27]

> The most stable democracy is one in which men disagree, without intensity and within a narrow range, on specific issues, widely share basic orientations, and have politically weak segmental identifications.

Eckstein found that even Norway did not come very close to fitting this model because of sharp segmental cleavages, but that it was democratic for other reasons. Investigations of other democracies find that they are even further from the model. If for no other reason, this examination of the New Zealand case may provide some empirical indications that the model of the ideal stable democracy should be retained because in many respects New Zealand approaches it. In terms of providing reference points along a continuum of stable-to-unstable democracy, examination of New Zealand may indicate that the previously expected empirical parameters of the possible should be raised. Three aspects of New Zealand political culture-and-personality will be examined, the affective linkages between the polity and the citizen in terms of participation, the consensus on the polity's goals, and the affective linkages between the polity and the citizen with regard to the subject side of government.

Participatory Linkages Between Citizens and Polity

Diffuse positively affective orientations toward the polity are prevalent in New Zealand. They can be inferred from the fact that 77 percent of an urban sample of voters disagreed with the following statement: "I don't think politicians care much what people like me think."[28] In comparison, the rate of American[29] disagreement in 1964 with a similar item was considerably lower, 61 percent. However, the American statement, "I don't think public officials care much what people like me think," could be interpreted as including administrators, whereas the New Zealand item was limited to politicians. Whether including the administrators in the statement in New Zealand would have materially affected the rate of disagreement is problematical. As another example, a very strong sense of citizen duty is indicated by the disagreement of 95 percent of the New Zealand sample with the item: "So many other people vote in a general election that it doesn't matter much whether I vote or not."[30] Eighty-nine percent of the Survey Research Center's 1960 American sample disagreed with the item from the Citizen Duty Scale: "So many other people vote in the national elections that it doesn't matter much to me whether I vote or not." However, it should be noted that the insertion of the phrase "to me" in the American statement changes the focus of the question from the systemic consequences of non-voting to the individual consequences and possibly affected the pattern of response.

Even though the New Zealand scores on these two questions were somewhat higher than the American, they were similar in direction. I would suggest that they may have a somewhat different meaning. Almond and Verba's conclusion based on similar data for the U.S. (and Britain) was that "there exists a gap between the actual political behavior of our respondents, on the other hand, and their perceptions of their capacities to act and their obligations to act, on the other."[31] The existence of this high level of "subjective political competence" in the civic cultures was viewed as important to their stability, but their citizens' behavioral quiescence was partially rationalized as helping to "provide the power that governmental elites need if they are to make decisions."[32] I would contend, although precisely similar data do not exist,[33] that this gap is considerably narrower in New Zealand, and that the closer correspondence between ideal and behavior is a source of stability for the polity, although it certainly affects the output structures by making them more sensitive to inputs.

One way of measuring the participatory linkages is through examining the subjective matter of party identification. The respondents were asked: "Apart from the way you felt about this election, we'd like to know whether you usually think of yourself as a supporter of one of the parties on this list, or as not supporting any party?" Table 1 indicates that the incidence of party identification in New Zealand is considerably higher than in the other countries for which we have comparable data. It should be noted that as in the other cases cited, this figure was obtained without adding the supplementary question for those who did not immediately identify with the two major parties, "Do you usually think of yourself as closer to the Labour Party or to the National Party?" It is of great interest that the New Zealand interviewers placed only one person in their category 8, Apolitical (e.g. "I never vote"), out of their 861 respondents.

Only 3.4 percent of the sample were Social Credit supporters, so that 90.1 percent identified with one of the two major parties. The consequences of subjective party identification have been thoroughly discussed in the literature cited above, but the fact that

Table 1
Comparative Extent of Subjective Party Identification in Six Countries[34]

Country	Percent Identifiers
New Zealand	93.5
Great Britain	79.0
Germany	76.5
United States	76.0
Norway	73.0
France	45.0

all but 6.5 percent identified with one or another party must be stressed.

Each cell in Table 2 indicates the percent of each party's supporters which identified themselves as *strong* supporters. The data indicate that the pattern of intensity of party support for the left party is greater in New Zealand than it is in the United States, but that the relationship is reversed, for the right party. (However, the difference between the strength of support for the right parties in the two countries is small.) In a general sense, the data indicate that the earlier measure of party identification has a comparable meaning between the countries and that, for both, the left party has more strong supporters than does that of the right. However, the level of intensity of support for neither New Zealand party is high enough to lead to instability.

This pervasive willingness to identify with one of the political parties is not merely subjective. Actual popular participation in the political parties is in a comparative sense widespread. Robinson has estimated that for the National Party in an election year paid membership is roughly 40 percent of its voters.[36]

Positive orientations toward citizen participation were also strongly visible in the elite interviews. For example, the members of Parliament tended to have an unusual perception of their role. They did not know that they were supposed to respond to my role question in terms of whether they considered themselves as a "trustee, delegate, or politico." Consequently, they predominantly responded in terms of a role con-

Table 2
Percent of Strong Identifiers per Party in New Zealand and
the United States[35]

Country	Left Party	Right Party
New Zealand	Strong Labour 57%	Strong National 43%
United States	Strong Democrat 49%	Strong Republican 45%

ception seeming to be that of a communications channel, rather than in terms of one of the three "approved" roles. The data may yet be coded along different dimensions, but very common responses contain phrases such as "link to the people," "social worker," "helping my constituents," "father confessor," and "looking after my people." They normally have a "surgery" each week in their constituency to get feedback; only one or two of the 80 seemed to be uninterested in citizens' problems. They were also asked an open ended question about their opinions on the extent of political participation in New Zealand. They often opined that it was high, but *not high enough!*

Various output structures are oriented toward receiving advice and complaints from the public and some specialize in that function. There is, for example, a Parliamentary Petitions Committee and the Scandinavian Ombudsman was adopted in 1962. The point should also be emphasized that pressure groups are considered legitimate and that they have a crucial role in the governmental process. Perhaps the extent of their influence can best be illustrated by the following Ministerial response to an opposition question about a minor bill:

> The member for Timaru asked who had had discussions on this draft. I would inform him that the following organisations have been consulted in the drafting of this Bill: The New Zealand Municipal Association; the New Zealand Society of Master Plumbers; the New Zealand Plumbers, Gasfitters, and Related Trades Industrial Union of Workers; the Auckland Metropolitan Drainage Board; the Christchurch Drainage Board; the Dunedin Drainage Board, the North Shore Drainage Board; the chief plumbing and drainage inspector, Wellington City Council; the Hutt Valley Drainage Board; the

New Zealand Counties Association; the New Zealand Trades Certification Board; the New Zealand Employers' Federation; the New Zealand Institute of Health Inspectors; the New Zealand Gas Council; and the New Zealand Institute of Engineers. I give him an assurance that the term "sanitary plumbing" has been revised with the complete agreement of all those people interested in this matter.[37]

This degree of consultation with relevant groups is very common, and any other course would be viewed by all as illegitimate. It is particularly significant that the department would have provided the minister with this information in advance, anticipating the question. To conclude, the affective participatory linkages between the citizen and the state are well developed in New Zealand, both from the point of view of the citizen's feelings and behavior, and from that of the sensitivity of governmental mechanisms to demands.

Mutual Consensus on the Goals of the Polity

Traditional political theorists have assumed that a high level of consensus is necessary to the functioning of a democratic state. However, political scientists have examined this proposition operationally for the United States, and have been unable to find consensus in the sense in which it has been assumed to exist. Prothro and Grigg[38] concluded after their fruitless attempt to find consensus in American society on *specific* political propositions that consensus only had meaning when it was related to very broad principles, such as "Democracy is the best form of government."

They even found that with regard to specific propositions their respondents were "closer to perfect discord than to perfect consensus on over half the statements." These findings have been well digested by American political scientists, and it may have been assumed by some that political consensus is a meaningless term, a condition unattainable by political man.

Some important differences between the pattern of consensus in New Zealand and in the United States, both on certain specific social goals, and on the proper use of the mechanism of the State, are apparent from the data in Table 3. The two questions upon which the table is based were similar but not identical. The New Zealand statement was "The government has a definite duty to see that everybody has a job and a decent standard of living." The U.S. question was a part of the 1964 Survey Research Center's study and read: "In general, some people feel that the government in Washington should see to it that every person has a job and a good standard of living. Others think the government should just let each person get ahead on his own. Have you been interested enough in this to favor one side over the other?" The addition of "definite" seems to make the New Zealand statement considerably more demanding. New Zealanders very clearly expect government to be used to achieve important social goals to a degree that many Americans would find most surprising. As one might predict, these goals are not very congenial to most Americans. The extremely high New Zealand rate of agreement, coupled with the phenomenally low degree of no opinion, reveals a depth of consensus on the crucial specifics that is probably without parallel among developed nations.

However, it is possible that this general agreement with the statement could mask important differences in the intensity of agreement, particularly between the two political parties. Table 4 investigates this possibility, and indicates that it does not pertain. More supporters of *both* parties *strongly* agreed than simply agreed! Also, National Party identifiers did not cluster (if such a term can be used with such small numbers) at the strongly disagree pole. In an analysis separate from the table it was further found that only 4.7 percent of the strong National Party identifiers disagreed with the statement, and only one of them disagreed strongly! This seems to represent consensus according to even the most stringent definition.

Agreement on this is so apparent in New Zealand that it is a tribute to the devisers of the questionnaire that they included such an "obvious" question. As a *mea culpa,* I must report that I was so seduced by its obviousness that unfortunately I decided not to make space for the item in my elite questionnaire. It would have been theoretically relevant to "prove" the degree of mass-elite agreement, although some interesting party differences may have emerged.

In pursuing these goals, New Zealanders have created a very active government, deeply involved in society. The ubiquitous welfare state may come into direct contact with individuals on such matters as installing a telephone, granting a pension, obtaining a loan on a house, or writing a last will and testament. These and many other disparate services require a

Table 3
New Zealand and U.S. Attitudes on Government Responsibility for Employment and Living Standards

Attitude	New Zealand	United States
Agree that both are government's responsibility	95%	31%
Disagree that both are government's responsibility	5%	43%
No Opinion (N.Z.); Other, Don't Know, No Interest (U.S.)	1%	25%
Total*	101%	99%

*Totals are greater or less than 100% because of rounding.

Table 4
New Zealand Partisan Attitudes on Government Responsibility for Employment and Living Standards*

Party Identification	Strongly Agree $N = 453$	Agree $N = 358$	No Opinion $N = 8$	Disagree $N = 37$	Strongly Disagree $N = 5$	Total $N = 861$
Labour N = 337	60%	38%	0%	2%	0%	100%
National N = 438	48%	44%	2%	6%	1%	101%
Other N = 86	44%	47%	1%	6%	2%	100%
Total N = 861	53%	42%	1%	4%	1%	101%

*Some totals are greater than 100% because of rounding.

large governmental establishment, and New Zealand has the world's highest percentage of its working-age population employed by its various government and public enterprises.[39] Considerable financial resources are also required, and New Zealand's extractive as well as distributive capabilities are well developed. It is the third or fourth ranking nation and is close to the leaders in the measure (by different methods) of both governmental revenue and expenditure as a percentage of the Gross National Product.[40] The extent of the instrumental use of the state[41] is such that it would make many Americans gasp and confidently predict that the extension of the welfare state would mean the end of freedom. However, unhampered by theoretical preconceptions about the "proper" role of the state, it would seem foreign to New Zealanders to worry about the possibility that a grasping government could theoretically use a projected scheme to subvert their liberties.[42]

Having established the existence of this consensus, it is now possible to introduce some data that may, at first, seem not to support it. Both the popular sample and the elite sample were given the following item: "We have taken the welfare state too far; it's discouraging initiative and enterprise to a dangerous degree." Table 5 depicts the responses. The statement is, of course, very heavily loaded in favor of an affirmative response. Here the pattern of the relationship between the party elites and their supporters is clear, and the differences between the parties is in the expected direction.[43] It is of interest that the National Party's ministers, charged with the responsibility of adminis-

tering the welfare state, are almost evenly divided over the statement. Whether through late adult political socialization or through some quirk in the recruitment process (e.g., self-selection), their rate of agreement is substantially lower than that of their Backbench colleagues. It is interesting that, in spite of their apparent vested interest, the administrators are almost exactly equally divided. Perhaps this is an interesting indication of their near identity of opinion with their ministers.

It should be stressed that the above data indicate only in a relative sense that there is a current of opinion which believes that the pursuit of equality through the mechanism of the State should not be taken too far. *Equality* remains a most valued goal and equality means exactly that in New Zealand, whereas when the term is used in the United States in reference to a social goal, what is meant is *equality of opportunity*. The government shares this popular orientation, and truly impressive strides have been made in increasing the minimum levels in areas such as income, housing, health care, and education. Though New Zealand is a "developed" society, it is not economically rich; existing financial resources are very equitably distributed. For example, in 1966[44] only 1.4 percent of those with any income reported one of over $8,000 N.Z.; only 6.9 percent had an income of over $4,000 N.Z. Thus, this survey indicates that there is substantial consensus upon the basic goals of the state in New Zealand and about the means to attain them. Though there is party conflict[45] about the extent to which the goals should be pursued, the major thrust

Table 5
Attitudes on Taking Welfare State Too Far and Thus, Danger-
ously Discouraging Initiative and Enterprise, by Popular and
Elite Respondents*

Respondents	Grouping		Agree	Disagree
National Party	Popular Supporters	N = 438	57.0	30.2
	Members of Parliament	N = 26	76.9	23.1
	Ministers of the Crown	N = 16	52.2	47.8
Permanent Heads of Administrative Departments		N = 19	50.7	49.3
Labour Party	Popular Supporters	N = 337	26.4	51.9
	Members of Parliament	N = 36	16.7	83.3

*Elite respondents were not given a separate don't know option as was the
popular sample so there is no separate column. However, D. K. responses,
no response, etc., were taken into account in the base before figuring all percentages. The total N for the politicians is 78 because the Prime Minister and
heads of the Opposition were not asked this question.

of the polity's output structures is devoted to the process of pursuing them.

Subject Linkages Between Citizen and Polity

According to the "safety-valve" theory of democracy,[46] the very high level of political participation in New Zealand should produce intense pressures on elites, political instability, and "banana republic" conditions.[47] This has not occurred; New Zealanders recognize that they must pay the price of reducing their freedoms, especially economic freedom, in order to attain certain economic goals; this they are willing to do in pragmatic fashion. Table 6 records the samples' responses to the statement: "The government ought to cut taxes, even if it means putting off some things that need to be done." It should be recalled that the following attitudes are held in a situation in which the rate of taxation is higher than in the United States and in which, even before taxes, income is likely to be below or near the official American definition of poverty.

Note that the supposedly profligate Labour voters are more in favor of reducing taxes and delaying programs than are the theoretically more "capitalistic" National voters. It could be hypothesized that the higher status National voters have a clearer realization that most social goals cost money gained through taxation, while Labour voters might hope that a Labour government could get the money in some other way than from their paychecks. However, the really striking thing about the data in the table is the degree of intra-party consensus they reveal. Most voters have an opinion on the issue, and the majority of each party feel that individual economic freedoms must be sacrificed to attain desired social goals. In a similar spirit the other controls of the welfare state are also tolerated.

In a list of items that related to the general images of the two political parties, supporters were asked their perceptions of the parties' attitudes towards state interference with the individual's activities—a matter even more directly related to New Zealanders' orientation toward the subject side of the polity. The data in Table 7 indicate that Labour was viewed as the most interfering government by both parties' voters. National voters were very unified in this opinion, and nearly half of the Labour voters also accepted this image as accurate. Exactly half of the Labour voters perceived National as the party of controls and restrictions; 31 percent of the National voters agreed with this image.

Table 6
Attitudes on Reducing Taxation and Delaying Achievement of Social Goals

Attitude		Labour Voter N = 337	National Voter N = 438	Total (Includes all other responses) N = 861
Favor cutting taxes and delaying goal achievement	N = 304	43%	32%	35%
Against cutting taxes and delaying goal achievement	N = 472	50%	58%	55%
No opinion	N = 85	7%	11%	10%
Total	N = 861	100%	101%*	100%

*Total exceeds 100% because of rounding.

Table 7
Images of Liberty Under the National and Labour Parties

Attitude		Labour Voters N = 338	National Voters N = 438	Total N = 776
I. "The Labour Party means controls and restrictions."				
Agree	N = 519	47%	83%	67%
Disagree	N = 161	37%	8%	21%
No Opinion	N = 96	16%	9%	12%
Total	N = 776	100%	100%	100%
II. "The National Party means controls and restrictions."				
Agree	N = 306	50%	31%	40%
Disagree	N = 362	33%	57%	47%
No Opinion	N = 108	17%	12%	14%
Total	N = 776	100%	100%	100%

Explorations of perceived differences in voters' images of the parties are worthwhile, but for present purposes the extent of electoral agreement that the implementation of New Zealand political party programs means controls and restrictions is most interesting. It can be computed from the entire table that fully 53 percent of the whole sample believed that a vote for one party or the other or for either party, was a vote for state interference. Further, it is most important to note that 47 percent of the Labour voters and 31 percent of National's (38 percent of the whole sample) believed that in voting for their own party they cast a ballot for controls and restrictions. Thus,

it is apparent that a party's perceived stance of interference with the individual was often not a deciding factor in voting preference. Rather than rationalizing away or reinterpreting events, this large proportion of the electorate seemed to be intellectually aware that it was bartering away some of its freedoms and independence. This sacrifice, it was hoped, would be compensated for by the furthering of other social goals, such as governmental efficiency, economic security, or equality.

Not only are New Zealanders willing to make economic sacrifices to attain social goals and to accept government controls, but also the data of Table 8 suggest that they are positively oriented toward one aspect of governmental performance, that of their member of Parliament. It is apparent that the members of each political party would prefer to be represented by one of their own, but only 41 percent and 28 percent of the out-of-office party in the respective electorates disparaged the performance of the sitting member. The fact that those responding "no opinion" in each electorate greatly outnumbered those who thought that the member had *not* been energetic enough indicates that this issue was not vitally salient and that satisfaction, or at least acquiescence, was widespread.

In short, the attitudes of the "good citizen" and the satisfied consumer of government are prevalent. These attitudes are usually matched by behavior; New Zealand is a very peaceable, law-abiding society,[48] and disobeying a police officer is considered a serious offence. One expatriate Kiwi has said of his brethren's propensity to defer, "There is no one more docile in the face of authority."[49] Professor David Ausubel has contrasted American and New Zealand attitudes as follows:

When confronted face-to-face with the arbitrary pronouncements of officialdom, instead of questioning their wisdom and challenging them publicly, the adult New Zealander tends to comply with little or no open show of protest. Unlike the American who conforms under similar circumstances because it is expedient to do so, he seems to be *genuinely* overimpressed with the omniscience of authority figures, and to believe that they are *really* wiser than he. Intellectually, of course, he may think that they are all wrong, but emotionally he stands in awe – as a child – of their right to make unchallengeable decisions and cannot bring himself to demur in their presence.[50]

While it would be erroneous to describe New Zealand as a country in which citizens put themselves in thrall to the state, the extent of their deference to authority is striking and an attempt must be made to explain it. The working hypothesis is advanced that the personality trait of authoritarian submissiveness[51] is widely distributed in New Zealand. Because of a lack of comparative data,[52] it is advanced quite tentatively.

Table 8
Opinions of the Adequacy of Member of Parliament's Representation of District*

Opinion		Labour N = 136	National N = 216	Total (Including other) N = 393
National Electorate				
Adequate Job	N = 160	20%	52%	38%
Inadequate Job	N = 91	41%	13%	23%
No Opinion	N = 151	38%	34%	38%
Total**	N = 393	99%	99%	99%
Labour Electorate		N = 201	N = 222	N = 468
Adequate Job	N = 216	63%	40%	46%
Inadequate Job	N = 88	8%	28%	19%
No Opinion	N = 164	27%	33%	35%
Total**	N = 468	98%	101%	100%

* The actual wording of the statement was "The local M.P. (Mr. _____) hasn't been looking after the interests of this district energetically enough."

** Totals are greater than or less than 100% because of rounding.

Suggestions of a widespread ambivalence between liberty and authority can be discerned in the responses of representative voter samples to the two following statements: "Belonging to the Communist Party should be made a criminal offence" and "People guilty of serious sexual crimes should be flogged." The first is interpreted as being a test of tolerance of unpopular political opinion. The Communist Party has a very small following in New Zealand; its estimated membership in 1965 was only about 400 members;[53] and New Zealand did not undergo a period similar to the McCarthy era in the United States. Agreement with the statement would seem to indicate attitudes inimical to the free expression of political preference, hence undemocratic. The second statement suggests a method of punishment that would be regarded by libertarians as harshly punitive and intolerant of the psychological problems of offenders.[54] Agreement with this statement is interpreted as representing an intolerant preference for a form of punishment now considered archaic by the civilized world. The two questions seem to be theoretically related, and in the absence of any more reliable data, such as a number of similar items that could be combined to form a scale; answers to them are interpreted as partial indicators of libertarian or authoritarian orientations.

The results of Table 9 point to a seeming discrepancy; while 61.2 percent of the respondents were willing to tolerate Communists, only about half of that number 32.8 percent favored continued liberal treatment of one class of criminals. Also, note that the low rate of "no opinion" on the second item indicates the greater polarization of opinion on it. According to the cross-tabulation, only slightly more than one-quarter of the respondents were libertarian on both questions. The table indicates that a total of 47.6 percent of the respondents were consistent in offering libertarian, authoritarian, or no opinion replies to both of the statements; thus, the *majority* were inconsistent. The largest single group of respondents, 30.3 percent, believed that sexual offenders should be flogged, but also that Communist Party membership should *not* be made a criminal offence. It is possible that these questions may not measure the same attitudinal dimension, but the results seem to be indicative of an extensive distribution of authoritarian personality traits.

The widespread political participation discussed above should not be taken to imply that the New Zealanders are a gregarious people. Far from it; they tend to be reserved and introverted. They would also clearly distinguish themselves from "brash" Americans and Australians. Differences tend not to be discussed openly (except in the stylistic arena of Parliamentary debate); instead, a widespread New Zealand inclination would be to work quietly behind the scenes to attempt to resolve a disagreement. Nevertheless, they tend to form groups easily and to work well to-

Table 9
Cross-Tabulation of Tolerance for Communists and for Sexual Offenders (N = 861)

Sexual Offenders Should Be Flogged	Communist Party Membership Should Be Made Illegal			
	Libertarian Answer	Authoritarian Answer	No Opinion	Total
Libertarian Answer	26.1%	3-6%	3.1%	32.8%
Authoritarian Answer	30.3%	19.4%	9.2%	58.9%
No Opinion	4.8%	1.2%	2.1%	8.1%
Total	61.2%	24.2%	14.4%	99.8%*

*Total is less than 100% because of rounding.

gether as a team. Despite the fact that normally New Zealanders passively comply with the dictates of governmental authorities, as Professor Harold Bourne, a British psychiatrist, has cogently pointed out, this compliance does not tell the entire story:

> Typically, he seldom questions authority, and he never opposes it head on, but if its back be turned, he follows his own inclinations. . . . As for evading authority, when concealed, this is done as a simple matter of course. . . . After-hours trading is illegal, but inspectors can't be everywhere, so the grocer will oblige. . . . In short, the New Zealander is both a tame conformist and an habitual law-breaker, but the third course, changing the decree, seldom occurs to him — he is not a reformer and he is not a radical. If the early settlers brought any of the English radical tradition with them in their baggage, there is little sign of it that I can see now.[55]

Faced with the necessity of living among many thousands of restraints upon his activities, the New Zealander responds by covertly evading those which seem irksome to him and whose violation he thinks is undetectable.

This set of traits, which have been called authoritarian submissiveness, seem to have their origin in or to be reinforced by the rigid disciplinary practices in the home and in the secondary school.[56] However, it should be observed that New Zealand was settled almost entirely by working class English migrants and that most of the population could be ascribed to the working class today as could the society. Thus, following Lipset, we could describe the pattern as one of working class authoritarianism. He has described "the making of an authoritarian" as follows:

> The lower-class individual is likely to have been exposed to punishment, lack of love, and a general atmosphere of tension and aggression since early childhood — all experiences which tend to produce deep-rooted hostilities expressed by ethnic prejudice, political authoritarianism, and chiliastic transvaluational religion.[57]

This portrait is clearly overdrawn for New Zealand, for we are suggesting only a mild authoritarianism. In addition to this socio-economic variable, the low "salience" — to use Czudnowski's term — of New Zealand politics may have an impact upon personality formation. It would be most interesting to inquire into the conditions under which such low salience encourages authoritarian submissiveness rather than liberal tolerance.

Whether or not this hypothesized pattern of authoritarian submissiveness can be found to be important, and it is hoped that it will be tested further, the fact that New Zealanders are highly loyal subjects is incontestable. As has been established above, the polity's output structures are highly sensitive and are oriented toward the provision of services for the citizenry. However, the fact that the widespread personality trait of authoritarian submissiveness tends to orient individuals toward the acceptance of authority is quite important. It provides governments with a considerable sphere of "reserve support"[58] and thus allows considerable freedom of action. Nevertheless, New Zealand governments have not tended to take advantage of these potential opportunities. Probably the most serious instance of such an attempt was the conservatives' decision to postpone for a year the election that was scheduled for 1934, while hoping for a more favorable trade balance. They were decisively defeated, but were functionally accepted as the legitimate government for the extra year. Such behavior, however, is certainly not normative.[59]

Conclusion

This exploration of some theoretical perspectives on the ideal of stable democracy through the application of a political culture-and-personality focus to the New Zealand polity suggests that New Zealand approaches Eckstein's ideal type. First, the participatory linkages between the citizen and the polity were determined to be well-developed. The predominant orientations are positively affective, and political behavior is both congruent with them and results in frequent interaction with a large proportion of the citizens. The polity's output structures are also designed to facilitate feedback and are very sensitive to the comparatively high loads of demands placed upon them.

Second, the level of shared consensus between the citizen and the polity on both the goals and the instrumental use of the state are quite high. New Zealanders are principally oriented toward materialistic and egalitarian goals both theoretically and behaviorally, and their government's output structures are also closely attuned in that direction. Within this broad consensus party conflict is played out over subsidiary goals and means.

Third, I have contended that the subject linkages between the state and citizen are also crucial. If there is any empirical justification for the assumption that a high level of political participation creates tendencies toward instability, such tendencies are ameliorated by the widespread orientation to defer to political authority. This authority, I have argued, reaches the level of a personality trait that we may call authoritarian submissiveness among a certain distribution (of unknown size) of individuals. New Zealand is, of course not entirely homogeneous, nor is it the embodiment of the rational ideal of democracy. However, its very high consensus and lack of the basic segmental cleavages that seem to characterize other stable democracies may indicate that scholars have tended to limit unnecessarily the expected horizons of "political man." The usefullness of this preliminary analysis of this near polar type of a stable democracy will be greatly enhanced by comparable analyses of other systems.

Notes

[1] Gabriel Almond, "Comparative Political Systems," *Journal of Politics* 18 (August, 1956), p. 396.

[2] *Ibid.*

[3] Samuel H. Beer and Adam B. Ulam (eds.), *Patterns of Government* (New York: Random House, 1958), p. 12. Italics in original.

[4] Sydney Verba, "Conclusion: Comparative Political Culture," in Lucian W. Pye and Sidney Verba, eds., *Political Culture and Political Development* (Princeton: Princeton University Press, 1965), p. 513.

[5] Lucian Pye, "Political Culture," *International Encyclopedia of the Social Sciences* 12: 218.

[6] Gabriel Almond and Sydney Verba, *The Civic Culture: Political Attitudes and Democracy in Five Nations* (Princeton: Princeton University Press, 1963), pp. 14–15.

[7] The exception is that in the United States the measure used was the subjective one of party identification. See Table 1, p. 125.

[8] For example, Table 14, p. 320, "Percentage of Respondents Who Scored Highest in Subjective Competence Among Members of One or More Organizations, by Nation and Education."

[9] For example, Table 6, p. 254, "Percent Who Report Belief that Elections Are Necessary Among Three Groups of Subjective Competents, by Nation and Education."

[10] See J. David Singer, "Man and World Politics: The Psycho-Cultural Interface," *Journal of Social Issues* 24 (1968): p. 136.

[11] Francis L. K. Hsu (ed.), *Psychological Anthropology: Approaches to Culture-and-Personality* (Homewood, Illinois: Dorsey, 1961), p. 6.

[12] See, for example, Almond and Verba, p. 34. An important exception is Moshe M. Czudnowski, "A Salience Dimension of Politics for the Study of Political Culture," *American Political Science Review* 62 (September, 1968): p. 884. See also Henry S. Albinski and Lawrence K. Pettit, eds., *European Political Processes: Essays and Readings* (Boston: Allyn and Bacon, 1968), pp. 1–2. The authors discuss "structural components" of political culture, yet these are usually noninstitutional.

[13] Singer, p. 150.

[14] See Fred I. Greenstein, *Personality and Politics* (Chicago: Markham, 1969), pp. 133–39 for a discussion of this problem.

[15] It is pertinent that no survey has yet been done using the American States as a sampling base. Thus, when—not until 1968—Samuel C. Patterson wrote his innovative article, "The Political Cultures of the American States" *Journal of Politics* 30 (February, 1968): 187–209, it was definitely a pioneering piece. Research now underway at the University of North Carolina will hopefully fill this gap.

[16] The other is Hadley Cantril, *The Pattern of Human Concerns* (New Brunswick, N.J.: Rutgers University Press, 1965). While based upon various stratification criteria rather than random national samples, Alex Inkeles' article, "Participant Citizenship in Six Developing Countries," *American Political Science Review* 63 (December, 1969): p. 1120–41, is an important contribution to the literature.

[17] Patterson's study cited above follows this mold; he uses survey data wherever it exists, interpretations of other analysts, such as Key, Gunther, and Tocqueville, and inferences from institutions.

[18] Possibly the most relevant treatment of the national character concept for political scientists is Alex Inkeles, "National Character and Modern Political Systems," in Hsu (ed.), pp. 172–209. One has difficulty in recognizing there the simplistic "straw man" supposed to be typical of this genre.

[19] Harry Eckstein, *Division and Cohesion in Democracy: A Study of Norway* (Princeton: Princeton University Press, 1966), pp. 3–10.

[20] In 1966 New Zealand's population was about 2.7 million,

similar to the state of Oklahoma. The land area is about equal to that of the state of Colorado.

21 Gary L. Buck and Alvin L. Jacobson, "Social Evolution and Structural-Functional Analysis: An Empirical Test," *American Sociological Review* 33 (June, 1968): 348. The "evolutionary universals" examined were technology, bureaucracy, cultural legitimation, money and market, economy, stratification, communications, democratic association, religion, kinship, and generalized universalistic norms.

22 David C. McClelland, *The Achieving Society* (New York: Free Press, 1961), pp. 90–91. The scale relates the n achievement level (as observed in socialization stories in children's textbooks) to electricity produced in kilowatt-hours per capita and to national income in International Units per capita.

23 "Correlations Among Political and Social Indices," in Bruce M. Russett (ed.), *World Handbook of Political and Social Indicators* (New Haven: Yale University Press, 1964), Table B. 2, p. 298.

24 Of course, New Zealand has long been regarded as a laboratory in a somewhat different sense—as a "laboratory for democracy." Prominent among such innovations that either originated there or were adopted comparatively early have been (1) the neglected and dependent children legislation, 1867; (2) the establishment of the Government Life Insurance Department, 1869; (3) the creation of the Public Trust Office, 1872; (4) women's suffrage, 1893; (5) Court of Arbitration introduced, 1894; (6) Old Age Pensions Act, 1898; (7) Family Allowances Act, 1926; (8) Government health care program implemented, 1938–41; (9) Unicameral Legislature adopted, 1950; and (10) the Ombudsman, 1962. See the Chronological Table in J. L. Robson (ed.), *New Zealand: The Development of its Laws and Constitution,* 2nd ed. (London: Stevens, 1967), pp. xv–xx.

25 Three limited reports have been published using this data base. See A. D. Robinson and A. H. Ashenden, "Mass Communications and the 1963 Election: A Preliminary Report," *Political Science* (Wellington) 16, no. 2 (September 1964); A. H. Ashenden, R. H. Brookes, and A. D. Robinson, "Attitudes Toward Liquor Among New Zealand Voters," *Political Science* 18, no. 2 (March 1966); and R. H. Brookes and A. H. Ashenden, "The Floating Vote in Wellington and Palmerston North 1960–63," *Political Science* 19, no. 1 (July 1967).

26 The following treatment of aspects of New Zealand politics is highly tentative. Several of the ideas presented here have been developed with Alan D. Robinson of the Victoria University and will be explicated in a later joint enterprise. However, Professor Robinson should not be held accountable for the interpretations given here. The best corollary reading, particularly that likely to be available to Americans, for the present paper is Robinson's contribution, "Class Voting in New Zealand: A Comment on Alford's Comparison of Class Voting in the Anglo-American Political Systems," in Seymour M. Lipset and Stein Rokkan (eds.), *Party Systems and Voter Alignments* (New York: Free Press, 1967), pp. 95–114.

27 Eckstein, p. 38.

28 Cited in Robinson, "Class Voting . . . ," p. 105.

29 All otherwise unidentified U.S. data reported here were originally collected by the Survey Research Center of the University of

Michigan and were made available by the Inter-University Consortium for Political Research. The author is indebted to Professor Samuel Kirkpatrick of the University of Oklahoma for obtaining it. None of the sources bears any responsibility for the analysis or interpretation.

30 Cited in Robinson, p. 105.

31 Almond and Verba, p. 479.

32 *Ibid.,* p. 481.

33 One piece of evidence in support of the claim is that over 90 percent of the registered electors normally vote in general elections. (Registration is compulsory, but not voting). Also the incidence of voluntary group and political pressure group activity is very high. When that data is analyzed I would suspect it may be the highest for any nation. Furthermore, New Zealanders do attempt in great numbers to influence their legislators (though this is less important than in the U.S. because of rigid party discipline), and they are very active in complaining to the government. See Larry B. Hill, "The New Zealand Ombudsman's Authority System," *Political Science* 20 (September 1968): 40–51.

34 The British number has been "derived by projecting survey findings," by Richard Rose, *Politics in England* (Boston: Little, Brown, 1964), Table IV. 2, p. 89. The 1961 German figure was provided in Werner Zohlnhofer's German language text. A section is translated by Kurt Shell and reprinted in *The Democratic Political Process,* (Waltham, Mass.: Blaisdell, 1969), p. 156. The American results are for 1958 and are cited in Angus Campbell et al., *The American Voter: An Abridgment* (New York: Wiley, 1964), p. 69. The Norwegian source is Angus Campbell and Henry Valen, "Party Identification in Norway and the United States," *Public Opinion Quarterly* 25 (Winter, 1961): 510. The French data comes from Philip E. Converse and Georges Dupeux, "Politicization of the Electorate in France and the U.S.," *Public Opinion Quarterly* 26 (Spring, 1962): p. 9.

35 United States data are compiled from Campbell et. al., p. 69.

36 A. D. Robinson, "Notes on New Zealand Government and Politics: Note 2," Victoria University, 1968, mimeo, p. 3. In comparison, Jean Blondel has estimated that only about 20 to 25 percent of the British Conservative Party's electors are members. See *Voters, Parties, and Leaders: The Social Fabric of British Politics* (Baltimore: Penguin, 1963), p. 90.

37 *New Zealand Parliamentary Debates* 338 (June 19, 1964): 176.

38 James W. Prothro and Charles M. Grigg, "Fundamental Principles of Democracy: Bases of Agreement and Disagreement," *Journal of Politics* 22 (May, 1960): 276–94. See also Herbert McClosky, "Consensus and Ideology in American Politics," *American Political Science Review* 63 (June, 1964): 361–82.

39 Russett (ed.), Table 19, p. 70.

40 *Ibid.,* Table 14, p. 62; Table 15, p. 63; Table 16, p. 64; and Table 17, p. 65. For a thorough discussion of the welfare state, see C. Westrate, *Portrait of a Modern Mixed Economy: New Zealand* (Wellington: Sweet and Maxwell, 1959).

41 James Bryce's interpretation (Modern Democracies, Vol. 2 (New York: Macmillan, 1924), p. 324) of this New Zealand characteristic, which he made before World War I when German metaphysical conceptions of the State were so highly visible, has re-

mained accurate: "If the most obvious way to avert some evil or obtain some good seems to lie in involing the State's action, they invoke it. 'What is the State but ourselves? It is ours to use; why be jealous of it?' There is in this none of the German deification of the State as Power. The State is not to them a mighty organism in which national life is to be centre, and by which national life is to be moulded and controlled, but rather an instrument ready at hand to be employed for diffusing among themselves and their neighbours comfort and prosperity, the things they really care for. . . ."

[42] The following personal reference is apropos: While lecturing on American government to students at the Victoria University this author found it despairingly difficult to get them to believe the extent of the emotional attachment Americans have for such "paper" guarantees against governmental interference with individual liberties as the Constitution and Bill of Rights. (New Zealand has no written constitution. She and Britain seem now to be the only two countries that do not.) Nor could they understand how millions of Americans could subscribe to such dicta as "That government is best which governs least."

[43] The pattern faithfully follows that found by Herbert Mc-Closky, Paul J. Hoffman and Rosemary O'Hara, and will not be discussed further here. See "Issue Conflict and Consensus Among Party Leaders and Followers," *American Political Science Review* 54 (June, 1960): 406–27. See especially pp. 419–23.

[44] Cited in *New Zealand census of Population and Dwellings— 1966: Summary Results,* Department of Statistics, Wellington, p. 8. The N.Z. dollar is worth about $1.12 U.S.

[45] The stress here on consensus should not blur the existence of party conflict. Robinson, "Class Voting . . ." found a high level of class voting.

[46] This is explained in the popular textbook, Charles R. Adrian and Charles Press, *The American Political Process* (New York: McGraw Hill, 1965), pp. 268–69.

[47] See Seymour M. Lipset, *Political Man: The Social Bases of Politics,* (New York: Doubleday, 1963), pp. 226–29, for a balanced review of this literature as of 1963. Since then these theories have been increasingly employed as a rationalization for the low degree of participation, interest, and so on shown by the electorate in American politics.

[48] During the five-year period from 1957 to 1961 a mean of only 1.6 convictions and sentences for the crime of murder were handed down each year. Compiled from *New Zealand Statistics of Justice*

—1965, Department of Statistics Publication, Wellington: Government Printer, 1967, Table 13, p. 16. Precisely comparable statistics are not available, but estimates are that a comparable figure for the State of Oklahoma (which has a similar population) might be about 200!

[49] Bill Pearson, "Fretful Sleepers: A Sketch of New Zealand Behavior and Its Implications for the Artist," *Landfall* (September, 1952), p. 202.

[50] David P. Ausubel, *The Fern and the Tiki: An American View of New Zealand National Character, Social Attitudes and Race Relations* (New York: Holt, Rinehart, and Winston, 1960), p. 111.

[51] See Erich Fromm, *Escape From Freedom* (New York: Reinhart, 1941), p. 141 and T. W. Adorno et al., *The Authoritarian Personality* (New York: Harpers, 1950), p. 433.

[52] We do not have any representative data on TAT, Rorchach tests, or the F Scale, for example. The concept of authoritarian submissiveness is not altogether satisfactory, for other aspects of authoritarianism do not seem to be present. Perhaps some new concept is needed.

[53] H. Roth, "The Communist Vote in New Zealand," *Political Science* 17 (September, 1965): 33. In 1960 the Party got 0.89 percent of the total vote in the nineteen seats contested.

[54] Two similar items have been suggested by H. J. Eysenck, *Sense and Nonsense in Psychology* (Baltimore: Penguin, 1957), pp. 304–05, as measuring both conservatism on a radical-conservative scale and toughness on a tough-tender scale.

[55] Harold Bourne, "Authority and the New Zealander," *New Zealand Listener* (October 4, 1957).

[56] Patterns of discipline in the primary schools are more relaxed on the American model, whereas the secondary level they are modeled upon the harsh pattern of the Victorian British schools. See Ausubel, pp. 88–107. Some of his interpretations should be taken with a grain of salt.

[57] Lipset, p. 114.

[58] For an early formulation of the concept of reserve support see David Easton, "An Approach to the Analysis of Political Systems," *World Politics* 9 (April, 1957): 396–97.

[59] It is interesting that in my hundreds of hours of discussion with the political elite and with academics the subject was never once mentioned.

5

Political Socialization

Plato, in his *Republic,* discussed at length the political requirements of the educational system. His advocacy of civic indoctrination followed from a belief that behavior appropriate to political roles should be conciously taught and learned. Doubtless the term, "political socialization," still suggests to some readers a form of official indoctrination through which a ruling ideology is imparted—along with forced quiescence—to "loyal" subjects. To be sure, in some societies political instruction is a conscious objective of the state, and the "proper" political philosophy is learned in much the same manner as one learns physics or the calculus.

To modern political science, however, political socialization is a more embracing term. It refers more generally to the development of a "political self"; to the learning and acquiring of an orientation toward politics. The process of political socialization, which is life-long and continuous, involves one's internalization of the prevailing knowledge, values, norms and beliefs which contribute to the uniqueness of his political culture. Yet the process involves more than the internalization of values, for the individual not only engages in role taking but also in role making. He plays an active role in processing these values and norms, thereby contributing to some changes in social structures and cultural values. And within a given political culture there will be a wide range of individual differences in the learning of political attitudes, and in how persons relate to the political system. Moreover, in addition to general socialization, there are formal and informal procedures for acquainting elites with the special expectations associated with leadership roles.

We associate the concept "culture" most readily with the concerns of anthropology and many of the earlier studies of political learning were rooted in the anthropologists' interest in the intergenerational transmission of culture. In its political context the transmission of culture serves to strengthen ties of loyalty and affection, and, in the words of Easton and

Dennis, to create and sustain "sentiments of legitimacy and compliance."[1] The psychoanalytic theory of Sigmund Freud and others has also influenced the study of political learning. Freud, of course, stressed the importance of infant experience in explaining adult behavior. The role of society and its authority agents, beginning in the family, is to suppress socially forbidden impulses in the child. This, of course, may include instruction in "acceptable" or "unacceptable" political behavior, or the effects of suppression may have civic consequences later in the form of rebellion or other antisocial behavior. Personality is very much a product of socialization, and personality, as we have seen in Chapter 2, can affect political orientation and behavior.

Cognitive and Affective Components

Form and content of political socialization vary, but generally we can speak of both *cognitive* and *affective* aspects of one's political orientation. The cognitive component refers to the development of beliefs and the acquisition of knowledge about politics. A child might learn rather early in life, for example, that the United States is a "democracy," and he might develop the belief that his country is strong and powerful in relation to other nations. This kind of political learning usually occurs at the simplest role level. Perhaps later the same person will acquire a capacity for conceptual learning, and will appreciate the subtle and complex character of such terms as "democracy" and "power." In the process of learning to conceptualize, one is refining and enlarging his "cognitive map," and perhaps to some extent modifying his political orientation.

The affective side of one's political being has to do with *feelings, emotional attachments,* and judgments respecting good and bad, or right and wrong. For example, one might believe that the federal government is becoming more powerful in relation to the states. Such a belief may be neutral in that the believer reserves judgment on whether such a trend is "good." But if the holder of such a belief is either elated or discomfitted by the belief, then he is investing the belief with affect. Similarly, one might learn a simple affective response to one's country, characterized by the unexamined patriotism of "my country, right or wrong." Or, he might develop a cognitive orientation toward patriotism in which loyalty is predicated on the rationale of belief or the assurance of knowledge. The essential point here is that people learn and acquire a combination of cognitive and affective postures toward government and politics, and

[1] See David Easton and Jack Dennis, *Children in the Political System* (New York: McGraw-Hill Book Company, 1969).

that one's relationships and experiences are crucial in determining the substance and tone of his political attitudes.

Manifest and Latent Learning

In addition to the cognitive/affective distinction, the content of political socialization may differ with respect to the obviousness of its political character. Some learning has a specifically political content, such as that associated with "civics" courses, or that absorbed through some forms of political participation and media exposure. But most politically relevant learning is what we call "latent." Several scholars have examined the learning experiences, for example, that contribute to the formation of "authoritarian" or "democratic" characters, which in turn affect the nature of one's political consciousness. One scholar mentions the need in socialization research to acknowledge transference and generalization to politics from nonpolitical learning, and uses as an example the various ways in which one acquires feelings about political authority.[2]

Psychological and Political Focus

The content of learned or acquired political attitudes may vary in two additional ways. First, at the *psychological level* political attitudes may be basic—such as feelings of national loyalty—or, on the other hand, what Jennings and Niemi refer to as the "secondary and tertiary values which tend to distinguish the political behavior of individuals." We know that basic feelings of loyalty and identification are formed earliest in life, and are the kinds of political attitudes which are most resistant to change. Secondly, the *political focus* may vary, in Easton's terms, from the government, to the regime, to the political community.

Agents

There are several possible agents of socialization or political learning. Most research has been devoted to the family and the school, with some attention having been given to the way in which later socializing agents either elaborate or attenuate the influence of earlier agents. Clarke and

[2] Jack Dennis, "Major Problems of Political Socialization Research," *Midwest Journal of Political Science* 12 (1968): 85–114.

Soule in a selection below analyze the importance of an external event as an agent of socialization. The relationship between the socializing agent and the subject can be of three types, as described by Robert Lane in a study of father-son relationships several years ago:[3] there can be overt *indoctrination;* the agent provides a *social context* that helps to define appropriate political responses; and the general character of *interpersonal relations,* not overtly political, can have consequences in the development of political attitudes and orientations toward political authority.

Even though political content learned early in life is usually the most tenacious, it is still an open empirical question whether the family is the single most important socializing agent. This is not to gainsay the importance of the family. Research on the backgrounds of radical dissenters among college students, for example, has shown them to be drawn predominantly from the same kind of environments with upper-middle-class, professional, permissive parents.[4] Such students apparently find it difficult to adjust to either structured or arbitrary authority, or to restrictive social conventions with respect to personal tastes and behavior. Note, on the other hand, the finding of Jennings and Niemi: there was little correspondence between the attitudes of twelfth-graders and their parents with respect to their positions on political issues, evaluations of sociopolitical groupings, degree of political cynicism, or religious views—even though there was great similarity in the party identifications of the students and their respective parents. They suggest that the family's role is essentially to support basic orientations of loyalty and beliefs which are part of the national consensus, and to influence partisan attachment.

Since political socialization continues to develop over the life cycle it is obvious that postfamilial influences play a role. Schools inculcate a sense of national identity, and develop the habits of venerating national heroes and observing national holidays. Often the "civics" content in precollege education is noncritical and blindly laudatory of the national experience. In addition, the pattern of one's identifications in terms of socioeconomic status, religion, race, ethnicity, geographic region, and so on—affects the style and content of his political learning. Note below the significant racial and socioeconomic status differences in children's reaction to the assassination of Martin Luther King as discussed by Clarke and Soule. Yet demographic changes alone do not produce changes in behavior and reactions to political violence. As the Sears and McConahay research on the Watts riots suggests there are social-psychological changes—age and racial socialization—that mediate demographic effects and influence riot behavior.

[3] "Fathers and Sons: Foundations of Political Belief," *American Sociological Review* 24 (1959): 502–11.

[4] See generally, Kenneth Keniston, *The Uncommitted* (New York: Harcourt, Brace and World, 1965).

The three selections to follow present what we believe to be a useful synopsis on the topic of political learning. They offer perspectives on the transmission of values from family to child with a focus on orientations to such conventional political objects as parties and issues, and the impact of socialization on orientations to less conventional forms of reaction and protest.

Selected Additional Readings

Apple, Dorian. "Learning Theory and Socialization." *American Sociological Review* 16 (1951): 23–27.

Bender, Gerald. "Political Socialization and Political Change." *Western Political Quarterly* 20 (1967): 390–407.

Clausen, John A., ed. *Socialization and Society*. Boston: Little, Brown & Company, 1968.

Dawson, Richard. "Political Socialization." In ed., *Political Science Annual* I: 1–84. Edited by James Robinson. New York: Bobbs-Merrill, 1966.

Dawson, Richard, and Kenneth Prewitt. *Political Socialization*. Boston: Little, Brown & Company, 1969.

Easton, David, and Robert Hess. "The Child's Political World." *Midwest Journal of Political Science* 6 (1962): 229–46.

Easton, David, and Jack Dennis. "The Child's Acquisition of Regime Norms: Political Efficacy." *American Political Science Review* 61 (1967): 25–38.

Easton, David, and Jack Dennis. *Children in the Political System*. New York: McGraw-Hill Book Company, 1969.

Eulau, Heinz, et al. "The Political Socialization of American State Legislators." *Midwest Journal of Political Science* 3 (1959): 188–206.

Froman, Lewis A., Jr. "Personality and Political Socialization." *Journal of Politics* 23 (1961): 341–52.

Greenberg, Edward S. "Orientations of Black and White Children to Political Authority Figures." *Social Science Quarterly* 51 (1970): 561–71.

Greenberg, Edward S. "Black Children and the Political System." *Public Opinion Quarterly* 34 (1970): 333–45.

Greenstein, Fred. "The Benevolent Leader: Children's Images of Political Authority." *American Political Science Review* 54 (1960): 934–44.

Greenstein, Fred. *Children and Politics*. New Haven: Yale University Press, 1965.

Harvey, S. K., and T. G. Harvey. "Adolescent Political Outlooks: The Effects of Intelligence as an Independent Variable." *Midwest Journal of Political Science* 14 (1970): 565–95.

Hess, Robert D., and David Easton. "The Child's Changing Image of the President." *Public Opinion Quarterly* 24 (1960): 632–44.

Hess, Robert D., and Judith V. Torney. *The Development of Political Attitudes in Children*. Chicago: Aldine Publishing Company, 1967.

Hyman, Herbert. *Political Socialization*. Glencoe: The Free Press, 1959.

Jaros, Dean, Herbert Hirsch, and Frederic J. Fleron, Jr. "The Malevolent Leader: Political Socialization in an American Sub-Culture." *American Political Science Review* 62 (1968): 564–76.

Jennings, M. Kent. "Pre-Adult Orientations to Multiple Systems of Government." *Midwest Journal of Political Science* 11 (1967): 291–317.

Kornberg, Allan, and Norman Thomas. "The Political Socialization of National Legislative Elites in the United States and Canada." *Journal of Politics* 27 (1965): 761–75.

Langton, Kenneth P., and M. Kent Jennings. "Political Socialization and the High School Civics Curriculum in the United States." *American Political Science Review* 62 (1968): 868–78.

Langton, Kenneth P. *Political Socialization*. New York: Oxford University Press, 1969.

Prewitt, Kenneth, Heinz Eulau, and Betty H. Zisk. "Political Socialization and Political Roles." *Public Opinion Quarterly* 30 (1966–67): 569–82.

Rogers, Harrell R., and George Taylor. "Pre-Adult Attitudes Toward Legal Compliance: Notes Toward a Theory." *Social Science Quarterly* 51 (1970): 539–51.

Sigel, Roberta. "Image of a President: Some Insights into the Political Views of School Children." *American Political Science Review* 62 (1968): 216–26.

Sigel, Roberta, ed. *Learning About Politics: A Reader in Political Socialization*. New York: Random House, 1970.

The Transmission of Political Values

from Parent to Child

M. Kent Jennings
Richard G. Niemi

In understanding the political development of the pre-adult one of the central questions hinges on the relative and differentiated contributions of various socializing agents. The question undoubtedly proves more difficult as one traverses a range of polities from those where life and learning are almost completely wrapped up in the immediate and extended family to those which are highly complex social organisms and in which the socialization agents are extremely varied. To gain some purchase on the role of one socializing agent in our own complex society, this paper will take up the specific question of the transmission of certain values from parent to child as observed in late adolescence. After noting parent-child relationships for a variety of political values, attention will be turned to some aspects of family structure which conceivably affect the transmission flows.

I. Assessing the Family's Impact

"Foremost among agencies of socialization into politics is the family." So begins Herbert Hyman's discussion of the sources of political learning.[1] Hyman explicitly recognized the importance of other agents,

M. Kent Jennings and Richard G. Niemi, "The Transmission of Political Values from Parent to Child," *American Political Science Review* 62 (1968): 169–84. Reprinted with permission.

but he was neither the first nor the last observer to stress the preeminent position of the family. This viewpoint relies heavily on both the direct and indirect role of the family in shaping the basic orientations of offspring. Whether the child is conscious or unaware of the impact, whether the process is role-modelling or overt transmission, whether the values are political and directly usable or "nonpolitical" but transferable, and whether what is passed on lies in the cognitive or affective realm, it has been argued that the family is of paramount importance. In part this view draws heavily from psychoanalytic theory, but it is also influenced by anthropological and national character studies, and by the great emphasis on role theory in sociological studies of socialization. In part the view stems also from findings in the area of partisan commitment and electoral behavior indicating high intergenerational agreement. Unfortunately for the general thesis, such marked correlations have been only occasionally observed in other domains of political life. Indeed, other domains of political life have been rarely explored systematically with respect to the central question of articulation in parent-child political values.[2] Inferences, backward and forward extrapolations, and retrospective and projective data have carried the brunt of the argument.

A recent major report about political socialization during the elementary years seriously questions the family's overriding importance. In contrast to the previously-held views that the family was perhaps preeminent or at least co-equal to other socializing agents stands the conclusion by Robert Hess and Judith Torney that "the public school is the most important and effective instrument of political socialization in the United States," and that "the family transmits its own particular values in relatively few areas of political socialization and that, for the most part, the impact of the family is felt only as one of several socializing agents and institutions."[3] Hess and Torney see the primary influence of the family as the agent which promotes early attachment to country and government, and which thus "insures the stability of basic institutions."[4] Hence, "the family's primary effect is to support consensually-held attitudes rather than to inculcate idosyncratic attitudes."[5] The major exception to these conclusions occurs in the area of partisanship and related matters where the family's impact is predictably high.

The Hess and Torney argument thus represents a major departure from the more traditional view. They see the family's influence as age-specific and restricted in its scope. In effect, the restriction of the family's role removes its impact from much of the dynamic qualities of the political system and from individual differences in political behavior. The consensual qualities imparted or reinforced by the family, while vital for comprehending the maintenance of the system, are less useful in explaining adjustments in the system, the conflicts and accommodations made, the varied reactions to political stimuli, and the playing of diverse political roles. In short, if the family's influence is restricted to inculcating a few consensual attributes (plus partisan attachment), it means that much of the socialization which results in individual differentiation in everyday politics and which effects changes in the functioning of the political system lies outside the causal nexus of the parent-child relationship.

The first and primary objective of the present article will be to assay the flow of certain political values from parent to child. Our attention will be directed toward examining the variation in the distributions of the offsprings' values as a function of the distribution of these same values among their parents. This is not to say that other attitudinal and behavioral attributes of the parents are unimportant in shaping the child's political orientations. For example, children may develop authoritarian or politically distrustful attitudes not because their parents are authoritarian or distrustful but because of other variables such as disciplinary and protection practices.[6] Such transformations, while perhaps quite significant, will not be treated here. Rather, we will observe the degree to which the shape of value distributions in the child corresponds to that of his parent. Most of the values explored do not reflect the basic feelings of attachment to the political system which supposedly originate in the early years,[7] but much more of the secondary and tertiary values which tend to distinguish the political behavior of individuals and which contribute to the dynamics of the system.

Study Design

The data to be employed come from a study conducted by the Survey Research Center of the University of Michigan in the spring of 1965. Interviews were held with a national probability sample of 1669 seniors distributed among 97 secondary schools, public and nonpublic.[8] The response rate for students was 99 percent. For a random third of the students the father was designated for interviewing, for another random third the mother was designated, and for the other third both parents were assigned. In the permanent absence of the designated parent, the other parent or parent surrogate was interviewed. Interviews were actually completed with at least one parent of 94 percent of the students, and with both parents of 26 percent of the students, or 1992 parents altogether. Among parents the response rate was 93 percent.[9] Two features of the student and parent samples should be underscored. First, since the sample of students was drawn from a universe of 12th graders, school drop-outs in that age cohort, estimated at around 26 percent for this time period, were automatically eliminated. Second, due mainly to the fact that more mothers than fathers constitute the head of household in single-parent families, the sample of parents is composed of 56 percent mothers.[10]

Our basic procedure will be to match the parent and student samples so that parent-student pairs are formed. Although the actual number of students for whom we have at least one parent respondent is 1562, the base number of pairs used in the analysis is 1992. In order to make maximum usage of the interviews gathered, the paired cases in which both the mother and father were interviewed (430) are each given half of their full value.[11] A further adjustment in weighting, due to unavoidably imprecise estimates at the time the sampling frame was constructed, results in a weighted total of 1927 parent-student pairs.[12]

Using 12th graders for exploring the parental transmission of political values carries some distinct characteristics. In the first place, most of these pre-adults are approaching the point at which they will leave the immediate family. Further political training from the parents will be minimal. A second feature is that the formal civic education efforts of society, as carried out in the elementary and secondary schools, are virtually completed. For whatever effect they may have on shaping the cognitive and cathectic maps of individuals, these various formal and informal modes of citizenship preparation will generally terminate, although other forms of educational preparation may lie ahead, especially for the college bound. A final consideration is that while the family and the educational system have come to some terminal point as socializing agents, the pre-adult has yet to be much affected by actual political practice. Neither have other potentially important experiences, such as the establishment of his own nuclear family and an occupational role, had an opportunity to exert their effects. Thus the 12th grader is at a significant juncture in his political life cycle and it will be instructive to see the symmetry of parental and student values at this juncture.

Adolescent Rebellion

It should be emphasized that we are not necessarily searching for patterns of political rebellion from parental values. Researchers have been hard-pressed to uncover any significant evidence of adolescent rebellion in the realm of political affairs.[13] Pre-adults may differ politically from their parents—particularly during the college years—but there is scant evidence that the rebellion pattern accounts for much of this deviance. Data from our own study lend little support to the rebellion hypotheses at the level of student recognition. For example, even of the 38 percent of the student sample reporting important disagreements with their parents less than 15 percent placed these disagreements in a broadly-defined arena of political and social phenomena. And these disagreements do not necessarily lie in the province of rebellion, as one ordinarily construes the term.

There is, furthermore, some question as to whether adolescent rebellion as such occurs with anything approaching the frequency or magnitude encountered in sociological writings and the popular literature. As two scholars concluded after a major survey of the literature dealing with "normal" populations:

> In the large scale studies of normal populations, we do not find adolescents clamoring for freedom or for release from unjust constraint. We do not find rebellious resistance to authority as a dominant theme. For the most part, the evidence bespeaks a modal pattern considerably more peaceful than much theory and most social comment would lead us to expect. 'Rebellious youth' and 'the conflict between generations' are phrases that ring; but, so far as we can tell, it is not the ring of truth they carry so much as the beguiling but misleading tone of drama.[14]

To say that rebellion directed toward the political orientations of the parents is relatively rare is not to say, however, that parent and student values are consonant. Discrepancies can occur for a variety of reasons, including the following: (1) Students may consciously opt for values, adopted from other agents, in conflict with those of their parents without falling into the rebellion syndrome. (2) Much more probable are discrepancies which are recognized neither by the parent nor the offspring.[15] The lack of cue-giving and object saliency on the part of parents sets up ambiguous or empty psychological spaces which may be filled by other agents in the student's environment. (3) Where values are unstable and have low centrality in a belief system, essentially random and time-specific responses to stimuli may result in apparent low transmission rates. (4) Another source of dissonant relationships, and potentially the most confounding one, is that life cycle effects are operative. When the pre-adult reaches the current age of his parents, his political behavior might well be similar to that of his parents even though his youthful attitudes would not suggest such congruency. This is an especially thorny empirical question and nests in the larger quandry concerning the later life effects of early socialization.

II. Patterns of Parent-Child Correspondences

Confronted with a number of political values at hand we have struck for variety rather than any necessary hierarchy of importance. We hypothesized a range of correlations dependent in part on the play of factors assumed to alter the parent-student associations (noted above). We have purposely deleted values dealing with participative orientations and, as noted previously, those delving into sentiments of basic attachment and loyalty to the regime. The values selected include party identification, attitudinal positions on four specific issues, evaluations of sociopolitical groupings, and political cynicism. For comparative purposes we shall glance briefly at parent-student congruences in the religious sphere.

To measure agreement between parents and students we rely primarily on correlations, either of the product-moment or rank-order variety. While the obvious alternative of percentage agreement may have an intuitive appeal, it has several drawbacks. Percentage agreement is not based on the total configuration of a square matrix but only on the "main diagonal." Thus two tables which are similar in percentage agreement may represent widely differing

amounts of agreement if deviations from perfect agreement are considered. Moreover, percentage agreement depends heavily on the number of categories used, so that the degree of parent-student similarity might vary for totally artificial reasons. Correlations are more resistant to changes in the definition of categories. Finally, correlations are based on relative rankings (and intervals in the case of product-moment correlations) rather than on absolute agreement as percentage agreement usually is. That is, if student scores tend to be higher (or lower) than parent scores on a particular variable, but the students are ranked similarly to their parents, a high correlation may be obtained with very little perfect agreement.

Party Identification

Previous research has established party identification as a value dimension of considerable importance in the study of political behavior as well as a political value readily transmitted from parents to children. Studies of parent-youth samples as well as adult populations indicate that throughout the life cycle there is a relatively high degree of correspondence between respondents' party loyalties and their parents'. Our findings are generally consistent with those of these earlier studies.

The substantial agreement between parent and student party affiliations is indicated by a tau-b (also called tau-beta) correlation of .47, a statistic nearly unaffected by the use of three, five, or all seven categories of the party identification spectrum generated by the question sequence.[16] The magnitude of this statistic reflects the twin facts of the presence of a large amount of exact agreement and the absence of many wide differences between students and parents. When the full 7×7 matrix of parent-student party loyalties is arrayed (Table 1), the cells in which parents and students are in unison account for a third of the cases. The cells representing maximum disagreement are very nearly empty. Despite our earlier contention, collapsing categories and considering percentage agreement in the resulting table does make

Table 1
Student-Parent Party Identification

Parents	Strong Dem.	Weak Dem.	Ind. Dem.	Ind.	Ind. Rep.	Weak Rep.	Strong Rep.	Total
				Students				*Total*
Party Identification								
Strong Dem.	9.7%	8.0	3.4	1.8	.5	.9	.5	24.7%
Weak Dem.	5.8	9.0	4.2	2.6	.7	1.6	.7	24.7
		(32.6)[a]		(13.2)		(3.6)		(49.4)
Ind. Dem.	1.6	2.1	2.1	1.7	.8	.7	.2	9.3
Ind. Ind.	1.1	1.6	1.6	2.7	1.2	.9	.5	9.7
Ind. Rep.	.1	.5	.8	.9	.9	1.3	.5	4.9
		(7.0)		(12.7)		(4.1)		(23.9)
Weak Rep.	.3	2.1	1.6	2.3	1.9	5.0	1.9	15.0
Strong Rep.	.2	.9	.8	.8	2.4	3.3	3.5	11.7
		(3.4)		(9.7)		(13.6)		(26.7)
Total	18.8%	24.2	14.5	12.8	8.4	13.6	7.7	100.0%
		(43.0)		(35.7)		(21.3)		
			tau-b = .47				N = 1852	

[a] The full 7 × 7 table is provided because of the considerable interest in party identification. For some purposes, reading ease among them, the 3 × 3 table is useful. It is given by the figures in parentheses; these figures are (within rounding error) the sum of the numbers just above them.

good substantive sense with regard to party identification. In this instance the collapsed categories have a meaning beyond just broader segments of a continuum, and are associated with a general orientation toward one party or the other or toward a neutral position between them. Thus arrayed, 59 percent of the students fall into the same broad category as their parents, and only *seven* percent cross the sharp divide between Republicans and Democrats.

The observed similarity between parents and students suggests that transmission of party preferences from one generation to the next is carried out rather successfully in the American context. However, there are also indications that other factors (temporarily at least) have weakened the party affiliations of the younger generation. This is most obvious if we compare the marginal totals for parents and students (Table 1). The student sample contains almost 12 percent more Independents than the parent sample, drawing almost equally on the Republican and Democratic proportions of the sample. Similarly, among party identifiers a somewhat larger segment of the students is but weakly inclined toward the chosen party. Nor are these configurations simply an artifact of the restricted nature of the parent sample, since the distribution of party identification among the parents resembles closely that of the entire adult electorate as observed in November, 1964 (SRC 1964 election study).

A number of factors might account for the lesser partisanship of the students, and we have only begun to explore some of them. On the one hand, the students simply lack their parents' long experience in the active electorate, and as a consequence have failed as yet to develop a similar depth of feeling about the parties.[17] On the other hand, there are no doubt specific forces pushing students toward Independence. The experience of an ever-widening environment and the gradual withdrawal of parental power may encourage some students to adopt an Independent outlook. The efforts of schools and of teachers in particular are probably weighted in the same direction. If these forces are at work, high school students may be gradually withdrawing from an earlier position of more overt partisanship. But, whatever the exact nature of the causes, they clearly draw off from the partisan camp a small but significant portion of the population as it approaches full citizenship.

Opinions on Specific Issues

One way in which political values are expressed is through opinions on specific issues. However, as Converse has shown, many opinions or idea elements not only tend to be bounded by systems of low constraint but are also quite unstable over relatively short periods of time among mass publics.[18] Hence in comparing student responses with parent responses the problem of measurement may be compounded by attitude instability among both samples. Rather than being a handicap instabilities actually sharpen the test of whether significant parent-to-child flows occur. One would not expect unstable sentiments to be the object of any considerable political learning in the family. It seems unlikely that many cues would be given off over matters about which the parents were unsure or held a fluctuating opinion. Even in the event of numerous cues in unstable situations, the ambivalent or ambiguous nature of such cues would presumably yield instability in the child. In either case the articulation between parent and child beliefs would be tempered.

We have selected four specific issues for examination. Two involve public schools; given the populations being studied, schools are particularly relevant

attitude objects. Furthermore these two issues envelope topics of dramatic interest to much of the public—integration in the schools and the use of prayers in schools. After an initial screening question weeded out those without any interest at all on the issues, the respondents were asked if they thought the government in Washington should "see to it that white and Negro children go to the same schools" or if the government should "stay out of this area as it is none of its business." On the prayers in school question the respondents were asked if they believed "schools should be allowed to start each day with a prayer" or that "religion does not belong in the schools."[19] Taken in the aggregate the high school seniors proved less likely to sanction prayers in school than did the parents (although a majority of both answered in the affirmative) and more willing to see the federal government enforce segregation than were the adults (with both yielding majorities in favor). These differences are moderate; no more than 14 percentage points separate like-paired marginals on the prayer issue and no more than 10 points on the integration issue. The cross-tabulation of parent and student responses produces moderately strong coefficients, as shown in the first two entries of Table 2.

Table 2
Correlations between Parent-Student Attitudes on Four Issues

Federal government's role in integrating the schools	.34[a]
Whether schools should be allowed to use prayers	.29
Legally elected Communist should be allowed to take office	.13
Speakers against churches and religion should be allowed	.05

[a]Each of the correlations (tau-b) in this table is based on at least 1560 cases.

Combining as they do some very visible population groupings along with topics of more than usual prominence in the mass media and local communities, it would be surprising if there were not at least a moderate amount of parent-student overlap. The wonder is not that the correlations are this high, but rather that they are not higher. If correlations no higher than this are produced on issues which touch both generations in a manner which many issues assuredly do not, then one would speculate that more remote and abstract issues would generate even less powerful associations.

This hypothesizing is borne out by the introduction of two other issues. Both parents and students were asked to agree or disagree with these two statements: "If a Communist were legally elected to some public office around here, the people should allow him to take office"; and "If a person wanted to make a speech in this community against churches and religion, he should be allowed to speak." In general, the pre-adults took a slightly more libertarian stance on the two issues than did the parents, but the differences in any of the like-paired marginals do not exceed 14 percent. These similarities mask extremely tenuous positive correlations, however, as the second pair of items in Table 2 reveals.

These two issues carry neither the immediacy nor the concreteness which may be said to characterize the two issues dealing with integration and prayers in the schools. Indeed, one might question whether the two statements represent issues at all, as the public normally conceives of issues. At any rate it is improbable that the students are reflecting much in the way of cues emitted from their parents, simply because these topics or related ones are hardly prime candidates for dinner-table conversation or inadvertent cue-giving. Nor do they tap some rather basic sentiments and attitude objects which permeate the integration and prayers issues. Such sentiments are more likely to be embedded in the expressive value structure of the parents than are those having to do with some of the more abstract "fundamental" tenets of democracy as exemplified in the free speech and right to take office issues. That adults themselves have low levels of constraint involving propositions about such fundamental tenets has been demonstrated by McClosky, and Prothro and Grigg.[20] Given this environment, the lower correlation for the two more abstract propositions is predictable.

Although the issues we have examined by no means exhaust the variety of policy questions one might

pose, they probably exemplify the range of parent-student correspondences to be found in the populace. On all but consensual topics—which would perforce assume similar distributions among virtually all population strata anyway—the parent-student correlations obtained for the integration and prayer issues probably approach the apex. In part this may be due to unstable opinions and in part to the effects of agents other than the family. It is also possible that the children will exhibit greater correspondences to their parents later in the life cycle. But for this particular point in time, the articulation of political opinions is only moderately strong on salient, concrete issues and virtually nil on more abstract issues.

Evaluations of Socio-Political Groupings

Collectivities of people which are distinguished by certain physical, locational, social, religious, and membership characteristics (the list is obviously not exhaustive) often come to serve as significant political reference groups for individuals. While distinguishable groups may carry affective neutrality, it seems to be in the nature of mass behavior that these groups most often come to be viewed with greater or lesser esteem. The intersection of group evaluations and the political process comes when claims or demands are made by or upon significant portions of such groupings. The civil rights movement of the past decade is perhaps the most striking contemporary example. As Converse has suggested, social groupings are likely to have greater centrality for mass publics than abstract idea elements per se.[21] Thus when particular issues and public policies become imbued with group-related properties, the issues acquire considerably more structure and concreteness for the mass public than would be the normal case.

To what extent is the family crucial in shaping the evaluations of social groupings and thus—at a further remove—the interpretation of questions of public policy? Some insight into this may be gained by comparing the ratings applied by the parents and students to eight socio-political groupings. While the groups all carry rather easily recognized labels, they do differ in terms of their relative visibility and their inclusive-exclusive properties. They include Protestants, Catholics, Jews, Negroes, Whites, Labor Unions, Big Business, and Southerners.

To measure the attitudes toward these groups, an instrument dubbed the "feeling thermometer" was used. The technique was designed to register respondents' feelings toward a group on a scale ranging from a cold 0 to a warm 100. In the analysis we will treat this scale as interval level measurement. We have also examined the data using contingency tables and ordinal statistics; our conclusions are the same regardless of the method used.

Turning first to the mean ratings, given in Table 3, we find a striking similarity in student and parent aggregate scores. The largest difference is five points and the average difference is only 2.2 points. Additionally, the standard deviations for the two samples (not shown) are extremely similar across all groupings. Nor were there significant tendencies for one sample to employ more than the other the option of "unawareness" or "no feelings" (a reading of 50 on the thermometer) about the groupings. Moreover, the aggregate differences which do occur are not immediately explicable. For example, students rate Southerners slightly lower than parents, as we expected, but the difference in ratings of Negroes is negligible, which was unanticipated. Students rate Whites and Protestants somewhat lower than parents. This is not matched, however, by higher evaluations of the minority groups—Jews, for example.

Given these extraordinarily congruent patterns it is rather startling to see that they are patently not due to uniform scores of parent-child pairs. As shown in Table 3, the highest correlation between the parent and student ratings is .36 and the coefficients range as low as .12. Even the highest correlation is well below that found for party identification (where the product-moment coefficient was .59 for the sevenfold classification), and for several groupings the relationships between parent and student scores are

Table 3

Correlations between Parent-Student Group Evaluations

Group Evaluated	Parent-Student Correlations	Mean Ratings	
		Parent	Student
Catholics	.36[a]	72	70
Southerners	.30	66	62
Labor Unions	.28	60	60
Negroes	.26	67	69
Jews	.22	67	63
Whites	.19	84	83
Protestants	.15	84	79
Big Business	.12	64	63

[a] Each of the product-moment correlations in this table is based on at least 1880 cases. The corresponding tau-b's are (top to bottom) .28, .22, .22, .20, .18, .19, .13, .08.

very feeble. If the child's view of socio-political groupings grows out of cue-giving in the home, the magnitude of the associations should exceed those observed here.

It is beyond the task of this paper to unravel thoroughly these findings. The range of correlations does provide a clue as to the conditions under which parent-student correspondences will be heightened. In the first place the three categories producing the lowest correlations appear to have little socio-political relevancy in the group sense. Whites and Protestants are extremely inclusive categories and, among large sectors of the public, may simply not be cognized or treated in everyday life as groupings highly differentiated from society in general. They are, in a sense, too enveloping to be taken as differentiated attitude objects. If they do not serve as significant attitude objects, the likelihood of parent to child transmission would be dampened. In the third case—Big Business—it seems likely that its visibility is too low to be cognized as a group qua group.

As the parent-student correlations increase we notice that the groupings come to have not only highly distinguishable properties but that they also have high visibility in contemporary American society. Adding to the socio-political saliency thereby induced is the fact that group membership may act to increase the parent-student correlations. One would hypothesize that parent-student pairs falling into a distinguishable, visible grouping would exhibit higher correlations in rating that same grouping than would nonmembers. Taking the four groupings for whom the highest correlations were obtained, we divided the pairs into those where both the parent and the child—except in the case of labor unions—were enveloped by the groupings versus those outside the groupings. Although none of the hypothesized relationships was contravened, only the coefficients for evaluations of Southerners provided a distinct demarcation between members and nonmembers (tau-b = .25 for Southern pairs, .14 for non-Southerners). It is quite possible that measures capturing membership identification and intensities would improve upon these relationships.

As with opinions on specific issues, intrapair correlations on group evaluations are at best moderately positive, and they vary appreciably as a result of sociopolitical visibility and, to a small degree, group membership characteristics. What we begin to discern, then, is a pattern of congruences which peak only over relatively concrete, salient values susceptible to repeated reinforcement in the family (and elsewhere, perhaps), as in party identification and in certain issues and group evaluations. It is conceivable that these results will not prevail if we advance from fairly narrow measures like the ones previously employed to more global value structures. We now turn to an illustrative example. It so happens that it also provides an instance of marked aggregate differences between the two generations.

Political Cynicism

Political cynicism and its mirror image, trust, offer an interesting contrast to other variables we are considering. Rather than referring to specific political issues or actors, cynicism is a basic orientation toward political actors and activity. Found empirically to be negatively related to political participation, political cynicism has also been found to be positively correlated with measures of a generally distrustful outlook

(personal cynicism).[22] Political cynicism appears to be a manifestation of a deep-seated suspicion of others' motives and actions. Thus this attitude comes closer than the rest of our values to tapping a basic psychopolitical predisposition.

Previous research with young children suggests that sweeping judgments, such as the essential goodness of human nature, are formed early in life, often before cognitive development and information acquisition make the evaluated objects intelligible. Greenstein, and Hess and Easton, have reported this phenomenon with regard to feelings about authority figures; Hess and Torney suggest similar conclusions about loyalty and attachment to government and country.[23] Evaluative judgments and affective ties have been found among the youngest samples for which question and answer techniques are feasible. This leads to the conclusions that the school, mass media, and peer groups have had little time to influence these attitudes.

It seems to follow that the family is the repository from which these feelings are initially drawn. Either directly by their words and deeds or indirectly through unconscious means, parents transmit to their children basic postures toward life which the children carry with them at least until the development of their own critical faculties. Although our 12th graders have been exposed to a number of influences which could mitigate the initial implanting, one should expect, according to the model, a rather strong correspondence between parent and student degrees of political cynicism.

To assess the cynicism of parents and students, a Guttman scale was constructed from five questions asked of both samples. All questions dealt with the conduct of the national government.[24] In each sample the items formed a scale, with coefficients of reproducibility of .93 and .92 for parents and students, respectively. The aggregate scores reflect a remarkably lesser amount of cynicism among students than among parents. This is apparent in the marginal distributions in Table 4, which show the weight of the parent distributions falling much much more on the cynical end of the scale. Similarly, while a fifth of the students were more cynical than their parents, three times

Table 4
Relationship between Parent-Student Scores on
the Cynicism Scale

| | Students | | | | | | | |
| | Least Cynical | | | Most Cynical | | | Row Totals | Marginal Total[a] |
Parents	1	2	3	4	5	6		
Least Cynical — 1	25%	27	33	13	1	2	101%	8%
2	19	28	38	9	1	5	100	12
3	18	28	37	10	3	4	100	33
4	16	23	41	13	3	4	100	17
5	15	19	35	19	3	9	100	9
Most Cynical — 6	12	22	36	18	4	8	100	21
Marginal Totals[a]	17%	25	37	13	3	5		100%

tau-b = .12   N = 1869

[a] Marginal totals show the aggregate scaler patterns for each sample.

this number of parents were more cynical than their children. The students may be retreating from an even more trusting attitude held earlier, but compared to their parents they still see little to be cynical about in national political activity.

Here is a case where the impact of other socialization agents — notably the school — looms large. The thrust of school experience is undoubtedly on the side of developing trust in the political system in general. Civic training in school abounds in rituals of system support in the formal curriculum. These rituals and curricula are not matched by a critical examination of the nation's shortcomings or the possible virtues of other political forms. Coupled with a moralistic, legalistic, prescriptive orientation to the study of government is the avoidance of conflict dimensions and controversial issues.[25] A direct encounter with the realities of political life is thus averted or at least postponed. It would not be surprising, then, to find a rather sharp rise in the level of cynicism as high school seniors move ahead in a few years into the adult world.

Students on the whole are less cynical than parents; relative to other students, though, those with distrustful, hostile parents should themselves be more suspicious of the government, while those with trusting parents should find less ground for cynicism. Against the backdrop of our discussion, it is remarkable how low the correspondence is among parent-student pairs. Aside from faint markings at the extremities, students' scores are very nearly independent of their parents' attitudes (Table 4). The cynicism of distrustful parents is infrequently implanted in their children, while a smaller group of students develops a cynical outlook despite their parents' views. Political cynicism as measured here is not a value often passed from parent to child. Regardless of parental feelings, children develop a moderately to highly positive view of the trustworthiness of the national government and its officials.

These findings do not mean that parents fail to express negative evaluations in family interaction nor that children fail to adopt some of the less favorable attitudes of their parents. What is apparently not transmitted is a *generalized* cynicism about politics. Thus while warmth or hostility toward specific political objects with high visibility may be motivated by parental attitudes, a more pervasive type of belief system labelled cynicism is apparently subject to heavy, undercutting influences outside the family nexus. These influences are still operative as the adolescent approaches adult status.

Working with another encompassing set of values we encountered much the same patterns as with cynicism. After obtaining their rank orderings of interest in international, national, state, and local political matters the respondents were allocated along a 7–point scale of cosmopolitanism-localism through an adaptation of Coombs' unfolding technique.[26] On the whole the students are considerably more cosmopolitan than the parents, and the paired correlation is a modest .17. Both life cycle and generational effects are undoubtedly at work here,[27] but the central point is that the students' orientations only mildly echo those of their parents.

What results from juxtaposing parents and their children on these two measures of cynicism and cosmopolitanism-localism is the suspicion that more global orientations to political life do not yield parent-student correspondences of greater magnitude than on more specific matters. If anything, the opposite is true—at least with respect to certain specifics. It may be that the child acquires a minimal set of basic commitments to the system and a way of handling authority situations as a result of early experiences in the family circle. But it appears also that this is a foundation from which arise widely diverse value structures, and that parental values are an extremely variable and often feeble guide as to what the pre-adult's values will be.

Religious Beliefs

Up to this point we have traversed a range of political and quasi-political values, and have witnessed varying, but generally modest degrees of parent-student correspondences. To what extent does this pattern also characterize other domains of social values? For comparative purposes we can inject a consideration of religious beliefs. Like party preference, church affiliation among pre-adults is believed to be largely the same as parental affiliation. Such proves to be the case among our respondents. Of all parent-student pairs 74 percent expressed the same denominational preference. That this percentage is higher than the agreement on the three-fold classification of party identification (Democrat, Republican, Independent) by some 15 percent suggests that by the time the pre-adult is preparing to leave the family circle he has internalized the church preference of his parents to a moderately greater extent than their party preference.

There are some perfectly valid reasons for this margin. To a much greater extent than party preference, church preference is likely to be reinforced in a number of ways. Assuming attendance, the child will usually go to the same church throughout childhood; the behavior is repeated at frequent intervals; it is a practice engaged in by greater or lesser portions of the entire family and thus carries multiple role-models; formal membership is often involved; conflicting claims from other sources in the environment for a change of preference are minimal except, per-

haps, as a result of dating patterns. Religious affiliation is also often imbued with a fervid commitment.

In contrast, party preference is something which the child himself cannot transform into behavior except in rather superficial ways; reinforcement tends to be episodic and varies according to the election calendar; while the party preference of parents may vary only marginally over the pre-adult years, voting behavior fluctuates more and thus sets up ambiguous signals for the child; other sources in the environment—most noticeably the mass media—may make direct and indirect appeals for the child's loyalty which conflict with the parental attachments. Given the factors facilitating intrafamilial similarities in church preference, and the absence of at least some of these factors in the party dimension, it is perhaps remarkable that cogruity of party identification approaches the zone of church-preference congruity.

We found that when we skipped from party identification to other sorts of political values the parent-student correlations decreased perceptibly. May we expect to encounter similar behavior in the realm of religious values? One piece of evidence indicates that this is indeed the case. Respondents were confronted with a series of four statements having to do with the literal and divine nature of the Bible, ranging from a description of the Bible as "God's word and all it says is true" to a statement denying the contemporary utility of the book.

Both students and parents tended to view the Bible with awe, the parents slightly more so than the students. But the correlation (tau-beta) among parent-student pairs is only a moderately strong .30. As with political values, once the subject matter moves out from central basic identification patterns the transmission of parental values fades.[28] And, as with political values, this may be a function of instability—although this seems less likely for the rendering of the Bible—the impingement of other agents—particularly likely in this case—or the relative absence of cue-giving on the part of the parents. The more generalizable proposition emerging from a comparison of political and religious orientations is that the correlations obtained diminish when the less concrete value orientations are studied.

III. Family Characteristics and Transmission Patterns

We have found that the transmission of political values from parent to child varies remarkably according to the nature of the value. Although the central tendencies lie on the low side, we may encounter systematic variations in the degree to which values are successfully transmitted according to certain properties of family structure. That is, whether the transmittal be conscious and deliberate or unpurposive and indirect, are there some characteristics of the family unit which abet or inhibit the child's acquisition of parental values? We shall restrict ourselves to a limited set of variables having theoretical interest.

In order to dissect the parent-student relationships by controlling for a variety of independent variables, we shall retain the full parent-student matrices and then observe correlations within categories of the control variables.[29] The political values to be examined include party identification, political cynicism, political cosmopolitanism, four specific political issues, and the ratings assigned to three minority population groupings—Catholics, Negroes, and Jews. This makes ten variables altogether, but for some purposes the issues and the group ratings are combined into composite figures.

Parent and Student Sex Combinations

Various studies of adolescents have illustrated the discriminations which controls for sex of parent and sex of child may produce in studying the family unit.[30] Typically these studies have dealt with self-development, adjustment problems, motivational patterns, and the like. The question remains whether these discriminations are also found in the transmission of political values.

Part of the common lore of American political behavior is that the male is more dominant in political matters than the female, in his role both of husband and of father. And among pre-adults, males are usually found to be more politicized than females. While our findings do not necessarily challenge these statements, they do indicate the meager utility of sex roles in explaining parent-student agreement. The correlations between parent-student values show some variation among the four combinations of parent and student sex, but the differences are usually small and inconsistent across the several values. Of the sixty possible comparisons for the ten political variables (i.e., $\binom{4}{2} = 6$ pairs of correlations for each variable), only eight produce differences in the correlations greater than .10, and thirty-three fall within a difference of less than .05. The average parent-student correlations for these variables are: Mother-Son, .22; Mother-Daughter, .24; Father-Son, .20; Father-Daughter, .22. Thus the values of the father are not more likely to be internalized than those of the mother; nor do sons register consistently different rates of agreement than daughters. Finally, the particular sex mix of parent and child makes little difference. We also found that the use of sex combinations as controls on other bivariate relationships usually resulted in minor and fluctuating differences. Whatever family characteristics affect differential rates of value transmission, they are only marginally represented by sex roles in the family.

Affectivity and Control Relationship

Another set of family characteristics employed with considerable success in studies of the family and child development has to do with the dimension of power or control on the one hand, and the dimension of attachment or affectivity on the other.[31] One salient conclusion has been that children are more apt to use their parents as role models where the authority structure is neither extremely permissive nor extremely autocratic and where strong (but not overprotective) supportive functions and positive affects are present.

Although these dimensions have been employed in various ways in assessing the socialization of the child, they have rarely been utilized in looking at value transmission per se. In the nearest approach to this in political socialization studies, college students' reports suggested that perceived ideological differences between parent and child were higher when there was emotional estrangement, when the parental discipline was perceived as either too high or too low, and when the parent was believed to be interested in politics.[32] Somewhat related findings support the idea that affective and power relationships between parent and child may affect the transferral of political orientations.[33]

Affectivity and control relationships between preadults and their parents were operationalized in a number of ways, too numerous to give in detail. Suffice it to say that both parent and offspring were queried as to how close they felt to each other, whether and over what they disagreed, the path of compatibilities over the past few years, punishment agents, perceived level of parental control, parent and student satisfaction with controls, the nature and frequency of grievance processing, and rule-making procedures.

In accordance with the drift of previous research we hypothesized that the closer the student felt to his parent the more susceptible he would be to adopting, either through formal or informal learning, the political values of the parent. This turned out to be untrue. The closeness of parents and children, taking either the parent's report or the child's report, accounts for little variation in the parent-student correlations. This is true whether closeness to mother or father is considered and regardless of the student's sex. Similarly, other measures of affective relationships give little evidence that this dimension prompted much variation in the correlations among pairs.

Turning to the power relationships between parent and child we hypothesized two types of relationships: (1) the more "democratic" and permissive these relationships were the greater congruency there would

be; and (2) the more satisfied the child was with the power relationships the greater would be the congruency. Where patterning appears it tends to support the first hypothesis. For example, those students avowing they have an "average" amount of autonomy agree slightly more often with their parents than do those left primarily to their own resources and those heavily monitored by their parents. More generally, however, the power configuration—either in terms of its structure or its appraised satisfactoriness—generated few significant and consistent differences. This proved true whether we relied on the parent's account or the student's.

As with sex roles, the affective and control dimensions possess weak explanatory power when laid against parent-to-student transmission patterns. In neither case does this mean that these characteristics are unimportant for the political socialization of the young. It does mean that they are of little help in trying to account for the differential patterns of parent-student congruences.

Levels of Politicization

Another set of family characteristics concerns the saliency and cue-giving structure of political matters within the family. One would expect parents for whom politics is more salient to emit more cues, both direct and indirect. Other things being equal, the transmission of political values would vary with the saliency and overt manifestations of political matters. Cue-giving would structure the political orientations of the child and, in the absence of rebellion, bolster parent-student correspondences. The absence of cue-giving would probably inject considerable instability and ambiguity in the child's value structure. At the same time this absence would invite the injection of other socializing agents whose content and direction might vary with parental values. In either event parental-offspring value correspondences should be reduced in the case of lower political saliency and cue-giving.

Turning to the data, it is evident that while the

hypothesis receives some support for party identification and political cynicism, it does not hold generally. Illustratively, Table 6 provides the parent-student correlations for party identification, cynicism, cosmopolitanism, averaged group evaluations, and two pairs of issues. The two politicization measures capture different elements of family politicization—the extent of husband-wife conversations about politics (reported by parents) and the frequency of student-parent conversations related to political affairs (reported by students). The correspondence between parent and student cynicism is mildly related to both of these measures, while party identification is clearly affected by parental conversations, but not by student-parent political discussions. The other opinions and values show no consistent relationships with either measure of politicization. Similar results were obtained when politicization was measured by the general political interest among parents and students, parent-student disagreements regarding political and social matters, and parents' participation in political campaigns.

That the level of family politicization affects somewhat the flow of party identification and cynicism but is unrelated to the transmission of other variables should not be ignored. The extremely salient character of party loyalties, which results in the higher overall parent-student correlation, and the summary nature of the cynicism variable suggest characteristics that may determine the relevancy of family politicization for the transmission of political values. The essential point, though, is that the level of politicization does not uniformly affect the degree of parent-student correspondence. Students with highly politicized backgrounds do not necessarily resemble their parents more closely than students from unpoliticized families. Whether it is measured in terms of student or parent responses, taps spectator fascination with or active engagement in politics, or denotes individual-level or family-level properties varying amounts of politicization do not uniformly or heavily alter the level of correspondence between parent and offspring values.[34]

Since our findings are mostly on the null side, it is

Table 6
Family Politicization and Parent-Student Agreement on a Range of Political Values[a]

Frequency of:	Party Identification	Political Cynicism	Cosmopolitanism-Localism	Group Ratings[b]	Prayer and Integration Issues[c]	Freedom Issues[c]
Husband-Wife Political Conversations						
Very often	.54	.19	.22	.20	.36	.13
Pretty often	.49	.15	.11	.20	.30	.10
Not very often	.45	.11	.14	.24	.28	.06
Don't talk	.32	.08	.22	.23	.32	.08
Student-Parent Political Conversations						
Several times/week	.49	.16	.17	.22	.32	.08
Few times/month	.45	.12	.16	.21	.35	.14
Few times/year	.41	.10	.18	.30	.18	−.05
Don't talk	.47	.02	.12	.20	.26	.06

[a] Each tau-b correlation in this table is based on at least 82 cases.
[b] Average ratings of Negroes, Catholics, and Jews on the "feeling thermometer."
[c] See p. 168 for a description of these issues.

important to consider the possibility that interaction effects confound the relationship between family characteristics and transmission patterns. Previous work suggests that affectivity and power relations in the family will be related to parent-child transmission primarily among highly politicized families. Only if politics is important to the parents will acceptance or rejection of parental values be affected by the parent-child relationship. In order to test this hypothesis, student-parent agreement was observed, controlling for family politicization and affectivity or power relations simultaneously. No strong interaction effects emerge from this analysis. The affectivity and power dimensions sometimes affect only the highly politicized, sometimes the most unpoliticized, and at other times their effect is not at all dependent on the level of politicization.[35] The lack of impressive bivariate relationships between family characteristics and the transmission rate of political values is not due to the confounding influence of multiple effects within the family.

With hindsight, reasons for the failure of the hypothesized relationships bearing on family structure can be suggested. But to give a clear and thorough explanation and test alternative hypotheses will be difficult and time-consuming. One exploratory avenue, for example, brings in student perceptions of parental attitudes as an intervening variable. Another is concerned with the relative homogeneity of the environment for children of highly politicized backgrounds versus youngsters from unpoliticized families. A third possibility is the existence of differential patterns of political learning and, in particular, a differential impact of the various socializing agents on children from politically rich versus those from politically barren backgrounds.[36] It is also possible that knowledge about later political development of the students would help explicate these perplexing configurations.

IV. A Concluding Note

In our opening remarks we noted the conflicting views regarding the importance of the family as an agent of political learning for the child. This paper has been primarily concerned with a fairly narrow aspect of this question. We sought evidence indicating that a variety of political values held by pre-adults were induced by the values of their parents. Thus our test has been rather stringent. It has not examined the relative impact of the family vis-à-vis other socializing agents, the interaction effects of the family and other agents, nor the other ways in which the family may shape political orientations.

Having said this, it is nevertheless clear that any model of socialization which rests on assumptions of pervasive currents of parent-to-child value transmissions of the types examined here is in serious need of modification. Attitude objects in the concrete, salient, reinforced terrain of party identification lend support to the model. But this is a prime exception. The data suggest that with respect to a range of other attitude objects the correspondences vary from, at most, moderate support to virtually no support. We have suggested that life cycle effects, the role of other socializing agents, and attitude instabilities help account for the very noticeable departures from the model positing high transmission. Building these forces into a model of political learning will further expose the family's role in the development of political values.

A derivative implication of our findings is that there is considerable slack in the value-acquisition process. If the eighteen-year old is no simple carbon copy of his parents—as the results clearly indicate— then it seems most likely that other socializing agents have ample opportunity to exert their impact. This happens, we believe, both during and after childhood. These opportunities are enhanced by the rapid sociotechnical changes occurring in modern societies. Not the least of these are the transformations in the content and form of the mass media and communication channels, phenomena over which the family and the school have relatively little control. It is perhaps the intrusion of other and different stimuli lying outside the nexus of the family and school which has led to the seemingly different *Weltanschauung* of the post-World-War-II generation compared with its immediate predecessor.

The place of change factors or agents thus becomes crucial in understanding the dynamics at work within the political system. Such factors may be largely exogenous and unplanned in nature, as in the case of civil disturbances and unanticipated consequences of technical innovations. Or they may be much more premeditated, as with radical changes in school organization and curriculum and in enforced social and racial interaction. Or, finally, they may be exceedingly

Notes

* Revised version of a paper delivered at the annual meeting of the American Political Science Association, New York, September, 1966. Financial support for the study reported here comes from The Danforth Foundation and the National Science Foundation. We wish to acknowledge the assistance of Michael Traugott in the preparation of this paper.

[1] Herbert Hyman, *Political Socialization* (New York: Free Press of Glencoe, 1959), p. 69.

[2] Most of these few studies, cited by Hyman, *op. cit.*, pp. 70–71, are based on extremely limited samples and nearly all took place between 1930–50.

[3] Robert D. Hess and Judith V. Torney, *The Development of Basic Attitudes and Values Toward Government and Citizenship During the Elementary School Years, Part I* (Cooperative Research Project No. 1078, U.S. Office of Education, 1965): pp. 193, 200.

[4] *Ibid.*, p. 191.

[5] *Ibid.*, p. 192.

[6] Illustrative of this argument is Frank A. Pinner's careful rendering in "Parental Overprotection and Political Distrust," *The Annals* 361 (September, 1965): 58–70. See, in the same issue, Fred I. Greenstein, "Personality and Political Socialization: The Theories of Authoritarian and Democratic Character," pp. 81–95.

[7] In addition to the Hess and Torney report, evidence for this is supplied by, *inter alios*, Fred I. Greenstein, *Children and Politics* (New Haven: Yale University Press, 1965); and David Easton and Jack Dennis, "The Child's Image of Government," *The Annals* 361 (September, 1965): 40–57.

[8] Of the original ninety-eight schools, drawn with a probability proportionate to their size, eighty-five (87 percent) agreed to participate; matched substitutes for the refusals resulted in a final total of ninety-seven out of 111 contacted altogether (87 percent).

[9] Additional interviews were conducted with 317 of the students' most relevant social studies teachers and with the school principals. Some 21,000 paper-pencil questionnaires were administered to all members of the senior class in 85 percent of the sample schools.

[10] In any event, initial controls on parent (as well as student) sex suggest that parent-student agreement rates on the values examined here differ little among parent-student sex combinations. This will be discussed in more detail below.

diffuse factors which result in numerous individual student-parent differences with no shift in the overall outlook of the two generations. Our point is that the absence of impressive parent-to-child transmission of political values heightens the likelihood that change factors can work their will on the rising generation. Shifting demands on the political system and shifting types of system support are natural outgrowths of these processes.

[11] The alternative to half-weighting these pairs is to subselect among those cases where both mother and father were interviewed. Half weighting tends to reduce the sampling variability because it utilizes more data cases.

[12] It proved impossible to obtain accurate, recent figures on 12th grade enrollment throughout the country. Working with the data available and extrapolating as necessary, a sampling frame was constructed so that schools would be drawn with a probability proportionate to the size of the senior class. After entry was obtained into the sample schools and precise figures on enrollments gathered, differential weights were applied to correct for the inequalities in selection probabilities occasioned by the original imprecise information. The average weight equals 1.2.

[13] Hyman, *op. cit.*, p. 72, and n. 6, p. 89. See also Robert E. Lane, "Fathers and Sons: Foundations of Political Belief," *American Sociological Review* 24 (August, 1959): 502–11; Eleanor E. Maccoby, Richard E. Matthews, and Anton S. Morton, "Youth and Political Change," *Public Opinion Quarterly* 18 (Spring, 1954): 23–39; Russell Middleton and Snell Putney, "Political Expression of Adolescent Rebellion," *American Journal of Sociology* 68 (March, 1963): 527–35; and Robert H. Somers, "The Mainsprings of the Rebellion: A Survey of Berkeley Students in November, 1964," in Seymour Martin Lipset and Sheldon S. Wolin (eds.), *The Berkeley Student Revolt* (Garden City, N.Y.: Doubleday, 1965), p. 547.

[14] Elizabeth Douvan and Martin Gold, "Modal Patterns in American Adolescence," in Lois and Martin Hoffman (eds.), *Review of Child Development Research* (New York: Russell Sage Foundation, 1966), vol. 2, p. 485.

[15] For an analysis of students' and parents' knowledge of each other's political attitudes and behavior, see Richard G. Niemi, "A Methodological Study of Political Socialization in the Family" (unpublished Ph.D. thesis, University of Michigan, 1967).

[16] This figure is based on parent-student pairs in which both respondents have a party identification; eliminated are the 2 percent of the pairs in which one or both respondents are apolitical or undecided. The product-moment correlation for these data is .59. The standard SRC party identification questions were used: see Angus Campbell, Phillip E. Converse, Warren E. Miller, and Donald E. Stokes, *The American Voter* (New York: Wiley, 1960), Ch. 6.

[17] This is suggested by an analysis of different age groups among the active electorate: see *Ibid.*, pp. 161ff. For evidence that the depth of adult attachment to party is not necessarily uniform across

electoral systems see M. Kent Jennings and Richard G. Niemi, "Party Identification at Multiple Levels of Government," *American Journal of Sociology* 72 (July, 1966): 86–101.

[18] Philip E. Converse, "The Nature of Belief Systems in Mass Publics," in David E. Apter (ed.), *Ideology and Discontent* (New York: Free Press of Glencoe, 1964), pp. 206–61. The following section borrows from Converse's discussion. Robert E. Agger takes a somewhat different view of instabilities in "Panel Studies of Comparative Community Political Decision-Making," in M. Kent Jennings and L. Harmon Zeigler (eds.), *The Electoral Process* (Englewood Cliffs: Prentice-Hall, 1966), pp. 265–89.

[19] Sizeable proportions of both parents and students elected to state a middle or "depends" response, particularly on the first question. Such responses occupy a middle position in our calculation of the rank order correlations. On the first issue 10 percent of the pairs were dropped because either the parent or child opted out on the initial screen; the corresponding figure for the second issue is 19 percent.

[20] Herbert McClosky, "Consensus and Ideology in American Politics," *American Political Science Review* 58 (June, 1964): 361–82; and James W. Prothro and Charles W. Grigg, "Fundamental Principles of Democracy: Bases of Agreement and Disagreement," *Journal of Politics* 22 (May, 1960): 276–94.

[21] Converse, *op. cit.*

[22] Robert E. Agger, Marshall N. Goldstein, and Stanley A. Pearl, "Political Cynicism: Measurement and Meaning," *Journal of Politics* 23 (August, 1961): p. 490; and Edgar Litt, "Political Cynicism and Political Futility," *Journal of Politics* 25 (May, 1963): 312–23.

[23] Greenstein, *op. cit.*, Ch. 3; Robert D. Hess and David Easton, "The Child's Changing Image of the President," *Public Opinion Quarterly* 24 (Winter, 1960): 632–44; and Hess and Torney, *op. cit.*, pp. 73ff.

[24] The items are as follows:

(1) Do you think that quite a few of the people running the government are a little crooked, not very many are, or do you think hardly any of them are?

(2) Do you think that people in the government waste a lot of the money we pay in taxes, waste some of it, or don't waste very much of it?

(3) How much of the time do you think you can trust the government in Washington to do what is right—just about always, most of the time, or only some of the time?

(4) Do you feel that almost all of the people running the government are smart people who usually know what they are doing, or do you think that quite a few of them don't seem to know what they are doing?

(5) Would you say that the government is pretty much run by a few big interests looking out for themselves or that it is run for the benefit of all the people?

[25] These are old charges but apparently still true. After a survey of the literature on the subject and on the basis of a subjective analysis of leading government textbooks in high schools, Byron G. Massialas reaches similar conclusions: see his "American Government: 'We are the Greatest,'" in C. Benjamin Cox and Byron G.

Massialas (eds.), *Social Studies in the United States: A Critical Appraisal* (New York: Harcourt, Brace, & World, Inc., 1967), pp. 167–95.

[26] A description of this operation and some results are given in M. Kent Jennings, "Pre-Adult Orientations to Multiple Systems of Government," *Midwest Journal of Political Science* 11 (August, 1967): 291–317. The underlying theory and technique are found in Clyde Coombs, *A Theory of Data* (New York: Wiley, 1964), esp. Ch. 5.

[27] This is discussed in more detail in Jennings, *op. cit.*

[28] To compare directly the amount of correspondence on interpretation of the Bible with church membership information, which is nominal-level data, we used the contingency coefficient. Grouping parent and student church affiliations into nine general categories, the coefficient is .88, compared to .34 for the Bible question.

[29] A more parsimonious method is to develop agreement indexes and to relate the control variables to these indexes. This results in a single statistic and contingency table for each control variable rather than one for each category of the control variable. Experience with both methods indicates that similar conclusions emerge, but retaining the full matrices preserves somewhat better the effects of each category of the control variable.

[30] See, e.g., Charles E. Bowerman and Glen H. Elder, "Adolescent Perception of Family Power Structure," *American Sociological Review* 2 (August, 1964): 551–67; E. C. Devereux, Une Bronfenbrenner, and G. J. Suci, "Patterns of Parent Behavior in the United States of America and the Federal Republic of Germany: A Cross-National Comparison," *International Social Science Journal* 14 (UNESCO, 1963): 1–20; and Morris Rosenberg, *Society and the Adolescent Self-Image* (Princeton: Princeton University Press 1965), Ch. 3.

[31] A discussion of these dimensions is found in Murray Straus, "Power and Support Structure of the Family in Relation to Socialization," *Journal of Marriage and the Family* 26 (August, 1964): 318–26. See also Wesley C. Becker, "Consequences of Different Kinds of Parental Discipline," in Martin and Lois Hoffman (eds.), *Review of Child Development* (New York: Russell Sage Foundation, 1964), vol. 1, pp. 169–208; William H. Sewell, "Some Recent Developments in Socialization Theory and Research," *The Annals* 349 (September, 1963): 163–81; Glen H. Elder, Jr., "Parental Power Legitimation and Its Effects on the Adolescent," *Sociometry* 26 (March, 1963): 50–65; and Douvan and Gold, *op. cit.*

[32] Middleton and Putney, *op. cit.*

[33] Lane, *op. cit.*; and Maccoby et al., *op. cit.*

[34] Nor was the intensity of parental feelings related in any consistent fashion to the amount of parent-student correspondence.

[35] There is a moderate tendency for those children feeling most detached from their parents to exhibit greater fluctuation in agreement with their parents—at various levels of politicization—than is true of those feeling most attached to their parents.

[36] At another level, the explanation may be in the lack of validity of students' and parents' reports of family structure. See Niemi, *op. cit.* Ch. 11 and pp. 184–85.

Political Socialization, Racial Tension and the Acceptance of Violence: Reactions of Southern Schoolchildren to the King Assassination

James W. Clarke
John W. Soule

The assassin's bullet which abruptly ended the life of Martin Luther King on April 4, 1968 evoked a public response among black Americans that remains unparalleled in our long history of such tragic events. King's death again dramatized the racial hostility and tension in this country. This event precipitated the violence which erupted in many cities and on a number of black university campuses. In the absence of such tension this violence would not have occurred.

One of the most important sources of tension in American society is the racial hostility which has divided this society as no other issue since the Civil War. The dimensions of this tension are well known: A persistent antipathy between blacks and whites which is reinforced by discrimination in education, employment and housing, as well as other areas of human concern.

It comes as no surprise that our findings confirm that racial tensions persist among black and white school children. We have documented the attitudes one might expect from such a group in the aftermath

of the violent death of this nation's most prominent black leader. More important is the fact that these school children—black and white—give indications that violence is recognized, tolerated, and in some cases, a preferred means of accomplishing one's objectives. Neil J. Smelser has suggested that "if hostility is to arise from conditions of strain ·[tension] these conditions must exist in a . . . setting which is either permissive of hostility or prohibitive of other responses, or both."[1] Our findings suggest that significant numbers of young black and white students accept the use of violence as a legitimate alternative for political actions. We are suggesting here that this acceptance of violence is an important consequence of what social scientists have called "political socialization."

For the past ten years, social scientists have devoted a great deal of attention to the political socialization of young Americans, i.e., how children learn politically relevant behavior. This research has been plagued with a number of substantive or methodological problems of which we shall deal with only one. Studies of how children acquire political beliefs from their parents have been limited to only those beliefs which are supportive of the existing political system.[2]

The research to date does support generally the hypothesis that children transfer feelings they have toward their parents to political figures. However, as a result of the heavy emphasis placed upon the influence of the family and the schools as agents of socialization, we have overlooked the effect that public events, e.g., economic crises and assassinations, have on the acquisition of the child's political beliefs. It is our contention that external events, which are highly publicized and emotional in character, interact with parental and peer group beliefs to constitute a significant factor in the political socialization of young people. It is also conceivable that such events have an independent influence on socialization, i.e., apart from family and school influences.

The heavy reliance in previous socialization research on psychoanalytic hypotheses has directed attention away from the influence of external events.[3] It is our contention that the psychoanalytic focus overly accentuates children's reactions to parental authority. The determination of influential agents of political socialization is an empirical question. The psychoanalytic focus ignores this point. The result is a static or status quo view of political socialization. It does not explain the dynamics of change in political cultures.

Our study is concerned with the impact that Martin Luther King's slaying had upon public school children. We have examined children's reaction to the assassination from cognitive and affective perspectives which include their perceptions of their parents' attitudes; their thoughts concerning just punishment (or reward) for the unknown assassin; and a comparison with reactions following President Kennedy's assassination. The evidence shows that this assassination had a substantial impact on these students. Among black students, reactions indicate that this event reinforces doubt and suspicion of existing legal means of apprehending and punishing criminals. White student reactions suggest that the assassination reinforces an attitude that violence is an acceptable means to a preferred end. While our data are only suggestive, the response to the King slaying suggests the probability of important dysfunctional consequences for the American political system.

Methods and Sample

A sample of 165 white and 217 black students was drawn from seventh, ninth, and eleventh grade classes of four public schools. The schools were located in two metropolitan communities in north and southeast Florida. With the exception of the eleventh grade classes, these students attend schools which are essentially segregated. Questionnaires were distributed and administered to each class by the regular classroom teacher. We, as two white university professors, avoided any contact with the students in an effort to minimize any bias which may have been introduced by our presence. Every effort was made to avoid any disruption of the normal classroom situation.

One major consideration in selecting the sample was simply to include a comparable number of black and white students within each grade level. Our desire to determine the reaction to the King assassination as soon after the event as possible, precluded the implementation of more rigorous sampling techniques. The data were collected within a twelve-day period immediately following the assassination. Meetings with school officials to explain and secure approval for the study accounted for this delay. No claim is made for the representativeness of our sample. It was impossible, given the nature of the event, the crucial time factor, and the sensitivity of school officials, to approach the problem in any other way. Although we have no reason to believe that our respondents are atypical Southern school children, there is no attempt to generalize beyond the data reported here.

Initial Reactions

Data in Table 1 indicate a clear difference between races in their critical reactions toward King's assassination. Responses were elicited by asking students the open-ended question: "How did you feel when you first heard of Dr. King's death?" Reactions varied from a deep sense of sorrow and grief to feelings of elation and happiness. Mixed between such polar reactions were feelings of indifference, incredulity, and anger. Fifty-nine percent of the white students surveyed expressed indifference or elation. Conversely, 96 percent of the black respondents expressed profound shock and grief. Clearly, black and white students responded quite differently to the assassination. While this finding is not surprising, the realization that a majority of white students were, at best, indifferent or unconcerned about the assassination, suggests an alarming callousness among these youngsters concerning such acts of violence.

Table 1
Results: Initial Reaction to Dr. King's Assassination by Race*

Initial Reaction	Black N = 189 %	White N = 141 %
Shocked, grieved, saddened, or angry	96	41
Indifferent or pleased	4	59
	100%	100%

* A total of 52 students did not answer these particular questions and were excluded from analysis in computing percentages. The fluctuations in the marginals of future tables are due to "don't know" and "no responses" on the item or items being considered. In this and in future tables, no answer/don't know responses are excluded except where inclusion is specifically noted. In investigating student attitudes, particularly young students, a substantial number of "no responses" are to be expected.

The reaction of white males and females are shown in Table 2. White males were clearly less sympathetic than their female counterparts. Seventy-three percent of the white males were indifferent or pleased. Over half of the white females registered a sympathetic response. Virtually no differences in reactions were revealed between black males and females. Black students of both sexes were greatly disturbed by the assassination.

Perceived Parental Reactions and Social Class

That parents transmit their attitudes and values to their children has been well-documented in behavioral

Table 2
Initial Reaction to Dr. King's Assassination by Sex Among White Students

Initial Reaction	Males N = 70 %	Females N = 71 %
Shocked, grieved, saddened, or angry	27	55
Indifferent or pleased	73	45
	100%	100%

research.[4] One scholar offers the following explanation for this relationship: "The family is the most prominent environmental source not only of what may be deemed its inherent function of providing affection, but also of satisfying other needs. This is probably the central reason that the individual comes to think and act like his family more than he thinks and acts like those who are less regularly relevant to his need satisfactions."[5]

Convincing evidence of this relationship is shown in Table 3. More interesting, however, is the fact that fully 30 percent of the sample who reported their own feelings were unable or unwilling to report their perceptions of their parent's attitudes. This finding lends support to the hypothesis that events like assassinations have an effect on young people that is independent of family influence.

Table 3
Correspondence between Perceived Parental Reactions and Children's Reactions to Dr. King's Assassination (Combined Black and White)

Children's Reaction	Perceived Parental Reaction Felt Bad N = 111 %	Indifferent or Glad N = 80 %
Felt bad	97	17
Indifferent or glad	3	83
	100%	100%

The class dimensions of racial prejudice are well-known, i.e., that lower status whites tend to be more prejudiced than higher status whites.[6] Our findings regarding the King assassination tend to confirm these views. We found marked differences in the reactions of white students whose fathers hold different occupational statuses. Table 4 shows the relationship between father's occupation and the initial reaction of white students. The data indicate considerably more indifference and pleasure among white students with fathers in clerical, skilled, and unskilled occupations compared to other white students with fathers in managerial, professional, and official occupations. Furthermore, 65 percent of these children from higher status families expressed sadness or sympathy. It seems clear from these results that there are class differences in the expected direction among white students with regard to their reaction to the assassination.

Table 4
Initial Reaction to Dr. King's Assassination by Father's Occupational Status among White Students

	Father's Occupation	
	Managers, Professionals, and Officials	Clerical, Sales, Skilled, and Unskilled
Students' Initial Reaction	N = 65 %	N = 51 %
Shocked, grieved, saddened, or angry	65	18
Indifferent or pleased	35	82
	100%	100%

Further evidence of class differences are observed when race is controlled and parental reactions to the assassination are considered with regard to occupation in Table 5. Table 5, in conjunction with Table 4, shows that children share essentially the basic class biases of their parent. Sixty-three percent of the white children, whose fathers are employed in lower level occupations, were either pleased or indifferent about King's death. Fewer parents of white children in higher level occupations (25 percent) shared these attitudes. More disturbing is the fact that in both the upper and lower occupational categories, childrens' responses to the news of King's assassination were

less compassionate than their perceptions of their parents' response. This finding raises some unsettling questions concerning the socialization of Southern white children. The fact that children are less compassionate than their parents suggests that some other influence—perhaps the school, the community or the cultural milieu of the South—is affecting their attitudes.[7] These are questions which cannot be answered in this study. Again, black students were overwhelmingly saddened by the event without regard to class differences, as were their parents.

Table 5
Parental Reaction to Dr. King's Assassination by Father's Occupational Status

	Managers, Professionals and Officials		Clerical, Sales, Skilled and Unskilled	
	Black	White	Black	White
Parental Reaction	N = 40 %	N = 65 %	N = 101 %	N = 56 %
Felt bad	73	34	73	12
Pleased and indifferent	2	25	2	63
Not sure	25	41	25	25
	100%	100%	100%	100%

Religion

Another indicator of student reaction was ascertained by asking respondents: "Did you say any special prayer or attend a memorial service for Dr. King?" As expected, 70 percent of the Negro students as compared to 17 percent of the white students reported that they had done so. Following the Kennedy assassination, Sheatsley and Feldman reported that three-fourths of a national sample of adults answered positively to this same question.[8] Although black students were found to attend church more regularly than whites, church attendance seemingly had little bearing on whether blacks or whites prayed following the assassination. Most blacks did pray and most whites did not, regardless of their past record of church attendance. Similarly there was no relationship between religious preference and either the black or white reaction.

Who Is to Blame?

The extent to which the King assassination was viewed in racial perspectives was explored by asking, "Who or what do you think is to blame for his [King's] death?" Black and white responses to this question are reported in Table 6. It is not surprising to note that more blacks than whites identified the assassin as a white man. Furthermore, 41 percent of the white students felt that King himself was to blame for his own death. Only 4 percent of the black students felt that way. The following is typical of the white response blaming King:

> 11th-grade white male: "Himself (He is to blame). He went around stirring up trouble."

Most of these responses described King as a man who "started riots," "pushed too hard," or "was stupid." Twenty-five percent of our sample refused to speculate on who the assassin might be—16 percent of the whites and 29 percent of the Negroes.

Table 6
Who Is to Blame for Dr. King's Slaying? (by Race)

	Race	
	Black	White
	N = 154	N = 138
Blame Placed Upon	%	%
A white man	35	12
Killer's color not mentioned	34	30
King himself is to blame	4	41
A prejudiced, racist, sick society	27	17
	100%	100%

Some of the children in our sample viewed the assassination in a much broader perspective. After President Kennedy's assassination, not one child— white or black—was reported as saying that "We are all to blame."[9] Our findings are sharply divergent. Twenty-seven percent of the blacks blamed a "racist society" for the tragedy as did 17 percent of the whites. An important difference in this response was the fact that white students tended to generalize more about

the ills of American society, whereas blacks tended to identify specifically the racist character of this society.

When these results were analyzed by grade level, we found that as their grade level increased, blacks were much more likely to blame a racist society for King's death. For example, one eleventh-grade black girl, struggling for words, expressed it this way: "I feel that the blame for his death is that white people don't want the Negroes to be said as good as they are. . . . Negroes is better than white if you want my opinion of it, because we have done white people's labor long enough." Another young black ninth grader said, "I think hate is to blame for his death . . . the hate for Negroes and thinking of them getting their freedom." Younger blacks tended to view the event in a more limited perspective, i.e., they were more likely to blame simply "a white man." Among the white students, as grade level increased, blame was increasingly attributed to King himself. Sixty-six percent of the white eleventh graders blamed King for his own assassination.

Punishment for the Assassin

A further inquiry involved the question, "What do you think should be done to the person who shot Dr. King?"[10] Again, the data reveal a clear distinction between the races as to the fate of the assassin (Table 8). Sixty-five percent of the black students responded with hostility or a desire for revenge. Typical responses were:

> 7th-grade black: "He should be hanged by the neck on public TV."

> 9th-grade black: "He should be shot by Mrs. King or King's brother."

> 11th-grade black: "He should be taken out and beaten. Why don't they set him loose on . . . [a black university] campus. We would do the job on him—but good!"

Conversely, sixty-five percent of the whites felt the assassin whould be accorded the due process of law.

More disturbing, however, is the finding that 17 percent of the white students felt the killer should be rewarded for his deed. For example, respondents said:

7th-grade white: "He should go free."

9th-grade white: "He should get the Congressional Medal of Honor for killing a nigger."

11th-grade white: "We should try him in court and find him not guilty. He did what lots of us wanted to do, he had the guts."

Table 7
What Do You Think Should Happen to Guilty Person? (By Race)

	Black N = 198 %	White N = 151 %
Imputed Fate		
Tried, punished by courts	35	65
Death	65	18
No punishment, freed, congratulated	0	17
	100%	100%

Moreover, among whites, sympathy for the killer increased with grade level, i.e., about 30 percent of the white eleventh graders favored no punishment for the assassin compared with only 4 percent of the white seventh graders.[11] An opposite reaction was noted among black students. As grade level increased blacks were much more likely to elicit "due process" responses as opposed to extra-legal, violent or revengeful responses. Whereas 74 percent of the seventh grade blacks expressed a desire for violent sanctions for the killer, this percentage declined to 50 percent among eleventh grade blacks.[12] However, it is important to note that at all grade levels a majority of blacks favored some form of violent death for the assassin with no mention of established legal procedure. In their view, King's death could only be atoned through the violent and, in some cases, sadistic execution of his killer.

Two Assassinations: Some Comparisons

Studies made following President Kennedy's assassination revealed that blacks—adults and children—expressed more sorrow over the President's death than whites. A number of the same items used in Sigel's study of reactions to the Kennedy assassination were included in our questionnaire for comparative purposes. (See Table 8.)

The data reveal that the contrast between black and white student reactions are sharp. Invariably the white students expressed less sympathy, were less ashamed and upset, and were less disturbed that such violence could occur in this country. Following President Kennedy's assassination both black and white students responded sympathetically.

The extent and intensity of the black response to King's death is evidenced by the fact that black students expressed a greater emotional loss, more anger, shame, and vengeance at his death than they did when President Kennedy was killed. (It is generally accepted that President Kennedy enjoyed considerable popularity among blacks.) Again, this response indicates the decided effect King's death had upon black school children.

Conclusions

In our introduction, we outlined several components of social behavior which have political relevance. Subsequently, we have shown the extent to which both racial tension and attitudes conducive to the use of violence exist among black and white school children. This volatile combination of situation and attitudes provide sufficient conditions for inter-racial conflict.

While Martin Luther King's death served as a precipitant for the violence which followed immediately, his death might also be viewed as an important event in the long-range socialization of young blacks.

Table 8
Reaction of Children by Race Toward Both the King and Kennedy Assassinations (In Rounded Percentages)

| | This Is How I Felt | | | |
| | King Reactions | | Kennedy Reactions[a] | |
	Black N = 217 %	White N = 165 %	Black N = 342 %	White N = 1006 %
Felt the loss of someone very close	89	15	81	69
Worried what would happen to our country	88	85	74	63
Felt so sorry for his wife and children	98	63	91	94
Felt worried how the Civil Rights movement would carry on	89	45	—[b]	—[b]
Felt angry that anyone should do such a terrible thing	95	47	84	81
Hoped the man who killed him would be shot	76[c]	20[c]	54	36
Felt ashamed that this could happen in my country	77	63	75	86
Was so confused and upset I didn't know what to feel	40	15	40	44
Felt in many ways it was King's (Kennedy's) own fault	10[c]	49[c]	18	15

[a] These data were taken from Roberta Sigel, op. cit., p. 211.

[b] This item was not included in the study of President Kennedy's assassination.

[c] The differences between these responses and the responses presented in Tables 6 and 7 are explained by the fact that a larger number of students responded to the items which appear in this table.

Sixty-five percent of these children wanted revenge, beyond punishment by law, for his death. Some evidence of this and other factors may be reflected in the increasing militancy of young blacks.

The King assassination has revealed also that prejudice and hostility are important dimensions of the attitudes of significant numbers of the white children studied. Fifty-nine percent of these children were indifferent or pleased upon hearing of King's death. These children, at best, were not concerned that a man had been killed because his views were contrary to the views of many white Americans.

The revengeful attitudes of blacks and the callousness of whites suggest what may be an alarming dimension of racism in the United States. Violence appears to be increasingly recognized and accepted—by both blacks and whites—as a legitimate means of settling grievances.

Notes

[1] Neil J. Smelser, *Theory of Collective Behavior* (New York: The Free Press, 1962), pp. 224–25.

[2] See, for example, Lewis A. Froman, Jr., "Learning Political Attitudes," *Western Political Quarterly;* R. E. Dawson, "Political Socialization" in *Political Science Annual,* James A. Robinson, ed., (New York: Bobbs-Merrill, 1966), pp. 1–84; Robert D. Hess and David Easton, "The Child's Changing Image of the President," *Public Opinion Quarterly* 24 (1960): 632–44; Fred I. Greenstein, "Children's Political Perspectives: A Study of the Development of Political Awareness and Preferences among Preadolescents," Yale University Library, 1959, unpublished doctoral dissertation; and Dean Jaros, "Children's Orientations toward the President: Some Additional Theoretical Consideration and Data," *Journal of Politics 29 (1967): 368–87.*

[3] Froman, *loc. cit.*

[4] See, for example, Frederick Elkin, *The Child and Society: The Process of Socialization* (New York: Random House, 1960).

[5] James C. Davies, "The Family's Role in Political Socialization," *The Annals of the American Academy of Political and Social Science* 361 (September, 1965): p. 12.

[6] The explanations offered for this are complex, involving personality attributes associated with lower class backgrounds and socio-economic insecurity. For a more detailed discussion see, George Eaton Simpson and J. Milton Yinger, *Racial and Cultural Minorities: An Analysis of Prejudice and Discrimination* 3rd. ed. (New York: Harper and Row, 1965), pp. 103–8.

[7] Also, it may be that this deviation means nothing more than that we are simply comparing people at different stages of the socialization process at a given point in time, i.e., the attitudes of these children may change substantially by the time they reach the age of their parents. At this point, we cannot predict either the magnitude or direction of attitudinal change over time.

[8] Paul Sheatsley and Jacob J. Feldman, "A National Survey of Public Reactions and Behavior," *Public Opinion Quarterly* 28 (1964): 189–215.

[9] Roberta Sigel, "Television and Reactions of School Children to the Assassination," in *The Kennedy Assassination and the American Public,* B. Greenberg and E. Parker, eds. (Stanford, Calif.: Stanford University Press, 1965).

[10] Responses were coded into three categories: included in the first category were those who thought the killer should be accorded the due process of law; respondents included in the second category expressed a desire that extra-legal sanctions be brought against the killer; our third category contained those persons who felt the killer should not be punished, or who, in fact, felt this person should be rewarded in some way for his deed.

[11] Relationships involving grade level as a control variable are not shown in tabular form.

[12] A fourth variable, father's occupational status, was added as a control in analyzing black and white responses to the killer by grade level. It was possible that occupational status was an intervening variable. While the cell sizes became very small when this control was introduced, the relationship remained unchanged.

Racial Socialization, Comparison Levels, and the Watts Riot

David O. Sears

John B. McConahay

One of the reasons most Americans have been so disturbed by the urban race riots of the 1960s is that they are such an utterly new phenomenon in twentieth-

century America. There has been virtually no precedent whatever for these mass eruptions by the black population in the United States. The long years of slavery were only infrequently, and ineffectually,

David O. Sears and John B. McConahay, "Racial Socialization, Comparison Levels, and the Watts Riot," *Journal of Social Issues* 26 (1970): 121–40. Reprinted with permission.

The research on which this paper is based was conducted under a contract between the Office of Economic Opportunity and the Institute of Government and Public Affairs at UCLA. The coordinator of the Los Angeles Riot Study was Nathan E. Cohen. Some of the data have appeared in an earlier technical report

(Sears and McConahay, 1970). We wish to express our gratitude to the many people who worked on the study, particularly to Diana TenHouten, Paula Johnson, T. M. Tomlinson, Ronald Abeles, and Esther Spachner. Computing assistance was obtained from the Pomona College Computing Center and the Health Sciences Computing Facility at UCLA.

punctuated by slave rebellions. The abrupt relaxation of institutionalized slavery brought with it relatively few instances of violence perpetrated by newly freed blacks upon their former masters. And the 100 long years since Emancipation, filled with almost uninterrupted frustration and privation for black Americans, witnessed only rare outbreaks of mass violence by blacks against whites and against the white-dominated social system. Historically, mass violence by American blacks against their oppressors has been rare, and until recently it has never posed an important threat to the stability of American society. In this context, the riots of the mid-1960s are novel and shocking.

Population Changes

To learn what has caused this sharp departure from historical passivity, let us look at how black Americans have changed in other respects. Most obviously, there have been major demographic changes. In the late nineteenth century, the black population of America was rural, agrarian, Southern, only semiliterate, and had been residentially stable for many years. Today, it is urban, industrial, national, moderately well educated, and residentially mobile. Although this change is by now well known, it is easy to forget just how dramatic it has been.

Region. In 1910, at the beginning of the major migration from South to North, only 11 percent of the American Negro population lived outside the South. By 1966, this had increased to 45 percent. Migration to the Pacific states such as California was particularly late, so that California was less than 1 percent black in 1910. As late as 1940 only 1 percent of the nation's blacks lived in all the Western states; by 1966, 8 percent did (Bureau of Labor Statistics, 1967; Taeuber and Taeuber, 1966).

Urbanization. Most of this migration has been to the large urban centers of the North and West, and from the rural South to Southern cities. Consequently a predominantly rural population became highly urbanized: in 1910, 29 percent of the Negroes lived in metropolitan areas; and in 1966, 69 percent did.

Whites, more urban to begin with (48 percent in 1910), have become urbanized at a much slower rate (64 percent in 1966). And in the North and West, the areas most responsible for the riots, Negroes have become almost completely urbanized: in 1960, 93 percent lived in metropolitan areas (whereas fewer than 70 percent of the whites did). And today the migration into Northern cities is no longer from the farms: of the nonwhites who moved to Los Angeles in the 1955–60 period, 72 percent came from some other metropolitan area (Taeuber and Taeuber, 1966).[1]

Education. The deficiencies in Negroes' educational opportunities are now well known. However, recent increases in educational attainments are dramatic. In 1940, Negro males aged 25 to 29 averaged 6.5 years of education; by 1962, the average was 11.0 years. This has not eliminated the racial differential, but it has reduced it: in 1940, whites had on the average 4.0 more years of education than blacks, but by 1962 the difference was only 1.5 years (Taeuber and Taeuber, 1966). The number of years does not provide an adequate index to the quality of education, of course, but this considerable increase in the average length of a black man's time in school is bound to affect his literacy and his sophistication.

Youth. The higher birth rate of Negro mothers has produced a black population markedly younger than the white. In 1966 the median age of Negroes was 21.1 years, and of whites, 29.1 years (Kerner, O. et. al., 1968, p. 238).

To summarize, then, the Negro population has become much more urbanized, Northernized, and considerably better-educated. It is a young and physically vigorous population. Yet it remains highly segregated, crammed into relatively small and deteriorated urban areas, underemployed, and underpaid. It is also a population generally regarded as inferior by the white majority.

Riot Participation and the New Urban Black Man

Have these demographic changes been responsible, in part, for the rioting? One test is simply to determine whether or not the young Northern urban better-educated blacks have been more prominent in the rioting than those representing the earlier pattern of Negro life.

Our data come from a sample survey conducted in the South Central black ghetto in Los Angeles during late 1965 and early 1966, soon after the Watts riot of August, 1965. Two samples will be discussed here: a representative sample of adults (age 15 and up) living in the area cordoned off during the riot (the "Curfew Zone sample," $n = 586$), and an accidental sample of blacks arrested during the riot, contacted through lawyers providing free legal aid ("Arrestee sample," $n = 124$). All the respondents were interviewed by black interviewers living in the Curfew Zone.[2] Persons who were most involved in the riot were identified in three ways: (1) Arrestees; (2) in the Curfew zone sample, those "active" in the riot by self-report; and (3) also in the Curfew Zone sample, those reporting they had seen at least four of the following five events: shooting, stone-throwing, burning of stores, looting of stores, and crowds in the street.

The young were considerably more likely than the old to be involved in the Watts riot, both in terms of self-reported activity and in viewing riot events. Table 1 gives the data for the Curfew Zone sample. The Arrestee sample was primarily composed of young people, and was considerably younger than either the Curfew Zone sample or the South Central Los Angeles area as a whole (Sears and McConahay, 1969).

Those who were native to Los Angeles were considerably more likely to have been active in the rioting than Southern migrants and in-migrants from Northern cities. This too is shown in Table 1. Reported elsewhere (Sears and McConahay, 1970) are data which indicated that recency of migration also diminished participation. Considering the youngest of our age groups (age 15–29), 37 percent of those who had been born in Los Angeles or who arrived before age 7 claimed activity, while only 17 percent of those who had arrived in Los Angeles within the previous five years said they had been active.

With respect to education, on the other hand, there was little or no relationship to riot participation. In

Table 1
Riot Participation as a Function of Current Age and Region of Origin

	Age			
	15–29	30–44	45+	All Ages
Percent reporting themselves active				
Natives	37%[a]	9%	0%	28%
Northern migrants	19	17	17	19
Southern migrants	24	21	15	20
All origins	32%	18%	14%	
Percent high in events witnessed				
Natives	52%	43%	25%	48%
Northern migrants	37	21	17	26
Southern migrants	20	28	21	25
All origins	41%	30%	20%	

Note. – "Natives" are those born in Los Angeles or arriving before age 17. N on which these percentages are based is 586.

[a]The entry is the proportion active in the riot of those meeting the age and migrancy conditions specified. Thus, 37 percent of young natives reported themselves active, the remaining 63 percent said that they were not.

fact, there was virtually no relationship between riot participation and any such indices of socio-economic status.[3]

The Social Psychology of the New Urban Black Man

The rioters thus seem to fit the portrait of the new urban black man. Whereas the Southern rural "Negro" of 1900 was not likely to go to war against the ruling white population, the young Northern urban blacks of the 1960s are geared for battle and for confrontation.

Demographic changes do not by themselves produce behavioral changes, however. What social psychological changes might they have produced that would mediate their effects on behavior? More specifically, what social psychological changes have occurred that were sufficiently profound to spur a sudden surge of rioting? Here, we wish to focus particularly upon the effects of age and of area of socialization. The remainder of this paper is devoted to spelling out possible changes in the attitudinal effects of early socialization and in comparison levels, and to some preliminary tests with our data from the Watts riot.

First, the socialization of blacks in the rural South of years gone by emphasized repression of hostility against whites and against institutions dominated by white authority. It did not, needless to say, encourage outspoken criticism, disagreement, or confrontation. And this socialization had lifelong effects upon the behavior of Negroes. We hypothesize that black socialization has become substantially more militant, especially in the North. Perhaps open anti-white feeling has always been less dangerous in the North; but partly, as well, the young of today are imitating the open confrontations with authority seen in the civil rights battles of the late 1950s and early 1960s. According to this view, then, the riots represent just one manifestation of a wider tendency to express open hostility against whites, and to become more independent of their wishes.

Second, migration from the rural, poverty-stricken South to the more affluent and better educated North has raised blacks' expectations. Hence the possibility arises that disappointments in the North yield a sense of relative deprivation. We wish to test for evidence of relative deprivation and for its possible role in instigating rioting.

A third possible consequence of being reared in Northern ghettos is one that ought to be raised, but is unfortunately not one we can directly address with empirical evidence. The residential segregation of Northern metropolitan areas has largely restricted blacks to small, deteriorating, compact urban ghettos. Among the numerous effects this could be expected to have is an exceptional lability of attitudes bearing on matters of common concern. For example, one might expect parental influence over racial attitudes to be diluted, on the grounds that peers are so accessible that youngsters spend much more time with their friends and correspondingly less with their families than in more isolated suburban areas. Hence it would

seem likely that inter-generational attitude change would occur more readily with changes in events, that norms would change more rapidly, that consensuses could form and reform more quickly, and so on. For these reasons one might expect a more widespread "generation gap" between older, Southern-reared parents and young ghetto-reared offspring than in less densely concentrated residential areas.

Racial Socialization

The psychology of enduring dispositions. To test the possibility that contemporary Northern urban socialization was a key factor in the rioting, we must first consider more generally the question of the enduring effects of socialization. From the growing mass of data on attitudes of the American public at our disposal, it is beginning to appear that certain kinds of attitudes represent enduring dispositions. Other attitudes appear to be much more transitory and meaningless, even declining to the status of what one writer has called "non-attitudes (Converse, 1963)." Let us consider this contrast in more detail.

One might pose a number of criteria by which long-standing attitudinal dispositions could be contrasted with transitory and ephemeral preferences: (1) acquisition earlier in life; (2) greater stability; (3) greater internal consistency; and (4) ability to control opinion formation on other issues. As research has accumulated, it has begun to appear that most attitudes fitting these criteria refer either to groups or to persons. In contemporary America, most salient among these are, perhaps, those attitudes referring to political party, to racial issues, to nation, and to some particularly well-known political personalities. Let us here merely suggest some of the evidence for this contention (see Sears, 1969a, for a more detailed treatment).

There is now convincing evidence of the early acquisition of racial attitudes (Proshansky, 1966), nationalism (Hess and Torney, 1967), and political partisanship (Greenstein, 1965; Hess and Torney, 1967). Whether or not children acquire these in anything like their adult form is not so clear; still, most children do not acquire attitudes on other political and social matters until later on (Sigel, 1968), and these early preferences show a certain stability, consistency, and ability to determine other opinions (Hess and Torney, 1967; Sears, 1969a). And it seems clear that early familial influence is more marked on the child's racial attitudes and party identification than in a whole host of other areas, partly because the parents' racial and partisan attitudes are a good deal clearer to the child than any of their other political and social attitudes (Jennings and Niemi, 1968; Niemi, 1969). The same holds for parents' presidential preferences; these probably are the political and social attitudes most clearly communicated by parents to their children.

By these several standards, then, it appears that attitudes referring to political party, race, nation, and some public personalities are acquired earlier than are other social and political attitudes. These attitudes appear also to be more stable over both long and short terms. Panel studies have demonstrated short-term stability most convincingly. For example, Converse (1964) has shown that racial attitudes and party identification are more stable over two or four year periods than are any of a variety of other political attitudes tested. The stability of presidential preferences through a campaign is well known (Lazarsfeld, Berelson, and Gaudet, 1948; Benham, 1965).

Longer-term stability is more of an unknown, since longitudinal studies of attitudes have been conducted only on a few rather specialized, and usually highly politicized, samples (cf. Bloom, 1964; Newcomb et al., 1967). Retrospective reports can yield some information, and relatively few respondents do report having changed parties (Campbell et al., 1960, p. 147). Another imperfect, but somewhat edifying, test of stability is to look at persons subjected .to major environmental changes, especially changes from one attitudinally homogeneous environment to another. For example, social and geographic mobility may not influence party or racial attitudes as much as is generally believed (Barber, 1965; Campbell et al., 1960; Sears, 1969a). Marriage may have substantial effects

and thus may be an exception in this respect, but the change of environment it involves is considerably more proximate and immediate, and the affective ties more complex, than is the case for most other environmental changes—even so, the data on its effects are not yet very clear (Sears, 1969a).

Systematic tests of the relative internal consistency or controlling power of various kinds of attitudes have been less common. What indications are available suggest that by both criteria, the predispositions described above tend to be more coherent and powerful (Converse, 1964; Sears, 1969a).

Contemporary northern socialization vs. earlier southern socialization. It seems, then, that group-related predispositions are acquired rather early in life and are maintained with considerable persistence. To account for adult differences in attitude, consequently, one must look first at differential socialization experiences in childhood and adolescence. What specifically differentiates the contemporary socialization of Northern urban blacks from that of the rural South of an earlier era?

There are few hard data on this point, but there are many impressionistic accounts. Let us consider Pettigrew's (1964) representative treatment. He contrasts Northern and Southern socialization in terms of differential mechanisms for coping with the hostility engendered by white authority and white racism. Open expression of hostility against whites has traditionally been quite dangerous in the South, and so traditional Southern socialization of Negroes emphasized its repression. It was expressed only in the very muted and diluted forms he describes as reflecting "moving away from the oppressor": aggressive meekness, spiritualism, passivity and withdrawal, passive acquiescence to whites, social insulation, and such extreme forms of escapism as addiction to drugs or alcohol. In some cases excessive denial of aggression against whites has produced "emotional dullness."

In contrast, Northern socialization has placed less premium upon the control of hostility against white authorities. Northern blacks generally agree that police brutality is widely practiced (see Raine, 1970;

Campbell and Schuman, 1968; among others). Even so, the norms for black behavior in the North do not restrict assertiveness as much as they do in the South.

Systematic data to document this contrast are not very plentiful. Brink and Harris (1966) found Southern Negroes more contented than Northern Negroes on a wide variety of measures (e.g., regarding housing, school integration, transportation, police, white business, etc.). Northerners also were more likely to favor "black power," and to say that the struggle for Negro rights was going "too slow." Beardwood (1968) has presented more recent data showing that Southern Negroes feel less anti-white and are less likely to feel that violence is necessary. So it appears that currently there is less discontent in the South, and also less militancy. Whether or not this is a consequence of differential socialization is hard to tell without more detailed analysis. Our data below will address this question.

A related hypothesis is that the younger generation is being socialized into a more militant frame of mind, from a variety of sources, than were its elders. There is some evidence that dramatic public events have a more marked effect upon youthful attitudes than they do upon the attitudes of older people (Wolfinger, 1965; Sheatsley, 1966; Campbell et al., 1960). One would therefore expect young Negroes to have been more profoundly influenced by the very visible and salient confrontations of the late 1950s and early 1960s between blacks and unsympathetic white authority. The televised civil rights marches, the publicity about court cases, and the confrontations between federal authority and Southern obstructionists very likely contributed to greater radicalism and militancy among Negro youth.[4] Presumably they also had some effect, but perhaps not as dramatic, upon older blacks.

Our analysis tests these hypotheses in terms of two predictions: (1) the young Northern-reared black man is more disaffected toward conventional institutions and their white incumbents than are older and migrant Negroes; and (2) the Watts riot occurred in part because of widespread feelings that conventional mechanisms of grievance redress were not responsive to the needs of ghetto residents.

The disaffection of the new urban black man. Our data reveal considerable evidence of the greater disaffection of the young Northern urban blacks. Their mistrust of elected officials is a clear example. Our respondents were asked whether or not one could trust "elected officials" and "Negro elected officials." Both youth and Northern socialization were closely related to mistrust. Among the young natives (those aged 15–29 who arrived in Los Angeles before they were 7), 38 percent felt they could trust both kinds of officials. At the other extreme, 66 percent of the old migrants (those aged 45 and over who arrived in Los Angeles at age 30 or later) said they could trust both kinds of officials.[5]

The pattern is the same, though not always quite so marked, on numerous other dimensions of attitude toward white authority: a generalized scale of political disaffection (e.g., "How do you feel about the way you are represented?"), attitudes toward white liberals (e.g., California Governor Brown, or the Democratic party), evaluations of white officeholders (e.g., President Johnson, Los Angeles City Councilman Gibson, or Los Angeles County Supervisor Hahn) and of legislative bodies (Congress, the state legislature, etc.). In all cases, the young proved to be more disenchanted with government, though not significantly so in each case; in most cases those brought up in Los Angeles were more disaffected than the migrants, though significantly so only in the case of generalized disaffection.

There were two important exceptions to this pattern. One concerns aspects of local government: evaluation of local welfare agencies (e.g., Bureau of Public Assistance), perceived discrimination in local agencies (e.g., school system, fire department), attitude toward the local political structure (e.g., the Mayor and City Council), and perceived fairness of mass media in covering Negro problems. Migrancy affected none of the four scales generated to measure these concerns; age had only a marginally significant effect upon evaluations of the local political structure ($p < .10$) and no effect in the other cases.

However, a closer look reveals that youth and nativity alike contribute to hostility toward the most salient white incumbents in local politics. For example, the young natives were more antagonistic than the old migrants toward Los Angeles Mayor Yorty and Chief of Police William Parker, each of whom had a wide reputation for being unsympathetic to Negro demands (Sears, 1969b). These data appear to indicate that genuine, reality-based grievances about the failures of local government agencies (see Jacobs, 1966) produce disaffection from local government among older and migrant citizens that approaches the more intense generalized disaffection of the young native. A mother of five children, aged 40, does not have to be a sophisticated political ideologue to be embittered about the Aid to Dependent Children program or to perceive racial discrimination in a school system that is a model of *de facto* segregation. Thus, the greater immediacy of and familiarity with the failures of local government appear to override the usual disposition of the somewhat older and migrant Negro not to criticize white authority very much.

Attitudes toward black leadership constituted the other exception to the generational and origin gap in militancy. Four evaluation scales were used: (1) militancy (e.g., the Black Muslims), (2) local black politicians (e.g., Congressman Hawkins, Councilman Bradley), (3) civil rights groups (e.g., NAACP, SNCC), and (4) assimilationists (e.g., Ralph Bunche, Thurgood Marshall). The young were more militant, did not differ from the old regarding black politicians or civil rights groups, and were less favorable to assimilationists. Thus, the younger blacks were not more disaffected than their elders toward black leadership, with the sole exception of traditional assimilationist leaders. And they were in fact *more* enthusiastic than their elders about such militant groups as the Muslims.

Natives also were not more disaffected than migrants toward black leadership. In fact, they were *slightly (p < .10)* more favorable to black politicians and assimilationists than were migrants, though they did not differ in terms of Muslims or civil rights groups.

Finally, the young natives were significantly more likely to endorse the use of violence in redressing Negroes' grievances. When given a choice of violent protest, nonviolent protest, or negotiation, the young natives were twice as likely as young migrants to choose violence. This is a further indication of the young native's greater willingness to assert himself and aggress openly against white authority.

In short, the young natives were more politically disaffected in a variety of respects than older and migrant respondents. However, the new generation was not particularly disaffected with respect to black leadership, and young and old respondents alike expressed considerable unhappiness with the work of local government.

Rioters' attitudes toward mechanisms of grievance redress. The second question is whether or not this disaffection in fact had some causal role in precipitating the rioting. Such causal relations cannot be established in any rigorous sense from retrospective correlational data. However, if disaffection was essentially uncorrelated with rioting, it would seem much less likely to have played a causal role. What in fact was the relationship between riot participation and the several versions of disaffection cited above? Here we shall merely present some representative findings; for a more complete presentation of the data, the reader is referred to our original report (Sears and McConahay, 1970).

The riot participants differed from nonparticipants both in being more disaffected in general terms, and in being particularly disaffected from local government. The generalized disaffection is illustrated by the fact that 35 percent of those who said they trusted neither elected officials nor Negro elected officials were active in the riot, by self-report; whereas only 14 percent of those who said they trusted officials on both items were active. Thirty-eight percent of the Arrestees, against 50 percent of the Curfew Zone sample, said they trusted elected officials.

Each of our indexes of disaffection with local government (see above) was also closely related to riot participation. Self-reported riot activity was strongly related to disaffection from the local political structure, unfavorable evaluations of local welfare agencies, perceived discrimination in local government, and unfavorable evaluations of the fairness of local media in dealing with Negro problems.

Perhaps the most graphic demonstration of the

special disaffection rioters had with local mechanisms of grievance redress is given by the item, "If you were treated unfairly by the police, what would you do about it?" Replies were divided into those reflecting conventional civics-course trust in the system (e.g., report it to the authorities, take it to court, file a complaint with the police department) and those reflecting despair and cynicism (e.g., do nothing, what can you do, self-defense, take revenge). Self-reported riot activity was considerably higher among those giving the cynical response (30 percent active) than among those giving the trusting response (18 percent), and the cynical answer was much more likely to emerge from Arrestees (41 percent) than Curfew Zone respondents (29 percent).

However, this appears to reflect a despair about the process of redressing grievances rather than simply hostility against the rioters' adversaries in the disturbance, such as the police. Self-reported riot activity was only marginally related to our scale measuring belief in widespread police brutality against Negroes ($p < .10$), unrelated to attitudes toward the police chief, and modestly related to the view that the authorities handled the riot badly. The fact that attitudes toward the police do not clearly differentiate participants and nonparticipants implies two things: that the special antagonism expressed by riot participants toward local government is not simply a rationalization for their rioting, because the police would be an even more convenient target for rationalization; and that, in addition, grievance against the police was more widespread than that against any other civic agency (the rioters were not alone in expressing it).

There is some other evidence suggesting the causal role of this disaffection toward local government and its services. Some of the more salient alternative explanations for the correlation can be ruled out by our data. First, as indicated above, it does not seem to be simply a rationalization for counter-normative behavior (the rioters were not much more antagonistic to the police than nonrioters, and the police would have been a convenient target). Additional evidence that it is not merely post facto rationalization is that rioters did not adopt more than non-rioters the various

complex mythologies that justified the riot, e.g., that the riot was a directed protest against white racism (Sears and Tomlinson, 1968; Tomlinson, 1970). For example, 66 percent of the Arrestees, 68 percent of the active in the Curfew Zone sample, and 62 percent of the inactive in the Curfew Zone sample agreed that it was a "Negro protest."

Moreover, the special disaffection of the rioters focused upon the local situation. Rioters and non-rioters alike generally had praise for the national administration, for the Democratic party, for the poverty program, and so on. The differential disaffection did not show up there. Nor did it emerge with respect to black leadership. Self-professed riot activity was related to antagonism toward assimilationists, but only marginally related to attitudes toward black politicians, and not at all related to evaluations of civil rights groups. And the riot participants actually approved of the Muslims significantly more than did nonparticipants. So the hostility of the rioters toward local white authority and institutions did not merely reflect a generalized biliousness; it tended to be specific to local white authority and institutions.

The participants were also distinctive in feeling that the riot had been aimed at specific persons and institutions rather than at impersonal conditions. As mentioned above, they joined in the general feeling that it had been a deliberate, purposeful protest. The rioters' personalizing of the protest provides some further evidence for the role of disaffection from local authority structures. And, finally, those respondents who were most disaffected about local institutions were also most optimistic about the outcome of the riot; they expected the riot to bring whites to their senses, and that it would make whites more attentive to Negro problems (Sears and McConahay, 1970).

Relative Deprivation and Comparison Levels

A basic assumption in theories of relative deprivation and social evaluation is that a state of deprivation or unfavorable evaluation has motivating properties (Pettigrew, 1967). It is here proposed that one motivating force for the violent outbursts of the mid-1960s was an unfavorable comparison between the attainments of the young Northern natives and those which they expected or thought they deserved.

That blacks in general felt relatively deprived in the early 1960s seems clear. Pettigrew (1967) has shown that in 1963 the American black community was generally in a state of rising expectations regarding their general life situation and with regard to such specific areas as income, housing, and education for their children. At the same time, black Americans were not satisfied with their current status. Our hypothesis is that the combination of this relative deprivation and the widespread feeling that the social structure allowed no means of improving outcomes or redressing grievances led to an attack upon the symbols of the white social structure. Here we wish to consider what light this perspective can shed on the general finding that the young natives were most involved in the rioting.

First, let us consider a somewhat more formalized version of the relative deprivation hypothesis, deriving from Thibaut and Kelley's (1959) notion of "comparison level" (CL). This concept was proposed to account for the manner in which an individual evaluates his outcomes in a given social interaction. It embodies all of the usual features of the relative deprivation idea, emphasizing evaluation of one's life situation not in terms of its absolute value, but in terms of the way one's present condition compares with the condition of salient others. In addition to this, however, Thibaut and Kelley have proposed that such evaluations are also affected by the outcomes one has experienced in the past. They have defined the CL (1959, p. 81) as being "some modal or average value of all outcomes known to the person (by virtue of personal or vicarious experience), each outcome weighted by its salience (or the degree to which it is instigated for the person at the moment)." This modal or average value, the CL, is a neutral point on a scale of satisfaction and dissatisfaction. Outcomes falling above CL will be satisfying (regardless of how the "independent observer" might evaluate them), and those falling below will not be satisfying.

Among the variables Thibaut and Kelley hypothe-sized to affect CL, two are most important for our understanding of the riots. *First,* experienced outcomes are expected to be highly salient and hence to carry great weight in the location of the CL. *Second,* perceived extent of control over one's outcomes is proposed to affect the range of groups and other persons whose outcomes vicariously influence an individual's CL.

Comparison levels and relative deprivation of northern and southern blacks. We might expect the joint operation of the experience and perceived control (power) factors to produce the following effects: (1) Northern natives should have a higher CL than Southern-reared migrants to the North, and (2) Northern natives should be in a state of relative deprivation (outcomes below CL), while Southern migrants should be in a state of relative satisfaction (outcomes above CL).

The first of these expected effects rests upon the further assumption that outcomes are objectively worse for black people in the South than in the North. This has been demonstrated in numerous studies, and there is a consensus in the black community that this is so. When asked, "Do you think that Negroes are generally better off in Los Angeles than in the South?", 67 percent of our respondents replied that things were better in Los Angeles, while only 6 percent thought things were worse in Los Angeles than in the South. The black man growing up in the South experiences only these lesser outcomes and brings a lower CL with him when he migrates to the North. Blacks reared in the North have experienced the better outcomes for most of their lives. Thus, their CL's are likely to be higher than those of Southern migrants.

Indeed, most empirical studies do show Northern blacks to have considerably higher expectations and aspirations than Southern blacks. Parker and Kleiner (1966) found that the Northern-reared aspired to higher status occupations than did the Southern-reared. When residents of Philadelphia were offered a hypothetical choice between a low-paying white collar job and a high-paying blue collar job, 57 percent of the Southern migrants chose the white collar position, but 69 percent of the native-born and 78 percent of the Northern migrants preferred the white collar job.

Furthermore, the Northern- and Southern-reared young people in our sample (those 15–29 years of age) differed significantly in their optimism regarding the attainability of additional education they desired. Over 90 percent of both groups said that they wanted more education, both Northern- and Southern-reared young people wanting an average of four additional years of schooling. However, 83 percent of the Los Angeles natives felt they would reach this goal, as compared with only 63 percent of the Southern migrants ($p < .005$).

The second expected effect, a difference in relative deprivation between Northern natives and Southern migrants, derives from the difference between the two groups with regard to the social structure of the region in which they received their socialization. Thibaut and Kelley proposed that greater perceived control over one's outcomes affects the CL by increasing the number of reference groups whose outcomes one vicariously experiences. One implication of this is that in societies with heavy emphasis upon ascribed status, the range of persons and groups whose outcomes contribute to an individual's CL is quite limited, whereas in achieved status systems the range is much broader. Thus, we might propose that the individual reared in the North, where there is more emphasis upon achieved status and where the caste lines are blurred, would compare himself with a greater range of persons, including affluent white society, than would a black person reared in the South.

When he came to the North, the Southern migrant would evaluate his new experiences by using a CL which was low, not only because of his poor past outcomes, but also because of the narrow range of the people and groups (mostly Negro) with whom he compared himself while in the South. Since his new outcomes would be well above his CL, he would (temporarily, at least) be in a state of relative satisfaction.

On the other hand, the young Northern urban black person's CL would be higher than the Southern migrant's because of his past experiences, and above

his actual outcomes because he compares himself with whites as well as blacks. For example, a black person who compared himself to whites with similar educational attainments would find his outcomes below those of this reference group; e.g., in 1966, whites with a grade school education earned an average of $1,099 more than blacks with the same education. Furthermore, as education increased, whites' advantage increased to $3,095 among those with a college degree (Bureau of Labor Statistics, 1967).

To examine the relative deprivation hypothesis further, we constructed a measure of deprivation by combining the responses to two questions: "What kind of work are you doing?" and "If you could have any job, what would you most like to do?" The responses to each question were grouped into nine steps according to the NORC prestige ratings of the occupations given. The rank of the present job was subtracted from the rank of the job the respondent would most like to have, creating a nine-step distribution ranging from 0 (wanted a job of the same rank or less compared to his present job) to 8 (wanted a job which was 8 ranks above his present job). Those scoring 0 on this measure (30 percent) were said to be satisfied; those scoring 1–3 were said to be moderately deprived (35 percent); and those scoring 4–8 were said to be highly deprived (35 percent). Los Angeles natives and migrants to Los Angeles from other Northern areas were significantly more deprived on this measure than were Southern migrants ($\chi^2 = 28.86, 4df, p < .001$). Among the young, the effect of region of socialization was even more pronounced. Natives (36 percent) and Northern migrants (32 percent) were almost twice as likely as Southern migrants (17 percent) to score as highly deprived.

Thus, it appears that Northern natives and Southern migrants to the North differ in their aspirations, their optimism, and their satisfaction with their life experiences. The natives have higher aspirations, are more optimistic, and feel more deprived of the rewards they see whites getting than do their brothers who have recently arrived from the South.

Relative deprivation and riot participation. Now we turn to the question of whether or not this state of relative deprivation is related to participation in the riot. We know that the strains of higher aspirations can produce psychopathology (Parker and Kleiner, 1966). It appears that these strains can also produce social violence. Of those who were optimistic about attaining additional education, 29 percent reported themselves active in the riot, and 42 percent scored high on the events-witnessed scale. The pessimists were lower on both indexes: 15 percent on self-reported activity and 24 percent on events witnessed. The differences were highly significant ($p < .001$ in each case).

Relative deprivation, as we measured it, was also related to riot participation. Sixteen percent of the satisfied reported themselves active. This increased to 25 percent of the moderately deprived and 31 percent of the highly deprived ($\chi^2 = 9.89$, $2df$, $p < .01$). Among the young, the differences between the deprived and the satisfied were even greater (20 percent, 40 percent, and 44 percent, respectively). The deprived and satisfied did not differ significantly on the events-witnessed index. As deprivation increased, the number of events witnessed also increased. However, the differences were not large enough to be significant.

The role of powerlessness, or lack of control over one's outcomes, has already been alluded to above. Respondents who felt they could not trust local authority, or who felt they could "do nothing" if abused by the police, tended more often to be involved in the riot. This corroborates findings reported by others. Ransford (1968), in another survey of blacks in South Central Los Angeles, found the greatest endorsement of violence among those who felt dissatisfied relative to the treatment accorded whites and other reference groups, who felt powerless, and who had little social contact with whites.[6] Crawford and Naditch (1968) extended this analysis, proposing that degree of perceived powerlessness would determine whether the dissatisfied would strike out in violence, or would attempt to use conventional procedures of grievance redress. They reanalyzed Ransford's data and found that the dissatisfied who felt subjectively powerful were indeed more likely to have engaged in civil rights

demonstrations, whereas endorsing violence was most common with dissatisfaction and felt powerlessness.

Summary

The basic hypothesis offered here is that the outbreak of mass violence was an almost inevitable consequence of the major population changes that American Negroes have been undergoing in recent years.

(1) The most important of these population changes have been the movement from the South to the North, the movement from rural areas to the largest metropolitan centers, and the rapid rise in the average level of education, in combination with the extreme youth of the black population.

(2) Individuals from the "new" background (the young natives of Northern cities) were considerably more active in the riots than were those from the "old" background (the older, migrants from the South).

(3) Two principal socio-psychological mediators were offered to explain this finding: the attitudinal and behavioral effects of changes in black racial socialization, and of differential comparison levels.

(4) Evidence was presented that early racial socialization produces predispositions that tend to endure through life. For Negroes, contemporary Northern socialization is generally thought to involve more abrasive and assertive norms of behavior toward white authority and white-dominated social institutions than does Southern socialization, particularly that of earlier times. Data from the Watts riot suggest that young Northern natives were more disaffected from the political structure, and were more likely to endorse violence, than were older and migrant residents. The disaffected were also considerably more likely to have been involved in the riot.

(5) The Northern natives also appear to feel more deprived than do the Southern blacks. And dissatisfaction in this sense was related to participation in the riot.

It goes without saying that no single explanation or set of explanations is likely to be adequate for such complex and massive social events as the recent race riots. However, the evidence presented here suggests that fundamental and irreversible social changes in the location and characteristics of the black population have produced important social-psychological changes within individual blacks. These, in turn, have increased enormously the probability that blacks will respond to white racism with intransigence, vigorous protest, and even violence.

The further implication is that the apparently centrifugal movement represented by the Deacons, the Black Panthers, and the wavering attachment of some young militants to the American political and economic system are not epiphenomena; nor are they merely representative of a small minority's peculiar and disreputable ideas. They symbolize, although in more extreme form, the direction being taken by young ghetto natives throughout the country. Our data suggest that the direction and thrust of this movement are irreversible without extreme measures that white Americans presumably would not condone. The question appears to be whether or not institutional America, and the white population more generally, are prepared to accept the new "black man" as a replacement for the old "Negro." There seems to be little chance that the latter will return.

References

Barber, J. A., Jr. "Social Mobility and Political Behavior." Unpublished Ph.D. dissertation, Stanford University, 1965.

Beardwood, R. "The New Negro Mood." *Fortune* 78 (1968): 146 passim.

Benham, T. W. "Polling for a Presidential Candidate: Some Observations on the 1964 Campaign." *Public Opinion Quarterly* 29 (1965): 185–99.

Bloom, B. S. *Stability and Change in Human Characteristics.* New York: Wiley, 1964.

Brink, W., and L. Harris. *Black and White.* New York: Simon and Schuster, 1966.

Bureau of Labor Statistics. *Social and Economic Conditions of Negroes in the United States.* BLS Report 332. Washington, D.C.: Government Printing Office, 1967.

Campbell, A., P. E. Converse, W. E. Miller, and D. E. Stokes. *The American Voter.* New York: Wiley, 1960.

Campbell, A., and H. Schuman. "Racial Attitudes in Fifteen American Cities." *Supplemental Studies for the National Advisory Commission on Civil Disorders.* Washington, D.C.: Government Printing Office, 1968.

Converse, P. E. "Attitudes and Non-attitudes: Continuation of a Dialogue." Paper presented at the meeting of the International Congress of Psychology, Washington, D.C., August, 1963.

Converse, P. E. "The Nature of Belief Systems in Mass Publics." *Ideology and Discontent.* Edited by D. E. Apter. New York: Free Press, 1964.

Crawford, T. J., and M. Naditch. "Unattained and Unattainable Goals: Relative Deprivation, Powerlessness, and Racial Militancy." Paper presented to the American Psychological Association Convention, September, 1968.

Greenstein, F. I. *Children and Politics.* New Haven: Yale University Press, 1965.

Hess, R. D., and J. V. Torney. *The Development of Political Attitudes in Children.* Chicago: Aldine, 1967.

Jacobs, P. *Prelude to Riot: A View of Urban America from the Bottom.* New York: Random House, 1966.

Jennings, M. K., and R. G. Niemi. "The Transmission of Political Values from Parent to Child." *American Political Science Review* 62 (1968): 169–84.

Kerner, O. et al. *Report of the National Advisory Commission on Civil Disorders.* New York: Bantam, 1968.

Lazarsfeld, P. F., B. Berelson, and H. Gaudet. *The People's Choice.* 2nd ed. New York: Columbia University Press, 1948.

Murphy, R. J., and J. M. Watson. "The Structure of Discontent: The Relationship Between Social Structure, Grievance, and Support for the Los Angeles Riot." *The Los Angeles Riots: A Socio-Psychological Study.* Edited by N. E. Cohen. New York: Praeger, 1970.

Newcomb, T. T., K. E. Koenig, R. Flacks, and D. P. Warwick. *Persistence and Change: Bennington College and Its Students After 25 Years.* New York: Wiley, 1967.

Niemi, R. G. "Collecting Information About the Family: A Problem in Survey Methodology." *Political Socialization: A Reader of Theory and Research.* Edited by J. Dennis and F. W. Frey. New York: Wiley, 1969.

Parker, S. and R. J. Kleiner. *Mental Illness in the Urban Negro Community.* New York: Free Press, 1966.

Pettigrew, T. F. *A Profile of the Negro American.* Princeton, N.J.: Van Nostrand, 1964.

Pettigrew, T. F. "Social Evaluation Theory: Convergences and Applications." *Nebraska Symposium on Motivation.* Edited by L. Levine. Lincoln: University of Nebraska Press, 1967.

Proshansky, H. M. "The Development of Intergroup Attitudes." *Review of Child Development Research*. Vol. 2. Edited by L. W. Hoffman and M. L. Hoffman. New York: Russell Sage Foundation, 1966.

Raine, W. J. "The Perception of Police Brutality in South Central Los Angeles." *The Los Angeles Riots: A Socio-Psychological Study*. Edited by N. E. Cohen. New York: Praeger, 1970.

Ransford, H. E. "Isolation, Powerlessness, and Violence: A Study of Attitudes and Participation in the Watts Riot." *American Journal of Sociology* 73 (1968): 581–91.

Sears, D. O. "Political Behavior." *Handbook of Social Psychology*. Edited by G. Lindzey and E. Aronson (Revised ed.). Reading: Addison-Wesley, 1969. (a).

Sears, D. O. "Black Attitudes Toward the Political System in the Aftermath of the Watts Insurrection." *Midwest Journal of Political Science* 13 (1969): 515–44. (b)

Sears, D. O. and J. B. McConahay. Participation in the Los Angeles Riot." *Social Problems* 17 (1969) no. 1: 3–20.

Sears, D. O., and J. B. McConahay. "The Politics of Discontent: Blocked Mechanisms of Grievance Redress and the Psychology of the New Urban Black Man." *The Los Angeles Riots: A Socio-Psychological Study*. Edited by N. E. Cohen. New York: Praeger, 1970.

Sears, D. O., and T. M. Tomlinson. "Riot Ideology in Los Angeles: A Study of Negro Attitudes." *Social Science Quarterly* 49 (1968): 485–503.

Sheatsley, P. B. "White Attitudes Toward the Negro." *Daedalus* 95 (1966): 217–38.

Sigel, R. S. "Image of a President: Some Insights into the Political Views of School Children." *American Political Science Review* 62 (1968): 216–26.

Taeuber, K. E., and A. F. Taeuber. "The Negro Population in the United States." *The American Negro Reference Book*. Edited by J. P. Davis. Englewood Cliffs, N.J.: Prentice-Hall, 1966.

Thibaut, J. W., and H. H. Kelley. *The Social Psychology of Groups*. New York: Wiley, 1959.

Tomlinson, T. M. "Militance, Violence and Poverty: Ideology and Foundation for Action." *The Los Angeles Riots: A Socio-Psychological Study*. Edited by N. E. Cohen. New York: Praeger, 1970.

Tomlinson, T. M., and D. TenHouten. "Method: Negro Reaction Study." *The Los Angeles Riots: A Socio-Psychological Study*. Edited by N. E. Cohen. New York: Praeger, 1970.

Wolfinger, R. E. "The Development and Persistence of Ethnic Voting." *The American Political Science Review* 59 (1965): 896–908.

Notes

[1] Migration to Southern cities still tends to be from rural areas. In the same period, only 29 percent of those moving to Atlanta came from metropolitan areas.

[2] For a more detailed account of the procedure, see Tomlinson and TenHouten (1970).

[3] This greater participation of Northern natives and the absence of substantial relationships between indicators of social class and riot participation have been typical findings of recent riot studies.

See the *Report of the National Advisory Commission* (Kerner et al., 1968), and Murphy and Watson (1970).

[4] Sheatsley (1966) has argued that these events had a conservatizing effect on the same generation of young Southern whites.

[5] These data and the others to be presented in this section are given in considerably greater detail in Sears and McConahay (1970). Our purpose here is to illustrate the findings rather than present them exhaustively.

[6] See Murphy and Watson (1970) for additional discussion of the role of interracial contact.

6

Political Perception

The process of perception is the means by which the individual sees and takes account of objects in his environment. It is the way in which one views those objects subjectively and thereby treats them as objective reality. In our context, these objects are primarily political, e.g., parties, candidates, enemies, slogans, events; and they constitute a set of specific stimuli which translate generalized attitudes into political opinions. Perception is therefore a link between environmental stimuli and political opinions. It is a screening process which is shaped by sets of predispositions, such as physiological and psychological needs and one's existing belief system, and it acts to filter political stimuli.[1] This screening is necessary for the individual to make sense out of a multitude of stimuli, since we are each limited in our capacity for understanding and assimilating complex events and objects in our environment. It is therefore an important process which enables one to cope with his surroundings.

Nature of the Object

The operation of this *perceptual screen* and the extent to which it enables a match of objective and subjective realities, a filtering out of certain stimuli, distortion and misperception, is part of the cognitive process of acquiring attitudes and it depends on a variety of factors. Two important factors are the *nature* of the object being perceived and the *physiological*

---

[1] For an elaboration of this theme see Lester W. Milbrath, *Political Participation: How and Why Do People Get Involved in Politics?* (Chicago: Rand McNally & Company, 1965), pp. 33ff.

capacities of the individual. All perception, whether of physical objects or social processes, is dependent upon physiological characteristics (e.g., neurological, sensory mechanisms), yet the type of object shapes the nature of that perception. When we speak of physical and visual perception we realize that the process *is* different from the perception of social and political processes and objects. In the world of politics the screening process is more adaptive and flexible; there are few political objects so intrusive as a loud noise or strong odor. Whereas these more physical stimuli cannot be easily avoided in everyday life, political objects are readily subject to avoidance and misperception. In political perception we are often perceiving people (e.g., candidates, leaders) and this implies that we are perceiving something similar to ourselves and can thereby look within to understand others. Furthermore, our perception of political objects is rarely based on one characteristic of the object (as a perception of color) but on a pattern of attributes and diverse observations.

The Context of Perception

In addition to the nature of the object, the process of perception is influenced by the *context* in which it is observed, the form of communication and the strength of the stimulus. When political and social objects are perceived, a larger range of attitudes and evaluations result than from the process of perceiving, for example, a chair. Political stimuli evoke stronger feelings than physical objects, and the strength of this stimulus is partially determined by the context in which it occurs. Our perception of a chair is invariant over a range of contexts, but our perception of political candidates varies by the content of the campaign and the social interaction of the individual. The situation, whether viewed in broad environmental terms (e.g., culture) or in terms of a more immediate and intimate environment (e.g., peer groups), as well as the manner in which one defines these relationships, influences perception. One's intimate environment, such as family or peer group, will have a more immediate impact on perception. Yet the individual's entire range of social relationships, his group memberships, his roles and his social status are also influential. Often these sociological conditions, particularly in the intimate environment, will even influence one's capacity for perceiving physical objects. In a famous experiment Solomon Asch found that perception of the length of lines was shaped by group norms and a group consensus on their length.[2] Another component of the situation is the nature of the process by which political objects are communicated to the individual. If

[2] "Effects of Group Pressure Upon the Modification and Distortion of Judgment," in H. Guetzkow, ed., *Groups, Leadership, and Men* (Pittsburgh: Carnegie Press, 1951).

the source of this communication is a trusted source within a primary group, there is less filtering of the perception than if the source is the mass media. Therefore, social factors (e.g., one's social characteristics and group identifications) are not only directly linked to perception, but they are also means by which political object-specific stimuli are communicated to the individual.

Belief System

The nature of one's existing belief system is also a primary determinant of perception and its accuracy. The cognitive network gradually defines credibility, affecting the manner of perceiving a source as credible. The individual tends to perceive on the basis of existing beliefs, and later perception builds upon and reinforces these beliefs. The perceptual screen is therefore more likely to filter out or distort those political stimuli which are not consonant with, or do not reinforce the existing beliefs. Often political objects are placed beyond one's range of acceptance and, based upon existing beliefs, they will be perceived as more discrepant than they actually are. This "contrasting" is a function of the degree of ego involvement (high involvement, greater contrast), the properties of the communication process by which stimuli are introduced (ambiguous communications are more subject to contrast), and the context of the immediate situation.[3]

Socialization, Personality, and Culture

We have suggested that the nature of the object, the strength of the stimulus, the form of the communication and the social context within which it occurs, as well as the existing belief system all help to shape the process of political perception. Yet there are three additional factors which also play an important role. (1) The process of *political socialization,* including the modes of adapting which the individual learns, is actually a process of learning to perceive. The individual will perceive in ways that are characteristic of the discriminating ability passed on to him by the agents of socialization. For example, a child reared in an authoritarian family structure will be socialized to simple cues of right and wrong, and his ability to make fine distinctions in the perception process will thereby be hampered. (2) It follows that the individual *personality*

[3]Carolyn W. Sherif, Muzafer Sherif and Roger E. Nebergall, *Attitude and Attitude Change* (Philadelphia: W. B. Saunders Co., 1965), pp. 226ff.

structure will also shape perceptions; not only will visible personality attributes be influential, but, more important, the individual will also perceive as a function of his needs. (3) On a much broader level, the *cultural environment* of the individual, the norms, prescriptions, proscriptions, and myths, and the communications systems within the culture (e.g., language, media) not only influence his perceptual capabilities, but they also determine the salience of political objects in his environment.

Balance Model

The various components discussed above are often interrelated to form theories of perception. While these theories and the arguments over them are not a primary concern here, there are several general models which have guided research on perception, particularly political perception. The most frequently used model is what Sigel (below) refers to as *perceptual balance*. This model is based on theories of stress reduction which postulate that in order to avoid stress, the individual will perceive what is favorable and distort what is unfavorable. That is, perception is perceiver-determined, resulting in a comfortable balance of perception for the individual. This model has enhanced our understanding of political perception, and it has encouraged political scientists to focus on misperception and the avoidance of stress. In attempting to understand voting behavior and the system-level implications of perception, i.e., patterns of cleavage and consensus on political parties, issues and candidates, Berelson and his associates (below) have paid explicit attention to the process of perception. They are concerned with those factors that influence the lack of congruence between the "pictures in our heads" and objective reality. Relying on perceptual balance and the functions which it performs (e.g., avoidance of stress), they view perception as a defense against things complex and uncomfortable. They find that the voter oversees the favorable and distorts or denies the unfavorable; a political campaign is perceived so that it is satisfying to the individual. Although one may change existing opinions to achieve balance, he may perceive only what he wants to perceive in order to *avoid* stress. This process of selective perception contributes to psychological rationality, since perception can maximize agreement with one's own candidate and maximize disagreement with the opposition, i.e., the vote decision appears rational to the individual. Through the use of such mechanisms as rationalization, generalization, exclusion and denial, the perception process makes for greater intraparty consensus and less interparty consensus. Voters exaggerate the support of groups for their own party, i.e., the closer the voter is to a particular group (in status or contact), the more likely he is to perceive them as voting his way; voters hostile to certain groups (e.g., racial) assign them to the opposition. In addition, Berelson and his colleagues show that misperception of a candidate's position on issues is prevalent among two-thirds of the voters in their study. The more intense a voter is in his choice of a candidate, the more likely he is to misperceive that candidate's position; and if he disagrees with both candidates, he will offer more support for his own party's candidate than will a voter who agrees with both candidates.

Related research achieves refinements of this scheme by attempting to treat factors related to one's misperceiving a party's stand on *issues*.[4] By examining two types of issues, position issues, or those basically material (e.g., public ownership), and style issues, or those basically idealistic (e.g., war and peace, civil rights), it has been found that misperception varies according to the type of issue. It is greater on style issues because these are issues on which the parties are more alike in objective reality, and therefore perceptions about them are more influenced by one's party loyalty. This loyalty is a way for the individual to create perceived differences between the parties, and it is more likely to occur among citizens with low education. In contrast, misperception on position issues is more likely to occur among those with weak party attachment. This finding has led to the recommendation that candidates should appeal to their own partisans on the basis of style issues, but appeal to the opposition on position issues. This recommendation is based on the assumption that broad generalizations will be more persuasive with supporters but much less persuasive with opponents. Individuals in the opposing party perceive their party as the one of peace and prosperity (style), therefore a candidate should stress position issues when appealing for their support, so that they will suppose the candidate to be an exception to their usually perceived party differences. It is the weak party identifier in the opposition party who is most confused about which party will fulfill his position-issue needs; it is these people who are most likely to be persuaded or converted by the opposition-party candidate.

Transactional Model

Another approach similar to the balance model is one referred to as "transactional."[5] This model views perception as a *choice* or even a guess

[4] Lewis A. Froman, Jr., and James K. Skipper, "Factors Related to Misperceiving Party Stands on Issues," *Public Opinion Quarterly* 26 (1962): 265–72; and Lewis A. Froman, Jr., "A Realistic Approach to Campaign Strategies and Tactics," in M. Kent Jennings and L. Harmon Zeigler, eds., *The Electoral Process* (Englewood Cliffs: Prentice-Hall, Inc., 1966), pp. 1–20.

[5] Joseph DeRivera, *The Psychological Dimension of Foreign Policy* (Columbus: Charles E. Merrill Publishing Company, 1968), pp. 20–22.

about the objective reality of a political object or stimulus. For any political object a large number of choices exist, and those choices are dependent on other elements in the belief system, i.e., beliefs about related objects. The final choice or perception is one which is consonant with other beliefs. This is not only important for the individual in the mass public, but also for all political actors, some of whom are important decision makers in the political system, and therefore their perceptions may have immediate policy consequences. If an event occurs in Hanoi—perhaps a sincere peace offer is made public—and a top decision maker in the United States who distrusts Hanoi perceives that event, his perception is likely to require the least reorganization of his existing belief system. From this example it is possible to surmise how many chances for peace might be lost by inaccurate perception. Local community leaders are equally subject to misperception, and it has been found that they are most likely to misperceive community opinions in areas where their personal preferences are different from the preferences of constituents.[6] These leaders misperceive and *selectively* perceive in order to *balance* perceptions and play their leadership role properly.

Image Model

Even another theory is investigated in the essay by Roberta Sigel: *image theory*. This theory postulates that one's images are stimulus-determined (vs. perceiver-determined), e.g., by the candidate, and that the image conveyed accounts for the individual's perception. She finds that perception is stimulus-determined when it focuses on objective characteristics of candidates (e.g., personality, appearance) but perceiver-determined on political traits (e.g., political views of candidates).

Political Actors and Objects

While the first two readings to follow focus on perceptions of political candidates and parties, the remaining readings treat perceptions of the enemy (Soviet Union) and perceptions of a rhetorical political object (black power). In a case study of one political actor, John Foster Dulles, Ole Holsti explores cognitive processes that tend to sustain images of the Soviet Union. His framework treats the relationship of *belief systems* to

[6] Roberta A. Sigel and H. Paul Friesema, "Urban Community Leaders' Knowledge of Public Opinion," *Western Political Quarterly* 18 (1965): 883–95.

perception, viewing the belief system as a filter or a lens for environmental stimuli. He also relies on balance concepts to investigate the consequences of belief inconsistencies and various modes of imbalance resolution relevant to the perception process. The author attempts to combine several of the factors shaping perceptions as discussed above by examining the content and source of incoming discrepant information, the nature of the situation and the personality of the actor.

A final selection in the readings (Aberbach and Walker) brings together a variety of factors influencing perceptions of a political slogan—black power. This is a relatively new political object, emerging as a result of controversy over the proper role of a black minority in the United States. The authors' basic premise is that one's definition of the slogan provides important information about how one defines himself politically. The modal interpretation of white respondents is one of "hysterical response" related to fears of black rule over whites. On the other hand, blacks are more likely to relate black power to black unity or a fair share for blacks. When factors influencing a favorable perception of black power are examined for black citizens, few differences are found on the basis of age or SES—casting doubt on "riffraff" or generation gap theories. Other factors emerge as significant influences: differences in cultural environment and socialization, evident in less favorable interpretations among southern blacks who migrate to the north; the impact of religious influences, leading to more favorable reactions to black power among those who have broken with the church; and the role of political trust, with a tendency for those with highest trust to offer less favorable interpretations. In addition, the authors offer a detailed discussion of a factor mentioned earlier in this chapter: the impact of an existing belief system on perceptions of a new political object and the degree of interrelationship among those beliefs.

Selected Additional Readings

Lippman, Walter. *Public Opinion.* Pp. 15ff. New York: Macmillan, 1960.

McGrath, J. E., and M. F. McGrath. "Effects of Partisanship on Perceptions of Political Figures." *Public Opinion Quarterly* 26 (1962): 236–48.

Milbrath, Lester W. *Political Participation.* Pp. 29–47. Chicago: Rand McNally & Company, 1965.

"Misperception and the Viet Nam War." *Journal of Social Issues* 22 (1966): entire issue.

Robinson, John P., and Robert Hefner. "Perceptual Maps of the World." *Public Opinion Quarterly* 32 (1968): 273–81.

Sears, David O., and Jonathan L. Freedman. "Selective Exposure to Information: A Critical Review." *Public Opinion Quarterly* 31 (1967): 194–213.

Sigel, Roberta A., and H. Paul Friesema. "Urban Community Leaders' Knowledge of Public Opinion." *Western Political Quarterly* 18 (1965): 883–95.

White, Ralph K. "Misperception of Aggression in Vietnam." *Journal of International Affairs* 1 (1967): 123–40.

Political Perception

Bernard Berelson

Paul Lazarsfeld

William McPhee

The modern political party in a town like Elmira has an effective existence more in the minds of the partisans than in the local community's formal political organizations. . . . This existence is primarily expressed through differences in attitudes toward political issues of the day.

But this is not the only way in which the partisans differentiate themselves. There is also the fact of political perception—how the voter *sees* events in the political world. Specifically, we are concerned here with how voters in 1948 saw the issues of the campaign and what difference that made in their political behavior.

Now this is not simply a nice psychological problem with little relevance for the political situation. The process of political perception can operate to increase cleavage or consensus within the community. It undoubtedly contributes directly to a "real" definition of the differences between the parties, in terms of what might be called their "political norms."

For political beliefs and perceptions have a strongly "normative" quality. They not only state that "this is the way things are," but they also imply that "this is their customary or natural state" and therefore what

they "ought" to be. The parties are not only what their leaders do or say; the parties are also what their followers believe they are, expect them to be, and therefore think they should be.

Once again we encounter a brief glimpse of the spiral of cause and effect that constitutes political history—in this case the history of political issues: What the parties do affects what the voters think they are and what the voters think they are affects what they subsequently do. Out of this interaction between subjective perception and objective reality, mutually affecting one another over decades, emerges not only our Definition but the reality of a political party's role. The popular image of "what Republicans (or Democrats) are like" helps to define and determine what they "really" are. Today's subjective unreality in the voters' minds affects tomorrow's objective reality in the political arena.

About thirty years ago an analyst of public opinion gained lasting distinction by elaborating the differences between "the world outside and the pictures in our heads." Walter Lippmann discussed what many theorists—philosophers, psychologists, sociologists, political scientists, anthropologists—have noted and documented before and since: subjective perception does not always reflect objective reality accurately. Selective perception—sampling the real world—must be taken into account. The mirror that the mind holds up to nature is often distorted in accordance with the subject's predispositions. The "trickle of messages from the outside is affected by the stored-up images, the preconceptions, and the prejudices which interpret, fill them out, and in their turn powerfully direct the play of our attention, and our vision itself. . . . In the individual person, the limited messages from outside, formed into a pattern of stereotypes, are identified with his own interests as he feels and conceives them."[1] Another student of public opinion put it similarly: "Each looks at, and looks for, the facts and reasons to which his attention points, perceiving little, if at all, those to which his mind is not directed. As a rule, men see what they look for, and observe the things they expect to see."[2]

The world of political reality, even as it involves a presidential campaign and election, is by no means simple or narrow. Nor is it crystal-clear. Over a period of six months, and intensively for six weeks, the electorate is subjected to a wide variety of campaign events. Even if all the political events were unambiguous, there would still be a problem of political perception; but, as it is, the campaign is composed (often deliberately) of ambiguous as well as clear elements.

Perception and Voting

Just how clear was the objective field to be perceived in 1948? Some propagandists, and some students of propaganda, believe that ambiguity often promotes effectiveness, since each subject is then free to define the matter in terms satisfactory to himself. While a sharply clear statement may win some friends by its very decisiveness, it may also lose some people for the same reason. Now Truman and Dewey had both been public figures for some time and had taken public stands on many political matters; yet their positions on the issues in the campaign were not equally clear.

In 1948 Truman took a more straightforward and more aggressive position on these issues than Dewey (Table 1). The latter spoke to a large extent on the need for unity, peace, and freedom, while Truman specified his position *for* price control and public housing and *against* the Taft-Hartley Law. And Truman used quite vigorous language in stating his position, whereas Dewey employed a more lofty rhetoric. Except perhaps for the Russian issue (which became involved with the spy and domestic Communist issue), there can be no question but that, objectively, Dewey's position was more amenable to misperception than Truman's.

And this is reflected in the extent of nonperception of the candidates' stands.[3] On the four issues the proportion of respondents who do not know the candidates' stands average about 10 percent for Truman and about 25 percent for Dewey. (This also reflects the fact that Truman's official position brought him before the public on such issues on numerous occasions; but a counterconsideration is that Dewey's position as governor of New York made him especially familiar to Elmirans.)

Perception and Party Preference

More importantly, the voter's perception of where the candidates stand on the issues is not uniformly affected by partisan preference—only selectively so (Fig. 1). It is not marked on the central issues of price control and the Taft-Hartley Law. Republicans and Democrats agree that Truman is for price control and against the Taft-Hartley Law and that Dewey is for the Taft-Hartley Law and against price control (although on this last there is by no means a clear perception of where Dewey stood). On public housing (and, as we saw earlier, on the Russian problem) the difference between the parties was greater.

Why should the partisans agree in perception on some issues and disagree on others? For one thing, of course, perception varies with the ambiguity of the situation. The less ambiguous the objective situation (e.g., Truman's position on price control), the less disagreement. But, for another, perception seems to vary with the degree of controversiality of the issues in the community. On price control and the Taft-

Table 1

Positions Taken by Dewey and Truman on Four Issues During the Campaign

	Dewey	*Truman*
Price Control	Causes of high prices were war, foreign aid, the administration's discouragement of production, governmental mismanagement Remedies: cut government spending, reduce national debt, increase production No reference to imposition of controls Only one major reference	Republicans would not act against inflation in Eightieth Congress or special session; they rejected the administration's program Called for price controls or anti-inflation measures on several occasions
Taft-Hartley Law	Referred to it as "Labor-Management Relations Act of 1947," never as "Taft-Hartley Law" Made abstract remarks about "labor's freedoms" which would be "zealously guarded and extended" Approved the law in general ("will not retreat from advances made") but left door open for improvements ("where laws affecting labor can be made a better instrument for labor relations . . .")	Made the "shameful" and "vicious" law a major issue; recalled that Republicans passed it over his veto: "It ought to be repealed" Took this position in at least ten major campaign speeches during October
Policy Toward U.S.S.R.	Took a strong anti-communism position; linked communism to administration Made this a major issue in about seven campaign speeches	Took an anti-communism position; major references twice
Public Housing	Only minor references to need for more housing (Republican platform called for housing financed by private enterprise, with federal "encouragement" when private industry and local government were unable to fill need)	Republicans "killed" Taft-Ellender-Wagner Bill Called for public housing sponsored by government in at least ten major campaign speeches

Hartley Law the respondents with opinions divided about 60–40; on the other two issues (including firmness toward Russia), in Elmira the split is about 90–10. In the latter case, then, there is virtual agreement within the community—which means that one side of the issue is considered "right" and the other side "wrong." Hence there is, so to speak, a standard to guide misperception—and each side pulls its own candidate toward the "correct position" and pushes the opponent away from it. On the two central issues,

however, the controversy is too visible to allow a designation of "rightness" for one or the other side, and as a result there is less motive for or gain in misperception. If the voter gets nothing for his misperception (e.g., being "right"), there is less reason for him to engage in it. Deviation or misperception requires a certain degree of ambiguity in the objective situation being perceived, but it also requires a psychic indulgence for the misperceiver. Where this opportunity is not present, perception is likely to be more accurate.

Dewey's Stand / Truman's Stand

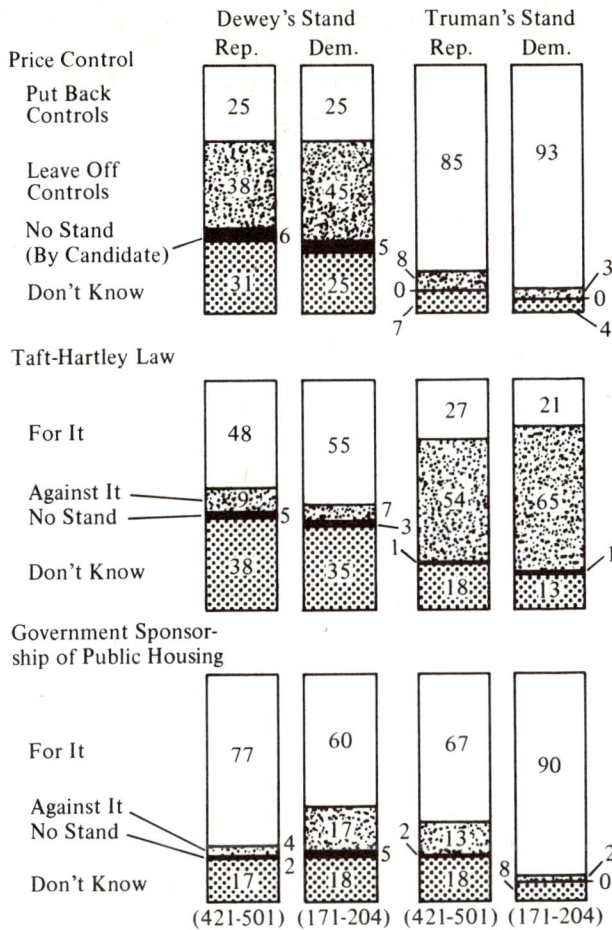

Fig. 1. Party preference does not particularly affect the voter's perception of where the candidates stand on some campaign issues

Perception and Own Stand

This suggests that perception of the candidates' stands on issues may be affected by the respondents' own stands on them. The voters can thus manage to increase the consistency within their own political position, or at least the apparent consistency. And this is clearly the case. In almost every instance respondents perceive their candidate's stand on these issues as similar to their own and the opponent's stand as dissimilar—whatever their own position (Fig. 2). For example, those Republicans who favor price control perceive Dewey as favoring price control (70 percent), and few who oppose price control perceive Dewey as favoring controls (14 percent). And the Republicans who are against controls perceive Truman as favoring them somewhat more than the Republicans who are for them. As with their perception of group support, so with their perception of the issues: the partisans manage to "pull" their own candidate and "push" the opposing candidate with considerable consistency. Overlaying the base of objective observation is the distortion effect—distortion in harmony with political predispositions. As Schumpeter says, "Information and arguments in political matters will 'register' only if they link up with the citizen's preconceived ideas."[4]

At the same time, some voters maintain or increase their perceptual defense on political issues by refusing to acknowledge differences with one's own candidate or similarities to the opposition candidate. Such denial of reality, a defense utilized against uncongenial aspects of the environment, is well documented by case studies and laboratory experiments in the psychological literature of neurosis. Here we have evidence on its operation in the midst of a political campaign where motivation is less strong.

Take the two major issues of price control and the Taft-Hartley Law, on which the candidates took relatively clear positions. Objectively, an observer would say that Truman was for and Dewey against price control and that Truman was against Dewey for the Taft-Hartley Law. Yet, when our respondents are asked where the candidates stand, a certain proportion of them do not know or profess not to know. But—and this is the point—the "Don't knows" are more frequent among partisans who themselves take a different position from their own candidate or the same position as the opponent (Fig. 3).

Perception and Strength of Feeling

This tendency to "misperceive" issues in a favorable direction does not operate in a uniform fashion

Percentage of Those
with Opinions Who
Think the Candidate Is

	Among Republicans Who Are:				Among Democrats Who Are:			
	For the Policy	Against the Policy			For the Policy	Against the Policy		
For Price Control								
Dewey	(144) 70	14 (155)		(146)	(107) 32	43 (30)		
Truman	(223) 87	97	(207)		(99) 99	88 (41)		
For Taft-Hartley Law								
Dewey	(175) 96	54 (46)		(26) 85		95 (62)		
Truman	(224) 27	43 (75)		(47) 40		10 (73)		
For Public Housing								
Dewey	(273) 98	77 (56)		(143) 78	(Too few cases)	(7)		
Truman	(258) 82	89 (65)		(171) 99		(7)		

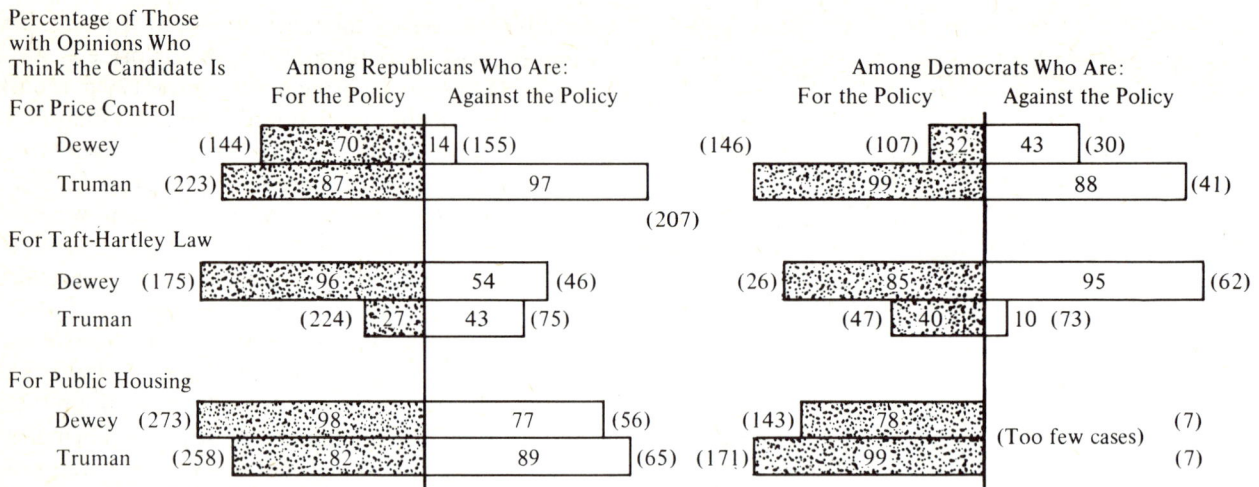

*For simplification and clarity, the "No stand" and the "Don't know" responses have been omitted from this chart. The omission does not affect the point of the data.

Fig. 2.   The voters' own stands on the issues affect their perception of the candidates' stands*

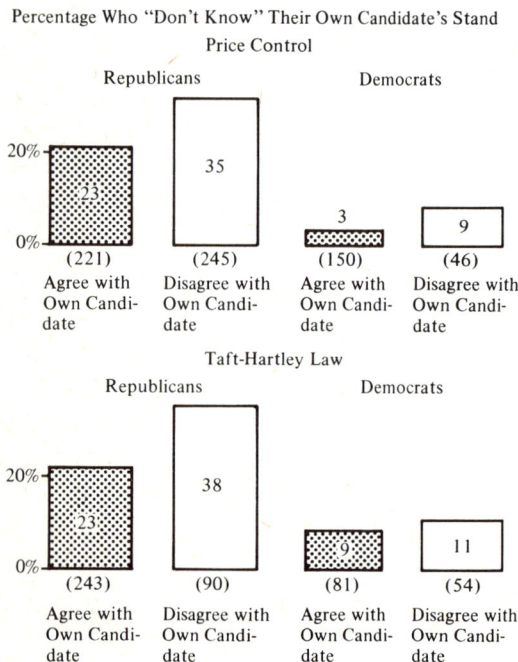

Percentage Who "Don't Know" Their Own Candidate's Stand

Price Control

Republicans		Democrats	
23	35	3	9
(221)	(245)	(150)	(46)
Agree with Own Candidate	Disagree with Own Candidate	Agree with Own Candidate	Disagree with Own Candidate

Taft-Hartley Law

Republicans		Democrats	
23	38	9	11
(243)	(90)	(81)	(54)
Agree with Own Candidate	Disagree with Own Candidate	Agree with Own Candidate	Disagree with Own Candidate

Fig. 3.   Partisans tend not to perceive differences with their own candidate or similarities to the opposition candidate

within the electorate. The degree of affect attached to the election, in the form of intensity upon one's vote intention, also influences perception. Those voters who feel strongly about their vote intention perceive political issues differently from those who do not feel so strongly about the matter (Fig. 4). With remarkable consistency within each party, the intensely involved "pull" their own candidate and "push" the opponent more than the less involved. (Incidentally, it is probably not too much to suggest that this "pull" and "push" are equivalent to the psychological defense mechanisms of generalization and exclusion.)

For example, when objectively they are *not* in agreement with their own party, *strong* Republicans and Democrats perceive their candidate's stand on the issues as more in harmony with their own stand than do weak Republicans and Democrats in the same situation. But, by no means is this a general tendency to see everyone in agreement with themselves. When they objectively disagree with the *opposition* candidate, the strong partisans are quickest to perceive that disagreement. The stronger the partisanship, the *greater* the (mis)perception of agreement with one's own side and the *less* the (mis)perception of agreement with the opposition. Presumably, misperception makes for partisanship, and the reverse. Thus, the people strongest for a candidate — the ones most interested in and active for his election, the ones who make up the core of the party support — are the ones who take the least equivocal position on what their party stands for. And, at the same time, those who favor the party position as they see it are more likely to support the candidate strongly.

In the course of the campaign, then, strength of party support influences the perception of political issues. The more intensely one holds a vote position, the more likely he is to see the political environment as favorable to himself, as conforming to his own beliefs. He is less likely to perceive uncongenial and contradictory events or points of view and hence presumably less likely to revise his own original position. In this manner perception can play a major role in the spiraling effect of political reinforcement.

Necessarily, such partisanly motivated perception increases the recognized or believed differences be-

tween the parties. Strong Republicans and Democrats are farther apart in perception of political issues than weak Republicans and Democrats; they disagree more sharply in their perception of campaign events. Among the strongly partisan, then, the process of perception operates to make the opponent into more of an "enemy" and thus to magnify the potential for political cleavage.

But all this should not be taken to exaggerate the effect of perception (or issues). Regardless of their perception of the issues, important social groups still follow their own voting tradition.[5] An index of agreement was constructed between the position of each respondent and the position he perceived each candidate to be taking. Here again Catholics vote more strongly Democratic regardless of the degree of their ideological agreement with Truman or Dewey (Fig. 5). But why does agreement with Dewey make more difference for Catholics, and agreement with Truman for Protestants?

Now when these two indexes of agreement are combined into one, this curious effect of perceived agreement sharpens. If Protestants and Catholics

Among Those Objectively in Disagreement with the Given Candidate

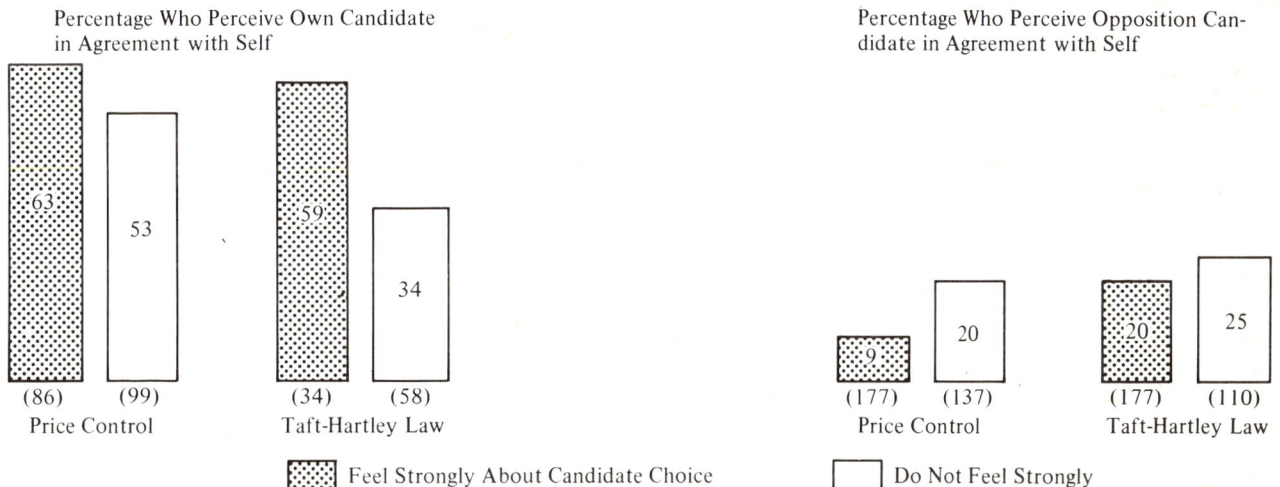

Percentage Who Perceive Own Candidate in Agreement with Self

Percentage Who Perceive Opposition Candidate in Agreement with Self

Feel Strongly About Candidate Choice   Do Not Feel Strongly

*Analogous results are obtained for the housing and "firmer with Russia" issues. This same tendency appears in the case of perception of the support given the candidates by various socioeconomic and ethnic groups. In almost every case strong partisans "pull" approved groups more than weak partisans.

Fig. 4.   **The stronger the political affiliation, the greater the tendency to perceive political issues favorably to oneself**[*]

agree with "their own group's" candidate and disagree with the opponent, then the vote is overwhelmingly for one's own candidate; and, if the situation is reversed, so is the vote—though not so strongly (see Fig. 6). But what of those people who agree with both candidates, as perceived, or with neither? The answer is that voters who *disagree* with both candidates' stands on the issues, as they perceive them, end by supporting their group's "proper" candidate (more strongly than those who agree with both). If they disagree with both candidates, they seem to have no alternative. So they remain loyal, "at home." If they *agree* with both, however, they are more likely to try the other side. When the grass is green in *both* yards, it seems a little greener in the other fellow's!

Accuracy of Perception

The question of "correct" and "incorrect" perception has been implicit in our discussion thus far, since differentiation in perception requires a degree of misperception on the part of some perceivers (assuming a definition of objective reality). But the question has not been given explicit consideration. Without retracing our steps, let us now summarize from this vantage point.

Analysis of the perception that occurs during a presidential campaign requires a definition of what is "correct" perception. In the case of political issues, perceiving the candidates' stands as they predominantly appear in the campaign speeches should serve. Since some stands are ambiguous, or at least contain an element of propagandistic vagueness, we use here two stands of Truman and Dewey that are reasonably straightforward and clear—those on the Taft-Hartley Law (with Truman against and Dewey for) and on price control (with Truman for and Dewey against).

→

Fig. 5. Social differences in voting remain regardless of perceived agreement with candidates

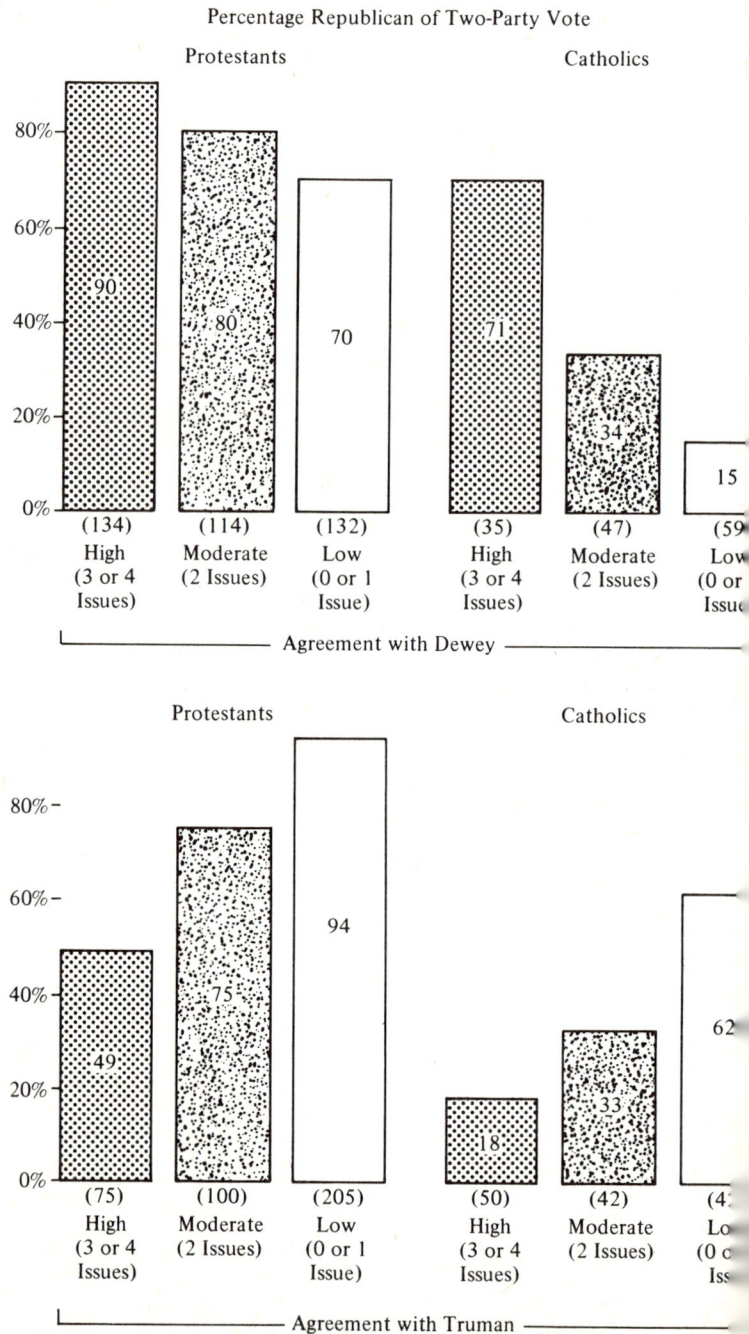

Percentage Republican of Two-Party Vote

Agreement with Dewey

Agreement with Truman

Protestants and Catholics

Percentage Voting for
"Own Group's" Candidate

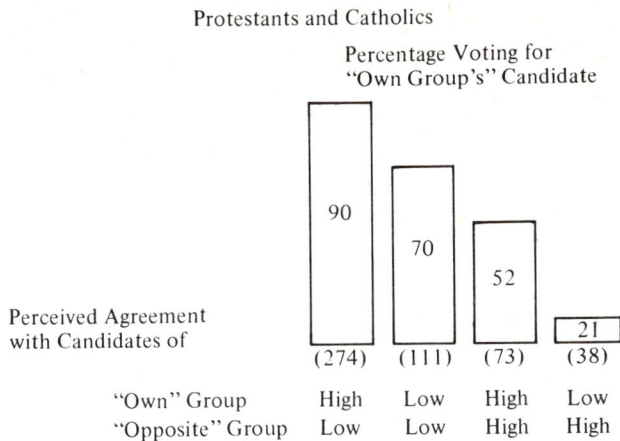

Perceived Agreement
with Candidates of

	High	Low	High	Low
"Own" Group	High	Low	High	Low
"Opposite" Group	Low	Low	High	High

Fig. 6

amount of correct perception, regardless of the barrier presented by the voter's party preference (and despite the fact that those who do most of the reading and listening also feel most strongly for their candidate and are hence more amenable to selective perception). The more that people are *exposed* to political material, the more gets through.

Other characteristics also make for accurate perception. The intellectual training received in the classroom enables the voter to make clearer discriminations in the political arena. And, despite greater affect toward campaign affairs, the interested people manage to maintain a clearer view of the issues (see Fig. 8). In addition, accuracy of perception is a function of cross-pressures. Voters cross-pressured on class and religion are less accurate than those not so cross-pressured (34 percent high to 41 percent); and voters

The index of correct perception on the issues is based upon the number of correct responses given out of the four possible.

In the first place, the amount of correct perception in the community is limited. Only 16 percent of the respondents know the correct stands of both candidates on both issues, and another 21 percent know them on three of the four. Over a third of the respondents know only one stand correctly or none at all. And these are crucial issues in the campaign, much discussed in the communication media. Thus, a good deal less than half the political perception in the community is reasonably accurate, by such definitions.[6]

But any such arbitrary measure is less useful for its absolute than for its relative value. Who are the people more and less likely to perceive political issues correctly? For example, what of attention to the campaign in the press and radio? Do the people who read and listen about politics more than others perceive more correctly, or does selective perception get in the way? It seems that communication exposure clarifies perception probably more than any other factor (Fig. 7). This is an important consideration: the more reading and listening people do on campaign matters, the more likely they are to come to recognize the positions the candidates take on major issues. It is as though the weight of the media is sufficient to "impose" a certain

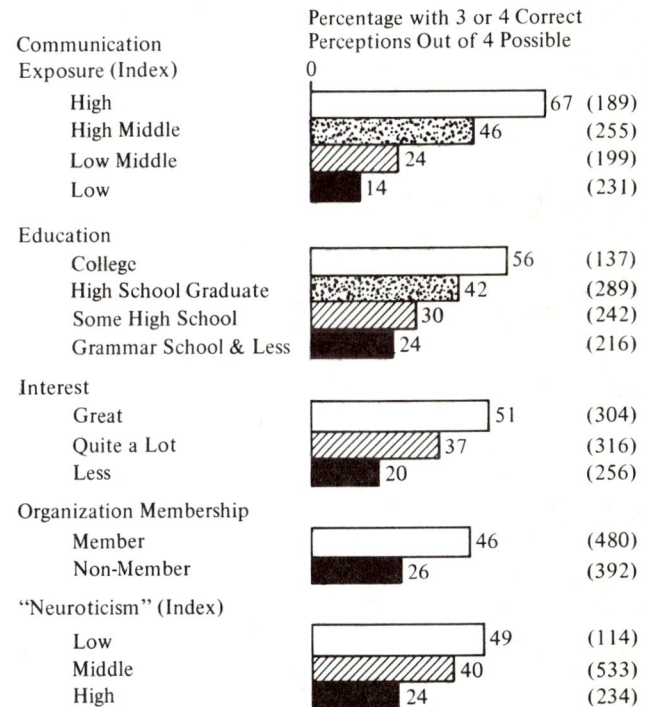

*Each of these characteristics works independently of the others.

Fig. 7. Several characteristics are associated with accurate perception of the candidates' stands on issues*

cross-pressured (inconsistent) on price control and Taft-Hartley are less accurate than those not so cross-pressured (42 to 65 percent). But, of all these factors, the strongest is communication exposure. It is more effectively related to accurate perception of where the candidates stand than either education or interest. Reading and listening must make a difference.

Inferences: Psychological and Political

What are the implications of this perceptual situation? Broadly speaking, there are two sets of conclusions which can be drawn.

The first deals with the psychology of political perception. For perceptual selection must serve a definite psychological function for the individual voter. As in other spheres of activity, so in the political: one function must be to avoid potential stress. The voter must do this, even though unconsciously, by using his perceptual opportunities as a defense or protection against the complexities, contradictions, and problems of the campaign. Indeed, the extent and nature of

Percentage with 3 or 4 Perceptions Correct

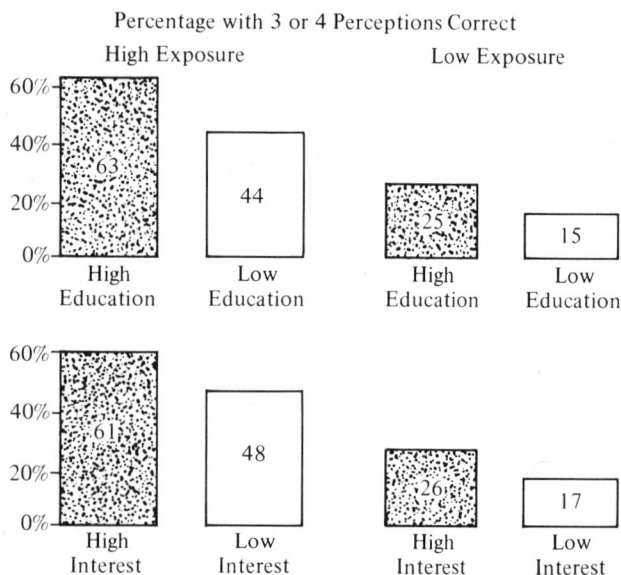

Fig. 8

misperception suggests that the voter may even be aware of the attitudinal cross-pressures to which the campaign subjects him and from which he gains escape through perceptual processes. For the greater his affect toward the election (in terms of strength of feeling toward the candidates), the greater the degree of psychic protection. The voter tends to oversee or to invent what is favorable to himself and to distort or to deny much of what is unfavorable. This must leave him fewer internal conflicts to resolve—with, so to speak, a favorable balance of perception. In any event, the voters manage to use the materials of politics, even of a presidential campaign, for their own psychological protection—for the avoidance of some inconsistencies in their beliefs that otherwise would be manifest.

Then there are certain political implications of the patterning of perception. First, there are in a sense two political campaigns. One is the objective campaign that is carried on in the "real" world, and the other is the campaign as perceived. There is no one-to-one correspondence between them. Given the chance, some voters transform the objective campaign into a subjective one more satisfying to them. The campaign waged by the candidates—even when deliberately unambiguous—is not the one perceived by all the voters, but this does not make it any less "real" for the voters themselves. "If men define situations as real, they are real in their consequences."

Second, there is the meaning of perception for rational political judgment. Here its role must make the voter's political judgment *seem* more rational to him because it maximizes agreement with his own side and maximizes disagreement with the opposition. In other words, perception often operates to make the differences between the parties *appear* greater than they actually may be—and thus to make the voter's decision *appear* more rational (in one sense) than it actually is. In this way, paradoxical though it may seem, misperception contributes to a seeming "rationality" in politics.

Third, perception must reduce or even eliminate certain political cross-pressures before they come to the level of visibility—before they start pressing. If the voter finds himself holding opinions championed by opposing parties, it has been thought that he could do one of two things: remain in this "inconsistent" position (which is, of course, altogether legtimate) or remove the "inconsistency" by changing one opinion to fit the other. But he has another out: he can perceptually select, out of the somewhat ambiguous propaganda of the campaign, those political cues which remove the problem by defining it away. He can "see" that the candidates do not disagree on the issue at hand or that his candidate really agrees with him or that the opponent really disagrees or that he cannot tell where his candidate stands. Just as the process may reduce the voter's level of psychological tension, so may it reduce his political inconsistency.

Finally, this serves to introduce the major political implications of our perceptual material—its implications for the problem of cleavage and consensus in the democratic community. In an earlier section we dealt with this problem in the *evaluation* of political affairs; now we meet it in perception. The over-all effect of political perception is to increase the amount of political consensus *within* the parties and to increase the amount of political cleavage *between* the parties— once again, homogeneity within and polarization between. Both are achieved by something like the mechanisms of generalization, exclusion, and denial— through the perceptual enlargement of the area of agreement with one's own candidate (generalization); through the misperceived rejection of the opponent's position (exclusion); and through the professed lack of knowledge of one's candidate's stand where disagreement is likely (denial).

Let us close this chapter by comparing it briefly with the chapter on the perception of groups. In each case the perceptions are likely to help voters to maintain their own position, without being too much concerned by contradiction. In the social case it is harmony with people; in the present case it is a harmony with ideas. With groups the matter was fairly simple: each respondent is surrounded by a primary group in which the large majority thinks like himself. No wonder, then, that he infers that "everyone" will vote as he does. (Of course, this tendency is tempered by a strong sense of reality; misperception is only superimposed upon it.) In the case of the candidates' stand, the voter gets his information from reading, listening, and discussion. This is subject to *selective* gathering of information, forgetting of disturbing elements, reinterpretation of what the candidate "really" means—all mechanisms familiar in social psychology. Probably, even, social selection reinforces the selective collection of information, as a result of discussion between like-minded people.

In a way, both phenomena can be subsumed under one heading. Voters cannot have contact with the whole world of people and ideas; they must *sample* them. And the sampling is biased. People pick the people and the ideas to suit their personal equilibrium and then project that sample upon the universe. First. selective perception, then misperception, then the strengthening of opinion, and then, in turn, more selective perception. Fortunately, there are realities, competing concerns, and corrosion of existing beliefs that, under normal circumstances, do not permit this process to get far out of bounds.

In sum, then, the actual operation of political perception during a presidential campaign decreases tension in the individual and increases tension in the community—one might almost say, *by* increasing tension in the community. The voters, each in the solitude of his own mind, wish to see the campaign in a favorable way, and they use their perception of where the candidates stand to this end. "Democracy in its original form never seriously faced the problem which arises because the pictures inside people's heads do not automatically correspond with the world outside."[7]

Summary

Perception and Voting

1. Party preference does not particularly affect the voter's perception of where the candidates stand on the issues.

2. The less ambiguous the objective situation, the more agreement in perception between the two sides.

3. Partisans tend to perceive the candidate's stand on the issues as favorable to their own stand. (1) They perceive their candidate's stand as similar to their own and the opponent's stand as dissimilar. (2) They tend *not* to perceive differences with their own candidate or similarities to the opposition candidate.

4. Voters who feel strongly about their choice are more likely to misperceive the candidates' stands on the issues as favorable to their own positions.

5. Social differences in voting are largely maintained regardless of perceived agreement with the candidates.

6. Voters who disagree with both candidates' stands, as perceived, support their own candidate more strongly than those who agree with both.

Accuracy of Perception

7. Only about one-third of the voters are highly accurate in their perception of where the candidates stand on the issues.

8. Accuracy of perception is affected by communication exposure, education, interest, and cross-pressures—with communication exposure probably the strongest influence.

Notes

[1] Walter Lippmann, *Public Opinion*, p. 21.

[2] A. Lawrence Lowell, *Public Opinion in War and Peace*, p. 22.

[3] The questions followed this form: "From what you know, is Truman (Dewey) for the Taft-Hartley Law or against it?" The respondent could say "Don't know" or state that the candidate had not taken any stand on the issue. The perception questions were asked in August, before the campaign proper; replies may have been different in October.

[4] Joseph Schumpeter, *Capitalism, Socialism, and Democracy,* p. 263.

[5] Nor was perception related to *changes* in voting. We hypothesized that voters might maintain stability by means of misperception, but there were no differences in the data on voting changes subsequent to the asking of perception questions. If perception questions had been repeated, then one would expect perception to adjust to vote more often than the reverse.

[6] To repeat: these figures apply to the early campaign period of August. Similar data for October, at the end of the campaign, would almost certainly raise these estimates.

[7] Walter Lippmann, *Public Opinion*, p. 21.

Effect of Partisanship on the Perception

of Political Candidates

Roberta S. Sigel

How voters perceive political candidates and issues "is not simply a nice psychological problem with little relevance to the political situation. The process of political perception can operate to increase cleavage or consensus within the community."[1] In fact, it tends to influence the whole process of political behavior. A definitive answer to the question of how voters perceive political candidates would greatly enhance our understanding of voting behavior.

Since the 1944 publication of Lazarsfeld's *The People's Choice,* social scientists have increasingly turned their attention to the study of the above problem, and they have developed two contradictory theories to explain it.

One theory leans heavily on theoretical and empirical work in social psychology, especially social perception, and has been referred to as the perceptual balance theory.[2] It holds that political perception

. . . must serve a definitive psychological function for the individual voter. As in other spheres of

activity, so in the political: one function must be to avoid potential stress. . . . The voter tends to see or to invent what is favorable to himself and to distort or to deny much of what is unfavorable. This must leave him fewer internal conflicts to resolve—with, so to speak, a favorable balance of perception.[3]

From this theoretical formulation it follows that political perception is perceiver-determined. In order not to experience inbalance or stress, partisans, especially, will see in a preferred candidate what they wish to see—even if it is unrelated to objective reality.

A second explanation is the image theory, which holds that the image voters have of a candidate is not perceiver-determined but candidate- or stimulus-determined. This theory maintains that candidates, by their appearance, speeches, stands on issues, etc., convey a specific image. The image emanating from the candidate accounts for the public's perception of that candidate, not the sterotyped "pictures inside people's heads [which] do not automatically correspond with the world outside."[4] The candidate who casts the most popular image wins the election.

The image thesis has as yet not been subjected to much empirical study. However, results from a recent investigation by McGrath and McGrath reported in this journal indicated that "perceptions of political figures are stimulus-determined rather than perceiver-determined for a large number of attributes. Thus there seems to be much support for the image theory

Roberta S. Sigel, "Effect of Partisanship on the Perception of Political Candidates," *Public Opinion Quarterly* 28 (1964): 483–96. Reprinted with permission.

Support for this study came from the Science of Society Division, Monteith College, Wayne State University, where the survey was designed and conducted under the author's directorship. I wish to express appreciation to Dr. Irving E. Sigel, Merrill-Palmer Institute, and Professor Ross Stagner, Wayne State University, for a critical reading of the manuscript and valuable editorial assistance.

of political perception."[5] The authors tested for the presence or absence of the image principle by means of an interpersonal-perception questionnaire administered to members of the Young Republicans and the Young Democrats at the University of Illinois. Each respondent was asked to rate himself, Kennedy, and Nixon on a fifty-item questionnaire, which contained personal attributes that only by inference—if at all—could be perceived as political. On a majority of items Republicans and Democrats differentiated themselves from the candidates and also differentiated the two candidates from each other. Furthermore, all respondents agreed on the nature of the Kennedy and Nixon images. These findings, especially coming from highly partisan respondents, lend support to the image theory.

It is possible, however, to argue that such image differentiations do *not* furnish conclusive evidence for the image theory, because the differentiations discovered by the McGraths were not the kind likely to produce stress, which would be produced only in politically relevant areas. To cite two examples, a voter may perceive a candidate as "sensitive" and himself as "rugged" without experiencing stress. Republicans and Democrats could agree with each other on Kennedy being "more light," and Nixon being "more heavy"[6] without experiencing stress. Only if image differentiation were found in politically relevant and therefore stressful areas could we accept such differentiation as evidence in support of the image theory.

Moreover, image differentiation may conceivably support the perceptual balance theory rather than the image theory, if this differentiation occurs by bringing the political image of the preferred candidate into perceptual balance with one's own political predilections. This would happen, for example, when the respondent sees the preferred candidate in the image of his preferred party. It is *political* differentiation and similarity that must be assessed in explaining political perception. To obtain meaningful explanations of political behavior, studies testing the image theory or any other theory of political perception must be examined in a political frame of reference. The study we are about to report attempts to do this.

Procedure

In October 1960 a face-to-face interview was conducted with 1,350 registered voters constituting a random sample of the Detroit electorate. Our sampling procedures yielded the following: 59 percent Democrats, 19 percent Republican, 20 percent independents, and 2 percent miscellaneous, a distribution consistent with Detroit voting patterns and party affiliations.[7]

The interview contained a list of ten traits that our respondents considered to be important in a President and hereafter referred to as the idealized image. The list included qualities related to job competency as well as personal ones.[8]

Next, respondents were asked to rank their preferred and nonpreferred candidates on the same list of attributes. They were asked to judge each candidate as to which of the qualities he possessed and which he lacked.

Toward the end of the interview, after intervening questions of a different nature, we asked four open-ended questions dealing with a reason why the respondent wanted to vote for his preferred candidate and a reason why he might not wish to vote for him. The same questions were then repeated for the nonpreferred candidate.

Respondents were also asked their party affiliation. We classified as partisans those who identified themselves as Republican, Democrat, Socialist, etc. Nonpartisan designations were assigned to those voters who identified themselves as independents.

Since, as the McGraths state, "differentiation between the two candidates is a necessary condition for either the perceptual balance theory or the image theory to be supported,"[9] the data were analyzed to test for (1) the presence or absence of image differentiation and (2) the specific conditions under which such differentiation occurred or failed to occur. The partisans' idealized image of the President was therefore compared (1) to their image of the preferred candidate and (2) to their image of the nonpreferred candidate. Next we tested to see if Republicans and Democrats had the same or different views of Nixon and Kennedy. The nonpartisans' images of both candidates were also compared with their idealized view and with the candidate images held by Republicans and Democrats.

To test for the difference in images, we assigned ranks to each of the presidential qualities on the basis of the frequency with which respondents attributed these qualities to a given candidate and to the idealized image. Rank-order correlations were computed to assess the relationship between the idealized image of the President and the qualities assigned to the preferred candidate; similar rank orders were computed for intercandidate comparisons (Nixon image as seen by Republicans and Democrats; Kennedy image as seen by Republicans and Democrats).

Not to lose sight of the *content* of the candidate's image, we analyzed the candidate image by examining what *specific* qualities voters attributed to candidates.

The Logic of the Analysis

A comparison of a respondent's ideal image with his image of his preferred and nonpreferred candidates seems a good test of the perceptual balance theory. The preferred candidate's image should be similar to the idealized image in order for a voter not to experience stress. The perceptual balance theory would be supported if there is a positive correlation between idealized and preferred-candidate images and a negative one between idealized and nonpreferred-candidate images.

Further evidence for the perceptual balance theory would result if a comparison of nonpartisans with partisans showed nonpartisans to be more stimulus-determined. We would expect to find greater image differentiation between nonpartisans' idealized images and their images of both candidates, because the fact that respondents identify themselves as independents indicates a lack of involvement with either party. This, in turn, should permit them to see candidates in a much more reality-determined and less perceiver-

determined way than do partisans. Consequently, they can vote for a candidate perceived as not ideal without suffering cognitive dissonance, or stress. We would thus expect to find no correlations between nonpartisans' idealized views and their views of *either* candidate.

Validation of the perceptual balance theory could be further enhanced from respondents' views of the candidates as obtained from the *open-ended questions*.[10] For the perceptual balance theory to be operative, we would expect respondents to perceive candidates in a way that avoided stress or imbalance. One way of avoiding inbalance would be for a respondent to see the preferred candidate's political image and views as similar to his own. In the case of partisans, such image balance could be brought about by seeing close similarity between preferred candidate and preferred party. We would consider the perceptual balance theory to be validated if candidates were seen as possessing party-typical attributes and if these attributes were cited as reasons for voting for or against a candidate.

Validation for the image theory, on the other hand, would be established if partisans and independents agreed on the extent to which both candidates conformed or deviated from the idealized image. In such a case, it would be concluded that voter perception is stimulus-(i.e. candidate-image) determined. If, however, stimulus-determined responses were limited exclusively to nonpolitical attributes, such as the candidate's appearance, age, or speaking ability, this would not be proof of the image theory per se but merely proof of its effectiveness in a restricted nonpolitical area.

Results

Comparisons of ideal image with candidate image. As Table 1 shows, the total sample judged the following qualities to most essential for a President:

Table 1

Qualities Considered Most Essential to Presidential Candidates, from Selected List, by Political Affiliation (in percent)

Quality	Democrats (775)	Republicans (246)	Independents (263)	Other (10)	No Answer (48)	Total Population (1,342)
Honesty	75.2	87.8	79.1	80.0	77.1	78.4
Intelligence	51.2	61.8	61.2	80.0	41.7	55.2
Independence	44.0	45.5	47.9	30.0	43.8	44.8
Careful spender of public money	33.9	42.7	33.0	40.0	39.6	35.8
Ideas	25.8	18.7	23.6	40.0	25.0	23.9
Sympathy with little man	25.9	7.7	14.8		18.8	20.2
Humility	7.4	13.8	14.1	20.0	8.3	9.7
Friendliness	9.8	5.3	6.8		12.5	8.2
Good speaker	10.3	3.7	3.8	10.0	8.3	7.5
Other (specify)	4.8	5.7	6.1		6.3	5.2
Good television personality	2.1	2.0	0.8		2.1	1.5
No answer	1.3	0.4	0.8		2.1	1.5

Note: Percentages are based on number of respondents, not on number of responses, and therefore exceed 100 percent.

honesty (78 percent), intelligence (55 percent), and independence (45 percent).[11]

Republicans, Democrats, and independents had the same idealized image. Rank-order correlations were positive for (1) the ideal Republican and the ideal Democratic image ($\rho = .890 < .02$), (2), the ideal independent and the ideal Democratic image ($\rho = .981 < .02$), and (3) the ideal independent and the ideal Republican image ($\rho = .988 < .02$).[12]

Comparison of candidate image to idealized image, however, found sharp disagreement among the three groups (see Table 2). The image Democrats held of the ideal President correlated positively with their image of Kennedy ($\rho = .697 < .04$). The Republican ideal image correlated positively with their image of Nixon ($\rho = .870 < .02$). The Democratic view of Nixon did not relate significantly to their idealized image of the President ($\rho = .273$). The same held true for the Republicans' image of Kennedy ($\rho = .164$). No significant correlations were obtained when the independents' ideal image was compared to that of either candidate (Kennedy $\rho = .225$; Nixon $\rho = .455$).[13]

These findings are consistent with the perceptual balance theory. To maintain balance and avoid stress, people who have commitments, like the partisans, bring about perceptual congruence between their ideal and preferred-candidate images but do not do so for their ideal and nonpreferred-candidate images. Independents do not have this commitment and do not have to create congruence. No relationship was found between their ideal image and their candidates' images.

In view of the above, it is not surprising to find that partisans showed a great deal more image differentiation than independents when comparing the two candidates. No statistically significant rank-order correlations were obtained when comparing the Republican or Democratic view of either candidate; i.e. the Nixon seen by Republicans was a different Nixon from the one seen by Democrats, and the same for Kennedy. Following logically from it, Democrats and Republicans saw little if any similarity between Nixon and Kennedy. This type of image differentiation tends to corroborate the perceptual balance theory.

An item-for-item comparison of the above rank

Table 2
Rank-order Comparison of Ideal Image and Candidate Image, by Political Affiliation

Qualities	Democrats	Republicans	Independents
Possessed by Kennedy:			
Honesty	1	5	2
Intelligence	2	2	1
Independence	3	7	6
Careful spender of public money	9	10	9
Lots of ideas on how to solve problems	7	6	7
Sympathy with little man	6	8	8
Humility	10	9	10
Friendliness	5	4	3
Good speaker	4	1	4
Good television personality	8	3	5
Possessed by Nixon:			
Honesty	4	1	2
Intelligence	1	2	1
Independence	8	3	5
Careful spender of public money	5	4	6
Lots of ideas on how to solve problems	6	5.5	7
Sympathy with little man	10	9	10
Humility	9	8	9
Friendliness	3	7	4
Good speaker	2	5.5	3
Good television personality	7	10	8
*Lacking in Kennedy:**			
Honesty	9	5	8
Intelligence	10	10	10
Independence	4	2	2
Careful spender of public money	1	1	1
Lots of ideas on how to solve problems	5	6	4
Sympathy with little man	6	4	5.5
Humility	2	3	3
Friendliness	8	8	9
Good speaker	7	7	7
Good television personality	3	9	5.5
*Lacking in Nixon:**			
Honesty	3	9	6
Intelligence	10	10	10
Independence	2	4	3
Careful spender of public money	5.5	8	5
Lots of ideas on how to solve problems	4	7	4
Sympathy with little man	1	5.5	1
Humility	8	2.5	7.5
Friendliness	9	5.5	9
Good speaker	7	2.5	7.5
Good television personality	5.5	1	2

 * Respondents were offered the same list twice and asked first to name the three qualities the candidate showed and then the three the candidate lacked. The order in which the qualities are ranked in the bottom half of the table is not exactly the opposite of the order in the top half because some respondents refused to name as many as three qualities.

orders demonstrates this even more clearly. The preferred candidate was rated high with regard to the possession of the three job-crucial attributes (which were assigned ranks 1 through 3), while the nonpreferred candidate was ranked high with respect to the possession of personal attributes (such as speaking ability, friendliness, etc.). Only on the two policy or issue attributes was there some agreement among partisans. Republicans and Democrats, for example, ranked Nixon similarly with regard to fiscal conservatism. In all other instances, the nature of the image differentiation, i.e. the fact that the preferred candidate was ranked politically high and the nonpreferred was not — was such as to suggest further corroboration for the perceptual balance theory.

For the independents, a positive rank-order correlation between the Kennedy and Nixon images was found ($\rho = .808 < .02$). This shows that independents held much less highly differentiated candidate images than did partisans.

The highly differentiated images held by partisans and the less differentiated images held by nonpartisans seems to be further — though only inferential — evidence for the perceptual balance theory. Partisans cannot "afford" to perceive much similarity between opposing candidates, but nonpartisans can.

The independents occupied a curious position in another way: in all but one instance (the Republicans' view of Nixon's weaknesses, $\rho = .327$) they agreed with the views of both Republicans and Democrats. Significantly positive correlations were obtained for the partisans' image and the independents' image of preferred and nonpreferred candidate. The rhos for these relationships ranged from .800–912. All of them were significant at the .02 level of confidence or less. Independents, apparently, are more ambivalent in judging candidates and see each candidate simultaneously as the opposition sees him and as the endorsing party sees him. Maybe that is one reason why they *are* independents and why they seem more stimulus-determined.

Up to this point the evidence from pre-structured questions suggests that partisan political perception is for the most part perceiver-determined,[14] but nonpartisan perception is largely stimulus-determined.

Content of political image. Another assumption in this study is that the candidate image is politically potent only in terms of political attributes. The findings from the open-ended questions verify this. Table 3 shows that voters' reasons for voting for or against a candidate were mainly political and not based on personal characteristics of the candidate. In explaining their voting intentions, voters did not often refer to such personal qualities as intelligence or honesty but rather referred to highly specific political views or stands of the candidate, bearing out our assumption that the salient aspects in perception of candidates were the perceiver's political attitudes.

In this part of our interview we found a great deal more image similarity among the three subgroups than we did in the structured part. Analysis yields two findings: (1) Democrats, Republicans, and independents agreed on the Nixon and the Kennedy images. The degree to which all subgroups chose similar attributes to characterize the two candidates is impressive. In fact, some qualities (between five and ten for each candidate) recurred with extraordinary frequency and will form the basis of our analysis. (2) The two candidate images were highly differentiated from each other. Each candidate presented a unique constellation of attributes. From our data, Nixon's greatest asset appears to have been his experience and his training under Eisenhower. His political views, especially on foreign affairs and fiscal matters, also featured prominently. Kennedy's greatest assets were his political views, especially on domestic questions, such as his concern for the "little man" and his party affiliation. He was young and hence would "get things done." To condense the image even further, we might say Nixon was seen as the man of experience and fiscal prudence and Kennedy as the young man of action representing the common people. No mirror image of the two candidates here! (A comparison in Table 3 of the five most frequently mentioned assets for each candidate illustrates the high degree of agreement among partisans and nonpartisans with regard to the candidates' chief assets.)

Agreement on candidate liabilities was not as consistent among partisans. Partisans often failed to agree on what constituted a candidate's greatest weakness,

Table 3
Assets and Liabilities Attributed to Presidential Candidates in Open ended Questions

Kennedy's Assets, As Seen by:

Democrats:

Democrat	23.5
More capable than Nixon	23.5
Represents common people	20.4
Political views (domestic)	18.2
Young: Will get things done	13.4
	(N = 679)

Republicans:

More capable than Nixon	26.0
Young: Will get things done	15.0
Personality	15.0
Views (domestic)	12.3
Determined	10.9
	(N = 73)

Independents:

More capable than Nixon	24.3
Views (domestic)	23.1
Sincere, honest	20.7
Represents common people	12.8
Congressional record	8.5
	(N = 164)

Kennedy's Liabilities, As Seen by:

Democrats:

Catholic	28.7
Inexperienced	15.8
Views (domestic affairs)	12.2
Too young	11.5
Humility	5.7
Affiliations	5.7
	(N = 139)

Republicans:

Views (domestic affairs)	18.9
Inexperienced	16.7
Spends too much	12.9
Democrat	11.8
Too young	11.8
	(N = 185)

Independents:

Views (domestic affairs)	19.1
Spends too much	16.5
Catholic	14.7
Inexperienced	13.0
Can't do what he promised	7.8
	(N = 115)

Nixon's Assets, As Seen by:

Democrats:

More experience	38.6
Views (foreign affairs)	17.0
More capable	14.4
Sincere, honest	10.3
Personality	4.9
	(N = 223)

Republicans:

More experience	46.4
More capable	23.7
Views (foreign affairs)	17.9
Sincere, honest	13.0
Republican	11.6
Trained under Ike	11.6
	(N = 224)

Independents:

More experience	43.9
Views (foreign affairs)	20.0
More capable	16.8
Trained under Ike	10.3
Sincere, honest	9.7
	(N = 155)

Nixon's Liabilities, As Seen by:

Democrats:

Republican	31.0
Views (foreign affairs)	14.9
Doesn't represent common man	12.5
Not independent	10.5
Not sincere	9.0
	(N = 522)

Republicans:

Views (foreign affairs)	33.3
Not independent	10.0
Past record and performance	6.7
Less capable than Kennedy	6.7
Personality	6.7
Religious slander used in campaign	6.7
Too fast	6.7
	(N = 30)

Independents:

Views (foreign affairs)	22.0
Not independent	17.8
Not sincere, honest	10.2
Past record and performance	9.3
Republican	8.5
	(N = 118)

which contradicts the McGraths' findings. We have no data to explain this but can infer that what kept a Republican from voting for Kennedy, for example, was not the same as what deterred a Democrat. To cite an example, our Republican respondents were concerned about Kennedy's lack of thrift but showed no concern about his religion. For Democrats it was the other way around. Independents showed a great deal of agreement with the views of both partisan groups and were in the curious position of agreeing with both Democrats and Republicans even when Republicans and Democrats did not agree with each other.

Although such concise image differentiation seems to substantiate the image thesis, closer examination of the two images raises considerable doubt as to that interpretation. The candidates' images (in their political aspects) were almost identical to the images the public customarily has of the candidate's own *party*.[15] Kennedy was seen by Democrats and Republicans much as the Democratic Party is seen by the public at large; Nixon, similarly, was seen in the image of the Republican Party.

If this is true, how justified are we in attributing these different images to the two candidates; might not much of this image conciseness actually be the result of a public projecting its very definite party preferences onto the candidates? Our data suggest that the different images of the two parties are deeply engraved on the perception of voters and influence their candidate perception more than do the candidates themselves. Our data do not permit us to argue that voters responded to candidates solely, or even preponderantly, in terms of the unique attributes of the candidates.

Given two nonincumbents about equally well known, and the absence of any large-scale, immediate crisis, it may well be that the image voters have of candidates is mostly the party's image and only partially the candidate's image. To put it another way, given two fairly well-known candidates, neither of whom has yet had an opportunity to show how he would proceed as President, and given the public's conviction that both are reasonably competent, the voter will choose the one who is endorsed by his party, since he perceives his party as furthering his self-interest.

Where our findings do substantiate the stimulus-determined thesis is in the area of the candidate's *personal* image. Respondents attributed many qualities to the candidates that appear to be neither perceiver- nor party-determined but objective realities. For example, some people referred to Kennedy's religion, his wealth; others referred to Nixon's apprenticeship in the Cabinet, his speech mannerisms, etc. Apparently, perception is stimulus-determined when perceivers look at a candidate's personality, appearance, objectively verifiable circumstances, etc., but it is perceiver-determined when respondents view the candidate's political traits. Since the political image is cited more frequently as the reason for voting intentions, we must conclude that it has more salience than the candidate's personalized image.

More intensive analysis of our data casts further doubt on the image thesis, because so many voters seemed "imageless." The proof of the image thesis in our study and the McGraths' was provided by people who *had an image* of preferred and nonpreferred candidates. In our survey, however, respondents also had an opportunity *not* to give us a candidate image by volunteering answers such as "everything good," "nothing good," or simply the time-honored "I don't know." "Imageless" or inarticulate people constituted a majority of our sample (except when asked to list Kennedy's assets; only 30 percent remained vague then) (see Table 4). These people, however, were not imageless across the board. They were, on the contrary, highly partisan in their imagelessness. Thus the majority of Democrats (74 percent), when asked for Nixon's good points, could not think of any, while most Republicans could see nothing good in Kennedy (72 percent). Conversely, Democrats saw few *bad* points in Kennedy (82 percent refused to cite any) and Republicans saw few in Nixon (88 percent refused to cite any).

What Table 4 demonstrates is that most partisans did not have very articulate images: they could easily think of attributes that made their preferred candidate attractive but could not conjure up a negative image of him. They were at a loss to see anything good in the opposition candidate but found it easy to find fault with him. People like these are not imageless, but their image is biased and highly stereotypic. We question whether such selectivity of perception is a function of candidate stimulus; rather, it seems due to the perceiver's predilection. Could these be people who never "acquainted" themselves with the Kennedy or Nixon image ("All that counts for me"—in the words of one of our respondents—"is his party; that is good")? Perhaps many such imageless people never attended carefully to either candidate but rather prejudged them in the image of the particular party. It is therefore impossible to classify their perception as stimulus-determined.

Table 4
Percentage of Respondents Failing to Attribute Specific Qualities to Candidates

	Kennedy	Nixon
No Specific Asset Cited:		
Democrats	16	74
Republicans	72	10
Independents	40	46
Total population	30	54
	(N = 408)	(N = 718)
No Specific Liability Cited:		
Democrats	82	36
Republicans	26	88
Independents	56	57
Total population	63	51
	(N = 854)	(N = 680)

The independents seemed to bear us out. They were at a loss for candidate images and thus seemed less perceiver-determined and more prone to influence by candidate stimuli. (A majority could cite good points for both candidates.) More independents than partisans had clear images of both the strengths and weaknesses of each candidate (see Table 4). Far fewer independents than partisans could see only good or only bad in a candidate. It is the greater imagelessness and the highly biased imagelessness of our partisan sample—in contrast to the independents—that

casts doubt on the operation of the image thesis. After all, when 70 or 80 percent of the sample can think of nothing bad in their preferred candidate and of nothing good in the nonpreferred one, it is hard to believe that voters' perception is exclusively or even largely a function of stimuli emanating from the candidate. Rather, it would seem that political perception is to a large extent a function of the perceiver's personal cognitive political map. Party loyalty might account for as much, if not more, of this political map than any other phenomenon, including the candidate's own image.

Discussion

It may well be that neither the perceptual balance theory nor the image theory provides exhaustive explanations of political perception, since both fail to take into account the crucial role of political party identification.

It is by now well known that in the United States political party has high salience in determining political attitudes and voting decisions.[16] It seems only logical, therefore, to assume that party preference would greatly affect a voter's perception of candidates. After all, a presidential candidate is the standard-bearer of his party, and the voter usually knows this. Even those who are not highly partisan have some image—no matter how vague and general—of the two major parties. Undoubtedly, they must carry this image with them when evaluating the candidates. The candidate thus is hardly ever seen just as an individual to whom voters may respond or on whom they may project as they see fit. Rather, he stands both for himself and for his party, and often the image is intensely interwoven. How often have our respondents expressed realization of the role of party when making statements such as, "He can't deliver what he promises; the party won't let him," or "He won't be able to handle the world situation; Democrats always cause war!" The latter statement, particularly, shows the fusion of party and man to the point of indistinction.

In 1960 millions of Americans got a close personal

look at both candidates via the TV cameras and thus were in an excellent position to be affected by the candidate's image and to lose sight of the candidate's party, as they could never have done so easily before. And yet our data bring out that, even in a highly personalized campaign, party image featured prominently in the sample's political perception. The only inference to be drawn from this finding is that the image voters have of candidates is influenced by their party images.

Future research on political perception and voting preferences must take into consideration the degree to which candidate perception is influenced by party perception. We must discover the intensity of party identification; the extent to which voters have been exposed to candidates, as opposed to the party and its position; the role they attribute to partisanship; etc. No theory of political perception can offer much

promise that fails to take cognizance of the role of parties in voters' political imagery. Nor should we overlook another intervening variable: the impact of political events on voters' political perception. Events such as unemployment, controversies over segregation, or the threat of war may affect a voter's perception at the expense of candidate- or self-image. Theories of political perception must take account of the *political* context in which political perception occurs. They must never lose sight of the fact that political perception, like candidate images, needs to be multidimensional, because perceiver, external events, party, and candidate all participate in determining the total image. Any theory that overlooks the intrinsic complexity of the topic and operates in the realm of one-to-one cause-and-effect relationships loses sight of the reality of American political life.

Notes

[1] Bernard Berelson and William McPhee, *Voting* (Chicago: University of Chicago Press, 1954).

[2] Cf. F. Heider, "Attitudes and Cognitive Organization," *Journal of Psychology* 21 (1946): pp. 107–12, and J. E. and M. F. McGrath, "Effects of Partisanship on Perceptions of Political Figures," *Public Opinion Quarterly* 26 (1962): 236–48.

[3] Berelson and McPhee, *op. cit.,* p. 83.

[4] Walter Lippmann, *Public Opinion* (New York: Macmillan, 1922), p. 21.

[5] McGrath and McGrath, *op. cit.,* p. 246.

[6] Items from the McGraths' questionnaire.

[7] Roberta S. Sigel, "Race and Religion as Factors in the Kennedy Victory in Detroit, 1960," *Journal of Negro Education* 31 (1962): 436–47.

[8] We had in mind that three schools of thought existed on what was important to the voter in a President. One held that personality counted most; one held that political stands counted most (i.e. what group does he represent?); and the last held that personal ability and statesmanship counted most. We developed eight items to test for the absence or presence of these preferences. We also included two items (good speaker and good TV personality) appropriate to the 1960 election.

[9] McGrath and McGrath, *op. cit.,* p. 240.

[10] One may reasonably argue that the structured and unstruc-

tured questions do not tap the same dimensions of the candidate's image, because a voter might have been aware of certain undesirable attributes in his favorite candidate and yet this "image" might not enter into the determination of his voting decision.

[11] These data were previously reported in Roberta S. Sigel, "Presidential Leadership Images," paper read before the 1962 Annual Meeting of the American Political Science Association, Washington, D.C.

[12] Such agreement among all three subgroups on the nature of the ideal President precludes the possibility that voters responded to questions about the ideal President in terms of the candidate they intended to vote for.

[13] However, Republicans and Democrats agreed among themselves that *both* candidates ranked in the upper part of the rank order with regard to two traits held essential for a President, namely honesty and intelligence. In this sense both candidates apparently possessed job competence or suitability even in the eyes of voters who did not intend to vote for them.

[14] Except for the partisans' agreement that both candidates are competent to fill the job (see footnote 13 above).

[15] For data from public opinion polls on the American's image of the two parties, cf. V. O. Key, *Public Opinion and American Democracy* (New York: Knopf, 1961), Chap. 17.

[16] Cf. Berelson and McPhee, *op. cit.* For a discussion of the relative importance of party vs. issues vs. candidates, cf. Angus Campbell, P. Converse, W. Miller, and D. Stokes, *The American Voter* (New York: Wiley, 1960).

Cognitive Dynamics and Images of the Enemy

Ole R. Holsti

I

It is a basic theorem in the social sciences that "if men define situations as real, they are real in their consequences." Stated somewhat differently, the theorem asserts that an individual responds not only to the "objective" characteristics of a situation, but also to the meaning the situation has for him; the person's subsequent behavior and the results of that behavior are determined by the meaning ascribed to the situation.[1]

This theorem can be applied more specifically to the concept of the enemy. Enemies are those who are defined as such, and if one acts upon that interpretation, it is more than likely that the original definition will be confirmed: "It is an undeniable privilege of every man to prove himself in the right in the thesis that the world is his enemy; for if he reiterates it frequently enough and makes it the background of his conduct, he is bound eventually to be right."[2]

If the concept of the enemy is considered from the perspective of attitudes, one interesting problem is the manner in which attitudes about the enemy are maintained or changed. The history of international rela-

tions suggests two contradictory tendencies. On the one hand, just as there are no permanent allies in international relations, there appear to be no permanent enemies. During its history, the United States has fought wars against Britain, France, Mexico, Spain, Germany, Italy, and Japan, all of which are currently allies to some degree. Even the most enduring international antagonisms — for example, between France and Germany — have eventually dissolved. Thus, it is clear that attitudes toward enemies do change.

Although hostile relationships at the international level are not eternal, it is also evident that they tend to endure well past the first conciliatory gestures. This resistance to changes in attitudes may be attributed to a number of factors, not the least of which is an apparently universal tendency to judge the actions of others — and particularly of those defined as enemies — according to different standards than those applied to oneself. Because friends are expected to be friendly and enemies to be hostile, there is a tendency to view their behavior in line with these expectations. When the other party is viewed within the framework of an "inherent bad faith"[3] model the image of the enemy is clearly self-perpetuating, for the model itself denies the existence of data that could disconfirm it. At the interpersonal level such behavior is characterized as abnormal — paranoia. Different standards seem to apply at the international level; inherent-bad-faith models are not considered abnormal, and even their underlying assumptions often escape serious questioning.

This paper reports a case study of the cognitive

This paper is drawn from sections of a full-scale study published in David J. Finlay, Ole R. Holsti, and Richard R. Fagen, *Enemies in Politics* (Chicago: Rand-McNally, 1967). Owing to space limitations, quantitative content-analysis data used to test a number of propositions have been omitted from this paper. The reader interested in the data and techniques used to obtain them should consult the book.

dynamics associated with images of the enemy. The basic hypothesis—that there exist cognitive processes that tend to sustain such images—will be examined through study of a single individual, former Secretary of State John Foster Dulles, and his attitude toward a single "enemy," the Soviet Union. One point should be made explicit at the outset: there is no intent here to indicate that Secretary Dulles' attitudes or behavior were in any way "abnormal." It is precisely because of the assumption that his attitudes and behavior were within the normal range of high-ranking policymakers that he was selected for intensive study. Thus, though Dulles was a unique personality in many respects, this research was undertaken on the premise that the findings may have implications for foreign-policy decision-making in general.

Primary data for this study were derived from the verbatim transcripts of all publicly available statements made by Dulles during the years 1953–59, including 122 press conferences, 70 addresses, 67 appearances at Congressional hearings, and 166 other documents. This documentation was supplemented by contemporary newspapers, secondary sources, questionnaires sent to a number of Dulles' closest associates, and memoirs written by those who worked closely with him.[4]

II

The theoretical framework for this study has been developed from two major sources. The first and more general of these is the literature on the relationship of an individual's "belief system" to perception and action. The belief system, composed of a number of "images" of the past, present, and future, includes "all the accumulated, organized knowledge that the organism has about itself and the world."[5] It may be thought of as the set of lenses through which information concerning the physical and social environment is received. It orients the individual to his environment, defining it for him and identifying for him its salient characteristics. National images may be considered as subparts of the belief system. Like the belief system itself, these are models that order for the observer what would otherwise be an unmanageable amount of information.

All images are stereotyped in the trivial sense that they oversimplify reality. It is this characteristic that makes images functional—and can render them dysfunctional. Unless the *content* of the image coincides in some way with what is commonly perceived as reality, decisions based on these images are not likely to fulfill the actor's expectations. Erroneous images may also prove to have a distorting effect by encouraging reinterpretation of information that does not fit the image; this is most probable with such inherent-bad-faith models as "totalitarian communism" or "monopolistic capitalism," which exclude the very types of information that might lead to a modification or clarification of the models themselves. Equally important is the *structure* of the belief system, which, along with its component images, is in continual interaction with new information. In general, the impact of this information depends upon the degree to which the structure of the belief system is "open" or "closed."[6]

Further insight and more specific propositions concerning the relationship between the belief system and new information can be derived from the theoretical and experimental literature on the cognitive dynamics associated with attitude change, and more specifically, from those theories that have been described as "homeostatic" or "balance theories." Among the most prominent of these are theories that postulate a "tendency toward balance," a "stress toward symmetry," a "tendency toward increased congruity," and a "reduction of cognitive dissonance."[7] Despite terminological differences, common to all these theories is the premise that imbalance between various components of attitude is psychologically uncomfortable.

Attitudes, which can be defined as "predispositions to respond in a particular way toward a specified class of objects," consist of both cognitive (beliefs) and affective (feelings) components.[8] Beliefs and feelings are mutually interdependent. A person with strong positive or negative affect toward an object is also likely to maintain a cognitive structure consistent with that affect. The reverse relationship is also true. Thus new information that challenges the pre-existing balance between feelings and beliefs generates intrapersonal tension and a concomitant pressure to restore an internally consistent belief system by reducing the discrepancy in some manner, *but not necessarily through a change in attitude.*

A stable attitude about the enemy is one in which feelings and beliefs are congruent and reinforce each other. An interesting problem results when information incongruent with pre-existing attitudes is received. What happens, for example, when the other party is perceived to be acting in a conciliatory manner, a cognition that is inconsistent with the definition of the enemy as evil? According to the various balance theories, a number of strategies may be used to reduce this discrepancy between affect and cognition. The source of discrepant information may be *discredited,* thereby denying its truth or relevance. However, denial may be difficult if it involves too great a distortion of reality; denial is perhaps most likely to occur when the discrepant information is ambiguous, or when its source is not considered credible. Receipt of information not consistent with one's attitudes may lead to a *search for other information* that supports the pre-existing balance. The challenge to pre-existing attitudes about an object may lead a person to *stop thinking* about it, or at least to reduce its salience to a point where it is no longer uncomfortable to live with the incongruity. This strategy seems most likely if the attitude object has low ego-relevance for the person. It has been pointed out, for example, that the remoteness of international relations for most individuals places them under very little pressure to resolve incongruities in their attitudes.[9] The person whose beliefs are challenged by new information may engage in *wishful thinking* by changing his beliefs to accord with his desires. The new information may be *reinterpreted* in a manner that will conform with and substantiate pre-existing attitudes rather than contradict them. The process of reinterpreting new and favorable information about a disliked person is illustrated in the following dialogue:

Mr. X: The trouble with Jews is that they only take care of their own group.

Mr. Y: But the records of the Community Chest show that they give more generously than non-Jews.

Mr. X: That shows that they are always trying to buy favor and intrude in Christian affairs. They think of nothing but money; that is why there are so many Jewish bankers.

Mr. Y: But a recent study shows that the percent of Jews in banking is proportionally much smaller than the percent of non-Jews.

Mr. X: That's just it. They don't go in for respectable business. They would rather run night clubs.[10]

Discrepant information may also be *differentiated* into two or more subcategories, with a strong dissociative relationship between them. Whereas strategies such as discrediting discrepant information appear to be most germane for situations of limited and ambiguous information, differentiation is likely to occur in the opposite situation. Abundant information "equips the individual to make minor (and hair-splitting) adjustments which minimize the degree of change in generalized affect toward the object. . . . Upon receipt of new information, a person is more agile in producing 'yes, but . . .' responses when he is well informed about an object than when he is poorly informed."[11]

Finally, the new and incongruent information may be accepted, leading one to *modify or change his pre-existing attitudes* so as to establish a new, balanced attitude-structure.

One difficulty with balance theories as described to this point is that any and all data—attitude change or resistance to attitude change through a variety of strategies—appear to support them. If the theories are to be meaningful, they should enable the investigator to predict which of the outcomes discussed above is likely to take place under specified circumstances. At least four factors related to persuasibility have been identified: the *content* and *source* of the discrepant information, the *situation,* and the *personality* of the recipient.[12] A further discussion of these four factors in conjunction with their relevance to John Foster Dulles will permit the development of specific propositions about his attitudes toward the Soviet Union and the effects of new information on these attitudes.

Content Factors

All discrepant information does not create an equal pressure to reduce dissonance. Attitudes about central values will be more resistant to change because of the introduction of discrepant information than those at the periphery of the belief system. Tolerance for incongruity is lowest and, therefore, the pressure for dissonance reduction is highest if the attitude object is highly salient for goal attainment. Attitudes that support important values, such as self-acceptance, tend to remain unchanged even in a high dissonance situation. Thus predictions concerning the effects of incongruent information about an attitude object presuppose some knowledge of the person's belief system and the relationship of the attitude object to central values in the belief system.

In his memoirs, Anthony Eden describes Dulles as "a preacher in a world of politics."[13] Of the many attributes in Dulles' belief system it is perhaps this "theological" world view that was most germane to his conception of the enemy. It is clear that the Soviet Union represented the antithesis of the values that were at the core of his belief system. An associate recalled that "the Secretary's profound and fervent opposition to the doctrine and ambitions of communism was heightened by the fact that communism was atheistic."[14] The distinction between moral and political bases for evaluating the Soviet Union was blurred, if not totally obliterated. The more Dulles' image of the Soviet Union was dominated by moral rather than political criteria, the more likely it would be that new information at odds with this model would be rein-

terpreted to conform with the image, leaving his basic views intact.

Situational Factors

An individual may hold inconsistent attitudes without discomfort if he is not compelled to attend to the discrepancy. But he may find himself in a situation that continually forces him to examine both information at odds with his attitudes and any inconsistency arising therefrom.

That Dulles' position as Secretary of State constantly forced him to examine every aspect of Soviet foreign policy is a point requiring no further elaboration. As a result, any discrepancies in his attitudes toward the Soviet Union were continually brought to his attention, presumably creating some pressure to reduce the dissonance created by incongruent information. Persons who are required to express their attitudes in public may be under greater constraint to maintain or restore a balance between components of attitudes; this pressure may be heightened if the situation is one in which a high social value is placed on consistency.[15] Again it is clear that the office of Secretary of State required frequent public interpretations of Soviet policy. These statements were in turn scrutinized and evaluated for consistency by the press, Congress, interested publics, and allies. Thus situational factors would have made it difficult for Dulles to withdraw his attention from any discrepancies in those attitudes.

Source Factors

Responses to new information are related to the perceived credibility of the communicator; the higher the credibility of the source and the more he is esteemed, the more likely is the audience to be persuaded.[16]

Dulles considered Soviet communicators to be generally unreliable, an opinion sustained both by the record of Soviet propaganda and by his judgment that "atheists can hardly be expected to conform to an ideal so high"[17] as truth. The fact that much of the information which might be at odds with Dulles' image of the U.S.S.R. originated with the Soviets themselves tended to diminish rather than enhance the probability of attitude change; unless the truth of the information was beyond question, it was likely to be discredited owing to its source.

Personality Factors

Persuasibility exists as a factor independent of content.[18] That is, certain personality types can be more easily persuaded than others to change their attitudes. Individuals also appear to differ in their tolerance for dissonance and tend to use different means to re-establish stable attitudes. There is also evidence that persons with low self-esteem and general passivity are more easily persuaded to alter their attitudes. With such persons, "a previously stabilized attitude will be maintained at low levels of certainty and confidence. Such persons will also be more likely to 'submit' to others who claim for themselves some status as authority or expert."[19] On the other hand, persons with high self-esteem are inclined to decrease their search for information under stress.[20]

Data on attributes of Dulles' personality that might be relevant to the problem of attitude change are necessarily fragmentary and anecdotal rather than systematic. The problem is perhaps compounded by the controversy that surrounded him. Both critics and admirers seem to agree, however, that Dulles placed almost absolute reliance on his own abilities to conduct American foreign policy. He felt, with considerable justification, that his family background and his own career had provided him with exceptional training for the position of Secretary of State. Intensive study of the Marxist-Leninist classics added to his belief that he was uniquely qualified to assess the meaning of Soviet policy. This sense of indispensability carried over into the day-to-day operations of policy formulation, and during his tenure as Secretary of State he showed a marked lack of receptivity to advice. One of his associates wrote:

He was a man of supreme confidence within himself. . . . He simply did not pay any attention to staff or to experts or anything else. Maybe in a very subconscious way he did catalog some of the information given him but he did not, as was characteristic of Acheson and several others of the Secretaries of State with whom I have worked, take the very best he could get out of his staff. . . .[21]

Using this summary of content, situational, source, and personality factors as a base, a number of specific predictions about Dulles' attitudes toward the Soviet Union can be derived. It seems clear that Dulles' role was one that placed a high premium on consistency between elements of his attitudes toward the Soviet Union. At the same time, despite information that might challenge his beliefs, any fundamental change in attitude would appear unlikely. As long as the Soviet Union remained a closed society ruled by Communists, it represented the antithesis of values at the core of Dulles' belief system. Furthermore, information that might challenge the inherent-bad-faith model of the Soviet Union generally came from the Soviets themselves—a low-credibility source—and was often ambiguous enough to accommodate more than one interpretation. Finally, the sparse evidence available is at least consistent with the theory that Dulles had a low-persuasibility personality.

Thus, on the basis of the theoretical framework developed earlier, three strategies for restoring a balance between his belief system and discrepant information appear most likely to have been used by Dulles: discrediting the source of the new information so as to be consistent with the belief system; searching for other information consistent with pre-existing attitudes; and differentiating between various elements in the Soviet Union.[22]

III

Dulles' views concerning the sources of Soviet foreign policy provide an almost classic example of differentiating the concept of the enemy into its good and bad components to maintain cognitive balance. His numerous statements indicate that he considered Soviet policy within a framework of three conflicting pairs of concepts: ideology vs. national interest; party vs. state; and rulers vs. people.

After Dulles had been temporarily retired to private life by his defeat in the New York senatorial election in 1949, he undertook his most extensive analysis of Soviet foreign policy in his book *War or Peace*. The source of that policy, he stated repeatedly, was to be found in the Stalinist and Leninist exegeses of Marx's works. In particular, he cited Stalin's *Problems of Leninism,* which he equated with Hitler's *Mein Kampf* as a master plan of goals, strategy, and tactics, as the best contemporary guide to Soviet foreign policy. From a careful reading of that book, he concluded, one could understand both the character of Soviet leaders and the blueprint of Soviet policy. Characteristically, he placed special emphasis on the materialistic and atheistic aspects of the Communist creed, attributes that he felt ensured the absolute ruthlessness of Soviet leaders in their quest for world domination. By the time Dulles took office as Secretary of State in 1953 he had clearly adopted the theory that Soviet policy was the manifestation of ideology. His six years in office appear to have confirmed for him the validity of that view; it changed only in that it became stronger with the passing of time.

The second dichotomy in Dulles' thinking concerning the sources of Soviet foreign policy—the Russian state vs. the Communist Party—paralleled the concepts of national interest and Marxist ideology. He often pointed to the existence of a conflict of interests and, therefore, of policies between party and state. It was to the Communist Party rather than to the Russian state that he attributed Soviet aggressiveness, asserting that the state was simply the tool of the party. During his testimony at the hearings in early 1957 on the Eisenhower Doctrine for the Middle East, the following dialogue took place.

Secretary Dulles: I say countries controlled by international communism.

Senator Jackson: Yes. Well, they are synonymous [with 'Soviet'] but for the purpose —

Secretary Dulles: No, it is much broader. . . . international communism is a conspiracy composed of a certain number of people, all of whose names I do not know, and many of whom I suppose are secret. They have gotten control of one government after another. They first got control of Russia after the first World War. They have gone on getting control of one country after another until finally they were stopped. But they have not gone out of existence. . . .

Senator Jackson: Would you not agree on this: that international communism has been used as an instrument of Russian foreign policy since 1918?

Secretary Dulles: I would put it the other way around. Russian foreign policy is an instrument of international communism.[23]

From the distinction between party and state Dulles deduced that Soviet hostility toward the United States existed only on the top level of the party hierarchy and that, but for the party, friendly relations between Russia and the United States could be achieved.

The third dichotomy in Dulles' theory of Soviet foreign policy was that of the Russian people vs. the Soviet leaders. As in the case of the distinction between party and state, in which he equated the former with hostility toward the United States, he believed that the enmity of the Soviet leadership was in no way shared by the Russian people. At no time did he suggest anything but the highest degree of friendship between the Russian people and the free world. Typical of his view was the statement that: "There is no dispute at all between the United States and the peoples of Russia. If only the Government of Russia was interested in looking out for the welfare of Russia, the people of Russia, we would have a state of non-tension right away."[24] By asserting that the rulers of the Soviet Union, as Communists, enjoyed little public support, Dulles laid the groundwork for the further assumption that, were Soviet leaders responsive to Russian public opinion, Soviet-American differences would be negligible.[25]

This theory, however, directly contradicted another of his propositions concerning Soviet foreign policy. Discussing Khrushchev's sensational revelations about the Stalin era in 1956, he commented that a Stalinist dictatorship was tolerated as long as it was gaining external triumphs, as was true from 1945 to 1950.[26] That interpretation, made in the course of a declaration that Soviet policy had gone bankrupt in the face of free-world firmness, is not wholly compatible with a theory of absolute divergence of interests between people and rulers.

Dulles' views regarding the sources of Soviet foreign policy lend support to the proposition that a stable attitude-structure can be maintained by differentiating the concept of the enemy. Moreover, it was consistent with Dulles' proclivity for viewing the world in moral terms that the various characteristics of the Soviet Union were differentiated into the categories of good and evil. The former, which in his view played little part in actual Soviet policy-formulation, consisted of the policy of the Russian state, grounded in a concern for Russia's national interest and representing the aspirations of the Russian people. Rarely, if ever, did he represent these as being hostile toward the free world. The second set of interests that Dulles felt were represented in actual Soviet policy were Marxist ideology, the international conspiratorial party, and the Soviet rulers. These factors had completely dominated his thinking by the latter part of his term in office, and it was in them that he located the source of Soviet-American enmity.

A theory such as Dulles', which postulated a divergence of interests between party and state and between elites and masses, is pessimistic for short-term resolution of conflict. At the same time, the theory is optimistic for the long-term, for it suggests that competing national interests are virtually nonexistent. It assumes that, but for the intransigence of the Communist elite, Russia and the United States would coexist in harmony (Table 1). In this respect, his theory was in accord with what has been described as "the traditional American assumption that only a few evil leaders stood in the way of a worldwide acceptance of American values and hence of peace."[27]

Table 1
Dulles' Conception of Conflict Between the Soviet Union and the Free World

Parties to Conflict		Level of Conflict	Conflict Resolution
Free World	Soviet Union ruled by International Communists	Moral	No resolution possible
Free World	Russia ruled by national elites	Political	Resolved by traditional methods
Free World	Russian people	No conflict exists owing to moral consensus	

IV

The proposition that information consistent with pre-existing attitudes is more readily accepted than that which is incongruent can be illustrated by a more detailed examination of Dulles' views concerning various elements of Soviet capabilities: military, technological, political, economic, popular support, and external support. Two further factors beyond Dulles' belief system must also be considered: How ambiguous was the information, and how easily could it be confirmed by data from sources other than the Soviet Union? Because Dulles considered the Soviets a low-credibility source, there should be a tendency to discount information on Soviet strength unless independent verification was available.

On the basis of Dulles' belief system it was predicted that information about those elements of Soviet strength that contribute to and sustain the inherent-bad-faith model and that can be verified would be accepted most readily. Technological and military elements of strength meet both requirements; such capabilities are compatible with the image of a hostile and threatening enemy, and are relatively easily verified by independent data. On the other hand, those attributes of the Soviet system about which information is most ambiguous, or which tend to lend "legitimacy" to the regime, would be perceived as weak. Such factors as morale, loyalty, prestige, and goodwill — all of which are implied in the categories of "internal support" and "external support" — are difficult to evaluate, in part owing to the paucity of independent sources of data. Moreover, a high assessment of Soviet strength on these factors would be at odds with that aspect of Dulles' image of the Soviet Union which predicted an absolute divergence between the Russian people and their Communist rulers. In summary, then, the hypothesis predicts an evaluation of Soviet capabilities that would be most compatible with the image of a garrison state with ample capabilities for aggression, but internally weak owing to the absence of economic strength, political stability, and support for the regime from within or without. A more precise explication of the hypothesis is presented in Table 2.

Dulles' evaluation of Soviet armed forces and military strength was consistently high. Without disregarding Soviet capabilities in atomic weapons, he repeatedly pointed to the huge land forces at the disposal of the Kremlin as the major threat to the West, a threat heightened by the mobility of these forces within the perimeter of the Sino-Soviet world. He felt that neither in size nor in mobility could the more dispersed armies of the West match those of the Soviet Union and its satellites. This assessment was in large part the underlying rationale for the Dulles doctrine

of "massive retaliation," which was designed to neutralize the preponderant Communist strength for conventional and guerrilla types of warfare.

If Dulles had any doubts about the military strength of the Soviet Union they were, as might be expected, with respect to its loyalty. In 1952 he stated that the "Communist leaders of Russia are almost as afraid of the Red Army as we are."[28] These doubts notwithstanding, Dulles' statements on the Soviet military are notably lacking in the ringing pronouncements of impotence that often characterized his assessment of other elements of Soviet power.

Dulles generally had a high regard for Soviet technology, particularly for that sector with implications for military strength. As with many Americans, any doubts about Soviet capabilities disappeared after the successful launching of Sputnik I in the autumn of 1957. In 1953 he had expressed some skepticism about the first Soviet claim to having exploded a hydrogen bomb, but four years later, when questioned about the veracity of the announced claim of a successfully tested intercontinental ballistic missile, he replied, "I would assume that there are facts which underlie this statement. *In general the Soviet statements in this area have had some supporting facts.*"[29]

During the middle years of his term in office, Dulles perceived Soviet strength as deteriorating markedly, a decline attributed largely to economic weakness. He insisted that the Soviet Union was staggering under an impossible economic burden that had forced its leadership to seek a respite in the cold war. It was in this area that Dulles located the major cause of the im-

Table 2
Hypothesized Assessment of Soviet Capabilities

Element of Soviet Power	Congruity with "Inherent Bad Faith" Model	Ambiguity of Information	Sources of Independent Data	Hypothesized Assessment by Dulles
Military	High	Low	Many	Strong
Technology	High	Low	Many	Strong
Economy	Intermediate	Intermediate	Intermediate	Intermediate
Political	Intermediate	Intermediate	Intermediate	Intermediate
Popular Support	Low	High	Few	Weak
External Support	Low	High	Few	Weak

pending "collapse" of the Soviet regime; one of his associates recalled that Dulles "felt it [the Soviet system] would eventually break on the rigidities of its economic system."[30] This belief was clearly revealed in his Congressional testimony just before the Geneva summit meeting of 1955.

> They [the Soviets] have been constantly hoping and expecting our economy was going to collapse in some way, due to what they regard as the inherent defects in the capitalistic system, or due to overexpenditure, and the like. *On the contrary, it has been their system that is on the point of collapsing.*[31]

Hence he was initially quite optimistic concerning the Soviet shift toward the use of economic tactics in foreign policy. His first reaction was that Soviet offers of aid to underdeveloped areas were a bluff to force the United States into bidding against the Soviet Union and, in the end, into spending itself into bankruptcy. He characterized that economic offensive as an admission of weakness rather than a sign of strength, stating that the Soviet Union had neither the intention nor the ability to carry out all of its foreign-aid commitments. At the December 1955 meeting of the NATO Council, Dulles predicted that the free world would defeat Soviet economic moves in the Middle East because the Soviet Union had a deficit in its balance of trade. Under these circumstances it was agreed to offer Colonel Gamal Abdul Nasser of Egypt a loan—80 percent to be financed by the United States —for building a dam at Aswan, in order to reap some of the propaganda advantages that had accrued to the Soviet Union through far less grandiose projects.

The Egyptian government, however, contracted for the purchase of Soviet-bloc arms, recognized the Peoples' Republic of China, and made unfriendly gestures toward both Israel and the Suez Canal. Although Dulles had been tolerant of Egyptian diplomacy only weeks earlier, stating that Nasser was "actuated primarily by a desire to maintain the genuine independence of the area,"[32] Nasser's increasing reliance upon Soviet aid was not so easily forgiven.

With the tacit support of a Congress increasingly uncomfortable about the prospects of competition from higher Egyptian cotton production and the precarious survival of Israel, he decided upon Egypt as the place to call the bluff of Soviet economic aid. C. D. Jackson, a presidential foreign-policy adviser, revealed that the Aswan offer was cancelled to provoke a showdown with the Soviet Union.[33] Thus, partly on the basis of his evaluation of Soviet economic weakness, he abruptly cancelled the Aswan Dam offer, setting off a chain of events that was to culminate in the tripartite invasion of Egypt.

In many respects, Dulles' conduct during the Middle East crisis was most revealing of certain facets of his personality and belief system. It was based upon an almost unshakeable conviction that the Soviet Union was economically weak and upon a belief in the efficacy of "brinkmanship" to defeat Soviet policy. It was a period during which he relied largely upon his own instincts rather than upon the advice of others. Henry A. Byroade, American Ambassador to Egypt, was never consulted, perhaps because he had made known his opposition to the cancellation of the Aswan offer. In fact, Byroade did not know of the decision until he read of it in Cairo newspapers. Byroade called the Aswan Dam "a feasible project" that would be beneficial to our relations with Egypt and the Middle East, the cancellation of which was "a mistake."[34] The French Ambassador's attempts to warn Dulles of the probable consequences of his decision, two days prior to the cancellation, were greeted by Dulles with derision. The announcement of cancellation was made in such a manner as to maximize the humiliation of Colonel Nasser by casting doubts on the ability of the Egyptian economy to absorb the American aid. And finally, after the tragic episode had run full cycle, Dulles was prepared—as he had not been after his earlier "triumphs at the brink"—to give full credit to the Senate Appropriations Committee, which he claimed had forced him to cancel the Aswan offer.[35]

As much as a year after the Suez episode, Dulles was still adamantly insisting that the Soviet economy was weak because of serious imbalances. He was especially inclined to suggest that the effort to gain rocket and missile parity with the United States had placed an intolerable burden upon the economy, a contention for which, however, he relied upon such evidence as the low Russian automobile production figures. Thus, it was largely in the realm of economics that he located the "fatal weakness" in the Soviet regime.

Only during his final year in office was Dulles' estimate of Soviet economic strength revised upward. The continuing Russian economic offensive, which proved to be more than mere bluff, the increased evidence of a rising Russian standard of living, coupled with Premier Khrushchev's contention that he would "bury" the free world under the products of his economy, appear to have had a marked effect upon his attitude. By mid-1958, he referred to a Russian "economic breakthrough" and to the Soviet intention to become the world's greatest producer of consumer goods.

Why did Dulles' evaluation of the Soviet economy change so dramatically in 1958, while other aspects of his attitude remained constant? In terms of the typology presented in Table 2, the evidence beyond mere Soviet claims was so overwhelming that denial of its validity was no longer possible. Even Dulles must have recognized that his predictions of economic collapse, made only three years earlier, were no longer tenable.

Dulles' evaluation of Soviet political and diplomatic strength was an ambivalent one, in which he perceived both institutional strengths and weaknesses as well as varying capabilities among individual leaders. He felt that Soviet goals were institutionalized in the Communist Party and in the works of Marx, Lenin, and Stalin, and not, like those of the Nazis, dependent upon the idiosyncracies of one unstable man. Following the death of Stalin, however, his estimate changed in that his attention was focused more on the intra-Kremlin cliques and the "despotic disarray" among Stalin's heirs. Dulles' reaction to such events was a curious mixture of hope and fear. On the one hand, he welcomed maneuverings for personal power within the Kremlin on two grounds: they tended to confirm his theory of weakness and instability within the Soviet Union, and he interpreted much of the infighting as a challenge by those who represented the

forces of enlightenment within the Soviet Union (national interest and more consumer goods) against the forces of evil (international Communism and continued emphasis on heavy industry). On the other hand, he appeared to fear the consequences of de-Stalinization on the Western Alliance. When Beria was arrested in mid-1953, Dulles told the Cabinet: "This is the kind of time when we ought to be *doubling* our bets, not reducing them—as all the western parliaments want to do. This is the time to *crowd* the enemy—and maybe *finish* him, once and for all. But if we're dilatory, he can consolidate—and probably put us right back where we were."[36]

Dulles' most unequivocal assessment of Soviet weakness was in the area of popular and external support. Not one of his recorded statements indicates that he believed there was any support whatever by the masses of the Russian people for the Soviet regime. This was completely consistent with his prior assumption that there was no conflict of interest between the Russian people, who were basically friendly to the free world, and the United States. The corollary to this premise was that Soviet hostility and aggressiveness derived only from the designs of a small clique of leaders. Thus, the Russian people were assumed to be not only dissatisfied with domestic conditions but also opposed to the Soviet orientation in foreign policy.

Dulles had mixed feelings about the increment added to Soviet power by other Communist nations. His most serious criticism of the Truman Administration during the 1952 campaign had been against the "sterile" policy of containment, which did not envision an offensive to liberate the captives of international Communism. The proclaimed policy was based upon the premise that moral support from the free world would enable patriots within the Communist world to bring "nationalist" regimes to power. Despite his sometimes intemperate language—he was reprimanded by General Eisenhower during the campaign for his failure to qualify his discussion of liberation with the word "peaceful" in one of his speeches[37]—it is highly unlikely that he ever intended the "rollback" to be accomplished by the force of arms.

The meaning of liberation received its first test in June 1953 when riots in East Germany threatened to destroy Soviet control of that satellite state. By October 1956, just prior to the Hungarian Revolution, Dulles spoke as one who, trapped by his own campaign slogan, had come to realize the truth in the London *Economist's* assertion that, "Unhappily, 'liberation' entails no risk of war only when it means nothing." On October 21, 1956, when questioned about events in Eastern Europe, Dulles devoted a great deal of time to emphasizing that the Soviet Union could *legally* as well as practically move troops into the area and that there was little the United States was prepared to do in any eventuality. Six days later he made a special point of stressing peaceful American intentions in Eastern Europe. He refused, however, to consider any bargain that would involve Soviet withdrawal of troops from the area in exchange for some American concessions.[38] The events of November 1956 removed all doubts about the meaning of liberation, confirming what had become obvious in 1953 when the East German rioting was met with offers of Red Cross food packages to the Ulbricht government.

Thus Dulles' evaluation of Soviet capabilities was consistent with his thinking on other aspects of the Soviet Union. His assessment of Soviet military and technological capabilities was consistently high, and there is evidence that he interpreted new information, such as the breakthrough in Soviet rocketry, with a realism not always shared by his colleagues. As was suggested in the hypothesis, new information in the military area of Soviet power was least ambiguous and most easily verified by external sources. At the same time, such information was not inconsistent with his pre-existing attitude toward the Soviet Union.

On the other hand, certain other elements of Soviet capabilities were consistently rated as weak. Dulles' overall evaluation of Soviet strength may have been valid in many respects. However, there is some question whether his views on the Soviet economy or popular support were totally realistic, even admitting the unevenness of Soviet economic development and the certainty of some dissatisfaction with Soviet dictatorship—be it of the harsh Stalinist type or of the more relaxed Khrushchevian model. In both cases, he appeared far more prone to accept information tending to confirm his beliefs of economic impotence and popular resistance than information to the contrary. He readily accepted, for example, almost any hint of agricultural trouble within the Soviet Union, but it was a long time before he regarded Soviet foreign aid as anything but a sign of weakness and failure. Not until long after the disaster of Suez did he reassess his earlier evaluation; only then did he conclude that the Soviet economy had achieved a "breakthrough." Whereas his attitude regarding the Soviet economy had changed by 1958, he never rejected his long-standing theory that the Soviet regime was wholly without support from the Russian people.

V

These findings concerning Dulles' views on the Soviet Union are generally consistent with research on attitude change carried out within the framework of "cognitive balance" theories under rigorous experimental conditions. But the relevance of either the theory or the findings for international politics is somewhat less evident.

At the beginning of this paper it was asserted that "enemies are those whom we define as such." This is not to say, however, that images of the enemy are necessarily unrealistic or that they can be attributed solely to an individual's belief system.[39] Soviet policy itself was clearly an important source of Dulles' images, and his definition of the Soviet Union as an enemy was in many respects a realistic one. During his tenure of office, from 1953 to 1959, the Soviet Union did represent a potential threat to the United States; the cold war was not merely a product of Dulles' imagination, nor can the development of Soviet-American relations during the period be explained solely by reference to his belief system.[40]

Another question also arises: To what extent do

policy decisions reflect attributes of those who made them? The assertion that personal characteristics are crucial to politics because political decisions are made by individuals is as trivial as it is true. If it were demonstrated that other factors (role, organization, culture, and the like) account for an overwhelming proportion of the variance in the formulation of foreign-policy decisions, then findings about individual behavior would be peripheral to international politics.

Although a decision-maker carries with him into office a complex of personal values, beliefs, and attitudes, even a high-ranking official such as the Secretary of State is subject to bureaucratic constraints. These range from constitutional and legal requirements to informal, but nevertheless real, limitations rooted in the expectations of his associates. The organizational context may influence the premises and information upon which the incumbent makes his decisions in a number of ways: organizational goals tend to endure beyond the tenure of a single individual; pressures for policy continuity can affect the interpretation of new information; colleagues and subordinates can serve as important sources of values and information; and the tendency of groups to impose conformity on its members is well documented. These constraints establish boundaries that restrict to a greater or lesser degree the scope of the incumbent's decisions and the criteria used to make them.

How much latitude is there, then, within which a single official's values and attitudes may significantly affect foreign-policy decisions?[41] In part this may depend on the nature of the situation and the ambiguity of relevant information. Decisions requiring only the application of well-established procedures are likely to reflect institutional routines rather than personal values. On the other hand, during an unanticipated situation in which decision time is short and information is ambiguous, the attitudes of a small group or even a single official will take on added significance.

The manner in which each decision-maker interprets his sphere of competence and perceives constraints upon it is also important. If he defines his role in narrow terms—for example, if he perceives his primary responsibility to be that of administering the Department of State rather than the formulation of policy—his influence on many issues will be concomitantly decreased. On the other hand, by defining his sphere of competence in broad terms, the decision-maker can increase his authority.

Dulles' admirers and critics agree that his impact on American foreign policy was second to none. Richard Rovere's judgment that "Mr. Dulles has exercised powers over American foreign policy similar to those exercised by Franklin D. Roosevelt during the war"[42] is supported by most students of the Eisenhower Administration. His brilliant mind and forceful personality, combined with an almost total reliance upon his own abilities and the strong support of the President, served to magnify his influence.

Dulles was keenly aware of the power structure in which he operated and was a zealous guardian of his position within it. He was most careful to ensure that no competing centers of influence were established. All four of President Eisenhower's White House aids on foreign policy—C. D. Jackson, Nelson A. Rockefeller, William Jackson, and Harold Stassen—left the government after clashing with Dulles, who perceived that they might become a threat to his position; he "watched these specialists intently and, at the first sign of what he suspected to be a possible threat to the tight and straight line-of-command between himself and the President, he straightened out the difficulty."[43] Nor did he brook any competition within his own department. It was reported that Henry Cabot Lodge's direct access to the President, through his unprecedented invitation to attend Cabinet meetings, was a source of friction between Lodge and Dulles. Also indicative is Christian Herter's remark that as Undersecretary he had been "No. 2 man in a one-man show."[44]

Dulles' care in guarding the prerogatives of his office was neither unique nor by itself incompatible with the active enlistment of alternative sources of premises, values, and information into the policy process. But during his tenure traditional sources of information—ambassadors and foreign-service officers—played a markedly less significant role, partly because he pre-empted some of their functions as the most widely traveled Secretary of State in history. Moreover, the Dulles-sanctioned "purge" of foreign-service personnel during the zenith of Senator Mc-Carthy's power was a deterrent to accurate reporting by any but the imprudent or the very brave. The severe punishment—loss of careers and often public disgrace—meted out to those who had years earlier warned of difficulties in the Nationalist Government in China did little to encourage frankness in the foreign service. At any rate, there is considerable evidence that the advice of subordinates was neither actively sought, nor, when tendered, was it often of great weight in the making of policy decisions.

Although it is not implied that American foreign policy and the will of John Foster Dulles were identical, a number of factors tended to enlarge the influence of his beliefs on policy decisions. Dulles' conception of his role, buttressed by the consent and support of President Eisenhower, by frequent crises, by the ambiguity of information concerning the Soviet Union, and by his tendency to make decisions with little consultation provided him with wide latitude in the conduct of foreign policy. Consequently, his interpretation of the Soviet Union and its foreign policy assumed considerable importance.

The decision-maker also operates within the somewhat broader and less clearly defined limits delineated by public opinion. In many respects Dulles' attitudes toward the Soviet Union resembled those of the public; opinion surveys have consistently revealed a tendency to view the Soviet Union in black-and-white terms not dissimilar to aspects of Dulles' views. This is not to say, however, that his attitudes merely reflected public opinion. Although public opinion may set broad limits on policy beyond which the decision-maker cannot move, it is also true that public attitudes are in large part shaped by decision-makers.

The role of "educator" was a challenge that Dulles recognized and accepted with characteristic vigor. His distaste for negotiation with the Kremlin derived in part from the fear that Soviet-American agreement on such matters as arms control might have an adverse effect on the public, which could lead to a relaxation of the American defense posture. Yet if his fear of uninformed public opinion was legitimate, his own contribution to its education was often niggardly. Even allowing a generous discount for political partisanship, there was more than a grain of truth in Senator Fulbright's complaint that in respect to the Soviet Union, Dulles "misleads public opinion, confuses it, feeds it pap, tells it that, if it will suppress the proof of its senses, it will see that Soviet triumphs are really defeats and Western defeats are really triumphs."[45] By painting a picture of the world in bold strokes of black and white, interlaced with periodic claims of spectacular American triumphs and calamitous Soviet defeats, he contributed to the latent tendency of the public to view the enemy of the moment in one-dimensional terms.

The extent to which Dulles' assessment of the Soviet Union was correct will become clearer with the passage of time; evaluations of his contemporaries ran from "unerring" to "absurd."[46] Yet some significant errors of judgment, *interpretations that appear to have derived directly from his belief system,* can be identified; these arose not from his "hard-headed" view of Soviet-American differences, but rather from inferences regarding developments in Soviet policy that did not appear to fit the model of an implacable enemy. The situation during the period from 1953 to 1959 was such that any American official would have regarded the Soviet Union as a major threat to the security of the United States; in this respect Dulles' initial premise coincided with those of even his most persistent critics. But no imperative of the situation, role, organization, or public opinion made other aspects of Dulles' beliefs about the Soviet Union inevitable. For example, his premise that Soviet and American interests were in deep conflict on most issues was surely accurate, but whether a similar conflict existed between the Soviet government and the Russian people is open to debate. Certainly, events in the Soviet Union during the years since Dulles' death have produced no evidence to support his conviction. The validity of his view that the Soviet Union possessed the military strength to threaten American security is beyond question, but his prediction that the Soviet system was on the verge of economic collapse—an estimate that contributed to the series of decisions leading to disaster at Suez—remains unfulfilled.

If, as the evidence appears to suggest, at least part of Dulles' attitudes about the Soviet Union can be traced to personal factors, how far can one generalize from these findings? It seems reasonable to suppose that his manner of perceiving and interpreting the environment is not unique among decision-makers. Like Dulles, many Soviet officials have interpreted their adversaries' actions within a rigid inherent-bad-faith model, that of "monopoly capitalism." Many other examples could be cited. If this premise is correct, the implications for international politics are somewhat sobering.

When decision-makers for both parties to a conflict adhere to rigid images of each other, there is little likelihood that even genuine attempts to resolve the issues will have the desired effect. Such a frame of reference renders meaningful communication with adversaries, much less resolution of the conflict, almost impossible. Even the British, whom Dulles tended to distrust, often found it difficult to get their views across to him by conventional methods: "As a result the British themselves occasionally felt bound to resort to non-diplomatic methods for getting their views across to the Secretary of State; one was to plant them on American secret service agents in the knowledge that they would then get back to Allen Dulles, who would pass them on to his brother, who would take them at their face value."[47] To the extent

that each side undeviatingly interprets new information, even conciliatory gestures, in a manner calculated to preserve the original image of the adversary, they are caught up in a closed system with little prospect of changing the relations between them.

Because every decision-maker is in part a prisoner of beliefs and expectations that inevitably shape his definition of reality, to judge Dulles or any individual against a standard of omniscience or total rationality is neither fair nor instructive. Decisions based on less-than-perfect knowledge are unavoidable and will continue to be a source of potential danger as long as foreign policies are formulated by human beings. The avoidable hazards are those that arise from reducing complexities to simplicities, ruling out alternative sources of information and evaluation, and closing off to scrutiny and consideration competing views of reality. On these counts Dulles is open to legitimate criticism.

Modern technology has created an international system in which the potential costs of a foreign policy based on miscalculation have become prohibitive; one of the cruel paradoxes of international politics is that those decisions that require the most serious consideration of alternative interpretations of reality often carry with them the greatest pressures for conformity to stereotyped images. Wisdom in our world consists of maintaining an open mind under such pressures, for a realistic assessment of opportunities and risks in one's relations with adversaries appears to be at least a necessary, if not a sufficient, condition for survival.

Notes

[1] Robert K. Merton, *Social Theory and Social Structure*, rev. ed. (New York: The Free Press of Glencoe, 1957), pp. 421–22.

[2] "X" (George F. Kennan), "The Sources of Soviet Conduct," *Foreign Affairs* 25 (1947): 569.

[3] This term, derived from Henry A. Kissinger, *The Necessity for Choice* (Garden City: Doubleday & Co., 1962), p. 201, is used here to denote a conception of the other nation by which it is defined as evil *whatever* the nature of its actions—"damned if it does, and damned if it doesn't." The reverse model is that of appeasement; all actions of the other party, regardless of their character, are interpreted as non-hostile. Despite some notable examples of appease-

ment, such as the Munich settlement prior to World War II, misinterpretation deriving from the appeasement model seems to be relatively rare at the international level.

[4] For example, Sherman Adams, *Firsthand Report* (New York: Harper, 1961); Emmet John Hughes, *The Ordeal of Power* (New York: Atheneum, 1963); and Andrew Berding, *Dulles on Diplomacy* (Princeton: Van Nostrand, 1965). Berding, Assistant Secretary of State for Public Affairs, took extensive shorthand notes that reveal a remarkable similarity between Dulles' public and private views. The Eisenhower and Nixon memoirs have also been consulted, but these are notably lacking in any insight into Dulles' personality or beliefs.

[5] George A. Miller, Eugene Galanter, and Karl H. Pribram, *Plans and the Structure of Behavior* (New York: Holt, 1960), p. 16.

See also, Kenneth E. Boulding, *The Image* (Ann Arbor: University of Michigan Press, 1956).

[6] Milton Rokeach, *The Open and Closed Mind* (New York: Basic Books, 1960), p. 50.

[7] Fritz Heider, "Attributes and Cognitive Organization," *Journal of Psychology* 21 (1946): 107–12; Theodore M. Newcomb, "An Approach to the Study of Communicative Acts," *Psychological Review* 60 (1953): 393–404; Charles E. Osgood and Percy H. Tannenbaum, "The Principle of Congruity in the Prediction of Attitude Change," *Psychological Review* 62 (1955): 42–55; Leon Festinger, *A Theory of Cognitive Dissonance* (Evanston, Ill.: Row, Peterson, 1957).

[8] Milton J. Rosenberg, "Cognitive Structure and Attitudinal Affect," *Journal of Abnormal and Social Psychology* 53 (1956): 367–72; and Milton J. Rosenberg, "A Structural Theory of Attitude Change," *Public Opinion Quarterly* 24 (1960): 319–40. The definition of attitude used here is derived from Rosenberg, Carl I. Hovland, William J. McGuire, Robert P. Abelson, and Jack W. Brehm, *Attitude Organization and Change* (New Haven: Yale University Press, 1960), p. 1.

[9] William A. Scott, "Rationality and Non-rationality of International Attitudes," *Journal of Conflict Resolution* 2 (1958): 8–16.

[10] Gordon W. Allport, *The Nature of Prejudice,* quoted in Robert B. Zajonc, "The Concepts of Balance, Congruity, and Dissonance," *Public Opinion Quarterly* 24 (1960): 281.

[11] Theodore M. Newcomb, quoted in Richard E. Walton and Robert B. McKersie, *Attitude Change and Intergroup Relations,* Herman C. Krannert Graduate School of Industrial Administration, Purdue University, Institute Paper No. 86, Oct. 1964, p. 53.

[12] Rosenberg et al., *op. cit.,* pp. 215–21.

[13] Anthony Eden, *Full Circle* (Boston: Houghton-Mifflin, 1960), p. 71.

[14] Berding, *op. cit.,* p. 162. See also, Hughes, *op. cit.,* 204–6.

[15] Rosenberg et al., *op. cit.,* pp. 220–21.

[16] Carl I. Hovland, Irving L. Janis, and Harold H. Kelley, *Communication and Persuasion* (New Haven: Yale University Press, 1953), pp. 19–55.

[17] John Foster Dulles, *War or Peace* (New York: Macmillan, 1950), p. 20.

[18] Irving L. Janis et al., *Personality and Persuasibility* (New Haven: Yale University Press, 1959).

[19] Ivan D. Steiner and Evan D. Rogers, "Alternative Responses to Dissonance," *Journal of Abnormal and Social Psychology* 66 (1963): 128–36.

[20] Margaret G. Hermann, *Stress, Self-Esteem, and Defensiveness in an Internation Simulation* (China Lake, California: Project Michelson, 1965), p. 77.

[21] Letter to author, Aug. 25, 1961.

[22] Only some of these techniques are illustrated in this paper. For further evidence, see Finlay, Holsti, and Fagen, *op. cit.,* Chap. 2.

[23] Senate Committees on Foreign Relations and Armed Services, *Hearings* (Jan. 15, 1957), pp. 176–77.

[24] John Foster Dulles, "Interview in Great Britain," *State Department Bulletin* (hereafter cited as *SDB*) 39 (Nov. 10, 1958): 734.

[25] This is precisely the position that the Soviet leaders have taken toward the nations of the free world. For example, after the U-2 incident Khrushchev stated: "Even now I profoundly believe that the American people, with the exception of certain imperialists and monopolist circles, want peace and desire friendship with the Soviet Union. . . . I do not doubt President Eisenhower's earnest desire for peace. But although the President is endowed with supreme executive power in the U.S.A., there are evidently circles that are circumscribing him." Nikita Khrushchev, "May 5 Report," *The Current Digest of the Soviet Press* 12, no. 18 (June 1, 1960): 17, 19. A detailed review of Soviet images of the United States may be found in Ralph K. White, "Images in the Context of International Conflict: Soviet Perceptions of the U.S. and the U.S.S.R.," *International Behavior,* ed. by Herbert C. Kelman (New York: Holt, Rinehart & Winston, 1965), pp. 236–76.

[26] John Foster Dulles, "News Conference of June 27, 1956," *SDB* 35 (July 9, 1956): 48.

[27] Eric F. Goldman, *The Crucial Decade—And After* (New York: Vintage Books, 1960), p. 250.

[28] *Congressional Record,* 82nd Cong., 2nd Sess., p. 1801.

[29] John Foster Dulles, "News Conference, Aug. 12, 1953," *SDB* 29 (Aug. 24, 1953): 236 (italics added); and Dulles, "News Conference, Aug. 27, 1957," *SDB* 37 (Sept. 16, 1957): 458.

[30] Letter to author, Aug. 25, 1961.

[31] House Subcommittee of the Committee on Appropriations, *Hearings* (June 10, 1955): 10. Emphasis added.

[32] John Foster Dulles, "News Conference, Apr. 3, 1956," *SDB* 37 (Apr. 16, 1956): 640.

[33] *Toronto Globe Mail,* Mar. 13, 1957, 1: 2–5.

[34] Senate Committees on Foreign Relations and Armed Services, *Hearings* (Feb. 7, 1957), pp. 708, 714, 717, and 752.

[35] Senate Appropriations Committee, *Hearings* (Aug. 19, 1957), pp. 610–11.

[36] Cabinet meeting of July 10, 1953, quoted in Hughes, *op. cit.,* p. 137. Emphasis in the source.

[37] Hughes, *op. cit.,* pp. 70–71; and Adams, *op. cit.,* p. 88.

[38] Hans J. Morgenthau, in *An Uncertain Tradition,* ed. by Norman A. Graebner (New York: McGraw-Hill, 1961), p. 293; John Foster Dulles, "Face the Nation" (Oct. 21, 1956), mimeo., pp. 1–7; Dulles, "The Task of Waging Peace," *SDB* 35 (Nov. 5, 1956): 698–99; and G. Barraclough, "More than Dulles Must Go," *Nation,* 186 (Jan. 25, 1958): 69.

[39] Except, of course, in abnormal cases such as paranoia. These are, however, outside the scope of this paper.

[40] More generally, a socio-psychological approach would provide an all-encompassing theory of international politics only if the prior assumption was made that all conflict results from distorted images of nations. Such a premise—in effect denying the existence of contradictory and mutually exclusive interests—is clearly untenable. For further elaboration of this point, see Herbert C. Kelman, "Social-Psychological Approaches to the Study of International Relations: The Question of Relevance," in Kelman (ed.), *op. cit.,* pp. 565–607.

[41] The assumption that the individual decision-maker has no freedom of action is often one aspect of the stereotyped images that Russians and Americans have of each other. According to the orthodox Marxist view of American politics, political figures of both parties are interchangeable, for they all represent the narrow interests of the capitalist ruling class. Similarly, Americans often tend to assume that all Societ leaders are interchangeable cogs in a monolithic party-state structure. Dulles himself seemed to alternate between this view of the Soviet political process and the theory that the Kremlin was split between factions representing the "friendly Russian nationalists" and "hostile Communists."

[42] Richard Rovere, "Dulles," *The New Yorker* 35 (Apr. 25, 1959): 95.

[43] Adams, *op. cit.*, p. 91. See also *The New York Times,* Feb. 25, 1953, 9: 1, and Feb. 2, 1958, 1: 4, 56: 3.

[44] Thomas C. Kennedy, "The Making of a Secretary of State: John Foster Dulles," M.A. thesis, Stanford University, 1959, p. 21.

[45] Quoted in *The New York Times,* Feb. 8, 1958, 7: 2.

[46] *Time* 26 (Feb. 4, 1957): 16; Senator Hubert Humphrey, quoted in V. M. Dean, "Two Worlds: Could Both Be True," *Foreign Policy Bulletin* 35 (Mar. 15, 1956): 104.

[47] Richard Goold-Adams, *The Time of Power: A Reappraisal of John Foster Dulles* (London: Weidenfeld and Nicolson, 1962), p. 309.

The Meanings of Black Power: A Comparison of White and Black Interpretations of a Political Slogan

Joel D. Aberbach

Jack L. Walker

I. Introduction

Angry protests against racial discrimination were a prominent part of American public life during the 1960's. The decade opened with the sit-ins and freedom rides, continued through Birmingham, Selma, and the March on Washington, and closed with protests in hundreds of American cities, often punctuated by rioting and violence. During this troubled decade the rhetoric of protest became increasingly demanding, blanket charges of pervasive white racism and hostility were more common, and some blacks began to actively discourage whites from participating either in protest demonstrations or civil rights organizations. Nothing better symbolized the changing mood and style of black protest in America than recent changes in the movement's dominant symbols. Demonstrators who once shouted "freedom" as their rallying cry now were shouting "black power"—a much more provocative, challenging slogan.

The larger and more diverse a political movement's constituency, the more vague and imprecise its unifying symbols and rallying cries are likely to be. A slogan like black power has no sharply defined mean-

Joel D. Aberbach and Jack L. Walker, "The Meanings of Black Power: A Comparison of White and Black Interpretations of a Political Slogan," *American Political Science Review* 64 (1970): 367–88. Reprinted with permission.

Thanks are due to the National Institute of Mental Health for the grant which made this study possible; to James D. Chesney, Katherine S. Luken, Douglas B. Neal and all our associates at the Institute of Public Policy Studies who assisted in the analysis of the data; to the coding section of the Survey Research Center for their exceptional patience and industry; and to our colleagues Ronald D. Brunner, Philip E. Converse, Steven L. Coombs, Robert D. Putnam and Herbert F. Weisberg who commented upon earlier versions of this paper.

ing; it may excite many different emotions and may motivate individuals to express their loyalty or take action for almost contradictory reasons. As soon as Adam Clayton Powell and Stokely Carmichael began to use the phrase in 1966 it set off an acrimonious debate among black leaders over its true meaning. Initially it was a blunt and threatening battle cry meant to symbolize a break with the past tactics of the civil rights movement. As Stokely Carmichael put it in one of his early speeches:

> The only way we gonna stop the white men from whippin' us is to take over. . . .
> We've been saying freedom for six years and we ain't got nothin.' What we gonna start saying now is black power, . . . from now on when they ask you what you want, you know to tell them: black power, black power, black power![1]

Speeches of this kind not only were a challenge to the white community; they also were attacks on the currently established black civil rights leaders, especially those who had employed more accommodating appeals or had used conventional political and legal channels to carry on their struggle. Carmichael's speeches brought a swift, negative response from Roy Wilkins:

> No matter how endlessly they try to explain it, the term black power means anti-white power. . . . It has to mean going it alone. It has to mean separatism. Now separatism . . . offers a disadvantaged minority little except a chance to shrivel and die. . . . It is a reverse Mississippi, a reverse Hitler, a reverse Ku Klux Klan. . . . We of the NAACP will have none of this. We have fought it too long.[2]

Although not so adamant and uncompromising as Wilkins, Martin Luther King expressed the doubts of many moderate leaders when he said:

> It's absolutely necessary for the Negro to gain power, but the term "black power" is unfortunate because it tends to give the impression of black

nationalism. . . . We must never seek power exclusively for the Negro, but the sharing of power with the white people. Any other course is exchanging one form of tyranny for another. Black supremacy would be equally evil as white supremacy. My problem with SNCC is not their militancy. I think you can be militantly nonviolent. It's what I see as a pattern of violence emerging and their use of the cry "black power," which whether they mean it or not, falls on the ear as racism in reverse.[2]

This disagreement over the implications of the black power slogan was caused partly by a clash of personalities and ambitions, but it was also the result of fundamental differences over the proper role of a black minority in a society dominated by white men. Should the ultimate goal be complete assimilation and the development of an essentially "color blind" society, or should blacks strive to build a cohesive, autonomous community, unified along racial lines, which would be in a stronger position to demand concessions and basic social changes from the whites? For American Negroes, who bear the brutal legacy of slavery and are cut off from their African heritage, this is a terribly difficult choice. As James Baldwin said when he compared himself with the lonely, poverty-stricken African students he met in Paris: "The African . . . has endured privation, injustice, medieval cruelty; but the African has not yet endured the utter alienation of himself from his people and his past. His mother did not sing 'Sometimes I Feel Like a Motherless Child,' and he has not, all his life long, ached for acceptance in a culture which pronounced straight hair and white skin the only acceptable beauty."[4] The slogan black power raises all the agonizing dilemmas of personal and national identity which have plagued black Americans since the end of slavery; the current dispute over its meaning is echoed in the speeches of Frederick Douglass, Booker T. Washington, W. E. B. DuBois, and Marcus Garvey.

Those, like Harold Cruse,[5] interested in a comprehensive social theory to guide black development in the United States are not particularly impressed with the term black power because:

it is open to just as many diverse and conflicting interpretations [as the former abstractions Justice and Liberation]. While it tries to give more clarity to what forms Freedom will assume in America as the end-product of a new program, the Black Power dialogue does not close the conceptual gap between shadow and substance any more than it plots a course for the program dynamic.[6]

Cruse hopes for the development of a synthetic political ideology in the classic sense which brings together economic, cultural and political factors; black power, at this point in time, is a label for a series of ideas which fall far short of this goal.

Whatever interpretation may be given it, black power is a provocative slogan which causes excitement and elicits strong responses from people. Even though, as Charles Hamilton says, "in this highly charged atmosphere it is virtually impossible to come up with a single definition satisfactory to all,"[7] the definition an individual selects may tell us a great deal about how he defines himself politically in a society torn by racial strife. His definition is a way for him to bring together his views on leaders and events in the environment. If he agrees with Stokely Carmichael and Charles Hamilton, he sees black power as "a call for black people in this country to unite, to recognize their heritage, to build a sense of community."[8] He may also see it as a call for anything from "premeditated acts of violence to destroy the political and economic institutions of this country" to "the use of pressure-group tactics in the accepted tradition of the American political process."[9]

We know that community leaders have strong reactions to the black power slogan, but little is known of its impact on ordinary citizens, both black and white. As we shall demonstrate, for the white citizen the slogan usually provokes images of black domination or contemporary unrest which he cannot understand or tolerate. For the black citizen, it is more likely to raise subtle issues of tactics and emphasis in the racial struggle. In this essay we will examine how blacks and whites in a large urban center define black power, why they define it as they do, and whether

their view of the slogan is part of a coherent set of interpretations and evaluations, a racial ideology, which they used to define the role of blacks as political and social actors in our society.

II. The Data

Our analysis is based on data gathered in a survey of Detroit, Michigan, completed in the fall of 1967. A total of 855 respondents were interviewed (394 whites and 461 blacks). In all cases whites were interviewed by whites, blacks by blacks. The total N came from a community random sample of 539 (344 whites and 195 blacks) and a special random supplement of 316 (50 whites and 266 blacks) drawn from the areas where rioting took place in July, 1967.[10] Since there are few meaningful differences between the distributions or the relationships of interest in the random and riot-supplement samples, we have employed the total N in the analysis so that a larger number of cases are available when controls are instituted.

III. A Profile of Community Opinion

Since there is such confusion and uncertainty over the meaning of black power among the writers, spokesmen and political leaders of both races, we might wonder if the slogan has had any impact at all on average citizens. The first questions we must ask are simply: do our respondents recognize the term, have they formed an elaborate reaction to it, and if so, what meaning do they give it?

Because of the lack of consensus among community leaders about the precise meaning of black power or even agreement on a common framework for discussing the slogan, we were reluctant to use a close-ended question to capture our respondents' interpretations of the term. In order to avoid the danger of biasing responses or eliciting a random choice we used a simple, open-ended question: "What do the words 'black power' mean to you?" This has the advantage of permitting people to speak with a minimum of clues, but it also has disadvantages which we recognized. Respondents may not have given the term a great deal of thought and their answers may be unreliable indicators of their opinion (or lack of opinion). Use of the vernacular at times inhibited interpretation of the answers.[11] It was sometimes difficult to judge whether a respondent was sympathetic or unsympathetic to black power as he interpreted it. For example, a small number of Negro respondents (N = 3) could only define black power as "rebellion." We can guess their feelings about this word from the context of the interview, but this carries us a step away from their answers.

Fortunately, the answers were generally quite comprehensible and when we asked the same open-ended question of a subsample of the original respondents one year later (1968) we received answers consistent with their first response from a majority of the people.[12] In addition, in 1968 we supplemented the question on the meaning of black power with a close-ended item: "Do you approve or disapprove of 'black power'?" This provided a means of checking the criteria we developed in 1967 from the open-ended question for deciding whether respondents had a favorable or unfavorable view of the black power slogan. The correlation between our scoring as favorable or unfavorable of the 1968 respondents' interpretations of black power on the open-ended question and their own assessment, on the close-ended question, of their position was (Gamma) .99 for blacks and .97 for whites.[13]

Table 1 presents a simple profile of Detroit community responses to our question on black power. As noted above, since there were no appreciable differences for either race in the interpretations given by respondents in the riot or non-riot areas, we have included all our respondents in the analysis.[14]

Interpretations indicating a favorable or unfavorable attitude toward black power are marked off for the convenience of the reader. As we go through the

Table 1
Black Power Interpretations, by Race

(*Question: What do the words "black power" mean to you?*)

Interpretation	Blacks	Whites
Unfavorable		
Blacks Rule Whites	8.5%	38.6%
Racism	3.9	7.3
Trouble, Rioting, Civil Disorder	4.1	11.9
"Nothing"	22.3	5.3
Negative Imprecise Comments (ridicule, obscenity, abhorrence)	6.5	11.7
Other*	4.3	5.9
	49.6	80.7
Favorable		
Fair Share for Black People	19.6	5.1
Racial (Black) Unity	22.6	5.6
	42.2	10.7
Don't Know, Can't Say	8.2	8.6
	100%	100%
	(N = 461)	(N = 394)

* "Other" responses were scattered and inconsistent, although generally negative. They include references to black power as communism, radicalism, a return to segregation and a sophisticated failure to define the concept because of a perception that it has contradictory meanings. The latter answer was given by one black and five white respondents.

various categories the reasons for our designations will be explained in detail.

Almost 40 percent of the whites believe black power means black rule over whites, while only 9 percent of the black respondents hold this view. This attitude of the whites is clearly *not* a function of a rational projection that the increasing black population in the city of Detroit (now about 40 percent) will soon elect a black mayor, but is an almost hysterical response to the symbolism of the slogan. White people in this category usually refer to blacks taking over the entire country or even the world:[15]

(white, male, 47, 12 grades) Nasty word! That the blacks won't be satisfied until they get complete control of our country by force if necessary.

(white, male, 24, 12 grades plus) Black takeover—Take over the world because that is what they want to do and they will. There's no doubt about it. Why should they care? I'm working and supporting their kids. In time they'll take over—look at how many there are in Congress. It's there—when they get to voting age, we'll be discriminated upon.

(white, female, 28, 12 grades plus) The colored are going to take over and be our leaders and we're to be their servants. Yes, that's exactly what it means.

(white, female, 28, 12 grades) They want the situation reversed. They want to rule everything.

(white, male, 32, 11 grades) The Negro wants to enslave the white man like he was enslaved 100 years ago. They want to take everything away from us. There will be no middle class, no advancement. He is saying, "If I can't have it neither can you." Everything will be taken away from us. We'll all be poor.

(white, female, 40, 12 grades) I don't like the sound of it. Sounds like something coming to take you over.

Most of our black respondents *do not* interpret black power in this way. Blacks who were coded in this category were usually also hostile to black power. For example:

(black, male, 28, 12 grades plus) It means dominating black rule—to dominate, to rule over like Hitlerism.

(black, female, 38, 11 grades plus) It means something I don't like. It means like white power is now —taking over completely.

(black, male, 29, no answer on education) It means to me that Negroes are trying to take over and don't know how.

A few others gave this answer because they have very vague ideas about the concept:

(black, female, 50, 9 grades) Sounds like they want to take over control.

There were only seven people in this group of 37 blacks who saw black domination over whites as the definition of black power and whose answers could possibly be interpreted as approval of this goal.

A small number of whites and blacks simply defined black power as racism or race hatred. The comments of blacks holding this view were especially scathing:

(black, female, 57, 11 grades) It's like the Ku Klux Klan and I don't like it.

(black, female, 38, 12 grades) It means something very detrimental to the race as a whole. This is the same tactic the whites use in discriminating.

The black power definitions of about 12 percent of the white population and 4 percent of the blacks sampled were directly influenced by the violence of the 1967 Detroit disorders. Terms like "trouble" and "rioting" were commonly used by these individuals, especially blacks in the riot areas and whites outside of it. Clearly, however, the vast majority of black people sampled do not see black power as a synonym for violence and destruction, racism or even black rule over whites, while 57.2 percent of the whites do.

Two views of black power predominate among our black respondents. One represents a poorly articulated negativism or opposition to the term and the other a positive or approving interpretation of the concept and its meaning. Roughly 23 percent of the black respondents indicated that the term meant "nothing" to them. This category was coded separately from the "Don't Know," "Can't Say," and "No Answer" responses because the word "nothing" is generally used as a term of derision, especially in the black community. Some examples of extended responses give the proper flavor:

(black female, 39, 10 grades) Nothing! (Interviewer probe) Not a damn thing. (further probe) Well, it's just a word used by people from the hate school so it don't mean nothing to me.

(black, male, 52, 12 grades plus) It means nothing! (probe) A word coined by some nut. (further probe) There is only one power and that is God.

(black, female, 60, 5 grades) It doesn't mean nothing. (probe) Biggest joke in the 20th century.

It is, of course, possible that some people use "nothing" as a synonym for "I don't know." We have two major pieces of evidence which indicate that this is not so for the major proportion of blacks giving the response: (1) while direct expressions of ignorance ("don't know," "can't say," etc.) are a function of educational level, "nothing" is used in the same proportion by blacks no matter what their academic accomplishments; (2) blacks use the expression more than four times as often as whites (22 percent to 5 percent) in trying to express what black power means to them; and (3) almost 90 percent of the respondents who interpreted black power in this way in 1968 also expressed disapproval of the term on our close-ended question.[16]

There are other individuals who give less ambiguous, clearly negative interpretations of the term. A small proportion of our respondents (1.3 percent of the blacks and 0.7 percent of the whites) found profanity indispensable as the sole expression of their definition. Others (5.2 percent of the blacks and 11.0 percent of the whites) were slightly more articulate in their condemnation, although their definitions were still imprecise. Often, especially for the whites, they reflect a general abhorrence of power in any form:

(white, female, 52, 12 grades) I hate the expression because I don't like power. It's very domineering and possessive and (they) have only themselves in mind.

(white, male, 54, 4 grades) No more than the words white power mean. They should cut that word out.

(black, female, 37, 9 grades) Black power and white power means the same to me which is no good. Man should be treated as a man.

(white, female, 55, 12 grades) Disaster! You know what you can do with your black power.

(white, female, 53, 12 grades) Scare! Why should there be black power any more than white power? Don't the blacks agree that all races are equal?

The last remaining major category of answers clearly distinguishes the black from the white community in its views of black power. In their statements 42.2 percent of our black respondents as compared to 10.7 percent of the whites emphasized a "fair share for black people" or "black unity." We coded all those answers which stressed blacks getting their share of the honors and fruits of production in society, exercising equal rights, bettering their living conditions or gaining greater political power into our "fair share" categories. Definitions stressing black unity or racial pride were coded separately.[17] Since only 7 blacks and 2 whites mentioned racial pride specifically, we will refer in the text to "black unity" or "racial unity" only. We felt that a definition of black power in terms of black people gaining political power in areas where blacks are in the majority fell under our fair share concept, but there were only two statements of this type. This definition may be implicit in the statements made (or in some of our black unity interpretations), but virtually all references are to justice and equity rather than exclusive control of a geographical area.

Fair share answers were given by almost twenty percent of our black respondents. People whose responses fall into this category see the black power slogan as another statement of traditional Negro goals of freedom, equality and opportunity. Respondents often take pains to reject notions of blacks taking advantage of others:

(black female, 47, 12 grades plus) That we should have blacks represent us in government — not take over, but represent us.

(black, male, 40, 9 grades plus) Negroes getting the same opportunities as whites when qualified.

(black, male, 24, 12 grades) Negroes should get more power to do the same things which whites do.

(black, female, 52, 12 grades plus) Give us an equal chance.

(black, male, 41, 0 grades) To me it means an open door into integration.

(black male, 39, 12 grades) Equal rights to any human being.

(black, female, 54, 7 grades) That America is going to have a new power structure so black people can have a share.

(black, male, 23, 10 grades) Getting in possession of something — like jobs and security.

(black, male, 55, 12 grades) It means equal opportunities for both races. What's good for one is good for the other.

About 23 percent of our black respondents gave "black unity" responses.[18] These were more militant in tone than the fair share definitions, sometimes extremely nationalistic, but always (as in the fair share answers) concerned with bettering the situation of the black man and not putting down the white man. In fact, the data suggest to us that blacks who are most favorably disposed towards black power simply do not see the political world as one where blacks can gain something only at the expense of whites and vice versa. As we have seen, however, large numbers of whites do see things this way. For them one group or the other must tend to "take over."

The major difference between the "fair share" and "black unity" groups is that the former places heavy stress on blacks as equal participants in the total society, while the latter emphasizes black togetherness and achievement without the same attention to the traditional symbols of Negro advancement. We know from extended answers to our black power question and others that individuals giving black unity responses want equality and a just share of America's goods, but "thinking black" and speaking militantly and with pride are given primacy when talking about black power.[19] It is not that they are against white people; they are simply *for* black people and deeply committed to the idea of black people working together:

(black, male, 35, 9 grades) People getting together to accomplish things for the group.

(black, male, 36, 12 grades plus) Negroes have never been together on anything. Now with the new movement we gain strength.

(black male, 24, 12 grades) We people getting together, agreeing on issues and attempting to reach a common goal.

(black, male, 28, 12 grades) Sounds frightening, but really is what whites, Jews, Arabs and people the world over do—divided we fall united we stand.

(black, female, 41, 12 grades plus) Togetherness among Negroes; but it means you can get along with others.

(black, female, 37, 10 grades) It means being true to yourself and recognize yourself as a black American who can accomplish good things in life.

(black, female, 57, 10 grades) The white man separated us when he brought us here and we been that way ever since. We are just trying to do what everybody else has—stick together.

As we have noted, the number of whites giving either the fair share or black unity response is small—just over 10 percent of the white sample. To most whites, even those who think of themselves as liberals, the concept of black power is forbidding. The 1967 riot is certainly one factor that might account for this, but we found little evidence of it. Only 5 whites in the entire sample (one percent) gave answers like the following:

(white, female, 23 college) It's gotten (away) from the original meaning. Means violence to me now.

In addition, as we shall see, even whites who have very sympathetic views about the causes of the disturbances can hardly be described as favorable to black power. The negative presentations of black power in the mass media may be responsible, but Detroit Negroes are also attentive to the same media and their views are quite different. The evidence presented in Table 1 points strongly towards a simple conclusion—the overwhelming majority of whites are frightened and bewildered by the words black power. Some of this seems rooted in abhorrence of stark words like power, but the term *black* power is obviously intolerable. The words conjure up racial stereotypes and suspicions deeply ingrained in the minds of white Americans. The slogan presents an unmistakable challenge to the country's prevailing racial customs and social norms; for precisely this reason it seems exciting and attractive to many blacks.

In summary, the vast majority of white people are hostile to the notion of black power. The most common interpretation is that is symbolizes a black desire to take over the country, or somehow deprive the white man. Blacks, on the other hand, are almost evenly divided in their interpretations with 42.2 percent clearly favorable to black power and 49.6 percent defining it in an unfavorable way. Those blacks who are favorable to black power see it as another call for a fair share for blacks or as a rallying cry for black unity, while those who are negatively inclined tend to see it as empty and meaningless (our "nothing" category, for example). Blacks certainly do not interpret the term the way the whites do. They do not see it as meaning racism, a general black takeover, or violence, and those few blacks who do define the term in this way are negative about such meanings. It is evident that "black power" is a potent slogan which arouses contradictory feelings in large numbers of people. Interpretations of the term may differ, but the slogan clearly stimulates intense feelings and may be exciting enough to move men to purposeful action.

Although these data invite many different forms of analysis, we have decided that an attempt to understand the sources of favorable reactions to the black power slogan is of primary importance. We have, accordingly, conducted a detailed investigation of factors which predispose an individual to give a "fair share" or "black unity" response to our question on the meaning of black power. In the case of blacks, we are confident that all such definitions indicate a favorable attitude and for whites we know that they usually represent a positive attitude and always indicate at least a grudging respect or admiration. Certainly, as indicated above, we will miss a few black people who are favorable to black power if we follow this procedure, but the number is very small. In most cases, in order to keep the tables and text from becoming inordinately complex, we will combine the fair share and black unity categories and speak of individuals favorably interpreting black power, but where differences between respondents giving these two answers are of great importance we will consider them separately.

IV. The Appeal of Black Power: Social Change, Socialization and Deprivation

Many social scientists in recent years have been struggling to understand the increasing militancy within the black community and the concurrent rise in popularity of slogans like black power. To date, most systematic social science research in this area has centered on the "conventional militancy" of the early 1960's[20] or the backgrounds and attitudes of rioters and those who sympathize with them.[21] The civil disturbances of the mid-1960's were clearly watersheds in American racial history, but most scholars concentrating on the riots would agree that there is more to the current upheaval in the black community — symbolized by the slogan black power — than violence. Recent calls for racial pride, black unity and black self-esteem, and programs to promote these ends, are meant to reach members of the community and help them to become a constructive force in their own behalf.

This section is devoted to a discussion of the factors which predispose an individual to interpret black power favorably. The major emphasis in our analysis will be on our black respondents, but at times we will compare them to whites in order to highlight certain points. The relative lack of support for black power among white respondents prevents a more elaborate analysis of their views in this section stressing favorable versus unfavorable interpretations of the term.

It is probably best to begin by laying to rest the so-called "riffraff" theory, which has been the favorite target of many riot researchers, as a possible explanation for the appeal of the black power slogan. The riffraff theory, drawn from the report of the McCone Commission on the Watts riots of 1964,[22] holds that urban unrest is a product of a deprived underclass of recent unassimilated migrants to the cities. We will discuss the issue of migration below, but neither education (Gamma $= -.02$)[23] nor income (Gamma $= -.06$) nor occupation (Gamma $= .00$) is a very potent predictor of favorable interpretations of black power for blacks. For whites, on the other hand, education (Gamma $= .32$), income (Gamma $= .23$) and occupation (Gamma $= .48$ are associated with positive views of black power, but here it is the upper status elements who interpret the slogan favorably.[24] It is clear that any notion that black power appeals strictly to the less privileged in the black community is without foundation.

Some scholars, and many journalists and politicians, have adopted the clash between generations as a principal explanation of the growing popularity of the black power slogan.[25] The riots in Detroit and Los Angeles are seen as only one manifestation of a worldwide revolt of youth against the established order. The young are said to be more impatient and less willing to accept marginal gains than their elders.

When we divided our respondents according to age, however, we did not find great differences over the interpretation of black power within either racial group, although age was a better predictor for whites (Gamma = −.26) than for blacks (Gamma = −.11). Among blacks, 51 percent of those in their twenties gave the racial unity or fair share interpretations, but almost the same percentage of thirty, forty and fifty-year-olds gave similar responses. Approval of black power drops off among sixty and seventy-year-old blacks, but they constitute a small percentage of our sample. As noted above, age is a better predictor for whites with individuals forty and older somewhat less likely to offer an approving interpretation of black power than those under forty.

A. Social Change and Socialization: Breaking the Traditional Mold

One might assume after examining this relationship that the much discussed "generation gap" is not very wide, especially in the black community. But that conclusion would be unwarranted. Differences among blacks exist, not between youth and age, but between those who grew up in Michigan and those who were born and grew up in the South. Blacks who were born in Michigan are much more likely to give the racial unity or fair share interpretation of black power than those born in the South (Gamma = .33).[26] When we related age and attitudes toward black power with regional background controlled (Table 2), we found that the background factors clearly predominated. Those in our sample who were born in Michigan are much younger, on the average, than the rest of our respondents (78 percent are under 40 years old and 98 percent are under 50), but definitions of black power

Table 2
Percentages of Black Respondents Favorably Interpreting Black Power* According to Their Ages and Regions of Birth

Present Age (In Ten's)	Southern Born (Arrived in Michigan After Age 21)	Southern Born (Arrived in Michigan Before Age 21)	Born in Michigan
10's	**	33%(6)	67%(12)
20's	39%(13)	46%(26)	59%(41)
30's	21%(19)	44%(45)	58%(24)
40's	52%(25)	64%(31)	55%(20)
50's	35%(20)	63%(19)	**
60's	17%(12)	33%(12)	**
70's	33%(12)	**	**
	(Gamma = −.02)	(Gamma = .15)	(Gamma = −.12)

* For economy of presentation and because of the complexity of our black power code, we display only the percentages of respondents favorably interpreting black power, that is, those who gave fair share or black unity interpretations of black power.

** Percentages are not displayed if N is less than 5.

are almost invariable for this group between age categories. There is also very little variance between age categories for those who were born in the South and came to Michigan after they were 21 years old, although, of course, there is much less approval for black power in this group. In both cases, it is regional background and not age which is the most powerful explanatory factor. Further confirmation of this conclusion comes when we examine those respondents who were born in the South, but arrived in Michigan before they were 21.

Within this group we find that the percentage of those voicing approval of black power actually increases along with age from the teens to the fifties, and then decreases again for the small number who are in their sixties.

It might be thought that regional differences mask a more fundamental difference between blacks who were born in cities and those raised in rural areas. This is not the case. Thirty-nine percent of Southern-born Negroes who grew up on farms and in small towns favored black power; the percentage giving fair share or black unity interpretations is only 4.3 percent higher (43.3 percent) for respondents raised in the large Southern towns and cities (Gamma = .03).

This evidence leads us to conclude that, for all but the very old, it is primarily the experience of life in Michigan and not the respondent's age which helps determine his reaction to black power.[27] A great migration began during World War II which brought thousands of black workers to the auto plants and foundries of Detroit. Their children are coming of age in the 1960's. It is not their youth, however, which leads them to see black power as a call for racial unity or a fair share for their race; it is their experience with the culture of the urban North. It seems that the further one is from life in the South, and the sooner one experiences life in a city like Detroit, the more likely one is to approve of black power.

Life in the Northern city brings to bear on a black person forces which lead him to reject the traditional, subservient attitudes of Southern Negroes, particularly if these forces represent his major socializing experience. Away from the parochial, oppressive atmosphere of the South, he is born into or slowly appropriates the more cosmopolitan, secularized culture of the North. The new life in the promised lands of Detroit, New York and Chicago is exciting and disillusioning at the same time. It brings new hopes and the promise of a better life, and disappointments when achievements do not live up to expectations.

The Southern migrant arrived in the "promised land" to find bigotry, filth, and a more sophisticated form of degradation. With time, he grasps sufficient information about the urban paradise. Traditional attitudes of deference and political passivity fade as a militant social and political stance gains approval in the community.[28] This is the atmosphere for the emerging popularity of fair share and racial unity interpretations of slogans like black power.

Just as the trip North represented an attempt to find deliverance, so the Negro church was another traditional avenue of entry into the "promised land." Most blacks who break with the church are more likely to define black power in fair share or unity terms.[29] This relationship holds even with region con-

trolled (Table 3). In fact, membership and place of birth exert an independent effect. Michigan-born church members are about mid-way between Southern-born church members and Southern non-members in their approval of black power. Retention of a church affiliation acts as a brake on the effects of being raised in the Northern urban environment. It represents a strong tie to the traditional Negro culture.[30]

Table 3
Percentages of Black Respondents Favorably Interpreting Black Power by Church Affiliation with Brithplace Controlled

	Place of Birth	
Affiliation	South	Michigan
Church Member	33%(143)	39%(58)
Non-Member	48%(107)	67%(33)
	(Gamma = −.32)	(Gamma = −.52)

Another aspect of traditional Negro culture is the unique measure of esteem granted the federal government and its personnel. Through the years the federal government, for all its shortcomings, has been the black man's special friend in an otherwise hostile environment. It won him his freedom, gave him the best treatment he received in his worst days in the South, provided relief in the Depression and in the difficult periods which have followed, and has done the most to secure his rights and protect him during his struggle for equality.[31] In addition, it has been the symbol of his intense identification with and "faith in the American Dream."[32] Evaluation of local government in the North has been less positive, but still higher than evaluation of local government in the South.

Systematic research on political trust is rather recent, but what does exist indicates that blacks have always had at least the same distribution as whites on answers to political trust questions focused on the federal government.[33] In fact, when one takes into account the extraordinary amount of interpersonal distrust present in the black community,[34] the level of trust in the federal government has always been remarkable. Our data indicate that this pattern is now breaking down, at least in cities like Detroit. Using the Standard University of Michigan Survey Research Center political trust questions, we found blacks less trusting of both the federal and Detroit governments than whites.[35] These differences in levels of political trust are not a function of education, income or other non-racial status discrepancies.

Let us assume that the black power slogan strikes a most responsive chord in the minds of black people who want to break their traditional ties with paternalistic friends and allies. For them, expressing distrust of government, especially the federal government, is in fact a rejection of dependency—an assertion of self-worth and non-utopian thinking about the realities in the United States.[36] As we can see in Table 4, expressions of political trust and approval of black power are indeed inversely related. The higher a person's score on the various trust indices, the less likely he is to favorably interpret black power. This relationship is especially strong for trust in the federal government which has traditionally been granted unique esteem in the black community.

When we consider all three indicators of traditionalism together—place of socialization, church affiliation and level of political trust—we see that each is important in its own right (Table 5). The combined explanatory power of these variables is substantial. Only 20 percent of the Southern-born church members who exhibit high levels of trust give approving interpretations of black power compared to 77 percent of the Northern-born non-members who are distrustful of government. Michigan-born church members are a particularly interesting group for further study in that church membership significantly depresses the effects of political trust. Our future research will

Table 4
Gamma Correlations for Blacks between Measures of Political Trust and Favorable Interpretations of Black Power

	Trust Detroit Government**	Trust Federal Government***	General (Combined) Measure of Political Trust****
Black power interpretation*	−.22	−.52	−.39

* A negative coefficient indicates that the higher a person's score on the various trust indices (high score equals high trust), the less likely he is to favorably interpret black power.

** The Trust Detroit Government measure is a simple additive index of answers to the following questions:

1. How much do you think we can trust the government in Detroit to do what is right: just about always, most of the time, some of the time, or almost never?
2. How much do you feel having elections makes the government in Detroit pay attention to what the people think: a good deal, some, or not very much?

*** The Trust Federal Government measure is a simple additive index of answers to the following questions:

1. How much do you think you can trust the government in Washington to do what is right: just about always, most of the time, some of the time, or almost never?
2. Would you say that the government in Washington is pretty much run for the benefit of a few big interests or that it is run for the benefit of all the people?
3. How much do you feel that having elections makes the government in Washington pay attention to what the people think: a good deal, some, or not very much?

**** The General Political Trust Measure runs from 0 to 4 and equally weights the Trust Detroit Government and Trust Washington Government answers.

Table 5

Percentages of Black Respondents Favorably Interpreting Black Power According to Church Affiliation, Place of Birth, and Levels of Trust in Government

Level of Trust in Government*	Place of Birth:	South		Michigan	
	Church Membership:	Member	Non-Member	Member	Non-Member
High (2–4)		20%(76)	29%(65)	38%(16)	58%(26)
Low (0–1)		55%(40)	66%(73)	44%(16)	77%(31)

*The General Political Trust measure was employed in this table.

emphasize the impact of socialization into the secular political culture of the Northern black communities, with special attention to the development of more refined indicators which will help us to understand better this acculturation process.

B. Deprivation: Dissatisfaction and Discrimination

We asked our respondents to tell us about "the life you would most like to lead, the most perfect life as you see it." Once they had described this kind of life they were shown a picture of a ladder with ten rungs and asked to imagine that their ideal lives were at the top of the ladder, on rung number ten. They were then asked to rank, in comparison with their ideal, their present lives, their lives five years ago, and what they expected their lives to be five years in the future.[37] Answers are therefore based on standards meaningful to the individual, with no simple objective indicator of achievement such as education, income or occupation serving as a substitute for his subjectively defined goals.[38]

This question revealed a great deal of current dissatisfaction in the black community, but also substantial optimism about the future. When asked to rank their lives five years ago only 13 percent of our black respondents put themselves in the top four categories (7, 8, 9, and 10); when asked to rank their present lives 23 percent place themselves within the top four ranks; but 64 percent chose the top four categories to describe their lives as they expected them to be five years in the future.

As Table 6 indicates, both current dissatisfaction

and, to a greater extent, pessimism about the future are strongly related to approval of black power in the zero-order case. When we control for level of education, however, the relationship only holds for the lower education group. The same general trend holds true for reports of experiences of discrimination. However, the differences are less pronounced. Experience of discrimination is a more powerful predictor of fair share or racial unity interpretations of black power for the lower than the upper education group, but it still

Table 6

Correlations (Gamma) for Blacks Between Ladder Positions on the Self-Anchoring Scales, Experiences of Discrimination, and Approval of Black Power, by Level of Education

Scales	Order	Low Education*	High Education*
Present Life**	−.27	−.34	.06
Future Life**	−.40	−.47	−.05
Reported Experiences of Discrimination***	.30	.34	.20

* Respondents in the low education group (N = 322) include all those who have completed high school (but had no additional training), while those in the high education group (N = 122) have, at minimum gone beyond high school to either specialized training or college. We chose education as a status indicator and dichotomized the sample so as to preserve the maximum number of cases for the analysis.

** The ladders were trichotomized as follows: 1–3 = 0; 4–7 = 1; 8–10 = 2. Therefore, a negative coefficient means that the higher a person's score on the ladder the *less* likely he is to give a fair share or racial unity interpretation of black power.

*** This is a simple additive index of reports of personal experiences of discrimination in Detroit in obtaining housing, in the schools, from a landlord, or in obtaining, holding or advancing on a job.

has a noticeable effect for the upper education group.[39]

These data fit a general pattern which we have discussed in detail elsewhere.[40] For lower education blacks, approval of black power is strongly influenced by dissatisfaction with one's current lot and pessimism about the future as well as by reported experiences of discrimination. For blacks with higher levels of educational attainment, however, personal dissatisfaction with present achievements or prospects for the future do not help us to understand favorable interpretations of black power. Even reported personal experiences of discrimination are only moderately related to approval of the slogan. The views on black power of this higher education group are more strongly influenced by their identification with others in the community—their feelings for the group.

Upper status blacks who have broken free from traditional moorings become a part of a *black political community* which includes persons from all social classes. The responses of these upper status blacks to questions about the interpretation of significant events and the evaluation of leaders are most strongly affected by their sense of empathy and identification with their racial community than by their feelings of achievement or even their personal expectations about the future. They share a set of beliefs and a mood of protest about racial issues with those lower status segments of the black community who have also assimilated the secular culture typical of the urban North.[41] The major difference between the two groups is that dissatisfaction with one's current lot and prospects for the future interact with church membership, region of socialization and political trust in determining interpretations of black power for the lower education group, but not for the upper education group.

V. The Black Power Ideology

So far our attention has been concentrated on the demographic and attitudinal correlates of approval of black power. Some scholars have argued that interpretations of this kind of slogan stem from a more comprehensive belief system, a "riot ideology," which is said to be developing within the black community.[42] We found that knowledge of the black power slogan has diffused widely through the black community of Detroit. There are many different interpretations of the slogan, but only about 8 percent of the population were unable to respond when asked about its meaning. The question remains whether an individual's reaction to black power, be it positive or negative, is related in any logical way to his attitudes about other issues of racial policy, his interpretation of significant events, and his choice of leaders or representatives. In order to investigate this question, we turned to our data in search of evidence of a coherent or constrained belief system on racial matters within Detroit's black community; something we might justifiably call a racial ideology.

Black Power by	Low Education	High Education
Church Membership	−.38	−.42
Place of Birth	.31	.34
Political Trust	−.39	−.37

Anyone acquainted with recent research on public opinion might doubt the existence of a set of ideas resembling a racial ideology among any but a small activist fringe in the black community. Public attitudes about political leaders or questions of public policy are usually fragmentary and contradictory. Citizens readily express opinions about public issues, but these beliefs seldom hang together in a coherent system; knowing an individual's position on one issue does not allow one to predict his positions on other, related issues. The classical liberal or conservative ideologies may often be employed by political activists or leaders as a guide to policy making, but most citizens seem to use as a guide some form of group identification or other considerations of self interest when formulating their attitudes toward political questions.[43]

Converse argues that the degree of constraint in a belief system is determined most directly by the amount of information the individual has acquired about the issues involved. Levels of information, in turn, are usually affected by the relative centrality or importance of the issues to the individual. The more deeply concerned the individual becomes about a subject, the more likely he is to seek information about it, and, as time passes, to form consistent or comprehensive beliefs about the issues involved. Converse, of course, has dealt most often with liberalism and conservatism in their American incarnations. Comprehensive belief systems of this sort generally "rest upon the kinds of broad or abstract contextual information about currents of ideas, people, or society that educated people come to take for granted as initial ingredients of thought."[44] This form of contextual or background information is usually accumulated after extensive, formal education, a factor which seems to be a prerequisite to ideological thinking, in most cases. Since only a small minority of the public possesses this important educational prerequisite, ideological thinking is said to be rare.

Since our respondents share the educational limitations of average Americans, and do not have any special access to political information, we would not expect them to be capable of broadly ideological thinking. As Converse suggests at several points, however, it would be unwarranted to infer from this fact that average citizens are incapable of consistent thinking about all areas of public affairs. Even without a grasp of classical liberalism or conservatism and with a minimum of formal education, respondents might have consistent belief systems concerning subjects which they found to be of inescapable personal importance, and which also involved the social groupings with which they most strongly identify.

Bearing in mind the possibility that considerable structure might be uncovered in the social and political thought of our respondents if the proper issues could be identified, we asked openended questions at several points in our interview about topics we thought might be salient for our respondents. Using these methods we discovered clear indications that a coherent belief system dealing with racial matters has developed within Detroit's black community. This belief system seems well organized and serves as a guide for most of our respondents in formulating their answers to our questions about racial problems. The high degree of constraint existing among the elements of this belief system is displayed in Table 7 where we present a matrix of correlations of answers by our black respondents to five questions concerning racial issues.[45] The coefficients appearing below the diagonal are for all those with a high school education, or less, while above the diagonal are findings for those who have, at minimum, progressed beyond high school to either specialized training or college. The relatively high correlations in this table make us feel justified in referring to this set of opinions as a racial ideology.

One of the most significant aspects of Table 7 is the attitudinal consistency existing among those with lower educational achievements. A careful examination of the table shows that the two educational groups display almost the same levels of constraint. Associations among the upper education group are slightly higher, as earlier research on ideology might lead one to expect, but only by .02, on the average. Further, as we shall establish, respondents in our sample are not only capable of consistency, but display, as well, an impressive amount of knowledge about these questions, and demonstrate the capacity to make several subtle distinctions among leaders and political symbols.

The results of Table 7 are even more significant in view of the fact that three of the five items in the matrix were completely open-ended questions. We have already discussed our open question on the meaning of black power and the way in which we constructed our code and identified favorable and unfavorable responses. The question on the word used by the respondents to describe the riot was also open-ended. At the beginning of each interview respondents were asked what word they would use to describe the events "that occurred in Detroit between July 23rd and July 28th" of 1967, and that word was used by the interviewers throughout the interview. Although some responses were quite unorthodox (one young woman called it a "steal-in" and an older woman called it "God's vengeance on man"), we found it

Table 7

Correlations (Gamma) among Responses to Racial Issues by Black Respondents, by Education*

		High Education (N = 122)				
		1.	*2.*	*3.*	*4.*	*5.*
		Approval of Black Power	*Word to Describe Riot*	*Sympathy for the Rioters*	*Reasons for the Riot*	*Leader Who Represents You*
	1. Approval of Black Power**	X	.34	.46	.32	.29
Low Education (N = 322)	2. Word to Describe Riot**	.36	X	.40	.58	.22
	3. Sympathy for the Rioters**	.45	.30	X	.62	.49
	4. Reasons for the Riot**	.64	.37	.48	X	.41
	5. Leader Who Represents You**	.41	.29	.32	.35	X

* Respondents in the low education group include all individuals who have completed high school (but had no additional training), while those in the high education group have, at minimum, gone beyond high school. Correlations for the high education group are recorded above the diagonal, and those for the low education group are below the diagonal.

** The following items make up this table:

1. What do the words "black power" mean to you? For this table only the signs on the black power code are reversed so that all coefficients are positive.
2. What would you call the events that occurred in Detroit between July 23 and July 28? What word would you use? Open-end question coded as follows: (1) Insurrection, (2) Riot, (3) Disturbance, (4) Lawlessness.
3. Do you sympathize with the people who took part in the (Respondent's term for the event)?: (1) yes, (2) somewhat, (3) no.
4. Which of the following comes closest to explaining why the (Respondent's term for the event) took place?: (1) people were being treated badly; (2) criminals did it; (3) people wanted to take things.
5. What single national or local leader best expresses your views on relations between the races? Open-ended question coded as follows: (1) Militant Black Leaders; (2) Other Black Leaders, excluding Martin Luther King; (4) White Leaders, excluding Robert F. Kennedy.
   A militant is defined here as someone who unequivocally endorsed black power before the time of our interviewing (September, 1967). Persons identifying Robert F. Kennedy were not considered in the calculation of coefficients for this question because of the special nature of his partisans. See below (footnotes to Table 11) for a discussion of this.

possible to code most of the answers into four categories: revolt, riot, disturbance, and lawlessness, which roughly form a dimension from an understanding of the events as an expression of political demands, to a belief that they were an anomic, lawless outburst. We also asked our respondents, without supplying any cues, to name "the single national or local leader who best expresses your views on relations between the races." The list of leaders mentioned were then arranged according to their publicly stated views on black power. This arrangement was made on the basis of our knowledge of these leaders and their public statements.[46]

Open questions require respondents to formulate their own answers, a formidable challenge to those with limited powers of expression. Some error may

be introduced by interviewers when recording answers to open questions, and once they have been
recorded, they must be coded. It is extremely difficult,
both to construct comprehensive codes for responses
of this kind, and to complete the coding process
without introducing even further error. In view of all
these difficulties, the relatively strong associations
we have found among the items in Table 7 are strong
evidence of the existence of a racial ideology. We
believe that the success of these techniques and the
high degree of consistency in our respondents' opinions was due to their intense interest and concern with
racial issues. It would seem that the relative salience
of an issue for an individual, or his interest in a subject,
is more important than his educational level or his
ability to manipulate abstractions in determining the
coherence of his beliefs.[47] Our findings confirm the
proposition that where issues of sufficient personal
importance are concerned, even the poorly educated
are capable of developing relatively sophisticated,
inter-related, ideological belief systems.

A. Black Power Ideology and Integration

Some of our respondents may not have an advanced
understanding of the justifications for their views,
but we are certain that the questions in our matrix
require a choice among legitimate alternatives; they
are not being translated by our black respondents into
simple tests of racial loyalty. An inspection of our
questions will show that we are not asking merely if
they are sympathetic or unsympathetic toward the
aspirations of blacks in America. Our respondents
are being called upon to identify and evaluate political
leaders as representatives, interpret the causes of the
Detroit riot, and define the meaning of a controversial
political slogan. One can be closely identified with his
racial group and greatly concerned for its welfare, and
yet be either *positive* or passionately *negative* about
black power, the riot, or many black political leaders.
Our black respondents are prevented from employing
some simple form of racial chauvinism as a guide for
answering our questions because of the necessity of

choosing sides in fundamental disputes over the role
of blacks in American society which have traditionally
divided their racial community.

Some symbols and ideas, of course, seem to be accepted by virtually all members of the black community. Had questions concerning these topics been
included in our matrix we would not have such strong
evidence of a racial ideology, because our responses
could then be interpreted as mere expressions of support for the black community. This would have been
true, for example, of any questions dealing directly
with racial integration. In order to find how both racial
groups felt about this issue, each of our respondents
was asked whether he favored "racial integration,
total separation of the races, or something in between." In response to this question, 27 percent of
our white respondents endorsed integration, 17 percent favored total separation, and 54 percent chose
"something in between." Even the most sympathetic
whites overwhelmingly disapprove of black power,
but as we can see in Table 8, approving interpretations of black power came most often from those
whites who endorsed integration. The relationship
was matched by a separate finding that whites who
reported having friends among blacks were somewhat
more approving of black power, although blacks who
reporting having white friends did not differ appreciably from others in their interpretation of the slogan.
All of the aversion of whites toward black power cannot be attributed to an aversion toward blacks; some
of it grows out of a fear and dislike of the general use
of power to achieve social ends, and an unease and
resentment of all forms of protest. Nevertheless, it is
our impression that when most whites are asked about
symbols like black power and integration, they are
less likely to respond directly to the complicated issues being raised, but are tempted to translate the
questions into the much simpler issue of whether they
are favorable or unfavorable toward black people.[48]

When our black respondents were asked the same
question about racial integration, 86 percent endorsed
integration, while only 1 percent chose separation.
Years of struggle against institutionalized segregation
and great efforts by opinion leaders in both racial

communities for almost a century have made integration a potent, positive symbol for blacks. Asking for an endorsement of this idea is almost akin to asking for an expression of loyalty to the black community. Since we recognized the emotional connotation of these terms we substituted the word "separation" for "segregation" in our questions, but even in this form the positive attraction of integration proved overwhelming. The consensus on the desirability of integration includes most black writers and intellectual leaders as well as the average citizens. Debate over the idea has remained sharp and vigorous, but it has primarily concerned the question of whether integration ultimately should result in virtual assimilation, or in some form of social pluralism.[49]

In view of the special status of integration as a symbol within the black community, it is not surprising that we should find conclusive evidence that approval for black power among blacks *does not* imply approval of racial separation. In Table 8 there are no appreciable differences in approval for black power between black respondents who endorse integration and those who do not.

Table 8
Percentages of Respondents Favorably Interpreting Black Power, by Race, According to Attitudes Toward Integration

Form of Race Relations Preferred	Percent Favorably Interpreting Black Power	
	Whites	Blacks
Integration	25%(96)	46%(364)
Something in Between	8%(197)	46%(54)
Separation	5%(65)	*
	Gamma = −.57	Gamma = .01

* N is less than 5.

The racial ideology we have identified, even though not merely an expression of racial loyalty, may still ave social rather than purely intellectual origins. An individual's status or the role he plays in the economy may prompt him to adopt the beliefs of the leaders of his social group because he is convinced that this is a way to advance his own interests. This form of intellectual emulation would be most likely among those, like many of our respondents, who have little education or experience with abstract thinking, and also have a strong sense of group identification. Several beliefs may be appropriated by an individual under these circumstances which may appear to him as natural collections of interdependent ideas, even if he does not have the intellectual capacity to make a similar synthesis of his own. In other words, he may know that several different elements of his belief system naturally go together, and he may also know that certain kinds of responses are considered appropriate for certain kinds of questions, without having any notion of why.[50]

Our respondents' racial ideologies may have originated through this process of social diffusion and group mobilization, but we find enough subtlety in the responses to conclude that many individuals have developed a surprisingly elaborate understanding of the applicability and meaning of the beliefs they hold. For example, although virtual unanimity exists within the black community about the desirability of integration as an ultimate goal, there is considerable disagreement over how soon it might occur. As we can see in Table 9, those who believe that realization of the goal is in the distant future are more likely to approve of black power than those who believe it will soon appear. In analyzing our data we have found that the perception of obstacles to racial progress, or the actual experience of some form of discrimination, is related to approval of black power. Table 9 demonstrates that the more pessimistic respondents are also more likely to interpret black power as an appeal for racial unity rather than a call for a fair share or an equal opportunity. There is evidence in this table, and in others we shall present, that the capacity for subtle shifts of emphasis and interpretation is not merely confined to the community's activist minority, but instead is widely diffused among a large segment of Detroit's black population.

Table 9
Percentages of Black Respondents Favorably Interpreting Black Power According to When They Believe Integration Will Occur

Time for Integration	Favorable Interpretations of Black Power		
	Fair Share	+ Black Unity	= Total
Near Future	18%	16%	34%(140)
Distant Future	22%	33%	55%(206)

B. Black Power Ideology and the Detroit Riot

The Detroit riot of July, 1967 caused fear and anxiety among almost all the citizens of the city, both black and white. Immediate reactions to the event ranged from those who believed it was a sign that the Negro citizens of the city were rising up in revolt against discrimination and injustice to those who saw it as an uncivilized expression of lawlessness and hooliganism. If, as we have suggested, responses to black power are a part of an individual's basic orientation toward race relations, there should be a strong relationship between his response to this slogan and his evaluation of the causes and consequences of the riot.

In Table 10a we can see that in both races those who use the word "revolt" to describe the events were much more likely to express approval for black power. In Table 10b where the black respondents are divided according to whether they gave racial unity or fair share responses we find that racial unity interpretations clearly predominate among those who see the riot as a protest against injustice. This is another demonstration of the shift in emphasis that occurs among those who are most aware and resentful of discrimination and inequality. The more convinced our black respondents are of the existence of injustice, the more they begin to interpret black power as a call for racial solidarity.

Table 10
Percentage of Respondents Favorably Interpreting Black Power, by Race, According to Word They Use to Describe the Riot

a. Total Sample

Word Used to Describe Riot	Percent Favorably Interpreting Black Power	
	Whites	Blacks
Revolt	32%(28)	62%(51)
Riot	10%(212)	50%(194)
Disturbance	0%(19)	33%(42)
Lawlessness	8%(25)	27%(33)

b. Black Respondents Only

Word Used to Describe Riot	Interpretation of Black Power		
	Fair Share	+ Racial Unity	= Total
Revolt	25%	37%	62%(51)
Riot	23%	27%	50%(194)
Disturbance	19%	14%	33%(42)
Lawlessness	21%	6%	27%(33)

C. Black Power Ideology and the Choice of Leaders

Our respondents were asked to name "the single national or local leader who best expresses your views on relations between the races." This question, like the one on black power, was completely open ended. Table 11 displays the relationship for Negroes between the selection of various leaders and fair share or black unity interpretations of black power.

The list of leaders is arranged so that the percentage totals of respondents favoring black power are in descending order. The table seems to us to indicate the validity of our measure since respondents identifying with militant black leaders are the most favorably disposed towards black power while those choosing white leaders are least positive. In addition, the assumptions we made earlier about the meaning of the "black take-over" and "nothing" responses also seem warranted as individuals who identify with the least militant leaders most often give responses of this kind.

Table 11

Percentage of Black Respondents Favorably Interpreting Black Power According to Their Selection of a Leader Best Representing Their Views on Race Relations

Leader Best Representing Respondent*	Black Power Interpretation		
	Fair Share	+ Racial Unity =	Total
Militant Black Leaders (N = 59)	26%	50%	76%
Robert F. Kennedy (N = 17)	12%	47%	59%
Other Black Leaders, excluding Martin Luther King (N = 107)	17%	34%	51%
"No One" (N = 20)	10%	30%	40%
Martin Luther King (N = 150)	28%	10%	38%
White leaders, excluding Robert F. Kennedy (N = 30)	11%	13%	24%

*Question: What single national or local leader best expresses your views on relations between the races?

N's in parentheses are the bases for the calculation of percentages, i.e., persons giving don't know or no answer responses to the black power question were not used in the table.

Total N's for the categories on leadership are given in the explanations of the leader classifications below:

A militant black leader (N = 61) is defined here as someone who unequivocally endorsed black power before the time of our interviewing (September, 1967). They include: Muhammed Ali (N = 3); H. Rap Brown (N = 9); Stokely Carmichael (N = 15); State Senator James Del Rio (N = 13); Dick Gregory (N = 6); Floyd McKissick (N = 3); Adam Clayton Powell (N = 8); and Rev. Albert Cleage (N = 4). Del Rio and Cleage are local figures.

Robert F. Kennedy (N = 21).

Other black leaders, excluding Martin Luther King (N = 111) mentioned were: Senator Edward Brooke (N = 16); Ralph Bunche (N = 3); U.S. Representative John Conyers (N = 31); U.S. Representative Charles Diggs (N = 17); Detroit Common Councilman Nicholas Hood (N = 10); Detroit Urban League Head Francis Kornegay (N = 1); Judge Thurgood Marshall (N = 4); Carl Rowan (N = 1); Roy Wilkins (N = 17); State Senator Coleman Young (N = 1); Whitney Young (N = 5); Hood, Kornegay and C. Young are local figures.

"No One" (N = 21).

Martin Luther King (N = 165).

White Leaders, excluding Robert F. Kennedy (N = 33), mentioned were: Senator Dirksen (N = 1); President Eisenhower (N = 1); TV Commentator Lou Gordon (N = 1); Vice President Humphrey (N = 1); President Johnson (N = 14); President Kennedy (N = 9); Walter Reuther (N = 3); Governor Romney (N = 3). Gordon is a local figure.

The total N = 412. Of the remaining 49 individuals in our black sample, 27 could not answer the question and 22 mentioned their minister (no name given), coach or assorted persons (including themselves) we could not categorize with confidence on a leadership spectrum.

There are some more subtle differences revealed in this table. Negroes who felt best represented by black leaders other than the late Martin Luther King favored racial unity over fair share definitions of black power by a ratio of two to one. Dr. King's partisans, however, heavily emphasized fair share definitions. In addition, the likelihood of a favorable definition of black power is a direct function of the type of black leader selected. As a general rule, the more militant the leader who represents the respondent, the greater the chance of a positive orientation toward black power.

Over seventy-five percent of our Negro respondents chose a black leader who best represented their views, but there were white leaders selected as well and instances where the interviewee could make no selection. The number of respondents who could not name a leader is small and we have divided them into two groups. "No one" is a category for individuals who decisively stated that they had no representative. This tiny group was often cynical about black power (and everything else) with over one-third saying that black power meant "nothing" to them. When they did define the slogan, however, black unity was the dominant theme. Another small group (N = 25) simply could not think of any person who represented them and they were also unlikely to answer the question about black power (i.e., they were coded in the don't know or no answer category on black power). These individuals were not visibly cynical about racial leaders or approaches; they were simply uninformed.

Thirty-one respondents identified with white leaders other than the late Senator Robert F. Kennedy. They were generally negative about black power, showing no meaningful preference for either positive interpretation. Over fifty percent of the black respondents who selected Senator Kennedy, however, gave favorable definitions of black power and they were disposed towards racial unity definitions of the term by a ratio of four to one. While the number of people who named Senator Kennedy is small, his importance as a link with the more militant elements in the black community should not be underestimated. The severing of this connection between the white and black worlds is a major tragedy. In the next phase our research we will explore the impact of the deaths of both Kennedy and King on the beliefs of their followers.

D. Black Power Ideology: An Overview

Black power has no direct, generally accepted meaning, but the slogan still provokes strong responses from both blacks and whites. The power of all effective political slogans lies in "the emotional charges or valences they carry, the very elements that make cognitions dissonant or consonant," and in "their associative meanings, the very ambiguities that permit them, like Rorschach ink blots, to suggest to each person just what he wants to see in them."[51] In their efforts to shape a meaning for black power, our black respondents have fallen back upon fundamental sets of beliefs which have spread throughout all sectors of their racial community. Many of those who share these beliefs may be unaware of their most profound implications, but the beliefs are consistently organized in the minds of our respondents primarily because they are securely focused on the issue of racial injustice in America, a problem faced by most blacks in one form or another virtually every day of their lives.

When Converse speaks of ideological thinking, of course, he usually refers to "belief systems that have relatively wide ranges and that allow some centrality to political objects."[52] The racial ideology we have identified has a much narrower range. Given the limitations of our data, we cannot be sure that individuals holding a consistent racial ideology would also have consistent opinions about federal aid to education, or governmental measures designed to ensure full employment. Those with a racial ideology might be able to think in coherent ways only about questions of public policy which bear some relationship to the status of blacks in American society, but not about the general relationship between government and private business, or about America's relations with foreign countries.

The ideology of black power is not a wide ranging, highly elaborated, political world view. Nevertheless, the tone and quality of American political life in the latter 1960's was profoundly altered by the development of this belief system and its exceptionally wide diffusion among black Americans. In its radical form, as it is developing among our more disillusioned black respondents, the belief system includes doubts about the possibilities of realizing the goal of integration in the near future, sympathetic explanations of the July, 1967 disturbances in Detroit and a revolutionary label for them, selection of a militant leader as a spokesman, skepticism about improvements in the quality of life in the future, and a definition of black power which stresses the need for greater racial solidarity. This system of beliefs does not arm many of our respondents with concrete programs of social and economic reform, but in spite of its limited scope, its existence is of great potential significance. Its impressively wide diffusion is a striking indication of the growing mobilization and increasing sense of group identification within the black community.

VI. Summary and Conclusions

Black power is a potent, meaningful slogan for most of our respondents. Some react with fear, others with cynicism, many with warm approval or strong disapproval, but in most cases reactions are intense and interpretations of the idea's meaning are related to an individual's basic orientation toward social and political problems. Whites have an overwhelmingly negative reaction to black power. The slogan is seen by most whites as an illegitimate, revengeful challenge. Among blacks, however, about forty-two percent of our sample see the term either as a call for equal treatment and a fair share for Negroes, or as an appeal for racial solidarity in the struggle against discrimination.

The partisans of black power among Negroes are somewhat younger than the rest of the black community, but neither their age nor other standard demographic factors, such as income, occupation, and education, are very helpful in explaining the distributions we have found. Sharp divisions exist within the Detroit black community, but they are not merely the result of a clash between young and old; instead, they represent a clash between those who have appropriated the cosmopolitan, secularized culture typical of the North and those whose social outlook and political attitudes are rooted in the paternalistic culture of the South. Approval for black power, as our analysis has shown, comes most often from those who were born or grew up in Detroit, are not members of churches, and have begun to doubt the trustworthiness of government in both Detroit and Washington.

Black power is the rallying cry of a generation of blacks whose fathers fled from the South to seek a new life in the "promised lands" of Detroit, New York, or Chicago. The move from the grinding poverty and overt oppression of the South to the cities of the North was seen as a great step forward by the original pioneers. But most of their children cannot be satisfied by these changes. In the words of Claude Brown:

> The children of these disillusioned colored pioneers inherited the total lot of their parents—the disappointments, the anger. To add to their misery, they had little hope of deliverance. For where does one run to when he's already in the promised land?[53]

This modern generation finds little compensation or hope in the evangelical, "old time religion" of their parents, nor do they share the traditional faith of Southern Negroes in the ultimate benevolence of white men. Many are distrustful of government, unimpressed with most of the civic notables and established political leaders of both the black and white communities, and increasingly pessimistic about their chances to achieve a satisfactory life in this country. They have not surrendered the ultimate aim of social equality and racial integration, but they have begun to doubt that the goal will be reached in the foreseeable future.

We encountered few racist, anti-white interpretations of black power among our black respondents and most of those came from respondents who were *not* sympathetic to black power. There was chauvinism and some glorification of blackness, especially among those who interpret black power as a call for racial unity or solidarity, but most were pro-black rather than anti-white. Black unity definitions of black power are not disguised appeals for separation from American society; at least, not at the present moment. If insufficient progress toward racial accommodation is made in the future and tensions continue to mount, separationist sentiments might begin to spread within the black community. Today, we find, instead, a deep concern with the rights of and desires for respect within the American black community. These feelings are most eloquently expressed in the interpretation of black power given by one of our young respondents:

> (black male, 19, 12 grades) It means mostly equality. You know, to have power to go up to a person, you know, no matter what his skin color is and be accepted on the same level, you know, and it doesn't necessarily have to mean that you gotta take over everything and be a revolutionary and all this; just as long as people are going to respect you, you know, for what you are as a person and not, you know, what your skin color has to do with the thing.

Restraining ties with the traditional culture of the South are being steadily eroded as the percentage of blacks who were born and grew up in the North increases, the influence of the church wanes, and faith in the benevolence of paternalistic friends and allies weakens. The children born in Detroit since World War Two are coming of age politically in the midst of a social revolution. Events as diverse as the Detroit riot, the dominance of black athletes in every major American spectator sport, the collapse of colonial empires in Asia and Africa, the total integration of the American armed forces, and the murders of Martin Luther King and Robert Kennedy are all accelerating the break with traditional modes of thought and accommodation. The reservoir of potential supporters for black power is bound to grow.

The social revolution now in progress has resulted

in a more unified, more highly mobilized black political community. Franklin Frazier's accommodating, apolitical "black bourgeoisie"[54] is rapidly disappearing as the sense of empathy and racial identification among the black middle class grows stronger. This developing racial community is profoundly restless and is searching for new forms of political expression and participation. The result of this search is likely to be increased activity of all kinds, both conventional and unconventional. Our data indicate a willingness to participate in political campaigns and elections on the part of even the most militant advocates of black power. Their involvement in this activity, however, would not preclude their taking part in other, more flamboyant, forms of protest.

No single, dominant tactical stance is likely to evolve among blacks; questions about the feasibility and utility of tactics are major sources of disagreement within the black community. Most of our black respondents, for example, believe the Detroit riots of 1967 were an understandable reaction to social injustice, and there is some sympathy for the individuals who actually did the rioting, but there is almost no approval of the sniping and fire bombing that took place. Extreme violence of this kind is presently thought of as a legitimate or useful expression of grievances by only a tiny minority of blacks in Detroit, but many others express considerable ambivalence about the utility of violent protests. For example, when we asked our black respondents, "Can you imagine any situation in which you would take part in a _____ (respondent's term for the events of July, 1967)?" a majority said no, but, as we can see in Table 12, respondents who expressed ambivalence were even more supportive of black power than those who said they definitely would participate. This undecided group is a substantial proportion of our sample, they have made the sharpest break with traditional forms of social thought, they are the most sympathetic toward the black power ideology, and they are wavering.

The outcome of this search by blacks for acceptable modes of political expression will depend primarily on the behavior of whites, both those who control all the public and private institutions that matter, and the average citizens who must adjust to changes in prevailing customs. If Detroit's future is to be

Table 12
Percentages of Black Respondents Favorably Interpreting Black Power According to Their Willingness to Take Part in a Riot

Would You Riot*	Percent Favorably Interpreting Black Power
No:	35%(262)
Yes:	57%(60)
Maybe:	69%(93)

* Question: Can you imagine any situation in which you would take part in a _____ (respondent's term for the events of July, 1967)?

peaceful, ways must be found to pull down the barriers to equal opportunity which now exist, and there must be radical improvement in the prospects for personal advancement of the city's black population. Although success in these efforts depends, in large measure, on the flexibility and compassion of the whites, it also depends on the capacity of many public and private governmental institutions to mobilize the resources necessary to create a decent, livable, urban environment.

Some of the most important decisions about Detroit's future will not be made in the city, but in Washington, in suburban city halls, or in the state capitol in Lansing; the policies adopted by labor unions, businesses and manufacturers in the city will probably be more important than anything done by the officials of city government. This complex, decentralized system of social choice, with its elaborate checks and balances and its many barriers to radical change, will be faced during the next decade with an insistent challenge from a new generation of black Americans. To successfully meet their demands large efforts will have to be made toward the creation of a truly inter-racial society. Depending on the extent and success of these efforts, this new black generation could either become a persuasive and creative new influence within the democratic system, or a force bent on the violent disruption of American urban life.

Notes

[1] William J. Brink and Louis Harris, *Black and White* (New York: Simon and Schuster, 1966), p. 50.

[2] *New York Times,* July 6, 1966, p. 14.

[3] *Ibid.,* July 6, 1966, p. 15, and July 9, 1966, p. 8.

[4] James Baldwin, *Notes of a Native Son* (Boston: Little, Brown, 1955), p. 122.

[5] Cruse, for example, in his provocative series of essays, *The Crisis of the Negro Intellectual* (New York: William Morrow, 1967), p. 557, says that "the radical wing of the Negro movement in America sorely needs a social theory based on the living ingredients of Afro-American history. Without such a theory all talk of Black Power is meaningless."

[6] *Ibid.,* p. 545.

[7] Charles Hamilton, "An Advocate of Black Power Defines It," *New York Times Magazine,* April 14, 1968, pp. 22–23, 79–83, reprinted in full in Robert L. Scott and Wayne Brockriede, eds., *The Rhetoric of Black Power* (New York: Harper and Row, 1969), pp. 178–94. This statement is found on p. 179.

[8] Stokely Carmichael and Charles V. Hamilton, *Black Power: The Politics of Liberation in America* (New York: Vintage Books, 1967), p. 44.

[9] Hamilton, *op. cit.,* p. 179. For a view of the concept from a broader perspective see, Locksley Edmondson, "The Internationalization of Black Power: Historical and Contemporary Perspectives," *Mawazo* (December, 1968): 16–30.

[10] Riot areas were defined by a location map of fires considered riot-related by the Detroit Fire Department.

[11] See our discussion below of "nothing" as a response.

[12] The correlation between interpretations of black power on the open-ended question in 1967 and interpretations in 1968 is (Gamma) .54 for blacks and .78 for whites. We will be gathering data from the same respondents once again in September, 1970, and will report our findings in detail after the third round is completed.

[13] We will present our codings below. A more conservative coefficient for demonstrating the relationship between interpretations of black power on the open-ended question and approval or disapproval on the close-ended question would be Kendall's tau-beta. See Leo A. Goodman and William H. Kruskal, "Measures of Association for Cross Classification," *Journal of the American Statistical Association* (December, 1954). The tau-beta correlations are .86 for blacks and .60 for whites. The lower coefficient in the white case reflects the relatively large percentage of whites who give favorable interpretations of black power but disapprove of the slogan. This will be discussed in more detail in the text.

[14] For the blacks, the riot area respondents gave a greater emphasis to black unity as opposed to fair share interpretations of black power, but the differences are not great. Non-riot area respondents actually were slightly more favorable to black power if we consider unity and fair share responses as indicators of positive feelings.

[15] The quotes presented here are typical examples of black power definitions coded in each category. Respondents are identified by race, sex, age and educational attainment for the benefit of the reader. In cases where the respondent has some specialized training, he is coded with a "plus" after his grade level.

[16] All of the few whites who interpreted black power as "nothing" in 1968 were negative about the slogan.

[17] In a few cases (N = 20) respondents stressed black unity in order to achieve a fair share. We are considering first mentions here and in our analysis, but will probe this in detail when we have more time.

[18] We will combine black unity definitions with the few racial pride references for purposes of analysis.

[19] See footnote 17. About 20 percent of the black respondents mentioning racial unity saw it as a means of achieving equality. For example:

> (*black, male, 42, 12 grades*) *Negroes getting together and forcing whites to realize our importance — our worth to the United States. Gaining respect and equality.*

The more articulate members of the black unity group are concerned with ends as well as means. See Carmichael and Hamilton, *op. cit.,* pp. 46–47.

[20] The best example of work in this area is Gary T. Marx, *Protest and Prejudice: A Study of Belief in the Black Community* (New York: Harper and Row, 1967). Marx defined "conventional militancy" by the standards of civil rights activists and organizations at the time of his study (1964). All were (pp. 40–41) "urgently aware of the extensiveness of discrimination faced by the American black man. All called for an end to discrimination and segregation and demanded the admission of the Negro to the economic and political mainstream of American life. And they wanted these changes quickly — 'Freedom Now.' In pursuit of this end, participation in peaceful demonstrations was encouraged."

[21] Riot research is widespread. See, especially, David O. Sears and John B. McConahay, "Riot Participation," and Raymond J. Murphy and James M. Watson, "The Structure of Discontent: Grievance and Support for the Los Angeles Riot," *Los Angeles Riot Study* (Los Angeles: Institute of Government and Public Affairs, University of California, 1967); Nathan S. Caplan and Jefferey M. Paige, "A Study of Ghetto Rioters," *Scientific American* (August, 1968): 15–21, also reported in the *Report of the National Advisory Commission on Civil Disorders (The U.S. Riot Commission Report).* Washington: United States Government Printing Office, 1968); *Supplemental Studies for the National Advisory Commission on Civil Disorders* (Washington: U.S. Government Printing Office, 1968), especially Angus Campbell and Howard Schuman, *Racial Attitudes in Fifteen American Cities,* Chapters 5–6 and Robert M. Fogelson and Robert B. Hill, *Who Riots: A Study of Participation in the 1967 Riots;* and Louis H. Masotti and Don R. Bowen, eds., *Riots and Rebellion: Civil Violence in the Urban Community* (Beverly Hills: Sage Publications, 1968). Studies which emphasize aggregate data can be found in Ted R. Gurr and Hugh D. Davis, eds., *The History of Violence in America* (New York: Bantam Press, 1969).

[22] *Violence in the City — An End or a Beginning? A Report by the Governor's Commission on the Los Angeles Riots* (Los Angeles: McCone Commission Report, 1965).

[23] In the calculations which follow, unless otherwise noted, the

black power variable is dichotomized with a favorable interpretation ("fair share" or "racial unity") scored *one* and unfavorable interpretations scored *zero*. Respondents with "don't know" or "no answer" responses were not used in the analysis. In this association, for example, those with low educational achievement were slightly less likely to approve of black power (give the "fair share" or "racial unity" interpretations) than those with substantial educational achievement.

[24] We do not think that this is simply because their higher level of education makes them more aware of the content of the actual debate over black power. Relative youth, education, and support of integration are all intertwined and each of these factors is related to a favorable interpretation of black power.

[25] See Jerome H. Skolnick, *The Politics of Protest* (New York: Simon and Schuster, 1969), p. 162, and *The U.S. Riot Commission Report, op. cit.*, especially p. 93 where "a new mood among Negroes, particularly among the young" is described. "Self-esteem and enhanced racial pride are replacing apathy and submission to 'the system.' Moreover, Negro youth, who make up over half of the ghetto population, share the growing sense of alienation felt by many white youth in our country. Thus, their role in recent civil disorders reflects not only a shared sense of deprivation and victimization by white society but also the rising incidence of disruptive conduct by a segment of American youth throughout the society."

[26] We have defined the South as the 11 states of the Confederacy (N = 255) and the border states of Kentucky, Maryland, Oklahoma, and West Virginia (N = 49). Blacks born in border states were actually less likely to interpret black power in fair share or black unity terms than those born in the former states of the Confederacy, although the differences are small. One hundred and seven of our black respondents were born in Michigan (coded *one*). This accounts for only 412 respondents. Of those remaining, 43 were born in the United States, but outside of Michigan and the South, 1 in Canada, 1 in the West Indies and 1 in Puerto Rico. We lack information on 3 individuals. The 43 respondents born in the U.S., but not in Michigan or in the South, come from a wide variety of places. They are more favorably disposed toward black power than the Southerners but less so than the Michigan-born.

[27] Other bodies of data and our own show that almost all riot participants are young and that age does have an impact on favorable attitudes toward violence, especially for young men. This is not surprising in light of the physical attributes helpful to a participant in a disturbance and the bravado of the young. However, age is unrelated to more general notions of whether riots helped or hurt the black cause (Murphy and Watson, *op. cit.*, p. 82) as well as to attitudes toward black power. It is clear that age is an important variable in the study of our recent strife, but by itself it does not explain contemporary militancy or even sympathy for those who participate in civil disturbances.

[28] See Samuel P. Huntington, *Political Order in Changing Societies* (New Haven: Yale University Press, 1968), pp. 280–83 for a discussion of the potential for "political radicalism" of second generation slumdwellers. Claude Brown makes the same points in the graphic Foreword to his autobiography, *Manchild in the Promised Land* (New York: Macmillan, 1965). We will make some distinctions between the effects of dissatisfaction on lower and upper status groups in the section on deprivation below.

[29] The sample was divided into church (coded *one*), non-members (coded *zero*) and members of groups, usually action groups, connected with a church (not included in the analysis). People in the latter category (N = 25) chose to emphasize their group above their church affiliation in answering our open-ended question on membership in "church or church-connected groups." They were about as likely as the non-members to approve of black power and should be the subject of intensive study because of their pivotal position in the black community.

For a detailed discussion of the similar influence of religion on conventional militancy among blacks, including consideration of denomination and religiosity, see: Gary T. Marx, "Religion: Opiate or Inspiration of Civil Rights Militancy Among Negroes," *American Sociological Review* (1967): 64–72.

[30] The impact of region as a variable will surely diminish over time as the effects of national black leadership and the messages of the media and relatives are diffused throughout the nation. However, church affiliation is likely to remain important.

[31] For example, see William Brink and Louis Harris, *The Negro Revolution in America* (New York: Simon and Schuster, 1964), pp. 131 and 232–33 on black attitudes towards various political institutions and figures.

[32] See Louis E. Lomax, *The Negro Revolt* (New York: Harper and Row, 1962), p. 250, and also Gunnar Mydral, *An American Dilemma* (New York: Harper and Row, 1944), pp. 3–5, 880 and 1007 on blacks as "exaggerated Americans."

[33] Donald E. Stokes, "Popular Evaluations of Government: An Empirical Assessment," in Harlan Cleveland and Harold D. Lasswell, (eds.), *Ethics and Bigness* (New York: Harper and Brothers, 1962), pp. 61–73 and Joel D. Aberbach, *Alienation and Race* (unpublished Ph.D. Dissertation, Yale University, 1967), pp. 119–26.

[34] Lee Rainwater's "Crucible of Identity—The Negro Lower-Class Family" in *Daedalus* (1966), especially pp. 204–5 and 215 is very insightful on this point, but this distrust is not confined to lower class ghetto dwellers. See Aberbach, *op. cit.*, pp. 104–14 for a detailed discussion.

[35] For a detailed discussion of our findings and a critique of the existing literature on Political Trust see Joel D. Aberbach and Jack L. Walker, "Political Trust and Racial Ideology," a paper delivered at the 1969 Annual Meetings of the American Political Science Association, especially pp. 2–7. A revised version appeared in *American Political Science Review* 64 (1970): 1199–1219.

[36] Political trust has complex roots. See *ibid.*, pp. 7–13 for an analysis of its origins.

[37] This is the famous Cantril Self-Anchoring Scale which indicates the discrepancy between an individual's definition of the "best possible life" for him and his past, present, or future situation. See Hadley C. Cantril, *The Pattern of Human Concerns* (New Brunswick: Rutgers University Press, 1965). Our respondents were given the following set of questions:

Now could you briefly tell me what would be the best possible life for you? In other words, how would you describe the life you would most like to lead, the most perfect life as you see it? (Show R card with a Ladder)

Now suppose that the top of the ladder represents the best possible life for you, the one you just described, and the bottom represents the worst possible life for you.

"Present Life" A. *Where on the ladder do you feel you personally stand at the present time?*

"Past Life" B. *Where on the ladder would you say you stood five years ago?*

"Future Life" C. *Where on the ladder do you think you will be five years from now?*

[38] In the black community sample, for example, level of education is correlated (Gamma) .06 with scores on the past life ladder, .09 with the present life ladder and .29 with the future life ladder. Education is, therefore, only important as a predictor of assessments of future prospects and even here other factors are obviously at work. Income and occupation work much the same way. It is clear that people's evaluations of their achievements vary more within than between objectively defined status groupings.

[39] Reported experiences of discrimination are unrelated to education (Gamma = .01).

[40] Aberbach and Walker, *op. cit.,* (1969), especially pp. 11–16.

[41] The correlations (Gamma) between church membership, place of birth and approval of black power are actually slightly higher in the upper education than in the lower education group.

[42] T. M. Tomlinson, "The Development of a Riot Ideology Among Urban Negroes," *American Behavioral Scientist* (1968): 27–31.

[43] The best single statement is Philip E. Converse, "The Nature of Belief Systems in Mass Publics," in David E. Apter (ed.), *Ideology and Discontent* (New York: Free Press, 1964), pp. 206–62. For a brief review of this literature see: Lester W. Mibrath, *Political Participation* (Chicago: Rand McNally, 1965); and Herbert McClosky, "Consensus and Ideology in American Politics," *American Political Science Review* (1964): 361–82. For some recent work see: Robert Axelrod, "The Structure of Public Opinion on Policy Issues," *Public Opinion Quarterly* (1967): 49–60; and Norman R. Luttbeg, "The Structure of Beliefs Among Leaders and the Public," *Public Opinion Quarterly* (1968): 398–410.

[44] Converse, *op. cit.,* p. 255.

[45] To judge the relative strength of these relationships, see a similar matrix for a national cross-section sample in Converse, *op. cit.,* p. 228.

[46] The two remaining questions in the matrix were close-ended and provided respondents with a set of alternative answers from which to choose. See the footnotes of Table 7 for their exact wording.

[47] See Converse, *op. cit.;* and Roy T. Bowles and James T. Richardson, "Sources of Consistency of Political Opinion," *American Journal of Sociology* (1969), who argue on p. 683, that "interest in politics is a more powerful predictor of both ideological conceptualization and consistency of opinion than is ability to use abstract ideas."

[48] The issue of the nature of racial ideology among whites will be explored in Joel D. Aberbach and Jack L. Walker, *Race and the Urban Political Community* (Boston: Little, Brown, forthcoming).

[49] Strong advocates of black power are almost uniformly in favor of social pluralism and reject cultural assimilation as resting on the demeaning "assumption that there is nothing of value in the black community." (Carmichael and Hamilton, *op. cit.,* p. 53). However, they do not endorse separatism holding that black power is "ultimately not separatist or isolationist." (Hamilton, *op. cit.,* p. 193). The basic idea is that after the black man develops "a sense of pride and self-respect . . . if integration comes, it will deal with people who are psychologically and mentally healthy, with people who have a sense of their history and of themselves as whole human beings." (Hamilton, *op. cit.,* p. 182). Detailed discussion on the meanings of assimilation can be found in Milton M. Gordon, *Assimilation in American Life* (New York: Oxford University Press, 1964).

[50] Converse discusses this possibility in a section called "Social sources of Constraint." Converse, *op. cit.,* pp. 211–13. For other treatments of the origins of ideology, see William H. Form and Joan Rytina, "Ideological Beliefs on the Distribution of Power in the United States," *American Sociological Review* (1969): 19–30; Samuel H. Barnes, "Ideology and the Organization of Conflict," *Journal of Politics* (1966), 513–30; Richard M. Merelman, "The Development of Political Ideology: A Framework for the Analysis of Political Socialization," *American Political Science Review* (1969): 750–67; Everett C. Ladd, Jr., *Ideology in America* (Ithaca: Cornell University Press, 1969), pp. 341–50; and Robert E. Lane, *Political Ideology* (New York: Free Press, 1962), pp. 213–439.

[51] Robert E. Lane, *Political Thinking and Consciousness* (Chicago: Markham, 1969), p. 316.

[52] Converse, *op. cit.,* pp. 208–9.

[53] Claude Brown, *op. cit.,* p. 8.

[54] E. Franklin Frazier, *Black Bourgeoisie* (New York: Free Press, 1957).

7

Political Belief Systems:
Function and Structure

Each of the previous chapters has focused on sets of factors which shape political belief systems. In addition, the readings to this point have often treated the direction and intensity of political opinions as a function of smaller sets of these factors. Although the substance of these opinions is very important (and therefore pervades the book), we now turn our attention to the structure of one's political opinions and the manner in which they serve basic psychological needs.

Neither the word, "system," nor the word, "structure," should be taken to imply that beliefs are organized coherently or rationally.[1] The average man does not intellectualize his reactions to political stimuli, nor is he informed sufficiently to determine the logical or historical relationship between elements of his or another's political orientation. A belief system, as defined by Converse, is simply a configuration of ideas and attitudes in which the elements are bound together by some form of "constraint." In this context "constraint" is defined as "functional interdependence," a concept to which we shall return below as we discuss the structure of belief systems. For now, the reader should understand that to speak of the "functional interdependence" of belief elements is to refer to the way in which the elements interrelate *in the mind of the believer.* When we refer to the functions of a belief system, however, we have in mind the way in which beliefs fulfill certain *psychological needs of the believer.*

Functions

Humans develop thought processes, such as categorization, to reduce stimuli to manageable units and, therefore, to impose order and meaning

---

[1] See Milton Rokeach, *The Open and Closed Mind* (New York: Basic Books, 1960), pp. 33ff.

on the world around them. What Lane calls the "pursuit of meaning" should not be confused with what has been called a "quest for knowledge." Not all men seek knowledge and truth, but all men do seek meaning in the emanations which come their way. The beliefs that one forms in what Smith (Chapter 2) labels the process of "object appraisal," help to make sense out of one's political world.

The lack of meaning has been discussed by various social scientists as having several political consequences. For example, "meaninglessness" has been considered by some to be one dimension of a broader psychological condition, "alienation." Others have suggested that the bewildered and disaffected are the most susceptible to the appeals of extremist movements in both politics and religion.[2] Such movements promise hope and deliverance; they often provide a ready-made belief structure to enable the faithful to interpret and evaluate political elements and thus to achieve meaning in their relationship with the political world.

More efficacious persons confront the need to understand on a more individualistic basis, but all of us rely to some extent on cues and definitions from the reference groups which we regard as significant. The more elaborate one's belief structure, the more easily he can accommodate subtle distinctions and discern shades of meaning in political phenomena.

The self-anchoring need is served by beliefs which aid in the social adjustment process and in defining one's position vis-a-vis significant others. Lane mentions the dependence that we all have on the approval and affection of others. In any case, political beliefs and attitudes help to define friends and rivals. Moreover, depending on the extent of our personality needs, we may develop summary attitudes of respect or hostility toward large categories of persons, thus simplifying the formation of subsequent evaluations and beliefs. The so-called "ethnocentric," for example, forms a positive attitude toward his own primary reference group, and is hostile and suspicious in his orientation toward "outsiders"—or all other persons.

Ego defense is one of the most basic needs served by political beliefs. One's need for self-esteem, for example, might very likely lead to the formation of beliefs by which one externalizes—or projects onto other persons or categories of persons—certain negative attributes which one fears are characteristic of himself. Lane speaks of political participation as possibly resulting in the relief of "intrapsychic tensions" which stem from sexual drives, feelings of hostility or aggression, and so forth. Beliefs, as well as participation, can help resolve inner conflicts through externalization or projection. One who is bothered by the self-recognition of a homosexual impulse, for example, can repress the forbidden impulse and

---

[2] For example, see the research of Aberbach reported in Chapter 2.

reduce psychic tension by projecting the attribute onto others. He may, consequently, develop the belief that the U. S. Department of State is honeycombed with homosexuals. A variety of ego-alien impulses can be similarly managed. The highly prejudiced person, more than a tolerant man, is likely to knit a belief system which incorporates elements of projection and externalization.

Structure

In addition to fulfilling certain functions for the personality of the believer, one's beliefs adhere interdependently to a system which has a discernible structure. The selection by Converse is the seminal work on the structure of political belief systems. Note again the definition of "constraint" as it is discussed at the beginning of this section. To us as individuals our beliefs somehow hang together, and often are experienced by us as "logically constrained idea clusters," no matter how illogical they are in fact. The "logic" of belief systems may follow from a major premise embedded in a "superordinate value," or an unquestioned element of faith. Note that Converse regards *ideology* as the kind of belief system in which constraint is highly developed, abstract, and quasi-logical.[3]

In rare instances logic can truly be a source of constraint for belief systems, but more often the sources are sociological. Most social niches are associated with certain interests and types of information, predisposing the occupants of such niches toward corresponding idea clusters whose quasi-logic they tend to reinforce. The social logic associated with a given perspective acts to bind together belief elements whose conjunction is illogical in the abstract. The individual is given socially provided cues regarding "what goes with what." As Converse remarks, understanding *why* certain idea elements "go together" requires a higher level of information.

The discussion is not meant to imply that belief systems are alike. They differ markedly in important respects. Dawson does show that persons who think alike on the Viet Nam war issue tend to have similar organizations of beliefs which support their views. But the "pro" and "con" respondents rank the importance of the belief elements in almost opposite fashion from one another. Some belief systems will be much more highly developed than others, with a greater range of referents. Converse points out also that constraint is far weaker among those of lower education and

[3] For a discussion of the interrelationships between ideology and general belief systems see Giovanni Sartori, "Politics, Ideology, and Belief Systems," *American Political Science Review* 63 (1969): 398–412.

political experience. As we move down in level of education and political experience, belief systems become narrower, and the "central idea objects become increasingly simple, concrete, or 'close to home.'" The importance of the above observation is as a guard against generalizing to the mass-public elite-based assumptions about "natural" belief combinations.

The selections which follow elaborate the points made here and provide the reader with some of the most cogent work relating to the functions and structures of political belief systems.

Selected Additional Readings

Brown, Steven R. "Consistency and The Persistence of Ideology: Some Experimental Results." *Public Opinion Quarterly* 34 (1970): 60–68.

Field, John O., and Ronald E. Anderson. "Ideology in the Public's Conceptualization of the 1964 Election." *Public Opinion Quarterly* 33 (1969): 380–99.

Fishbein, Martin, ed. *Readings in Attitude Theory and Measurement.* New York: John Wiley & Sons, Inc., 1967.

Holsti, Ole R. "The Belief System and National Images: A Case Study." *Journal of Conflict Resolution* 6 (1962): 244–53.

Holsti, Ole R. "Cognitive Dynamics and Images of the Enemy." *Journal of International Affairs* 1 (1967): 16–39.

Jahoda, Marie, and Neil Warren, eds. *Attitudes.* Baltimore: Penguin Books, 1966.

Katz, Daniel. "The Functional Approach to the Study of Attitudes." *Public Opinion Quarterly* 24 (1960): 163–76.

Lane, Robert E. *Political Life.* New York: The Free Press, 1959.

Lane, Robert E. *Political Ideology.* Glencoe: The Free Press, 1962.

Lane, Robert E. *Political Thinking and Consciousness.* Chicago: Markham Publishing Company, 1969.

Luttbeg, Norman R. "The Structure of Beliefs Among Leaders and the Public." *Public Opinion Quarterly* 32 (1968): 398–410.

McClosky, Herbert. "Consensus and Ideology in American Politics." *American Political Science Review* 58 (1964): 361–82.

Minar, David W. "Ideology and Political Behavior." *Midwest Journal of Political Science* 5 (1961): 317–31.

Prothro, James W., and Charles W. Grigg. "Fundamental Principles of Democracy: Bases of Agreement and Disagreement." *Journal of Politics* 22 (1960): 276–94.

Rokeach, Milton. *The Open and Closed Mind.* New York: Basic Books, Inc., 1960.

Rokeach, Milton. *Beliefs, Attitudes and Values.* San Francisco: Jossey-Bass, 1968.

Rosenberg, Milton J., et al., eds. *Attitude Organization and Change.* New Haven: Yale University Press, 1960.

Sartori, Giovanni. "Politics, Ideology and Belief Systems." *American Political Science Review* 63 (1969): 398–412.

Smith, M. Brewster, Jerome Bruner, and Robert W. White. *Opinions and Personality.* New York: John Wiley & Sons, Inc., 1956.

Smith, M. Brewster. "Opinions, Personality and Political Behavior." *American Political Science Review* 52 (1958): 1–26.

Stouffer, Samuel. *Communism, Conformity and Civil Liberties.* New York: John Wiley & Sons, Inc., 1955.

Wilker, Harry R., and Lester W. Milbrath. "Political Belief Systems and Political Behavior." *Social Science Quarterly* 51 (1970): 477–93.

Wolfinger, Raymond, et al. "America's Radical Right: Politics and Ideology." In David E. Apter (ed.), *Ideology and Discontent.* Pp. 262–93. New York: The Free Press, 1964.

Meeting Needs in Political Life

Robert E. Lane

What Conscious Needs are Served by Participation in Political Life?

Economic, Social, and Intellectual Needs

Of what use to a man is his politics? As Graham Wallas points out, it is unfruitful to say that men in politics are self-interested.[1] That only leads to the further question: which interests? He criticizes the over-rational approaches of the utilitarians, and deals instead with the political expression of such "impulses" as affection, fear, laughter, the desire for property, the "fighting instinct," "suspicion, curiosity, and the desire to excel."[2] Lasswell concurs in the impulse theory, but believes that their expression in politics represents a displacement from areas of private life.[3]

Another possible approach is through the study of values: Which values do men pursue through political instruments? Lasswell suggests that these values are: power, wealth, well-being, skill, enlightenment, affection, rectitude and respect—and it is true that men do seek these values in politics.[4] It is said that men join social movements because some object, person, or idea has become "ego-involved"—and this idea of the extension of the self to include selected features of society is useful.[5] Smith, Bruner, and White believe that men develop their political opinions to meet three needs: (1) to understand the world and to control events, (2) to get along well with others, and (3) to express psychic tensions.[6]

Reprinted with permission of The Macmillan Company from *Political Life* by Robert E. Lane. © The Free Press, a Corporation, 1959.

While all of these views are partially true, and frequently useful, it has served our purposes to develop the following grammar of political motives. These are the needs served by men's political activity.

1. Men seek to advance their economic or material well-being, their income, their property, their economic security through political means.

2. Men seek to satisfy their needs for friendship, affection, and easy social relations through political means.

3. Men seek to understand the world, and the causes of the events which affect them, through observing and discussing politics.

4. Men seek to relieve intra-psychic tensions, chiefly those arising from aggressive and sexual impulses, through political expression.

5. Men seek power over others (to satisfy doubts about themselves) through political channels.

6. Men generally seek to defend and improve their self-esteem through political activity.

These are not mutually exclusive motives, they are overlapping and leave lacunae, but they are "real" in the sense that their connection with political acts can be traced, and they are at the focus of attention of those who have discussed human nature in politics in the last thirty or forty years.

Politics and the Pursuit of Economic Gain

Here lies the substance of the older economic interpretations of politics: a man adopts those opinions and undertakes those activities which advance his material well-being. He protects his property by an interest in governmental economy implemented by a contribution to the local taxpayers' research bureau. He advances his security (certainty of income) by writing a letter to the President urging an extension of social security for the self-employed. He votes for a candidate because that candidate seems to be "for people like me"—a motive which combines many elements but includes the hope that the voters' economic interests will be favored. There is no doubt that, along with the political pursuit of other needs, men pursue economic gain through political activity.

Conceptualization in this area is clouded by certain irrelevancies which confuse the issue. Problems regarding the relation of the "cultural superstructure" to the economic basis of society, dialectical materialism in history, rationality of economic choice, etc., must be set aside as only tangential to the study of economic needs served by political activity. What is needed at this point is something less ambitious, a classification of the nature of the gratifications to be achieved by political pursuit of economic gain.

Perception of economics in politics. From survey material there accumulates evidence that relatively few people believe that national elections will "affect me personally"—only three out of ten in 1944.[7] Observers and interpreters of the political scene, relying on more impressionistic material, have come to the same conclusion. "We must not ignore the fact that political involvement may supply the individual with . . . the practical gratification of satisfying some material need. But psychologically speaking, the less obvious 'meanings' of politics are probably more influential in determining political behavior."[8] The articulation in the mind of the individual voter of economic life and political affairs is loose. But it is not altogether missing, and it takes devious routes.

One reason for this low perception is the individualized means whereby men in America satisfy their needs. If a man wants housing, lower prices, or other material satisfactions, he generally tries to gratify these needs individually by shopping around in the existing market, rather than through political organization. As one Ithaca citizen said, "I don't think politics or election results will or do affect my own life very much. Regardless of who is in power, I'll keep my job and my home."[9] Even Tocqueville noted something of this sort when he said, "The discharge of political duties appears to them [Americans] to be a troublesome impediment, which diverts them from their occupation and business. These people think they are following the principle of self-interest, but the idea they entertain of that principle is a very crude one. . . ."[10] Thus, in at least one crucial respect, the interpretation of economic man in the political arena is different from the view of the species in the marketplace. The relations of his acts to his needs in politics are even more obscure than usual to him.

Level of economic need. Economic theory tells us that the more money a person has, the less will each additional dollar contribute to his total satisfaction; money, like everything else, has a diminishing marginal utility. That is, for those with more money a 10 percent increase in spendable income has less utility than has a 10 percent increase for those with less, although the range within which this is true has never been specified. In any event, one cannot account for political activity on this basis since such activity shows a positive correlation with income. The less money a person has, the less likely he is to pursue economic or any other gain through political activity. The possibility exists, however, that the economic rewards of politics are more salient for the lower income groups: to the extent that they are interested at all in politics, they may see it more in economic terms. There is some evidence that this is true from a study of public attitudes toward Roosevelt, in which personal economic gain was more salient for the lower income groups than for the middle income groups.[11] This relatively greater salience of personal economic gain and loss for lower income groups is also supported by analysis of values in senatorial mail on the conscription issue. Here it was found that while 32 percent of the low income group referred to conscription in terms of its effect upon their economic situation, only 16 percent of the high income group made this kind of reference. The high income group was, on the other hand, much more likely to refer to "freedom," or civil liberties, or other generalized social values.[12] This greater focus of interest on personal-economic problems in lower income groups not only reflects greater marginal utility of money but also lower interest in general policy matters, lower capacity for handling abstractions, and generally lower horizons of knowledge and awareness.

There are, on the other hand, reasons for believing that lower income groups, instead of relating their economic well-being to political decisions more closely than others, in fact are less likely to perceive this relationship. At least in 1944 fewer lower status than upper status people expected the presidential election of that year to affect them personally.[13] And for a very good reason. Businessmen receive more individualized benefits from government: contracts, tariffs, tax abatements, etc. For them, therefore, there is an opportunity to relate personal gain to individual effort. Others, and especially workers, receive benefits only as members of larger groups and therefore see the rewards of effort as more tenuous and less probable. Under these circumstances, the salience of personal economic stakes in political decisions would be greater for businessmen (and to some extent farmers) than for urban laborers and white collar workers. Thus, there are both theoretical and empirical reasons for believing that the political perspectives of lower income persons have a higher than average economic content and reasons for believing the opposite.

From the findings, combined with our evidence[14] that electoral turnout is not in the least related to economic depression, it seems clear that level of income, awareness of economic implications of political decisions, and individualized incidence of economic benefit are so intertwined as to make a *general* relationship between economic need and political participation unlikely.

Reference groups and the perception of economic need. Almost everyone is better off than someone he knows and worse off than someone else. Almost everyone has unfulfilled desires which might be fulfilled if he had greater income. How, then, does he determine, in his own mind, whether he is underprivileged or privileged, whether he is economically deprived or

not. Of course, such a determination is a complex matter to which personality variables make a contribution, as do a host of circumstantial factors. Among these factors, however, the location and relative wealth of the individual's significant reference groups make considerable difference. In the armed services it was found that a person's estimate of his deprivation depended upon whom he compared himself with. If he was behind the lines overseas, his sense of deprivation was greater if he compared himself with others back home, and less if he compared himself with those in the front lines.[15] The perception of economic deprivation undoubtedly follows the same pattern. Those who compare themselves with parents who were or are less well off, or with their own status in their years of apprenticeship, may be less likely to perceive politics as a means of satisfying economic needs. Those who compare their status with more prosperous college friends, or with the image of exaggerated success their parents held out to them, may see everything, including politics, in terms of their economic needs.

Self and group. Most, but not all, political decisions which re-allocate resources affect selected classes of the population: importers, owners of natural gas wells, the unemployed, and so forth. Thus, when a person appraises politics in terms of the satisfaction of his economic needs, he is confronted with a group gain or loss and his perception of the group, and his identification or disidentification with the group, will color his attitudes toward the politico-economic decisions involved. When Beard reports that of the members of the Constitutional Convention of 1787, "The overwhelming majority of members, at least five sixths, were immediately, directly, and personally interested in the outcome of their labors at Philadelphia,"[16] a mixture of motives is apparent: loyalty to the class of men who were involved and satisfaction in the group gain along with the personal satisfaction in the individual's own gain.

Individual economic gain from political activity, of course, still persists in the form of patronage positions, assured contracts, or legal protection. In this form, however, the sanctions of the society tend to be brought to bear upon the individual, for the difference between group gain and individual gain usually coincides with the boundaries of what is loosely called political morality. With respect to individual gain, then, the desire for economic gain must be strong enough to cross the threshold imposed by concepts of unethical practice and hence a stronger economic orientation is likely to be implied.

When considering the decisions of group members on group-related issues, not only ethics but conflicting group memberships and political beliefs must be considered. In a study dealing with public attitudes toward government personnel problems, it was found that veterans were only slightly more in favor of veterans' preference provisions than were the general public.[17] Similarly, college educated respondents were only a little more favorable than respondents with less education to preference for educated persons in government hiring policies. Herring points out that cultural items favoring equality of opportunity interfere here with the college graduates' self-interest.

Economic values as instrumental to other values. One of the great difficulties in the kind of politico-economic analysis which has prevailed in this area of politics and economics is the illusion of economic gain as a terminal value. Beyond certain minima, economic gain is inevitably associated with prestige and status, self-validation called "success," opportunities for assertion against others, autonomy from disliked persons, tasks, or situations, and so forth. What gives economics its power to command such energy as is invested in the pursuit of gain is often its instrumental value as a means to some other objective. Money buys more than commodities; it buys psychic gratifications of all sorts—although never so completely as the money-seeker thinks it will. The pursuit of income through politics, then, may be preliminary or auxiliary to the gratification of other needs mentioned in this section.

The dynamics of politico-economic pursuits. We have said that money and wealth often become libidinized, so to speak, because of their instrumental values. There are two ways in which this investment

of wealth with high priority may be achieved. Society may do it by making certain equations between income and success or income and prestige. In some instances, as may be seen in the favored position of the middle-class child in public schools, income and morality tend to be equated[18]—a hideous perversion of the Calvinist doctrine first applied to the Puritan adult. Thus, social transfusion of value takes place, creating economic needs where there were none before.

The second method is the psychic process of displacement or generalization which will be discussed more systematically below. We need not accept, nor deny, the identification of thrift and miserliness with early training in cleanliness, though there is considerable case material to support this view. But considering only the processes of displacement in the mature adult, we may find that an individual substitutes pursuit of economic gain for the pursuit of sex objects, or of aggressive activity forbidden by the society. In this latter regard there are social gains, as Keynes notes in remarking that it is better for a man to tyrannize over his bank account than over other people.[19] We shall discuss below Lasswell's formula for political displacement, but we may note here that one might express this displacement in the economic sphere in similar terms: private emotions displaced onto an economic object and rationalized into an economic theory equals Economic Man. The explanation of the pursuit of economic needs through political activity, then, might examine the terms of the rationalization (human nature requires the profit motive), or the economic object (oil wells, pensions), or the private emotions (a desire to defeat the father in cross-generational competition). Out of such material, in the abundant society, are fashioned economic drives which may be pursued through political participation at every level.

That they are so pursued needs little documentation. Perhaps it is most clearly seen in the stakes of the ward leader or precinct committeeman. In King County, Washington, about an eighth of the group worked for the government and therefore had economic stakes in electoral outcomes; in Elmira, New

York, about a third of the ward leaders were in this position.[20] The precinct and ward leaders in Chicago in the late thirties and forties freely admitted their economic interests in their political work, and in Detroit volunteer workers included "several hundred paid workers" in 1952.[21] On certain kinds of issues, notably the tariff, the mail tends to emphasize economic self-interest or thinly disguised generalizations about the welfare of those whose jobs are jeopardized by low tariffs.[22] And in the various analyses of financial contributions to campaign funds, the economic self-interest of the contributors is stressed by most authors on the subject.[23]

In summary, then, we may say:

Political participation in pursuit of economic needs is impeded by the obscure relation of political decisions to the gratification of these needs. Paradoxically, this obscurity may be more characteristic of the American political system, where economic orientation is said to be high, than other cultures.

Political participation to satisfy economic needs is unrelated to level of income in the American culture.

Political participation to satisfy economic needs is related to the perception of needs mediated by the selection of reference groups.

Political participation to satisfy economic needs is usually associated with group gain or loss and the gratifications involved are related to attitudes toward the group. Where the gains and losses from political activity are individual, rather than group, the culture usually attributes some immorality to the transaction and hence motivation must be strong enough to overcome this cultural stigma.

Economic needs motivating political participation are usually instrumental to the gratification of some other psycho-social needs, such as status, power, or self-validation.

The investment of economic goals with emotional intensity is a product of (a) cultural equations between economic success and other values, and (b) the displacement onto economic objects of emotions and drives arising from unconscious needs and wishes of the individual.

Social Adjustment

Political interests and activity may facilitate easy interpersonal relations, and so satisfy a person's needs for social adjustment. Common political beliefs lay the groundwork for sharing equivalent emotions of anger, sympathy, and distress; common interests improve the opportunities for small talk; common activities create bonds of friendship. Politics may offer to the lonely man new opportunities for association with others—the excuse may be politics, the need may be fear of isolation. In short, political interests and activity may "lubricate" social relations and create opportunities for association in many areas.[24]

The effect of political disagreement is just the reverse. Interests or attitudes which diverge from those held by a person's friends may cause him to withdraw from politics and turn his attentions elsewhere. It is possible, at least, that one reason for American political apathy is that American political preferences frequently cut across class, religious, and ethnic lines so that without a clear orientation on the attitudes of one's social groups, the expression of political opinions offers risks of social friction rather than opportunities for social adjustment.

How strong is the need for agreement! The "strain toward agreement" (for most, but not all, people), and the fear of disagreement has been examined in experiments and field observations for over twenty years.[25] Persons viewing *together* an illusory movement of a fixed point of light give estimates of movement within a narrow range, whereas when persons view the illusion *separately,* there is a much broader range of reported movement. Furthermore, those who have established a standard in viewing the illusion alone, adjust their standard when they hear the reports of others in a second trial so that their standards come closer to the group norms.[26] Opinions on relative lengths of real objects, where there is no illusory effect, are subject to group pressure in such a way that many people will refuse the evidence of their senses in order to avoid an isolated opinion—although when given even a small minority with which to agree they become much more resistant to this pressure.[27]

College students who are oriented toward the college group adopt the favored attitudes of the college community;[28] members of a cooperative housing project have been shown to adjust their views on Russia to what they conceive to be the group mode.[29]

The facts of the situation seem clear. But the private meanings of these acts of opinion adjustment for social purposes may differ in each individual. Among these meanings, perhaps the instrumental need of the group's support for some personal project or goal, say election to office, is the most "objective." Other such needs turn directly upon the manner in which interpersonal relations are interpreted by the individual himself. Fear of conflict may be the motivating force in the politicization of a non-political person in a political group. Or social adjustment may serve as a needed counterweight to a nagging sense of personal inadequacy, perhaps as a reminder that one's private idiosyncratic behavior does not cut one off from other people as much as is sometimes feared. Whatever it is, it has a private meaning deriving from the individual's experiences and personality structure.

To some extent, perhaps, the problem of adequate integration in a human group is universal: all adults have experienced in some manner the "separation anxiety" which comes with growing up.[30] But in different societies this expresses itself in different ways. The mode of life and cultural pressure of the time creates, among most Americans, a need to "get along" with other people in a superficially harmonious manner but without deep personal emotional commitment.[31] This is the "other-directed" person, low in affect and high in facile competence in interpersonal relations. In a sense, this is a corollary to Lewin's diagnosis of American personality—a relatively small core of private "self" surrounded by a larger area of public "self" which is exposed to view and not so easily hurt. (This is in contrast to the German personality where the public area is much smaller and the private area larger).[32] The needs which such personality constellations reveal in abundant measure are adjustment needs; not the need for personal integrity, not the need for propitiating a stern super ego, but the need to get along socially without friction.

Horney makes this point in her discussion of the relation between culture and neurotic symptoms in the present era. She says, "One of the predominant trends of neurotics of our time is their excessive dependence on the approval and affection of others," a condition partly attributable to the highly competitive terms of existence in a laissez-faire industrialized society.[33] If this is true, group life will reflect these mutual demands for affection, or at least acceptance, to an unusual degree. The social adjustment function of politics will, in such a period, serve needs which have been culturally intensified.

The history of the past four hundred years is a history of increasing "individuation," the destruction of the primary group bonds of the individual.[34] This is true of the individual's family connections, religious connections, his class and status connections, his occupational connections, and, with the kind of mobility in America, the ties which bind him to a town or region. It is also true of political connections, particularly in America where "independence" is so highly valued. Fromm believes that man cannot endure such negative freedom, the loosening of old institutional bonds, and he seeks constantly to establish new ones which will relate him to his friends and his work and his beliefs either in a "positive" autonomous manner, or, failing that, in a destructive or dependent manner. Many persons do not have the capacity to make such bonds for themselves, to create a relationship which was once created ready made in the order of things. For them political life may serve acute needs for social adjustment and integration.

Toward whom does a person need to adjust? Authoritarians seek adjustments with people of higher status and power, content to ignore those with relatively less of these qualities. In much the same manner the ethnocentric, the snob, and often the merely insecure, define their adjustment needs in such a way that much of the population is excluded. The question of social adjustment is intricate in detail and specific in content for each individual.

We have suggested that such social adjustment needs may lead people to join political parties—although they may also lead them to avoid joining where this might antagonize others who are important. In a similar manner, the need for social adjustment, the need to make friends and keep their friendship on an easy frictionless plane, may lead them to join other organizations and to contribute to the political process in this way. Indeed the pluralistic basis of American politics may be dependent upon the prevalence of acute social adjustment needs in the population. Joining organizations and seeking friends, in turn, will lead to political discussion where this is not divisive, the kind of discussion referred to above as a reinforcement of mutually agreed upon views. Furthermore, social adjustment needs may lead to other forms of political behavior, such as financial contributions to parties. For some doners to political parties, the salient motive is to be a "good fellow" combined with a fear of the impression which refusing to "go along with the boys" may make upon friends and acquaintances.[35] Similarly, for party workers, door to door canvassing may be a "social event" whose primary meaning lies in the increased rate of visiting and gossiping.[36]

In summary, then, the following hypotheses reflect the ideas set forth.

Participation is a function of the individual's need for social adjustment with others in his community, although such adjustment has a variety of idiosyncratic meanings and functions for each person.

In all societies, some common ends and directives contribute to the mental health of the members of that community; hence behind the adjustment function there lies the powerful pressure towards consensus in some significant areas of life.

Persons brought up in the American culture are more likely to employ their participation as an aid to social adjustment than persons socialized in other Western cultures.

Gemeinschaft politics (particularly totalitarian movements) serve as especially suitable vehicles for participation for those with social adjustment needs arising from feelings of alienation.

Historically, the individualization or atomization of persons in society has tended to leave unsatisfied the drives for social adjustment, leaving available a powerful unfulfilled need for political movements.

Participation based upon the need for social adjustment will be differentiated according to the nature of the adjustment needs toward (a) people of differing status and power, (b) inclusively or exclusively defined groups.

Periods of crisis for societies, as for individuals, are likely to produce a "regressive" mode of satisfying social adjustment needs in politics.

The Need to Understand

"On a priori grounds one might suppose that a person's attitudes toward any topic serve the important function of sorting out his world of experience into a predictable order that can provide the background for an orderly existence."[37] An understanding of political events is a tool for living, an instrument whereby other goals are achieved. But, more than that, there is satisfaction in understanding which does not depend upon its utility in achieving further goals. "Quite apart from the pressure of particular emotions, we continually seek to extract meaning from our environment. There is, so to speak, intellectual pressure along with the emotional. To find a plausible reason for a confused situation is itself a motive. . . ."[38] An interest in public affairs and opinions about the world around us serves this motive and represents a response to this pressure. The results may be grotesque, as Lippmann's discussion of stereotypes suggests, but it is the very need to understand that partially accounts for the oversimplified image which causes "Mrs. Sherwin of Gopher Prairie" to think of a world war in terms of a personal duel.[39]

The pressure to have opinions on remote political topics is not just the vestige of days when opinions and influence went hand in hand. It is not just social pressure; it is, even for the ignorant, internal and personal.[40]

The nature of the "meanings" extracted from the environment varies. In a study of attitudes toward Russia, some people were more projective than others in their interpretation of events, making the meanings and opinions serve their wishes; others did not.[41] Some seek syntheses of many variables in an over-all world view, and nothing short of a comprehensive ideology is satisfactory. Others extract extremely limited meanings. As shown in recent studies, rational arguments are assimilated by some individuals relatively easily; others are blocked in their understanding of such arguments by overriding emotional needs. Furthermore, persons fearful that their interpretations, if stated aloud, will reveal their ignorance, will be inhibited from exercising their curiosity and asking questions about politics.[42]

The basis of this curiosity, like its products, has many facets. Animal psychologists, finding that rats who have satisfied all of the so-called "basic" drives (hunger, thirst, sex, relief from pain, etc.) may still be active, have included curiosity as an additional drive. This interpretation would give the phenomenon a biological basis. Good maternal care is said to be the basis for developing curiosity, and therefore educability, in the human child. Freud found sexual curiosity to be the beginning of intellectual curiosity. And it is said that "High school and college foster an abstract orientation and an involvement in the superpersonal. Hence educated people feel at home in the company of political ideas which partake of the abstract."[43] No doubt all these factors (and many more) may explain differential efforts to extract meaning from the political environment.

What does this pursuit of meaning lead people to do in the political sphere? People who seek to satisfy this need are undoubtedly more attentive to the media and are relatively well informed. An example of this behavior is the following response from a person who was deprived of his daily paper by a strike of newspaper dealers.[44]

I don't have the details now, I just have the results. It's almost like reading the headlines of the newspaper without following up the story. I miss the detail and the explanations of events leading up to the news. I like to get the story behind the news and the development leading up to—it's more penetrating. . . . I like to analyze for myself why things do

happen and after getting the writers' opinions of it from the various newspapers, in which each one portrays the story in a different manner, I have a broader view and a more detailed view when I formulate my own opinion.

Does the pursuit of meaning lead beyond this to active political behavior? One study of the factors associated with participation in grass roots civic meetings on a college campus shows that both a superior academic record and a capacity for critical thinking (as measured by a special test) were positively related to such participation.[45] This does not necessarily mean that going to civic or political meetings was prompted by the need to think through a problem, but this is at least a possible interpretation.

In a broader sense, it seems to have other results. In one analysis the pursuit of meaning forms one of the two most important psychological bases for participation in social movements (the other being the need for self-esteem).[46] It is reflected in almost all the interviews and psychoanalytic material dealing with Communists and former Communists.[47] Thus it seems to be a feature of both modal and deviant politics, of both active and "spectator" political participation.

Although political opinions may be functional, they may be dysfunctional as well. Ignorance has psychic utility too, and there are at least five circumstances in which a man will cling tenaciously to ignorance of public affairs. The first of these, *conflict-avoidance ignorance,* is illustrated by the businessman who remarked that he preferred not to study economics because it might undermine his faith in a system with which he had to work. Such a businessman is, of course, in a position similar to the Catholic who permits his reading to be guided by the Index, or a Communist who studies only Marxist social science. All of them are avoiding mental conflict before it begins to work upon them, rather than wait and, possibly, withdraw from the painful conflict after it has been initiated.

The second variety of useful ignorance exists when a person has discovered some tension relief in a belief which would be threatened by new knowledge, a variety which may be thought of as *cathartic ignorance*. For those to whom Red Russia has provided a legitimate target for the discharge of hostile emotions, a scientific treatment of the Soviet Union must be threatening—not because such a treatment would not provide evidence to feed their hatred, but the balanced tone of the discussion would suggest that their emotional investment was inappropriate. Similarly, the anti-intellectualism of the ethnocentric serves to ward off any study of ethnic relations which would jeopardize his, to him, useful hostilities. The very term selected by the anti-aliens of the 1850's— "Know-nothings"—although chosen for another reason, reflects a frame of mind where ignorance is positively valued.

In the third place, those who defend the *status quo* do not need to go to the trouble of producing evidence about it to the same extent as those who propose a reform. If this is an economic conviction they can rest upon the assumption that the challenger must make the case. If it is a psychic conviction that whatever is is best, inquiry is dangerous and should be suppressed. "A man who is prone to identify himself *a priori* with the world as it is has little incentive to penetrate it intellectually and to distinguish between essence and surface."[48]

A variation of this view, and an additional set of reasons for ignorance, is suggested by the fact that political affairs, for many people, meet few direct and urgent needs; they are "remote from the direct concerns of daily life."[49] Thus the person who is immersed in getting along in his own world from day to day avoids the political. His own private status quo, like the larger social status quo, does not require him to be politically informed. This kind of drive to exclude political information from what is learned may be termed *apathetic ignorance*.

Fourth, political views may alienate friends, neighbors, customers, and group members, as we have noted before. Better then, not to hold them. Ignorance from such a motive may be termed *socializing ignorance* (about which, more later). And a fifth situation, where ignorance of public affairs serves some

personal function, occurs when the drive to politicize men and saturate their lives with community, partisan, or social meaning becomes fatiguing and a person experiences the longing to privatize his life. This suggests a kind of *privatizing ignorance*.[50]

To summarize these views on the pursuit of meaning, the following hypotheses may be set forth:

Political participation and involvement are products of the need for meaning, both as a source of satisfaction in itself and as a means of satisfying other needs.

The pursuit of meaning is said to be based on (a) a physiological drive apparent in animals, (b) early socializing experiences and particularly the treatment of sexual curiosity, (c) education and other experiences awakening interests and developing skills for handling abstractions.

The pursuit of meaning leads to exposure, attention, and absorption of knowledge (with feedback effects) and, in some circumstances, to civic and political participation.

The reverse of the pursuit of meaning, clinging to ignorance, serves other needs: (a) avoidance of knowledge which might create internal conflict (conflict-avoidance ignorance), (b) avoidance of knowledge which might deprive a person of needed tension-releasing opinions (cathartic ignorance), (c) apathy about knowledge which fulfills no useful purpose (apathetic ignorance), (d) avoidance of knowledge which would disrupt social relations (socializing ignorance), and (e) avoidance of knowledge in order to protect interest and attention in other, and private affairs (privatizing ignorance).

How Are Unconscious Needs Expressed in Politics?

In the previous section we examined certain personal needs which are frequently directed into political channels. These are needs, which in some form, are likely to be recognized by the conscious mind and often explicitly stated. Of course they need not be conscious. Society puts a premium upon rationalizations of all personal needs in terms of the general welfare or the public interest. In addition, the individual may prefer not to examine his needs for social adjustment or his need for increments of goods and services for these may raise painful thoughts in his mind. But they are distinguishable from the needs discussed in this section not only in their substance, but also on the grounds of accessibility to consciousness.

The Relief of Intra-Psychic Tensions

An important function served by political participation is the relief of intra-psychic tensions. We do not mean here the conflicts at a more or less conscious level between identification with this or that reference group, or between pursuing one conscious goal or another.[51] Rather, we are dealing with conflicts which occur, partially at least, at the subconscious level, conflicts between impulse and control mechanisms, or between conflicting impulses, or between the unconscious super-ego and the rational mind.

In the first place, such conflicts may tend to produce a withdrawal from politics and almost complete self-absorption rather than political interest and participation. For example, those who rate high on a simple index of neuroticism ("I often find myself worrying about the future," "A lot of people around here ought to be put in their place," etc.) tend to listen to and read about politics less than others.[52] Certainly this is a possible solution for the person in conflict. But even if he does adopt a position of withdrawal in his general "social cathexis" this may not mean a political withdrawal. "Insofar as inner conflict does lead to withdrawal tendencies, it does not necessarily follow . . . that those objects that constitute the staple of public opinion studies will necessarily lose cathexis."[53] In other words, a person fatigued by inner conflict may withdraw from family life but endow political interests with increased attention. If, as so often happens, the inner conflict is closely connected with family life (and here the sex theme is particularly

important), withdrawal from family life will be rewarding and immersion in politics will provide a plausible excuse. In such a situation, inner conflict produces a withdrawal in one sphere and displacement of emotion into another sphere. This seems to be true of many of the Communists whose case histories have been analyzed by social scientists.[54] In these instances, moreover, withdrawal from the party was often a subsequent event of psychic origin occasioned by the subsidence of the internal conflict.

When the inner conflict is expressed by social (as contrasted to familial) withdrawal, participation is, of course, bound to be a casualty of the conflict. Indifference to politics may be the result of a "major expenditure of energy on internal emotional struggles."[55] Corroborating evidence on this theme is provided by clinical studies revealing the utter fatigue of many neurotic individuals. At this point, moreover, the theory of psychic conflict joins company with a theory of the withdrawal tendencies of the individual who is cross-pressured by his various group memberships or other social forces. Withdrawal is, of course, only one of the many possible responses to such a situation, but, when it does occur, it may be that the social conflict involved in cross-pressures is reinforced by, or is even congruent with, internal psychic conflicts.

There is some evidence to show that, in fact, the politically apathetic individual, more than the participant, is likely to be someone who suffers from intrapsychic conflict and, as a consequence, tends to fear any searching self-examinations.[56] A study of college students, contrasting those who were interested in national and local politics and intended to participate in political activities after college with those who were not interested and didn't expect to be, found that the typical apathetic could be characterized as follows:[57]

Inability to recognize personal responsibility or to examine—or even accept—his own emotions and feelings; vague, incomprehensible feelings of worry, insecurity, and threat; complete, unchallenging acceptance of constituted authority (social codes, parents, religion) and conventional values . . .

relative absence of responses emphasizing self-expression, ego-strivings and satisfactions or warm interpersonal relationships.

Thus political expression (on a college campus) which implies responsibility for what takes place, and which leads into areas where authority and conventionality are challenged (either by yourself or someone else) is not only alien but inadmissable to this group.

The politically active group, on the other hand, shows an over-all pattern of willingness to assume responsibility for one's own — and other's — destiny:[58]

> There is an emphasis on strivings for ego-satisfaction, independence, maturity, and personal happiness. Instead of vague, unmanageable feelings of threat which form part of the passive pattern, active attempts to achieve self-understanding, (many responses in categories pertaining to self-examination, self-awareness, and consciousness of shortcomings) . . . sensitivity to other's feelings and emotions. . . . The final aspect of this coherent pattern, the active group's great social consciousness and emphasis on social contribution and love-giving, involves a positive, active relationship with society generally.

It should be stressed, however, that social consciousness is not the *cause* of political activity — rather a personality orientation which stresses the active self-aware role in life is the cause of a general behavior pattern which includes social consciousness and political activity.[59]

Yet, plausible as these findings are, and they are supported by a range of statistically significant relationships, they nevertheless reveal only one of the lines of behavior for the person with feelings of "worry, insecurity, and threat." Here, in a conformist middle-class college campus, he withdraws and he accepts. He devotes his energies to the "management" of his psychic life. But under other circumstances where channels are available for expressing his conflict, displacing his aggressive feelings, and finding release in joining some alienated group, a different resolution is possible, at least for some so-called

apathetics.[60] The political resolution of psychic conflict then, is shaped by circumstances, and, partly for this reason, indeterminate.

If the intra-psychic tension does, in fact, find political expression, how does this come about? Two means are particularly relevant: first, the use of political participation as a means of blocking out the tension, distracting the individual from his personal troubles, and, second, the use of political participation as a means of expressing the troublesome impulse, or as a means of rationalizing the resolution of the conflict in socially acceptable terms. The first is illustrated by the case of the woman who, unable to adjust to her hostility toward her children (for whatever reason), assumed important responsibilities in the political life of her community. These took her out of the home and preoccupied her mind so that she did not have to "think" about her home problems. Or again, there is the incipient drug addict who, because of certain intra-psychic difficulties, could not face the problem and chose, instead, to keep busy with committee meetings or public affairs which removed him from temptation. Unable to accept the death of a person on whom he had grown dependent, a third person plunges into politics to keep from indulging his suicidal fantasies.[61]

More usual, however, since political expression is a product of total personality, is the case of the person who expresses his ego-alien impulses through political means. The political discharge of such intra-psychic tensions, on the whole, has two main themes, precisely the same themes which occur most frequently in clinical cases. These themes turn on the question of expression of hostile, aggressive feelings and the expression of sexual drives. It is for a very good reason that these are the core of the problem for they are the areas of expression which society most closely controls in adult life and most vigorously represses in childhood. An additional theme of frequent importance lies in the expression of dependency needs.

Aggression. The sources of aggression are, of course, multiple. According to one of the most commonly accepted views, it is the product of frustration: frustration is always followed by some form of aggression, aggression is always preceded by some form of frustration.[62] Since aggression may be impounded and expressed later, or may be directed against some irrelevant target such as an innocent bystander or the self, the channels of this relationship are difficult to trace. Learning theorists would add that aggression is a learned form of expression, rewarded at some time in the past and extinguished only when it ceases to be rewarding—with a time lag which may be of considerable importance. Whatever the source, it is a significant factor in political life and, because of the cultural control of this type of behavior, is almost always associated with problems of self-control and inner conflict.

My own case studies have led me to believe that persons who have a capacity for externalized aggression are more likely to become politically oriented than those for whom such external expression is inhibited.[63] Being *against* somebody, some group, or some thing is more easily turned into political channels than being impartial, or being *for* something. Aggression can almost always find an appropriate political target, and so become rationalized in socially and personally more acceptable terms. This is particularly true in those situations where the actual impact of politics is small—as is the case on a college campus. In those life situations where a political decision may in fact create a severe frustration of desired goals, aggressive responses have a totally different meaning. The concept of the "appropriate" expression of emotion, however vague, is often a necessary ingredient in such a theory. For the bulk of the electorate, however, intense political interests are certainly facilitated by a capacity to externalize aggression.

The political expression of outwardly directed aggression may take place in the context of deviant radical parties, where, in the American and British scheme of things, aggressiveness is the rule.[64] In this context, a particular source of aggression, such as sibling rivalry of an intense nature, may produce a continuing and habitual aggressive state with completely opposite forms of political expression. Au-

thoritarians of the right (Fascists) who feel they were victimized by their siblings, tend to deny this, idealize their actual siblings in a "phoney" way, and express their hostility toward others in their politics. The authoritarians of the left (Communists) who feel that they were victimized by their brothers and sisters, may admit their hostility toward their actual siblings, but then over-react by talking about the brotherhood of man, somewhat after the manner of Mr. A., portrayed by Harold Lasswell in his *Psychopathology and Politics*.[65]

Of course, the political expression of such aggression may also take place within the framework of more orthodox politics, as the "total" acrimony between certain McCarthy Republicans and selected liberal Democrats in the early 1950's reveals. The rivalry between nations, as in a cold war, and to a lesser extent all of foreign policy, presents ideal opportunities for those with aggressive impulses searching for a socially approved target. This is even more true of movements, such as those sponsored by the less responsible veterans' organizations, which pick out some unpopular group for attack in their own communities.

Although less usual, if such aggression is turned inward, nurtured by a sense of guilt, politics offers opportunities for expression of these feelings, too. These may, for example, take the form of atonement, expiation for the sins weighing upon a person's mind. Not a few of the active members of the Society for the Prevention of Cruelty to Animals, World Federalists, and even the white members of the National Association for the Advancement of Colored People are motivated more by unendurable feelings of guilt than by the objective requirements of their cause. Society is lucky when personality tensions erupt in this way, rather than in scapegoatism or even suicide.

Thus a person may reveal his characteristic manner of handling aggressive feelings by withdrawal and apathy or by launching into some outburst against a political figure, or by acts of atonement and dedication to a political cause.

Sex. The relationship between sex and politics is less quickly perceived for several reasons. One of the more important of these is the tabu which society places upon the discussion of sexual matters and the internal reflection of this in the anxiety which such discussion causes in each individual. But another reason is that the manner in which repressed sexual feelings, normal or perverted, are expressed politically is much more devious and the mechanisms are somewhat less well understood. One way to strike through these difficulties is to oversimplify the situation and present hypothetical cases in which sexual conflict finds its way into intense political beliefs. Two such hypothetical cases are presented by Money-Kyrle in a book on *Psychoanalysis and Politics*.[66] These are not presented for their life verisimilitude, but as theoretical models.

First, consider the case of a single woman "with no great desire or aptitude for marriage." After a hard struggle she has become a teacher or a civil servant. She is a socialist with deep humanistic feelings for those who have been thwarted or deprived in life, and this contributes to her politicization, but she also has a very intense hatred of the well-to-do or the managerial classes in society, regardless of their personal attitudes or their role in the "exploitation" of the poor. This also adds fuel to her political interests and it is this hatred, quite irrespective of persons, which needs explaining. According to Money-Kyrle, if a psychoanalyst were to pursue this line with her "he might well find that as a child she had been one of those girls who had desperately wanted to be a boy, that she had never outgrown this grievance, and that it was the unconscious source of her hatred of the overprivileged." A confusion of sex role, then, combined with a sense of her own sexual deprivation is the explanation given for her intense hatred of "the owning classes."[67]

The hypothetical conservative, identifying with upper status groups, traveled a different route. For him, freedom is erected into the highest value and hence a bureaucratic state is a threat. Such an attitude would politicize a person, but his politics would be endowed with a special intensity because of his intense hatred and suspicion of all those on the other side, regardless of their motives and the success of their acts in actually increasing certain areas of liberty. Psychoanalysis, according to Money-Kyrle, might very well find that this intense hatred towards bureaucrats and laborites stems from early fears of deprivation as a child, fears which were generalized into habitual thinking in these terms. The practical the rational fear of economic deprivation by the conservative, then, as it is so often the case, is said to fuse with an earlier fear, and intense emotions expressed in the political sphere are a possible result.[68]

Of course, these two cases are grossly oversimplified, but they are intended to illustrate the way in which conflicts and drives with a sexual origin *may* give to political life an intensity of emotion (and an aura of pathology) which can become a significant source of overt political activity.[69]

If this is the model, what are the realities? On this topic we have available some material gathered from psychoanalysts treating Communists or former Communists.[70] What psychic services did membership in the Communist Party perform for these patients? In the answers to this question it was apparent, at least to the analysts, that the Party met their patients' needs, not only for legitimizing the expression of aggression, but also for accommodating deviant sex roles. Thus, in the Party, dependent and passive men (often with latent or overt homosexual tendencies) were able to profit from a situation where they were told what to do, what to think, and how to live their lives. Here they were permitted to slough off the masculine role of an independent and responsible group (family) leader. For women with sexual confusion, the Party offered masculine roles where aggression, dominance, and even masculine clothes and manners were appropriate.

But one need not go so far to discover the way in which sexual needs stimulate political activity. Earlier, we referred to political discussion which takes the form of scandal mongering or rumor. It has long been known that the passing on of rumors with sexual content (Senator blank is having an affair with so and so) serves the vicarious gratification of sexual needs. In another context, one need not imply anything sinister or indeed much beyond the ordinary in noting some generalized libidinal theme in the reply of one of Al Smith's backers who reported that he contributed to Smith's campaign for the "affection and love" he bore the man.[71] Lasswell speaks too broadly, but with insight, when he says "Political life seems to sublimate many homosexual trends. Politicians characteristically work together in little cliques and clubs, and many show marked difficulties in reaching stable heterosexual adjustment."[72] To the extent that this is true at all, it is more likely to be true of the unsuccessful politicians, and the pool house "corner boys" or ward heelers. On a more general level, the similarities between White House mail and "fan" letters with quasi-romantic themes may be noted for what they reveal of the sexual basis of political behavior. Behind the empty phrase, "I vote for the man, not the party," lies a prevalent libidinization of a leader. But perhaps more important than any of these, will be the channeling into politics of "blocked" sex drives: the unmarried middle-aged woman in the League of Women Voters, the homely girl who, for want of a date, sits in the party office at election time and stuffs envelopes, the young man who flees from the college dances into the "youth movement," and so forth. Escape from sex or the enforced sublimation of sex, rather than the direct expression of it, is a normal and perhaps even frequent source of political drive.

Dependency. A third kind of need which arises within the psyche to disturb the individual and whose satisfaction may lead along political paths may be said to be dependency needs. Like sex and aggression, the American society tends to repress these needs, to deny them, and to encourage tension where they are expressed in undisguised form.[73] This is because in America the male, at least (and also the female to a considerable extent), is expected to show independence, to "stand on his own two feet," to have a "strong character," and to assume responsibility for himself and his family no matter what happens. Since this is true, people will tend to repress their dependency needs and to disguise them in some more acceptable form, perhaps in the postures of conformity. Here, then, is another source of conflict, which, like other

conflicts, may find expression in apathy or in sublimation and flight into politics.

The nature of these needs in the political area comes most readily to light in analyzing the responses of the public to Eisenhower and Franklin D. Roosevelt. When asked about Eisenhower in 1952 more of the public mentioned his "leadership" and personality than any other feature of his candidacy.[74] Moreover, at an earlier point Eisenhower was most attractive to those members of both parties who were directionless or politically indifferent.[75] Although not all such leadership-oriented responses imply dependency needs, when they are unaccompanied by any idea of an appropriate direction for the leadership to go, when they are "blind followership," so to speak, they are assuredly an expression of a personality constellation including dependency needs and wishes.

This facet of political orientation was even more clearly brought out in the attitudes toward Roosevelt of a panel of about nine hundred Philadelphians.[76] For a large proportion of this public, particularly those in the working class and Negro groups, the major feature of their orientation to the New Deal-FDR complex was one of personal dependence and gratitude for what might be called "sustenance." This sustenance was not merely economic; it was also psychological in the sense that FDR seemed to give them reassurance that "everything would be all right" and so to relieve their anxieties. From such material as this it appears that very often the strongest motive in bringing people into the political arena is precisely this dependency motive — a need for a man in charge who will give to his constituency (one might almost say, his "flock") this sense of being taken care of by a person deemed appropriate for such a mission. For such people politics offers a dilemma: how to be *active* for a candidate who will serve one's need to be taken care of, that is, to be *passive.*

Following these themes, some of which we shall return to later in the discussion of displacement and generalization, we may tentatively set forth a few hypotheses as follows:

Political participation may offer assistance in the

handling of intra-psychic conflicts through offering (a) a means of repressing the forbidden impulse or quieting the insistent conscience, or (b) offering "legitimate" channels for expressing the forbidden impulse, or (c) facilitating a life style embodying a particular compromise solution to the psychic conflict, but:

Political participation in non-deviant politics is generally inhibited by intrapsychic conflict since such conflict absorbs energy and impairs decision-making, interfers with successful inter personal relations, and weakens appropriate ego-strivings. Most commonly the sequence is: Thteatening impulses and nagging consciences create anxiety, and anxiety impedes successful political participation.

Political participation (it follows) is related both to a (a) healthy self-expression by the person who accepts himself and his emotions, and (b) the neurotic expression of the person with intra-psychic conflicts which are "engaged" with political phenomena.

Politics offers easy legitimation for aggressive drives since it is the area of controversy, electoral contests, scapegoating, and, particularly in foreign affairs, war and hatred.

Political participation is facilitated by a capacity for extra-punitiveness and externally expressed aggression; but, in a minority of cases, political participation may express intra-punitive needs for atonement.

Political participation may be the sublimation and rechanneling of blocked sex drives arising from the frustration of normal sex relations. It may be used to express broad sexual or libinal impulses in candidate orientation, "fan mail," and close interpersonal relations involved in work in a Common Cause.

Political participation offers means of expressing certain resolutions of Oedipal and other childhood situations involving fears of deprivation, mutilation, and restitution, and their symbolic continuation in the adult mind.

Dependency needs whose expression is discouraged by the culture create conflicts for the individual; these conflicts may be expressed in apathy or in political activity oriented toward "nurturant" political leaders.

The Pursuit of Power

In discussions of politics, the pursuit of power is often considered a primary motivating force. Thus Hobbes states:

> So that in the first place, I put for a general inclination of all mankind, a perpetual and restless desire of Power after power, that ceaseth only in Death.[77]

This is, of course, Nietzsche's theme, and it is implied by those modern political theorists who think of politics as the study of power, although it should be noted that these later analyses evaluate the power drive differently.[78]

At the outset we must eliminate from consideration instrumental uses of power appropriate to achieving some other goal. We focus instead on the enjoyment of power as a satisfaction in itself. The discussion divides into two parts, one constituted by the view that there is a separate political type whose motives are unusually concentrated upon achieving power over others; the other, while not denying this, focuses upon the power drives as one of a number of forces accounting for the selection of interest and behavior of those active in politics.

The idea of a distinctive type of person, political man, is attractive in many ways: If there were such a type, it would do much to clarify the problems of leadership selection, circulation of elites, and so forth. Spranger's work is illustrative of this approach, for he contends that in every personality there is a dominant value which makes its influence felt in wide areas of a person's life.[79] By the isolation and description of these dominant values, Spranger contended, some clarity could be given to the nature of men who might combine several values at once in real life. One of these values is power, and the type for which this is the supreme value is called the political type. Of this type, Spranger says:

> The purely political type makes all value regions of life serve his will to power. Cognition is for him only a means for control . . . voir pour savoir, savoir pour prevoir, prevoir pour regler.[80]

He uses other men as means to his end; he is realistic, amoral, and ruthless; in short, Machiavellian.

A modification of this idea appears in Allport's attempt to define twenty-one significant variables in personality, one of which is labeled, "political interest."[81] But here again the main reference is to the power value (other factors are the aesthetic interest, the economic interest, and so forth), revealing the orientation of the life-striving of the individual.

Lasswell develops the power motif in a more modern style, although, still, with a heavy emphasis upon the concept of a particular type of person who can be called political man. Thus, he states, the political man

1. Accentuates power

2. demands power (and other values) for the self (the primary ego plus incorporated symbols of other egos)

3. accentuates expectations concerning power

4. acquires at least a minimum proficiency in the skills of power.[82]

This is, of course, a relative concept and, as Lasswell points out, the "accentuation" of power must start from a cultural base line to be meaningful.

In these terms, political man is a person who gives priority to power values and craves deference, employing power to achieve deference and whatever other subsidiary values he cherishes. "The conception of a political type is that some personalities are power seekers, searching out the power institutions of the society into which they are born and devoting themselves to the capture and use of government."[83] The origins of such an orientation may lie in a sense of deprivation of respect and affection at an earlier age and some success in employing coercive measures (as the child interprets them) to restore the deprivation. As a consequence all perspectives are colored by the power relationship. Adopting one attitude toward such power, the child (adult) succumbs and becomes a completely passive person—a political apathetic, perhaps. Adopting the other alternative, the child (adult) asserts himself in a manner denying reciprocity (no power for the other person) and becomes rebellious and domineering.

These drives and attitudes do occur in persons in our culture with considerable frequency. In a sense they are like the needs for the expression of aggression, sex, and dependency which emerge in political form, that is, intra-psychic tensions which direct a person toward certain political goals. Like other such needs, the need for power is expressed in politics in sublimated or disguised form, rather than directly. The person who seeks power of the kind described cannot say so, but instead must rationalize this search in other terms. Analysis of the motives of some persons who wrote their Senators, on the conscription issue, brought to light their underlying satisfaction in an exercise of influence combined with a fear of genuine responsibility.[84] Extensive interviews with ward chairmen who ranked high in "authoritarianism" and pleasure in the exercise of power, as measured by certain projective questions, revealed that their own rationales of their jobs were limited to party support, issues, and images of the public welfare.[85] A need for power expressed in the area of public affairs may be concealed in a self-image of intellectual superiority and foresight based upon *knowing* names, dates, and places in the news.[86]

We have said that while it is true that power drives do find expression in politics, they do so only in a rationalized and sublimated manner. Now to what extent is it possible, even with this qualification, to accept the idea of political man as the man who has a higher than average power orientation. At the level of the electorate this is not a likely pattern. As indicated above in the reference to ward leaders, the power-oriented personality is close to the authoritarian personality in many ways. Yet in studies of authoritarianism, it appears that the latter do not vote more than others (nor do they vote less than others) and they tend to electioneer somewhat less than others and to have a lower level of political interest.[87] Furthermore, they are less likely than others to join quasi-political groups and to be selected as leaders of those they do join.[88] In the study of apathetic and active college students discussed above, it appears that the political activists on the campus have many more of the characteristics which go with a low power orientation than do the apathetics.[89] All of these findings tend to cast doubt upon the positive relationship of a power value and political activity. Why should this initially plausible hypothesis not be true?

To be successful in politics a person must have sufficient interpersonal skills to relate himself effectively to other men and must not be so consumed with power drives that he loses touch with reality. A person with a raging desire for power who "attaches great importance to imposing himself on others" will constantly alienate his supporters, thereby making the achievement of power impossible for him. On the whole, persons with this value orientation are relegated to minor roles in a democracy, and the top positions go to people who value power as an implement to other life goals.[90]

The low interpersonal skills of the power-oriented person may represent one of the impediments to his ascendance in politics, but there are several others. One of the most common sources of the need for power over others is the deeper need for reassurance about the self—"I am not weak," "I am not insignificant," "I am not dependent." This need for reassurance is, of course, related to lack of self-confidence, feelings of unworthiness, or low self-esteem. Now, as we shall see in discussing political attitudes related to participation, a feeling of personal effectiveness is highly related to political participation. With this in mind, it is most logical to expect that persons who seek to achieve power over others, but who are fighting doubts about their own effectiveness, might resolve these conflicts in different ways; some of them seek reassurance more actively, others give way to their feelings of insignificance more often. Political man, defined in these power terms, then, is an unpredictable political unit.

Other reasons come to mind. A democracy is built upon mutual trust but the power-oriented person lives in an untrustworthy jungle world; his cynicism may flush away his desire for participation. Much of the political activity of a democracy carries little or no power and very little prestige. Authoritarians are less likely to say they will serve on civic committees, but more likely to say they will be willing to "head up a committee."[91] Democratic political activity may be unattractive to the power seeker for these reasons. And in any event, the power seeker may have his eyes on areas of life where power is less controlled and sometimes more effective than in the political arena.

On the basis of twenty student case studies of the etiology of political preferences in an Eastern university, we conclude that the search for power is just as likely to be expressed in non-political areas as in political areas. Indeed, among these students the power-oriented individual was somewhat more likely to seek expression for his needs on the student newspaper or in fraternity life, which were the real centers of power on the campus, rather than in student political groups. Similarly, in adult life the search for the jugular of power may very likely lead to the world of finance, journalism, or industry instead of politics.

Finally, it should be noted that there are anachronistic traces of two earlier approaches to politics in the search for a relationship between power values and politics. For one thing, the orientation strongly suggests the trait approach of earlier leadership studies, a search for universal traits which in all or most situations would set a leader apart from others. Today, the particular context, the substance of the task for which leadership is required, the qualities and needs of the followers are recognized as vitally important in defining leadership selection. And, in the second place, there is the suggestion that political life is an area where the need for exercising power over others is given greatest expression. This may have some roots in the still widely accepted view that the distinguishing mark of government is its "monopoly of force," a view which, to this author, has never proved to be a useful criterion for distinguishing government from other institutions.

For these and other reasons, one must phrase the relationship of the need to exercise power over others to political activity with great care. The hypotheses which emerge from this discussion, then, should be both negative and positive.

Among the leaders of a democracy there is little tendency for a higher-than-average concentration of persons with needs to exercise power over others. There is also little tendency of this sort among the active group in the electorate.

Among persons with needs to exercise power over others there is (in American democracy) little, if any, tendency to select activity in one of the major parties as a vehicle for exercising power. There is a tendency for power-oriented persons to find a vehicle for their needs in extremist or deviant political groups.

Among the qualities of those who are active in political life, a *moderate* desire to impose one's views and wishes on others, and skill in doing it, contribute to a person's willingness and capacity for political participation.

Politics and the Need for Self-Esteem

The need for self-esteem is best conceived as an ingredient in all need systems, permeating and modifying the needs for economic gain, understanding of the environment, social solidarity and the various unconscious needs. It is universal, although the fulfillment of this need takes many forms. Yet the need for self-esteem is not merely a generalized form of other needs; it is an independent need, the crucial feature of a person's self-image. Indeed, in one analysis of social motivation, the enhancement and maintenance of self-esteem (self-regard), together with the pursuit of meaning, comprise the total sum of motivating factors.[92] The self-aware person can validate the significance of the need for self-esteem through a moment's introspection.

It is a need of wide reference and great intensity: "The individual's desire for personal status is apparently insatiable. Whether we say that he longs for *prestige,* for *self-respect, autonomy,* or *self-regard,* a dynamic factor of this order is apparently the strongest of his drives."[93] It serves as one of the more important of Horney's concepts, an ingredient in the normal personality which is easily distorted by the social pressures of today.[94] In Fenichel's concept of the need for "narcissistic supplies," the need for self-esteem is well supported.[95]

In a very important sense, life is devoted to the protection of the ego, the care and promotion of the self. Nor is the definition of what is ego or ego-involved confined to the body, or even to wholly personal attributes. On the contrary, it tends to be extended to people, symbols, ideas, and objects which in some way are associated with some aspect of the person. The selection of these ego-involved objects is the product both of social designation and idiosyncratic personal preference, the operation of the two factors making for individuality within a common framework. Self-esteem, then, inevitably rises and falls with the "fortunes" of the ego-involved objects. The socially determined sources of self-esteem have been termed "status," and the individually determined sources as "self-integrity." In reinforcing self-esteem from these sources, people fall back upon rationalizations as protective devices, as well as upon misperception, withdrawal, denigration of the opposition, and so forth.[96]

The need for self-esteem may be gratified by political participation in many ways. Merely having opinions or knowing bits and pieces of information tends to show a person off in a better light; he is "educated," *"au courant,"* "on the ball." On the other hand, to venture an opinion or even to entertain one privately, is to expose oneself to possible hurt and ridicule, for "An attack on a man's principles may often be seen as a blow to his self-esteem."[97] Thus a person may be torn between a desire to enhance his reputation for knowledgeability and a fear that his views will be attacked—both drives deriving from his need for self-esteem.

Self-esteem, of course, may be a prisoner of a moral sense or some other over-riding orientation. Where a person is dominated by a nagging super-ego, or in milder cases of moral orientation, his self-esteem will be enhanced by performing moral acts, or doing his duty. In this way, the sense of civic duty discussed below is tied to concepts of self-esteem. "Many people receive substantial superego gratification from political interest."[98]

Social motivation in general, then, and political motivation in particular, can be traced to an effort to maintain or enhance self-esteem. This effort lies behind identification with ethnic groups, social classes, regions, and social cliques which are ego-involved. Nothing reveals this more clearly than the pride in the achievements of the "old country" on the part of immigrant Americans. It is a prime force behind the emotional attachment to a party label of many political partisans here and abroad. We see it at work in the explanations of those who write letters to their congressmen, as in the case of the frail farmer's son who cannot do the chores about the farm and is fighting to achieve some life role which fulfills his need to think of himself as an "able" person. He says, in this connection, "an able person ought to take care of the opportunity to share in government. Many people are too lazy to think enough."[99] It is apparent in the reasons people give for serving as precinct chairmen,[100] and in the reasons for being merely "interested" in politics.[101]

Historically, social movements have been nurtured by the needs of men whose status was jeopardized by social developments. In the United States, the Progressive Movement of the Theodore Roosevelt era was heavily supported, not so much by the working class, as by the lawyers, ministers, teachers, and small businessmen whose status, relative to others, seemed threatened.[102] Abroad, the support by the lower middle class of the National Socialist movement was prompted, in large part, by their sense of status deprivation relative to the organized working class. Thus the undervaluing by the community of an individual or a group tends to lead such people into politics to redress their situation.

Not only may a discrepancy between the way a society esteems a person and his own sense of worth lead to active political involvement, it is also true that a discrepancy between a person's personal aspiration level and his achievement level has this effect.[103] It isn't the underprivileged who revolt, it is those whose privileges, status, and opportunities do not correspond to their expectations. The impetus behind the National Association for the Advancement of Colored People comes from the Northern Negro much more than from the less privileged Southern Negro.

In summary, then, the need for the maintenance of self-esteem is related to political participation in the following ways:

Political participation is encouraged by the need for self-esteem whenever politically linked objects (persons, ideas, groups, or symbols) become ego-involved, that is, whenever their fate is psychically linked to the fate of the self.

Political objects become ego-involved for an individual when (a) society invests them with a *status* attribute accepted by the individual, and (b) whenever the individual identifies with such objects in the pursuit of his private goals.

Political participation is increased by needs for self-esteem when political acts are socially valued. It is decreased by these needs when a political act exposes a person to charges of ignorance or socially disapproved deviance.

The need for self-esteem may lead to political participation through satisfying the super-ego of the individual who seeks participation as a duty.

Situations which tend to link political objects with the need for self-esteem include (a) discrepancies between social valuation of a person or his group and private or group self-valuation, and (b) differences between a person's aspiration level and his achievement level.

The "Overdetermination" of Political Participation

If any single lesson has been driven home by the investigations of the behavioral sciences in the past twenty years, it is the idea that all social acts are determined by multiple forces. In studying the genesis of neuroses Freud referred to a similar principle as "overdetermination", meaning that a symptom was the product of the culmination of influences; rarely, if ever, only one. Two things would follow from such a principle in the present context: (a) any one political movement will be attractive to persons whose needs differ from each other, and (b) any one person participates in politics in order to gratify a variety of personal needs. Something of this multiplicity of need fulfillment may be illustrated by reference to the Townsend movement in the thirties.[104]

The Townsend movement was nourished by the most severe depression in American history with attendant insecurity for all groups but especially for the young and the elderly. It was a movement which rapidly gained adherents, organized in Townsend Clubs, throughout the United States and developed an intensity of partisanship which approached the devotion of militant religious groups. Why did men and women join in such numbers and what functions did the movement serve for them?

In the first place, it immediately enhanced the self-esteem of people who had felt rejected and prematurely "shelved." It gave the elderly a voice and a "place in the scheme of things"—it gave the more active an opportunity for expression and a sense of usefulness. Thus it contributed immediately to the defense of a fragile ego for many persons whose egos had been cruelly injured.

The self-esteem motives became important in another sense. Many of the alternatives of the time—socialism, technocracy, native fascist movements—were identifiable as "foreign ideologies" or in some other way subversive. But the Townsendites, being elderly and conservative, could not identify with movements in this vein and retain their cherished image of themselves. By being Townsendites they could seek substantial reform, but in no way challenge private property, or the Constitution, or "the American way." In this way they could preserve their "self-respect."

Second, the movement offered future economic rewards for persons whose life status was almost always below the anticipations that they had built up during their lifetime. Their economic situations and their aspirations were at variance—hence discontent

over economic values and vulnerability to the political appeals of the Townsend movement.

In the third place the Townsend Plan was so simple that it could be grasped by those who disliked and shrank from discussions of economic reform, monetary problems, world trade, and matters of that nature. It served to structure the world and offer meaning to those who sought it. Because it was simple it fitted easily into a naive frame of reference: tax commerce to pay pensions to the elderly; the money spent by the elderly will create prosperity. The politicization of discontent was thus given a broad clear channel of operation.

Fourth, the movement offered opportunities for renewed solidarity with others. The tragic isolation of the elderly in the American family was mitigated by the social interaction involved in the movement. As one community leader said, "We have meetings once a week and card parties once in a while. You have to have activities to hold people's interest in the Clubs."[105]

Fifth, some of the leaders, including Dr. Townsend himself, found expression for their needs to exercise power, to impose themselves on others. Perhaps the power drive of some of the leaders could be most clearly seen in the alliance of the leaders with Father Coughlin and Gerald L. K. Smith in the Union Party of 1936.

And finally, in the working out of intra-psychic difficulties many Townsendites found the movement a source of assistance and a vehicle for expression. Some of the dependency needs of the Townsendites are suggested by the terms used by the Townsend *Weekly:* "We believe Dr. Townsend's perception of such an idea is not an accident but rather an answer to the prayers of tens of millions of organized children of God lost in a wilderness of doubt."[106]

In this sense a political movement, like a political party, can, without hypocrisy, be all things to all men.

Notes

[1] This is the Benthamite formula. Even the critics of Bentham, like Macaulay, assumed that men adapted their politics to serve

conscious self-interest. "When we see the actions of a man, we know with certainty what he thinks his interest to be," quoted in Graham Wallas, *Human Nature in Politics* (Boston: Houghton Mifflin, 1909), p. 22. On this see David Riesman's discussion of "self-interest: death of a motive," in his *Faces in the Crowd* (New Haven: Yale University Press, 1952), p. 33.

[2] Wallas, *op. cit.,* pp. 21–38.

[3] Harold D. Lasswell, "Psychopathology and Politics," reprinted in *The Political Writings of Harold D. Lasswell* (Glencoe, Ill.: Free Press, 1951), pp. 74–77.

[4] Harold D. Lasswell, *The World Revolution of Our Time* (Stanford, Cal.: Stanford University Press, 1951), p. 6.

[5] Hadley Cantril, *The Psychology of Social Movements* (New York: Wiley, 1941); Muzafer Sherif and Hadley Cantril, *The Psychology of Ego-Involvements* (New York: Wiley, 1941).

[6] M. Brewster Smith, Jerome Bruner, and Robert White, *Opinions and Personality* (New York: Wiley, 1956), p. 41; see also Smith, "The Personal Setting of Public Opinions: A Study of Attitudes Toward Russia," *Public Opinion Quarterly* 11 (1947): 516–23.

[7] Gerhart H. Saenger, "Social Status and Political Behavior," *American Journal of Sociology* 51 (1945): 104.

[8] Morris Rosenberg, "The Meaning of Politics in Mass Society," *Public Opinion Quarterly* 15 (1951): 8.

[9] Morris Rosenberg, "Some Determinants of Political Apathy," *Public Opinion Quarterly* 18 (1954–55): 363.

[10] Alexis de Tocqueville, *Democracy in America,* The Henry Reeve Text, edited by Phillips Bradley (New York: Knopf, 1945), p. 141.

[11] Fillmore Sanford, "Public Orientation to Roosevelt," *Public Opinion Quarterly* 15 (1951): 189–216.

[12] Rowena Wyant and Herta Herzog, "Voting via the Senate Mailbag, Part II," *Public Opinion Quarterly* 5 (1941): 607.

[13] G. H. Saenger, *op. cit.,* p. 104.

[14] See *Political Life,* pp. 329–30.

[15] Robert K. Merton and Alice S. Kitt, "Contributions to the Theory of Reference Group Behavior," in Merton and Paul F. Lazarsfeld, eds., *Studies in the Scope and Method of "The American Soldier"* (Glencoe, Ill.: Free Press, 1950), pp. 42–70.

[16] Charles A. Beard, *An Economic Interpretation of the Constitution of the United States,* rev. ed. (New York: Macmillan, 1948), p. 149.

[17] E. Pendleton Herring, "How Does the Voter Make Up His Mind?" *Public Opinion Quarterly* 2 (1938): 32–33.

[18] August de B. Hollingshead, *Elmtown's Youth* (New York: Wiley, 1949).

[19] John Maynard Keynes, *The General Theory of Employment, Interest, and Money* (New York: Harcourt Brace, undated [c. 1936]), p. 374.

[20] Hugh A. Bone, *Grass Roots Party Leadership: A Case Study of King County* (Washington, Seattle: University of Washington, 1952, (mimeographed); Bernard R. Berelson, Paul F. Lazarsfeld, William N. McPhee, *Voting* (Chicago: University of Chicago Press, 1954), p. 164.

[21] H. Gosnell, *Machine Politics, Chicago Model* (Chicago: University of Chicago Press, 1937); Sonya Forthal, *Cogwheels of Democracy, A Study of the Precinct Captain* (New York: William

Frederick Press, 1946); Peter J. Turano, *Organization and Operation of the Democratic Party in Wayne County, Mich.* (Ann Arbor, Mich.: Edwards, 1953, paper bound), p. 103.

[22] Lewis A. Dexter, "What Do Congressmen Hear: The Mail," *Public Opinion Quarterly* 20 (1956): 16–27; Frank Bonilla, "When is Petition Pressure?" *Public Opinion Quarterly* 20 (1956): 39–49.

[23] James D. Pollack, *Party Campaign Funds* (New York: Knopf, 1926), pp. 113, 126, Louise Overacker, *Money in Elections* (New York: Macmillan, 1932), pp. 169–93; V. O. Key, *Politics, Parties, and Pressure Groups,* 3rd ed. (New York: Crowell, 1952), pp. 537–42.

[24] See Rosenberg, "The Meaning of Politics in Mass Society," pp. 6, 11.

[25] See Theodore M. Newcomb, "The Prediction of Interpersonal Attraction," *American Psychologist* 11 (1956): 575–86.

[26] Muzafer Sherif, *The Psychology of Social Norms* (New York: Harper, 1936).

[27] Solomon E. Asch, "Effects of Group Pressure upon the Modification and Distortion of Judgments," reprinted in Dorwin Cartwright and Alvin Zander, eds., *Group Dynamics* (Evanston, Ill.: Row, Peterson, 1953), pp. 151–62.

[28] Theodore M. Newcomb, *Personality and Social Change* (New York, Dryden, 1943).

[29] Raymond L. Gorden, "Interaction between Attitude and the Definition of the Situation in the Expression of Opinion," *American Sociological Review* 17 (1952): 50–58.

[30] See Sebastian de Grazia, *The Political Community* (Chicago: University of Chicago Press, 1948).

[31] Riesman, *op. cit.*

[32] Kurt Lewin, *Resolving Social Conflicts* (New York: Harper & Bros., 1948), pp. 1–31.

[33] Karen Horney, *The Neurotic Personality of Our Time* (New York: Norton, 1937), pp. 35, 284.

[34] Erich Fromm, *Escape from Freedom* (New York: Rinehart, 1941).

[35] Overacker, *op. cit.,* pp. 169–95.

[36] Berelson and associates, *op. cit.,* p. 165.

[37] Smith, *op. cit.,* p. 521.

[38] Gordon W. Allport and Leo Postman, "An Analysis of Rumor," *Public Opinion Quarterly* 10 (1946–47): 503.

[39] Walter Lippmann, *Public Opinion* (New York: Macmillan, 1922), p. 8.

[40] David Riesman and Nathan Glazer, "The Meaning of Opinion," *Public Opinion Quarterly* 12 (1948): 631–48.

[41] Smith, *op. cit.,* pp. 516, 521.

[42] Rosenberg, "Some Determinants of Political Apathy," p. 353.

[43] Rosenberg, "The Meaning of Politics in Mass Society," p. 7.

[44] Bernard R. Berelson, "What 'Missing the Newspaper' Means," in Paul F. Lazarsfeld and Frank N. Stanton, eds., *Communications Research, 1948–49* (New York: Harper and Bros., 1949), pp. 111–29.

[45] Everett K. Wilson, "Determinants of Participation in Policy

Formation in a College Community," *Human Relations* 7 (1954): 287–312.

[46] Cantril, *op. cit.,* pp. 53–77.

[47] Gabriel Almond, *The Appeals of Communism* (Princeton: Princeton University Press, 1954).

[48] T. W. Adorno and associates, *The Authoritarian Personality* (New York: Harper & Bros., 1950), p. 658.

[49] Rosenberg, "Some Determinants of Political Apathy," p. 363.

[50] Ernst Kris and Nathan Leites, "Trends in Twentieth Century Propaganda," in Geza Roheim, ed., *Psychoanalysis and the Social Sciences* (New York: International Universities Press, 1947), pp. 393–410.

[51] For an adaptation of learning theory to psychic conflict in humans see John Dollard and Neal E. Miller, *Personality and Psychotherapy* (New York: McGraw Hill, 1950), pp. 352–68.

[52] Bernard Berelson and associates, *Voting* (Chicago: University of Chicago Press, 1954), p. 241.

[53] Herbert Goldhamer, "Public Opinion and Personality," *American Journal of Sociology* 55 (1950), p. 350.

[54] Herbert E. Krugman, "The Role of Hostility in the Appeal of Communism in the United States," *Psychiatry* 16 (1953): 253–61; Gabriel Almond, *The Appeals of Communism* (Princeton: Princeton University Press, 1954); Morris Ernst and David Loth, *Report on the American Communist* (New York: Holt, 1952).

[55] H. Goldhamer, *op. cit.,* p. 350.

[56] Paul H. Mussen and Anne B. Wyszynski, "Personality and Political Participation," *Human Relations* 5 (1952): 65–82.

[57] *Ibid.,* p. 78.

[58] *Ibid.,* p. 79.

[59] Although not on the specific subject of political participation, a study by Harrison Gough on extra-curricular "social participation" in high school offers some relevant findings. Gough found that the students who participated more in the extra-curricular life of the school could be characterized, on the basis of interviews and attitudes tests, as follows:

1. Greater candor and frankness, unpretentiousness.
2. Selfdisciplined, but tolerant of others.
3. Broader cultural and intellectual interests.
4. Sense of identification with and acceptance of the group.
5. Poise, assurance, and more effective social skills.
6. Greater optimism, drive, and "zest for life."

See Harrison Gough, "Predicting Social Participation," *Journal of Social Psychology* 35 (1952): 227–33.

[60] On this point Mussen and Wyszynski take too narrow a view: "The dissatisfied and hostile apathetic individual . . . must devote his energies to repressing his hostile feelings and conforming to conventional standards; hence he cannot become generally concerned with others or with the general welfare," *op. cit.,* p. 81.

[61] Andrew Bonar Law, the leader of the British Conservative Party for a number of years and Prime Minister of Great Britain suffered an enormous personal loss when his wife, upon whom he had been heavily dependent, died in 1909. He plunged into even more active participation in politics as a means of distracting him-

self from his anguish. His biographer notes that for him to abandon politics at the time of his wife's death would have been "folly," as it was the only thing which could occupy his mind and prevent him from becoming obsessed with his grief. The success of this expedient was so great that Bonar Law became the leader of his party within twenty-four months. Robert Blake, *Unrepentant Tory: The Life and Times of Andrew Bonar Law* (London: St. Martin's Press, 1956), pp. 61, 62.

[62] See John Dollard and associates, *Frustration and Aggression* (New Haven: Yale University Press, 1939).

[63] These views are based on twenty cases of political self-analysis by college men between nineteen and twenty-one years of age. It should be noted that these findings apply to persons who have personal stakes in political decisions of a more remote and less visible nature than is true of working adults.

[64] Gabriel Almond, *op. cit.*

[65] Edward A. Shils, "Authoritarianism: 'Right' and 'Left,'" in Richard Christie and Marie Johoda, *Studies in the Scope and Method of "The Authoritarian Personality"* (Glencoe, Ill.: Free Press, 1954), p. 39; Harold Lasswell, *Psychopathology and Politics,* reprinted in *The Political Writings of Harold Lasswell* (Glencoe, Ill.: Free Press, 1951), pp. 78–105.

[66] R. E. Money-Kyrle, *Psychoanalysis and Politics. A Contribution to the Psychology of Politics and Morals* (New York: Norton, undated, c. 1950), pp. 150–72.

[67] *Ibid.,* pp. 150–51.

[68] *Ibid.,* pp. 152–53.

[69] It must be noted at this point that these statements of the sexual basis of an inappropriately intense degree of political feeling leave something to be desired. They do not carry conviction to some people who have studied the mechanisms of the mind and the manner in which emotional life is expressed. They have no *prima facie* plausibility. But in their favor two considerations must be stated: a surprisingly large number of psychoanalysts, with very substantial amounts of empirical evidence to draw upon, have come to roughly the same conclusions. Of all people, they have probed most deeply into the sequence of causes which erupt into adult behavior. Secondly, there is as yet no better explanation for some of the emotional investment in politics which has been examined in certain instances. To the outsider this intensity of emotion is wholly inappropriate to the situation; sometimes it is directly contrary to a person's professed beliefs. There is no emotion without a cause. If sexual origins do not have anything to do with the situation, someone will come forward with a better explanation. In the meantime it is the part of prudence to lend a sympathetic ear to the sexual theories of social acts, but to maintain a polite reserve in the matter.

[70] Herbert E. Krugman, *op. cit.*

[71] Louise Overacker, *Money in Elections* (New York: Macmillan, 1932), pp. 169–93.

[72] Harold D. Lasswell, "Psychopathology and Politics," reprinted in *The Political Writings of Harold Lasswell* (Glencoe, Ill.: Free Press, 1951), p. 178.

[73] There is said to be a class difference in the repression of dependency feelings, the working class repressing these more than the middle class, while the middle class, on the other hand, represses

aggressive feelings somewhat more. See Else Frenkel-Brunswik, "Interaction of Psychological and Sociological Factors in Political Behavior," *American Political Science Review* 46 (1952): 44–65.

[74] Angus Campbell and associates, *The Voter Decides* (Evansville, Ill.: Row Peterson, 1954), p. 59.

[75] Herbert H. Hyman and Paul B. Sheatsley, "The Political Appeal of President Eisenhower," *Public Opinion Quarterly* 17 (1954–55): 443–60.

[76] Fillmore H. Sanford, "Public Orientation to Roosevelt," *Public Opinion Quarterly* 15 (1951): 189–216.

[77] Thomas Hobbes, *Leviathan,* reprint of 1st ed. (1651) (Cambridge, England: Cambridge University Press, 1904), p. 63.

[78] See Friedrich Nietzsche, "The Will to Power," in *The Complete Works of Friedrich Nietzsche,* Oscar Levy, ed. (New York: Macmillan, 1924), vols. 14, 15; Harold Lasswell, *Power and Personality* (New York, Norton, 1948); Charles E. Merriam, "Political Power" reprinted in Lasswell, Merriam and T. V. Smith. *A Study of Power* (Glencoe, Ill.: The Free Press, 1950).

[79] Eduard Spranger, *Types of Men,* translated from the fifth German edition by Paul J. W. Pigors (Halle: M. Niemeyer, 1928).

[80] *Ibid.,* pp. 190–91.

[81] Gordon W. Allport, *Personality, A Psychological Interpretation* (New York: Holt, 1937), pp. 229–30.

[82] Harold Lasswell, *Power and Personality,* p. 57.

[83] *Ibid.,* p. 20.

[84] See Rowena Wyant and Herta Herzog, "Voting Via the Senate Mailbag—Part II," *Public Opinion Quarterly* 5 (1941): 616–24.

[85] Louise Harned, *Participation in Party Politics: A Study of New Haven Committeemen.* Unpublished Ph.D. dissertation, Yale University Library, 1956.

[86] This variation of "the neurotic need for power" is developed by Horney in her discussion of "the neurotic need to control self and others through reason and foresight . . . in people who are too inhibited to exert power directly and openly." See Karen Horney, *Self-Analysis* (New York: Norton, 1942), p. 57.

[87] Robert E. Lane, "Political Personality and Electoral Choice,"

American Political Science Review 49 (1955): 178; Arthur Kornhauser, Albert J. Mayer, and Harold L. Sheppard, *When Labor Votes* (New York: University Books, 1956), pp. 172–73.

[88] F. H. Sanford, *op. cit.,* pp. 159–69.

[89] Mussen and Wyszynski, *op. cit.,* pp. 72–82.

[90] Harold Lasswell, "The Selective Effect of Personality on Political Participation," in Richard Christie and Marie Jahoda, eds., *Studies in the Scope and Method of "The Authoritarian Personality"* (Glencoe, Ill.: Free Press, 1954), pp. 197–225.

[91] F. H. Sanford, *op. cit.,* pp. 161–63.

[92] Hadley Cantril, *The Psychology of Social Movements* (New York: Wiley, 1941), pp. 30–52.

[93] Gordon W. Allport, "The Psychology of Participation," *Psychological Review* 52 (1945): p. 122.

[94] See Karen Horney, *The Neurotic Personality of Our Time* (New York: Norton, 1937), especially pp. 178, 286.

[95] See Otto Fenichel, *The Psychoanalytic Theory of Neurosis* (New York: Norton, 1945).

[96] Hadley Cantril, *op. cit.,* pp. 37–52.

[97] Morris Rosenberg, "Some Determinants of Political Apathy," *Public Opinion Quarterly* 18 (1954–55): p. 353.

[98] Morris Rosenberg, "The Meaning of Politics in Mass Society," *Public Opinion Quarterly* 15 (1951): 7.

[99] Wyant and H. Herzog, *op. cit.,* pp. 616–24.

[100] See Hugh Bone, *Grass Roots Party Leadership: A Case Study of King County* (Washington: Univ. of Washington, 1952).

[101] Unpublished material collected by Morris Rosenberg, 1956.

[102] Richard Hofstadter, *The Age of Reform* (New York, Knopf, 1952), pp. 131–72.

[103] H. Cantril, *op. cit.,* pp. 46–50.

[104] Adapted from Cantril, *op. cit.,* pp. 169–209.

[105] *Ibid.,* p. 199.

[106] *Ibid.,* p. 186.

Constraints on Idea Elements

Philip E. Converse

. . . We define a *belief system* as a configuration of ideas and attitudes in which the elements are bound together by some form of constraint or functional interdependence.[1] In the static case, "constraint" may be taken to mean the success we would have in predicting, given initial knowledge that an individual holds a specified attitude, that he holds certain further ideas and attitudes. We depend implicitly upon such notions of constraint in judging, for example, that, if a person is opposed to the expansion of social security, he is probably a conservative and is probably opposed as well to any nationalization of private industries, federal aid to education, sharply progressive income taxation, and so forth. Most discussions of ideologies make relatively elaborate assumptions about such constraints. Constraint must be treated, of course, as a matter of degree, and this degree can be measured quite readily, at least as an average among individuals.[2]

In the dynamic case, "constraint" or "interdependence" refers to the probability that a change in the perceived status (truth, desirability, and so forth) of one idea-element would *psychologically* require, from the point of view of the actor, some compensating change(s) in the status of idea-elements elsewhere in the configuration. The most obvious form of such constraint (although in some ways the most trivial) is exemplified by a structure of propositions in logic, in which a change in the truth-value of one proposition necessitates changes in truth-value elsewhere within the set of related propositions. Psychologically, of course, there may be equally strong constraint among idea-elements that would not be apparent to logical analysis at all, as we shall see.

We might characterize either the idea-elements themselves or entire belief systems in terms of many other dimensions. Only two will interest us here. First, the idea-elements within a belief system vary in a property we shall call *centrality,* according to the role that they play in the belief system as a whole. That is, when new information changes the status of one idea-element in a belief system, by postulate some other change must occur as well. There are usually, however, several possible changes in status elsewhere in the system, any one of which would compensate for the initial change. Let us imagine, for example, that a person strongly favors a particular policy; is very favorably inclined toward a given political party; and recognizes with gratification that the party's stand and his own are congruent. (If he were unaware of the party's stand on the issue, these elements could not in any direct sense be constrained within the same belief system.) Let us further imagine that the party then changes its position to the opposing side of the issue. Once the information about the change reaching the actor has become so unequivocal that he can no longer deny that the change has occurred, he has several further choices. Two of the more important ones involve either a change in attitude toward the party or a change in position on the issue. In such an instance, the element more likely to change is defined as less

Reprinted with permission of The Macmillan Company from "The Nature of Belief Systems in Mass Publics," by Philip E. Converse in David E. Apter, ed., *Ideology and Discontent* (New York: The Free Press of Glencoe, 1964). Copyright © 1964 by The Free Press of Glencoe, a Division of The Macmillan Company.

central to the belief system than the element that, so to speak, has its stability ensured by the change in the first element.[3]

In informal discussions of belief systems, frequent assumptions are made about the relative centrality of various idea-elements. For example, idea-elements that are logically "ends" are supposed to be more central to the system than are "means." It is important to remain aware, however, that idea-elements can change their relative centrality in an individual's belief-system over time. Perhaps the most hackneyed illustration of this point is that of the miser, to whom money has become an end rather than a means.

Whole belief systems may also be compared in a rough way with respect to the *range* of objects that are referents for the ideas and attitudes in the system. Some belief systems, while they may be internally quite complex and may involve large numbers of cognitive elements, are rather narrow in range: Belief systems concerning "proper" baptism rituals or the effects of changes in weather on health may serve as cases in point. Such other belief systems as, for example, one that links control of the means of production with the social functions of religion and a doctrine of aesthetics all in one more or less neat package have extreme ranges.

By and large, our attention will be focussed upon belief systems that have relatively wide ranges, and that allow some centrality to political objects, for they can be presumed to have some relevance to political behavior. This focus brings us close to what are broadly called *ideologies,* and we shall use the term for aesthetic relief where it seems most appropriate. The term originated in a narrower context, however, and is still often reserved for subsets of belief systems or parts of such systems that the user suspects are insincere; that he wishes to claim have certain functions for social groupings; or that have some special social source or some notable breadth of social diffusion.[4] Since we are concerned here about only one of these limitations—the question of social diffusion—and since we wish to deal with it by hypothesis rather than by definition, a narrow construction of the term is never intended.

I. Sources of Constraint on Idea-Elements

It seems clear that, however logically coherent a belief system may seem to the holder, the sources of constraint are much less logical in the classical sense than they are psychological—and less psychological than social. This point is of sufficient importance to dwell upon.

Logical Sources of Constraint

Within very narrow portions of belief systems, certain constraints may be purely logical. For example, government revenues, government expenditures, and budget balance are three idea-elements that suggest some purely logical constraints. One cannot believe that government expenditures should be increased, that government revenues should be decreased, and that a more favorable balance of the budget should be achieved all at the same time. Of course, the presence of such objectively logical constraints does not ensure that subjective constraints will be felt by the actor. They will be felt only if these idea-elements are brought together in the same belief system, and there is no guarantee that they need be. Indeed, it is true that, among adult American citizens, those who favor the expansion of government welfare services tend to be those who are more insistent upon reducing taxes "even if it means putting off some important things that need to be done."[5]

Where such purely logical constraint is concerned, McGuire has reported a fascinating experiment in which propositions from a few syllogisms of the Barbara type were scattered thinly across a long questionnaire applied to a student population. The fact that logical contingencies bound certain questions together was never brought to the attention of the students by the investigator. Yet one week later the questionnaire was applied again, and changes of response to the syllogistic propositions reduced significantly the measurable level of logical inconsistency. The conclusion was that merely "activating" these objectively related ideas in some rough temporal contiguity was sufficient to sensitize the holders to inconsistency and therefore to occasion readjustment of their beliefs.[6]

On a broader canvas, such findings suggest that simple "thinking about" a domain of idea-elements serves both to weld a broader range of such elements into a functioning belief system and to eliminate strictly logical inconsistencies defined from an objective point of view. Since there can be no doubt that educated elites in general, and political elites in particular, "think about" elements involved in political belief systems with a frequency far greater than that characteristic of mass publics, we could conservatively expect that strict logical inconsistencies (objectively definable) would be far more prevalent in a broad public.

Furthermore, if a legislator is noted for his insistence upon budget-balancing and tax-cutting, we can predict with a fair degree of success that he will also tend to oppose expansion of government welfare activities. If, however, a voter becomes numbered within his sphere of influence by virtue of having cast a vote for him directly out of enthusiasm for his tax-cutting policies, we cannot predict that the voter is opposed as well to expansion of government welfare services. Indeed, if an empirical prediction is possible, it may run in an opposing direction, although the level of constraint is so feeble that any comment is trivial. Yet we know that many historical observations rest directly upon the assumption that constraint among idea-elements visible at an elite level is mirrored by the same lines of constraint in the belief systems of their less visible "supporters." It is our argument that this assumption not only can be, but is very likely to be, fallacious.

Psychological Sources of Constraint

Whatever may be learned through the use of strict logic as a type of constraint, it seems obvious that few belief systems of any range at all depend for their constraint upon logic in this classical sense. Perhaps,

with a great deal of labor, parts of a relatively tight belief system like that fashioned by Karl Marx could be made to resemble a structure of ligical propositions. It goes without saying, however, that many sophisticated people have been swept away by the "iron logic" of Marxism without any such recasting. There is a broad gulf between strict logic and the quasi-logic of cogent argument. And where the elements in the belief system of a population represent looser cultural accumulations, the question of logical consistency is even less appropriate. If one visits a Shaker community, for example, one finds a group of people with a clear-cut and distinctive belief system that requires among other things plain dress, centrality of religious concerns, celibacy for all members, communal assumptions about work and property, antagonism to political participation in the broader state, and a general aura of retirement from the secular world. The visitor whose sense of constraint has been drawn from belief configurations of such other retiring sects as the Amish is entirely surprised to discover that the Shakers have no abhorrence of technological progress but indeed greatly prize it. In their heyday, a remarkable amount of group energy appears to have been reserved for "research and development" of labor-saving devices, and among the inventions they produced was a prototype of the washing machine. Similar surprise has been registered at idea-elements brought together by such movements as Perónism and Italian Fascism by observers schooled to expect other combinations. Indeed, were one to survey a limited set of ideas on which many belief systems have registered opposite postures, it would be interesting to see how many permutations of positions have been held at one time or another by someone somewhere.

Such diversity is testimony to an absence of any strict logical constraints among such idea-elements, if any be needed. What is important is that the elites familiar with the total shapes of these belief systems have *experienced* them as logically constrained clusters of ideas, within which one part necessarily follows from another. Often such constraint is quasi-logically argued on the basis of an appeal to some superordinate value or posture toward man and society, involving premises about the nature of social justice, social change, "natural law," and the like. Thus a few crowning postures—like premises about survival of the fittest in the spirit of social Darwinism—serve as a sort of glue to bind together many more specific attitudes and beliefs, and these postures are of prime centrality in the belief system as a whole.

Social Sources of Constraint

The social sources of constraint are twofold and are familiar from an extensive literature in the past century. In the first place, were we to survey the combinations of idea-elements that have occurred historically (in the fashion suggested above), we should undoubtedly find that certain postures tend to co-occur and that this co-occurrence has obvious roots in the configuration of interests and information that characterize particular niches in the social structure. For example, if we were informed that dissension was rising within the Roman Catholic Church over innovations designed to bring the priest more intimately into the *milieu* of the modern worker, we could predict with a high degree of success that such a movement would have the bulk of its support among the *bas-clergé* and would encounter indifference or hostility at the higher status levels of the hierarchy.

Of course, such predictions are in no sense free from error, and surprises are numerous. The middle-class temperance movement in America, for example, which now seems "logically" allied with the small-town Republican right, had important alliances some eighty years ago with the urban social left, on grounds equally well argued from temperance doctrines.[7] Nonetheless, there are some highly reliable correlations of this sort, and these correlations can be linked with social structure in the most direct way. Developmentally, they have status similar to the classic example of the spurious correlation—two terms that are correlated because of a common link to some third and prior variable. In the case of the belief system, arguments are developed to lend some more positive rationale to the fact of constraint: The idea-elements go together not simply because both are in the interest of the person holding a particular status but for more abstract and quasi-logical reasons developed from a coherent world view as well. It is this type of constraint that is closest to the classic meaning of the term "ideology."

The second source of social constraint lies in two simple facts about the creation and diffusion of belief systems. First, the shaping of belief systems of any range into apparently logical wholes that are credible to large numbers of people is an act of creative synthesis characteristic of only a miniscule proportion of any population. Second, to the extent that multiple idea-elements of a belief system are socially diffused from such creative sources, they tend to be diffused in "packages," which consumers come to see as "natural" wholes, for they are presented in such terms ("If you believe this, then you will also believe that, for it follows in such-and-such ways"). Not that the more avid consumer never supplies personal innovations on the fringes—he is very likely to suppress an idea-element here, to elaborate one there, or even to demur at an occasional point. But any set of relatively intelligent consumers who are initially sympathetic to the crowning posture turns out to show more consensus on specific implications of the posture as a result of social diffusion of "what goes with what" than it would if each member were required to work out the implications individually without socially provided cues.

Such constraint through diffusion is important, for it implies a dependence upon the transmission of information. If information is not successfully transmitted, there will be little constraint save that arising from the first social source. Where transmission of information is at stake, it becomes important to distinguish between two classes of information. Simply put, these two levels are what goes with what and why. Such levels of information logically stand in a scalar relationship to one another, in the sense that one can hardly arrive at an understanding of why two ideas go together without being aware that they are supposed to go together. On the other hand, it is easy to know that two ideas go together without knowing why. For example, we can expect that a very large majority of the American public would somehow have absorbed the notion that "Communists are atheists." What is important is that this perceived correlation would for most people represent nothing more than a fact of existence, with the same status as the fact that oranges are orange and most apples are red. If we were to go and explore with these people their grasp of the "why" of the relationship, we would be surprised if more than a quarter of the population even attempted responses (setting aside such inevitable replies as "those Communists are for everything wicked"), and, among the responses received, we could be sure that the majority would be incoherent or irrelevant.

The first level of information, then, is simple and straightfoward. The second involves much more complex and abstract information, very close to what Downs has called the "contextual knowledge" relevant to a body of information.[8] A well informed person who has received sufficient information about a system of beliefs to understand the "whys" involved in several of the constraints between idea-elements is in a better position to make good guesses about the nature of other constraints; he can deduce with fair success, for example, how a true believer will respond to certain situations. Our first interest in distinguishing between these types of information, however, flows from our interest in the relative success of information transmission. The general premise is that the first type of information will be diffused much more readily than the second because it is less complex.

It is well established that differences in information held in a cross-section population are simply staggering, running from vast treasuries of well organized information among elites interested in the particular subject to fragments that could virtually be measured as a few "bits" in the technical sense. These differences are a static tribute to the extreme imperfections in the transmission of information "downward" through the system: Very little information "trickles down" very far. Of course, the ordering of individuals on this vertical information scale is largely due to differences in education, but it is strongly modified as well by different specialized interests and tastes that individuals have acquired over time (one for politics, another for religious activity, another for fishing, and so forth).

Consequences of Declining Information for Belief Systems

It is our primary thesis that, as one moves from elite sources of belief systems downwards on such an information scale, several important things occur. First, the contextual grasp of "standard" political belief systems fades out very rapidly, almost before one has passed beyond the 10 percent of the American population that in the 1950s had completed standard college training.[9] Increasingly, simpler forms of information about "what goes with what" (or even information about the simple identity of objects) turn up missing. The net result, as one moves downward, is that constraint declines across the universe of idea-elements, and that the range of relevant belief systems becomes narrower and narrower. Instead of a few wide-ranging belief systems that organize large amounts of specific information, one would expect to find a proliferation of clusters of ideas among which little constraint is felt, even, quite often, in instances of sheer logical constraint.[10]

At the same time, moving from top to bottom of this information dimension, the character of the objects that are central in a belief system undergoes systematic change. These objects shift from the remote, generic, and abstract to the increasingly simple, concrete, or "close to home." Where potential political objects are concerned, this progression tends to be from abstract, "ideological" principles to the more obviously recognizable social groupings or charismatic leaders and finally to such objects of immediate experience as family, job, and immediate associates.

Most of these changes have been hinted at in one form or another in a variety of sources. For example, "limited horizons," "foreshortened time perspectives," and "concrete thinking" have been singled out as notable characteristics of the ideational world of the poorly educated. Such observations have impressed even those investigators who are dealing with subject matter rather close to the individual's immediate world: his family budgeting, what he thinks of people more wealthy than he, his attitudes toward leisure time, work regulations, and the like. But most of the stuff of politics—particularly that played on a national or international stage—is, in the nature of things, remote and abstract. Where politics is concerned, therefore, such ideational changes begin to occur rapidly below the extremely thin stratum of the electorate that ever has occasion to make public pronouncements on political affairs. In other words, the changes in belief systems of which we speak are not a pathology limited to a thin and disoriented bottom layer of the *lumpenproletariat;* they are immediately relevant in understanding the bulk of mass political behavior.

It is this latter fact which seems to be consistently misunderstood by the sophisticated analysts who comment in one vein or another on the meaning of mass politics. There are some rather obvious "optical illusions" that are bound to operate here. A member of that tiny elite that comments publicly about political currents (probably some fraction of 1 percent of a population) spends most of his time in informal communication about politics with others in the same select group. He rarely encounters a conversation in which his assumptions of shared contextual grasp of political ideas are challenged. Intellectually, he has learned that the level of information in the mass public is low, but he may dismiss this knowledge as true of only 10 to 20 percent of the voters, who affect the course of mass political events in insignificant ways if at all.[11] It is largely from his informal communications that he learns how "public opinion" is changing and what the change signifies, and he generalizes facilely from these observations to the bulk of the broader public.[12]

II. Constraints among Idea-Elements

. . . In our estimation, the use of such basic dimensions of judgment as the liberal-conservative contin-

uum betokens a contextual grasp of politics that permits a wide range of more specific idea-elements to be organized into more tightly constrained wholes. We feel, furthermore, that there are many crucial consequences of such organization: With it, for example, new political events have more meaning, retention of political information from the past is far more adequate, and political behavior increasing approximates that of sophisticated "rational" models, which assume relatively full information.

It is often argued, however, that abstract dimensions like the liberal-conservative continuum are superficial if not meaningless indicators: All that they show is that poorly educated people are inarticulate and have difficulty expressing verbally the more abstract lines along which their specific political beliefs are organized. To expect these people to be able to express what they know and feel, the critic goes on, is comparable to the fallacy of assuming that people can say in an accurate way why they behave as they do. When it comes down to specific attitudes and behaviors, the organization is there nonetheless, and it is this organization that matters, not the capacity for discourse in sophisticated language.

If it were true that such organization does exist for most people, apart from their capacities to be articulate about it, we would agree out of hand that the question of articulation is quite trivial. As a cold empirical matter, however, this claim does not seem to be valid. Indeed, it is for this reason that we have cast the argument in terms of constraint, for constraint and organization are very nearly the same thing. Therefore when we hypothesize that constraint among political idea-elements begins to lose its range very rapidly once we move from the most sophisticated few toward the "grass roots," we are contending that the organization of more specific attitudes into wide-ranging belief systems is absent as well.

Table 1 gives us an opportunity to see the differences in levels of constraint among beliefs on a range of specific issues in an elite population and in a mass population. The elite population happens to be candidates for the United States Congress in the off-year elections of 1958, and the cross-section sam-

Table 1

Constraint between Specific Issue Beliefs for an Elite Sample and a Cross-Section Sample, 1958[a]

Congressional Candidates	Employment	Domestic Education	Housing	F.E.P.C.	Economic	Military[b]	Foreign Isolationism	Party Preference
Employment	—	.62	.59	.35	.26	.06	.17	.68
Aid to education		—	.61	.53	.50	.06	.35	.55
Federal housing			—	.47	.41	−.03	.30	.68
F.E.P.C.				—	.47	.11	.23	.34
Economic aid					—	.19	.59	.25
Military aid						—	.32	−.18
Isolationism							—	.05
Party preference								—
Cross-Section Sample								
Employment	—	.45	.08	.34	−.04	.10	−.22	.20
Aid to education		—	.12	.29	.06	.14	−.17	.16
Federal housing			—	.08	−.06	.02	.07	.18
F.E.P.C.				—	.24	.13	.02	−.04
Economic aid					—	.16	.33	−.07
Soldiers abroad[b]						—	.21	.12
Isolationism							—	−.03
Party preference								—

[a] Entries are tau-gamma coefficients, a statistic proposed by Leo A. Goodman and William H. Kruskal in "Measures of Association for Cross Classifications," *Journal of the American Statistical Association* 49 no. 268, 749 (Dec., 1954). The coefficient was chosen because of its sensitivity to constraint of the scalar as well as the correlational type.

[b] For this category, the cross-section sample was asked a question about keeping American soldiers abroad, rather than about military aid in general.

ple represents the national electorate in the same year. The assortment of issues represented is simply a purposive sampling of some of the more salient political controversies at the time of the study, covering both domestic and foreign policy. The questions posed to the two samples were quite comparable, apart from adjustments necessary in view of the backgrounds of the two populations involved.[13]

For our purposes, however, the specific elite sampled and the specific beliefs tested are rather beside the point. We would expect the same general contrast to appear if the elite had been a set of newspaper editors, political writers, or any other group that takes an interest in politics. Similarly, we would expect the same results from any other broad sampling of politi-

cal issues or, for that matter, any sampling of beliefs from other domains: A set of questions on matters of religious controversy should show the same pattern between an elite population like the clergy and the church members who form their mass "public." What is generically important in comparing the two types of population is the difference in levels of constraint among belief-elements.

Where constraint is concerned, the absolute value of the coefficients in Table 1 (rather than their algebraic value) is the significant datum. The first thing the table conveys is the fact that for both populations, there is some falling off of constraint *between* the domains of domestic and foreign policy, relative to the high level of constraint *within* each domain. This result is to be expected: Such lowered values signify boundaries between belief systems that are relatively independent. If we take averages of appropriate sets of coefficients entered in Table 1 however, we see that the strongest constraint *within* a domain for the mass public is less than that *between* domestic and foreign domains for the elite sample. Furthermore, for the public, in sharp contrast to the elite, party preference seems by and large to be set off in a belief system of its own, relatively unconnected to issue positions (Table 2).[14]

Table 2
Summary of Differences in Level of Constraint within and between Domains, Public and Elite (based on Table 1)

| | *Average Coefficients* | | | |
	Within Domestic Issues	*Between Domestic and Foreign*	*Within Foreign Issues*	*Between Issues and Party*
Elite	.53	.25	.37	.39
Mass	.23	.11	.23	.11

It should be remembered throughout, of course, that the *mass* sample of Tables 1 and 2 does not exclude college-educated people, ideologues, or the politically sophisticated. These people, with their higher levels of constraint, are represented in appropriate numbers, and certainly contribute to such vestige of organization as the mass matrix evinces. But they are grossly outnumbered, as they are in the active electorate. The general point is that the matrix of correlations for the elite sample is of the sort that would be appropriate for factor analysis, the statistical technique designed to reduce a number of correlated variables to a more limited set of organizing dimensions. The matrix representing the mass public, however, despite its realistic complement of ideologues, is exactly the type that textbooks advise against using for factor analysis on the simple grounds that through inspection it is clear that there is virtually nothing in the way of organization to be discovered. Of course, it is the type of broad organizing dimension

to be suggested by factor analysis of specific items that is usually presumed when observers discuss "ideological postures" of one sort or another.

Although the beliefs registered in Table 1 are related to topics of controversy or political cleavage, McClosky has described comparable differences in levels of constraint among beliefs for an elite sample (delegates to national party conventions) and a cross-section sample when the items deal with propositions about democracy and freedom—topics on which fundamental consensus among Americans is presumed.[15] Similarly, Prothro and Grigg, among others, have shown that, while there is widespread support for statements of culturally familiar principles of freedom, democracy, and tolerance in a cross-section sample, this support becomes rapidly obscured when questions turn to specific cases that elites would see as the most direct applications of these principles.[16] In our estimation, such findings are less a demonstration of cynical lip service than of the fact that, while both of two inconsistent opinions are honestly held, the individual lacks the contextual grasp to understand that the specific case and the general principle belong in the same belief system: In the absence of such understanding, he maintains psychologically independent beliefs about both. This is another important instance of the decline in constraint among beliefs with declining information.

While an assessment of relative constraint between the matrices rests only on comparisons of absolute values, the comparative algebraic values have some interest as well. This interest arises from the sophisticated observer's almost automatic assumption that whatever beliefs "go together" in the visible political world (as judged from the attitudes of elites and the more articulate spectators) must naturally go together in the same way among mass public. Table 1 makes clear that this assumption is a very dangerous one, aside from the question of degree of constraint. For example, the politician who favors federal aid to education could be predicted to be more, rather than less, favorable to an internationalist posture in foreign affairs, for these two positions in the 1950s were generally associated with "liberalism" in American politics. As we see from Table 1, we would be accurate in this judgment considerably more often than chance alone would permit. On the other hand, were we to apply the same assumption of constraint to the American public in the same era, not only would we have been wrong, but we would actually have come closer to reality by assuming no connection at all.

All the correlations in the elite sample except those that do not depart significantly from zero exhibit signs that anybody following politics in the newspapers during this period could have predicted without hesitation. That is, one need only have known that Democrats tended to favor expansion of government welfare activities and tended to be internationalists in foreign affairs to have anticipated all the signs except one. This exception, the −.18 that links advocacy of military aid abroad with the Republican Party, would hold no surprises either, for the one kind of international involvement that Republicans came to accept in this period limited foreign aid to the military variety, a view that stood in opposition to "soft" liberal interests in international economic welfare. If these algebraic signs in the elite matrix are taken as the culturally defined "proper" signs—the sophisticated observer's assumption of what beliefs go with what other beliefs—then the algebraic differences between comparable entries in the two matrices provide an estimate of how inaccurate we would be in generalizing our elite-based assumptions about "natural" belief combinations to the mass public as a whole. A scanning of the two matrices with these differences in mind enhances our sense of high discrepancy between the two populations.

To recapitulate, then, we have argued that the unfamiliarity of broader and more abstract ideological frames of reference among the less sophisticated is more than a problem in mere articulation. Parallel to ignorance and confusion over these ideological dimensions among the less informed is a general decline in constraint among specific belief elements that such dimensions help to organize. It cannot therefore be claimed that the mass public shares ideological patterns of belief with relevant elites at a specific level

any more than it shares the abstract conceptual frames of reference.

Constraints and Overt Behavior

There is still another counter-hypothesis that deserves examination. This view would grant that the political belief systems of the less well educated may be more fragmented and chaotic. It would maintain at the same time, however, that this fact is inconsequential in the determination of behavior. The presence, absence, or incoherence of these "intervening" psychological states is thus epiphenomenal: Social structure commits behavior to certain channels quite independent of specific cognitions and perceptions of the actors themselves.[17] In other versions, researchable intervening mechanisms are suggested. The "opinion leader" model is one of them. If it is true that the mass of less knowledgeable people rely upon informal communication from a few more informed people for cues about desirable or appropriate behavior, then the lines of behavior choices followed in politics might indeed show strong sociostructural patterns, even though many uninformed actors have little of the opinion leaders' coherent and organized understanding of why one behavior is more appropriate than another. What these points of view have in common is the insistence that strong constraints can be expected to operate between sociostructural terms and conscious behavior choices quite apart from the presence or absence of appropriate intervening psychological "definitions of the situation."

Figure 1 is addressed to such arguments. The graphs indicate the varying degrees of association between objective class position and partisan preference in the 1956 presidential election, as a function of differences in the nature of political belief systems captured by our "levels of conceptualization."[18] If objective locations in the social structure served to produce behavioral consequences regardless of the presence or absence of relevant intervening organizations of conscious beliefs, then we would not expect any particular slope to the progression of bars

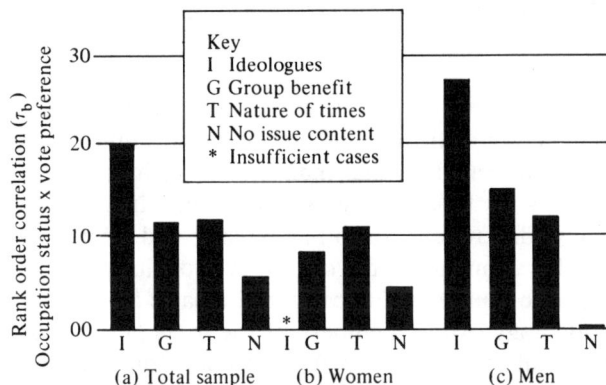

Fig. 1. The correlation of occupation and vote preference within levels of conceptualization

within each graph. As Fig. 1(a) shows for a sample of the adult electorate as a whole, however, the differences in intervening belief organization produce very marked and orderly differences in the degree to which partisanship reflects sociostructural position. Of course, from one point of view, this observation seems only common sense, yet the doctrinaire position that the intervening psychological terms are unimportant or epiphenomenal continues to be argued with more vehemence than empirical evidence.

Since it can be seen that a perfectly functioning opinion-leader model would also produce something approaching a rectangular distribution of bars in Fig. 1, the slope depicted in Fig. 1(a) can also be taken as a commentary on the practical imperfections with which opinion leader processes operate in this domain. That is, the "ideologues" and "near-ideologues" represented by the first bar of each graph are opinion leaders *par excellence*. While they tend to be disproportionately well educated, they nevertheless include representatives from all broad social *milieux*. Empirically they differ sharply from the less sophisticated in their attention to new political events and in the size of their store of information about past events. They get news firsthand and, presumably, form opinions directly from it. By their own report, they are much more likely than the less sophisticated to attempt to persuade others to their own political opinions in in-

formal communications. Finally, much social data leads us to assume that the bulk of these informal communications is addressed to others within their own social *milieu*. Since social-class questions are important for these opinion leaders and since their own partisan preferences are rather clearly geared to their own class, we would suppose that "opinion leading" should serve to diffuse this connection between status and behavior through less knowledgeable members of their *milieu*, whether or not the more complicated rationales were diffused. In other words, most of what goes on in the heads of the less informed of our respondents would indeed be irrelevant for study if the respondents could at least be counted upon to follow the lead of more informed people of their own *milieu* in their ultimate partisanship. And to the extent that they can be counted on to behave in this way, we should expect Fig. 1 to show a rectangular distribution of bars. The departure from such a pattern is very substantial.

Now there is one type of relationship in which there is overwhelming evidence for vigorous opinion-leading where politics is concerned in our society. It is the relationship within the family: The wife is very likely to follow her husband's opinions, however imperfectly she may have absorbed their justifications at a more complex level. We can do a fair job of splitting this relationship into its leader-follower components simply by subdividing our total sample by sex. As Fig. 1(b) suggests, our expectation that the presence or absence of intervening belief systems is of reduced importance among sets of people who are predominantly opinion followers is well borne out by the relatively flat and disordered progression of bars among women. Correspondingly, of course, the same slope among men becomes steeper still in Fig. 1(c).[19]

The fact that wives tend to double their husbands' votes is, from a broader "system" point of view, a relatively trivial one. If we are willing to consider the family as the basic voting unit, then Fig. 1(c) suggests that diffusion of the sociostructurally "proper" behavior without diffusion of understanding of that behavior through simple opinion-leading processes is a very feeble mechanism indeed across the society as a whole, at least where political decisions of this sort are concerned.[20] The organization of partisanship among those who give no evidence of intervening issue content shows no trace whatever of those residual effects that should be left by any systematic opinion-following (and that are visible among comparable women). Thus, while we are in no way questioning the existence of some opinion-leading, it seems doubtful that it represents the dominant, effective phenomenon sometimes supposed, a phenomenon that succeeds in lending shape to mass politics despite the absence of more detailed individual comprehension of the political context.[21]

Much more broadly, we have become convinced that this class of finding — the declining degree of constraint between a term representing social structure and one representing an important political choice as one moves from the more to the less politically sophisticated in the society — is a powerful and general one. It is powerful (for readers not accustomed to the statistics employed) in the simple sense that the variation in constraint as a function of sophistication or involvement is extremely large: There are no other discriminating variables that begin to separate populations so cleanly and sharply as these measures. It is a general finding in at least two senses. First, it replicates itself handsomely across time: In every instance within the span of time for which appropriate data are available, the finding is present where class and partisanship are concerned. Secondly, it has some incipient claim to generality where sociostructural terms other than "social class" are concerned: The same sharp finding emerges, for example, when the relationship between religion and partisanship (Protestant vs. Catholic) is examined.

And, of course, if class or religious membership is considered to constitute one set of idea-elements and the predispositions that lead to particular partisan preferences and final choice to form another, then the whole phenomenon takes its place as another large class of special cases of the decline of constraints and the narrowing of belief systems to which this paper is devoted. . . .

III. Summary

For the truly involved citizen, the development of political sophistication means the absorption of contextual information that makes clear to him the connections of the policy area of his initial interest with policy differences in other areas; and that these broader configurations of policy positions are describable quite economically in the basic abstractions of ideology. Most members of the mass public, however, fail to proceed so far. Certain rather concrete issues may capture their respective individual attentions and lead to some politically relevant opinion formation. This engagement of attention remains narrow however: Other issue concerns that any sophisticated observer would see as "ideologically" related to the initial concern tend not to be thus associated in any breadth or number. The common citizen fails to develop more global points of view about politics. A realistic picture of political belief systems in the mass public, then, is not one that omits issues and policy demands completely nor one that presumes widespread ideological coherence; it is rather one that captures with some fidelity the fragmentation, narrowness, and diversity of these demands.

Such a description is not particularly economical, and the investigator is confronted by the fact that, in coping with a poorly constrained system, he must choose between parsimony and explanatory power. This dilemma confronts him only in the degree that he insists upon dealing with the issue or ideological base of mass politics. That is, the very diffusion of this issue base at the mass level means that many of the threads cancel themselves out and can be ignored at one level of description. With good information on basic party loyalties in a population, with knowledge of sudden disruptions of economic expectations, and with freedom to treat other short-term perturbations in mass political behavior in terms of such inelegant factors as candidate popularity, there is no reason to feel that mass political phenomena are difficult to understand or predict in relatively economical terms.

But such accounts do not probe to the level that supplies for many the fundamental "why" of politics— its issue or ideological base.

If we insist on treating this base and choose economy over explanatory power, then we are likely to select one or two ideological threads to follow, with recognition that the consequences of substantial numbers of other threads must be ignored. If the limited threads are well chosen, this strategy has a number of strengths, and a "good" choice of threads is likely to involve visible and competing population groupings.

This latter strategy is essentially that employed by Lipset in tracing the imprint of social class upon mass political behavior across time and nationality in *Political Man*. His choice of threads is good, in part because of the ubiquity of social-class differences historically and cross-nationally and in part because, among issue threads, social class is one of the more reliably prominent. Despite the great diversity of issue concerns in the American public in the 1950s, if one were required to pick the single thread of ideological relevance most visible and persistent, it undoubtedly would be related to social class.

On the other hand, there is a major sacrifice of explanatory power here. For example, when we argue that social-class concerns represent the most prominent, unitary "issue" thread in mass American politics in the past decade, the scope of our statement should not be overestimated. Given the diversity and number of such threads, it need only mean (as is probably the case) that such concerns have made some greater or lesser contribution to the significant political behaviors—for the mass, largely in voting—of 20 to 40 percent of the American population in this period. This contribution is enough, of course, to leave a clear imprint on mass political phenomena, although it does not constitute even substantial explanation.[22]

Furthermore, it may well be that, in pluralist societies with other highly visible group cleavages, these cleavages may often have greater penetration into mass publics than do class differences, as far as consequences for political behavior are concerned.

Religious pluralism is a case in point. While class differences mark every society, not all current democracies contain fundamental religious differences. Where such differences exist and can in some measure be separated from social class differences—the Netherlands, Austria, and the United States are good examples—there is fair reason to believe that they are fully as important, if not more important, in shaping mass political behavior than are class differences. Even in current France, one can predict with great accuracy whether a citizen will be a partisan of the "left" or of the "right" by knowing his position on the "clerical question" than by knowing his position on the more central class issues typically associated with the left-right distinction. And this accuracy is possible despite several decades during which French elites have focused primary attention on other more gripping controversies and have frequently attempted to deflate the clerical question as a "phony" issue.[23]

Whatever problems are posed for description by the diffuseness of the issue base of mass politics, the most important insights are to be gained from the fact that ideological constraints in belief systems decline with decreasing political information, which is to say that they are present among elites at the "top" of political systems, or subsystems and disappear rather rapidly as one moves "downward" into their mass clienteles. We see the importance of this fact in a number of standard phenomena of both routine and crisis politics.

Perhaps the simplest and most obvious consequences are those that depend on the fact that reduced constraint with reduced information means in turn that ideologically constrained belief systems are necessarily more common in upper than in lower social strata. This fact in turn means that upper social strata across history have much more predictably supported conservative or rightist parties and movements than lower strata have supported leftist parties and movements.

These facts have further bearing on a number of asymmetries in political strategy, which typically arise between elites of rightist and leftist parties.

These elites operate under rather standard ideological assumptions, and therefore recognize their "natural" clienteles in the upper and lower strata of the society respectively. The cultural definitions that separate upper and lower in most if not all modern societies are such that the lower clientele numerically outweighs the upper. The net result of these circumstances is that the elites of leftist parties enjoy a "natural" numerical superiority, yet they are cursed with a clientele that is less dependable or solidary in its support. The rightist elite has a natural clientele that is more limited but more dependable.

Asymmetrical elite strategies therefore emerge. They are best summed up perhaps in terms of an increasingly *overt* stress on group loyalty and cohesion *per se* as one moves from right to left across party spectra in most political systems. This difference has a great number of concrete manifestations. For example, where political institutions encourage multiparty development, there is likely to be less party fragmentation on the left than on the right. Where political institutions permit interparty differences in the stringency of party discipline at the legislative level, it is common to find a rather steady progression in strength of discipline exacted as one moves from right to left. At an electoral level, rightist candidates are more likely to run as individual *notables,* dissociating themselves from party *per se* or claiming positions "above the parties" and priding themselves on the independence of their consciences from party dictation.

Entirely parallel asymmetries arise in the relations between party elites and elites of organized interest groups based "outside" the political order as it is narrowly conceived. These relations tend to be more overtly close as one moves from the right to the left. Trade unions have with some frequency created or coalesced with leftist parties, and, where such coalition has not occurred, trade unions (and particularly those with the less politically sophisticated member-

ships) publicize political endorsements that link them rather unequivocally with specific leftist parties. Associations of professional and business people, to the degree that they perform public political activity at all, tend toward non-partisan exhortations to "work for the party of your choice" and in other ways maintain or are kept at a "proper" distance from rightist parties so far as self-publicized connections are concerned. All these differences flow from the simple fact that, for leftist parties, the transmission of gross, simple, group-oriented cues is a functional imperative. For rightist parties, there is much to lose and nothing to gain in such publicity, for the basic clientele can be counted on for fair support without blatant cues, and the tactical needs are to avoid the alienation of potentially large-scale "haphazard" support from the lower-status clientele.

These simple social biases in the presence of ideological constraints in belief systems thus register to some degree in the calculations of practical political elites. Fully as interesting, however, are the miscalculations that arise when the low incidence of these constraints in the middle and lower reaches of mass publics is forgotten. While this forgetting is more common among academic commentators than among practical politicians, it is sometimes hard to avoid— particularly where an elite with a distinctive ideology captures a broad surge of mass support. Here it is difficult to keep in mind that the true motivations and comprehensions of the supporters may have little or nothing to do with the distinctive beliefs of the endorsed elite. Yet we believe that such hiatuses or discontinuities are common and become more certain in the degree that (1) the distinctive elements of the elite ideologies are bound up in abstractions or referents remote from the immediate experience of the clientele; (2) and that the clientele, for whatever reason, is recruited from the less informed strata of a population.

Notes

[1]Garner uses the term "constraint" to mean "the amount of interrelatedness of structure of a system of variables" when meas-

ured by degree of uncertainty reduction. Wendell R. Garner, *Uncertainty and Structure as Psychological Concepts* (New York, 1962), pp. 142ff. We use the term a bit more broadly as relief from such polysyllables as "interrelatedness" and "interdependence."

[2] Measures of correlation and indices of the goodness of fit of a cumulative scale model to a body of data are measures of two types of constraint.

[3] Definitions of belief systems frequently require that configurations of ideas be stable for individuals over long periods of time. The notion of centrality fulfills this requirement in a more flexible way. That is, once it is granted that changes in the perceived status of idea-elements are not frequent in any event and that, when change does occur, the central elements (particularly in large belief systems) are amply cushioned by more peripheral elements that can be adjusted, it follows that central elements are indeed likely to be highly stable.

[4] David W. Minar, "Ideology and Political Behavior," *Midwest Journal of Political Science* 5 (November, 1961): 317–31.

[5] See A. Campbell, P. E. Converse, W. Miller, and D. Stokes, *The American Voter* (New York, 1960), pp. 204–9.

[6] William J. McGuire, "A Syllogistic Analysis of Cognitive Relationships," in Milton J. Rosenberg, Carl I. Hovland, William J. McGuire, Robert P. Abelson, and Jack W. Brehm, *Attitude Organization and Change,* Yale Studies in Attitude and Communication, vol. 3 (New Haven, 1960), pp. 65–111.

[7] Joseph R. Gusfield, "Status Conflicts and the Changing Ideologies of the American Temperance Movement," in Pittman and Snyder, eds., *Society, Culture and Drinking Patterns* (New York, 1962).

[8] Anthony Downs, *An Economic Theory of Democracy* (New York, 1957), p. 79.

[9] It should be understood that our information dimension is not so perfectly correlated with formal education as this statement implies. Since educational strata have a more ready intuitive meaning, however, we shall use them occasionally as convenient ways of measuring off levels in the population. In such cases, the reader may keep in mind that there are always some people of lesser education but higher political involvement who are numbered in the stratum and some people with education befitting the stratum who are not numbered there because their interests lie elsewhere and their information about politics is less than could be expected.

[10] There is a difference, of course, between this statement and a suggestion that poorly educated people have no systems of belief about politics.

[11] This observation is valid despite the fact that surveys showing ignorance of crucial political facts are much more likely to run in a range from 40–80 percent "unaware." At the height of the 1958 Berlin crisis, 63 percent of the American public did not know that the city was encircled by hostile troops. A figure closer to 70 percent is a good estimate of the proportion of the public that does not know which party controls Congress.

[12] In this regard, it was enlightening to read the stunned reactions of the political columnist Joseph Alsop when, during the 1960 presidential primaries, he left the elite circuits of the East Coast and ventured from door to door talking politics with "normal" people in West Virginia. He was frank to admit that the change in perceived political worlds was far greater than anything he had ever anticipated, despite his prior recognition that there would be some difference.

[13] As a general rule, questions broad enough for the mass public to understand tend to be too simple for highly sophisticated people to feel comfortable answering without elaborate qualification. The pairing of questions, with those for the mass public given first, are as follows:

Employment. *"The government in Washington ought to see to it that everybody who wants to work can find a job." "Do you think the federal government ought to sponsor programs such as large public works in order to maintain full employment, or do you think that problems of economic readjustment ought to be left more to private industry or state and local government?"*

Aid to Education. *"If cities and towns around the country need help to build more schools, the government in Washington ought to give them the money they need." "Do you think the government should provide grants to the states for the construction and operation of public schools, or do you think the support of public education should be left entirely to the state and local government?"*

Federal Housing. *"The government should leave things like electric power and housing for private businessmen to handle." "Do you approve the use of federal funds for public housing, or do you generally feel that housing can be taken care of better by private effort?"*

F.E.P.C. *"If Negroes are not getting fair treatment in jobs and housing, the government should see to it that they do." "Do you think the federal government should establish a fair employment practices commission to prevent discrimination in employment?"*

Economic Aid. *"The United States should give economic help to the poorer countries of the world even if those countries can't pay for it." "First, on the foreign economic aid program, would you generally favor expanding the program, reducing it, or maintaining it about the way it is?"*

Military Aid. *"The United States should keep soldiers overseas where they can help countries that are against Communism." "How about the foreign military aid program? Should this be expanded, reduced, or maintained about as it is?"*

Isolationism. *"This country would be better off if we just stayed home and did not concern ourselves with problems in other parts of the world." "Speaking very generally, do you think that in the years ahead the United States should maintain or reduce its commitments around the world?"*

[14] We are aware that drawing an average of these coefficients has little interpretation from a statistical point of view. The averages are presented merely as a crude way of capturing the flavor of the larger table in summary form. More generally, it could be argued that the coefficients might be squared in any event, an operation that would do no more than heighten the intuitive sense of contrast between the two publics. In this format, for example, the elite-mass difference in the domestic-issue column of Table 2 would shift from .53 *vs.* .23 to .28 *vs.* .05. Similarly, that in the party column would become 15 *vs.* .01.

[15] Herbert McClosky, "Consensus and Ideology in American Politics," *American Political Science Review* 58, no. 2 (June, 1964).

[16] James W. Prothro and C. W. Grigg, "Fundamental Principles of Democracy: Bases of Agreement and Disagreement," *Journal of Politics* 22, no. 2 (May, 1960): 276–94.

[17] There is unquestionably a class of social behaviors for which this description is more rather than less apt, although one need not have recourse to mystical or unexplained terms to understand the processes involved. In any social system, some beliefs and behavior patterns are learned by the young in such a way that there is no awareness of the possibility of alternatives. Where beliefs are concerned, a phrase like "unspoken cultural assumptions" provides an appropriate description, and there are analogues in socially learned behaviors. Most of politics, however, involves competition between explicit alternatives, which means that conscious belief systems and conscious behavior choices have an important influence — which is *not* to say that these belief systems are not often better understood if one takes account of the sociostructural position of the actor who holds them. It *is* to say that, whether or not they are present is not a matter of indifference for the course of behavior, as we shall see.

[19] The reader is cautioned, in comparing Fig. 1(b) and 1(c), that women classed (for example) as "no issue content" are not necessarily the wives of husbands who are also "no issue content." Indeed, the point of the comparison is that wives tend themselves to be qualified at less elevated levels than their husbands but organize their behavior in terms of their husband's "opinion leadership."

[20] It should be remembered in assessing Fig. 1(c) that the complete absence of this kind of opinion-leading would not produce a graph with a single tall bar at the left and an absence of height for the three other bars. That is, opinion-leading quite aside, we should expect some kind of slope, albeit a steep one, since people represented by the second and (to a fainter degree) the third bars have cruder versions of the intervening images of politics that we are arguing have key behavioral importance. It is only the people represented by the fourth bar who give no evidence of this type of intervening organization at all.

[21] The empirical base for this argument becomes even more dramatic than is shown by Fig. 1 if we consider all the psychological terms that a class orientation in voting presupposes. That is, Fig. 1 treats the relationship between objective status and vote. To the degree that there are ideologues whose class identifications are not what their objective statuses would lead us to expect, they lower the degree of the association. Figure 13–3 of Campbell et al., *op. cit.,* p. 352, which is conceptually parallel to Fig. 1 of this paper, shows that ideologues with reported awareness of their social classes have a towering monopoly on the association of *subjective status* and vote partisanship.

[22] And if we take as a goal the explanation of political *changes* touched off by movements in mass political decisions in this period, as opposed to questions of more static political structure, then the explanatory utility of the social-class thread is almost nil, for the ideological class voters were least likely to have contributed to these changes by corresponding changes in their voting patterns.

[23] P. E. Converse and G. Dupeux, "Politicization of the Electorate in France and the United States," *Public Opinion Quarterly* 26 (Spring, 1962). For complementary evidence covering an earlier period, see Duncan MacRae, "Religious and Socioeconomic Factors in the French Vote, 1945–1956," *American Journal of Sociology,* 64, no. 3 (November, 1958).

The Structural Nature of Attitudes: an Experimental

Investigation of Attitudes toward the War in Viet Nam

Paul A. Dawson

I. Introduction

American social psychologists and sociologists have recently produced a voluminous literature

Paul A. Dawson, "The Structural Nature of Attitudes: An Experimental Investigation of Attitudes Toward the War in Viet Nam," *Experimental Study of Politics* 1 (1971): 61–86. Reprinted with permission.

concerning what they call "social attitudes"; the term is used to cover a multitude of facts of many kinds including almost every variety of opinion and

This research was supported by a grant from the United States Office of Education, Project No. 7-E-009 and by the generous support of the Department of Political Science and the Human Learning Research Institute, both of Michigan State University.

belief and all the abstract qualities of personality, such as courage, obstinancy, generosity and humility, as well as the units of affective organization which are here called "sentiments." I cannot see how progress in social psychology can be made without a more discriminating terminology.

(McDougall, 1933, p. 219)

Behavioral political scientists probably have the nagging suspicion that McDougall, were he writing today, would be equally critical of their use of the term "political attitude." The concept, to paraphrase Allport (1935), has become something of a factotum for political scientists who take its scientific meaning for granted rather than examine its worth with unusual care. Instead of taking "unusual care" with the conceptual meaning of the term, a strict operationalism is used which tacitly supports the view of an "attitude" as any respondent's answer to any researcher's question. For example, Shapiro has noted the absence of serious theoretical concern with the nature of attitudes in studies of voting behavior.

Most of the original data-gathering enterprises were guided by general theoretical frameworks which, for the most part, were not developed to a point where the ensuing analyses addressed themselves unambiguously to the original conceptions by which they were guided. (1969, p. 1106)

However, it seems unlikely that conceptualization could have "guided" data collection and analysis if the analysis did not in turn address itself unambiguously to the conceptualization. It seems more likely that the concept of attitude is reduced to a convenient label if attempts to measure attitudes are not preceded by, or at least coupled with, a serious concern with the nature of that which is being measured.[1]

This study adopts a particular theoretical view of attitudes to investigate the structural aspect of common attitudes toward the war in Viet Nam. Common attitudes, as distinguished from individual attitudes, are those "which are essentially uniform owing to the operation of similar environmental and cultural conditions upon similarly constituted human beings" (Allport, 1935, p. 826). This study began (in the spring of 1967) with the premise that the issue of the war in Viet Nam had become sufficiently salient so as to create structural uniformity in attitudes toward the war.[2] The research was designed first to determine whether similar attitudes toward the war exhibit similar structure; and second, to investigate the organization of such structures.

II. A Structural Theory of Attitudes

Attitudes are typically viewed as affective responses to objects.[3] This view would hold that the following are examples of "attitudes": (1) a positive feeling toward the President's handling of the war in Viet Nam; (2) an expression of agreement with a statement critical of U.S. policy in Viet Nam; (3) adoption of a pro position on the issue of unilateral withdrawal of U.S. forces from Viet Nam. Thus, in practice, the primary reference of the concept is any degree of emotive or affective response which is associated with some psychological object or situation. This view is desirable because it provides conceptual clarity. It is also desirable and necessary, however, to depart from this simple and somewhat restrictive view of attitudes. After all, an expression of affect is not an isolated free-floating response but rather a conglomerate response which summarizes the evaluative aspects of various cognitions which are associated with the attitude object. This conglomerate response may be derived from a number of sources. What is needed is some view which would identify (1) the cognitive elements which serve as sources of affective responses, and (2) the relationships among such cognitive elements. In other words, what is needed is a structural theory of attitudes.

What is commonly called an "attitude" is then more clearly and correctly seen as an *attitudinal affect*. Thus, a positive feeling toward U.S. policy in Viet Nam is nothing more than a positive attitudinal affect and not a positive attitude *per se*. An attitudinal affect is derived from two major sources. These are (1) beliefs about the object of the attitude (e.g., beliefs that Viet Nam is "not worth saving"), and (2) beliefs about the instrumentality or potentiality of the object for attaining or blocking the realization of valued states (e.g., beliefs that "saving Viet Nam will keep the rest of Southeast Asia from going Communist.")[4]

The structural view proposed here focuses on beliefs about the object of the attitude and is concerned with the organization of such beliefs which, by virtue of their evaluative aspects, underly and support an affective response toward the attitude object. This organization of beliefs may be analyzed in terms of a number of structural dimensions. However, this organization is most simply described in terms of a central-peripheral dimension "wherein the more central parts are conceived as being more salient or important, more resistant to change, and, if changed, as exerting relatively greater effects on other parts" (Rokeach, 1968b, p. 452). Beliefs organized in terms of a central-peripheral dimension therefore exhibit both static and dynamic constraint in a sense similar to Converse's (1964) use of the terms.[5]

The concept of *attitude* therefore refers to a complex organization of more simple cognitive phenomena, i.e., attitudinal affect, beliefs, and values. Attitudes are not therefore investigated directly. Attitudes are investigated by developing and testing theory about the identity and organization of the structural components of attitudes.

III. Operational Procedures

A. The first research problem is to determine whether similar organizations of supporting beliefs are associated with identical attitudinal affects toward the war in Viet Nam. It is hypothesized that, given the saliency of the war in Viet Nam, those who hold either pro or con positions on the issue will exhibit common attitude structures.

On the basis of general knowledge, it seemed that, in one way or another, both pro and con positions on the issue were based on beliefs about the following

aspects of American involvement: (1) the domino theory; (2) the political preferences of the Vietnamese; (3) the capacity of the United States to win the war; (4) the costs of fighting the war; (5) the democratic nature of the government of South Viet Nam; (6) the obligation of the United States actively to resist the spread of communism; (7) the feasibility of a peaceful settlement; (8) Vietnamese attitudes toward American soldiers; (9) the relative Vietnamese–American combat losses; (10) the behavior of Vietnamese youth toward American soldiers; (11) the honesty of Vietnamese governmental officials; (12) the killing of non-combatants; (13) the absolute level of American combat losses.

For each aspect of American involvement, two statements were devised. One statement expressed a belief supporting the pro position and the other expressed a belief supporting the con position on the issue. For example, on the topic of the domino theory, the following two statements expressed beliefs which supported pro and con positions, respectively: "If the communists win in Viet Nam, they will just go after other countries"; "Even if the communists win in Viet Nam, they will not go after other countries." The two belief statements were therefore logical reversals and expressed mutually inconsistent beliefs. This procedure was followed in order to devise two sets of thirteen statements. One set consisted of statements which, on the basis of face validity, expressed beliefs supporting the pro position on the issue of American involvement. Similarly, the second set expressed beliefs supporting the con position on the issue.[6]

The following procedure was used to determine whether those who adopt either the pro or con position on the issue would, as a group, exhibit a common attitude structure. In the early spring of 1967, 50 male and female students in grades nine through twelve of High School (P) completed a one page form on which they first indicated whether they agreed or disagreed with the statement that "The United States should stay and fight in Viet Nam until the communists stop trying to take over that country."[7] The thirteen statements which expressed beliefs supporting the pro position were placed under the "Pro" response and the thirteen statements which expressed beliefs supporting the con position were placed under the "Con" response. After indicating their own position, Ss read through the list of supporting statements and then ranked each in terms of its importance as a reason for holding their position.

B. The second research problem is to investigate the internal aspects of pro and con attitude structures. Two hypotheses are made about the nature of the organization of supporting beliefs in pro and con attitude structures: (1) Central beliefs are more resistant to change than are peripheral beliefs, i.e., organizations of beliefs exhibit a form of static constraint in the sense that initial knowledge of the relative centrality of a belief leads to success in predicting the relative likelihood of change in the belief; and (2) Beliefs are functionally interdependent in the sense that a belief is more likely to change given a change in an associated belief than it is otherwise. These two hypotheses are tested by the following experimental procedure.

In the late spring of 1967, 926 male and female high school students in grades nine through twelve of six public schools in five Michigan communities completed an original paper-and-pencil instrument.[8] Ss first indicated whether they agreed or disagreed with the statement that "The United States should stay and fight in Viet Nam until the communists stop trying to take over that country." Of the 926 students, 700 (76 percent) selected the pro position and 226 (24 percent) selected the con position on the issue. After indicating their own position, Ss were presented with a set of thirteen statements which tended to contradict their supporting beliefs. Each contradictory statement was written on a separate sheet of paper. The contradictory statements were not attributed to any source. Each contradictory statement was presented one at a time although Ss were able to tell that there were a total of thirteen such statements. The Ss received and reacted to each of these statements under the pretext that the researchers wanted them to answer some general (open-ended) questions about the Viet Nam situation. Ss were told that since the researchers realized that some students knew more than others about Viet Nam, all students would first read some statements about Viet Nam and then go on

to answer the general questions. After reading each contradictory statement, written instructions on the same page asked the subjects to judge how important they thought the statement was by indicating whether, given this information, they (1) changed their original position; (2) maintained their original position; or (3) were unsure one way or the other. After finishing the set of thirteen statements, Ss did go on and answer some general open-ended questions about the Viet Nam situation.

The identity and order of presentation of the contradictory statements (hereafter referred to as experimental statements) in the experimental situation were determined by the results reported above from students in a different community. The experimental statements presented to an S with a particular attitude were logical reversals of the beliefs of the same attitude. For example, Ss taking the pro position on the issue in the experimental situation were presented with logical reversals of the pro beliefs previously ranked by different Ss.[9] The order of presentation of experimental statements was also determined by the previous findings. The predetermined least central beliefs were challenged first and the most central beliefs were challenged last by the experimental statements. Since it was not feasible to first determine the attitude structures of the experimental Ss it was assumed that their attitude structures were comparable to those previously found. The research design therefore provided for one control group and six experimental groups. Once common organizations of supporting beliefs were identified for the control group, similar organizations were hypothesized and experimentally tested for in the other six groups.

IV. Results

A. The results of the first operational procedure support the hypothesis of common attitude structure. Of the 50 students in High School (P) who ranked supporting beliefs in terms of their perceived importance, 36 (72 percent) selected the pro position and 14 (18 percent) selected the con position. Analysis of assigned rankings yielded highly significant values of

W ($p < .001$) for both pro and con groups.[10] These values indicate that students who hold the same position also share very similar organizations of the supporting beliefs. At least in the case of this one issue, this is good evidence to justify the conceptualization of common political attitude structures organized in terms of a central-peripheral dimension.

Inspection of the rankings of particular beliefs for both pro and con positions yielded some interesting insights into each attitude structure. While persons with the pro position felt that their belief in the validity of the domino theory was the most important one supporting their position, persons with the con position on the issue felt that their belief in the falsity of the domino theory was the least important reason supporting their position. Similarly, while persons with the pro position felt that their belief that "Not very many Americans are getting killed" was their least important belief, persons with the con position felt that their belief that "Too many Americans are getting killed" was the most important one. An inspection of rankings within each position suggested that persons with pro positions may be primarily concerned with strategic and political considerations (the domino theory, political preferences of the South Vietnamese, the capability of the United States to win), while persons with con positions may be primarily concerned with the human and financial costs of involvement (a high absolute loss of American lives, the relative loss of American to Vietnamese lives—both combatant and non-combatant, and the worthfulness of our financial investment).[11]

B. The experimental results confirm both hypotheses about the organization of beliefs in the attitude structures.

First, more central beliefs in both pro and con attitude structures are more resistant to change than are more peripheral beliefs.[12] Tables 1 and 2 report the percentages of subjects with pro and con attitudes, respectively, who modified their supporting beliefs on trial 1 (most peripheral belief challenged) through trial 13 (most central belief challenged). These percentages are plotted for pro and con *Ss* as propor-

Table 1
Experimental Modification of Supporting Beliefs in *Pro* Attitude Structures

Subjects with Pro *Attitude* ($N = 698$)
Percentage Selecting "Uncertain," Opposite, and Either "Uncertain" or Opposite Response on Trials 1–13

Trial Number	"Uncertain" Response	Opposite Response	Either Defecting Response
1	15.90	8.45	24.36
2	20.20	14.33	34.53
3	18.48	3.58	22.06
4	15.19	8.17	23.35
5	17.48	15.19	32.66
6	15.19	15.04	30.23
7	21.78	19.34	41.12
8	17.19	7.59	24.78
9	15.33	6.45	21.78
10	13.32	12.61	25.93
11	13.90	10.03	23.93
12	16.90	11.60	28.51
13	10.46	6.30	16.17
Over all Trials	16.26	10.67	26.92

Table 2
Experimental Modification of Supporting Beliefs in *Con* Attitude Structures

Subjects with Con *Attitude* ($N = 226$)
Percentage Selecting "Uncertain," Opposite, and Either "Uncertain" or Opposite Response on Trials 1–13

Trial Number	"Uncertain" Response	Opposite Response	Either Defecting Response
1	30.09	30.97	61.06
2	17.26	35.84	53.10
3	26.99	17.70	44.69
4	25.22	24.34	49.56
5	22.19	20.80	42.92
6	24.34	19.03	43.36
7	20.35	22.12	42.48
8	17.26	11.50	28.76
9	25.66	40.26	65.93
10	21.24	15.04	36.28
11	18.14	10.18	28.32
12	24.34	12.39	36.73
13	12.83	11.50	24.34
Over all Trials	21.99	20.90	42.89

tions in Fig. 1 and 2, respectively. A t-test for stationarity indicated that the probability of change in the first six more peripheral beliefs was significantly greater than the probability of change in the second six more central beliefs.[13]

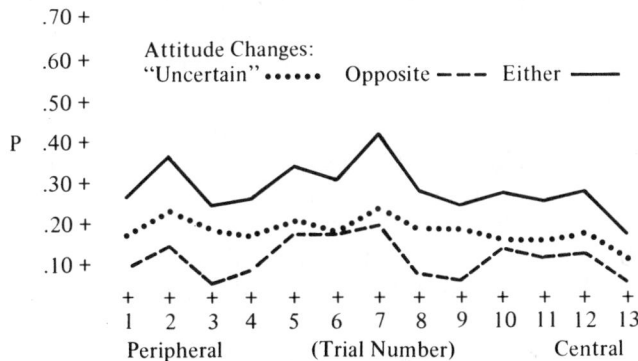

Fig. 1. Successfulness of experimental challenge as a function of centrality of supporting belief in *pro* attitude structures

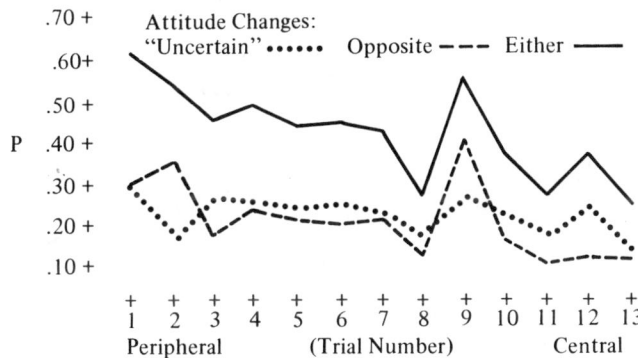

Fig. 2. Successfulness of experimental challenge as a function of centrality of supporting belief in *con* attitude structures

The relationship between centrality and likelihood of change of beliefs is also demonstrated by comparing the relative centrality of each belief with its relative likelihood of change. Accordingly, individual beliefs are ranked by centrality and successfulness of experimental challenge for pro and con attitude structures in Tables 3 and 4, respectively. Correlations between belief centrality and successfulness of experimental challenge are reported for pro and con attitude struc-

Table 3

Supporting Beliefs in *Pro* Attitude Structures Ranked by Centrality and Successfulness of Experimental Challenge

		Proportion of "Uncertain," Opposite, and Either "Uncertain" or Opposite Responses		
Belief	Centrality	"Uncertain"	Opposite	Either
if win, go after more	1	13	12	13
anti-communism of Vietnamese	2	6	6	5
U.S. can win	3	11	7	9
effort is worth cost	4	12	5	6
Viet Nam is a democracy	5	8	11	12
need to contain communism	6	5	10	7
peaceful agreement not possible	7	1	1	1
American soldiers liked	8	9.5	3	4
mostly a Vietnamese effort	9	4	2	3
American soldiers welcome	10	9.5	9	10
Vietnamese leaders honest	11	3	13	11
Communists being killed	12	2	4	2
not many Americans getting killed	13	7	8	8

tures in Table 5. For both attitude structures, there is a significant inverse correlation between the centrality of a belief and the likelihood that the belief was modified by the experimental challenge, where modification is measured by the subject changing from either a pro or con position to one of uncertainty. In addition, for con attitude structures, there is a significant inverse correlation between belief centrality and the likelihood that the experimental challenge resulted in adoption of the opposing position on the issue. A probable explanation for the absence of this relationship for pro attitude structures is that beliefs in pro structures are in general more central than are beliefs in con structures. On the average, pro Ss made 3.45 defecting responses (either "uncertain" or opposite responses) while con Ss made 5.55 defecting re-

Table 4
Supporting Beliefs in *Con* Attitude Structures Ranked by Centrality and Successfulness or Experimental Challenge

		Proportion of "Uncertain," Opposite, and Either "Uncertain" or Opposite Responses		
Belief	Centrality	"Uncertain"	Opposite	Either
too many Americans getting killed	1	13	11.5	13
mostly an American effort	2	5.5	10	9
effort not worth cost	3	10	13	12
innocent people are being killed	4	8	9	10
only desire peace	5	3	1	1
no need to contain communism	6	11.5	11.5	11
peaceful agreement possible	7	9	5	8
American soldiers not liked	8	5.5	7	6
Viet nam is not a democracy	9	7	6	7
American soldiers not welcome	10	4	4	4
Vietnamese leaders not honest	11	2	8	5
U.S. can't win	12	11.5	2	3
not go after more	13	1	3	2

sponses. A *t*-test of the difference between the two means is significant at the .001 level.

Second, the hypothesis of functional interdependence among beliefs in the attitude structures is confirmed by the experimental results. The hypothesis is tested by comparing the conditional probability of a change in belief $n + 1$ given change in belief n with the conditional probability of change in belief $n + 1$ given no change in belief n. For pro attitude structures, the conditional probability of change in belief $n + 1$ given change in belief n is 0.48 as compared with the conditional probability of change in belief $n + 1$ given *no* change in belief n of 0.19. Similarly, for con attitude structures, the conditional probability of change in belief $n + 1$ given change in belief n is 0.60 as compared with the conditional probability of change in belief $n + 1$ given *no* change in belief n of 0.26. The

results of the overall tests of interdependence of adjacent beliefs in pro and con attitude structures are reported in Tables 6 and 7, respectively. In both cases, significant ($p \ll .001$) χ^2 values confirm the hypothesis of functional interdependence.[14]

The finding of functional interdependence of adjacent beliefs in the two attitude structures can also be demonstrated for any pair of adjacent beliefs. The conditional probabilities of change in belief $n + 1$ given change and no change in belief n, along with the simple probability of change in belief $n + 1$, are plotted for pro attitude structures in Fig. 3 and for con attitude structures in Fig. 4. For all pairs of adjacent beliefs, significant (p at least $<.01$) χ^2 values confirm the hypothesis of functional interdependence.

Table 5
Spearman Rank Order Correlations of Belief Centrality and Successfulness of Experimental Challenge

Pro *Attitude Structures*
Successfullness of Experimental Challenge Resulting in . . .

	"Uncertain" Response	Opposite Response	Either Response
Belief Centrality	$r_s = - .68^a$	$- .13$	$- .33$
	$t = 3.07$	$.43$	1.16
	$p < .01$	n.s.	n.s.

Con *Attitude Structures*
Successfulness of Experimental Challenge Resulting in . . .

	"Uncertain" Response	Opposite Response	Either Response
Belief Centrality	$r_s = - .59^a$	$- .80^a$	$- .74$
	$t = 2.43$	4.42	3.66
	$p < .025$	$< .001$	$< .005$

[a]Corrected for ties, one-tailed tests of significance (df = 11).

VI. Conclusions

Since attitudes are inferred from the totality of an individual's affective responses, beliefs, values, and

Table 6
Interdependence of Adjacent Beliefs in *Pro* Attitude Structures

Pooled Transition Frequencies
Belief $n+1$

		Change	No Change	
	Change	1121	1205	2326
Belief n	No Change	1152	4898	6050
		2273	6103	8376

Probability (Change in Belief $n+1$ | Change in Belief n) = .48
Probability (Change in Belief $n+1$) = .27
Probability (Change in Belief $n+1$ | No Change in Belief n) = .19

$\chi^2 = 724.53$ df = 1 $p \ll .001$

Table 7
Interdependence of Adjacent Beliefs in *Con* Attitude Structures

Pooled Transition Frequencies
Belief $n+1$

		Change	No Change	
	Change	729	476	1205
Belief n	No Change	393	1114	1507
		1122	1590	2712

Probability (Change in Belief $n+1$ | Change in Belief n) = .60
Probability (Change in Belief $n+1$) = .41
Probability (Change in Belief $n+1$ | No Change in Belief n) = .26

$\chi^2 = 328.08$ df = 1 $p \ll .001$

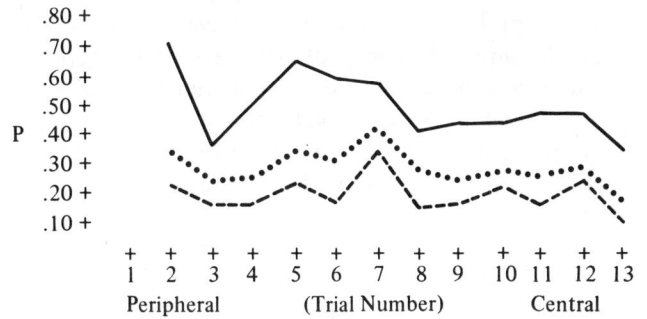

Fig. 3.   **Probability of change in belief $n+1$ given successfulness of challenge to belief n in *pro* attitude structures**

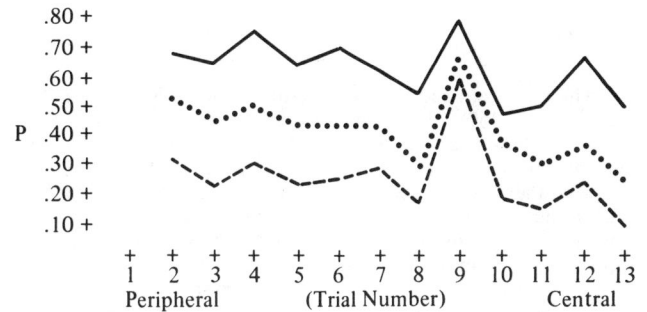

Legend (Fig. 3 and 4):
Probability (Change in Belief n+1/Change in Belief n) ——————
Probability (Change in Belief n+1) ••••••••••••••••••••••
Probability (Change in Belief n+1/No Chnage in Belief n)- - - - - -

Fig. 4.   **Probability of change in belief $n+1$ given successfulness of challenge to belief n in *con* attitude structures**

behaviors toward a psychological object, they cannot be investigated directly. An attitude is a conglomerate response summarizing various cognitions associated with an attitude object. Atheoretical or simplistic operational procedures are likely to lead to erroneous conclusions about the nature of attitudes and their relationships to political behavior. This research was not intended to investigate the relationship between attitudes and behavior directly, but rather to develop and test a particular theory about the structural aspects of attitudes. The latter objective was accomplished for the case of non-elite attitudes toward the war in Viet Nam.

The evidence presented here lends clear support to the view of an *attitude* as an organization of more simple cognitive phenomena, i.e., attitudinal affect and beliefs. Common or essentially uniform attitude structures are identified for aggregates of individuals who held similar positions on the issue of the war in Viet Nam. It is especially striking that these attitude structures were observed for relatively naive, uninformed non-elites. It seems true that there are some political issues—like the war in Viet Nam—which serve as sufficiently salient attitude objects so as to create common attitude structures about those objects. The process by which organization of attitude structures is created remains to be discovered.

The experimental phase of the investigation investigated the internal aspects of attitude structures. Two hypotheses were made about the organization of supporting beliefs in pro and con attitude structures. First, the hypothesis that more central beliefs are more resistant to change than more peripheral beliefs was, in general, confirmed. Second, strong support was found for the hypothesis of functional interdependence of beliefs within an attitude structure.

The results address themselves unambiguously to the theoretical concerns of this study. First, similar affective responses to some issues, like the war in Viet Nam, are associated with shared organizations of supporting beliefs. Second, an attitude can be viewed in structural terms as an organization of beliefs which, by virtue of their evaluative aspects, underly and support an affective response to an attitude object. Beliefs are organized in terms of a central-peripheral dimension so that (1) more central beliefs are more resistant to change than are more peripheral beliefs; and (2) all pairs of adjacent beliefs are functionally interdependent so that a change in a less central belief increases the probability of corresponding change in the next more central belief.

Notes

[1] The practical need for explicit attitude theory is recognized in Verba et al. (1967). The authors found that many of the "tried-and-true" variables (e.g. education, social class, party identification) did not satisfactorily account for the way individuals were able to organize their policy preferences on the war. Without explicit theory, they could do no more than conclude that organized policy preferences are patterned "by the respondent's cognitive and affective relationship to the war itself" (p. 331). For a demonstration of the practical value of explicit theory in formulating and testing rational models of individual voting decisions, see Shapiro (1969).

[2] Common attitudes toward culturally salient political objects are probably created by generally high levels of psychological involvement which minimize the influence of individualistic considerations (race, social class, occupation) as determinates of attitudes.

[3] This view of an attitude as a simple unidimensional concept referring to an affective response dates to the pioneering work of Thurstone (1931); can be favored, as it is by Fishbein (1967b) on the grounds that the concept is most often operationalized as though it were unidimensional, e.g. simply in terms of feelings or evaluations about attitude objects; and is to be preferred because it has provided a common frame of reference for research on attitudes.

[4] The first view of the sources of attitudinal affect is elaborated in Anderson and Fishbein (1965); Fishbein (1963); Fishbein (1965); Fishbein (1967a); Fishbein (1967b); Fishbein and Raven (1962); Kaplan and Fishbein (1969). The second view is developed in Carlson (1956); Peak (1955); Rokeach (1968a); Rokeach (1968b); Rosenberg (1956); Rosenberg (1960a); Rosenberg (1960b).

[5] Converse (1964) takes "static constraint" to mean "the success we would have in predicting, given initial knowledge that an individual holds a specified attitude, that he holds certain further ideas and attitudes" while "dynamic constraint" refers to "the probability that a change in the perceived status (truth, desirability, and so forth) of one idea-element would *psychologically* require, from the point of view of the actor, some compensating change(s) in the status of idea-elements elsewhere in the configuration." "Static constraint" as it is used here has the additional meaning of the success we would have in predicting, given initial knowledge about the centrality of a belief, the relative likelihood of change in the belief.

[6] It might be objected that this approach assumes that (1) the enumeration of beliefs on an *a priori* basis exhausts the set of meaningful beliefs which support either position on the issue, and (2) persons with pro or con positions on the Viet Nam issue have equal nunbers of supporting beliefs. The first assumption was not tested. The concern was not with exhausting such a set but with faithfully reproducing the most important elements of it. While this appeared accomplished, there was no direct test of it. The second assumption appears warranted in light of the finding that persons with pro and con positions on the Viet Nam war issue do not differ in the mean number of supporting and opposing arguments they can report for their positions (Feather, 1969).

[7] Intact classes in courses required for each of the grade levels participated in this procedure. The instrument was administered in a single high school in a small rural community (Community P) in mid-Michigan.

[8] Intact classes in courses required for each grade level participated in the experiment. The five communities differed mostly in terms of degree of urbanization and social class although no data was gathered on such characteristics.

[9] The full series of experimental statements will be provided on request.

[10] For a discussion of W, Kendall's coefficient of concordance, see Siegel (1956).

[11] This relative dominance of strategic over moral or human concerns is also demonstrated for college students (for the early 1960's) in Putney and Middleton, (1962). The authors found that a majority of a sample of about 1,200 college students regarded Communism "as a greater danger than war and (were) thus willing to accept the risks of nuclear war."

[12] It should be recalled that the relative centrality of beliefs in the experimental populations (High Schools, A, B, C, D, and E) was inferred from the rankings of supporting beliefs in the pre-test population (High School P).

[13] Stationarity exists when the probability of a particular re-

sponse remains constant at some value p over the entire series of trials. A t-test based on the mean difference scores of individual response sequences is preferred to a χ^2 test because the latter is not sensitive to trends within each individual's response sequence (Atkinson, Bower, and Crothers, 1965). In this case, a t value of 5.40 for pro S's was significant at $p < .001$ (df = 678) and a t value of 7.40 for con S's was significant at $p < .001$ (df = 225). The relatively high probability of change of some peripheral beliefs indicated that this finding is not simply due to Ss increasing their resistance to the experimental manipulation.

References

Allport, G. W. "Attitudes." In C. Murchison (ed.) *A Handbook of Social Psychology*. Worchester, Mass.: Clark University Press, Pp. 798–844.

Anderson, L. R. and M. Fishbein. "Prediction of Attitude from the Number, Strength, and Evaluative Aspects of Beliefs about the Attitude Object." *Journal of Personality and Social Psychology* 2 (September 1965): 437–42.

Atkinson, R. C., Bower, G. H., and E. J. Crothers, *An Introduction to Mathematical Learning Theory*. New York: Wiley, 1965.

Carlson, E. R. "Attitude Change through Modification of Attitude Structure." *Journal of Abnormal and Social Psychology* 52 (March 1956): 256–61.

Converse, P. E. "The Nature of Belief Systems in Mass Publics." In D. E. Apter (ed.) *Ideology and Discontent*. New York: Wiley, 1964. Pp. 206–61.

Feather, N. T. "Cognitive Differentiation, Attitude Strength, and Dogmatism." *Journal of Personality* 37 (March 1969): 111–26.

Fishbein, M. "An Investigation of the Relationships between Beliefs about an Object and the Attitude toward that Object." *Human Relations* 16 (August 1963): 233–39.

Fishbein, M. "A Consideration of Beliefs, and their Role in Attitude Measurement." In I. D. Steiner and M. Fishbein (eds.) *Current Studies in Social Psychology*. New York: Holt, Rinehart and Winston, 1965. Pp. 107–20.

Fishbein, M. "A Behavior Theory Approach to the Relations between Beliefs about an Object and the Attitude toward the Object." In M. Fishbein (ed.), *Readings in Attitude Theory and Measurement*. New York: Wiley, 1967. Pp. 389–400.

Fishbein, M. "Attitude and the Prediction of Behavior." In M. Fishbein (ed.). *Readings in Attitude Theory and Measurement*. New York: Wiley, 1967. Pp. 477–92.

Fishbein, M. and B. H. Raven. "The AB Scales: An Operational Definition of Belief and Attitude." *Human Relations* 15 (February 1962): 35–44.

Kaplan, K. J. and M. Fishbein. "The Source of Beliefs, their Saliency, and Prediction of Attitude." *Journal of Social Psychology* 78 (June 1969): 63–74.

McDougall, W. *The Energies of Men*. New York: Scribner's, 1933.

Peak, H. "Attitude and Motivation." In M. R. Jones (ed.), *Nebraska Symposium on Motivation*. Lincoln, Neb.: University of Nebraska Press, 1955. Pp. 149–88.

Putney, S. and R. Middleton. "Some Factors Associated with Student Acceptance of Rejection of War." *American Sociological Review* 27 (October 1962): 655–67.

Rokeach, M. "The Nature of Attitudes." In D. L. Sills (ed.), *International Encyclopedia of the Social Sciences*. New York: Macmillan and Free Press. Vol. I. Pp. 449–57. 1968a.

Rokeach, M. *Beliefs, Attitudes, and Values*. San Francisco, Calif.: Jossey-Bass, 1968.

Rosenberg, M. J. "Cognitive Structure and Attitudinal Affect," *Journal of Abnormal and Social Psychology* 53 (November 1956): 367–72.

Rosenberg, M. J. "Cognitive Reorganization in Response to Hypnotic Reversal of Attitudinal Affect." *Journal of Personality* 28 (March 1960): 39–63.

Rosenberg, M. "A Structural Theory of Attitude Dynamics." *Public Opinion Quarterly* 24 (Summer 1960b): 319–40.

Shapiro, M. J. "Rational Political Man: A Synthesis of Economic and Social-Psychological Perspectives," *American Political Science Review* 63 (December 1969): 1106–19.

Siegel, S. *Nonparametric Statistics*. New York: Wiley, 1956.

Thurstone, L. L. "The Measurement of Social Attitudes." *Journal of Abnormal and Social Psychology* 26 (December 1931): 249–69.

Verba, S. et al. "Public Opinion and the War in Vietnam." *American Political Science Review* 61 (June 1967): 317–33.

[14] Independence exists when the probability of a change in any belief is the same regardless of whether change or no change occurred on the preceding trial. The χ^2 test of independence essentially reduces to deciding whether the two conditional probabilities are equal (the probability of change in belief $n + 1$ given change in belief n and the probability of change in belief $n + 1$ given no change in belief n). If these two conditional probabilities are equal, the probability of change in any belief is independent of the probability of change in the preceding belief (Atkinson, Bower, and Crothers, 1965).

8

Political Belief Systems:
Conflict and Change

As we have treated sociological conflict and social cross-pressures as an intervening variable between social factors and political behavior, we now treat conflict within belief systems as a factor which tempers the impact of that belief system on behavior, subsequent attitudes, and the organization of the belief system itself. In short, attitudinal conflict itself has a direct impact on political behavior, changes in attitudes, and perceptions of others' belief systems.

In the previous chapter we discussed a functional theory of attitudinal organization: that attitudes form and change in the context of satisfying such needs as social adjustment and ego defense. Our model also implies that there are other factors which shape attitude organization, e.g., personality,[1] one's capacity for organizing and categorizing objects in the environment,[2] and a set of social influences including the role of primary group contacts and forms of communication.[3]

The Judgment-Involvement Model

One model of attitude organization and change which resembles a blend of conflict theories and social and personality influences is the Sherifs'

[1] T. W. Adorno, et al., *The Authoritarian Personality* (New York: Harper and Row, 1950).

[2] Muzafer Sherif and Carl I. Hovland, *Social Judgment: Assimilation and Contrast Effects in Communication and Attitude Change* (New Haven: Yale University Press, 1961).

[3] See Arthur R. Cohen, *Attitude Change and Social Influence* (New York: Basic Books, 1964); Elihu Katz and Paul Lazarsfeld, *Personal Influence* (New York: The Free Press, 1955).

judgment-involvement model.[4] Although many social psychologists have treated attitudes in terms of the position the individual maintains, Sherif prefers to specify the range of positions which the individual finds acceptable, the range of positions on which he is uncommitted, and the range of positions he must reject. That is, the individual categorizes positions as acceptable, unsure, and rejected, and these categories represent the individual's attitude. For example, an individual cannot have a preferred position on public policy without also being aware of a range of opinions he may also accept (latitude of acceptance), a range that he is uncommitted toward (latitude of non-commitment), and a range which he rejects (latitude of rejection).

Consistent with a conflict theme, when an individual is confronted with a discrepant communication there are two major factors that determine attitude change and reorganization. The first is *ego-involvement,* i.e., his involvement in the attitude being questioned. The political extremist who is highly ego-involved in his beliefs is likely to be beyond persuasion or change. The second factor is *judgment* or the extent to which an individual perceives a communication as disagreeing with his position. The degree to which a communication conflicts with the belief system is determined by the individual's perception of his beliefs, the communication and the distance between them. This judgment process is influenced by the ego-involvement factor so as to determine the latitudes of acceptance, non-committment and rejection. For example, as an individual becomes more ego-involved with his position, the latitude of rejection broadens, the latitude of non-commitment narrows, and the latitude of acceptance may narrow or remain the same. If some form of political communication (e.g., a candidate's policy position) falls within the latitude of acceptance, the individual will assimilate it into his own position; if it falls into the latitude of rejection, a contrast effect will occur and the individual will displace the communication away from his position.

Mediating Factors

Any conflict model of belief systems implies the reception of new and discrepant opinions, messages or information. The total situation in which a message is received determines how it will be perceived and what the individual's response will be. Elements of the situation include the nature of the message, the nature of the source, the group context of the communication, and internal factors relating to the individual's existing belief

[4] For a summary see Muzafer Sherif and Carolyn W. Sherif, "Attitude as the Individual's Own Categories: The Social Judgment-Involvement Approach to Attitude and Attitude Change," in Sherif and Sherif, eds., *Attitude, Ego-Involvement, and Change* (New York: John Wiley & Sons, Inc., 1967), pp. 105–39.

system. The nature of the discrepant message implies that its structure, such as a strong fear—arousing appeal; its organization, e.g., if it is a one-sided communication; and its order, such as those communications presented first, will each have a positive impact on attitude change.[5] In addition, the nature of the source and the individual's group context will influence attitude change. A trusted source, particularly one which interacts with the individual in an intimate environment, will be viewed as a credible source and therefore one likely to be effective in modifying opinions. Not only will friends and acquaintances have a direct impact on attitudes, but often individuals also need a high level of group support for their attitudes, and the perceived expectation of reference group reaction is itself an important component of opinion change.

A final group of mediating elements is that shaped by a person's existing belief system. For example, one's political belief system will shape the extent to which he only recalls information sympathetic to his beliefs (selective retention), the extent to which he misperceives or misinterprets unsympathetic communications and shapes them into supportive opinions (selective perception), and the extent to which he exposes himself to communications that are in accord with existing views (selective exposure).

Cognitive Consistency Theories

Several of the above factors are treated in the readings to follow, but the primary theoretical focus for this chapter is attitudinal conflict theories, collectively referred to as *cognitive consistency theories*. As we have seen in our examples of social cross-pressures within the intimate environment, conflict paradigms have become an integral part of social psychology. The fundamental roots stem from Lewinian conflict theory which posits psychological tensions as a result of conflict. Although it focuses primarily on attempts at conflict reduction before a decision is made, cognitive consistency theories usually focus on the reduction of tension after one has committed himself.[6] Despite these differences and the differences between a set of cognitive consistency theories, the theme is similar: that the individual has a tendency toward consistency in attitude structures, that he will avoid inconsistency-producing stimuli and maintain that balance, and when there is inconsistency, he will change his belief system or attempt to change the environment either psychologically

[5] See generally Paul F. Secord and Carl W. Backman, *Social Psychology* (New York: McGraw-Hill Book Company, 1964), pp. 135ff.

[6] Leon Festinger, ed., *Conflict, Decision and Dissonance* (Stanford: Stanford University Press, 1964), Chapter 2.

(e.g., misperception, rationalization) or behaviorally (so as to rectify an object causing that inconsistency) based upon his motivation to maintain inner harmony with himself and his environment. The basic assumption of cognitive consistency is therefore a striving toward a state of consistency between attitude-objects in one's environment. These objects may be such political objects as candidates, parties, events, or political groups, and, if inconsistency exists, belief-system reorganization, psychological mechanisms or behavioral acts will occur to reduce it.

In general, three models are subsumed under this conflict paradigm. (1) The balance model posits consistency between the individual, another person and an attitude object such that one's affect toward another person is balanced with one's affect toward an attitude object, to which the other person also relates.[7] (2) The congruity model can be viewed as a special case of the balance model with the same basic components: attitudes toward the source and assertions by the source about an object.[8] Whereas the balance model is frequently conceptualized as three points in a triad, one of which is the individual perceiver, congruity is viewed from the respondent's mind as a relationship between two other objects (e.g., a candidate and an issue). The focus is on the direction of attitude change: it occurs in the direction of increased congruity with the prevailing frame of reference. (3) Dissonance theory is not unlike the above models; yet it is more informal, less precise and less mechanistic. Its definition of cognitive elements is broad in scope: "any knowledge, opinions, or belief, about the environment, about oneself, or about one's behavior."[9] Unlike balance and congruity models, there is usually no explicit mention of persons, things, or objects, and the elements of dissonance theory are usually propositions expressed as sentences: e.g., I intend to vote Democratic. A dissonance situation exists when, in dealing with two elements, "the obverse of one element would follow from the other."[10] These non-fitting relations among cognitions lead to attempts at reducing the dissonance, and the situation will be particularly stressful if the objects are salient for the individual.

These inconsistency models may involve cases of logical inconsistency, e.g., "I favor Medicare, Democrats favor Medicare, I will vote Republican," or one specific opinion is sometimes included in a more general opinion, e.g., a Democrat who prefers a Republican candidate in a

[7] For a brief and simple analysis see Robert E. Lane and David O. Sears, *Public Opinion* (Englewood Cliffs: Prentice-Hall, Inc., 1964), pp. 45ff.

[8] See Robert B. Zajonc, "Balance, Congruity and Dissonance," *Public Opinion Quarterly* 24 (1960): 280–96.

[9] Leon Festinger, *A Theory of Cognitive Dissonance* (Stanford: Stanford University Press, 1957), p. 3.

[10] *Ibid.*, p. 13.

specific election; or dissonance may also arise from past experience or cultural morés, e.g., "I like candidate X, but he hates mint juleps." When inconsistency exists the individual may discredit the source, disbelieve the source, change his behavior and attitudes, or he may accept dissonant information and keep his existing belief structure, reducing the dissonance by rationalization or by emphasizing the importance of the consonant elements. A general means for reducing dissonance is to change an environmental element, i.e., changing the environment by changing the situation to which the element corresponds. Resistance to the reduction of dissonance occurs when a change may involve pain or substantial loss (e.g., political patronage), when present behavior may be satisfying (e.g., when the respondent has strong feelings about a candidate), or when a change may not be possible (e.g. when it is not time legally to change one's party registration).

Although there are definitional differences among the subsets of cognitive consistency theory, and although there may be situations where the individual seeks cognitive tension, the underlying principle of consistency has been found to be highly accurate and predictive in current social-psychological research. Variations on these themes are represented by the readings in this chapter.

Perceptions of Other's Beliefs

We have cited attitudinal consistency as a motivating force in attitude change, perception, and political behavior. The research reported by Eckhardt and Hendershot attempts to combine several of the theoretical approaches mentioned above in order to explain levels of political opinion awareness. They cite the need for a theory to incorporate both a sociological approach (social interaction and communication) and a psychological approach (attitudinal and personality components), based upon the assumption that individuals seek to validate opinions (and behaviors) and hold them consistent. This validation may occur by referring them to cognitive patterns (as they reflect the socialization process and political personality) or to group norms, or both.

The strain toward consistency means that one either reorganizes his cognitive set or changes reference group orientations. That is, there are two types of attitudinal conflict: (1) between individual opinions (or behaviors) and one's perception of other's opinions (e.g., public or group opinion); or (2) between individual opinion and one's cognitive set (past cognitions and existing belief system).

Within each type the individual may be consistent or inconsistent, and the two patterns of consistency/inconsistency mesh to provide a typology of relationships. For example, an individual may be congruent on group norms (e.g., with southern opinions on race), but dissonant with his cognitive set if he offers a discriminatory opinion on open housing when his belief system is basically non-prejudiced. An individual's expressed political opinion may therefore lack support from his cognitive set (psychological stress), his reference group or public opinion (social stress), or both. The authors find that those with social congruence but psychological dissonance will validate their opinions through the opinions of others and be more accurately informed of the group feelings. But those with social incongruity (i.e., their liberal or conservative stand on an issue is discrepant from the group) and psychological consonance will validate their opinions through their cognitive set, thereby avoiding social interaction on the issue. Also, if one is subjected to stress in both areas, public opinion will not be sought out and one's assessment of it will tend to be distorted.

Political Activity and Attitude Change

John Kessel hypothesizes relationships between political activity and cognitive organization defined as the amount of political information, one's ability to discriminate (differentiation) between components of information, logical consistency, ability to project into the future and scope of interests. Consistency in responses to questions about the most important problems facing the country, why they are important, and what should be done about them is therefore treated as one among several components of cognitive structure. Almost 70 percent of the respondents were consistent in their responses, and this consistency was moderately related to informational support, ability to differentiate, and concern with future problems. Each of these elements of cognitive structure was then related to various measures of political involvement and activity. Each element, except for scope of interests, was found to relate positively with political activity, yet many of the relationships were weak and not significant statistically. The closest ties were found to exist between cognitive structure and issue-oriented behavior (e.g., talking to others about issues), but the author suggests that the explanation may arise from the focus of the cognitive dimension on issues.

Following a similar theme, the Kirkpatrick study focuses on attitudinal consistency alone, but a variety of measures are incorporated across a national (vs. local) sample of the American population. Primary attention is paid to the relationship between a variety of inconsistency measures of political attitudes and the impact of those inconsistencies on issue and party intensity, the decision time for the vote choice, and political interest and participation. Particularly important relationships were found linking inconsistency with a late decision and with several forms of behavior. As a next step, several additional measures of consistency/inconsistency are examined over time in order to make inferences about attitude change. A variety of findings point to the relatively high level of consistency achieved on political objects, and when this does not exist, the tendency is to reduce that inconsistency in line with the theories postulated above.

Selected Additional Readings

Abelson, Robert P., ed. *Theories of Cognitive Consistency*. Chicago: Rand McNally, 1968.

Bennett, Stephen E. "Modes of Resolution of a 'Belief Dilemma' in the Ideology of the John Birch Society." *Journal of Politics*, 33 (1971): 735–72.

Bowles, Roy T., and James T. Richardson. "Sources of Consistency of Political Opinion." *American Journal of Sociology* 74 (1969): 676–84.

Boyd, Richard W. "Presidential Elections: An Explanation of Voting Defection," *American Political Science Review* 63 (1969): 498–514.

Brehm, Jack W., and Arthur R. Cohen. *Explorations in Cognitive Dissonance*. New York: John Wiley & Sons, Inc., 1962.

Cohen, Arthur R. *Attitude Change and Social Influence*. New York: Basic Books, Inc., 1964.

Feldman, Shel, ed. *Cognitive Consistency: Motivational Antecedents and Behavioral Consequents*. New York: Academic Press, 1966.

Festinger, Leon. *A Theory of Cognitive Dissonance*. Stanford: Stanford University Press, 1957.

Festinger, Leon, ed. *Conflict, Decision and Dissonance*. Stanford: Stanford University Press, 1964.

Finlay, David J., Ole R. Holsti, and Richard R. Fagen. *Enemies in Politics*. Chicago: Rand McNally and Co., 1967.

Hahn, Harlan. "The Political Impact of Shifting Attitudes." *Social Science Quarterly* 51 (1970): 730–42.

Halloran, J. D. *Attitude Formation and Change*. Leicester, England: Leicester University Press, 1967.

Hennessy, Bernard C. "Public Opinion and Opinion Change." In James A. Robinson, *Political Science Annual* 1: 243–96. New York: Bobbs-Merrill, 1966.

Hovland, Carl I., Irving L. Janis, and Harold H. Kelley. *Communication and Persuasion: Psychological Studies of Opinion Change*. New Haven: Yale University Press, 1953.

Jordon, Nehemiah. "Cognitive Balance, Cognitive Congruity and Attitude Change: A Critique." *Public Opinion Quarterly* 27 (1963): 123–32.

Kelman, Herbert C. "Processes of Opinion Change." *Public Opinion Quarterly* 25 (1961): 57–78.

Klapper, Joseph T. "Mass Communication, Attitude Stability and Change." In Muzafer Sherif and Carolyn W. Sherif, *Attitude, Ego-Involvement and Change*, pp. 297–309. New York: John Wiley & Sons, Inc., 1967.

Lipset, Seymour M., et al. "The Psychology of Voting: An Analysis of Political Behavior." In Gardner Lindzey, ed., *Handbook of Social Psychology*, pp. 1124–75. Cambridge: Addison-Wesley Publishing Co., Inc., 1954.

Maccoby, Nathan, and Eleanor E. Maccoby. "Homeostatic Theory in Attitude Change." *Public Opinion Quarterly* 25 (1961): 538–45.

McPhee, William N., Bo Anderson and Harry Milholland. "Attitude Consistency." In W. N. McPhee and W. A. Glaser, *Public Opinion and Congressional Elections*, pp. 78–120. New York: The Free Press, 1962.

Robinson, John P. "Balance Theory and Vietnam-Related Attitudes." *Social Science Quarterly* 51 (1970): 610–16.

Rosenberg, Milton J., et al., eds. *Attitude Organization and Change*. New Haven: Yale University Press, 1960.

Smith, Don. "Cognitive Consistency and the Perception of Others' Opinion." *Public Opinion Quarterly* 32 (1968): 1–15.

Stricker, George. "The Operation of Cognitive Dissonance on Pre- and Post-Election Attitudes." *Journal of Social Psychology* 63 (1964): pp. 111–12.

Sullivan, Denis. "Psychological Balance and Reactions to the Presidential Nominations in 1960." In M. Kent Jennings and L. Harmon Zeigler, *The Electoral Process*, pp. 238–64. Englewood Cliffs: Prentice-Hall, Inc., 1966.

Zajonc, Robert B. "Balance, Congruity and Dissonance." *Public Opinion Quarterly* 24 (1960): 280–96.

Zajonc, Robert B. "Cognitive Theories in Social Psychology." In Gardner Lindzey and Eliot Aronson, eds., *Handbook of Social Psychology*, rev. ed., pp. 320–411. Reading, Mass.: Addison-Wesley Publishing Co., Inc., 1968.

Dissonance-Congruence and the Perception of Public Opinion

Kenneth W. Eckhardt

Gerry Hendershot

Public opinion on social issues is seldom unanimous, and, while its development is a collective process, not all individuals contribute equally to its formation, nor are all members of the public equally informed as to the character and direction of the composite opinion.[1] The discrepancy between one's estimate of public opinion and the actual distribution of opinion in the community has been the focal point of research for several decades.[2] Working primarily within the traditions of their own fields, psychologists and sociologists have been developing complementary but disparate theories in an attempt to explain the differential assessments of public opinion held by individuals. Theorists approaching the problem within the framework of psychology have tended to emphasize attitudinal and personality components in their search for explanatory variables,[3] while theorists in the tradition of sociology have stressed interaction variables and especially the individual's position in the communication network.[4]

As the evidence has accumulated, it has become increasingly evident that as self-contained theories neither approach offers much promise. It is generally established that attitudinal and personality components enter into an individual's perception and

Kenneth W. Eckhardt and Gerry Hendershot, "Dissonance-Congruence and the Perception of Public Opinion," *American Journal of Sociology* 63 (1967): 226–34. Reprinted with permission of the authors and the University of Chicago Press, Copyright 1967 by The University of Chicago.

We gratefully acknowledge the financial assistance provided by the Committee on Faculty Development at the College of Wooster.

assimilation of information[5] and that situational and interactional variables influence the individual's exposure to communication.[6] What is required, therefore, if we are to move toward explaining the differential assessments of public opinion held by individual members, is a general theory which incorporates both perspectives. Such a theory must be flexible enough to include both psychological and sociological variables and yet remain logically consistent and empirically sound. In this paper we attempt to provide such a theory.

Our purpose is to present a theoretical model which generalizes the findings of past research and permits the deduction of empirically testable hypotheses. The body of the paper is divided into two sections: Part I is concerned with theory construction, while Part II presents empirical data supportive of the model.

I. General Theory

The model proposed herein is constructed on the basis of two familiar and widely accepted assumptions.[7] While it is recognized that the assumptions require qualification in certain contexts, they are stated in a universally valid form for purposes of discourse. Assumption 1: Individuals seek to validate their attitudes, opinions, and behaviors. Assumption 2: Individuals seek to make related attitudes, opinions, and behaviors consistent.

Assumption 1 accepts as valid the social psychological notion that individuals are continually engaged in a process of relating their ideas and behaviors to experience. When one speaks of an individual as seeking to validate his behaviors (mental or physical), the reference is to the notion that the individual is continually referring his behaviors to either (1) cognitive patterns he has developed through socialization, (2) group opinions, values, and norms which serve as points of reference, or (3) both cognitive patterns and group opinions, values, and norms.

The level of validation or support required by an individual is, of course, variable and is related to (1) the significance of the behavior to past cognitions and (2) the relevance and centrality of the behavior to membership-reference groups.

Assumption 2 provides the necessary motive power for the individual to either (1) reorganize his cognitive set or (2) orient himself to new reference groups if a discrepancy occurs between his action and sources of validation.

These assumptions and their implications permit the development of a four-cell paradigm which locates the position of an individual for any given point in time.[8]

Relationship of Behavior to Group Opinions, Norms, and Values	Relationship of Behavior to Cognitive Set	
	Consonant	Dissonant
Congruent	Consonant-congruent (situation a)	Dissonant-congruent (situation b)
Non-congruent	Consonant-non-congruent (situation c)	Dissonant-non-congruent (situation d)

An examination of the paradigm reveals that it is constructed on the basis of relationships which exist between the individual's behavior and (1) his past cognitions and (2) reference-group opinions, values, and norms. Where an individual's behavior finds support in his cognitions, the relationship is one of consonance; where it does not, it is one of dissonance. Where an individual's behavior finds support in group

opinions, values, or norms, the relationship is one of congruence; where it does not, it is one of non-congruence.

A hypothetical illustration of these events is provided below.

Type	
Consonant-congruent (situation a)	The discriminatory opinion of a prejudiced southern white is consonant with his cognitive set and congruent with southern public opinion.
Dissonant-congruent (situation b)	The discriminatory opinion of a non-prejudiced southern white is dissonant with his cognitive set but congruent with southern public opinion.
Consonant-non-congruent (situation c)	The liberal opinion of a non-prejudiced southern white is consonant with his cognitive set but non-congruent with southern public opinion.
Dissonant-non-congruent (situation d)	The liberal opinion of a prejudiced southern white is dissonant with his cognitions and non-congruent with southern public opinion.

According to the assumptions on which this paradigm has been constructed, the consonant-congruent individual is the only person who finds it possible to validate his opinion on both dimensions. Individuals who find themselves in any of the three remaining situations—(b, c, and d) dissonant-congruent, consonant-non-congruent, or dissonant-non-congruent—are in either a partial or total state of imbalance—that is, they lack support either from cognitive set or public opinion or from both.[9]

Since we have posited that the individual finds the state of imbalance psychologically and socially uncomfortable, we infer that the individual will attempt to reduce the imbalance in predictable ways. As we are primarily interested in the relationship between individual opinion and public opinion, we analyze the situation of an individual who holds an opinion which may or may not be in balance with his cognitive set and public opinion (group values and norms).

In situation a (consonant-congruent), the individual's opinion can be validated by reference to either his cognitive set or public opinion. Since his opinion is consonant with his cognitive set, he experiences no psychological strain, and since his opinion is congruent with public opinion, whatever interaction he has with others who share similar views only reinforces his own position. Unless his position in the social system requires an assessment of the public position, there exists little or no need for him to actively ascertain and assess the position of others.[10] In terms of psychological utility, the individual is under no pressure to determine accurately the distribution of public opinion, since such knowledge is of little reinforcement value.

In situation *b* (dissonant-congruent), the individual's opinion can be validated only along one dimension: its relationship to public opinion. As the individual has offered an opinion contrary to his cognitive set, he experiences discomfort. This discomfort or dissonance, however, can be reduced, if not eliminated, by seeking the support of others. Since we have posited a relationship of congruency, the individual finds it rewarding to assess the opinion of the public. In fact, the more aware he becomes of the congruence between his opinion and the opinions of others, the greater the validation or support he obtains for his own opinion. Other conditions being equal, therefore, individuals in a dissonant-congruent relationship have greater reason to be more aware of the distribution of public opinion than persons in a consonant-congruent relationship.

Persons in situations *c* and *d* differ markedly in their relationships from persons in situations *a* and *b*. In situation *c*, the individual's opinion and cognitive set are consonant, but he is non-congruent with public opinion. The more visible his deviance, the greater the negative sanctions he experiences from the public. Not only are negative sanctions increased with the visible display of deviance through interaction, but the greater extent to which the public serves as a reference group, the greater his psychological discomfort. His discomfort is reduced by validating his opinion with his cognitive set and by remaining ignorant of public opinion and avoiding interaction on this issue. Whatever motivation the individual origi-

nally possessed for determining public opinion is reduced through contact with the public. In a sense, awareness of public opinion is psychologically and socially punishing. Consonant-non-congruent individuals are therefore less likely to be informed concerning public opinion than consonant-congruents who in turn are less aware than dissonant-congruents.

Individuals who find themselves in situation *d* (dissonant-non-congruent) are confronted with a double dilemma. Validation for their opinions can be found neither through reference to their cognitive set nor through reference to public opinion. Persons in this situation are likely to be unstable in their opinions, cognitive sets, or reference groups. Precisely which relationship will change and under what conditions is subject to a variety of variables, and their examination is beyond the scope of this paper. For reasons developed above, however, the dissonant-non-congruent is unlikely to seek out public opinion, and his assessment of its distribution will be misinformed or distorted. As he is also confronted with a discrepancy between opinion and cognitive set, we can predict instability and a general unwillingness to consciously focus on the issue being discussed by the public.

The general hypothesis generated from the theory concerning the rank order of prediction is as follows: Assuming structural equivalence of social position and access to communication, dissonant-congruents should be the best estimators of public opinion, while dissonant-non-congruents should be the least informed. The rank-order prediction for persons in situations *a* and *c* is less clear since they are intermediate types, but the theory suggests that consonant-congruents should be better predictors of public opinion than consonant-non-congruents, since information acquired by the latter is punitive and serves only to increase discomfort. The rank order for prediction of public opinion is hypothesized to be as follows: best predictors: (1) dissonant-congruents, (2) consonant-congruents, (3) consonant-non-congruents; poorest predictors: (4) dissonant-non-congruents. Having developed the theory, the remainder of this paper is devoted to the presentation of empirical data testing the model.

II. An Empirical Test

In order to test the rank-order predictions generated by the theory, it was necessary to collect data on one dependent and two independent variables. The dependent variable was the accuracy of an individual's estimate of public opinion, while the independent variables were the individual's cognitive set and his opinion on a given issue.

Sample and Methodology

To collect the necessary data, a questionnaire was constructed and administered to a stratified random sample of two hundred undergraduates at a midwestern coeducational liberal-arts college in the fall of 1965. The variables under consideration were operationally defined and measured in the following ways.

Cognitive set. — Prior to the collection of data, a series of opinion items was submitted to a panel of judges composed of students and faculty ($N = 80$). From this series, the panel selected ten items which in their judgment formed a cognitive pattern, that is, were internally consistent along a liberal-conservative dimension. As a reliability check on adequacy and consistency, the items were pretested on seventy-five students. Respondents in the pretest were scored and Likert-scaled according to their responses on the items.[11] Using the upper and lower quartiles as test aggregates, the items were deemed adequate as an index to liberal-conservative cognitive set, since no item possessed a discriminative power of less than .90.

In similar manner, the two hundred respondents in the final sample were scored and Likert-scaled according to their responses to the test items. Respondents in the upper quartile of the Likert scale were classified as possessing a liberal cognitive set and respondents in the lower quartile as possessing a conservative cognitive set.

Individual opinion — Personal opinion for each respondent was measured by his response to the ten opinion items. Respondents were asked to indicate the strength of their opinions for each item on a four-point scale ranging from strong endorsement to strong opposition. Endorsement or non-endorsement of the item measured his opinion on the issue.

Public opinion — The distribution of public opinion for each issue considered by the sample was computed by summing individual opinions on the items. Using the random sample ($N = 200$) as a base, the parameters of public opinions in the college community ($N = 1482$) were estimated. By treating each item as a social issue around which publics were forming, the distribution of ten public opinions was ascertained.

Table 1 presents the items utilized in measuring cognitive set,[12] individual opinion, and the strength and direction of public opinion.

Public-opinion estimates. — For each item on which a respondent recorded his own opinion, he was also asked to estimate the percentage of students in the college community who would basically agree with the stated opinion. In this way it was possible to measure the strength and direction of public opinion of ten issues as they were perceived by the respondents in the sample.

Analysis and Findings

The first step in analysis consisted of classifying individuals according to the relationship between personal opinion and public opinion. The relationship was congruent when an individual's views were in the same direction on a given issue as the majority of the population. The relationship was non-congruent when an individual's views were in the opposite direction from the majority of the population.

This procedure entailed an important assumption. We assumed an empirical *equivalence* between the notion of reference group and public. Our decision to classify individuals as congruent or non-congruent to the public as a reference group follows from that assumption. From a theoretical perspective, the concepts "reference group" and "public" are neither con-

Table 1

The Distribution of Public Opinion on Ten Social Issues in the College Community ($N = 200$)

Direction of Majority Opinion	Strength of Majority Opinion (Percent)
Statements Majority Agreed with:	
A. The United States has a definite responsibility to the free world to prevent the spread of communism	36
B. Red China must be admitted to the United Nations if we are to move toward establishing a lasting world peace	70
C. The President of the United States should use the power of his office to influence the price policies of our major industries whenever necessary	53
D. The Medicare program would be a better program if it were not compulsory for all citizens	59
Statements Majority Disagreed with:	
E. Even if the majority of the members of the United Nations favor the admission of Red China, the United States should continue to oppose Red China's admission	74
F. The seat on the United Nations Security Council now held by Nationalist China should be given to Red China	74
G. Labor unions have a right to require new employees to join the local union	79
H. Management should be allowed to settle its differences with labor without government intervention	57
I. Medicare represents just one more step toward a socialized society where a government makes decisions which properly belong to the individual	54
J. The Medicare bill was a significant step toward meeting the needs of American citizens without encroaching on the sphere of individual freedom	53

terminous nor mutually exclusive. Standard usage in sociological theory indicates that reference groups are real or imaginary collectivities utilized by the individual for self-evaluation and goal direction,[13] while a public is viewed as a large number of persons interacting on a socially open issue through initiating and reacting to communications and opinions.[14] It follows that when public opinion is formed, individuals *may* utilize the public as a reference group. The empirical question is whether a particular public is serving as a reference group for the individual.

We have taken the position that, for our sample of college students, fellow student peers serve as both the public and the reference group. The utility of this assumption has been demonstrated in several articles in order to explain empirical findings.[15] The basis for assuming an identity between reference group and public in our own study stems from the characteristics of the institution and population from which the sample was drawn.[16]

From the theory developed in Part I of this paper, we hypothesized that congruents are more accurate estimators of the direction of public opinion than noncongruents. Table 2 presents the resulting distribution.

An examination of Table 2 reveals that congruents in general were more accurately informed than noncongruents concerning the distribution of public opinion. On the basis of interaction theory, congruents should be more aware of public opinion than non-congruents. Theoretically, non-congruents not only fail to receive support or approval for their own opinions but, since their actions are non-rewarding to others in the public, the result should be reduced communicative interaction.[17]

At this point we invite the reader's attention to an alternate interpretation which also accounts for these findings. It could be assumed that people project their views on others (in this case the public) and that non-congruents simply have the "wrong" opinions, thus resulting in misperception of public opinion. This assumption accounts for the observed differences between congruents and non-congruents, but it does not account for the observed variations *within* each group.

Some congruents perceived public opinion inaccurately, while some non-congruents perceived public opinion accurately. In the projection interpretation, these would have to be regarded as deviant cases. The theory we offer provides an explanation for the differences between congruents *and* non-congruents *and* for the differences within each group. Additional sup-

Table 2
Proportion Accurately Perceiving Public Opinion Among Congruents and Non-Congruents

Direction of Majority Opinion	Congruents and Non-Congruents Accurately Perceiving the Direction of Majority Opinion*					
	Congruents		Non-Congruents			
	Percent	N	Percent	N	χ^2	P
Statements Majority Agreed with:						
A	96	160	79	19	9.64	.01
B	63	129	64	53	0.03	.90
C	55	88	42	92	2.66	.20
D	74	106	49	74	9.22	.01
Statements Majority Disagreed with:						
E	61	136	55	47	.47	.50
F	80	132	60	50	7.92	.01
G	65	141	40	35	7.46	.01
H	47	106	27	71	7.45	.01
I	61	100	36	81	11.37	.001
J	53	92	38	87	2.60	.20

*Sample size varies, since not all respondents answered each item.

port for the dissonant-congruent model was obtained by correlating the proportion of non-congruents correctly perceiving public opinion with the size of the majority in the public. We hypothesized that if interaction was a significant variable, the proportion of non-congruents—those not agreeing with the majority—who failed to accurately perceive public opinion should decrease as the size of the majority increased. If projection accounts for the misperception of non-congruents, there should be little change within the category of non-congruents as a function of the strength of majority opinion. The latter interpretation did not find support, as $r = .74$ ($P < .01$). Thus the size of the majority constituting public opinion significantly influenced the ability of non-congruents to correctly identify public opinion.[18] In view of the supporting data and in the absence of a crucial test of the two theories, our interpretation seems to have greater explanatory power.

The next step was to determine whether introduction of the relationship between individual opinion and cognitive set had any impact on public-opinion awareness. This was accomplished by comparing the individual's opinion with the opinion predicted on the basis of his cognitive set. A respondent's cognitive set had previously been determined by the extent of his endorsement or non-endorsement of a series of liberal-conservative items. To strengthen the analysis, we selected only respondents classified as having a highly liberal or conservative cognitive set—the upper and lower quartiles of the liberal-conservative scale. We then compared the individual's opinion on a given item with his *predicted* opinion on the basis of his scale score and operationally defined the relationship as one of consonance or dissonance.

If the opinion was in the same direction as his cognitive set predicted, the relationship was defined as consonant; if the opinion was in the reverse direction, the relationship was defined as dissonant. This resulted in the classification of individuals into four role situations: consonant-congruents, dissonant-congruents, consonant-non-congruents, and dissonant-non-congruents. The percentage of individuals in each category correctly predicting the distribution of public opinion for each issue was then determined. These data are presented in Table 3.

Formally the hypothesis read: The rank-order prediction of public opinion would descend from dissonant-congruents to consonant-congruents, to con-

sonant-non-congruents, to dissonant-non-congruents. The data were organized according to the hypothesis and cast into the form presented in Table 4.

Examination of Table 4 discloses that the hypothesis was upheld. Of the ten items tested, two (*D* and *H*) resulted in perfect rank ordering of the four dissonant-congruent types, while four others (*A, C, I,* and *J*)

Table 3
Proportion Accurately Perceiving Public Opinion Among Dissonant-Congruents, Consonant-Congruents, Consonant–Non-Congruents, and Dissonant–Non-Congruents*

Item	Dissonant-Congruents I		Consonant-Congruents II		Consonant–Non-Congruents III		Dissonant–Non-Congruents IV	
	Percent	N	Percent	N	Percent	N	Percent	N
A	98	50	88	43	91	11	25	4
B	81	16	79	63	74	31	–	–
C	83	23	59	59	68	28	33	3
D	86	29	77	44	69	35	33	3
E	50	44	73	41	–	2	52	21
F	45	47	29	24	57	23	23	13
G	43	35	39	33	61	28	36	14
H	75	54	64	58	38	40	25	4
I	67	39	76	21	50	44	38	8
J	46	11	56	43	37	51	25	4

*The upper and lower quartiles of the liberal and conservative scales are used in this analysis. Group size varies, since not all respondents answered each item.

Table 4
Rank Order of Dissonant-Congruents, Consonant-Congruents, Consonant–Non-Congruents, and Dissonant–Non-Congruents Correctly Perceiving Direction of Public Opinion*

Item	Dissonant-Congruents	Consonant-Congruents	Consonant–Non-Congruents	Dissonant–Non-Congruents
A	1	3	2	4
B	1	2	3	–
C	1	3	2	4
D	1	2	3	4
E	3	1	4	2
F	2	3	1	4
G	2	3	1	4
H	1	2	3	4
I	2	1	3	4
J	2	1	3	4
Total	16	21	25	34

*Z score for number of successful rank orderings = 3.69; P < .001.

contained only one error. If these are defined as "successful" outcomes, then the probability of the observed ranked orderings is less than .001. It should be noted that dissonant-congruents always predict more accurately than dissonant-non-congruents but that the rank order for consonant-congruents and consonant-non-congruents is less stable.

III. Summary and Conclusions

In this study we have attempted to analyze the relationship between awareness of public opinion (dependent variable) and personal opinion and cognitive set (independent variables) according to a balance model related to the work of Festinger, Heider, and Osgood.[19] In many ways it parallels the efforts of Cartwright, Davis, Newcomb,[20] and others to develop a structural model embodying social psychological postulates.

By comparing personal opinion and cognitive set, we arrived at a structural relationship of consonance or dissonance; by comparing personal opinion and public opinion, we arrived at a structural relationship of congruence or non-congruence. Combining these relationships led to a typology of four types: dissonance-congruence, consonance-congruence, consonance-non-congruence, and dissonance-non-congruence. Given the assumption that people seek to balance these relationships, we derived a model which permitted prediction of which set of relationships led to accurate perception of public opinion.

The model was then tested on a series of public-opinion issues using a random sample of college students. Statistical analysis confirmed the hypotheses generated from the model. Although social position in the communication network was relatively uncontrolled, the theory permits these variables to enter into analysis by linking social psychological theory to the relationships between an individual and others.

The theory is an improvement on those models which explain awareness of group opinion solely on structural position. The latter, for example, fail to explain the differences between persons occupying a similar structural position, that is, why some leaders are more aware of group opinion than other leaders or why some non-leaders are better predictors than leaders.[21] In these instances it would seem necessary to introduce variables which account for the individual's failure to exploit his structural position or for his distorted percepton of public opinion. It is toward the solution of this type of problem that our theory appears to offer promise.

Notes

[1] Conceptually the term "public opinion" is ambiguous. Although most theorists recognize the social-interaction dimension in the development of public opinion, the concept has been operationally defined in a variety of ways, e.g., (1) as the summation of individual opinions on a social issue, (2) what individuals think are the opinions of others, and (3) what a collectivity of individuals has quasi-formally decided to be the "view" of the public. In this article we treat public opinion as the summation of individual opinions on a social issue as they have been shaped by social interaction. For discussions of the theoretical and methodological issues in the concepts "public" and "public opinion," see G. D. Wiebe, "Some Implications of Separating Opinions from Attitudes," *Public Opinion Quarterly* 17 (Fall, 1953): 328–52; H. H. Hyman, "Towards a Theory of Public Opinion," *Public Opinion Quarterly* 21 (Spring, 1957): 54–60; and E. Freidson, "Prerequisite for Participation in the Public Opinion Process," *Public Opinion Quarterly* 19 (Summer, 1958): 91–106.

[2] The most recent treatment of the problem appears to be W. Breed and T. Ktsanes, "Pluralistic Ignorance in the Process of Opinion Formation," *Public Opinion Quarterly* 25 (Winter, 1961): 382–92.

[3] An adequate review of psychological variables and processes is contained in Arthur R. Cohen, *Attitude Change and Social Influence* (New York: Basic Books, 1964).

[4] An enlightened sociological perspective is presented by J. W. Riley and M. W. Riley, "Mass Communication and the Social System" in R. Merton et al. (eds.), *Sociology Today* (New York: Basic Books, 1959), pp. 537–78.

[5] D. Kretch, R. S. Crutchfield, and E. Ballachey, *Individual in Society* (New York: McGraw-Hill Book Co., 1962), pp. 17ff.

[6] A summary of structural variables can be found in R. E. Lane and D. O. Sears, *Public Opinion* (Englewood Cliffs, N.J.: Prentice-Hall, Inc., 1964), pp. 33ff.

[7] These assumptions are drawn from the literature and are given extended treatment in the theories of Leon Festinger, *A Theory of Cognitive Dissonance* (Evanston, Ill.: Row, Peterson & Co., 1957); Fritz Heider, *The Psychology of Interpersonal Relations* (New York: John Wiley & Sons, 1958); and C. E. Osgood and P. H. Tannebaum, "The Principle of Congruity in the Prediction of Attitude Change," *Psychological Review* 62 (1955): 42–55.

[8] In this paper we are not concerned with the dynamics of opinion change but only the individual's ability to assess public opinion at a given time. Only in situation *a*, however, is the individual not under some pressure (either psychological, social, or both) to change his position.

[9] Here we are considering only the relationship between personal opinion and public opinion. Although the individual may lack support from the public, he may find support in other membership-reference groups.

[10] Clearly some individuals find it more necessary to be informed of group public opinion than others. See K. Chowdhry and T. M. Newcomb, "The Relative Abilities of Leaders and Non-Leaders to Estimate Opinions of Their Own Groups," *Journal of Abnormal and Social Psychology* 47 (1952): 51–57.

[11] W. J. Goode and P. K. Hatt, *Methods in Social Research* (New York: McGraw-Hill Book Co., 1952), pp. 270ff.

[12] Endorsement of items *A, D, E, H,* and *I* and opposition to items *B, C, F, G,* and *J* measured the conservative cognitive set, while the reverse pattern constituted the liberal cognitive set.

[13] See, e.g., Tamotsu Shibutani, *Society and Personality: An Interactionist Approach to Social Psychology* (Englewood Cliffs, N.J.: Prentice-Hall, Inc., 1961), pp. 249ff.

[14] Cf. Arnold Rose, "Public Opinion Research Techniques Suggested by Sociological Theory," *Theory and Method in Social Sciences* (Minneapolis: University of Minnesota Press, 1954), pp. 210–19.

[15] See, e.g., Theodore M. Newcomb, *Personality and Social Change* (New York: Dryden Press, 1943); Peter Blau, "Orientation of Students toward International Relations," *American Journal of Sociology* 59 (1953): 205–14; and James A. Davis, "The Campus as a Frog Pond," *American Journal of Sociology* 72 (1966): 17–31.

[16] The sample was drawn from a small, liberal-arts, residential institution which restricts the opportunity for students to interact with others and therefore to form significant membership-reference groups beyond the college community. The social-class and ethnic homogeneity of the student body further constrains the development of multiple student subcultures of the type available at larger, more heterogeneous universities. In a study of a similar type, Blau remarks on the social pressure of student peers: "These findings suggest that it is not primarily the logical inconsistency of a student's political ideology but rather the influence of his or her associates which induces a strain towards consistency" (*op. cit.*, p. 210).

[17] S. Schachter makes this point very clear in his article "Deviation, Rejection and Communication," *Journal of Abnormal and Social Psychology* 46 (1951): 190–207.

[18] M. J. Rosenberg and R. P. Abelson make this point indirectly when they suggest that another way of coping with imbalance is to "stop thinking" about the elements which have fallen into an imbalanced configuration. To "stop thinking" about the imbalance requires at a minimum avoiding communicative interaction about the discrepancy (M. J. Rosenberg, C. I. Hovland, W. J. McGuire, R. P. Abelson, and J. W. Brehm, *Attitude, Organization and Change: An Analysis of Consistency among Attitude Components* [New Haven, Conn.: Yale University Press, 1960]).

[19] Festinger, *op. cit.;* Heider, *op. cit.;* Osgood and Tannebaum, *op. cit.*

[20] Dorwin Cartwright and Frank Harary, "Structural Balance: A Generalization of Heider's Theory," *Psychological Review* 63 (1956): 277–93; James Davis, "Structural Balance, Mechanical Solidarity, and Interpersonal Relations," *American Journal of Sociology* 68 (1963): 444–62; and Theodore Newcomb, "An Approach to the Study of Communicative Acts," *Psychological Review* 60 (1953): 393–404.

[21] See, e.g., Chowdhry and Newcomb, *op. cit.*

Cognitive Dimensions and Political Activity

John H. Kessel

A model of public opinion that relies primarily on demographic characteristics and politically significant events is deficient in an important respect. It cannot explain why two individuals respond differently to the same environment. The job an individual holds, his opportunities for social mobility, and the speeches and news he hears are independent variables that may ultimately affect his behavior. However, we cannot neglect the intervening variables of perception and cognition if we wish to understand this behavior. Individuals have different ways of structuring external reality. Consequently, we must be aware of the distinctive ways in which people organize their awareness of events.

Too little attention has been devoted to cognitive dimensions—differentiation, hierarchy, space perspective, and so on—as a possible explanation for varying forms of political behavior. The literature has grown richer in recent years, but most of it has been based on experimental evidence rather than studies of larger populations.[1] There have been few attempts to relate cognitive or affective dimensions directly to political behavior.[2] Most survey data, of course, do not lend themselves to such analysis. There is no way of measuring any cognitive dimensions when the respondents are simply asked to tell whether the President is doing an excellent, good, fair, or poor job. This paper reports a study in which a number of steps were taken to make it possible to discern cognitive organization and relate this to political activity.

A series of open-ended questions was designed to give the respondent an opportunity to talk at some length. The first question—"What do you believe is the most important problem facing the country right now?"—gave the respondent a chance to select a topic with which he was familiar. Two follow-up questions—"Why do you think _____ is the most important problem facing the country right now? What do you think the government should do about this situation?"—encouraged him to discuss his view of the political world. The interviewers were given strict instructions to record the answers verbatim in order to obtain data rich enough to make analysis possible. A sample of 140 registered voters was drawn from upper-middle-class precincts located close to the University of Washington in the hope that the respondents would be well enough educated to have something to say about public affairs. A number of standard indices of political activity were included elsewhere in the schedule to permit comparisons between the cognitive dimensions and political behavior.

Cognitive Dimensions

It proved possible to order the data along five separate cognitive dimensions. The properties that could be measured were informational support, differentiation, logical consistency, time span, and space perspective. In two of these cases, it was necessary to select particular responses to serve as cutting points between successive magnitudes. Otherwise, it was

John H. Kessel, "Cognitive Dimensions and Political Activity," *Public Opinion Quarterly* 29 (1965): 377–89. Reprinted with permission.

possible to define the magnitudes in such a fashion that they were separate and exhaustive.

Informational support. Perhaps the most obvious attribute was informational support, the amount of information the respondent revealed in his answer. This was separated into three magnitudes by selecting two responses as boundaries. The answer that served as the cutting point between "little or no informational support" and "some informational support" was:

What do you believe is the most important problem facing the country right now? Oh, there are so many. Peace, I suppose . . .

Why do you think peace is the most important problem facing the country right now? To preserve mankind.

What do you think the government should do about this situation? It might be good if we straighten out our racial difficulties and set an example. Also carrying the big stick policy is good.

The demarkation between "some informational support" and "much informational support" was:

Problem? That's a good question. Probably the biggest thing is the economic problems developing because of automation, unemployment.

Why? We're going to have to increase work for these unemployed people. So many things stem from that. Political things stem from it.

How? Hmmmm. The government is the people. What should or can the people do about it? I think . . . one thing that might help would be the encouragement of smaller businesses. Tax aids of some sort would help these people.

If a response showed less information than the first cutting point, it was placed in the low magnitude. If it had more information than the first demarkation, but less than the second, it went into the middle magnitude. And if it had more information than the second cutting point, it was placed in the high magnitude.

Differentiation. The second property is the ability

to discriminate between distinct components of information. Following Zajonc, the number of discrete elements of knowledge in each response was taken as the indicator of the degree of differentiation. The low magnitude, little differentiation, was defined as that set of responses in which the respondent was unable to resolve his information into more than a single element. The next magnitude, moderate differentiation, was made up of the responses that contained two to six discrete components. Any answer containing more than six elements was classified as one exhibiting much differentiation.

Logical consistency. The third property is similar to differentiation in that both refer to the cognitive elements that compose the statement. The difference is that, while differentiation was defined on the basis of the number of components, logical consistency refers to the linkage between the components. The responses were divided into two classes, consistent and not consistent. This rudimentary scaling operation depended on one response that served as a cutting point:

Problem? Economic strength.

Why? Well, we have to provide . . . a . . . um . . . good life for our children.

How? Well, it should protect integrity of the dollar. It should . . . a . . . use the best wisdom for protection of the dollar.

Time span and space perspective. The last two attributes depended on the way the respondents discussed politics rather than on the content of their statements. The time span of a particular answer was scaled according to whether the concern of the respondent was with the events of the day, phenomena that would be important in the next few years, or problems of the next few decades. Space perspective was coded in a similar manner. If the effects, or reasons for concern, were essentially personal or local, the response was placed in the low magnitude. Statements with implications for national affairs were placed in the middle category. Responses concerning international affairs were placed in the high magnitude.

Table 1 contains the examples used in scaling in-

Table 1
Magnitudes Used in Scaling Cognitive Dimensions

Dimension and Magnitude	Example
Informational support:	
None	*Problem?* Gosh, I don't even think of such things. I don't want to answer anything like that.
Some	*Problem?* Foreign relations. *Why?* It seems like we're having trouble right now getting along with some countries like France and Russia and African countries. We need to improve our relations because we need all the friends we can get. *How?* I think we should try to get along better and stop forcing ourselves on others too much and try to see their viewpoint more. We should have more talks with the leaders of foreign countries.
Much	*Problem?* How to allocate our economic resources. *Why?* This determines what your effort is going to be in the military, and so forth. What the country puts its efforts to is going to be its policy ten or twenty years from now. *How?* Well, I'm a realist in politics. . . . I'd like to see the government determine their goals and then emphasize them to the people. . . . The Bowles Report on foreign aid. Should we have a security or economic type of foreign aid? We aren't trying to set up dictatorships in countries. . . . Kennedy has determined that juvenile delinquency is a problem and unemployment is a problem. He is trying to reach that now. . . . Tax reduction. Kennedy gave a little bit to everybody. I'm not idealist enough to think he could cut out all taxing.
Differentiation:	
Little	*Problem?* Spending the public's money so indiscriminately. *Why?* I believe in sound fiscal policy. Unsound finances are personally obnoxious to me. I don't conduct my own affairs that way. *How?* I don't know. Ummm . . . I think the government should appoint people who can balance a budget. And that people should elect representatives who can.
Some	*Problem?* Domestic economy. *Why?* Without a sound fiscal program we won't be able to worry about any other problems.

Dimension and Magnitude	Example
	How? Strive for a balanced budget and help to create a climate productive of reasonable profits in the private sector.
Much	*Problem?* Economics. *Why?* I think the Common Market has potential importance since I lived in England very very long, you know. We can't divorce ourselves from the economics of the world, you know. The tariffs are very important, for instance, in Germany and Japan. We cannot ignore these things in today's world. *How?* Well, that's a very tough question. . . . We can't do very much with DeGaulle acting as he is. We need more education. This I feel very strongly on. After all, I say, we do need education to handle our great technical fields. Without this we have nothing.
Logical Consistency:	
Not consistent	*Problem?* Cuba. *Why?* We should blast Cuba off the map. I don't care why. Just do it. It should be obvious why. *How?* It's hard to say really. I am really not one to say like my husband was. We should stop sending all our money to the Commies. And we should make all the draft dodgers and those Commies at U. W. [University of Washington] fight on the front lines some day. My ex-husband was a retired Army man, you know. . . .
Consistent	*Problem?* People wanting too much from the government. *Why?* It's forcing the government to grow too large. It's destroyed the people's will to do things for themselves. *How?* First of all I guess it should try not to get bigger. And try to restore the dignity of free enterprise and get over the campaign of making profit a dirty word.
Time Span:	
Immediate	*Problem?* Cuba. *Why?* Last evening's newspaper, and ah . . . the Russian statement about World War III.

Table 1 (continued)

Intermediate   *Problem?* The Cuban question.
            Why? The Cuban question holds the key to what the government can do to stop communism in the Western Hemisphere.
            How? We've got to completely isolate Cuba for one thing.

Long-range   *Problem?* To put our particular ideological system over to the rest of the world.
            Why? Because it will have important long-range consequences on the entire world.

How? The most important thing would be to practice what they preach and not to be inflexible toward possible social changes that would be under the heading of democratic socialism, even though I'm a capitalist. Give the world what they want in terms of socio-economic changes and do it in a democratic manner as opposed to an authoritarian manner.

Table 2
Frequency Distribution along Cognitive Dimensions

Dimension	(Number)	Percent*
Informational Support:		
Little or none	(64)	45.7
Some	(53)	37.9
Much	(20)	14.3
Differentiation:		
Little	(46)	32.9
Some	(63)	45.0
Much	(25)	17.9
Logical Consistency:		
Not consistent	(33)	23.6
Consistent	(97)	69.3
Time Span:		
Immediate	(48)	34.3
Intermediate	(47)	33.6
Long-range	(29)	20.7
Space Perspective:		
Personal or local	(17)	12.1
National	(45)	32.1
International	(70)	50.0

* Percentages do not add up to 100 because some responses could not be scaled, or served as cutting points.

formational support, differentiation, logical consistency, and time span.

Scaling the answers in this way resulted in having an adequate number of responses in each magnitude. The marginal distributions for informational support, logical consistency, and space perspective were skewed in one direction or the other. But, as a glance at Table 2 will show, there was a sufficient number of cases in each category to permit the analysis to go forward.

The final question about the scaling was whether the dimensions thus identified were independent of each other. The distributions of the marginals implied that they were, but these alone were not sufficient evidence. Therefore, rank-order correlations were computed for each pair of dimensions, using the gamma test for grouped data.[3] The results are shown in Table 3.

Table 3
Rank-order Correlations between Cognitive Dimensions

Dimension	Differentiation	Logical Consistency	Time Span	Space Perspective
Informational support	.92	.62	.31	.27
Differentiation		.55	.55	.30
Logical consistency			.56	−.10
Time span				.25

The only correlation high enough to raise a serious question about the independence of the attributes is between informational support and differentiation. However, the different relationships between these two dimensions and time span give some confidence that they are independent. And there should be a close relationship between these dimensions, since possession of information is a *sine qua non* for the ability to differentiate that information into distinct components. Otherwise, most of the relationships are strong enough to remind us that we are dealing with the cognitive characteristics of one set of individuals, but not so strong as to cause concern that we might be measuring the same phenomenon in five different ways.

Relationships between Cognitive Dimensions and Political Activity

In order to ascertain whether the cognitive dimensions had any bearing on political activity, a number of standard questions about forms of participation were included in the schedule. These included the Survey Research Center questions about voting frequency, campaign participation, political interest, and party identification; the Lazarsfeld-Katz pair of queries on opinion leadership; and some items on the respondent's voting history. When the data obtained from these questions were arrayed against the cognitive dimensions, relationships could be found for every cognitive attribute except space perspective.[4]

Opinion leadership. The strongest relationships between the cognitive dimensions and the varying forms of political activity were obtained in the case of opinion leadership. Following an extensive series of questions on issues, the respondents were asked the Lazarsfeld-Katz questions about the frequency of their discussions about issues and the role they played in these conversations.[5] Respondents who took part in such conversations occasionally and tried to convince others, and those who held discussions frequently and took at least equal part in these conversations were classified as opinion leaders. All others were categorized as not being opinion leaders. As Table 4 shows, the higher a person ranked on any of the four cognitive dimensions, the greater the likelihood that he was an opinion leader.

A similar question from the Survey Research Center series asked whether the respondent tried to talk any person into voting for any particular candidate

during the preceding campaign. Analysis of the answers to this question showed that a high ranking on any of the four cognitive dimensions was also associated with a tendency to argue in behalf of a favored party or candidate. The relationships were slightly weaker than those obtained for opinion leadership on issues, but they were perfectly consistent with the data in Table 4.

Table 4
Opinion Leadership in Terms of Cognitive Dimensions

| | Opinion Leadership | | | |
| | Yes | | No | |
Cognitive Dimension	Percent	(N)	Percent	(N)
Informational Support:				
Little or none	20.3	(13)	79.7	(51)
Some	37.7	(20)	62.3	(33)
Much	65.0	(13)	35.0	(7)
$\chi^2 = 13.13, p < .005$				
Differentiation:				
Little	21.7	(10)	78.3	(36)
Some	31.6	(20)	68.4	(43)
Much	64.0	(16)	36.0	(9)
$\chi^2 = 12.19, p < .005$				
Logical Consistency:				
Not consistent	15.2	(5)	84.8	(28)
Consistent	42.3	(41)	57.7	(56)
$\chi^2 = 7.69, p < .01$				
Time Span:				
Immediate	29.2	(14)	70.8	(34)
Intermediate	31.9	(15)	68.1	(32)
Long-range	55.2	(16)	44.8	(13)
$\chi^2 = 5.73, .10 > p > .05$				

Political participation. Nor was the apparent influence of the cognitive dimensions limited to opinion leadership. In the same series of questions that inquired whether the respondents tried to talk persons into voting for a candidate, the respondents also were asked whether they had given any money to a political organization, gone to any political meetings, belonged to any political organization, or displayed a campaign button or bumper sticker. The responses to these queries were combined into a scale reflecting participation in campaign activities.[6] Although the relationships between this scale and the cognitive dimensions were not statistically significant, there were positive associations between them. The same is true of the reported frequency of voting and the level of political interest between campaigns.[7] Table 5 shows the relationships between these forms of political participation and differentiation.

Partisanship. Data were gathered about both subjective party identification and the actual voting behavior of the respondents. Scales were constructed on the basis of these sets of data reflecting both direction of partisanship (Strong Republican to Strong Democrat) and strength of partisanship (Strong Partisan, Weak Partisan, Independent). Each of these scales was analyzed in terms of cognitive dimensions, but no relationships were found.

Discussion

Throughout the analysis, the strongest relationships were found between well-scaled cognitive dimensions and issue-oriented political behavior. The relationships were weak or nonexistent when scaling problems were encountered or when the activity had little to do with issues. For example, space perspective was not associated with any of the political activities. This may have been caused by scaling difficulties. It proved difficult to construct a space perspective scale so as to reflect the respondent's natural tendency rather than the content of the response. The basis of classification was supposed to be the reason the topic was thought to be of concern rather than the subject itself. Thus the subject of Cuba could exhibit personal space perspective if the respondent said he was afraid members of his family would be drafted, national space perspective if it was said that needed defense

Table 5
Political Participation in Terms of Differentiation

Number of Campaign Activities	Differentiation					
	Little		Some		Much	
	Percent	(N)	Percent	(N)	Percent	(N)
0	39.2	(20)	51.0	(26)	9.8	(5)
1	34.1	(15)	46.4	(20)	19.5	(9)
2–3–4	28.2	(11)	43.6	(17)	28.2	(11)
$\chi^2 = 5.16, .30 > p > .25$						
Political Interest:						
Follows politics not much at all	44.4	(8)	44.4	(8)	11.2	(2)
Follows politics fairly closely	32.4	(25)	51.9	(40)	15.7	(12)
Follows politics very closely	33.3	(13)	38.5	(15)	28.2	(11)
$\chi^2 = 3.93, .50 > p > .30$						
Voting Frequency:						
Some elections or no elections	53.8	(7)	38.5	(5)	7.7	(1)
Most elections	32.8	(24)	49.3	(36)	17.9	(13)
All elections	31.3	(15)	45.8	(22)	22.9	(11)
$\chi^2 = 3.98, .50 > p > .30$						

expenditures would cut the budget available for welfare programs, and international space perspective if the Cuban situation was considered in the light of hemispheric relations. But it requires a rather sophisticated argument to place an international problem in a domestic setting, and the fact that the space perspective scale is skewed in an international direction probably reflects the large number of people who mentioned some international problem, rather than their own cognitive sets.

The nature of the interview schedule may also have led to our finding strong relationships with issue-oriented activities rather than with other forms of political behavior. The data that were classified to form the cognitive dimensions, after all, were obtained by asking the respondents about issues. It should not surprise us that the cognitive dimensions thus established showed a close association with opinion leadership on issues and discussion of issues during the campaign. As the political activity became less and less proximate to issues, the relationships between the cognitive dimensions and the political behavior fell off. It is possible that a research instrument with a different focus might show stronger relationships between cognitive dimensions and other forms of political behavior. In short, this investigation seems to establish an association between certain cognitive dimensions and some forms of political activity. Variations in the design of future research may reveal additional linkages.

Representativeness of the Sample

Analyses of data concerning limited populations usually end at this point. There is a statement to the effect that if the sample drawn from San Antonio (or Peoria or Syracuse) may be taken as representative of the United States, then we may draw certain implications about the American political process. This is a risky assumption. Everyone who has been forced to rely on it knows that a sample drawn from a particular locality probably resembles the national population in some respects and differs in others. The problem is that we have not had sufficiently accurate estimates of the degree to which our limited samples correspond to more inclusive populations.

Happily, the organization of the Inter-university Consortium for Political Research has changed this situation for the better. Now that we have access to high-quality Survey Research Center data about national populations, comparison of local samples with national samples is a simple matter. We need but include some of the same questions in our interview schedules that the Survey Research Center uses in theirs. The resulting data tell us exactly how our local sample is different, and in what respects it can be relied on. Such a comparison is made in Table 6.

Table 6
Comparison of U.S. and Seattle Samples
(*in percent*)

	U.S.*	Seattle
Education:		
Grade school only	29.8	2.1
Some high school	18.7	2.9
High school graduate	23.9	12.9
Some college	13.3	30.0
College graduate	13.5	50.7
Reported income:		
Under $3,000	20.8	4.3
$3,000–$6,000	30.6	13.6
$6,000–$10,000	28.8	18.6
$10,000–$15,000	9.7	27.1
Over $15,000	4.9	28.6
Religion:		
Protestant	73.4	72.8
Catholic	20.1	12.9
Jew	3.4	7.1
Party Identification:		
Strong Democrat	24.0	8.6
Weak Democrat	24.3	9.3
Independent Democrat	7.5	13.6
Independent	8.1	7.9
Independent Republican	6.5	12.1
Weak Republican	16.9	21.4
Strong Republican	12.7	27.1

*Source: ICPR Survey, Fall 1962.

The crucial question about a limited population is whether the phenomena observed result from special characteristics of that population. The demographic characteristics in Table 6 tell us that our Seattle sample clearly is better educated, wealthier, and more Republican than the national population. Therefore we are led to ask whether the observed cognitive characteristics might have resulted from formal education. The answer is that they did not. The gamma rank-order correlations between educational level and the five cognitive dimensions are: informational support .10, differentiation .18, logical consistency .03, time span − .03, and space perspective .08. The cognitive dimensions are substantially independent of the level of formal education. Therefore, we may conclude that they do not result from educational attainment.

Now, what about the Seattlites' political activities? Our sample is much more interested in politics than a typical group of Americans, and they are much more extensively involved in politics. But, as Table 7 shows, this hyperactivity does not change the kinds of activity in which they are likely to engage. The ordering of the types of campaign activity is the same for the Seattle sample as for the national sample. With the exception of political contributions (which can be explained by the relative affluence of the Seattle residents), there is also a rough similarity in the proportions engaging in each activity. For example, in both samples about twice as many people engaged in discussion of issues or candidates as wore a campaign button or displayed a bumper sticker. So we can have some confidence that the selection of this particular

sample magnified the phenomenon in order that it could be studied on a statistical basis, but it did not distort its nature.[8]

There is one important respect in which our Seattle sample may reflect a regional rather than a national pattern. One of the most interesting findings in the national data resulted from an analysis by region of the responses to the query: "Did you talk to any people and try to show them why they should vote for one of the parties or candidates?" Eighteen and .3 percent of the respondents replied that they had, and this proportion accurately reflected the situation in the Midwest and the South. But in the East the percentage of those engaging in campaign discussions fell to 9.9 while in the West it rose to 30.8.[9] Politics is different in the West. This particular statistic summarizes much of the difference. In the East, party loyalty and political organization seem to set the tone of politics. In the West, the nonpartisan heritage is still strong and neighbors like to talk of the *men* they intend to support at election time.

All of this adds to our knowledge about the political stratum of society.[10] There is an apparent linkage between a well-informed, detailed cognizance of the political process and participation in various political activities. Whether this perspicacity leads to political involvement or whether acumen increases as a result of political experience, we do not know. Nor are we certain that we shall be able to find these relationships in a study of a more typical population. But on the basis of the evidence thus far, this certainly seems to be a vein worth exploring.

Table 7
Comparison of Campaign Participation of U.S. and Seattle Samples: Percentages Engaging in Specific Activities

	Discuss Parties or Candidates	Make Contribution	Wear Button or Display Bumper Sticker	Attend Meeting or Rally	Belong to Political Organization
U.S.	18.3	9.7	9.6	7.9	3.8
Seattle	47.1	42.1	26.4	24.3	10.0

Notes

[1] M. Brewster Smith, Jerome S. Bruner, and Robert W. White, *Opinions and Personality* (New York: Wiley, 1956); Daniel Katz, ed., *Public Opinion Quarterly* (Special Issue on Attitude Change) (Summer 1960); Robert B. Zajonc, "The Process of Cognitive Tuning in Communication," *Journal of Abnormal and Social Psychology* (1960): 159–167; and Robert E. Lane, *Political Ideology* (New York: Free Press of Glencoe, 1962). My own attention was drawn to the importance of this subject by lectures given by Herbert Hyman at Columbia University in 1954.

[2] An important exception is the work of Milbrath and Himmelstrand. See Ulf Himmelstrand, *Social Pressures, Attitudes and Democratic Processes* (Stockholm: Almquist and Wiksell, 1960); Lester W. Milbrath, "Latent Origins of Liberalism-Conservatism and Party Identification: A Research Note," *Journal of Politics* (November 1962): 678–88; and Milbrath and Himmelstrand, "A Proposal to Conduct a Cross-cultural Study of Constitutional Beliefs," April 1963, mimeographed.

[3] For a description of this measure, see Morris Zelditch, *An Introduction to Sociological Statistics* (New York: Holt, Rinehart & Winston, 1959), pp. 180–83, or L. A. Goodman and W. H. Kruskal, "Measures of Association for Cross-classifications," *Journal of the American Statistical Association* (1954): 732–34.

[4] Space perspective was the least satisfactory scale developed. As Tables 2 and 3 show, the distribution was badly skewed, and space perception had the weakest relationships with the other dimensions. In part, this is probably due to the subject matter of the responses. This is discussed below.

[5] "When you get together with your friends do you discuss topics such as these issues facing the nation and state frequently, occasionally, or never? I am going to read four statements to you. I'd like you to tell me which one best describes your role in these conversations. a. Even though I have my own opinions I usually just listen. b. Mostly I listen, but once in a while I express my own opinions. c. I take an equal share in the conversation. d. I do more than just hold up my end of the conversation; I usually try to convince others that I'm right."

[6] Although campaign discussion was part of the Survey Research Center series of questions, it was excluded from this scale because of the already identified relation between it and the cognitive dimensions. This avoided biasing the scale in favor of a relationship between campaign participation and the cognitive dimensions.

[7] The Survey Research Center question on this point specified politics "from day-to-day, when there isn't any big election campaign going on."

[8] An additional reason for confidence in generalizations drawn from these data is that earlier studies were conducted in a working-class precinct in Seattle and a suburban area in South Hadley, Massachusetts. The results were not of publishable quality, but it was apparent that there were some relationships between cognitive dimensions and political participation.

[9] Using the chi-square test, this relationship is significant at the .001 level.

[10] On the concept of political stratification, see V. O. Key, Jr., *Public Opinion and American Democracy* (New York: Knopf, 1961), Chap. 8; Robert A. Dahl, *Who Governs?* (New Haven: Yale University Press, 1961), Chap. 8; and Robert A. Dahl, *Modern Political Analysis* (Englewood Cliffs, N.J.: Prentice-Hall, 1963), Chap. 6.

Conflicts in Political Attitudes: Behavioral and Dynamic Consequences

Samuel A. Kirkpatrick

The role of perception and the attitudinal consequences of the perception of political objects has been of some concern to scholars of public opinion and the political process. However, political science has failed to develop a coherent body of knowledge about intrapersonal processes in the perception of political

Sections of this essay are reprinted from "Political Attitudes and Behavior: Some Consequences of Attitudinal Ordering," *Midwest Journal of Political Science* 14 (1970): 1–24 by permission of the Wayne State University Press, Copyright 1970, by Wayne State University Press; and from "Political Attitude Structure and Component Change," *Public Opinion Quarterly* 34 (1970), 403–407, with permission.

objects and the impact that these processes may have on the political system. Political pundits, normative theorists, and empirically oriented behavioralists have attempted to evaluate the individual as political man and as rational man in the context of an on-going political system. A body of prescriptions, proscriptions, guesses, and crude measures has developed by which we make generalizations of individual capacities in the political sphere. The following is an attempt to refine these measures and guesses in search for knowledge about the way in which the individual (modal) organizes his perceptual-attitudinal structure and its impact on his political behavior and attitudinal intensity, and its role in attitude change.

Normative political philosophers have been interested in rationality[1] (a component of consistency[2]); empirical political scientists have offered restatements and modifications of rationality assumptions based on survey research;[3] and theory has been constructed from these generalizations.[4] Social psychologists have focused on the assumption that the individual strives toward a state of consistency between attitude objects which he perceives in the environment, and if a state of inconsistency exists, cognitive reorganization will occur to reduce it. This approach has utilized balance models,[5] congruity approaches,[6] and dissonance theory.[7] Although these represent a related set of theories, there are theoretical and methodological distinctions between them.[8] The theoretical framework for the following analysis borrows heavily from the concept of structural balance. As it was originally formulated by Heider, the scheme contains an individual viewer (P), another person (O), plus an impersonal entity (X), with a focus on how P, O, and X are organized in P's cognitive structure. These elements of the model are linked by "relations" which are either positive, negative or null. More specifically, two types of information are included: affect or feelings, and cognitions or cognitive unit information. Therefore, "attitude" becomes the aspect of the cognitive unit that is a focal point for the balance principle. Generally, the theory deals with "the perception of social objects such as persons, ideas, and concepts."[9] Analytical attention is given to the perceiver (who,

below, is "outside" the attitude object triads) and to the relationships between the objects of perception. In the following analysis, these objects are treated broadly as persons, events, issues, groups, and combinations of feelings, beliefs or expectations associated with them. McGuire has reiterated the underlying hypothesis as follows: "The person tends to behave in ways that minimize the internal inconsistency among his interpersonal relations, among his intrapersonal cognitions, or among his beliefs, feelings, and actions."[10]

Although consistency concepts have been found to have high predictive power,[11] plus the advantages of generality and applicability to a large number of psychological problems,[12] the applications have occurred almost exclusively in the laboratory of the experimental social psychologist and in the context of attitude change. This focus has left questions unanswered about the impact of attitude orderings at one point in time. In spite of the criticisms leveled at researchers for an experimental bias,[13] and the claimed advantages of survey research (defined populations, natural settings, and generalizability), only a few attempts have been made at applying various aspects of balance-related theory to political data (and most of these are found in unpublished sources). Lewis Froman has tried to develop a theory of relationships between definitions, values and beliefs, and consistencies in values and beliefs about five political institutions based on responses from university students.[14] National Opinion Research Center data on value judgments of foreign policy have been analyzed to determine whether policy actions follow from basic value orientations and to test the rational quality of the public's views on foreign policy.[15] Other survey designs have measured congruencies between attitudes about the candidates and the political parties;[16] social cross-pressures and degrees of consistency on socio-political issues;[17] the impact of a mass communications campaign on consistencies in issue and party affect;[18] the relationship between attitude objects (candidate, party, religion) and the vote in the context of balance models;[19] the association between "logical consistency" in responses to questions about the country's problems and opinion leadership and political participation;[20] and incongruities in foreign affairs opinions.[21]

For the most part, the above attempts have failed to treat the specifics of balance theory (e.g., cognitive-affective distinctions); they have been based on either small, homogeneous samples or various parts of diverse samples; very specialized and diverse views of consistency have been adopted; and attitude objects have been defined narrowly (e.g., institutions,[22] issues[23]) without relevance to complexes of attitudes.

Index Construction

Social psychologists have hypothesized a strain toward consistency as a characteristic of human behavior, as well as a determinant of various forms of behavior. Zajonc comments that "it is significant that, although Heider drew upon Gestalt theory, he clearly recognized that cognitive inconsistency may have not only cognitive and attitudinal consequences, but "behavioral" consequences as well."[24] Political scientists have been somewhat concerned with "cognitive maps," yet they have neglected the concept of balance as an analytic and predictive tool. The experimental focus has been on induced discrepancies and syllogistic reasoning, and field research has focused primarily on issue consistencies to the point of avoiding other objects in the environment. The present research effort is an attempt to discover to what extent the theory has broader implications for political behavior. Objects are expanded to a treatment of candidates, issues, party identification, party affect, levels of conceptualization, political preferences, political expectations, knowledge, and various forms of political behavior. The data are from a sample of the national population,[25] there is an attempt to operationally separate affect and cognition, and attitude objects are treated as complexes of variables (multi-points in graph theory) with binary relations between them (e.g., likes-dislikes). The "attitudinal map" of respondents is conceptualized as a pattern of consistency and inconsistency relationships with regard to perceived political objects in the environment. In order to establish attitudinal map variables, a number of attitudinal responses were used to derive several indices of consistency-inconsistency at one point in time.

1. Total Partisan Affect — Party Identification — Political Preference Index (AIP)

The first balance model represents the direction of total partisan affect (for all indices the direction is either Democratic or Republican), party identification, political preference in 1964, and the extent to which these three attitudinal elements are consistent or inconsistent. In order to derive a level of consistency for each respondent on this index and any of the following indices, it was first necessary to measure the direction of affect (feeling) for each of the three elements.

The direction of total partisan affect[26] was estimated from a large number of unstructured (open-ended) questions asked the respondent about the parties and candidates. For example: What do you like about the Democratic Party? (five possible responses for each of these questions); What don't you like about the Republican Party? What do you like about Johnson? What don't you like about Johnson? What do you like about Goldwater? and What don't you like about Goldwater? Note that a single respondent could have as many as forty possible responses. These responses were summed for each individual (N = 1571) to yield an attitude toward each party and candidate, then combined to get one attitude toward parties and one attitude toward candidates, and the latter were summed to yield a total partisan attitude. The following symbolic representations indicate the steps involved in this process.[27]

Number of Pro-Democratic Party Responses (S_1)

Number of Anti-Democratic Party Responses (S_2)

Number of Pro-Republican Party Responses (S_3)

Number of Anti-Republican Party Responses (S_4)

Number of Pro-Democratic Candidate Responses (S_5)

Number of Anti-Democratic Candidate Responses (S_6)

Number of Pro-Republican Candidate Responses (S_7)

Number of Anti-Republican Candidate Responses (S_8)

Attitude toward the Democratic Party ($S_9 = S_1 - S_2 + 5$)

Attitude toward the Republican Party ($S_{10} = S_4 - S_3 + 5$)

Attitude toward the Democratic Candidate ($S_{11} = S_5 - S_6 + 5$)

Attitude toward the Republican Candidate ($S_{12} = S_8 - S_7 + 5$)

Combined Attitude toward the Parties ($S_{13} = S_9 + S_{10}$)

Combined Attitude toward the Candidates ($S_{14} = S_{11} + S_{12}$)

Total Partisan Attitude ($S_{15} = S_{13} + S_{14}$)

The direction of party identification was derived from a structured Survey Research Center (SRC) question, as was the respondent's candidate preference in 1964. Any affect other than Democratic (D) or Republican (R) was treated as "no affect"; therefore, if a respondent had no affect on any two of these three elements, he was dropped from the sample for purposes of this index. However, if a respondent had only one "no affect" he was judged to be consistent or inconsistent on the basis of the direction of the remaining two affects. For example, a respondent with a Republican total partisan affect, Republican party identification, and a preference for Goldwater was scored as totally consistent (TC), as was a respondent with two Republican affects and no affect (0) on a third

variable. An inconsistent (i.e., not totally consistent, NTC) respondent had a combination of Republican and Democratic responses.

Graph theoretic terms explain the index derivation more vividly.[28] Points in graph theory represent an affective, cognitive, or conative component, or a combination of these components (e.g., an attitude). Lines connecting points in a triad (three elements) denote the existence of a logical or rational relationship between points (attitudes) in the real world. A simple linear graph model for all of the indices, given three elements, can be represented as a triad of points:

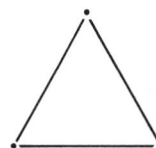

In order to make such a model attitudinally specific, the points can be identified as to their type, i.e., type of attitude. For example, point A = total partisan affect, point I = party identification, and point P = political preference:

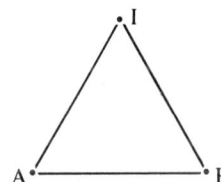

Internally, each respondent has an affective direction which he associates with the attitudinal points; therefore, let each point have a subscript which denotes Republican affect (r), Democratic affect (d), or no affect (o):

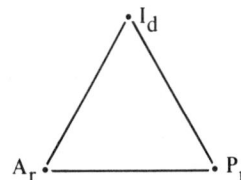

From the triads we can derive symbolic formulae (ordered sets) to indicate which combinations (cycles) or attitudes will be consistent (TC) or inconsistent (NTC). For example, in Table 1, the $A_r I_r$ bond represents a linkage of Republican total partisan affect and Republican party identification. It can be used as a guide to the way in which most indices were derived.

2. *Directional Conceptualization Index* (*CON*)

This consistency-inconsistency index measures the degree to which a respondent is consistently Democratic or Republican in his references to the parties and candidates, i.e., how consistent he is within the overall partisan index used to tap overall affect in the AIP index. It is a measure of the congruence between the levels of conceptualization that he used to evaluate the parties and candidates, that is, a measure of consistency in preference when preference is explained subjectively by different levels of conceptualization. These levels of conceptualization are similar to those derived in *The American Voter*.[29] From the unstructured questions about the parties and candidates, the SRC staff has developed an index of partisanship in Johnson references, an index of partisanship in Goldwater references, and indices of partisanship in references to groups, domestic issues, foreign issues, and the parties as managers of government. Each respondent has a Democratic or Republican affect (or no affect) on each of these levels of conceptualization. Therefore, in terms of graph theory, we have a six-point graph (six-attitudinal categories) with an affect associated with each point or attitude. To represent this symbolically, as in the AIP index, would require 729 ordered sets. If a respondent has six Republican affects or fewer than six Republican affects with a combination of no affects,

Table 1

Symbolic Representation of the Total Partisan Affect — Party Identification — Political Preference Index

Total Partisan Affect	*Affective Direction on:* Party Identification	Political Preference	*Symbolic Representation of Structural Balance*
R	R	R	$\{(A_r,I_r),\ (I_r,P_r),\ (P_r,A_r)\} = TC$
D	D	D	$\{(A_d,I_d),\ (I_d,P_d),\ (P_d,A_d)\} = TC$
R	R	O	$\{(A_r,I_r),\ (I_r,P_o),\ (P_o,A_r)\} = TC$
R	O	R	$\{(A_r,I_o),\ (I_o,P_r),\ (P_r,A_r)\} = TC$
O	R	R	$\{(A_o,I_r),\ (I_r,P_r),\ (P_r,A_o)\} = TC$
D	D	O	$\{(A_d,I_d),\ (I_d,P_o),\ (P_o,A_d)\} = TC$
D	O	D	$\{(A_d,I_o),\ (I_o,P_d),\ (P_d,A_d)\} = TC$
O	D	D	$\{(A_o,I_d),\ (I_d,P_d),\ (P_d,A_o)\} = TC$
R	R	D	$\{(A_r,I_r),\ (I_r,P_d),\ (P_d,A_r)\} = NTC$
R	D	R	$\{(A_r,I_d),\ (I_d,P_r),\ (P_r,A_r)\} = NTC$
D	R	R	$\{(A_d,I_r),\ (I_r,P_r),\ (P_r,A_d)\} = NTC$
D	D	R	$\{(A_d,I_d),\ (I_d,P_r),\ (P_r,A_d)\} = NTC$
D	R	D	$\{(A_d,I_r),\ (I_r,P_d),\ (P_d,A_d)\} = NTC$
R	D	D	$\{(A_r,I_d),\ (I_d,P_d),\ (P_d,A_r)\} = NTC$
R	D	O	$\{(A_r,I_d),\ (I_d,P_o),\ (P_o,A_r)\} = NTC$
D	O	R	$\{(A_d,I_o),\ (I_o,P_r),\ (P_r,A_d)\} = NTC$
O	R	D	$\{(A_o,I_r),\ (I_r,P_d),\ (P_d,A_o)\} = NTC$
D	R	O	$\{(A_d,I_r),\ (I_r,P_o),\ (P_o,A_d)\} = NTC$
R	O	D	$\{(A_r,I_o),\ (I_o,P_d),\ (P_d,A_r)\} = NTC$
O	D	R	$\{(A_o,I_d),\ (I_d,P_r),\ (P_r,A_o)\} = NTC$

he is consistently Republican. The same holds for Democratic affect. Any combination of Republican and Democratic affect is scored as a state of imbalance.

3. Expectation–Preference Index (EP)

This index measures consistency-inconsistency in terms of congruencies between a cognitively oriented expectation of who is likely to win the 1964 Presidential election and an affect oriented preference for a candidate (i.e., how the respondent expects to vote). Unlike the other indices, only two attitudinal elements are involved. If the respondent expects Johnson to win and prefers Johnson, or if he expects Goldwater to win and prefers Goldwater, he is consistent.[30] Other combinations are inconsistent and the existence of any "no affect" eliminates the respondent.

The Prevalence of Attitudinal Consistency at one Point in Time

Table 2 indicates the total levels of consistency and inconsistency in the 1964 sample of the national population as measured by three indices. All of these indices exhibit higher levels of consistency than inconsistency and most of them are well above any even probability level. However, one disclaimer must be made about the bias toward higher consistency

levels. In order to measure these psychological-attitudinal levels, an individual must give a sufficient number of responses so that his affect or cognition can be measured. That is, it is possible that some respondents who fail to indicate an affect or cognition on the questions used to formulate the indices do so on the basis of inconsistency avoidance. Although it is impossible to measure this bias, its movement in the direction of greater consistency is likely. Festinger contends that "a fear of dissonance would lead to a reluctance to take action—a reluctance to commit oneself."[31]

Using the Total Partisan Affect-Party Identification-Political Preference Index (AIP) as a criterion, Table 2 indicates that 86 percent of the population is consistent. This means that these respondents are consistent in the direction of their total partisan affect as measured by the index, their political party identification, and their political preference for a candidate in 1964. Some of these respondents are consistently Republican (24 percent), but most are consistently Democratic (62 percent). This finding represents, to some extent, the gross level of party identifiers in the electorate. Among all the indices, this one produces the highest consistency level. It is felt that this is representative of the most typical and vocal identifications and attitudes among the population. That is, the high total number of responses (N = 1538) indicates that the universe responds overwhelmingly on the items composing the scale. Most Americans have at least some degree of general feeling toward the political parties and candidates, and many have distinct

Table 2
The Existence of Consistency-Inconsistency in 1964

Index of Consistency	Level of Consistency-Inconsistency		
	% Consistent	% Inconsistent	Total N[a]
Total Partisan Affect-Party Identification- Political Preference (AIP)	86	14	1538
Directional Conceptualization (CON)	64	36	1521
Expectation-Preference (EP)	81	19	1087

[a]Deviance from a total N of 1571 is caused by omissions due to failures to respond or the existence of "no affects" in certain indices.

party identifications as well as political preferences. Nearly the entire population exhibits an affect on at least two of these attitude objects. More importantly, those who exhibit attitudes do so coherently along a Democratic-Republican continuum.

The Directional Conceptualization Index (CON) attempts to measure a related kind of consistency: consistencies in responses toward the parties and candidates, that is, consistencies within one of the elements (Total Partisan Affect) in the AIP Index. The attitudes toward the parties and candidates were separated in content based on levels of conceptualization (e.g., the parties as managers of government) and a directional affect (Democratic or Republican) was obtained for each of these levels. Table 2 indicates that 64 percent of the sample is able to arrange responses toward parties and candidates along a consistently Republican (15 percent) or a consistently Democratic (49 percent) continuum. These individuals can at least respond in a consistent fashion to questions which tap their attitude on any two levels of conceptualization. The percentage is substantially less than that displayed by the other indices, a probable reflection of the demand placed on the respondent and his difficulty in conceptualizing political objects on even these rather crude conceptual levels. In comparison with the other indices, the 36 percent who are inconsistent exhibit difficulty in making their evaluations of candidates and parties congruent.

The levels of consistency displayed by the Expectation-Preference Index (EP) are high (81 percent) and indicate a strong capability for individuals to align their expectations with their political candidate preferences. This index measures a cognitive element (expectation of which candidate is going to win the election) as well as an affective element (which candidate the individual prefers). The measure is remote from any indications of rationality or logical syllogism, but it does give an indication of psychological forces that tend to make an individual's expectations congruent with his preferences. That is, for those respondents included in the measure there is a strain toward cognitive-affective consistency at one point in time.

Political scientists have focused on psychological and behavioral frailties (e.g., the lack of ideology, knowledge, rationality, and objectivity) of members of the electorate. Social psychologists have focused on the individual, but not the individual as a political man, and concluded that there is a tendency for the individual to reduce states of imbalance. In general, each of the balance models indicates that relatively high levels of various forms of attitudinal consistency are prevalent in the population. The American electorate exhibits a strain toward consistency similar to that postulated in social-psychological cognitive consistency theories. Nevertheless, there are sufficiently high levels of attitudinal inconsistency to warrant an examination of the behavioral consequences of these levels. The rates of inconsistency indicate that there may be a segment of the population which fails to resolve structural imbalance or which seeks cognitive tension. It has been postulated that in certain circumstances, the organism may seek inconsistency and exacerbate levels of inconsistency in order to maximize satisfaction derived from the ultimate tension reduction. Furthermore, the respondent may seek inconsistency in order to hide more serious conflicts which are irresolvable through action (e.g., a passive person may seek cognitive excitement[32]). Research in political science has indicated that many citizens are able to tolerate high amounts of conflict,[33] that some people enjoy the tension of risk taking,[34] and that many respondents can hold inconsistent beliefs without trying to reconcile them.[35]

Attitudinal and Behavioral Consequences: Statistical Summary

In an attempt to measure the consequences of attitude orderings, three clusters of dependent variables were selected for cross tabulation with the three indices: issue and partisan intensity; the time for deciding how one is going to vote; and political interest, participation, and efficacy.[36] Table 3 indicates the significance level and direction of relationship for each of the indices.

Table 3
Attitudinal and Behavioral Consequences of Consistency-Inconsistency[a]

Consequences	Significance Level and Direction of Relationship For:		
	AIP	CON	EP
Issue Intensity for:			
General Power of the Federal Government	.89 0	.00* −	.00* −
Aid to Education	.34 −	.00* −	.00* −
Medicare	.84 0	.06 0	.14 −
Government Responsibility for Living Standards	.24 −	.63 0	.00* −
Government Ownership of Power Plants	.30 −	.00* −	.00* −
Equal Job Opportunities	.52 −	.20 −	.81 0
School Integration	.53 −	.23 0	.45 −
Integrated Public Accommodations	.21 −	.38 −	.90 0
Intensity of Partisan Identification	.00* +	.00* +	.25 +
Decision Time for Making up Mind About Vote Direction	.00* +	.00* +	.00* +
Political Interest and Participation:			
Interest in the Campaign (Asked Before Election)	.90 0	.00* −	.00* −
Attention Paid to the Campaign (Post-Election)	.64 +	.16 −	.00* −
Expect to Vote	.95 0	.05* −	.20 −
Turnout	.91 0	.27 −	.11 −
Mass Media Usage	.47 0	.00* −	.06 −
Talking to Others to Influence Them	.68 0	.03* −	.00* −
Attending Political Meetings	.60 0	.37 0	.01* −
Political Club Membership	.53 0	.66 0	.02* −
Using a Button or Bumper Sticker	.00* +	.02* +	.03* −
Giving Money	.30 +	.22 −	.00* −
Political Involvement Index	.01* +	.28 0	.13 −
Political Efficacy	.88 0	.06 −	.02* −

[a] See Appendix for coding procedures and table interpretation.

The table evidences a general lack of significant relationships for the AIP model, yet most of the issue intensity measures relate negatively to consistency. That is, the more consistent a respondent is in his ordering of partisan affect, party identification, and political preference, the less intense he is in his stand on domestic issues. However, intensity of party identification moves in the opposite direction. Seven of eleven political interest variables show no discernible relationship to attitudinal configurations; however, the direction for the decision time variables is clear. The time at which an individual makes up his mind about an important decision is a crucial element in the test of structural balance. The body of cognitive consistency theory postulates that an individual sub-ject to inconsistency delays his decision under the influence of conflicting psychological demands. The decision time for vote direction meets this test: most consistents make up their minds before or during the political conventions, whereas inconsistent respondents decide how they are going to vote during the post-convention campaign.

A clearer pattern of relationships is evident when consistency is measured by congruence in party direction when expressed as levels of conceptualization. Inconsistency is related to high issue intensity; however, as with the AIP Index, consistent respondents display higher degrees of intensity about their party identification. The time at which an individual decides how he is going to vote is also significantly related to levels of consistency: there is substantial evidence that individuals with conflicting affects will delay this decision. When most of the behavioral variables are examined, it can be seen that inconsistency is associated with political interest and action. For example, respondents with incongruous attitudes are more interested in the campaign and election, they are more likely to expect to vote and to actually vote, they use more forms of the mass media than do consistents, and they talk to others to influence them about the election. The only relationship which is contrary to the above set is that for participation involving a campaign button or bumper sticker. There is nothing inherent in the CON Index or the participation measure to give clues to this divergent relationship.

Table 3 also indicates that an individual who is inconsistent in his expectation of who is going to win the election and his preference for a candidate is most likely to take an intense stand on all but two of the measured domestic issues. In congruence with the other indices, the EP Index relates consistency to high partisan intensity, although it fails to meet the .05 probability level. The time for making up one's mind about how he is going to vote continues to be a strong variable in its association with consonance. In the face of structural imbalance, the above respondents also tend to take greater interest in the campaign, participate more, and express a higher degree of political efficacy about their influence on government.

Issue and Partisan Intensity

Although the AIP measure fails to evidence significant relationships, the indices all indicate that inconsistent respondents tend to be more intense in the stands they take on domestic issues. The AIP and CON indices are based on a foundation of similar variables: attitudes (open-ended) toward the parties and candidates are used by CON, and AIP includes these same attitudes plus structured responses to questions about party identification and candidate

choice. They exhibit a pattern of relationships which is similar, yet less powerful in their predictive force than the EP Index. The Directional Conceptualization Index relates consistency to lower intensity in a more statistically significant fashion than does the AIP Index, and the Expectation-Preference Index evidences more significant relationships than either the AIP or CON Index. Through the use of these indices, there is evidence to suggest the following: There is a tendency for respondents with mixed direction (combinations of Democratic and Republican) on their total affect toward parties and candidates, their party identification, and their preference for a candidate in 1964, to be more intense about domestic issues; respondents with mixed directions on their total affect toward parties and candidates (internally, according to Republican or Democratic affects attached to various levels of conceptualization) are more intense about domestic issues (strongly agree and strongly disagree); and individuals who prefer one candidate but expect another to win take more intense stands on issues.

The relationship between consistency and intensity of partisan identification is more stable than the relationships with issue intensity. According to all three indices, consistent respondents are more intense in their party identification. Although there is partisan identification bias in the measures (especially AIP), it appears that the fine distinction which inconsistent respondents make between elements in any consistency-inconsistency triad translate into more intense feelings about issues. Issues require these fine distinctions whereas intense party identification is a more prevalent and stable affect,[37] based on past partisan ties, and susceptible to strong feeling by respondents with broader (stereotypical and habitual) perceptual categories.

Decision Time about Vote Direction

The pattern of association which exists for the relationships between balance-imbalance and time of voter decision is stable across the indices: The indices indicate that there is a strong (and significant) positive association between consistency and an early decision on vote direction. Any incongruence between the elements of attitudinal triads (or dyads in the case of the EP Index) leads to a delay in the vote decision. For example, a respondent who has mixed affects (Democratic-Republican) toward the parties and candidates will tend to delay his decision, as will a respondent who prefers one candidate but expects another to win.

This is not the first instance in which a type of conflict situation related to a delay in decision time. Although Lazarsfeld, Berelson and Gaudet focused on social (versus attitudinal) cross-pressures and inconsistencies, they found that cross-pressured individuals arrive at a decision late:

> In the first place, it was difficult for them to make up their minds simply because they had good reasons for voting for both candidates. Sometimes such reasons were so completely balanced that the decision had to be referred to a third factor for settlement. The doubt as to which was the better course —to vote Republican or to vote Democratic— combined with the process of self-argument caused the delay in the final vote decision for such people. . . . In the second place, some of the people subject to cross-pressures delayed their final vote decision because they were waiting for events to resolve the conflicting pressures.[38]

Cross-pressures theory posits the existence of conflicts between or among determinants of behavior and its existence leads to avoidance, withdrawal and fluctuation. Although cross-pressures theory and cognitive balance theory share the same basic concerns, the focus for balance theory is the resolution of conflict rather than avoidance and withdrawal. Cross-pressures theory has been used in political science largely in a social rather than psychological-attitudinal context. It was recently tested in an attitudinal context[39] (most similar to the CON Index) and the focus was on one measure of consistency-inconsistency (conflict) which considered fewer relevant factors than

those incorporated here, yet the measure enabled the author to tap centrality and magnitude of dissonance. It was found that conflict is not the exclusive motivational principle of human behavior; that there are delays in decision time for cross-pressured respondents at high centrality (based on number of responses), more so than at medium or low centrality; and that there is a decrease in the rate of early decisions as magnitude of dissonance increases. That is, centrality acts as a separate and stronger factor than does tension reduction, and delays in decision time occur when the conflict has attained some strength. These findings are not unlike those presented here, yet the measures cannot tap centrality and magnitude. Furthermore, if there is any centrality bias to the data, it occurs in the direction of high centrality. That is, the elimination of "no affect" responses increases the chance that respondents will be highly central. This may be an explanation for the extraordinary strength of relationships between inconsistency and decision delays.

The data support the contentions of cross-pressures theory which postulate avoidance of decision (conflict) under strain. More importantly, they support cognitive balance theory. The psychological-attitudinal focus of the data and the similar focus for balance theory increases its conceptual importance over cross-pressures theory. Incongruent affects and cognitions about political objects produce psychological tensions which are sufficient to cause a delay in making a decision about vote direction.

Political Interest and Participation

Although the AIP Index lacks some degree of predictive ability, the remaining indices (CON and EP) relate inconsistency to high participation and interest. This is one area in which the possible interpretations according to cross-pressures theory and balance theory are in conflict. According to cross-pressures theory, inconsistency and conflict stimulate withdrawal, avoidance and reluctance. However, these data suggest modification of this inference. Cognitive consistency theory's emphasis on dissonance resolution is not necessarily congruent with cross-pressures theory's emphasis on withdrawal. For example, a way that an individual can solve his inconsistency between his political expectations and political preferences is to actively seek to alter one of these elements. According to the Expectation-Preference Index, a person who is inconsistent over whom he wants to win and who he thinks will win is very likely to be an active participant. He may participate in order to change his expectation of who is going to win so that a state of consistency can be achieved.[40] Although the short-term effects of the 1964 election seem to be operating, as evidenced by lower participation scores for the inconsistents who expect Goldwater to win but prefer Johnson,[41] there is no clear evidence about motivations beyond the strain toward consistency. For example, on all but two dependent variables (meetings and club membership), the E_dP_r link evidences the highest possible relationship to participation. There is evidence of an interactive effect between expectation and preference and their impact on the dependent variables. That is, the Republican (r) affect seems to play a more positive role vis-a-vis participation when it is combined with a Democratic cognition rather than a Republican cognition.

Except for the interaction effects, a similar pattern of relationships exists for the Directional Conceptualization Index. Given that an individual's affect toward parties and candidates (as tapped from unstructured questions) is the most relevant set of variables for his behavior,[42] any internal inconsistency in that set of variables will stimulate action. Although it was not measured directly in this index, it has been shown in a similar context[43] that inconsistent respondents have higher levels of centrality (based on the quantity of responses rather than the quality of responses) and therefore higher activation.

More specifically, the EP Index indicates that individuals who are inconsistent in their preferences and expectations tend to engage in social interaction as measured by political club membership, political meeting attendance, and talking to others. There is

supporting evidence to suggest that the existence of imbalance leads to the seeking of social support and the initiation of communications.[44] Festinger comments that "the existence of dissonance in a person leads to a process of social communication by which he attempts to reduce the dissonance,"[45] Therefore, there is reason to believe that an individual who prefers one candidate but expects another to win will seek social support to reduce his inconsistency. This social and political group support is in line with his desire to alter his expectation of who is going to win in order to make it congruent with his preference. A more conclusive answer could be given if data were available on the type of meeting he went to or the type of group he joined. This could then be related to his preferences and expectations to see if, for example, an individual who favored Goldwater, but expected Johnson to win, joined a Republican group.

On both the EP and CON Index, inconsistency is related to mass media usage. This should mean that inconsistents seek more information to resolve their unbalanced state. Although this may be the case, the mass media picture is rather complex. Festinger comments that: "If little or no dissonance exists, there would be no motivation (considering this source of motivation alone) to seek out new and additional information."[46] Yet there may also be no motivation to avoid new information. If a respondent is inconsistent he may seek out information which will introduce consonances, or he may avoid information which will increase the existing inconsistency. That is, inconsistency may mean attention or non-attention depending on the content of the information.[47]

Although some research has found a positive relationship between consistency and involvement, this research has either focused on social cross-pressures or it has defined consistency in a different manner. For example, Stein has found that individuals with conflicting or ambiguous opinions on some issues are likely to take only weak action. However, this discovery was made in the context of consistency defined in a more syllogistic (versus psychological) sense as "logical common sense-ness about goals."[48] In a similar context, Lane has found that involvement tends to be associated with greater stability of political attitudes over time, greater consistency in electoral preferences, and greater resistance to conflicting social pressures.[49]

Research has also indicated that the individual strives to confirm expectations: "the events that confirm expectancies are consonant, sought out."[50] The data presented here fail to support this finding because expectancies are accompanied by preferences. That is, the disconfirmation of expectancies may be a motivating factor in human behavior where one's preferences are inconsistent with one's expectancies. Although the exact means of tension reduction cannot be measured without time series data, the longitudinal data reported below indicate a tendency to change cognitive components (e.g., expectation) before affective ones (e.g., preference). This implies that there is an attempt to change the environment by changing the situation (the fact that the preferred candidate is an underdog) to which the cognitive element corresponds. Although this may be a difficult task, Festinger supports the possibility: "Changing the environment itself in order to reduce dissonance is more feasible when the social environment is in question than when the physical environment is involved."[51] The political environment *is* one which is susceptible to change.

Dynamic Aspects of Political Attitude Structure

To this point we have focused primarily on the behavioral consequences of conflicts in political belief systems. Although few political scientists have raised questions about the existence of congruent states at one point in time, even fewer have addressed themselves to the dynamic process of attitude change. Social scientists have generally dealt with gross changes in political attitudes over time[52] and with predictive factors associated with these changes.[53] Yet we know very little about the social psychology of political attitude change. According to cognitive consistency research and theory in social psychology, individuals who are originally consistent in their political attitudes are expected to remain consistent, whereas those who are inconsistent tend to become consistent over time. This homeostatic process is accomplished through various forms of attitude change that permit the establishment of congruent attitudinal structures.

This section focuses on attitude changes that occur between two points in time. The individual's "cognitive map" is again conceptualized as a complex set of consistent-inconsistent relationships vis-à-vis a set of perceived political objects. The data are from two samples of the national population organized in panel form.[54]

Four indices were used to assess attitude consistency at time 1 and time 2. They all attempt to measure consistency between an individual's stand on an issue (affect), the party which he perceives as most likely to follow his issue stand in terms of doing something about the problem (cognition), and his party identification.[55] The four issues were chosen for their domestic importance and because attitudes were tapped at both points in time: federal responsibility for employment, aid to education, electric power and housing, and school integration. Three theoretical points of interest are considered: the total prevalence of consistency at both points in time, the changes that occur over a two-year period, and the components of attitude structure which are changed.

Table 4 presents the proportion of respondents with consistent attitude structures at time 1 and at time 2. In general, it supports the hypothesis that attitudinal congruency is the rule: there are more consistents than inconsistents, and consistency ranges from 90 per cent to 83 percent. These levels indicate that respondents are well equipped to order their affect on issues, their party cognition, and their partisan identification. Furthermore, most of them correctly perceive the stands that the parties have taken and order their perceptions in line with their own stand and their own identification.[56]

In spite of high levels of consistency in both years, the total amount of consistency-inconsistency cannot yield information about individual changes in attitude structure. The necessary information is presented in

Table 4
The Prevalence of Consistency at Two Points in Time

Index of Consistency[a]	Time	% Consistent	N
Government responsibility for employment	1	86.7	264
	2	86.6	359
Aid to education	1	86.8	228
	2	90.0	220
Government responsibility for electric power and housing	1	83.9	224
	2	87.5	200
School integration	1	85.0	253
	2	83.3	270

[a]Each index consists of measures of the individual's stand on the issue, his cognition of the parties' stands on that issue, and his party identification.

Table 5. Although there has been an attempt to treat survey data in a quasi-experimental fashion, the number of respondents who answer questions with a discernible affect or cognition at both points in time becomes small.

Table 5 indicates that there is a tendency for consistents to remain consistent while inconsistents become consistent. Using employment as an example, 92 percent remain consistent and only 24 percent of the inconsistents at time 1 remain inconsistent at time 2. It may be possible for an individual to remain consistent over the two-year period yet adopt a different consistent stand. For example, he may change from a triad of Republican orientations to a triad of Democratic yet consistent orientations. For the most part this does not occur. On the employment index, 82 percent of the consistents who retain that state do so by keeping the same triad of relationships. This figure is 87 percent for education and 77 percent for electric power and housing.

Cognitive consistency theories also contend that inconsistents become consistent through a process of attitude change. That is, in order to become consistent, an individual must change one or more of the affective or cognitive elements in the triad. Conclusions about these changes are tentative because of the small number of inconsistents at time 1. However, there are

several clear patterns among those who change from inconsistent to consistent between the two surveys. When the employment issue is used, 54 percent of those who change do so by changing the second element of the triad: cognition. Fewer respondents (23 percent) change their stand on the issue and their cognition of which party will support their interests. The remaining 23 percent change their party identification alone or other elements in conjunction with it. For example, respondents who initially were in favor of the government taking more responsibility for employment, who thought the Democratic party shared their views, and who identified with the Republican party, would tend to keep their affect on the issue and their partisan identification the same, but to say at the second point in time that the Republican party actually was more likely to do something about jobs.

Table 5
Changes in Consistency between Time 1 and Time 2

	Time 1	
Time 2	% Consistent	% Inconsistent
Index 1[a]		
Consistent	92.2	76.5
Inconsistent	7.8	23.5
N	128	17
Index 2[b]		
Consistent	98.6	75.0
Inconsistent	1.4	25.0
N	69	8
Index 3[c]		
Consistent	89.1	70.0
Inconsistent	10.9	30.0
N	64	10
Index 4[d]		
Consistent	87.9	58.3
Inconsistent	12.1	41.7
N	99	12

[a]Government responsibility for employment.

[b]Aid to education.

[c]Government responsibility for electric power and housing.

[d]School integration.

When the aid to education issue is used, 67 percent of the inconsistents who become consistent change only their party cognition. The remainder change either their issue affect and cognition or their party identification. The percentages are similar for the electric power and housing issues. On school integration, 86 percent of the changers modify their issue affect and party cognition, and only 14 percent change their party identification.

The findings above manifest a tendency for individuals to change a cognitive element before they change their issue affect or party identification. A smaller number of individuals change both their stand on an issue and their notion of which party will pursue their interests in Washington. These findings support what much of the voting research has indicated for party identification: it is a stable element of the individual's cognitive-affective structure. In general, consistent respondents remain consistent over time, and inconsistent respondents become consistent by changing their cognitions rather than their affect or party identification.[57]

Although the data presented here indicate a strain toward inconsistency with resultant changes occurring after states of inconsistency, and a tendency for cognitive components to change most readily, there is a need for further research. Little is known about the general susceptibility of affective and cognitive elements to change.[58] Furthermore, if an individual's political actions and interests are based on his type of attitude structure, his political behavior should change if he changes his level of consistency. This relation between attitude structure and behavior also warrants investigation.

The Individual in the Polity

Characteristics of individual attitudinal structures do not exist in a state of intrapersonal isolation. After discussing the relationships between individual structures and the consequences of them, there remains a question of relevance for the polity. Man, with his cognitive-affective maps, lives in a total system where the mind and the environment interact. Herbert Hyman has commented that "cognitive processes underly [sic] political participation and party orientation and give meaning to these aspects of political behavior."[59]

The American population exhibits a high degree of consistency between cognitive and affective elements (as measured here) when these elements represent political objects in the real world. Furthermore, the data indicate a strain toward consistency after states of inconsistency have been encountered. When man is viewed as part of a total system of action, the goal of the strain toward inconsistency becomes an inner harmony with oneself and with the environment.[60]

Except for situations of incomplete knowledge, rationality implies cognitive consistency.[61] As an element of rationality, consistency between attitudes toward political objects exists at high levels in the population. The authors of *Voting* have contended that political preferences are not reasoned preferences.[62] Because the present research does not focus on vote direction, it does not attempt to judge this conclusion. However, preferences tend to be in line with sets of affects and expectations. The data presented in this paper support the findings of a small sample of respondents which were based on consistencies between party identification and candidate choice.[63] This early study by Lipset *et al.*, measured the most likely set of congruent attitudes (party and candidate). Although less likely sets of congruent attitudes have been included here, high rates of consistency have been found.

Nevertheless, there are inconsistents, some of whom fail to resolve inconsistency. For these individuals, psychic pleasure does not seem to be the crucial motivating force: The Benthamite calculus may not be relevant for all goals. For some, delayed gratification may be more important than immediate gratification. The higher an individual's education and self-acceptance, the greater the ability to tolerate ambiguity and to delay states of congruity.[64] Individuals who do not change their attitudinal structures in the face of unbalanced states over time possess infra-threshold intensity. That is, they have not met the threshold of intolerance for inconsistency. As has been suggested earlier, some individuals may actively seek states of imbalance (e.g., the internally passive). External pressures may force man to behave in ways inconsistent with his principles, and he may be presented with new information which is incongruous with previous beliefs.

Those writers critical of restatements of democratic theory are interested in the psychic satisfactions of man (e.g., Wolin).[65] Attitudinal balance is not unrelated to this gratification. Man can attain a form of psychic satisfaction through the strain toward consistency. For example, inconsistents who participate in order to reach a state of consistency may do so on the basis of a type of psychic gratification (yet consistency may be a secondary and instrumental goal to participation). If this inconsistency and the reduction of psychic tension is functional for participatory democracy described normatively, research on the inner man vis-a-vis his political world can assist in the bridge building that is necessary between empirical research and normative theory. Although complex multivariate techniques will give us a more complete picture of politically active man, it is suggested that there are conceptual and empirical foundations for the phenomenon of "ordering" and that we must begin to build a theory about the role of inconsistent attitude states, subsequent decision delays, and the pursuit of active or passive support in the attainment of congruent states. Despite the exploratory nature of the above findings, the relationship between any environmental socio-political homeostasis and man's inner homeostasis remains a fruitful research endeavor.

Notes

[1] For comprehensive statements see Bernard Berelson, "Democratic Theory and Public Opinion," *Public Opinion Quarterly* 16 (1952): 313–30; Henry Mayo, *An Introduction to Democratic*

Appendix

Key for the Interpretation of Tabular Analysis

Dependent Variables (coding)

Issue Intensity: high, low, no interest; Intensity of Partisan Identification: strong, not very strong, independent but learning toward one party, independent, apolitical; Decision Time for Making Up Mind about Vote Direction: knew all along, pre-convention, during convention, during campaign, within two weeks of election day, election day; Interest in the campaign: (before election) very much, somewhat, not much; Attention Paid to the Campaign: very much, fairly, slightly, no interest; Expect to Vote: yes, probably yes, questionable, probably no, no; Turnout: yes or no; Mass Media Usage: none through use of four forms of media; Talking to Others to Influence Them: yes or no; Attending Political Meetings: yes or no; Political Club Membership: yes or no; Using a Campaign Button or Bumper Sticker: yes or no; Giving Money: yes or no; Political Involvement Index: (based on whether the respondent cares who wins the election and whether he is interested in the campaign) 1 (high) to 8 (low); Political Efficacy Index: (based on the following statements: "People like me don't have any say about what the government does." "Voting is the only way that people like me can have a say about how the government runs things." "Sometimes politics and government seem so complicated that a person like me can't really understand what's going on." "I don't think public officials care very much what people like me think.") very low, moderate, high, very high.

Probability

Due to the low level of measurement necessarily assumed by most of the variables, significance level was determined by Chi-Square tests, with the Yates Correction Factor for 2 × 2 tables. * = significant at the .05 level. Exact probabilities have been rounded to two decimal places.

Direction of Relationship

+ = the positive association of consistency with "high" issue intensity, "high" intensity of partisan identification, an early vote decision, "high" participation and interest, and "high" efficacy. − = a negative association between consistency and the above levels of the dependent variables. 0 = no discernible relationship.

Theory (New York: Oxford University Press, 1960); William T. Bluhm, *Theories of the Political System* (Englewood Cliffs: Prentice Hall, 1965); and Richard E. Ashcraft, "Political Rationality and Democratic Values" (unpublished paper delivered at the Annual Meeting of the Western Political Science Association, Tucson, Arizona, March 17, 1967).

[2] Don D. Smith, "Cognitive Consistency and the Perception of Others' Opinion," *Public Opinion Quarterly* 32 (1968): 1–15; William A. Scott, "Rationality and Non-Rationality of International Attitudes," *Journal of Conflict Resolution* 2 (1958): 8–16; and R. B. Zajonc, "Balance, Congruity, and Dissonance," *Public Opinion Quarterly* 24 (1960): 280–96.

[3] Especially the interdisciplinary endeavors of Bernard Berelson, Paul F. Lazarsfeld, and William N. McPhee, *Voting* (Chicago: University of Chicago Press, 1954); Berelson, "Democratic Theory and Public Opinion"; Eugene Burdick, "Political Theory and the Voting Studies," in *American Voting Behavior,* ed. Eugene Burdick and Arthur Brodbeck (Glencoe: The Free Press, 1959), pp. 136–149; J. Plamenatz and G. Sartori, "Electoral Studies and Democratic Theory," *Political Studies* 6 (1958): 1–75; V. O. Key, Jr., *The Responsible Electorate* (Cambridge: Harvard University Press, 1966); and Hugh A. Bone and Austin Ranney, *Politics and Voters* (New York: McGraw-Hill, 1963).

[4] Robert A. Dahl, *A Preface to Democratic Theory* (Chicago: University of Chicago Press, 1956); Harry Eckstein, *A Theory of Stable Democracy* (Princeton: Princeton University, Center of International Studies, 1961); Charles Lindblom, *The Intelligence and Democracy* (New York: The Free Press, 1965); Gabriel A. Almond and Sidney Verba, *The Civic Culture* (Boston: Little, Brown & Co., 1965); Philip E. Converse, "The Nature of Belief Systems in Mass Publics," in *Ideology and Discontent,* ed. David E. Apter (New York: The Free Press, 1964), pp. 206–62; and Gabriel A. Almond, *The American People and Foreign Policy* 2nd ed. (New York: Frederick A. Praeger, 1960).

[5] Fritz Heider, "Attitudes and Cognitive Organization," *Journal of Psychology* 21 (1946): 107–12. Important explications have been developed by Dorwin Cartwright and Frank Harary, "Structural Balance: A Generalization of Heider's Theory," *Psychological Review* 63 (1956): 277–93; Julian O. Morrissette, "An Experimental Study of the Theory of Structural Balance," *Human Relations* 11 (1958): 239–54; and Milton J. Rosenberg and Robert Abelson, "An Analysis of Cognitive Balancing," in *Attitude Organization and Change,* ed. Carl I. Hovland and Milton J. Rosenberg (New Haven: Yale University Press, 1960), pp. 112–63.

[6] Charles E. Osgood and Percy H. Tannenbaum, "The Principle of Congruity in the Prediction of Attitude Change," *Psychological Review* 62 (1965): 42–55.

[7] Leon A. Festinger, *A Theory of Cognitive Dissonance* (Stanford: Stanford University Press, 1957); and Jack W. Brehm and Arthur R. Cohen, *Explorations in Cognitive Dissonance* (New York: John Wiley & Sons, Inc., 1962).

[8] Congruity is frequently viewed as a special case of balance, but finer distinctions are made about dissonance. See Samuel A. Kirkpatrick: "Social-Psychological Approaches to the Study of Political Phenomena" (unpublished paper delivered at the Annual Meeting of the Rocky Mountain Social Science Association, Lubbock, Texas, May 2–3, 1969).

[9] Robert B. Zajonc, "Cognitive Theories in Social Psychology," in *Handbook of Social Psychology,* ed. Gardner Lindzey and Elliot Aronson (2nd ed.; Reading, Mass.: Addison-Wesley Publishing Company, 1968), I, 339.

[10] William J. McGuire, "The Current Status of Cognitive Consistency Theories," in *Cognitive Consistency: Motivational Antecedents and Behavioral Consequents,* ed. Shel Feldman (New York: Academic Press, 1966), p. 1.

[11] Festinger, *A Theory of Cognitive Dissonance,* p. 1.

[12] Brehm and Cohen, *Explorations in Cognitive Dissonance,* p. vii.

[13] Carl I. Hovland, "Reconciling Conflicting Results Derived from Experimental and Survey Studies of Attitude Change," *American Psychologist* 14 (1959): 8–17; Karl E. Weick, "Promise and Limitations of Laboratory Experiments in the Development of Attitude Change Theory," in *Attitude, Ego-Involvement and Change,* ed. Carolyn W. Sherif and Muzafer Sherif (New York: John Wiley & Sons, Inc., 1967), pp. 51–75; and Bertram L. Koslin, "Laboratory Experiments and Attitude Theory," in *Attitude, Ego-Involvement and Change,* ed. Sherif and Sherif, pp. 76–87.

[14] Cognitive Consistency of Political Values and Beliefs" (unpublished Ph.D. dissertation, Northwestern University, 1960).

[15] Leonard S. Stein, "Consistency of Public Opinion on Foreign Policy" (unpublished Ph.D. dissertation, University of Chicago, 1962).

[16] Peter W. Sperlich, "Cross-Pressure and Conflict in Political Behavior" (unpublished Ph.D. dissertation, University of Michigan, 1966).

[17] Roy T. Bowles, "The Social Sources of Opinion Consistency" (unpublished Ph.D. dissertation, University of Oregon, 1965).

[18] William N. McPhee, Bo Anderson, and Harry Milholland, "Attitude Consistency," in *Public Opinion and Congressional Elections,* ed. W. N. McPhee and W. A. Glaser (New York: The Free Press, 1962), pp. 78–120.

[19] Denis Sullivan, "Psychological Balance and Reactions to the Presidential Nominations in 1960," in *The Electoral Process,* ed. M. Kent Jennings and L. Harmon Zeigler (Englewood Cliffs: Prentice-Hall, Inc., 1966), pp. 238–64.

[20] John Kessel, "Cognitive Dimensions and Political Activity," *Public Opinion Quarterly* 29 (1965): 377–89.

[21] Scott, "Rationality and Non-Rationality of International Attitudes."

[22] Froman, "Cognitive Consistency of Political Values and Beliefs."

[23] Samuel A. Kirkpatrick, "Issue Orientation and Voter Choice in 1964," *Social Science Quarterly* 49 (1968): 87–102.

[24] "Cognitive Theories in Social Psychology," p. 341.

[25] The data from the 1964 Election Study utilized here were made available by the Inter-University Consortium for Political Research. The data were originally collected by the Survey Research Center of the University of Michigan. Neither source bears any responsibility for the index construction or interpretation presented here.

[26] The index is a summary of cognitive unit information as well as affect.

[27] From "Construction of Don Stokes' Six-Predictor Master Code Indexes," Memorandum, University of Michigan, Survey Research Center, May 22, 1967.

[28] Graph theory is a branch of mathematics and is more general than indicated here. Joseph Berger et al., *Types of Formalization in Small Group Research* (Boston: Houghton Mifflin Company, 1961); Frank Harary, Robert Norman, and Dorwin Cartwright, *Structural Models: An Introduction to the Theory of Directed Graphs* (New York: John Wiley & Sons, Inc., 1965); and John G. Kemeny and J. Laurie Snell, *Mathematical Models in the Social Sciences* (Waltham: Blaisdell Publishing Company, 1962), pp. 95–108.

[29] Angus Campbell, et al., *The American Voter* (New York: John Wiley and Sons, Inc., 1960), Chapter 10.

[30] Due to the logical connotations of balance theory, this index is not unlike aspects of dissonance theory. See Bernard C. Hennessy, *Public Opinion* (Belmont: Wadsworth Publishing Co., 1965), p. 324.

[31] *A Theory of Cognitive Dissonance*, p. 31.

[32] Albert Pepitone, "Some Conceptual and Empirical Problems of Consistency Models," in *Cognitive Consistency*, ed. Feldman, pp. 257–97.

[33] Robert Lane, *Political Ideology* (New York: The Free Press, 1962), pp. 30–31.

[34] R. B. Zajonc, "Balance, Congruity and Dissonance," p. 295.

[35] Robert Dahl, *Who Governs?* (New Haven: Yale University Press, 1961), p. 319.

[36] Although the independent variables are complex indices, the advantages of parsimonious indices on the dependent variables were avoided for both theoretical and methodological reasons. For example, theoretically, there are important differences (information, personal interaction, and involvement) between various participation variables in the context of balance theory. A serious methodological problem which constrains such index construction is the reduction of N, particularly for issue intensity and specific forms of participation. These problems became evident in a Candidate-Party-Issue index discussed in Kirkpatrick, "Social-Psychological Approaches to the Study of Political Phenomena."

[37] McPhee, Anderson, and Milholland, "Attitude Consistency," views partisanship as a stable element which has the potential to increase consistency. Also see Converse, "The Nature of Belief Systems in Mass Publics."

[38] Paul F. Lazarsfeld, Bernard Berelson, and Hazel Gaudet, *The People's Choice* (New York: Columbia University Press, 1948), pp. 60–61.

[39] Sperlich, "Cross-Pressure and Conflict in Political Behavior," p. 130. This is clearly a departure from early cross-pressures theory.

[40] Related panel data reported below support the ease of changing a cognitive component over an affect.

[41] Generalizations about this cell are difficult because only 7 percent of the inconsistents were located here.

[42] Kirkpatrick, "Issue Orientation and Voter Choice in 1964," p. 99.

[43] Sperlich, "Cross-Pressure and Conflict in Political Behavior," p. 130.

[44] Dick H. Baxter, "Interpersonal Contact and Exposure to Mass Media During a Presidential Campaign" (unpublished Ph.D. dissertation, Columbia University, 1951). A more recent study of political data in this theoretical context is Fred W. Grupp, "Personal Satisfactions Derived From Membership in the Birch Society" (unpublished paper delivered at the Annual Meeting of the Southwestern Political Science Association, Houston, Texas, April 3–5, 1969).

[45] *A Theory of Cognitive Dissonance*, p. 204.

[46] *Ibid.*, p. 127.

[47] Although a content analysis of newspapers read might be helpful, a recent review of selective exposure research supports the inconclusive nature of hypotheses on information seeking and avoidance. David O. Sears and Jonathan L. Freedman, "Selective Exposure to Information: A Critical Review," *Public Opinion Quarterly* 31 (1967): 194–214.

[48] Consistency of Public Opinion on Foreign Policy," p. 14.

[49] Robert E. Lane, *Political Life* (New York: The Free Press, 1959), Chapter 10.

[50] Brehm and Cohen, *Explorations in Cognitive Dissonance*, p. 178.

[51] *A Theory of Cognitive Dissonance*, p. 20.

[52] See Charles Y. Glock, "Some Applications of the Panel Method to the Study of Change," in Paul F. Lazarsfeld and Morris Rosenberg, eds., *The Language of Social Research* (New York: Free Press, 1955), pp. 242–50.

[53] Leo A. Goodman, "Statistical Methods for Analyzing Processes of Change," *American Journal of Sociology* 68 (1962): 57–78; and T. W. Anderson, "Probability Models for Analyzing Time Changes in Attitudes," in Paul F. Lazarsfeld, ed., *Mathematical Thinking in the Social Sciences* (New York: Free Press, 1954), pp. 17–66.

[54] The data utilized are the 1956 and 1958 election studies originally collected by the Survey Research Center of the University of Michigan and made available by the Inter-University Consortium for Political Research. Neither source bears any responsibility for the analysis or interpretation.

[55] There are eight possible sets of triads for each issue. For example, a consistent respondent could respond favorably to aid to education, believe the Democrats favored it, and maintain a Democratic party identification, whereas an inconsistent triad would include a Republican party identification.

[56] For example, when "perceptual correctness" is ideologically defined as the association of Democrats with more liberal causes, the employment issue indicates that 69 percent of the consistents at time 1 and 78 percent at time 2 are "perceptually correct."

[57] Although candidate affect is not measured in this series of indices, there is weak evidence to suggest that supporters of a winning candidate maintain their original attitudes whereas supporters of the loser change their opinion (after the election) to achieve congruity. See George Stricker, "The Operation of Cognitive Dissonance on Pre- and Post-election Attitudes," *Journal of Social Psychology* 63 (1964): 111–12.

[58] See James Bieri, "Attitudes and Arousal: Affect and Cogni-

tion in Personality Functioning," in Carolyn W. Sherif and Muzafer Sherif, eds., *Attitude, Ego-Involvement and Change* (New York: Wiley, 1967), pp. 178–200; and Milton Rosenberg, "An Analysis of Affective-Cognitive Consistency," in Carl I. Hovland and Milton J. Rosenberg, eds., *Attitude Organization and Change* (New Haven: Yale University Press, 1960), pp. 15–64.

[59] *Political Socialization* (Glencoe: The Free Press, 1959), p. 20.

[60] Prescott Lecky, *Self-Consistency: A Theory of Personality* (New York: Island Press, 1945), p. 119.

[61] Scott, "Rationality and Non-Rationality of International Attitudes," p. 11; and Zajonc, "Balance, Congruity and Dissonance," p. 280.

[62] Berelson, Lazarsfeld, and McPhee, *Voting,* p. 311.

[63] Seymour M. Lipset et al., "The Psychology of Voting: An Analysis of Political Behavior," in *Handbook of Social Psychology,* ed. Gardner Lindzey (Cambridge: Addison-Wesley Publishing Company, Inc., 1954), pp. 1124–75.

[64] Samuel A. Kirkpatrick, "Toward a Theory of Political Dissonance" (unpublished paper delivered at the Annual Meeting of the American Political Science Association, New York, September 2–6, 1969).

[65] Sheldon Wolin, *Politics and Vision* (Boston: Little, Brown & Co., 1960), Chapter 10.

9

Political Motivation

There is probably no single component of a social-psychological model of political behavior so little understood as motivation. The concept itself, as it is borrowed from psychology and social psychology, reflects complexities of definition and contradictory theories in those disciplines. In addition, it has been seriously underresearched in political science and often used as a catch-all concept synonymous with behavior.[1] This is often a reflection of the difficulties inherent in operationizing definitions and constructing empirical measurements. It is not our purpose to resolve these difficulties here, but to provide a general introduction to the concept and its role in political behavior.

In Chapter one we mentioned that behavior is not always consistent with belief systems, but that it does follow from them. This relationship was described as a function of the characteristics of the belief system and a broader set of influencing factors present in our model. This model locates motivation as a threshold between political belief systems and subsequent behavior. To ask what "pushes" an individual across this threshold is not unlike asking what causes his behavior. Yet there are determinants specific to the concept of motivation, for in treating it as a threshold, we imply that there must be a certain combination of influencing forces which translate opinions into behavior. We will address ourselves to some of these forces in reviewing motivation from a social–psychological perspective.

---

[1] An early attempt to categorize research on motivation is further evidence of its use as a residual term. See Wendel Bell, Richard J. Hill and Charles R. Wright, *Public Leadership* (San Francisco: Chandler Publishing Co., 1961), Chapter 8.

Driving Forces and Goals

For many social psychologists the motivational concept is offered in terms of driving forces (e.g., wants, fears) that imply a goal for achievement. These driving forces are "indicating and sustaining forces of behavior,"[2] some of which are positive (e.g., wants) and some of which are negative (e.g., aversions). These forces imply an object or set of objects to which they are directed, i.e., approach objects and avoidance objects. Indeed, there appear to be certain political objects which fall into one of these categories more than the other. Most people belong to and have an identification with a political party as an object, but political office is an avoidance object for most. In either instance actions imply goals, and objects or circumstances are the goals of motivated behavior. The goals which are chosen express wants (or motives); these wants are closely tied to personality, and goals vary according to personality, social processes and cultural norms. These goals are highly dependent on the individual's self-conception (e.g., self-esteem) which is a function of personality and social interaction with others.

When we speak of motivation in social-psychological terms we view behavior as a reflection of wants and goals, yet this view also implies that it is shaped by social and cultural factors, the context of the situation, habit and attitudes. Furthermore, wants are dependent on physiological needs (e.g., sex and hunger), as well as personality and social needs developed over time through the socialization process. The existence of goals dependent on wants and needs also implies a hierarchy of goals, some of which are more important to the individual than others.

The achievement of political office may not be an avoidance object, but merely a goal which occurs ultimately at the top of a hierarchy of goals. For some, a common power want may be linked to different goals (e.g., the president of a political club or a candidate for political office). The individual moves toward or away from certain goals with degrees of persistence. This movement implies both direction and persistence of action. The direction of action may be toward joining a political party, yet a complex hierarchy implies a necessary persistence. These concepts of directionality[3] and persistence suggest that motivation is not merely an inducement to act or behave, but also to continue to do so in one direction. And as the Grupp article points out, the motivations for action (joining the John Birch Society) may be different from the motivation to persist or

[2] David Krech, Richard S. Crutchfield and Egerton L. Ballachey, *Individual in Society* (McGraw-Hill Book Company, Inc., 1962), p. 69.

[3] See Roger Brown, *Social Psychology* (New York: The Free Press, 1965), p. 422.

remain a member. The concept of directionality reflected in a pattern of behavior is not unlike working one's way through a maze. The progress through that maze of goals and achievements and reinforcements is a function of the intensity of motivation as it is reflected in the strength and endurance of directionality. The individual's motivations may change, and his goal objects may change at various points in that maze.

The Threshold Concept: Predisposition and Environment

A threshold concept of motivation implies a point at which a set of individual predispositions "take command" of the individual.[4] These predispositions include physiological and psychological needs and the existing belief system. Certain predispositions win out over others in controlling the organism. The number and quality of these predispositions, such as the strength of needs and the intensity of the belief system, are important. Yet environmental cues are necessary for arousing these predispositions. The effectiveness of cues or stimuli reflect the nature of the goal object (e.g., the political office), its availability and the individual's perception of its availability in the environment, the context of the situation, and the strength of the stimuli. A stimulus will be stronger if it has been reinforced and if the individual has been "rewarded" in the past. This reinforcement is inherent in the process of political socialization, as well as in the process of "maze wandering" in a hierarchy of goals based upon this socialization. A strong stimulus may even call up weaker predispositions which serve to catapult the individual over the threshold to act. An individual may have needs which are met in ways other than political participation, and his belief system may lack intensity and constraint; yet the strong stimulus of a vigorous political campaign may at least stimulate him to vote. Nevertheless, the interaction of these stimuli and predispositions may not be sufficient to stimulate broader and more intense forms of political participation. In many ways, motivation reflects a sensitization of the individual to the possibilities in his political environment.

Both predispositions and environmental stimuli contribute to the threshold of motivation for the individual. As we have stated previously, these predispositions include physiological and psychological needs and the existing belief system. The stimuli which interact with them are basically two-fold: non-political stimuli in the environment which contribute to these predispositions, and specific objects to which political motivation

[4] See Lester W. Milbrath, *Political Participation* (Chicago: Rand McNally & Company, 1965), pp. 30ff.

is directed. Crossing the threshold is a function of the strength of the stimuli, the context in which they occur, and the nature of the political goal object.

Cultural and Social Pressures

The non-political stimuli relevant for political motivation are as diverse as we have described them throughout the book. Cultural patterns help to define the roles and expectations of individual motivation; they often set boundaries which define behavioral proscriptions and therefore inhibit political motivation. Even cultural definitions of sex roles inhibit motivation toward certain political objects for women which are not so inhibited for men. In the American political culture the Jacksonian myth of political action contributes to the norms of behavior and the meaning of civic duty. In addition, a wide range of social factors, such as social status and group affiliation, shape access to information about political goal objects; they define the meaning of social cross-pressures which may serve to inhibit motivation; and they shape the context of the social situation through which goal objects are given meaning. An individual's social status contributes to the relevancy of political policy for the individual such that, e.g., those subjected to greater economic restrictions may be highly motivated to change that policy. We have previously noted that individuals with inconsistent statuses are highly motivated to change environmental conditions which contribute to those inconsistencies. Direct and immediate economic impact has also been found to play an important role. We know, for example, that money is of some importance (but not a single factor) in motivating individuals to assume the role of political party worker,[5] that patronage rewards have motivated political activity, and that generally secondary payoffs and favors encourage formal cooptation of businessmen into the political structure.

The Nature of Political Objects

The nature of political goal objects is also important for motivation. Many objects, such as high political office, are not readily available in the political system. Furthermore, motivation varies according to different goal objects. Although there are common factors contributing to moti-

---

[5] Bernard Berelson, Paul Lazarsfeld and William McPhee, *Voting* (Chicago: University of Chicago Press, 1954), pp. 164ff.

vation for political participation on the one hand, and motivation to seek political office on the other, the wants served by each may vary.

By saying that the nature of the goal object is important, we are recognizing that its nature is shaped by individual perceptions of the object. This implies that the most important influences on motivation are predispositional. Indeed, this is the meaning offered by most social psychologists and by the political scientists whose work is presented in this chapter. Physiological needs may stimulate this driving force, but psychological needs and the nature of the belief system are prime factors. Motivation is not necessarily tied to attitude, for some actions may reflect habit, yet the structure of the belief system, its intensity, constraint, and its components are directly influential. We have previously defined attitude as an admixture of cognitive and affective components, yet there is a further component recognized by social psychologists. This component is sometimes referred to as the *behavioral* or *conative* component — one that symbolizes readiness to act. It recognizes that attitudes have motivational qualities which can lead one to seek or avoid the political objects about which they are organized.[6] Each attitude toward a specific political object (candidates, policies) is a political opinion which contains a readiness to behave or a behavioral intention. When the conative component is weak or when it is not activated, there may be weak linkage between the cognitive and affective components on the one hand, and overt behavior on the other.

The activation of this conative component is highly dependent upon the final predispositional elements, personality and psychological needs. This dependence is a common theme of the readings in this chapter. It recognizes that needs not only shape attitudes, but motivation for action as well. These psychological needs may range from Lasswell's values of power and deference which reflect a primary need for self-concept, to the needs of relieving intrapsychic tension, understanding, knowing, and belonging.[7]

One of the earliest political science formulations of motivations focused on power drives. Lasswell postulated that the individual accentuates power over other values in his personality and that this emphasis in turn compensates for a low estimate of the self. The typical "political type" according to Lasswell, displaces these private motives onto the public sphere and rationalizes them in terms of civic duty or the public interest. Furthermore, we have previously seen how such personality traits as authoritarianism, alienation, and misanthropy can lead to varying degrees of political ineffectiveness.

---

[6] See Milton Rokeach, *Beliefs, Attitudes, and Values: A Theory of Organization and Change* (San Francisco: Jossey-Bass, Inc., 1968), pp. 114ff.

[7] See Harold D. Lasswell, *Power and Personality* (New York: The Viking Press, 1948); Robert E. Lane, *Political Life* (Glencoe: The Free Press, 1959).

Power Motivation

Lasswell's concept of power motivation is an integral part of the research recorded below by Browning and Jacob. By using a projective test
to measure power, achievement, and affiliative motivation, they are able
to test hypotheses about the presence of these motivations in politicians
and non-politicians. Although they find few differences between the two
groups in terms of motivation—a finding which is itself significant—they
proceed to examine the impact of political system characteristics on variations in motivational levels for politicians. The individual's motivation to
enter or remain in politics is not only a function of individual motivation
or the need for satisfaction, but also his perception of satisfaction in a set
of alternative activities. In turn, these motivations vary for different
political offices (e.g., men in positions of power have higher power motives) and between different political systems. The systems which they
examined offered different opportunities for power and achievement, and
they find that one city tends to attract more highly motivated men.

Organizational Behavior and Recruitment

Barber also takes a need-oriented approach to explain differences in
motivation to enter politics and remain there. His study focuses on the
political recruitment of state legislators, who lend themselves to a four-
fold typology based upon their level of legislative activity and their
commitment to the office (willingness to return):

(1) *The Spectator:* This legislative type displays a low level of legislative activity but a high willingness to return. He also enjoys the entertainment and drama aspect of legislative life; he is likely to come from a
non-competitive small town; and he is personally inadequate, a socializer
and only slightly involved in the substantive work of the legislature.

(2) *The Advertiser:* This individual is high in activity but low in willingness to return. His goal is to seek contacts which are occupationally
beneficial, and he tends to be a young upward-mobile lawyer who is linked
to politics through his occupation. As a consequence, he feels powerless
and anxious, and tends to dwell on his own suffering as a reflection of his
difficulty in accepting his place in the system.

(3) *The Reluctant:* This individual tends to be a hometown reliable,
recruited through a sense of civic duty from a non-competitive district.
He is low in legislative activity and low in his willingness to return, and
he tends to be bewildered by the legislative pace and its strange environment. His legislative work is hampered by his background, and, although

he has a high sense of moral responsibility, he often feels useless and tends to withdraw.

(4) *The Lawmaker:* This modal type is high in legislative activity and high in his commitment to the office. He tends to be young, mobile, attentive to substantive tasks, interested in issues, and interested in the legislature as a full-time job. Furthermore, his energies focus on bills, and he makes a significant contribution to the passage of legislation. Although he has a strong sense of individuality, he works cooperatively with others within the legislative system.

In the essay presented below, Barber offers an explanation of differing levels of motivation for the various legislative role types. He speaks of "motivational potentialities" as they exist long before candidacy as being a function of general interest in politics and, more importantly, a function of needs, e.g., power, display, which can be met (or perceived to be met) in political life. He therefore bases the legislator's motivation on "a collection of adjustive techniques or strategies by which he attempts to maximize the satisfaction of his needs." The pursuit of these strategies towards goal objects is not unlike our previously mentioned concept of pattern-behavior maze. These motivations are conditioned by the extent to which the political environment offers a means to satisfy needs or is perceived to offer such a means. Again, motivation reflects a sensitization of the individual to the possibilities in his environment.

Although most studies of political participation link behavior to high self-esteem, Barber finds two patterns operating when the object is political office. Three of his legislative types are low in self-esteem, and he suggests that they seek political office to compensate for their inadequacies. Yet the Lawmaker of high self-esteem is capable of managing the risk, strains, and threats of the office. He therefore finds that political candidacy is a form of deviant behavior "drawing toward it exceptional people—exceptional either in their high abilities or in their strong needs." These differences between needs and motivations, and the conflicts between the ideal and real self are examined in some detail.

The political object focus for the Grupp research is not on political office, but on membership in an extremist group: the John Birch Society. Membership in any group can be defined in terms of shared attitudes that reflect the need to be comfortable with peers. Generally, an individual is often motivated to join a group because it provides him with a perceptual screen which filters out dissonant information—it helps to shape his political alternatives, to articulate his interests, to translate attitudes into specific political opinions, to define facts, and to offer him a life-perspective or social identity.

In a more specific way, Grupp contends that people join a political group such as the John Birch Society in order to fulfill such basic needs as information, association, ideology, commitment, or religion. These needs are not unlike common needs discussed by others, e.g. Maslow's need to know and understand, and Lane's cognitive needs (learning, curiosity).[8] But the research reported below makes a distinction between motivation to join and motivation to remain a member. The author finds that most join for ideological reasons (e.g., to fight communism and moral decay) rather than to meet associational or informational needs. Yet some degree of motivation is necessary for one to remain in a political group, i.e., he must reach a threshold of satisfaction and his original motives must be satisfied, or he must rationalize his acts on the basis of new satisfactions. After one joins the John Birch Society, the major satisfaction is not ideological, and there is a shift from goal orientation to action orientation where political commitment is a primary motivation to remain.

Each of the readings to follow treat aspects of motivation, particularly those emphasizing a motive as an "engaged need," reflecting "latent conditions" and predispositions to act.[9] These subsequent actions are important inputs for the political system as they are mediated by the components of that system and result in public policy. These policies are the major outputs of the political system which in turn shape a host of environmental stimuli, which are crucial in the dynamic process of political life.

Selected Additional Readings

Bell, Wendel, Richard J. Hill, and Charles R. Wright. *Public Leadership,* Chapter 8. San Francisco: Chandler Publishing Co., 1961.

Berelson, Bernard R., Paul F. Lazarfeld, and William N. McPhee. *Voting.* Chicago: University of Chicago Press, 1954, *passim.*

Blum, Alan F., and Peter McHugh. "The Social Ascription of Motives." *American Sociological Review* 36 (1971): 98–109.

Bowen, Don R. *Political Behavior of the American Public.* Columbus: Charles E. Merrill Publishing Co., 1968.

Campbell, Angus, et al. *The American Voter.* New York: John Wiley & Sons, Inc., 1960, *passim.*

Campbell, Angus. "The Passive Citizen." *Acta Sociologica* 6 (1962): 9–21.

Conway, M. Margaret, and Frank B. Feigert. "Motivations, Incentive Systems, and the Political Party Organizations." *American Political Science Review* 62 (1968): 1159–73.

Crowne, Douglas P., and David Marlowe. *The Approval Motive.* New York: John Wiley & Sons, Inc., 1964.

Feldman, Shel, ed. *Cognitive Consistency: Motivational Antecedents and Behavioral Consequents.* New York: Academic Press, 1966.

Hennessy, Bernard C. "Politicals and Apoliticals: Some Measurements of Personality Characteristics." *Midwest Journal of Political Science* 3 (1959): 336–55.

Kornberg, Allan, Darwyn Linder, and Joel Cooper. "Understanding Political Behavior: The Relevance of Reactance Theory," *Midwest Journal of Political Science* 14 (1970): 131–38.

Krause, Merton, S. et al. "Some Motivational Correlates of Attitudes Toward Political Participation." *Midwest Journal of Political Science* 14 (1970): 383–91.

Lane, Robert E. *Political Life.* Glencoe: The Free Press, 1959.

Lane, Robert E. *Political Thinking and Consciousness.* Chicago: Markham Publishing Company, 1969.

Lasswell, Harold D. *Power and Personality.* New York: The Viking Press, 1948.

Maslow, A. H. *Motivation and Personality.* New York: Harper and Row, 1954.

Milbrath, Lester W. *Political Participation.* Chicago: Rand McNally & Company, 1965.

Rosenberg, Morris. "Some Determinants of Political Apathy." *Public Opinion Quarterly* 18 (1954–55): 349–66.

[8] A. H. Maslow, *Motivation and Personality* (New York: Harper and Row, 1954), pp. 80–98; Robert E. Lane, *Political Thinking and Consciousness* (Chicago: Markham Publishing Company, 1969), pp. 26–31.

[9] The terms are developed by Lane, *ibid.,* p. 22.

Personal Satisfaction Derived from Membership in the John Birch Society

Fred W. Grupp, Jr.

This study focuses on the recruitment and retention of members of the John Birch Society as perceived by the individual members.[1] What motivated the individual to join the Society? Why does he remain a member? And how can changes between the reasons for joining and the satisfactions derived from membership by the individual member be explained?

The Research

Responses to the question, "What is the single most important reason for your joining the Society?" were coded into these categories — become informed; associate with like-minded people; ideological; need for political commitment; religious; and other.[2]

The findings, presented in Table 1, indicate that three of every five Birchers were motivated to join the Society by ideological concerns. An additional sixth joined out of a desire to associate with people whose views were similar to their own; 11 percent sought to become informed; eight percent indicated

Fred W. Grupp, Jr., "Personal Satisfaction Derived from Membership in the John Birch Society," *Western Political Quarterly* 24 (1971): 79–83. Reprinted by permission of the University of Utah, Copyright holder.

An earlier version of this paper was presented at the Southwestern Social Science Association meetings in Houston, April 3–5, 1969.

a need to be politically involved, with the remaining few distributed among the other categories.

The data in Table 1 clearly reveal the shrinkage that takes place among the ideologically motivated members. Each of the other satisfaction categories shows an increase. Thus, many of the goal-directed respondents have come to prize their membership for other reasons. Long ago, Gordon Allport noted the "functional autonomy" of human motives.[3] His observation that individuals may tend to develop an attachment to the instrumental activity itself, rather than to the original goal, is particularly relevant to this study. Approximately one-third of the Birch members derive their satisfaction with membership from the activity associated with it. These political commitment members are action, rather than goal, oriented.

Other social scientists have discussed changing motivations among members of organizations. According to March and Simon, when the basic group goals are non-operational there is a tendency to evaluate group progress in terms of more operational sub-goals.[4] They cite several reasons for this change in emphasis. First, within the individual member, selective perception and rationalization tend to elevate in importance the operational sub-goals which may be only marginally related to the larger, non-operational, group goals. A second reason for the persistence of sub-goals is that in-group communications may serve to reinforce them.

Both processes are evidently at work in the John

Table 1

Most Important Reason for Joining and Personal Satisfaction of Membership among Birchers by Category (in percentages)

Category	Reasons for Joining	JBS Satisfaction	Change
Become Informed	11%	16%	+ 5%
Associate with Like-Minded People	17	19	+ 2
Ideological	61	19	−42
Need for Political Commitment	8	37	+29
Religious	1	2	+ 1
Dissatisfied	−	3	+ 3
Other (including Not Ascertained)	2	4	+ 2
Total	100%	100%	
Number of Cases	650	650	

Birch Society. The extent to which Society goals are non-operational is revealed in this excerpt from the *Bulletin:* "But it is the very purpose, and reason for existence, of The John Birch Society, to blaze a path of truth through the darkness of deception and immorality and cruelty and corruption, which now hovers over our whole earth — to a plateau of light and sanity and freedom and kindness, and honesty and peaceful labor, which other men may then behold with longing and with hope."[5] The Bircher who circulates an "Impeach Warren" petition perceives this activity as promoting Society goals and is praised for the effort by the Birch leadership.

Cognitive Dissonance Theory

The theory of cognitive dissonance provides a more complete explanatory framework for the data. According to Festinger and Aronson, dissonance may result from unrewarded striving. They wrote: "If an individual is in a situation in which he continues to expend effort in order to reach some goal, yet does not reach it, he will experience dissonance. His cognition that he is expending effort will be dissonant with his cognition that he is unrewarded.[6] The ideologically motivated Birchers should have been particularly susceptible to dissonance of this type at the time that the questionnaires were distributed — during the highly productive first session of the 89th Congress.

One way for the Birch member to reduce the dissonance caused by the unsuccessful pursuit of ideological goals is to come to regard favorably the activity itself, in much the same way that the golfing duffer expresses satisfaction with the exercise associated with a round of golf rather than with the score. This mode of dissonance reduction seems prevalent in the Birch Society. Over one-third of the 399 ideologically motivated Birchers satisfy a need for political commitment from the activity associated with membership.

In addition to valuing the effort rather than the unachieved goal, the individual can also reduce dissonance by obtaining social support from people who hold opinions similar to his own.[7] One of every five of the Birchers who joined for ideological reasons prizes his membership because it affords him the opportunity to associate with like-minded people, indicating extensive need for social support among these respondents.

These two modes of dissonance reduction were utilized by over half of the ideologically motivated respondents and account for almost three-fourths of the ideological joiners who find satisfaction from other than ideological reasons. Overall, 277 ideological joiners find non-ideological satisfaction from membership, while only 31 Birchers who joined for other reasons cite ideological satisfaction derived from membership.

Another way of reducing dissonance caused by unrewarded effort is to overvalue the group for whom the effort is being expended.[8] Four-fifths of the respondents consider their membership in the John Birch Society to be their most important group attachment. And the highest rates of valuing membership in the Birch Society are found among the respondents who derive their satisfaction from associating with like-minded people and those who fulfill their need for political commitment through membership. In other words, those who receive social support and those who value the activity associated with membership— both ways of reducing dissonance caused by unrewarded effort—are the ones who value their membership in the Society the most.

It is significant that these dissonance reducing processes are at work among the chapter leaders as well as among the ordinary members. While chapter leaders are somewhat more likely to have joined for ideological reasons than were nonleaders (67 to 60 percent) and slightly more likely to derive ideological satisfaction from membership (23 to 16 percent) the interesting and most relevant aspect of these figures is the similarity, not the difference, between them. Almost identical percentages of the leaders and followers who joined the John Birch Society for ideological reasons have come to value either the activity associated with membership or the social support from like-minded people, with the leaders tending to be activity oriented (42 to 36 percent) and the followers tending to prize the social support benefits (20 to 15 percent) of membership. Thus, among the ideologically motivated, leaders and non-leaders engage almost equally in these two forms of dissonance reduction.

There is some evidence that dissonance caused by unrewarded effort extends to the upper levels of the organizational elite as well. For example, in July of 1965, Robert Welch indicated some awareness of the lack of progress toward Society goals in this message to the membership:

> In the movement to impeach Warren, for instance, or in the long slow campaign to *Get us Out!* of the United Nations, we have not been strong enough, and hence have not yet made any effort, to meet the enemy head on. . . . In our efforts to expose the "civil rights" fraud, however, we are moving from a strategy of continuous skirmishes into the tactics of a direct engagement. We are now embarking, for the first time, on an undertaking which can do palpable damage in reasonably short order to an important front of the advancing Communist lines.[9]

The passage of the Voting Rights Act of 1965, just a month after Welch made these observations, and the subsequent enactment of the Civil Rights Act of 1968 cannot have gone unnoticed by Society members. The organizational elite, the chapter leaders, and the "ordinary" members must be aware that the Society's program to "fully expose the civil rights fraud and you will break the back of the Communist conspiracy"[10] was singularly unsuccessful. Hence the extraordinary effort in support of this project[11] should have produced dissonance among leaders and followers alike.

Conclusion

Research in cognitive dissonance has provided a theoretical basis for evaluating the reported changes between the motivations to join and the satisfactions derived from membership of the Birch respondents. The data reveal that chapter leaders are about as likely as the other members to engage in dissonance reduction. There is reason to believe that the same processes are at work among the national leadership of the Birch Society as well.

One implication of these findings for the Birch Society is that the leaders and followers can be expected to place their emphasis on the activity associated with membership rather than on the actual achievement of symbolic Society goals. Success, for Birchers, is measured in terms of more operational sub-goals— the number of new recruits, the number of study clubs formed, the number of signatures gathered, and the number of pamphlets distributed. In addition, the Bircher can be expected to overvalue his membership in the Society – "the finest body of men and women in the world"[12] – and his social relationship with other Birchers.

The data suggest that recruiting by the Birch Society will be less effective since the Nixon victory. The Society is most effective in recruiting among the ideologically dissatisfied and the presence of a Republican in the White House weakens the Administration as a target for ideological hostility.[13]

To generalize beyond the date, it seems likely that any organization, whose major goals are ideological, whose primary appeal is to the ideologically dissatisfied *and* which elects to remain within the "rules of the game" – that is, to utilize legitimate means, such as circulating petitions, organizing study groups, running candidates for office, or lobbying – will suffer the decline in ideological intensity predicted by dissonance theory. The capacity of the American political system to thwart, delay, and finally absorb radical change[14] insures that dissonance due to unrewarded striving will occur among ideological activists, whether they are New Leftists or Radical Rightists.

Notes

[1] The data come from a mail survey of a sample of the national membership of the John Birch Society conducted in July of 1965. The sample of 1,866 Birchers was drawn by the Society and resulted in 650 completed questionnaires for a response rate of 35 percent. Without access to the mailing list it was impossible to utilize normal follow-up procedures. Furthermore, the questionnaire was lengthy and contained several complex, open-ended questions. As a result, the responses may overrepresent the better educated, more literate segment of the Birch membership. In addition, chapter leaders and other officials of the Society comprised 21 percent of the respondents; they are obviously overrepresented.

A more complete discussion of methodological problems may be found in F. Grupp, "Social Correlates of Political Activists: The John Birch Society and the ADA" (Ph.D. dissertation, University of Pennsylvania, 1968), Appendix I.

[2] Typical responses in each category are these: A. Become Informed; "To learn the TRUTH"; "Become better informed." B. Associate with Like-minded People: "To be with people who see things the way I do"; "The JBS has the same views I do." C. Ideological: "Save the U.S. from Communism"; "Promote Individual Liberty." D. Need for Political Commitment: "Knowledge that I am doing something"; "I was concerned." E. Religious: "To fight the Anti-Christ"; "To work for God." F. Other: "Pressure of friends"; "To meet girls."

[3] G. Allport, "The Functional Autonomy of Motives," *American Journal of Psychology* 50 (1937): 146.

[4] J. March and H. Simon, *Organizations* (New York: Wiley, 1958), pp. 150–54.

[5] *Bulletin,* April 1965, pp. 1–2.

[6] L. Festinger and E. Aronson, "The Arousal and Reduction of Dissonance in Social Contexts," in D. Cartwright and A. Zander, eds., *Group Dynamics,* 2nd ed. (Evanston: Row, Peterson, 1960), pp. 218–19.

[7] *Ibid.,* p. 229.

[8] E. Aronson and J. Mills, "The Effect of Severity of Initiation on Liking for a Group," *Journal of Abnormal and Social Psychology* 59 (1959): 177–81.

[9] *Bulletin,* July 1965, p. 2.

[10] *Bulletin,* May 1965, p. 10.

[11] Six times as much space was given to this Society program as was expended on any other in the four monthly *Bulletins* (April–July) preceding the distribution of the questionnaires. In addition, the April issue was accompanied by a sixteen-page pamphlet, *Two Revolutions at Once,* which portrayed the civil rights movement as communist inspired and controlled. In May, one hundred copies of this pamphlet were mailed to each chapter for free distribution. See the *Bulletin,* May 1965, p. 11.

[12] *Bulletin,* April 1965, p. 2.

[13] Only 2 percent of the membership identified with the Democratic party. Another 3 percent considered themselves hyphenated Democrats – e.g., Goldwater Democrats. The overwhelming majority of Birchers are Republicans.

[14] An interesting journalistic view of this phenomenon is A. Kopkind, "Are We in the Middle of A Revolution?" *New York Times Magazine,* November 10, 1968, pp. 54–66.

Power Motivation and the Political Personality

Rufus P. Browning

Herbert Jacob

How important is the desire for power in the quest for political office? To what extent does it dominate the acts of politicians, of political leaders? The common assumption, reflected in many political biographies and in popular writing, is that the quest for power propels many into politics and is a most likely explanation for much of the politician's activity. Political scientists—especially in recent years—have been a bit more cautious. Harold D. Lasswell wrote fifteen years ago that political man accentuates power, demands power for the self, accentuates expectations concerning power, and acquires at least a minimum proficiency in the skills of power.[1] Yet a few years later, speaking of democratic political man, Lasswell noted that the power-hungry individual may be too compulsive and rigid to win power; he is more likely to be found at the fringes of the political system than at its center.[2] In reviewing what little evidence existed on the motivations of politicians, Robert Lane suggested that "among the leaders of a democracy there is little tendency for a higher-than-average concentration of persons with needs to exercise power over others."[3]

Reprinted by permission of the publisher and authors from Rufus P. Browning and Herbert Jacob, "Power Motivation and the Political Personality," *Public Opinion Quarterly* 28 (Spring, 1964): 75–90.

Research by Rufus P. Browning was supported by a Ford Foundation grant to Yale University for the study of business and politics. Helpful criticism and suggestions by Messrs. Robert A. Dahl, Dave Barber, and Fred Greenstein are gratefully acknowledged. Research by Herbert Jacob was made possible by a Ford Foundation Public Affairs Grant administered by Tulane University.

Little empirical work has been done in the field, for valid measures of power motivation have not been available.[4] In recent years, however, psychologists have developed a projective test that taps power motivation as well as achievement and affiliative motivation. They have given the test to experimental groups, students, businessmen, and armed forces personnel, and to a nationwide sample. One of the developers of the test has used it to expound a unique psychological theory of economic development.[5] This paper applies the test for the first time to politicians. We examine the intensity of power motivation (as measured by the test) displayed by politicians in two widely separated locales. The questions we ask are: (1) How strongly are politicians motivated to seek power, achievement, and friendship (affiliation) as compared with nonpoliticians? (2) To what extent do characteristics of the political system—specifically, the kinds of positions available and the opportunity structure of the community—make a difference in the motivations of the individuals attracted to politics?

The Test of Motivation[6]

The test we used is an outgrowth of the Thematic Apperception Test. Like the TAT, it assumes that respondents will reveal deeply rooted impulses in their imaginative responses to pictures. The form we used consisted of six pictures: an older man talking to a younger one in a rather old-fashioned office; a man sitting at what is apparently a drafting table with a picture of a woman and children in front of him; seven younger men around a table; a man working at a desk in an otherwise dark office, hat and coat piled at the side; a man in city clothes talking to a boy sitting on a farm fence; and a man leaning back in what many people interpret as a seat in an airplane with papers or a book on his lap.

These pictures sometimes evoke stories with clear political content, such as this one:

[This man] is organizing, no doubt, or joined an organization, giving his points or giving his political—giving out what he thinks is so, giving out his orders, or forming an organization. He's a leader. I have no doubt that he wants good government. If this is the same man in this picture, he has one thing in mind and that is to bring out the picture for generations to come. These people will go out, no doubt, this man is going out now to campaign. You've got four interested parties listening to him and they're going to bring charges against him.

The main character is an influential person, he is engaged in influencing activity, and he wants to be influential—all signs of concern about power. Power-oriented stories may also be present in an entirely nonpolitical context:

It looks like a group of young fellows in a club. One is pointing up some decision, trying to get the others to go along. One is not interested at all, and one is undecided. The man sitting down, pointing, is the one who is very strong with his thoughts. He is going to win out and get his point across.

The scoring system does not depend on the context of the plot but rather on the actions or feelings depicted. When a story involves attempts to control others, it is scored for power motivation. Additional points are scored if someone in the story is actually influencing others, anticipates doing so, shows joy or anguish about influencing others, states a need to influence, or overcomes obstacles in influencing others. The stories are scored in a like manner for achieve-

ment motivation when stories concern individuals trying to do well in any activity and for affiliative motivation when stories involve attempts to win or maintain friendly relationships with others.

The scoring system has been standardized to allow self-training with the use of a manual, so that a novice can quickly score stories expertly.[7] Each story is scored separately for each of the motives. A maximum possible score on the six-story test is 60 for power and affiliative motivation and 66 for achievement, but these are never attained; almost all of our scores lie in the 0 to 20 range.

The test is well validated, in several ways.[8] Versions of it have been experimentally validated (mainly with students), in that the test has been shown to measure individual responses to experimental situations that are presumed to arouse motivation. For instance, men who were told the test was a measure of ability and might affect their career chances scored higher in achievement motivation than men who were told it was just a graduate student's experiment. Candidates for campus office had higher power motivation scores while waiting for ballots to be counted than other students showed during an ordinary classroom session. Students who had just been rated for popularity by their fraternity brothers scored higher in affiliative motivation than a fraternity group that took the test routinely along with a food-rating test.

More substantial and theoretically much more interesting validations than these, however, stem from dozens of studies exploring relationships between motivation, on the one hand, and features of behavior, role, status, upbringing, and other variables, on the other hand.[9] Studies have shown that men with strong achievement motivation perform well in a variety of tasks, tend to persist longer, choose moderate, realistic risks rather than very safe or very doubtful ones, and perform better as the chances of success drop, apparently stimulated by the challenge of a difficult task. Achievement motivation in men is the result of quite specific patterns of relationships with the boy's father and mother, and these characteristic child-raising practices are related to the socio-economic class of the parents.

Somewhat fragmentary evidence indicates that men with strong power motivation are more argumentative and try to influence others more frequently.[10]

Studies of the behavioral correlates of affiliative motivation suggest that those who score high tend to seek approval more than others, but their peers rate them as relatively unpopular; they are also rated as overcautious and dependent on others for decisions. In contrast, men high in achievement motivation but low in affiliative motivation are rated as socially poised and adept, self-possessed, and consistent; this group is strong in such qualities as conversational facility and ability to communicate ideas effectively. Furthermore, this group (low in affiliative motivation) states a preference for working with people rather than with things.[11] Note that affiliative motivation—concern with warm, friendly relationships—is not necessarily an approach motive and apparently may often be a real barrier to dealing with people. It seems that strong concern for friendly personal relationships, perhaps accompanied by anxieties that interfere with attempts to relieve such concern, manifests itself in part in behavior that is usually not admired or liked—approval seeking, excessive caution, vacillation, etc. It is apparent that motive-generated acts may not lead to goal attainment and motive satisfaction. Affiliative motivation is not the same thing as sociability or liking to be with people. We should not expect the stereotype of the glad-handing politician to score high on this motive.

In short, these measures of motivation are associated with a large range of variables prominent in leadership recruitment and other behavior of leaders—e.g. risk taking, class background, dependence, consistency, sensitivity to opportunities to influence others. For instance, it would be surprising if the ability to assess risks and a willingness to take moderate, realistic ones were not important ingredients in the rise to high office and in the making of public policy decisions. As another obvious example, we are very often concerned about the degree of dependence of political executives on the people with whom they deal. It seems plausible that motivational factors are important in cases like these.

Administration of the Test

In the present application, the authors gave the test to politicians at the beginning of an hour-long interview on their political careers. It was introduced as a test of imagination, with no hint given that the purpose was to measure motivation. Stories respondents told were recorded in one case by shorthand (Browning) and in the other by tape recorder (Jacob), with respondents' consent. When the stories were scored, the identity of the respondent was effectively hidden.

We tested politicians in two places: a middle-sized Eastern city (Browning) and two parishes (counties) in Louisiana (Jacob). In Louisiana, the sample consisted of 50 elected local officials who represented 67 percent of all elected officials in their parishes.[12] In Eastern City, respondents were a random sample of 23 businessmen (not retired) who had been or were ward chairmen, had run for or held elective office (both local and state) in the city, or had held appointive patronage positions, usually only part-time in conjunction with political activity at the ward level.[13] In addition, the test was given in Eastern City to a sample of 18 politically inactive businessmen who matched 18 of the businessmen-politicians with respect to type and size of business, career level and specific occupation, religion, ethnic background, urban residence, average education, and age.

Motivations of Politicians

In the literature of political science, one can find almost as many reasons for expecting politicians to exhibit moderate power motivation as high power motivation. Although politics is frequently concerned with power, blatantly power-hungry individuals are distrusted in a democratic system. It is common, nevertheless, to suppose that all politicians have at least some basic traits in common, among them concern for power.[14]

Our evidence does nothing to support this image. In Table 1, Eastern City politicians have only slightly higher mean power motive scores than the matched nonpoliticians, and the variation within both groups is large. Indeed, in Louisiana, 12 of the 50 politicians scored zero on the test. In short, politicians we tested did not uniformly have any particular level of power motivation, and are not clearly different in power motivation from nonpoliticians of similar occupation and status.

The sociability of politicians has often been noted. The test permits us to assess concern for warm personal relationships. We hypothesized that politicians would score low on this trait, for much of politics is inimical to this kind of relationship. In contrast to sociability, i.e. a friendly manner, the real need for friendship and approval that characterizes a high level of affiliative motivation is probably incompatible with political activity. Politicking often requires single-minded attention to winning over others or manipulating them; it may also entail hurting some friends and helping others if one tends to regard political acquaintances and associates as potential friends.

The data in Table 1 show that this line of reasoning is apparently wrong—in Eastern City, businessmen-politicians as a group are *more* concerned with friendship than businessmen who are not politicians. In Louisiana, the degree of dispersion on this measure was about the same as in Eastern City. As with power, politicians apparently do not possess a uniform level of affiliative motivation and are not clearly different from nonpoliticians.

Familiar characterizations of politics as involving risk taking and persistence led us to hypothesize that politicians would score high on achievement motivation. But the Eastern City politicians did not in any sense score significantly higher than nonpoliticians (Table 1). In Louisiana, 10 of the 50 had zero scores, while others scored quite high.

In sum, our data indicate that none of the three motives are peculiarly characteristic of the total samples of politicians tested. When compared with a control group, politicians did not differ markedly from non-politicians. Moreover, in both Eastern City and

Table 1

Mean Motive Scores of Politically Active and Inactive Businessmen in Eastern City (18 Matched Pairs)

Motive*	Politicians	Non-politicians	Diff.	p of Diff.†
Power	6.5	5.2	1.3	.13‡
Affiliation	4.2	2.9	1.3	.28§
Achievement	7.4	6.1	1.3	.20‡

* Differences within groups between power, achievement, and affiliative motive scores do not signify that a group has, for instance, on the average "more" achievement than affiliative motivation; the evocation of motive-related imagery of various sorts is heavily dependent on the cues in the particular pictures used. Hence scores for each motive are comparable between individuals or groups, but not between motives in the same individual or group.

† From Wilcoxon matched-pairs signed-ranks test on ranked motive scores; hence the different p-values in spite of identical differences between means.

‡ One-tailed.

§ Two-tailed (difference not in predicted direction).

Louisiana, all three sets of motive scores showed considerable dispersion, indicating a lack of homogeneity in our samples with respect to motivation.

Motivation in the Context of the Political System

This variation in scores encourages us to look for factors that would lead individuals with different motives to enter or remain in politics. Two obvious sets of factors involve the characteristics of the political system, and within the system, the characteristics of the specific offices available. We believe that these characteristics engage the motivations of politicians in identifiable patterns that can help us explain the recruitment of certain individuals into politics.

Motivated behavior—for example, the choice of one activity over another less preferred—is the product of (1) the individual's underlying motivation, or need for a certain kind of satisfaction, and (2) his expectations or perception of motive satisfaction in the alternative activities.[15] A person highly motivated for power may choose to concentrate on business (or take it out on his wife) rather than get into politics. In some cases, this is the result of other motives—for instance, a desire to make a great deal of money, or a desire for prestige in a group in which business occupations are highly valued. But the choice is in part also the result of the individual's perceptions of business and politics. He may be quite ignorant of politics and expect opportunities for influence only in business. He may perceive opportunities in politics but expect, rightly or wrongly, that they are out of his reach. He may perceive political power but see politics as a dirty game in which one must deal with and accept as associates lower-class and perhaps even dishonest people. Choice depends on expectations or perceptions as well as on motives.

Many of the ingredients of the possible combinations of perceptions and motives are the consequence of the political system in which the individual finds himself. Is it easy or difficult to enter? Is accession to power closed to all outside a particular social, racial, or economic group? Are important decisions tightly controlled by a small, durable elite? Does political activity in the system involve considerable financial sacrifice? Is politics an arena where important decisions are in fact being made? Is politics a bitterly competitive activity in the community, or is it relaxed, easygoing, and friendly? The answers to this sort of question will help determine the kinds of satisfactions and dissatisfactions perceived in politics by individuals of varying socio-economic status who are motivated in varying degrees of power, achievement, and affiliation. Men who are strongly power-motivated, for instance, are likely to be attracted only to certain kinds of political systems, and then only to certain offices or roles within the system. Men intensely motivated for achievement will get into politics and seek office only when they perceive opportunities for achieving, with effort, whatever it is they define as achievement—perhaps getting a new school or new streets built, or initiating a redevelopment program, or perhaps simply running a businesslike city government. Where such opportunities are seemingly not available, strongly achievement-motivated men are not likely to enter politics on their own initiative.[16]

We shall consider relationships, first, between motivation and kind of office held or run for and, second, between motivation and characteristics of the political systems.

Motivational differences among offices. We made no systematic direct measurement of perceptions of power, achievement, and affiliative opportunities in the offices that appear in our samples, but we felt justified in dichotomizing the offices into positions with high and low potential for achievement and power (see Table 2). The division was carried out on the basis of our own impressions and of the impressions of others, including some of the respondents intimately familiar with the communities. For this purpose, we defined positions with high power potential as those from which any occupant would be perceived to have relatively plentiful opportunities for advancement to more influential positions or for influence over matters of public policy, party affairs, or the enforcement of laws, where enforcement was in practice a matter of discretion for the office holder.[17] Not all occupants of these positions were influential, but the positions were generally regarded as ones from which one *could* exercise influence, and all the men who we knew were influential were occupants of positions of this sort.

To classify the offices according to achievement potential, we defined achievement potential as opportunity to attain policy objectives or to advance to higher offices. The definitions of achievement and power potential are largely overlapping, in practice— attaining policy objectives is, in our dictionary, equivalent to influencing matters of public policy. Consequently, positions high in achievement potential are also high in power potential. The converse is *not true,* however. Positions high in power potential may not be high in achievement potential. For example, if some of the ward chairmen in Eastern City had been party leaders who were influential with respect to party nominations but not with respect to public policy, they would have been classified high in power potential but low in achievement potential. Similarly in Christian Parish, where gambling is nonexistent and justices of the peace have little control over

Table 2
Positions with High and Low Power and Achievement Potential in Eastern City and in Casino and Christian Parishes, La.

| | Power Potential | | Achievement Potential | |
	High	Low	High	Low
Eastern City	City Council State Representative State Senator	City Clerk Registrars of Voters, Vital Statistics Patronage, sinecure positions Ward chairmen	Same as for Power Potential	Same as for Power Potential
Casino Parish	Justice of the Peace Constable Parish Council Parish School Board State Representative Parish-wide (Sheriff, Assessor, etc.)	None	Parish Council Parish School Board State Representative Parish-wide	Justice of the Peace Constable
Christian Parish	Parish School Board Parish Council Parish-wide (Sheriff, Assessor, etc.)	Justice of the Peace Constable	Parish School Board Parish Council Parish-wide	Justice of the Peace Constable

anything, they are rated as low in both respects; in Casino Parish, we have classified them as high in power but low in achievement potential, for they made decisions that affected gambling but could not hope to rise to higher office.

It must be understood that our categorizations depend not on formal characteristics of the offices but on an estimate of the prevailing expectations about the offices. Moreover, the distinctions were drawn without reference to the motive scores of the incumbents. The discussion and data which follow must be interpreted within the limitations of these operational definitions, but we believe that they are accurate both in terms of the meaning of the test of motivation and, roughly, in terms of perceptions of political offices in the communities studied.

As Table 3 indicates, men in positions with high power and achievement potential in Eastern City had considerably higher power-motive scores and perhaps higher achievement-motive scores than those in low-potential positions. In Louisiana, the direction of differences in power and achievement motivation is the same as in Eastern City, but the difference in achievement motivation between high- and low-potential offices is relatively large; in power motivation, slight.

Since we have a nonpolitical control sample for the Eastern City politicians, we can check the implications of these data by comparing Eastern City politicians in high- and low-potential offices separately with their samples of matched political inactives. The hypothesis relating motivation of officeholders to the opportunities of the offices is strongly corroborated. Politicians in high-potential positions scored much higher in both achievement and power motivation than their matched sample (N = 9 pairs).[18] With each motive, only one non-politician scored higher than the politician he was matched to. In contrast, politicians in low-potential positions scored insignificantly lower in both motives than their matched inactives. In short, politicians in offices with high power and achievement potential are more strongly motivated for power and

Table 3
Mean Motive Scores of Non-School Board Politicians in Positions with High and Low Power and Achievement Potential

| | Position Potential | | | |
Motive	High (N)	Low (N)	Diff.	p of Diff.
Eastern City:				
Power	7.9 (10)	4.7 (13)	3.2	.02
Achievement	8.3	6.5	1.8	.13
Louisiana Parishes:				
Power	5.9 (26)	4.9 (10)	1.0	.26
Achievement	5.9 (14)	3.5 (22)	2.4	.06

NOTE: Combining Eastern City and Louisiana parishes and holding *place* constant, p-values of partial linear regression coefficients (*motive* on *position potential*) are: for power, .01; for achievement, .03. Other p-values from Mann-Whitney U test on ranked scores.

achievement than politically inactive men from the same occupational and socio-economic strata. The implication is that high-potential offices attract men with relatively strong achievement and power motivation.

A role-theory explanation—that holders of high-potential offices have developed strong power and achievement motivation over a period of years because of long exposure to power and achievement opportunities—does not account for these results. In Eastern City, where data were gathered on candidates as well as on officeholders, candidates for high-potential positions have the same distinctive motivational characteristics as long-time officeholders. Moreover, politicians in high-potential positions in spite of weak power and achievement motivation are more likely to drop out of politics than strongly motivated officeholders, according to our data. Apparently, motivation affects entry into the potential arena and willingness to remain in office, but officeholding does not determine underlying motivation (though it may serve to arouse existing motives). Some motive change may take place because of role learning, but these data do not support such a hypothesis.[19]

Fourteen school board members in the Louisiana parishes are excluded from Table 3 in order to make the data comparable to Eastern City figures, where school board members were not sampled. When school board members are examined separately, as in Table 4, we find that they score somewhat lower on power motivation and somewhat higher on achievement and affiliative motivation than other officials. The data are not conclusive, but they are suggestive. What might make school board members different from others who hold high-potential positions?

Table 4
Mean Motive Scores of Louisiana School Board Members and Other Louisiana Politicians in Positions with High Power and Achievement Potential

Motive	School Board (N = 14)	Other High Potential	(N)	Diff.	p of Diff.
Power	4.7	5.9	(26)	1.2	.13
Achievement	6.5	5.9	(14)	0.6	.34
Affiliation	3.0	1.7	(26)	1.3	.05

NOTE: Affiliative motive scores are for men in high-power-potential positions; p-values from Mann-Whitney U test.

In many localities, school board elections are not considered to be part of the ordinary political game. Elections to the board are often nonpartisan. The board usually does not serve organization maintenance functions for local parties in the sense that mayoralty office or the city council often do through their control over patronage and over a range of policies. School board politics usually seems less "political" in the sense that there is (or appears to be) less open competition for leadership and less clearly power-oriented behavior. Serving on the school board has more of the flavor of civic duty, in which one is expected to do what is best for all, than of political career.

In Louisiana, only a few of these considerations hold true. The elections are as partisan as those for parish council; school boards control important sources of patronage through the dispensation of custodial and bus-driving positions, through the award of contracts, and through the purchase of land. It is true that there is more public comment when the school board is used for partisan purposes than when power politics are played on the parish council; candidates for the board make some effort to dissociate themselves from partisan politics, whereas other officials do not. Nevertheless, there are grounds for suspecting that motivational differences between school board members and other officials are smaller in the Louisiana parishes than in many other localities. In cities that have both vigorous party or factional politics and a nonpartisan school board, we expect motivational differences between the two sets of officeholders to be greater.

Motivational differences between political systems. Opportunities for exercising power and for achieving — hence for satisfying relevant motives — vary not only among offices within local political systems but also from one system to another. What are the distinctive features of the two political systems we studied? Eastern City's parties compete vigorously, and alternation between them occurs even though each has dominated the scene for several terms at a time in recent decades. At the same time, each party is tightly controlled by a small and only slowly changing set of leaders, so that mobility within the local party structure is somewhat limited. This is not necessarily a sharp restriction on achievement and power opportunities, however, since expectations are prevalent that it is possible to go on to state legislative office or higher from the position of councilman or mayor. Recent city administrations have been vigorous, initiating very important new policies, such as large-scale urban redevelopment. The city government is the focus of demands from diverse groups, and the consensus, in a relatively stagnant economy, is that the city's future depends heavily on the initiative and ability of its political leaders. Opportunity in the economic arena is further restricted by the exclusion of several immigrant minority groups from the highest positions in industry and finance.

The Louisiana parishes, in contrast, have witnessed immense growth and industrialization in recent years. There is no consensus that the most important decisions are to be made in the political process; rather, opportunities for power and achievement abound in the commercial and industrial life of the area. Parish politics is factional, fragmented, shifting, personal. There are no parties competing on the basis of issues, defining important public problems, and mobilizing support for their stands. Factions and individuals compete, but there is little focus on matters of general interest or on public problems that might appear as a challenge to men who otherwise would be attracted to business or professional careers. Furthermore, political mobility upward to state or national offices from a background of parish officeholding is practically unheard of.

In sum, opportunity for power and achievement in local politics is smaller in the parishes than in Eastern City; opportunity for movement up to higher office is much smaller; opportunity for power and achievement in the economic arena is relatively greater. These quite striking differences between Eastern City, on the one hand, and the two parishes, on the other, suggest that Eastern City politics will attract more strongly power- and achievement-motivated men than will the politics of Christian and Casino Parishes. If, as we suggested above in relation to school board politics, concern for policy is likely to stem from at least moderate levels of affiliative motivation, Eastern City politicians may also be somewhat more motivated in this direction.

The hypothesis is supported by data in Table 5, in which Eastern City businessmen-politicians are compared with those Louisiana politicians who are also businessmen, with power and achievement potential of their offices held constant. The Eastern City politicians show substantially higher power, achievement, and affiliative motivation than their counterparts in Louisiana.[20]

Summary and Conclusions

Simply being a politician does not entail a distinctive concern for power, or for achievement or affiliation. For the communities studied our data show that businessmen in local politics do not differ in motiva-

Table 5
Mean Motive Scores of Businessmen-Politicians in High- and Low-
Potential Positions in Louisiana and Eastern City*

	Mean Motive Scores				p of Diff. between Communities
Position Potential	La. Parishes (N)		Eastern City (N)	Diff.	
		Power Motive			
For Power:					
High	5.8	(13)	7.9	(10)	2.1	
Low	2.0	(2)	4.7	(13)	2.7	.04
		Achievement Motive			
For Achievement:					
High	6.3	(9)	8.3	(10)	2.0	
Low	3.8	(6)	6.5	(13)	2.7	.04
		Affiliative Motive			
For Affiliation:					
High	1.5	(13)	3.0	(10)	1.5	
Low	3.5	(2)	4.3	(13)	0.8	.05

* School board men excluded.
NOTE: Affiliative motive scores are for men in high- and low-power-potential positions. The data in this table differ from those in Table 3 in that Louisiana politicians who are not businessmen are omitted to assure comparability with Eastern City data. All p-values are 1-tailed for partial linear regression coefficients for *motive* on *place* with *position potential* held constant as the second independent variable. Although 1-tailed significance levels of $\propto = .05$ are reached or nearly reached for all six coefficients (*place* and *position potential* for each of three motives), it is of interest to note that these two variables together account for only between 7.5 and 20 percent of the variance in motive scores.

tion from politically inactive businessmen. However, patterns of political and nonpolitical opportunities in different communities, and the distribution of opportunities among political offices, are related to the motivational make-up of officeholders. The data for Eastern City and the Louisiana parishes are consistent with the propositions that relatively plentiful opportunities for power and achievement in the economic arena channel strongly motivated men into economic rather than political activity; that in communities where politics and political issues are at the center of attention and interest, men attracted to politics are likely to be more strongly power- and achievement-motivated than in communities where politics commands only peripheral interest; that political systems

that offer upward political mobility attract men with relatively strong achievement and power motivation; and that concentration in a political system on matters of strictly party or factional organization and power, to the near exclusion of public policy concerns, tends to keep men with strong affiliative needs out of politics. Similar relationships hold for specific offices within the communities studied. Offices with high potential for power and achievement are occupied by men who are more strongly power- and achievement-motivated than politicians in low-potential offices.

The implications of data of this sort are not trivial, as a glance back to our summary of the behavioral correlates of these motives reminds. Groups of men who differ with respect to these traits will run a government in sharply different ways, we suspect. Furthermore, the pool of local politicians available for advancement to higher office is a major input to the pool of state and national leaders. Patterns of motivation in local politicians will determine in part what kinds of political leadership we experience in the future. What kind of political system is likely to recruit authoritarian leaders, men whose strong power motivation is untempered by affiliative concern? What sort of politics will produce leaders with high achievement motivation and the characteristics of high levels of performance,

response to challenge, and a propensity for moderate risk that go with it?

It is here that the significance of data on personality is apparent, in the decisions of political leaders, in their yielding to certain pressures rather than to others, in their acceptance of some decision premises over others. Information on the motives of politicians provides us with links between complex social, economic, and political variables, on the one hand, and patterns of the recruitment and behavior of leaders, on the other.

Notes

[1] Harold D. Lasswell, *Power and Personality* (New York: Norton, 1948), pp. 229–30.

[2] Harold D. Lasswell, "Effect of Personality on Political Participation," in R. Christie and M. Jahoda, editors, *Studies in the Scope and Method of "The Authoritarian Personality,"* Glencoe, Ill., Free Press, 1954.

[3] Robert E. Lane, *Political Life* (Glencoe, Ill.: Free Press, 1959), p. 128.

[4] Still unique in its effort to test such hypotheses is J. B. McConaughy, "Certain Personality Factors of State Legislators in South Carolina," *American Political Science Review* 44 (1950): 897–903.

[5] David C. McClelland, *The Achieving Society* (Princeton, N.J., Princeton University Press), 1961.

[6] The main sources of information and theory about the test are David C. McClelland et al., *The Achievement Motive* (New York, Wiley, 1953); McClelland, *The Achieving Society;* and John W. Atkinson, editor, *Motives in Fantasy, Action and Society: A Method of Assessment and Study* (Princeton, N.J.: Princeton University Press, 1958).

[7] See the scoring manuals in Atkinson, *op. cit.,* pp. 685–818. A score-rescore rank-order correlation of .90 indicates sufficient skill to use the results of the test for research purposes. Both authors attained this standard.

[8] See McClelland, *The Achievement Motive,* and Atkinson, *op. cit.,* Chaps. 3–6. The particular advantage of a validated psychological test in this research (in contrast, for example, to data from interviews) is that it provides an assurance that the same motives are being measured in many separate studies of a wide range of important dependent variables, ranging from class-related differences in child-raising practices to patterns of decision making. The network of theoretically meaningful empirical associations that attach to the test as the result of extensive research, and the repeated experimental validations, far outweigh in our opinion an unsuccessful attempt by Reitman to arouse achievement motivation in student subjects after the method of the original experimental validation

studies. See Walter R. Reitman, "Motivational Induction and the Behavior Correlates of the Achievement and Affiliation Motives," *Journal of Abnormal and Social Psychology* 60 (1960): 8–13. In addition, it should be noted that projective measures of motivation are subject to special limitations vis-à-vis test-retest reliability. However, "it would not appear wise to insist on high test-retest reliability before using such measures because it is so hard to replicate testing conditions—to put the subject back in the condition he was in before he made the first response. Instead, one can rely on other criteria, such as validity, for inferring stability of motivational dispositions indirectly" (McClelland, in Atkinson, *op. cit.,* p. 20). Test-retest checks have in fact yielded low correlations (about .4) (R. C. Birney, "The Reliability of the Achievement Motive," *Journal of Abnormal and Social Psychology* 58 (1959): 266–67).

[9] McClelland very briefly cites and summarizes conclusions from studies of the behavioral correlates of achievement motivation in "The Use of Measures of Human Motivation in the Study of Society," in Atkinson, *op. cit.,* p. 521, and much more extensively in *The Achieving Society,* Chaps. 6–8.

[10] J. Veroff, "Development and Validation of a Projective Measure of Power Motivation," in Atkinson, *op. cit.,* pp. 105–16, and "Power Motivation Related to Influence Attempts in a Two Person Group," Princeton, N.J., Princeton University, 1956, unpublished manuscript.

[11] T. E. Shipley, Jr., and J. Veroff, "A Projective Measure of Need for Affiliation," in Atkinson, *op. cit.,* pp. 83–94; J. W. Atkinson, R. W. Heyns, and J. Veroff, "The Effect of Experimental Arousal of the Affiliation Motive on Thematic Apperception," *ibid.,* pp. 95–104; and B. L. Grosebeck, "Toward Description of Personality in Terms of Configuration of Motives," *ibid.,* pp. 383–99.

[12] The remainder of the officials in the two parishes were accounted for as follows: 5.4 percent were located in remote fishing communities quite different from the rest of the parishes; 2.7 percent were women, for whom the test was not appropriate; 12.1 percent were respondents who took the test but for whom the tape recordings were defective; and 12.1 percent were officials who could not be contacted.

[13] Of a population of 32 businessmen-politicians, 27 were selec-

ted by a random process, 23 were interviewed. Of the 4 dropouts, 2 were out of town during the interviewing period, 2 refused to be interviewed.

[14] An earlier paper by one of the authors posited this view. H. Jacob, "Initial Recruitment of Elected Officials in the U.S.— A Model," *Journal of Politics* 24 (1962): 708–9.

[15] We are following here the suggestions of John W. Atkinson (*op. cit.,* Chap. 20).

[16] Inferring from high motive scores of certain officeholders that they sought office because of their motivation depends on the assumption that they initiated their own political activity rather than being recruited by their party. Our impression of the kind of men who are recruited by the parties for local and state offices is that they are likely to be less strongly power- and achievement-motivated than those who initiate their own activity; if so, motive scores of all those in office underestimate the role of motivation in self-recruitment.

[17] This last subcategory arises only in the case of some Louisiana justices of the peace and constables who exercised discretion over enforcement of gambling laws.

[18] These are the mean scores: power motive—politicians 8.3, nonpoliticians 5.2, p = .03; achievement motive—politicians 8.6, nonpoliticians 4.7, $p = .03$ (by Wilcoxon matched-pairs signed-ranks tests; see Sidney Siegel, *Nonparametric Statistics,* New York: McGraw-Hill, 1956).

[19] Still another explanation might attribute motive differences to differences in social class or class background: relatively high-status men are elected to high-potential offices, and their motivational characteristics are associated with their class rather than with the way they attain their political positions. In both localities, men in high-potential positions do come from somewhat higher-class families; they have somewhat more education (Louisiana only) and higher incomes. But those who rank highest with respect to these social characteristics do not account for the differences in motivation between men in high- and low-potential positions. Motivational differences remain when social class and class origin are held constant.

[20] We recognize that the data may also be interpreted as supporting either or both of two other hypotheses: (a) interviewer effects are responsible for the differences; (b) the relatively low motive scores of the Louisiana politicians simply mirror differences in the general populations of the two locales. Since there is no way of excluding these possibilities, our interpretation is only suggestive.

Motivations: Self-Esteem, Identification, and Politics

James David Barber

Long before a person faces a decision whether to undertake a particular candidacy, he may have developed certain motivational potentialities inclining him to office-seeking. I have suggested that these potentialities can be usefully classed as, first, personal needs of a general character, such as the need for power or display, which might be met in politics but are not so engaged at present; and, second, predispositions toward politics specifically, such as an interest in following political events in the press.

When we consider the first potentiality, we are immediately confronted with a contradiction. Many studies of political participation[1] indicate that there is a close correlation between high self-esteem and such activities as voting, discussing politics, and interest in elections and political news. Yet the Spectators, Advertisers, and Reluctants appear in the interviews as people with rather severe deficiencies in self-esteem. Furthermore, their low self-estimates seem to be linked in significant ways with their political participation. These legislators resemble more closely the political figures Harold Lasswell describes as suffering from marked feelings of personal inadequacy or inferiority, who seek out political opportunities for compensating for these feelings.[2] How is this disparity to be explained?

"The More, the More" Hypothesis

A hypothesis which would deny the validity of this last set of findings might be called "the more, the more": the more healthy, efficacious, and confident a person is, the more he participates in politics. The evidence for the validity of this hypothesis as regards a considerable collection of activities *short* of office-holding is impressive. By a process of extension one would expect that officials would show even more self-confidence than the politically active citizenry.

Yet the hypothesis is, it seems to me, based on certain assumptions that need examination. If it is to apply to the whole spectrum of political participation, from voting to holding high public office, it must posit a scale or continuum encompassing the full range. Individuals would then be ranked along this scale and these rankings compared with their scores on tests of self-esteem. How might such a scale be constructed? The most logical method would be to list the various forms of participation, score individuals on each of them, and then combine the scores into an overall index of participation. In this last step it would of course be necessary to weight each kind of participation (for example, discussing politics, or serving in the Senate) according to the amount of political activity involved. The emphasis in this measurement process is necessarily on the *quantity* of activity, whether indicated by frequencies of certain acts or by some other continuous (interval) measure.[3]

If we include public office-holding in this array, it is necessary to take great care in placing offices in a hierarchy of participation. There is no a priori reason for rating a judgeship, for example, higher or lower than a party chairmanship, the president of the local chamber of commerce or municipal union higher or lower than the state legislator. We know that within any collegial governmental body there is a wide range of participation, from virtually complete lethargy to the most intense activity. If possible, one would want to observe or measure directly the individual's activity rather than deduce it from the fact of office-holding. And it would be most desirable for this purpose to be able to distinguish his political acts from nonpolitical acts. Is the lobbyist acting politically when he addresses a legislative committee but nonpolitically when he addresses the members of his organization? And finally, since we are interested not simply in finding out who the socially active people are in the population, we should be specially concerned to locate individuals who spend an abnormal proportion of their social energies on politics.

Let us suppose that these difficulties could be overcome, perhaps through a series of approximations, and that we wind up with a positive correlation between self-esteem and political participation, official and nonofficial. Certain implications for the recruitment process are evident. It would be reasonable to expect that the incumbents of the highest-participation positions would be recruited from those most active at the next level, and so on down the line. From the finding on self-esteem we would similarly suppose that the topmost participants would be recruited from those at the next level who were most self-confident. These two flows of personnel would culminate at the top in a collection of very active persons who were very sure of themselves. In effect, the promotion from one level to another would depend on one's having high self-esteem.

If such findings could be accumulated, they would suggest that the evidence indicating low self-esteem among public officials is faulty or its interpretation in error. Our Lawmakers would find a place in the picture, but the Spectators, Advertisers, and Reluctants would be considered very doubtful cases.

The Specialization Hypothesis

An alternative way of looking at this contradiction would make room for both sets of actual findings. This approach emphasizes variations in the *nature* of participation as well as in its quantity or intensity. Questioning the utility of the general rubric "politics," it focuses on the specialized nature of various political activities. More specifically, it hypothesizes a marked

discontinuity between minor forms of political participation, on the one hand, and running for or holding
public office, on the other. The former represent a collection of relatively widespread, general activities,
while the latter are restricted to a small, specialized
segment of the population. There are reasons for believing that at the level of citizen politics, self-esteem
and participation are strongly related, while at the
official level the picture is mixed. But an explanation
of this point requires a brief detour.

Normal and Abnormal Politics

An individual's self-esteem probably both reflects
and enhances his general adaptation to the culture in
which he lives. Persons who, from childhood on, behave in accordance with cultural norms are rewarded
for such behavior and thus come to value themselves
more highly than those who are continually out of step
with their environment. Conversely, high self-esteem
increases the individual's ability to adapt successfully
to his culture.

Now the cultural norms with which we are concerned are of two kinds: general and specific. General
cultural norms consist of widely shared values regarding what everyone or nearly everyone should do. Being "straightforward" and "friendly" are American
examples. Specific cultural norms consist of widely
shared values about the characteristics and skills
appropriate for particular specialized roles in the
society. For example, a banker should possess above-
average "number" skills, a doctor should not be
squeamish about the sight of blood, etc. Such norms
insist not that everyone should be a banker or doctor
but only that those who undertake these occupations
have the appropriate characteristics.[4]

How do the general and special norms apply to
politics? It is clear that minor participation of the
citizen in politics receives strong support from the
general American value system. From an early age the
American citizen is taught—in the family, at school,
from the pulpit, through his organizations, over the

mass media—that it is a good thing to vote and take
an interest in his community, nation, and world.[5]
Indeed, the "ideal citizen" is, in our culture, practically indistinguishable from the "ideal man." Consistently those who are more "successful" in terms of
social status show higher rates of voting, discussing
politics, and the like. Minor political participation is
seen as a natural complement or extension of one's
other activities; the good father is a better one if he
takes time to vote in school board elections, the good
neighbor becomes more so when he attends a zoning
hearing. These activities, it appears, are valued in large
part for their own sake. That is, one is taught to "participate," "vote," "take an interest," without any
specification of the particular goals to be sought by
these activities. The conflict and uncertainty inherent
in the purposes of such activities are masked by consensus on the worthiness of participation as such.

The formality of the norm is evident in the fact that
a majority of those who say they have little interest
in a particular political campaign, "don't care at all"
which party wins a specific election, or think their vote
will make little or no difference nevertheless turn out
and vote.[6] In Erie County, Ohio, no fewer than 83
percent of the men who said they had no interest in
the 1940 election voted, as did nearly three-fourths
of those in a national sample who thought the outcome of the 1952 election of no importance to the
country.[7] By contrast, only a small fraction (13 percent in 1956) of American voters who lack a "sense
of citizen duty" bother to vote.[8] The general picture is
clear: Americans invest little of their emotional
energies in the tensions and conflicts of political issues
(although they may hold opinions on them), but nevertheless troop to the polls in impressive numbers. The
explanation appears to lie less in the fleeting appeals of
various candidates and programs than in a broad tradition of participation as valuable in its own right.[9]

The citizen participant, then, need make no special
explanations for these civic activities; he gets a pat
on the back for doing his part. The barriers to such
participation are low, requiring only a modicum of skill
and motivation to overcome them. We would expect,
therefore, that individuals who are generally best

adapted to their culture would also be best adapted to this aspect of it. And since such people will usually possess higher self-esteem than others have, there will be a positive correlation between participation and self-esteem.[10]

This argument can be reduced to the following proposition:

1. High self-esteem is associated with successful adaptation to general cultural norms.

2. These norms include a widespread positive evaluation of minor political participation.

3. Therefore high self-esteem and such participation are associated.

The dividing line between citizen politics and public office-holding is clear despite some uncertain middle-ground cases such as membership on a small-town government board—an office not much different, in terms of time and effort, from service on a Lion's Club committee. The distinction is most evident when we consider the degree to which the person's daily routine is disrupted. Even service in a state legislature requires a marked readjustment in one's round of life, alterations of a significantly different order from those required for attending an evening meeting every few weeks. In contrast to the act of voting—limited by law in some places to one minute—the legislature requires months of full-time work. It requires, during this period, a shift to another place, where one associates with a different set of people. In other words, it represents a change or disruption of one's normal role in job, home, and community, rather than a minor complement to this role.

For higher offices the contrasts are even greater. A senator or governor is not just doing more than the citizen who writes him letters. He is devoting his major daily efforts to a specialized political office while his scrivening constituent continues in his regular occupation.

Nor does office-holding enjoy a clearly positive popular evaluation. Obviously, running for political office is not the "normal" thing to do in the sense that voting is normal—that is, expected of and valued for everyone. The general value question regarding voting is, it seems evident, whether one should do it or not—and the answer is unambiguous. The question regarding a political career is very different: whether one should be a public official or pursue some other occupation.

One general attitude is relevant, however. While minor forms of participating such as voting, discussing politics, reading the news, and the like are seen as unquestionably "good," running for office has both a good and a bad dimension. It is true that the public accords remarkably high ranks to certain public offices and such[11] and that public officials are invariably overrepresented in poll choices of "most important" or "greatest" men. But at the same time there is in the public mind a dirty side to political candidacy, getting on the public payroll, taking part in political deals. No one has to explain why he votes. But every candidate probably has to explain to those who know him why he is getting mixed up in politics. The aura of risk, danger, temptation, and doubt that surrounds this kind of participation contrasts markedly with the clean-cut flavor of citizen politics.[12]

The move into political candidacy, then, in contrast to participation in citizen politics, does not receive unambiguous normative support in the general culture. Nor is it guided and justified by unambiguous *specialized* cultural norms. No clear image of what the office demands or what criteria the public thinks should be used in selecting candidates is evident. Take, for example, the apex of attention, the Presidency. The criteria applied in the 1952 selection of General Eisenhower were concerned in large measure with the pros and cons of his previous military experience.[13] The reelection of President Eisenhower turned much more on his personal qualities—his honesty, sincerity, and general likeableness versus his age and health. For some reason Governor Stevenson's divorce was of more concern to the voters in 1956 than in 1952; on both occasions the people were also concerned with his articulate or, as some thought, "highfalutin" speechmaking. Television viewers responded to the 1960 Kennedy-Nixon debates primarily in terms of which candidate agreed with their views and seemed better informed, more sincere, and more specific.[14] And there is good evidence that Mr. Kennedy's religion was considered a highly salient matter in 1960 by a great many voters.[15] There appears to be little consensus on the qualities the Presidency demands—although perhaps if voters were asked directly for a list of such qualities a consensus would emerge.[16] Yet the public probably has a much clearer idea of the Presidency than of any other public office. The specific norms applicable to legislators, sheriffs, governors, and the like are even more amorphous. It would be interesting to know what personal qualities the public thinks are necessary for one to be a good legislator. We would be safe in predicting considerable variety in the response.

The translation from citizen to politician, then, is not facilitated by definite cultural cues as to who has the appropriate qualifications. Nor is either the time of entry or the office to which entry is appropriate defined clearly.

One becomes a member of the electorate at a certain definite age. One becomes a lawyer, normally, upon graduation from law school. But politics as a career is a "late-entry, late-leaving" occupation.[17] No birthday or graduation ceremony automatically ushers one into an official role. The element of uncertainty and choice is considerably greater. Furthermore, if there is a typical course it is to move from an occupational role one has held for years over into a political role. Unlike the relatively uncommitted new graduate in law or business, the new politician enters late upon a political career by breaking off (or severely bending) his connections with a regular, recognized occupational role and status. This decision represents an interruption or diversion from a relatively long-standing *personal* identity which the individual has established in his work. In a sense his candidacy is a public admission that there was something incomplete or unsatisfactory about the course he was pursuing.[18]

The appropriate level or office of entry and the proper progression from office to office are also ill-defined.[19] One does not necessarily move through an apprenticeship as a party worker to some minor office at the local level, and on up the ladder to state and national office. A great many national officials have held no previous local or state office.[20] A number of governors have had little or no experience in other offices.[21] Probably a majority of state legislators enter that office without even having worked in their political parties.[22] And it is not at all unusual to find local candidates whose first political activity is their own campaign.[23] The starting points are as various as the starting time is indefinite.

Political candidacy is best seen not as a simple extension of citizen politics but as a shift into a different frame of reference, one involving a rearrangement of one's regular, normal commitments and, from a personal viewpoint, considerable uncertainty. Insofar as such a step depends on deeper motives, it is most likely to be taken by two kinds of people: those who have such *high* self-esteem that they can manage relatively easily the threats and strains and anxieties involved in this change; and those who have such *low* self-esteem that they are ready to do this extraordinary thing to raise it.

In the Lawmaker we have a person who can call upon exceptionally strong personal resources—particularly a deep sense of personal identity and self-acceptance—which enable him to handle this shift with a minimum of personal stress. Like Riesman's autonomous man, Lawmakers are freed to deviate from the common path precisely because they are in possession of powerful techniques for dealing directly with accompanying strains.[24] From among the ranks of the politically active in a community these persons are likely to select themselves for candidacy. They overcome with relative ease barriers that are much more difficult for others to surmount.

Those whose self-esteem is very low, cripplingly low, are unlikely to be available for political candidacy except in very unusual circumstances. But among the availables in and out of active community participation there are those whose self-doubt, while obvious, is not disabling. Our three less effective types of legislators, each in a different way, experience such doubts. Often they appear to have undertaken political office despite themselves; often they recognize their own lack of any preparation or special aptitude for the job. Our hypothesis must be that they are attracted to politics by forces strong enough to over-power all the objections they are aware of. Politics must offer them personal rewards that offset the strains involved in switching, often at an advanced age, from the regular, normal round of family, job, and community life to something as off-beat as running for the legislature.

On the motivational side, such deep-reaching appeals are very likely to be linked to the self system, to the fundamental need such people feel for getting or confirming a higher self-esteem. As we have seen, political office-holding can offer some strong and specific rewards to the damaged self, bolstering up an ego here, offering an extra chance there, conferring a moral blessing in another place. These rewards may compensate for much of the embarrassment, frustration, and confusion the unconfident person experiences in stepping out into politics. From among the politically available such attractions may entice candidates who are not socially active or whose social activities are inadequate compensation for their needs.

Political candidacy appears, then, as a form of deviant behavior, drawing toward it exceptional people—exceptional either in their high abilities or in their strong needs. Our tentative estimate regarding self-esteem must be that elected public officials possess either rather high or rather low levels of self-esteem compared with other persons who have the same social characteristics. In statistical terms, their dispersion around the mean on a scale of self-esteem will be greater.[25]

Translated into propositional form, this argument states:

1. Initial political candidacy represents a marked shift in the continuity of the person's regular life at work, in the home and community, a shift not clearly evaluated by general cultural norms nor clearly guided by special norms.

2. The changes involved in this shift pose strains for the individual that are of a different (higher) order of intensity compared to shifts involved in low-level political participation.

3. In order for a person to take a candidacy, he must be able either to manage these strains directly or find substitute, compensating need-

satisfactions that make up for them. Exceptionally high (but realistic) self-esteem may be an important resource in dealing directly with these strains; exceptionally low self-esteem may be the basis for a compensatory pattern.

4. Therefore the candidate population is likely to exhibit more variation in self-esteem than will be found among a matched group of noncandidates.

An Illustration from Another Game

These abstractions can perhaps be clarified by drawing a concrete hypothetical example from a completely different realm—the world of sports. Consider the following three baseball players. Mr. A played some sandlot baseball as an adolescent and made the college team in his junior year. After graduation he settled down to work and family, but retained a good deal of interest in baseball. He follows the sport in the newspapers, attends games occasionally, and refuses to be distracted by family complaints during World Series time. Many of A's friends share this interest and enjoy discussing it with him, particularly since he is unusually well-informed on batting averages, prominent players, the rules of the game, current controversies about managers, and stadium characteristics. A's wife encourages him in this hobby because she feels it helps him forget his cares and the perils of middle age. At last report A was attempting to organize a softball league among the office staff, to the delight of the company president, who believes that everyone should participate in some form of physical exercise. Secretly, A hopes to play pitcher and can be found practicing in his back yard most weekends.

Mr. B graduated from the state university a few years ago. He was captain of the varsity baseball team. B is an exceptional physical specimen, strong of arm and steady of nerve, wide awake and well-coordinated. After college he took a job with a sporting-goods company, continued to follow baseball in the press and television, and played with local teams from time to time. *B* likes his work but misses the intense effort and challenge of regular team play with others of comparable ability. Recently he approached an old friend of his, a big-league team manager, and asked to try out for the team. The manager, anxious about his prospects in the coming season and aware of *B's* collegiate record, jumped at the chance. *B's* employer is also enthusiastic; he is confident that *B* will do well and be a credit to the company.

Mr. *C's* intense interest in baseball dates back only to last year. *C* was a rather sickly child; he admired and envied school sports stars, but it seemed that every time he was drafted into a game he got hurt. At college *C* was known as a quiet, scholarly fellow, with little interest in sports. After graduation he found employment as an assistant librarian. Last spring the library's softball team lost its third baseman, and *C,* being the only male nonplayer on the staff, was asked to fill in for a season. *C* accepted. Since then he has become the most ardent baseballer in the building. He attends every practice session and insists on pitching, which he does very badly. His exertions leave him too physically exhausted to do his library work correctly and his supervisor continually reprimands him. At home *C* talks about nothing but baseball, to the dismay of his wife and friends. He continually nags his young son, whose interests run more to reading, to go out for the Little League team. Recently he announced his plan to quit library work and seek a position as pitcher for a minor-league team.

If we substitute political for baseball terms in these imaginary cases we can see the significance of thresholds for the selection of public officials. Mr. *A* is analogous to the interested, active political participant. In another context he would be found voting regularly, discussing politics, taking part in minor organizational activities. These activities, like *A's* baseball hobby, are supported by strong cultural norms. They dovetail nicely with middle-class job and family interests, supplementing and complementing these main concerns. For this kind of activity in this kind of culture the barriers to participation are low, and we would expect that those whose general life adjustment is good will be the ones who will most likely take part.

Mr. *A* was content with an occasional softball game; *B* and *C,* on the other hand, undertook to become professional players. In this culture big-league baseball players are generally admired. Similarly, although one supposes for different reasons, public officials are admired. But there is a great deal of difference between admiring someone and actually attempting to follow in his footsteps. This helps to account for the ambiguous finding that despite their admiration for public officials, few Americans want their sons to go into politics.

In the case of our hypothetical Mr. *B* we see a man who easily surmounts a threshold which is extremely high for most people, because *B* has special resources appropriate for the job. Similarly, the Lawmakers move into legislative candidacy and officeholding much more easily than do persons who lack the appropriate skills or are inhibited by deep-seated doubts. Lawmaker types select political alternatives freely, on the basis of their special characteristics and strengths appropriate for the position.

In the somewhat exaggerated case of *C,* the late-blooming baseball fanatic, we are at once led to suspect some special, obscure reason for his mysterious behavior. How can we explain it? In a culture that would encourage, perhaps, some slight part-time baseball activity on his part, there is certainly no support for his intense and inappropriate ambition. Not only does he lack the necessary skills but he also receives continual punishment in the course of participating. Nevertheless he chooses to seek even more of the same. The explanation is not evident, but it seems clear that some aspect of baseball playing has tapped some deep-seated personal need, providing rewards important enough to overcome the concomitant costs.

Latent Links to Politics

One kind of predisposition for political candidacy, then, may develop out of certain features of the person's basic self-image. These characteristics are, in some cases, linked to politics only at the time the opportunity for nomination presents itself. But in other cases the potential candidate has also developed, parallel with his self-image, an image of the political world that facilitates his recruitment. Whether or not he participates in any active way, he may take an observer's interest in certain facets of politics. The media continually bombard him with messages about even the most remote political events. While we would expect the Lawmaker to attend generally to these messages, it is probable that the other types perceive them in highly selective ways, focusing closely on some aspects and ignoring others. Such perceptions may accumulate, over a lifetime, to form latent links or bonds with politics that are activated at the time of recruitment. In deciding to run, the person calls upon his stored-up impressions of the political world; he "remembers" what politics is about and applies these memories in making his choice.

For the Lawmaker these impressions are quite consciously held and are linked with his own direct experience and participation. The other three patterns are more obscure in this regard. How might such latent links to politics develop in the person whose self-esteem is low?

When we speak of the person as having a low self-estimate, we refer to relations between two aspects of his self-concept.[26] Part of this is his ideal self, his image of what he should be like. This ideal self is largely the product of experience in the family leading the child to incorporate into his own personality a conception of himself as he ought to be. An important influence in this process of ideal-self development is identification: the person seeks to model his behavior after that of some other person. His ideal self appears originally in the form of perceived others "who seem to be more successful in gratifying their needs"[27] than he is.

The other part of the individual's self-concept is his perception of himself-as-he-is. This perception is heavily dependent on the person's experience in interacting with his environment. He learns who he is by the reactions he elicits from others. An important determinant of his perception of himself-as-he-is will thus consist of the rewards and punishments he experiences.

A low self-estimate, then, consists of an awareness (sometimes only partly conscious) of a disparity between ideal self and perceived self. Persons who are not completely overwhelmed by such feelings, yet experience them as painful, will seek to reduce this tension. In order for this seeking to gain significance for political participation, the person's problem must be translated in some sense into political terms. The individual must come to link up his ideal and/or perceived self with political objects and/or experiences. Much of this linkage process may be latent in the prerecruitment phase. That is, persons with low self-estimates may collect, at the periphery of attention, perceptions of politics that ready them to seek or accept candidacy when the chance arises.

Such predispositions may develop through identification with political figures.[28] One way for the person to close the gap between ideal and perceived selves is to imitate or get close to the ideal self, which is the product of an original process of identification. Links to politics may thus be established by the operation of a desire to approach (in the psychological sense) public figures who display the most important characteristics of the person's ideal self.

The legislators we have examined differ markedly in the particular bases for their low self-estimates. We would expect that the Advertiser, whose low self-estimate stems from the feeling that he should be powerful (perhaps as a result of early identification with a powerful father),[29] will be especially sensitive to political leaders who are strong and forceful. Consciousness of such leaders will be painful insofar as it highlights his own impotence, but one way of reducing this tension is to identify with them, attempt to be like them, try to find ways to share their power. Leaders who show lovable characteristics—kindness, sincerity, benevolence—are likely to attract the attention and imitation of persons like our Spectators, whose low self-estimates are based in part on an ideal self with these characteristics. The Reluctants, who see their failure as an inability to meet high standards of duty, service, and right moral conduct will be attracted to leaders who display these qualities.

The political scene can supply important objects

for such identifications. Of all the nonfictional personalities pictured in the mass media, top political leaders probably appear more frequently than any other single category. The political context is especially important because, in contrast to sports and entertainment figures, political leaders act in the real world in benevolent, powerful, and righteous ways. They are in a position, and are expected, to display a wide range of nurturant behavior, caring for the needs of large numbers of people.[30] They control the machinery for making and executing laws; their power is real, has widespread effects, and involves coercion. They are linked with the whole mythology of patriotism, public service, and the performance of a high duty. In all these respects, other available objects for identification tend to be at a disadvantage. One need only make a mental comparison between the President and the movie star, or the industrialist, or the great scientist, or the television personality, in regard to their roles in distributing general indulgences, exercising authoritative power, and manipulating the symbols of national duty, in order to see the possibilities for such linkages developing. Political leaders provide objects for identification in ways of special relevance for the person with a low self-estimate, according to the particular form that this problem takes for him. Other persons, less concerned with problems of self-esteem, are less likely to develop these particular links with politics. On the contrary, they tend to see political leaders instrumentally rather than as compensators.

Perhaps for some people politics is attractive precisely because it is a "dirty," forbidden thing to do. Erik Erikson notes that a person may form "a *negative identity* — meaning an identity which he has been warned *not* to become, which he can become only with a divided heart, but which he nevertheless finds himself compelled to become, protesting his wholeheartedness."[31] There are no doubt cases in which rebellious feelings that one cannot express directly toward his moral mentors break out indirectly in the form of political gang-joining and hell-raising. . . . But Robert Lane presents convincing evidence and argument that rebelliousness is dampened in the American family (even when the father is a drunken

tyrant) and is unlikely in any case to be channeled into politics.[32] In the main, the personal identifications of recruits to candidacy are likely to be positive ones.

But a second set of latent predispositions toward politics may develop out of experience in being punished or deprived by various political forces. Low self-estimates tend to be rooted not only in high ideals but also in a personal history of being rejected, dominated, or accused.[33] Such experiences teach the person that his "real" self is far below the ideal and, equally significant, instruct him as to the particular character of his shortcomings.[34] He develops special sensitivities to certain forms of deprivation, responding to those aspects of the situation that threaten him in familiar ways. Probably the most usual response to such threats is avoidance: the person attempts to keep himself out of situations in which the threat is intensified. But such avoidance may be extremely difficult to arrange. If the sense of failure is deeply ingrained in the personality — or, put another way, if the threatening forces have been internalized — the individual will experience attack and deprivation in many encounters that others do not interpret in this way. This predisposition to be hurt tends to turn every social situation into a punishing experience regardless of its objective character. In addition, avoidance is hampered when the person is actually in a position where escape is impossible or very difficult, either because the environments available to him are pervaded with threat ("no place to turn") or because the threat is concentrated in some central, indispensable environment that he can leave only at great cost. Under such conditions the person may attempt to alleviate his discomfort by approach rather than avoidance, by working on or through the source of threat itself, trying to correct or remove it. He attends to the depriving aspects of the situation and watches for ways to turn them to his own purposes.

Punishing experiences can be connected with politics in a variety of ways. In the small community especially, the political order tends to be mixed in with the general community system of status and prestige. Persons of ethnic or religious minority groups or of low economic status are discriminated against in most social organizations, including the political parties. Thus the Spectator may become aware of politics as one dimension of a general status system which accords him a low place, excludes him from the inner circles, and leaves him feeling rejected. The dominant party represents the social upper-crust, which also dominates church life, the service clubs, the PTA, etc. In a sense the person who is especially sensitive to social rejection may find himself surrounded by it. But in comparison with other alternatives politics may offer better opportunities to palliate the consequent anxieties through participation in party affairs, particularly since the parties cannot publicly set many restrictions on participation.[35] Social rejection, then, may predispose a person to political action.

The Advertiser appears to encounter politics primarily through the central dimension of his life—his occupation. Here the power aspect is the most significant one. The lawyer, the real estate operator, the insurance man all operate within a framework of extensive legal regulation. The rules are imposed on them from without; when the rules change, they must change their practices accordingly. Almost inevitably, the power-oriented person in such a situation becomes aware that politicians have a great deal to say about how he must go about his business. Thus in a way different from that of the Spectator, the Advertiser experiences a special political frustration in a central dimension of his life. Here again, however, politics offers a way out—the Advertiser can join those he cannot lick. The other major source of frustration in his life—a powerlessness to attract clients or customers and thus succeed in his occupation—has a less definite, more diffuse configuration, which offers no readily apparent target. His predisposition to participate in politics is intensified because he is dominated by politics, because he can clearly identify the dominators, and because he has ways of becoming one of them.

The Reluctant's milder self-denigration seems to be based on a consciousness of moral shortcomings. Politics probably entered his consciousness in a double form: inspirational sermons about heroic national leaders, and tales of political corruption told by the muckrakers of his day. Politics for the Reluctant, then, seems both very clean and very dirty. If the ideal side is likely to be linked with his need to identify with virtuous leaders, how does the corrupt side connect with his tendency to accuse himself? Primarily, I suggest, through his strong commitment to his community. Corruption in high places, communicated to him by the mass media, offends him as an American. But more immediately, corruption at home introduces a disturbing sense of guiltiness, which is made all the more severe by his feeling that he is somehow responsible for what goes on in his community. Judging from accounts of small-town politics in the interviews and other sources,[36] politics is a pervasive topic of conversation there, discussed in predominantly personalistic and moralistic terms. The "corruption" is likely to be insignificant by big-city standards but not by the standards of the village street corner. Reluctants, brought up in straitlaced families and strongly identified with the community, probably feel a certain sense of threat when they hear of shady dealings at home.

These themes can be generalized: politics offers, for many, a second chance. If things have gone poorly in one's occupational life (and judging from the occupational-choice literature disappointment is very likely),[37] or in the search for approval or respect, one may seek some extra way, some special departure from the ordinary, in order to break out of a wrong assignment. If politics is linked in some way with his troubles yet offers relatively better chances for improvement, the person may find his interests and inclinations drifting toward political opportunities.[38]

Notes

[1] See, for example, Lane, *Political Life*, pp. 154–55; Campbell et al., *The American Voter*, pp. 515–19; Morris Rosenberg, "Self-Esteem and Concern with Public Affairs," *Public Opinion Quarterly* 26 (1962): 201–11; Heinz Eulau and Peter Schneider, "Dimensions of Political Involvement," *Public Opinion Quarterly* 20 (1956): 128–42; Robert E. Agger, Marshall N. Goldstein, and Stanley A. Pearl, "Political Cynicism: Measurement and Meaning," *Journal of Politics* 23 (1962): 477–506.

[2] See especially Lasswell, *Power and Personality,* chap. 3, and *Psychopathology and Politics;* Alex Gottfried, "The Use of Socio-Psychological Categories in a Study of Political Personality," in Eulau et al., eds., *Political Behavior,* p. 129; George, *Woodrow Wilson,* pp. 317–22; Louise Harned, "Authoritarian Attitudes and Party Activity," *Public Opinion Quarterly* 25 (1961): 393–99. The assessment of interview responses as indicating low or high self-esteem remains a matter of inference, particularly as to the degree to which they show deep-seated, persistent or superficial, temporary feelings. That some low-self responses are due to challenges of a new environment is evident. In judging the relative importance of these situational elements, however, the reader should take into account (1) the respondent's own generalization of his self-estimate, (2) his tendency to react similarly to many environmental facets, (3) the apparently habitual character of his defenses, (4) the lack of tight correspondence between objective features of past social milieus and reactions to the new one, especially in Advertiser-Lawmaker comparisons, (5) findings from other research indicating persistence of personality and especially self-concepts through the life cycle. I am indebted to Philip Converse for noting this problem.

[3] Research by James E. Teele casts doubt on the validity of cumulative indices of "social participation." "Measures of Social Participation," *Social Problems* 10 (1962): 31–39. Cf. Arnold M. Rose, "Attitudinal Correlates of Social Participation," *Social Forces* 37 (1959): 202–6.

[4] Cf. Theodore Caplow, *The Sociology of Work* (Minneapolis: University of Minnesota Press, 1954), Chap. 6, "Occupational Ideologies." On "legitimizing characteristics" see Robert S. Weiss, "Factors Determining the Adoption of Decision-Making as a Role Behavior: A Study of Scientists in a Government Organization," in Albert H. Rubenstein and Chadwick J. Haberstroh, eds., *Some Theories of Organization* (Homewood, Ill.: Irwin, 1960); Lewis M. Terman, "Are Scientists Different?," *Scientific American* (Jan. 1955): 25. On "occupational-role identification" see Robert F. Winch, *Identification and Its Familial Determinants* (Indianapolis: Bobbs-Merrill, 1962), pp. 102–4. On the distinction between general and special norms in small groups see Richard Videbeck and Alan P. Bates, "An Experimental Study of Conformity to Role Expectations," *Sociometry* 22 (1959): 1–11.

[5] Cf. Key, *Public Opinion and American Democracy,* Pt. IV; Herbert H. Hyman, *Political Socialization* (Glencoe, Ill.: Free Press, 1959), Chaps. 4 and 5. That a good deal of this takes hold is evident. See Lane, *Political Life,* pp. 157–62. Gabriel A. Almond and Sidney Verba, *The Civic Culture* (Princeton: Princeton University Press, 1963) indicates that Americans put exceptional stress on "the obligation to participate." See pp. 146–47 and Chap. 6.

[6] Campbell et al., *The American Voter,* pp. 101–6.

[7] Lazarsfeld et al., *The People's Choice,* chart 16, p. 48; Angus Campbell, Gerald Gurin, and Warren E. Miller, *The Voter Decides* (Evanston: Row, Peterson, 1954), p. 39.

[8] Campbell et al., *The American Voter,* table 5–7, p. 106.

[9] Cf. Lane, *Political Life,* p. 93, and *Political Ideology,* pp. 343–45.

[10] Relationships among three dichotomized variables from the 1956 Survey Research Center election study support this interpre-tation. "Personal competence" is significantly related to "sense of citizen duty" (chi square $p < .001$) and the latter is significantly related to "political involvement" (chi square $p < .01$). I am indebted to Arthur Goldberg for this analysis. Cf. Morris Rosenberg, "Self-Esteem and Concern with Public Affairs," *Public Opinion Quarterly* 26 (1962): 201–11; Jeanne Clare Ridley, "Status, Anomie, Political Alienation, and Political Participation," *American Journal of Sociology* 68 (1962), 205–13. See also Wayne E. Thompson and John E. Horton, "Political Alienation as a Force in Political Action," *Social Forces* 38 (1960): 190–95.

[11] Cf. William C. Mitchell, "The Ambivalent Social Status of the American Politician," *Western Political Quarterly* 12 (1959): 683–98.

[12] Research on public attitudes toward elective office careers leaves a great deal to be desired. The questions asked often refer vaguely to "going into politics" or "entering politics," thus introducing an obviously pejorative term. As Mitchell suggests, p. 695, this is much like asking "whether they would like to see their sons become 'shysters' rather than lawyers, or 'quacks' rather than physicians." Fewer than half the Connecticut legislators agreed with a questionnaire item, "I am a politician." And of 85 *elected* local *government officials* I surveyed for another study, 68 percent were against political careers for their sons. Other effects of wording are evident in the following results: In November 1945 a national sample was asked: "If you had a son just getting out of school, would you like to see him enter politics as a life work?" 65 percent said no. A year later (December 1946) another national sample was asked: "Suppose a boy or girl asks your advice about entering politics. Would you advise him or her to plan to enter politics or keep away from politics?" The negative responses dropped to 45 percent. Explanations are speculative, but the second form differed in at least three ways: (1) an anonymous child rather than one's son is referred to; (2) the inappropriate timing of entry is dropped; and (3) the second-choice nature of politics (not "life work") is allowed for. The questions and figures are in Hadley Cantril and Mildred Strunk, *Public Opinion 1935–1946* (Princeton: Princeton University Press, 1951), pp. 534, 538. It is interesting to note that far more Germans (76 percent) and almost as many Englishmen (43 percent) responded in negative terms about political careers for their children. For a useful review of literature on "Attitudes toward Public Leaders" see Bell et al., *Public Leadership.* For critiques of simple interpretations of such questions as indicative of occupational "prestige," see the following: Joseph A. Gusfield and Michael Schwartz, "The Meanings of Occupational Prestige: Reconsideration of the NORC Scale," *American Sociological Review:* 28 (1963): 265–70; Albert J. Reiss and others, *Occupations and Social Status* (New York: Free Press of Glencoe, 1961); William A. Gamson and Howard Schuman, "Some Undercurrents in the Prestige of Physicians," *American Journal of Sociology* 68 (1963): 463–70; Kingsley Davis, "Reply," *American Sociological Review* 18 (1953): 397; Paul K. Hatt, "Occupation and Social Stratification," *American Journal of Sociology* 55 (1950): 533–43.

[13] The evidence on Eisenhower and Stevenson is from Campbell et al., *The American Voter,* pp. 55–59.

[14] Elihu Katz and Jacob J. Feldman, "The Debates in the Light of Research: A Survey of Surveys," in Sidney Kraus, ed., *The Great Debates* (Bloomington: University of Indiana Press, 1962), p. 198.

[15] Philip E. Converse et al., "Stability and Change in 1960: A Reinstating Election," *American Political Science Review* 55 (1961): 269–80.

[16] In 1939 a national sample was asked to specify the "youngest age at which a man should become President" and the age at which "a man becomes too old for the presidency." Medians were 40 and 65 respectively. Cantril and Strunk, p. 590. For a review of evidence on the variability of criteria applied by the public, see Bell, pp. 135–43.

[17] Super, *The Psychology of Careers*. See also Robert E. Agger, Marshall N. Goldstein, and Stanley A. Pearl, "Political Cynicism: Measurement and Meaning," *Journal of Politics* 23 (1961): 501.

[18] It is at least worth suggesting that for some of the more effective politicians, the period between school and entry to politics is one of cumulative experimentation and cogitation in which a strong personal identity is slowly being forged, while for the less effective types the period is one of relatively aimless drifting, reflecting an inability to come to grips with identity problems. Cf. Erikson, *Young Man Luther*, pp. 43, 176.

[19] Everett C. Hughes, "Institutional Office and the Person," *American Journal of Sociology* 43 (1937–38): 413. Cf. Leiserson, *Parties and Politics*, pp. 202–3. On the other hand, it is wise not to exaggerate the contrast with other occupations: many business careers seem to proceed in mysterious fits and starts. See Melville Dalton, "Informal Factors in Career Achievement," *American Journal of Sociology* 56 (1951): 209–18; Fred E. Katz, "Occupational Contact Networks," *Social Forces* 37 (1958): 52.

[20] C. Wright Mills notes that "From 1789 right up to 1921 generation after generation, the proportion of the political elite which has *ever* held local or state offices decreased from 93 to 69 percent. In the Eisenhower administration, it fell to 57 percent." Mills presents evidence that recruitment of the "political elite" from the House and Senate is on the wane, *The Power Elite* (New York: Oxford University Press, 1959), pp. 229ff. Of the United States Senators who served between 1947 and 1957, Matthews classifies 34 percent as "Amateur Politicians," 60 percent of them having been over 40 when they achieved their first public offices. A quarter of the amateurs had no prior public office experience. Matthews, *U.S. Senators and Their World*, p. 62.

[21] Of the 932 governors who served between 1870 and 1950, 86 had held no previous public office, and another 154 had spent only one to four years in public office. Joseph A. Schlesinger, "Lawyers and American Politics: A Clarified View," *Midwest Journal of Political Science* 1 (1957): 29. See also his *How They Became Governor* (East Lansing, Mich., Governmental Research Bureau, 1957).

[22] The following percentages of state legislators in four states reported that they had "no party office or work" prior to their legislative service: New Jersey, 41 percent; Ohio, 62 percent; California, 52 percent; Tennessee, 66 percent. Wahlke et al., *The Legislative System*, p. 97. Of the Connecticut legislators responding to the questionnaire (a group over-representing the more active members), 55 percent reported no previous elective public office, 58 percent no appointive office, and 45 percent no political party office. Derge reports that 51 percent of the Missouri legislators responding to a questionnaire reported "no prior political experience." David R. Derge, "The Lawyer as Decision-Maker in the American State Legislature," *Journal of Politics* 21 (1959): 416.

[23] Of 59 local government officials in Louisiana, 28 percent reported that they first participated in politics by "campaigning for oneself." Herbert Jacob, "Why Men Seek Political Office: Motivation and Social Status in the Recruitment of Locally Elected Officials," a paper delivered at the 1961 Annual Meeting of the American Political Science Association, p. 14. Samuel C. Patterson reports that "more than 40 percent of the county chairmen in Oklahoma have not run for public office, do not intend to run, and do not desire to run; and in this Democratic and Republican chairmen do not differ significantly. "Characteristics of Party Leaders," *Western Political Quarterly* 16 (1963): 345.

[24] Cf. Riesman, *The Lonely Crowd*, Chap. 12.

[25] This hypothesis is consistent with some findings reported by Lester W. Milbrath on the political activities of 98 North Carolinians who made monetary contributions to their parties. Milbrath develops a scale of "sociability" which appears to have a strong self-esteem dimension and is related significantly (.05 or better) with a variety of political activities, but *not* with holding public office or making a political contribution. "Predispositions toward Political Contention," *Western Political Quarterly* 13 (1960): 5–18. William Buchanan's "purposive voters" – "a tolerant, educated, experienced, active minority in community affairs" – "who see their vote as a tool for shaping their environment do not prefer the political to the social techniques; in fact, they are more likely to use the latter." "An Inquiry into Purposive Voting," *Journal of Politics* 18 (1956): 295.

[26] The following discussion has been facilitated by Arthur R. Cohen's chapter, "Some Implications of Self-Esteem for Social Influence," in Irving S. Janis et al., *Personality and Persuasibility* (New Haven: Yale University Press, 1959); Carl R. Rogers, "Some Observations on the Organization of Personality," *American Psychologist* 2 (1947): 358–68; Hall and Lindzey, *Theories of Personality*, Chap. 12, "Rogers Self Theory." Cf. Jacob Tuckman and Robert J. Kleiner, "Discrepancy between Aspiration and Achievement as a Predictor of Schizophrenia," *Behavioral Science* 7 (1962): 443–47, for a simple technique, using demographic variables, for estimating such discrepancies.

[27] Hall and Lindzey, p. 47, describing identification in Freud's psychoanalytic theory. Cf. Nelson N. Foote, "Identification as the Basis for a Theory of Motivation," *American Sociological Review* 16 (1951): 14–21; Shibutani, *Society and Personality*, Chap. 7 and Pt. IV; Helen Merrell Lynd, *On Shame and the Search for Identity* (New York, Science Editions, 1961), Chap. 5; White and Lippitt, *Autocracy and Democracy*, pp. 209–22; Winch, *Identification and Its Familial Determinants*; James C. Davies, *Human Nature in Politics* (New York: Wiley, 1963), pp. 37ff.

[28] For purposes of illustration I focus on identification with individual leaders, but similar things could be said about identification with political groups. Cf. Franz Neumann, "Anxiety and Politics," in Stein et al., eds., *Identity and Anxiety*, p. 276. On "positional" as contrasted with "personal" identification see Winch, p. 147. On "proximal" and "distal" groups in politics, see Davies, *Human Nature in Politics*, Chaps. 5 and 6. The identification con-

cept has its ambiguities, which are analyzed effectively by Nevitt Sanford, "The Dynamics of Identification," *Psychological Review* 62 (1955): 106–18.

[29] Cf. Leon J. Saul, *The Hostile Mind* (New York: Random House, 1956), Chap. 6, "Hostility and Politics."

[30] Cf. Fred I. Greenstein, "The Benevolent Leader: Children's Images of Political Authority," *American Political Science Review* 54 (1960): 934–43.

[31] Erikson, *Young Man Luther*, p. 102. Cf. Winch, pp. 13–14.

[32] Lane, *Political Ideology*, Chap. 17. This view is confirmed by Russell Middleton and Snell Putney, "Political Expression of Adolescent Rebellion," *American Journal of Sociology* 68 (1963), and by Philip Nogee and Murray B. Levin, "Some Determinants of Political Attitudes among College Voters," *Public Opinion Quarterly* 22 (1958–59): 449–63.

[33] Harold D. Lasswell, "Psychology Looks at Morals and Politics," in Ulmer, ed., *Introductory Readings in Political Behavior*, p. 26. Cf. William H. Sewell and A. O. Haller, "Factors in the Relationship between Social Status and the Personality Adjustment of the Child," *American Sociological Review* 24 (1959): 511–20.

[34] E. J. Cleveland and W. D. Longaker, "Neurotic Patterns in the Family," in Leighton et al., *Explorations in Social Psychiatry*, p. 171; Manford H. Kuhn, "Self-Attitudes by Age, Sex, and Professional Training," Sociological Quarterly 9 (1960): 39–55.

[35] Cf. Robert A. Dahl, "Who Participates in Local Politics and Why," *Science* 134 (Oct. 27, 1961): 9. At another level, Lasswell writes, "A general proposition is that *the accent on power rather than some other value in the social process has come because limitations upon access to other values have been overcome by the use of power*." "The Selective Effect of Personality on Political Participation," in Richard Christie and Marie Jahoda, eds., *Studies in the Scope and Method of "The Authoritarian Personality"* (Glencoe, Ill.: Free Press, 1954), p. 206 (emphasis in the original).

[36] Cf. Vidich and Bensman, *Small Town in Mass Society*, pp. 111–12.

[37] Cf. Anne Roe, *The Psychology of Occupations* (New York: John Wiley, 1956), Chaps. 21, 22. Relatively few occupational aspirations are fulfilled in fact. And apparently many people drift into careers for which they may or may not be suited, rather than making a definite, conscious occupational choice at some definite moment in time. Fred E. Katz and Harry W. Martin, "Career Choice Processes," *Social Forces* 41 (1962), 149–54. Cf. Lamar T. Empey, "Social Class and Occupational Aspiration: A Comparison of Absolute and Relative Measurement," *American Sociological Review* 21 (1956): 703–9; and Russell R. Dynes, Alfred C. Clarke, and Simon Dinitz, "Levels of Occupational Aspiration: Some Aspects of Family Experience as a Variable," *American Sociological Review* 21 (1956): 212–15. The latter two articles are reprinted in Stoodley, ed., *Society and Self*.

[38] Joan W. Moore, "Social Deprivation and Advantage as Sources of Political Values," *Western Political Quarterly* 15 (1962): 217–26. Cf. Robert K. Merton and Alice S. Kitt, "Contributions to the Theory of Reference Group Behavior," in Merton and Paul F. Lazarsfeld, eds., *Studies in the Scope and Method of "The American Soldier"* (Glencoe, Ill.: Free Press, 1950).